A New History of Asian America

A New History of Asian America is a fresh and up-to-date history of Asians in the United States from the late eighteenth century to the present. Drawing on current scholarship, Shelley Sang-Hee Lee brings forward the many strands of Asian American history, highlighting the distinctive nature of the Asian American experience while placing the narrative in the context of the major trajectories and turning points of U.S. history. Covering the history of Filipinos, Koreans, Asian Indians, and Southeast Indians as well as Chinese and Japanese, the book gives full attention to the diversity within Asian America. A robust companion website features additional resources for students, including primary documents, a timeline, links, videos, and an image gallery.

From the building of the transcontinental railroad to the celebrity of Jeremy Lin, people of Asian descent have been involved in and affected by the history of America. *A New History of Asian America* gives twenty-first-century students a clear, comprehensive, and contemporary introduction to this vital history.

Shelley Sang-Hee Lee is Associate Professor of Comparative American Studies and History at Oberlin College. She is the author of *Claiming the Oriental Gateway: Prewar Seattle and Japanese America*.

A New History
of Asian America

SHELLEY SANG-HEE LEE

Routledge
Taylor & Francis Group

NEW YORK AND LONDON

First published 2014
by Routledge
711 Third Avenue, New York, NY 10017

Simultaneously published in the UK
by Routledge
2 Park Square, Milton Park, Abingdon, Oxon OX14 4RN

Routledge is an imprint of the Taylor & Francis Group, an informa business

Library of Congress Cataloging-in-Publication Data
Lee, Shelley Sang-Hee, 1975–
   A new history of Asian America / Shelley Sang-Hee Lee.
     pages cm
   Includes bibliographical references and index.
   1. Asian Americans—History. 2. Asian Americans—Cultural assimilation. 3. Asian Americans—Politics and government. 4. United States—Race relations. I. Title.
   E184.A75L45 2013
   973'.0495—dc23   2013001775

ISBN: 978–0–415–87953–8 (hbk)
ISBN: 978–0–415–87954–5 (pbk)
ISBN: 978–0–203–44107–7 (ebk)

Typeset in Dante
by Keystroke, Station Road, Codsall, Wolverhampton

Contents

Acknowledgements

I am thankful to the many individuals whose support and encouragement made the completion of this book possible. First, are the numerous scholars, past and present, who have dedicated themselves to building and growing the field of Asian American history. This book stands on your shoulders. My editor Kimberly Guinta receives my utmost gratitude for her guidance, enthusiasm, and patience throughout the process. I cannot thank her enough. Students at Oberlin College were instrumental in the conceptualization and completion of this book, through their contributions in class, participation in "focus group" discussions about Asian American history, and helpful research assistance. The following deserve particular mention: Angus Chen, Laura Dellplain, Aki Gormezano, Aly Halpert, Rachel Ishikawa, Joelle Lingat, Tim Ng, Tuyet Ngo, Eric Oeur, Karl Orozco, Skylar Sweetman, and Ted Young. Colleagues at Oberlin provided a constant supply of good cheer, professional support, and intellectual camaraderie over the last five years, which helped sustain me through the writing of this book. They include Pablo Mitchell, Renee Romano, Gina Perez, Meredith Raimondo, Wendy Kozol, Marko Dumancic, Pawan Dhingra, and Len Smith. Other friends and fellow Asian Americanists to whom I owe a great debt for their advice and wisdom are Celine Shimizu, Karen Leong, Judy Wu, Scott Wong, Xiaojian Zhao, and Gordon Chang. Finally, I thank my family in California and in-laws in the Pacific Northwest and, as always, my husband, Rick Baldoz. This book is dedicated to our daughter Kaya.

Introduction

A New History of Asian America provides readers with an updated, interpretive synthesis of Asian American history. It was written primarily with undergraduate students and newcomers to the field in mind, but I hope that specialists will find the text useful and appreciate the ways in which this book pays tribute to their scholarship and visions.

Asian American history, a subset of the broader field of ethnic studies, has been a robust and dynamic area of study for nearly forty-five years. The study of Asians in America long precedes the late 1960s, but it was out of the struggle to establish ethnic studies curricula and uncover the "buried histories" of people of color in America that the first generation of "Asian Americanists" emerged and pioneered a field that has grown by leaps and bounds. In the early days of Asian American history, much of the work revolved around collecting community voices and histories and carving out a space for the field in the academy. The histories were new and the validity of this kind of inquiry not entirely accepted. When it came to engaging the broader field of U.S. history, Asian Americanists' efforts revolved around asserting that people of Asian descent had a place in the American past, whether as targets of racism or key players during important historical developments. There was also an urgency driving the early scholarship; the stories of old-timers still living needed to be recorded, the injustices of episodes like Japanese wartime internment and Chinese exclusion had to be stressed, and the stories of Asian people's contributions to building the nation needed to be told. Framing much of this work was the imperative to demonstrate that Asians in America were not foreigners, but rather a people with a long history in this country and hence a rightful claim to American identity and belonging.

Subsequent generations of Asian American historians have sustained and enhanced the vitality of the field while taking it in new directions and offering more challenging and critical interpretations of Asian American and U.S. histories. At times it is impossible to isolate much of the recent scholarship within a single genre of history, as scholars have done as much to develop Asian American history as they have to reinterpret such subjects as Reconstruction history, the history of the Cold War, legal history, and urban history. Additionally, the field has become increasingly theoretically and conceptually innovative, illuminating such analytical concerns such as transnationalism, diaspora, gender, sexuality, race, ethnicity, and class. More than just an interesting and distinctive narrative about people who crossed the Pacific to make new lives in America, Asian American history now compels us to view American history and society anew.

In *A New History of Asian America*, I have attempted to synthesize the older and recent literature to give an updated narrative of Asian American history. For the established histories and perspectives I mainly consulted the major textbooks in the field, namely Ronald Takaki, *Strangers from a Different Shore*; Sucheng Chan's *Asian Americans*; Roger Daniels, *Asian America*; and H. Brett Melendy, *Asians in America*. While differing in style and somewhat in thematic focus, they generally presented Asians as participants in "immigrant America," working against the traditional elision of this group from immigration, racial, and ethnic histories. While not seeking to supplant their narratives, *A New History of Asian America* supplements them by incorporating new and reconsidered insights drawn from the last twenty years of historical scholarship in Asian American history. In particular, the book extends the chronology both backwards and forwards, considering the years prior to major Asian immigration, and provides more detailed discussions of the history after World War II. It also gives greater attention to Filipinos, Koreans, Asian Indians, and Southeast Asians, whose experiences have been the subject of fewer historical studies than the Chinese and Japanese. While the book was not completely able to overcome the imbalance—as the current scholarship remains skewed due to a number of factors including accessibility and scope of sources—it has attempted to address it considerably. Finally, *A New History of Asian America* seeks to foreground new themes and narratives in Asian American history that go beyond the simple story of newcomers working, surviving, enduring hardship, and overcoming the odds. It is also a history about American power and inequality, interethnic tension and competition, glass ceilings and racial profiling, and economic, racial, and patriarchal privilege.

That said, I should also acknowledge what this book does not do. The scholarship I have drawn upon to incorporate into this synthesis reflects my view of the significant turns in the field. It is also selective and subjective. For instance, it does not employ post-national or transnational frameworks as organizing concepts and is primarily concerned with Asian American experience in and engagement with the United States, and American identity and institutions of power. One of the current and very exciting trends in Asian American history and American studies more broadly is the turn toward transnationalism. Asian Americanists have contributed much to this with research on the Pacific Northwest borderlands, comparative U.S.–Canada studies, and hemispheric approaches of migration and exclusion politics. While this work is generative and groundbreaking, I have chosen not to make such approaches central to this book due to the limitations of length and my belief that the U.S. nation and issues of national identity and policies remain highly salient and merit continued focus.

I believe a book like *A New History of Asian America* is needed now because over forty years since the founding of ethnic studies, the place of fields like Asian American history is at once entrenched and vulnerable. The field has made real strides and its leading practitioners are respected and recognized by both Asian American studies and history associations. They teach in ethnic studies, American studies, gender studies, and history departments. They also serve as deans and public intellectuals. Colleges and universities outside the West Coast continue to add Asian American history to their curricula. That said, plenty of signs indicate that these and other achievements remain limited and tenuous. Its impact on the broader public consciousness has been modest at best. This is seen, for instance, in the slowness with which Asian American history has appeared in high school curricula, and regular appearance of ill-informed articles by non-specialists on subjects like Japanese internment (when there are plenty of specialists who might be consulted for such pieces or perhaps even be asked to write them).[1] This suggests that much work remains to be done and to keep writing and teaching Asian American history. Another urgency that informs *A New History of Asian America* is the fact that ethnic studies is in danger. Among many administrators and faculty, it was never a legitimate field, but in today's climate of scarcity and cutbacks, its opponents are taking advantage of the circumstances to call for its reduction or elimination. Especially alarming is that many of the attacks are driven by xenophobia and narrow-minded thinking about what constitutes American history and identity, points of view that ethnic studies was established to interrogate and remedy.

In the vein of traditional immigration histories, *A New History of Asian America* seeks to tell stories of people who migrated to and made new homes in America. However, its ultimate objective is not to celebrate them, or to weave a narrative of progress or decline. Its main goal is to highlight the distinctiveness of Asian American experience and to interrogate, through the lens of Asian America, the salience of race in American history: its centrality to notions of American identity and citizenship, how it has oppressed and excluded people, how its meanings have changed, and how people have negotiated it. Chapter 1 explores Orientalism in Western thought and in early America, as a cultural and intellectual pre-history to major Asian migration. Chapter 2 gives a broad overview of early Asian immigration to the United States, focusing on Chinese, Japanese, Koreans, Asian Indians, and Filipinos and framing these migrations as functions of larger diasporic movements during the nineteenth and early twentieth centuries. Chapters 3 and 4 describe major facets of Asian American experience during the 1800s and early 1900s, with the former focusing on work and labor, and the latter on family, community, and social intimacy. Chapters 5 and 6 deal with anti-Asian racism, also during the pre-World War II decades, with attention on the mechanisms of racism and discrimination and how Asian Americans responded and resisted. Chapter 7 deals mainly with the interwar years and explores themes of modernity, youth culture, and the Great Depression. Chapter 8 examines Asian America during the World War II years with particular attention on how the experiences of Japanese Americans diverged from those of other Asian Americans, as well as how the United States came out of the war embracing an ethos of liberal multiculturalism. Chapter 9 traces how this ethos unfolded amidst Cold War fears and the shifting place of Asian Americans in 1950s and early 1960s America. Chapters 10 and 11 discuss major developments impacting Asian America from the late 1960s and 1970s, namely the post-Vietnam War Southeast refugee migration and the Asian American movement. Chapter 12 foregrounds the Immigration Act of 1965 and how this legislation heralded a new era for revived Asian immigration, and Chapter 13 surveys key developments in the closing decades of the twentieth century.

Supplemental pedagogical material can be accessed on the book's website, which includes additional images, study questions, primary documents, and an historical timeline.

Notes

1 For instance, see Edward Rothstein, "The How of an Internment, but Not All the Whys," *New York Times*, December 9, 2011. http://www.nytimes.com/2011/12/10/arts/design/heart-mountain-interpretive-learning-center-review.html?pagewanted=all.

Orientalism before Asian America

1

The question of when Asian American history begins is a complicated one. If looking for the first known presence of a person from Asia on American soil, we might consider the findings of a 2007 Canadian archaeological project, which theorized that North America's first inhabitants were seafarers from the Japanese islands who sailed the coastal waters of the North Pacific about 16,000 years ago.[1] Using this as a starting point for Asian American history, however, does little to illuminate the long and continuous presence of Asians in the United States and North America. We could instead begin with the appearance of discrete populations of Asians in what is now the United States. Here we might look to 1763, when Filipino sailors aboard Spanish galleons on the Manila–Acapulco trade jumped ship and settled in the New Orleans area. Yet another approach would be to start with more sustained and large-scale migrations that led to a permanent presence of Asians in America. In this case, the California gold rush, which drew tens of thousands of Chinese in the late 1840s and early 1850s, stands out. Finally, we could start when persons of Asian descent in the United States consciously identified themselves as "Asian American." This would make for a brief history, as it was not until the late 1960s that activists proclaimed an Asian American identity that rejected old labels, signaled pan-Asian solidarity, and made assertive claims to American belonging.

This is all to say that pinpointing when and where Asian American history begins, while an interesting exercise, can detract from a productive exploration of the subject. Rather than seeking to mark a definitive starting point for when Asians and Asian Americans become a presence in U.S. history, I suggest we first reflect upon what constitutes a presence. Here, it helps to consider ideas as well as bodies, and in this regard, it is important to note that traditions in Western thought about Asia, or the "Orient," long predating the nineteenth century migrations informed the Asian American experience. Having inherited much cultural baggage from Europe, white Americans, from the dawn of independence, displayed distinct attitudes about Asia and the differences between Europeans and Asians, which in turn would shape how they viewed and treated Asian people in America. While the particular ideas about Oriental–Occidental difference changed over time and place, they pivoted consistently on a presumption of Western superiority and evinced a simultaneous fascination with and revulsion of the "East." Such thinking not only shored up Western, European—and subsequently white—identity, but also helped to rationalize political, economic, and military domination and interventions over "weak" Asian powers.

I realize that Westerners' (i.e., white people's) perceptions of Asians in history may seem an unconventional way to begin an exploration of Asian American history. To do so might implicitly give too much weight to racism and the views of outsiders, and marginalize or make secondary the agency, distinctiveness, and vitality of Asian American people and their communities. This is not the book's intention, and as the reader will see in the chapters that follow, the lives and viewpoints of Asian Americans themselves are the centerpiece of *A New History of Asian America*. I do believe, however, that the discussions in this chapter are crucial because they underscore how Asian immigrants did not enter a blank slate. Their experiences were not shaped just by the baggage and expectations they brought with them, but also by the society they came into. Furthermore, while racism is not the only or most important theme in Asian American history, it is, I emphasize, a critical one that merits a sustained exploration.

As former colonial subjects, Americans in the late eighteenth century had a much different relationship with Asia than Europe did, although they inherited the outlook that Asia was an exotic and otherworldly place. As the young nation grew and matured over the nineteenth century, its perception of the "East" underwent numerous permutations, from a land of mysterious, ancient knowledge and desired luxury goods to a barbaric place to be opened, dominated, and civilized. However, more than just a far-flung part of the world and the site of Western civilization's opposite, Asia—its people and things—would become intimately tied up in notions of American freedom and nationhood at key historical junctures. Furthermore, these moments—during which dominant thought with respect to East–West difference and the inherent foreignness of people from the "Orient" crystallized—revealed stark intellectual and ideological boundaries that cast Asians and Asian Americans as outsiders from the national civic body.

European Orientalism

In his rumination on where Asian American history begins, the historian Gary Okihiro poses as a conceptual starting point the entry of Asians into the Western historical consciousness. "The when and where of the Asian American experience," he states, "can be found within the European imagination and construction of Asians and Asia."[2] Indeed, Europeans have been thinking about Asia for a long time, and while the content of that thought and the contours of Europe–Asia relations have constantly shifted, remaining remarkably consistent was the upper hand that Europeans presupposed or sought over Asia, culturally, politically, economically, and militarily. This authority was bolstered by the one-sided production and unidirectional flow of knowledge whereby Westerners wrote and spoke about and for the East without allowing the East to speak for itself. The theorist of Orientalism Edward Said has explained that the "Orient's" position as Europe's most recurrent "other" stems from its position as the site of Europe's "greatest and richest colonies, the source of its civilizations and languages, and its cultural contestant."[3] As such, Asia has been imagined variously as romantic, exotic, terrifying, and disgusting, but always otherworldly. Moreover, the function of such notions has been to root and substantiate Europe's identity rather than to understand Asia in an accurate or nuanced manner.[4]

Early Western articulations of the differences between Europe and Asia can be traced as far as the fourth century B.C.E. A nascent East–West awareness informs, for instance, ancient Greek plays such as *The Bacchae* by Euripides and *The Persians* by Aeschylus.[5] The physician Hippocrates, in ruminating on the area between the Mediterranean and Black Seas, said that the people of Asia were unlike Europeans in every respect. Asia's lush environment, he believed, produced monotony and indulgence amongst its inhabitants, while Europe, by contrast, had less natural abundance, and, thus, developed a more energetic and courageous people.[6] Divisions between savagery and civilization animated ancient Greeks' understandings of the East–West divide, solidified during encounters such as the Persia–Greece conflict in the fourth century B.C.E. Likewise, during his push into India in the third century B.C.E., Alexander the Great characterized his journey as a contest between civilization and barbarism. With civilization on their side, the Greeks triumphed over the undisciplined, slavish, and effeminate Asians. Echoing earlier writers, Alexander's exoticized descriptions of Asia were influenced by his belief in the "generative relationship between the environment and race and culture."[7]

Hundreds of years later, medieval writers reflected and reinforced the European awareness of the world as fundamentally divided between Eastern and Western civilizations, with their depictions of the East still entrenched in fantastical imaginings. Considered the most influential book about Asia from its publication in 1356 until the eighteenth century, *The Travels of Sir John Mandeville* captured the imaginations of Europeans for generations. Mandeville was a pseudonym for several authors who purportedly traveled from England to the Holy Land, Egypt, Arabia, and Cathay. Like Marco Polo before him, Mandeville described the "marvels and monsters of the East, from the bounties of gold, silver, precious stones, cloves, nutmeg, and ginger to the horrors of one-eyed and headless beasts, giants, pygmies, and cannibals."[8] Also emphasizing the bizarre physical appearance of Orientals, *Wonders of the East*, of which Alexander the Great is the hero, described Asian women with "boars' tusks and hair down to their heels and oxen's tails growing out of their loins. [They] are thirteen feet tall, and their bodies have the whiteness of marble, and they have camels' feet and donkeys' teeth."[9] During the thirteenth century, the Mongol invasions made immediately terrifying what to many Europeans had long been a strange but otherwise distant people. In 1225, Friar William of Rubruck described the Mongols as "swarming like locusts over the face of the earth" and bringing "terrible devastation to the eastern parts [of Europe], laying waste with fire and carnage."[10] Despite their military prowess, they remained a filthy and barbaric people.

Also by the medieval period, religion—more specifically Europeans' perceptions of the differences between Christians and non-Christians—had emerged as a major axis of East–West difference. Here, the rise of Islam in the Near East and parts of southern Europe and Asia in the seventh through fifteenth centuries framed European views of non-Christian others.[11] Islam was, Edward Said explains, to Europe "a lasting trauma," for until the end of the 1600s, the "'Ottoman peril' lurked alongside Europe to represent for the whole of Christian civilization a constant danger."[12] By the twelfth century, it was a common belief that Arabia was "on the fringe of the Christian world, a natural asylum for heretical outlaws," and that Mohammed, Islam's founder, was a "cunning apostate," for Islam itself, as the sixteenth-century Orientalist Barthelemy d'Herbelot maintained, was merely a "fraudulent version of Christianity."[13] Such assumptions explain depictions of Muslims in such works as Dante's *The Inferno*. In this fourteenth-century poem in which Dante journeys through the nine circles of hell, he encounters in the eighth circle "Maometto" (Mohammed) who is condemned to a fate in which he is "endlessly cut from his chin to anus." In the first circle, he meets a group of Muslims who, despite being "virtuous heathens," are nonetheless damned to hell because they have not experienced Christian revelation.[14]

As noted in some of the descriptions above, gender was a pronounced aspect of Europeans' understanding of East–West difference. This was apparent in ancient Greek representations of "soft men and erotic women," as well as "hard, cruel men and virile, martial women."[15] According to Arrian, the second-century Greek historian, the women of Asia were hypersexual, untamed, and wild. Marco Polo's writings also highlighted the unusual gender formations in Asian societies. There, he found "chaste women and diabolical men, and grotesque and wondrous objects and people, including unicorns, Amazons, dog-headed creatures, mountain streams flowing with diamonds, and deserts full of ghouls."[16] Yet Chinese women were "the most delicate and Angelique things, and raised gently, and with great delicacy, and they clothe themselves with so many ornaments and of silk and of jewels, that the value of them cannot be estimated."[17] Such observations spoke to the feminization of Asia in the European consciousness, which would be folded into perceptions of Asian inferiority and used to rationalize colonization from the sixteenth century onward.[18]

Over the centuries, accumulated impressions of Asia, drawn from direct encounters, the writings of others, and powerful stereotypes, developed into a self-reinforcing worldview in which the Orient and Occident represented separate categories of humanity. As noted earlier, this served to develop and refine European identity.[19] As historical relationships and the particular interests of Westerners in the "Orient" changed, what was remarkably enduring and took on the authority of "common sense" as late as the nineteenth century (and perhaps today) was the perceived East–West dichotomy and familiar set of images that the "Orient" evoked: backwardness, irrationality, sensuality, and stagnation. Orientalism flattens the Orient and gives authority to the Orientalist who claims to "know" the area. Furthermore, it enthralls and elevates the Western consumer with tales and objects from strange, faraway places. The power that Westerners have been able to draw from Orientalist practices always relied on the fact that the "Orient" did not have a voice of its own. "Orientalism," explains Said, "is premised . . . on the fact that the Orientalist, poet or scholar, makes the Orient speak, describes the Orient, renders its mysteries plain for and to the West. He is never concerned with the Orient except as the first cause of what he says."[20]

Ideology and Power

Western ideas about the "Orient" found in travel narratives, diaries, encyclopedias, and scholarly texts were not merely abstractions without material basis or expression. These ideas constituted a long tradition that eventually legitimized Western ambitions to dominate and appropriate Asia, administratively, economically, and militarily. This process began with Portugal's penetration of India, Southeast Asia, and Macao in the sixteenth century and proceeding in a systematic fashion by the late eighteenth century.[21]

European imperialism led to more extensive contacts across the Orient–Occident divide than what had occurred previously, leading to new Western "discoveries" of Eastern knowledge and languages, and in turn, the production of more texts, the formation of additional learned societies, and rise of new Orientalist authorities. This expansion of Western awareness and East–West interaction, however, also continued the production of difference while refining Europeans' understanding of how they were unlike Asians. With Europe's mastery over the globe via militarism and knowledge production, Westerners were less impressed and enthralled by contemporary Asia. If there was anything to be in awe of, it was Asia's past, and one of the underlying logics of modern empire building was that Europeans were "stirring an inert people" from "obscurity, alienation, and strangeness," and "raising them to their former greatness."[22]

As to why and how distorted perceptions persisted in the face of sustained contact from the eighteenth century on, it is important to consider the purpose and uses of knowledge. As long as the impulse to dominate, possess, or "know" the "Orient" framed Europe's relationship with Asia, then the primary function of knowledge produced and disseminated about it was to rationalize this interest by setting Europe apart from Asia as both *different* and *better*. Accuracy and thoroughness are, at best, secondary concerns. "Knowledge," says Said, "no longer [required] application to reality; knowledge is what [got] passed on silently, without comment, from one text to another."[23] Because knowledge about Asia has long been constructed and functioned within a framework of European desire, Orientalism has always been reductive, existing principally to affirm Western identity, expertise, and mastery. Its power derived from the long tradition of thought that it drew from, giving its tenets the power of "common sense." In other words, the Orient was backward because it was and people had been saying this for a long time. And although building empires required constant interaction between colonial authorities and subjects, most Europeans would never actually visit the "Orient" or encounter an Oriental person, and therefore remained reliant on the word of texts and purported experts. Because for most Europeans, encountering the "Orient" was limited to consuming objects and texts, there was little need or chance to understand its people as multidimensional beings. Nor was there much need for Orientalist consumers to update their knowledge. In his Introduction to a 1908 edition of Marco Polo's *Travels*, John Mansfield wrote that, "[Polo's] picture of the East is the picture which we all make in our minds when we repeat to ourselves those two strange words, 'the East,' and give ourselves up to the image which that symbol evokes."[24]

Orientalism in America

Turning to the significance of European Orientalism for Asian American history, we consider the migration of such ideas across the Atlantic from 1492 on. Gary Okihiro states, as European explorers "arrived in the New World carrying the baggage of the Old World, Americans developed their own projections and invented their own mythologies, peering from their 'clearing' into the 'wilderness.'"[25] There were significant differences in how Europeans and Americans related to and discussed Asia but we can nonetheless find striking similarities and connections that demonstrate that Americans did not begin with a blank slate, and drew on European thought to make sense of their circumstances.

Not only did the Europeans who sailed across the Atlantic to the Americas come with distinct ideas about the Orient and East–West difference, but their "discovery" and conquest of the Americas were also bound up with Orientalist projections. It was the desire to find a westward sea route to India, after all, that led Christopher Columbus to embark on his fabled journey. He had been thrilled by tales of the Orient he had read in the works of Mandeville and Marco Polo, so much that his impressions of the New World resembled their descriptions of India in tone and content.[26] Believing he was somewhere near China, Columbus described the Bahamas as a beautiful and rich land. He noted, for instance, that the mouth of the Orinoco River was shaped "like a woman's nipple," which echoed the sensuous and sexualized imagery of places in the Orient.[27] Regarding the people, he took particular notice of their nakedness. Even after they realized that the Americas were not Asia but entirely separate land masses, they continued to view this part of the world as an opposite of their civilization and persisted in calling native people "Indians," thus shedding some light on how similarities in Westerners' perceptions of the indigenous people of Asia and the Americas originated.

Subsequent generations of European settlers and their descendants in North America, while eventually molding a separate identity from Europeans, shared their view of the "Orient" as a distant, exotic place. In the pre-Revolutionary British North America, it was England, not the "Orient", that represented colonists' most immediate and pressing "other." By the late eighteenth century, the culture of the colonies embodied what John Tchen describes as a "hybridizing Anglo–American identity," consisting of "British symbolic meanings and American revolutionary character."[28] During these years of revolution and nation building, the "Orient" clarified Americans' social, economic, and cultural values in a number of ways. Explaining how Orientalism differed on either side of the Atlantic, Vijay Prashad says that Americans shared the European view in which the Orient and Occident were separate worlds, dividing along the Levantine coast and representing contrasting cultures and opposite historical trajectories. Yet while European Orientalists "felt that the twain (of East and West) would never meet," American Orientalists "hoped for some transfer of values to benefit their new republic and prevents its decline into the morass of materialism."[29]

China, "an imagined place of fabulous luxuries, an advanced civilization that the founding fathers and mothers sought to emulate," held a prominent place in the minds of revolutionaries.[30] Specifically, Chinese objects and ideas played an instrumental role in the formation of U.S. cultural and national identity. Americans shared Europeans' taste for and fascination with Chinese luxury goods, culture, and civilization, manifesting in their protest against British trade regulations. One of the flash-points leading to the War for Independence, we might recall, was a fight over access to Asian commodities when the Boston Tea party protested British tax policy that protected the East India Company by dumping its tea from China into Boston harbor. Rather than being an act of disdain toward Chinese goods, it was an expression of the colonists' desire for fair and unfettered access to the products of the Orient and elsewhere. If restricting the consumption of such goods amounted to tyranny, then opening it up became crucial to many revolutionaries' understanding of freedom, highlighting the interconnections of American capitalist identity, cultural independence, and desire for refinement.[31]

Identified with elite culture, luxury goods signaled a person's inherited or attained status, or at the least the aspiration to achieve such rank. George Washington exemplified the individual who elevated himself from relatively humble origins and demonstrated his new social status in part through the consumption and display of objects of refinement. By partaking in rituals as tea drinking and collecting porcelain, he performed the roles of a proper gentleman and revolutionary leader. Washington was known for his love of exotic luxuries, even keeping them close in the midst of the war against Britain. "[His] insistence on having Chinese tea sets, or Wedgwood queensware, certainly reminded him and his officers, in the heat of battle, of his status and authority," notes Tchen.[32] In the new republic, participating in this material culture allowed elites, old and new, to shore up their status and cement relations with one another. The practice of paying calls to private residents for tea and conversation amid stylized tables and fine China was a means of establishing one's credibility and worth. The exchange of desired luxuries, moreover, could foster bonds of intimacy, friendship, and power. In the new republic, where the individual, as opposed to the family or village, became an increasingly central unit, socializing and gift giving were ways to establish personal ties. For example, when Alexander Hamilton and Elizabeth Schuyler received a Chinese enameled punch bowl for their 1780 wedding, the gift symbolized the Schuylers' acceptance of Hamilton into their circle.[33] When passed through the generations, these objects—from family crests to Chinese porcelains—maintained elite status and were crucial in rituals of refinement.

In addition to material objects, ideas from China were likewise influential among early Americans. Having access to writings about the Orient, by way of European travelers, some of the founding fathers became interested in Confucianism, particularly as a philosophy that could shed light on the links between personal virtue and state affairs. One source from which they learned about China was Jesuit priest Jean Baptiste De Halde's book, *The General History of China*, which highlighted such achievements as the Great Wall as products of moral and civil authority. Americans also read the works of Enlightenment thinkers like Voltaire and Quesnay, who praised China's stable and prosperous agricultural economy as a model for the West.[34] Thomas Jefferson and Benjamin Franklin were known for their interest in China, which they both studied while in Paris. In his writings, Franklin noted Chinese flora and fauna, windmills, the use of mulberry trees, rice cultivation, central heating and silk production, and explored how these things might be adopted in America.[35] As he once wrote, "Could we be so fortunate as to introduce the industry of the Chinese, their arts of living and improvement in husbandry ... America might become in time as populous as China."[36] Jefferson took interest in Confucian moral statecraft and the ways in which American prosperity could grow from applying its principles. A reader of books such as Du Halde's as well as Count Destutt de Tracy's *Treatise on Political Economy*, he extended his curiosities about China to objects and aesthetics as others of his social rank did. He once planned to have a miniaturized Chinese pavilion and temple built in Monticello and enjoyed plays such as the *Orphan of China*, a popular production based on a twelfth-century work by a Yuan Dynasty playwright that was performed in New York during the late eighteenth century.[37]

As revolutionaries and citizens of a new republic, Americans' views of China were different from Britain's. Representing a powerful empire with a long history, the British did not share Americans' enthusiasm for Confucian antiquity nor see its connections with Western Enlightenment traditions. As "the British Empire's fortunes and power rose," Tchen explains:

the China of contemporary geopolitics came to be viewed as outdated . . . [over-zealous] monarchs in China were despotic . . . However, debt-ridden Americans could ill afford to take on such an imperious British attitude. For them China was still a place to be admired and envied, a source of luxuries and the hoped-for savior of the American economy.[38]

After independence, Americans confronted daunting challenges, among them developing the Revolution's vision of economic wealth and sustainability. For many, this hinged on establishing trade and visions quickly fixed upon China. Alexander Hamilton was an especially strong proponent of this in his writings. In contrast to Franklin and Jefferson, he thought about China primarily in terms of the global exchange of goods and resources. Following the Revolution, Americans learned more about the possibilities of the China trade through travel narratives. An important source in this regard was John Ledyard's 1783 narrative about his voyage with Captain James Cook. This was the first book published in the United States describing the people, places, and resources of the Pacific, and marked the "Americanization of direct Western knowledge of the Pacific world."[39] Ledyard gave detailed descriptions of goods made by Chinese artisans, and noted what Chinese merchants would pay for North American commodities such as furs.

In New England, a group of investors hoped to act on this vision of generating wealth through trade with China and formed the American India Company. The main players included Robert Morris of Daniel Parker and Company, New England speculator Daniel Parker, French entrepreneur John Holker, New Yorker William Duer, and other merchants from Boston. Duer, Holker, Parker, and Morris devised ambitious plans that eventually had to be scaled down to an operation consisting of two ships, the *Empress of China* and the *Emperor of China*. They discovered that China would trade for ginseng, a highly prized but prohibitively expensive commodity that grew abundantly in America's Atlantic Coast.[40]

Though organizing the expedition was costly and marred by the scheming and swindling of partners, it culminated on February 22, 1784, when the *Empress of China* disembarked from New York harbor and journeyed to China around Cape Horn. The journey literally opened up a new frontier for Americans; prior to independence, British navigation restrictions prohibited colonial subjects from engaging in international trade, which effectively barred Americans from visiting "Cathay." Even the sea captain of the *Empress* did not know precisely how to get to his destination.[41] Nonetheless, the *Empress*'s maiden voyage stood out for many Americans at the time as a pivotal moment, symbolizing the new nation's confidence and hope for future prosperity. Newspapers of the northern Atlantic brimmed with optimism, and when the ship returned some fifteen months later, carrying tea, silk, nankeens, porcelains, fans, and other items, it was greeted by a fanfare and a thirteen-gun salute.

By the early nineteenth century, the China trade flourished and transformed New York, the nation, and American commercial culture. The prosperity it generated helped establish New York as the nation's largest city and one of its most crucial ports and immigrant gateways. Moreover, the trade produced a new merchant elite that included immigrants like Stephen Girard and John Jacob Astor.[42] By the early 1800s, New York had no less than six major China trade houses, which arranged sailings, ordered shipments from agents in Canton, and sold goods at auction.[43] Others profited indirectly from the China trade. These included William Russell Grace, an Irish immigrant, who with his father, made a fortune chartering guano shipments to San Francisco and New York, a trade that owed its growth to the shipment of Chinese coolie labor to South America. The rise of men like Astor and Grace signaled the emergence of a nouveau riche and the gentrification of New York. This group forged a bourgeois culture reflected in the new mansions that dotted the urban landscape and showcased their elite distinction through display of luxury goods from China court culture such as Ming vases and embroidered silk robes.[44]

The establishment of the China trade in the late eighteenth century also marked a new phase in the United States' relationship with Asia and Americans' attitudes about Asian people. The *Empress of China*'s voyage initiated direct U.S. involvement with China, which also, explains Tchen, commenced a "continuous cross-cultural process of interaction against which Western social, economic, and political values were constantly measured and contrasted."[45] Possessing Chinese things remained a mark of distinction, but Americans' attitudes about Chinese people, with whom they now directly interacted, became less admiring. It did not need to be this way, as direct contact can generate understanding and camaraderie, but the interactions here were guided and inherently limited by their context of capitalist trade relations. "The closer Americans got to real Chinese, dispelling their imagined 'Orient,' the more their respect for and emulation of Chinese civilization diminished," says Tchen. When frustrated, for instance, by Chinese traders' insistence on prices or terms that were unfavorable to their interests, Americans decried Chinese "despotism" and clung to their "superior" claims of "free trade."[46]

American traders' descriptions of Chinese practices became increasingly racialized and ethnocentric, ultimately leading them to embrace an identity rooted in their occidentalism that shared affinities with the European traders they encountered in Asian ports.[47] Americans disdainfully noted the "cowardly" and "submissive" nature of Chinese people, whom they also characterized as "silly grunts" and "menaces." They returned home with tales of the bizarre foodways of Chinese (dogs, cats, rats), their odd music ("mass of detestable discord") and their theater ("disgracefully obscene").[48] One remarked that Chinese people were "grossly superstitious," that "gambling [was] universal" among them, that "they use pernicious drugs," and were as a whole a "people refined in cruelty, bloodthirsty, and inhuman."[49] Samuel Shaw, a businessman who was part of the first *Empress of China* expedition, returned from bargaining sessions with Chinese merchants ridiculing their pidgin and behaviors he found comical.[50] He noted two types of Chinese merchants, explains Tchen: "the lowly trickster Chinaman and the refined merchant gentleman, whom he called a 'mandarin,' adept at Western ways."[51]

Such dehumanizing views would be reinforced in the coming decades with Asian immigration. The writings of early nineteenth-century American Protestant missionaries gave some indication of the changing direction of Americans' perceptions of Asia. As Derek Chang has explained, their "evangelical nationalism" was central to both American religiosity and the discourse of race. The first Baptist missionaries to Asia, Adoniram and Ann Judson, were posted in Burma in 1813, and their descriptions of the "heathen" and "savage" Burmese would soon be applied to other Asians. In 1834, the *American Baptist Missionary* said China was a country "hardly penetrated with a single ray of light . . . Nowhere has Satan a seat on earth to be compared in extent with that which he holds in seeming triumph . . . in the . . . so-called 'celestial empire.'"[52]

American Orientalists

While much of what they initially presumed about Asia came from Europe, people in the United States developed their own Orientalist traditions, fostered by the establishment of learned societies, the publication of Asian texts, and the emergence of a homegrown corps of writers, missionaries, and other authorities. Such developments showed Americans' growing cultural and intellectual independence during the nineteenth century, although this independence remained tied to invoking the "East" to wrestle with and clarify issues of national identity. And while consuming oriental goods and texts remained a mark of refinement in American life in the 1800s, also emerging at this time was a popular Orientalism that emphasized spectacle and wider participation. Writings about Asia, furthermore, expressed admiration and romantic longing, especially in light of the rapid changes sweeping the nation due to industrialization and modernization, but they also conveyed repulsion and disdain.

Along with China, India, with whom the United States had also started trading in the late eighteenth century, became the object of much cultural fascination during the 1800s. Indian texts were being published in America as early as 1805, and in Boston, where interest in India had become a fixture of elite culture, the city's upper crust was known as the Brahmins, taking its name from the highest caste of Indian society. In 1842, Boston's Brahmins started the American Oriental Society for the "cultivation of learning in the Asiatic, African and Polynesian languages."[53] Its journal, published from 1843 to 1900, contained articles about ancient Indian literature and philology. The life of the city's cultural elite was also characterized by the reading of popular books about India, acquiring Bengal ginghams and Calcutta goatskins, watching plays like *The Raja's Daughter* and *Cataract of the Ganges*, and singing songs such as "The Hindu Girl."[54]

As for India itself, Americans had mixed feelings. On the one hand, writers believed it was socially and politically inferior to the West, but on the other, the same individuals were enthralled by its religions and cultures and believed that Americans could learn much from them. Ralph Waldo Emerson, a reader of translated Asian texts, saw India as a largely deplorable place overcome by poverty and famine that nevertheless showed glimmers of genius, especially with respect to ancient knowledge. He wrote, "All tends to the mysterious East," articulating the view that no matter how repugnant contemporary India and the East were, it remained the cradle of civilization.[55] In contrast, Henry David Thoreau, a frequent critic of U.S. actions abroad, nonetheless expressed relief that "no Hindoo tyranny prevailed at the framing of the world, but we are freemen of the universe, and not sentenced to any caste."[56]

Despite the Orient's perceived shortcomings, some intellectuals and writers believed that its religions, texts, and other sources of ancient knowledge held valuable insights from which Americans could benefit. Toward disseminating these insights, Emerson and Thoreau edited several volumes of the transcendental philosophy journal *The Dial,* with selections from Indian and Chinese texts.[57] Thoreau lamented conditions associated with modernity in the mid-1800s, such as agrarian suffering and the growing factory system, which had produced an excess of material and spiritual hardship. He had sought escape from these ills in the bucolic environs of Walden, but he also believed that all Americans could overcome their alienation by tuning to the cultural and spiritual wealth of India. Walt Whitman, who held a more positive view of industry and technology—he celebrated the completion of the Suez Canal and transcontinental railroad in 1869—nonetheless thought that the pure spiritualism of India should be preserved and could bring salvation to Americans.[58] In 1868 he wrote the poem, "Passage to India," which extolled the idea that India's wisdom could help Americans.[59]

By the mid-nineteenth century, consuming Asian things evolved into a pursuit not limited to intellectuals and elites. Perhaps because commercialization drove this "popular orientalism," the phenomenon was rooted in spectacle and accompanied by an exaggerated flattening and fetishizing of Asia that left its redemptive qualities less discernible. Thus, the general public's knowledge about India, for instance, rather than becoming more nuanced with time, instead drew increasingly on sources like the fantasy tales of *Arabian Nights*.[60] Besides reading popular stories, people could encounter the Orient by gazing at objects collected by whites who had traveled there. In 1847, for instance, Charles Huffnagle, a former U.S. consul in Calcutta, opened a museum called Springdale at his home in New Hope, Pennsylvania. There, visitors could see his collection of Brahman bulls, safari trophies, books, household objects, and other objects, and also taste crystallized Calcutta sugar and rare Assam teas.[61] The same year in New York, an Australian sea captain opened to the public a Chinese vessel called *Keying* in Castle Gardens. For 25 cents people could view goods from the China trade as well as the crew, which included a Chinese man called "Eesing" who was described as a "specimen of the second class of Mandarins."[62] The ship drew an estimated 50,000 people, and the *New York Herald* said that it "convey[ed] to us a better idea of the natives of China than all we could gather by reading a score of books on the subject."[63] The *Herald* commented on the strangest and most taboo aspects of the *Keying* exhibit, such as opium and the odd names and expressionless faces of the Chinese, perpetuating the view of China as quaint but backward.

As the United States grew into a confident young nation, Americans' relationship with the "Orient" changed as well. As described above, during the late eighteenth century, in consuming oriental luxuries and reading about its civilizations, American elites mimicked European practices, although they also held the Orient in awe for its longevity and how the new nation might learn from it. With industrialization, many continued to look to Asia, especially for things like the "pure spiritualism" of India as an antidote to what they felt was lacking or endangered in their own lives. Yet, as people remained enthralled and humbled by the "mysterious Orient," Americans also sought mastery over it, whether by collecting objects and creating exhibits, becoming literary experts, or undertaking missionary work to uplift its people, acts that in turn reinforced a growing confidence in American values and practices. By the late nineteenth century, this mastery extended to the production of Chinese objects. In 1876, at the Philadelphia world exposition, where Americans celebrated the nation's centennial, the items on display included the porcelain work of Karl Muller. This was a landmark exhibit, explains John Tchen, that exemplified American mastery of Chinese material culture and underscored how over the nineteenth century, "admiration [toward China] shifted first to emulation and then again to a sense of civilizational mastery."[64]

Slavery, Coolies, and Freedom

As shown above, during critical moments in the nation's history, the "Orient" was variously imagined as the source of objects and wisdom that would help Americans achieve their independence in the late 1700s or meet the challenges of modern life in the early to mid-1800s. It was also a useful "other" that affirmed American mastery and self-confidence against the backdrop of great transformations in the late nineteenth century. Another time that stands out is the 1860s when, amid sectional conflict and the reconstruction of the South, the presence—or *specter*—of Asians informed changing notions of freedom and citizenship, particularly with respect to race and labor. Moon-Ho Jung has discussed how the figure of the Chinese "coolie" loomed over debates between pro and anti-slavery forces before, during, and after the Civil War, clarifying their positions on and understandings of free and unfree labor. The term coolie referred to imported Asian contract laborers, mostly from China and South Asia, and worldwide demand for them intensified after 1807 when Britain banned the slave trade throughout its empire.[65] As other colonial powers followed suit or faced pressure to do so, slave owners searched for alternative labor sources to maintain their plantations, and many turned to coolies. Between 1838 and 1870 over five hundred thousand Chinese and South Asian men were shipped to labor in places such as Cuba, Peru, Mauritius, Demerara (British Guiana), Brazil, Trinidad, Jamaica, Natal, and Reunion.[66] Heralded as "free labor," coolieism seemed to depart from the worst aspects of slavery, as it purportedly relied on voluntary contracts and legal rights. In practice, however, the freedom of coolies was illusory. Procurers and employers used kidnapping, deception, and corporal punishment, and frequently coerced or tricked coolies into entering eight-year contracts for fixed wages. Conditions on ships were atrocious, and things were rarely better at their destinations. In Peruvian guano cultivation, for example, coolies worked in scorching heat alongside slaves, and the large amounts of ammonia they were exposed to often caused their eyes and skin to burn and their noses to bleed. Life was so unbearable that it was not uncommon for coolies to commit suicide.[67]

By the 1850s, as rising abolitionist sentiment in the United States stirred passionate debates about the future of slavery, just as coolieism was taking off in the Caribbean, the coolie trade increasingly drew the attention of Americans. Some engaged directly in the trade, as American ships were responsible for transporting tens of thousands of coolies between Asia and the Americas, and others benefited indirectly by trading goods produced by coolie labor (e.g., Pervian guano).[68] Meanwhile, defenders and opponents of slavery became intrigued and alarmed by the possibility of coolieism's extension to the American South, and this debate, which raged in publications and the halls of Congress for much of the 1860s, had lasting effects on notions of race and nation for many years after emancipation.

As a racialized category in between free and slave labor, coolies had no place in a nation headed toward emancipation and where free labor and immigration were touchstones of civic membership.[69] Popular nineteenth-century understandings of coolieism in America tended to conflate the practice with any form of imported Chinese labor, which not only made legislating against it difficult, but also shaped the perception that Chinese immigrant laborers threatened the dignity and wellbeing of the American—usually white, male—working class and hence American values of uplift and independence. An 1862 law prohibiting the coolie trade illustrated these dilemmas. In debates leading to its passage, members of Congress tried to distinguish between voluntary and coerced migration, with the intent to encourage the former and outlaw the latter. Representative Thomas D. Eliot of Massachusetts explained that Chinese cooliesm was "unchristian and inhuman, disgraceful to the merchant and the master, oppressive to the ignorant and betrayed laborers, a reproach upon our national honor, and a crime before God as deeply dyed as that piracy which forfeits life when the coasts of Africa supply its victims."[70] Other representatives, however, pointed out that Chinese migration to California was "voluntary and profitable mutually to the contracting parties." Despite these attempts to distinguish between free and unfree Chinese labor and gestures toward protecting the former, the final version of the anti-coolie bill was vague. It outlawed the shipping of Chinese subjects "known as coolies" abroad "to be held in service or labor," but did not provide a clear definition of what a coolie was. Despite initial intentions to include it, the phrase "against their will and without their consent" was stricken from the final legislation.[71] Though it specified that "any free and voluntary emigration of any Chinese subject" should continue, by not explicating how to determine who was involuntary and by singling out Chinese, the law contributed to the racialization of Chinese as a degraded class of labor.[72] Additionally the burden fell on Chinese migrants to prove that they were "free and voluntary." While this process would be detrimental for Chinese, it opened a channel for the acceptance of blacks and white immigrants (as freed people or free laborers) and shored up the centrality of free labor and immigration as cornerstones of American identity.[73] In other parts of America, the presence and specter of Chinese laborers, indiscriminately called "coolies," helped unite white wageworkers behind resisting cooliesm and other degraded forms of labor that the "Asiatics" represented. As Chapter 6 will discuss further, fears of "coolieism" and Chinese labor, while originating in emancipation, eventually dominated national debates and led to Chinese exclusion.

Manifest Destiny Across the Continent and the Pacific

By the late nineteenth century, Orientalism encompassed more than songs, books, and objects, having tangible impacts on U.S. diplomatic objectives and actions. One of the driving forces of Western territorial expansion was to bring Americans closer to the markets of Asia, and after reaching the Pacific Coast, they pushed on until, "the Far West [became] the Far East."[74] This phrase, coined by McKinley's Secretary of State John Hay, made explicit how Americans' pursuit of interests across the Pacific continued an ongoing process, a process whose roots lay in the European voyages of discovery. "America's manifest destiny," states Gary Okihiro, "was 'an additional chapter' in the Orientalist text of Europe's 'dominating, restructuring, and having authority over' Asia."[75] In this respect, the United States' relations with Asian countries in the second half of the nineteenth century might be called the second period of America's manifest destiny, informed by enduring assumptions about the "East" and driven by growing American confidence as a world power.

By the mid-1800s, after several decades of commercial relations with China and a burgeoning missionary enterprise, the United States turned its attention on Japan, with the intention of "opening" it to Western influence and domination, as Britain had with China after the Opium War. For Secretary of State William Seward, this would be a step toward building the United States' "empire of free trade" across the Pacific.[76] Despite their limited contact, Americans already held distinct views about Japan. The *American Whig Review* said it was so backward that its people "hardly go forward a year during the century," while the *North American Review* explained that this was the result of being closed off from much of the world, although it was possible the country could be rescued from its backwardness.[77] While such remarks reflected generally held views about the "Orient," people did distinguish between China and Japan, especially on the eve of an American expedition to the latter in the early 1850s. The *Atlantic Monthly*, for instance, said that China was corrupt and degraded, while Japan showed vigor, thrift and intelligence.[78]

In 1853, the United States sent Commodore Matthew Perry to Japan to open the country to commercial and diplomatic relations with the West. Faced with the threat of force—Perry arrived with warships—the emperor agreed to commence international trade. In the wake of this encounter, which had exposed Japan's weaknesses against Western imposition, a new government took power in 1868 and implemented a program of rapid modernization. Also following the Perry expedition, American writers depicted and took credit for Japan's "awakening." Henry M. Field's 1877 travelogue *From Egypt to Japan* purported to build bridges between Americans and foreigners, but did so with a condescending point of view that placed Japan within old Orientalist tropes. "If these pictures of Asia make it a little more real, and inspire the feeling of a common nature with the dusky races that live on the other side of the globe, and so infuse a larger knowledge and a gentler clarity then a traveller's tale may serve as a kind of lay sermon, teaching peace and good will to men."[79] Japan's opening was just the most recent chapter in the West's "civilizing" of the East. Britain, Field said, was educating India about justice, a noble cause considering "the Asiatic nature is torpid and slow to move, and cannot rouse itself to great exertion."[80] The latest to join in this civilization mission was the United States, and chronicling of Japan's "progress" helped to shore up Americans' authority and identity as Westerners bringing light to other parts of the world.

In 1870, the United States hoped to repeat its success in Japan and "open" Korea, despite the country's longstanding non-intercourse policy. In charge of the expedition was Frederick F. Low, a businessman whose experience as a congressman and governor of California—the state with the largest Chinese population—purportedly gave him insights about Koreans. American contact with Korea had been limited to few unofficial encounters, but this did not stop members of the expedition from making hard and fast conclusions about the country's people, as they believed that their knowledge about one group of Asians could be seamlessly applied to another. In a letter to his wife, Adm. John Rodgers, the expedition's commander, revealed his limited knowledge, writing, "The Coreans [sic] are a stiff necked people . . . but there are said to be two parties, the liberals and tory's. Those who wish their rules relaxed and those who would not give anything—but really we know very little about them."[81] He was not troubled, however, because as he wrote elsewhere, "Asians, whether in Singapore, Hong Kong, Japan, or Shanghai, [are] physically repugnant and their ways either disagreeable or childishly quaint."[82] Before he departed for Korea, he wrote to his wife that he and other Westerners in Shanghai were enjoying Bret Harte's "The Heathen Chinee," a popular poem that perpetuated stereotypes of Chinese deception and trickery, which shaped many readers' perceptions of Asian people before they ever encountered one in real life.[83]

Employing tactics similar to those used in Japan, the U.S. sent a force of five warships to Korea in spring 1871, but rather than having the same outcome, a short battle, which the *New York Herald* described as "Our Little War with the Heathen," ensued. The United States turned around and went home, achieving nothing but ill-will and misunderstanding.[84] The Koreans, meanwhile, believed they had defeated Western encroachment and vindicated their policy of seclusion. Americans disputed their version of events and compared the Koreans' fighting to that of animals, Indians, and demons. Insisting that he had taught the Koreans a lesson, Low ridiculed Korea as the "only nation on earth claiming to be civilized" that simultaneously refused to "hold intercourse of any sort with the Christian countries of Europe and America."[85] In the aftermath of the war, he and Rodgers doubled down on their conviction of the backwardness and inferiority of all of Asia, not just Korea. As Low said, "the Oriental civilization is as distinct from ours as darkness is from light. There is no similarity in our language or modes of thought."[86] He drew on his experience to become an ardent supporter of Chinese exclusion, testifying to a congressional committee in 1876. In 1882, the year that Chinese exclusion was achieved, the United States returned to Korea, this time successfully concluding a treaty.

The annexation of the Philippines after the Spanish–American War of 1898 culminated over a century of U.S. ambitions in Asia. With this step into formal empire, Americans drew on an extensive archive of ideas about the Orient and its people to justify its actions and rationalized annexation without upsetting the Orient–Occident divide. Americans claimed it was the "duty and destiny of the United States to share its talent for democratic development and save the Filipinos from civilizational ruin," although as Senator Albert Beveridge pointed out, the possibilities of spreading American commercial and naval influence also factored into the decision to take the Philippines.[87] Interestingly, arguments both for and against annexation turned on Filipino "otherness," as annexationists wanted to take on the work of "civilizing the savages," while opponents doubted such a backward population could be uplifted. "Not in a hundred years, nay, not in a thousand years can we lift the Philippine Islands and the mixed races that there inhabit to the level of civilization which this land, God-blessed, possesses," said Senator John Daniel from Virginia.[88] Because they had little, if any, direct interaction with the Philippines and its people, anti-imperialists relied on their shaky knowledge about other Asians to make their case. Representatives from western states, for instance, claimed that being from regions with large Chinese immigrant populations gave them an understanding of all "orientals." Francis Newlands of Nevada warned that Filipinos would be "invited here in swarms by speculators of labor, as were the Chinese," resulting in a foreign invasion.[89]

Through the annexation debates, as with earlier discussions about Chinese coolies and "opening" East Asia, U.S. officials and opinion-makers reflected on and defined the substance and boundaries of American civic identity. The Philippine episode reinforced the racialized dimensions of this identity and its grounding in the capacity for self-government and vague notions of "civilization." Casting the people of the Philippines outside the boundaries of potential U.S. national belonging allowed for the perpetuation of the Orient–Occident divide; the U.S. exercised its dominance over the territory, but in denying Filipinos there and in America equal legal standing, upheld barriers between the East and West.

Conclusion

With early U.S.–Asia contact established by traders and missionaries, a handful of Asian people took up opportunities to come to the United States in the late eighteenth to nineteenth centuries, mostly ending up on the East Coast and other places far from the traditional Asian immigrant population centers. According to John Tchen, the first documented visit of a Chinese person to New York City was by a merchant named "Chong," who came in 1808 to collect money owed to him by American business agents, although there is also evidence of Chinese domestic servants in the city as early as the 1790s.[90] The earliest known case of a Chinese person attaining naturalized U.S. citizenship was a Cantonese resident of Boston named Atit in 1845.[91] With regard to South Asians, trade had also resulted in the appearance of Indians in U.S. port cities. In Salem, Massachusetts, young Indians who had come to the United States with American sea captains were found as early as the 1790s, working on the wharves.[92] It is believed they married black women and joined the local African American community, eventually disappearing from the historical record.[93]

These early Asian arrivals usually came as servants of traders, students of missionaries, independent merchants, or entertainers, and if they did not assimilate into the larger society or nearby communities, they stood out as oddities whose presence catered to curious white Americans. American missionaries played a key role in bringing Asians this kind of attention, often with the goals of raising money and support for their missions. Among the pioneers in this regard was Rev. William J. Boone of South Carolina, founder of the American Episcopal Mission in China and China's first Episcopal bishop.[94] After being appointed a missionary to China by the Foreign Committee of the Board of Missions, he set off with his wife Sarah in 1837 to work among the Chinese in Batavia and Macao. After Sarah died in 1842, Boone returned to America with his children and two Chinese, a language teacher Sin Sy and servant Wong Kong Chai. He traveled with them along the east coast to raise interest in China missions, often referring to them and their homeland as "heathen."

Other Asians were presented in ways that catered to Americans' appetite for the exotic, and exhibits of "oriental curiosities" became quite commonplace over the nineteenth century. Afong Moy, believed to be the first Chinese woman to appear in the United States for an entertainment exhibition, was displayed in New York in 1834 under the title, "Chinese lady." Usually donning a Qing dynasty gown and surrounded by oriental objects, she appeared in theaters, often on bills with magicians and other entertainers. In addition to gazing at Moy and her "monstrous" bound feet, visitors could purchase engravings with her likeness.[95] In 1849, the merchant John Peters opened the Great Chinese Museum in New York, arguably the largest exhibition of curiosities outside of Asia and promoted by the *New York Herald* for offering visitors a chance to see Chinese life in person. The Museum conveyed mixed feelings about China, showing admiration for aspects of its government and culture, but also looking down on Chinese religions, the emperor, and patriarchal power. Not long after it opened, P.T. Barnum took over the Museum. Barnum, perhaps the most successful commercial orientalist of his time, had an "oriental villa" called Iranistan built in Fairfield, Connecticut, and one of his aims for the Museum was to make it more amenable for popular consumption. One of the changes he made toward this end was adding the display of a "Chinese lady," Pwan Yee Koo, and her "family."[96] Barnum was ambivalent about the "Orient" and China, once saying, "unlike the notions many of us have formed of the rising generation among the odd people, we are compelled to admit that these specimens of 'young China' are really pretty, graceful and intelligent."[97]

The most popular "oriental" performers from the nineteenth century were Chang and Eng Bunker. Also known as the "Siamese Twins," they were conjoined twins born in 1811 to a Chinese fisherman father and part-Chinese, part-Malaysian mother in Siam, and they thought of themselves as Chinese. They were "discovered" by Captain Abel Coffin in 1829, who, along with managers James Hale and Charles Harris, took them on tour across the United States and the world where they performed for overflow audiences. Chang and Eng usually appeared in venues decorated like Victorian parlors and would be dressed in elegant Western suits or Chinese costumes, sometimes even performing acrobatics during their shows, as if to bring attention to the abnormality of their bodies and racial backgrounds. Despite their fame, Chang and Eng never spoke in their own voice. Instead, their white handlers crafted their personas and identities to the public, representing them as upstanding yet childlike and inferior due to their race and origin. For instance, James Hale wrote a pamphlet stressing the backwardness of Siam and Chang and Eng's eagerness to become Americanized.[98]

As mentioned earlier, Americans were enthralled by the "pure spirituality" of India especially as a counterpoint to their own problems and excesses. It was just a matter of time, then, that they would seek out Indian people to impart their mystical knowledge. The best known of these was Vendatist Swami Vivekananda, who first visited the United States in 1893 at the World's Parliament of Religions in Chicago. Though his message may have been troubling to Christian missionaries, he became an instant celebrity and subsequently embarked on a tour of the United States. His success paved the way for other Indian swamis who preached to Americans and established Vendata centers.[99] Disturbed by the popularity of commercial orientalist entertainments, Vivekananda insisted that his appearances not be collapsed with "heathen shows," but he nonetheless played up the East–West divide. While the West was adept in matters such as business, the East's strength, he said, was spirituality, and he sought to carve out an authoritative, albeit essentialized, role for Indians as spiritual teachers for Americans, ushering in what Vijay Prashad has termed the "circus of the transcendental."[100]

With growing national confidence and greater, albeit still limited, contact with Asian people, Americans' perceptions of the "Orient" changed over the late eighteenth and nineteenth centuries. Once associated with refinement and civilization, Asian people were increasingly regarded as inferior peoples.[101] To be sure, there were subtle differences in how different groups and countries were perceived. Japan, for instance, while inferior and uncivilized, had potential (not equality) if it followed the Western model of modernization. India was more spiritually refined than the West, but this was owing to its static and pre-modern condition. Indeed, while the East was broadly inferior to the West, there were still things about the "Orient" that intrigued Americans, which captures one of the paradoxes of Orientalism. They wanted to encounter Indian "God men" whose ancient spirituality would make them more enlightened. They wanted to gaze upon the odd and monstrous bodies of Chinese people to quench their curiosity and reinforce their own normality. And they wanted to teach "heathens" whose transformation validated the Christian missionary enterprise. Ultimately such contacts helped to establish boundaries and define who and what Americans were by highlighting who and what they were not. Americans were modern, civilized, and

Figure 1.1   An engraving of the Bunker twins, also known as the "Siamese twins," 1839. Eng is to the left, holding a book, and Chang is to the right. For many Americans during the nineteenth century, the conjoined twins from Asia represented the ultimate exotic spectacle. (In the Chang and Eng Bunker Papers #3761, Southern Historical Collection, Wilson Library, University of North Carolina at Chapel Hill.)

forward moving. Asians could sometimes assist them by enriching their cultural lives, but they could not be one of them.

A final example illustrating how the dynamics of orientalism and empire solidified ideas about U.S. national identity and the foreignness of Asian bodies comes from the turn of the twentieth century. After the Spanish–American War, Americans still knew very little about the Philippines. One way that the inhabitants of the newly acquired territory were introduced to a larger public was by putting them on display, first at world expositions and then on national tours, sometimes as sideshow performers. In America, the first opportunity to see Filipinos in this manner was in 1904 when federal officials for the St. Louis world's fair organized an ethnological exhibit of natives. Called the "Philippine Reservation," it displayed 1,100 Filipinos and an array of artifacts and structures. Although the Filipinos were featured in varied settings, including a classroom, to demonstrate the possibility of uplift, the most popular exhibits were of the so-called savage tribes, the Negritos and Igorottes.[102] Described by the *Los Angeles Times* as "a most excellent place for the benevolent assimilation of ideas regarding the subjects of our first experiments in colonial government," this and similar exhibits marked the triumph of American mastery and power over these backward, dusky people of the East.[103]

As the discussions above have shown, from the U.S. perspective, a presumption of difference informed U.S.–Asia relations long before and during periods of Asian migration. Asia had exotic commodities that Americans wanted, ancient spirituality that would enhance their lives, or a backwardness that needed to be corrected. However, by the mid-nineteenth century, Americans took an additional interest in Asia; they wanted laborers from this part of the world, and to import them by the thousands to develop Hawaii plantations, build North American railroads, work in industrial factories, and cultivate the agricultural fields of the American West. In the face of mass migration, which the following chapter examines, the place of Asian people in America would change, although Americans' assumption of fundamental East–West difference endured well into the twentieth century.

Notes

1 "Asian Seafarers May Have Been North America's First Inhabitants," *Vancouver Sun*, August 20, 2007.
2 Gary Okihiro, *Margins and Mainstreams: Asians in American History and Culture* (Seattle: University of Washington Press, 1994), 7.
3 Edward Said, *Orientalism* (New York: Pantheon Books, 1978), 1.
4 Ibid., 3.
5 Ibid., 56.
6 In another example, the philosopher Aristotle explained the distinctiveness of Greek civilization, remarking that northern Europeans were "full of spirit, but wanting in intelligence and skill" and Asians were "intelligent and inventive," but lacked spirit, and were, thus, "always in a state of subjection and slavery." Greeks benefited from being in between the groups and were both "high-spirited and also intelligent." Okihiro, *Margins and Mainstreams*, 8.
7 Ibid., 9–10.
8 Ibid., 15.
9 In the story, Alexander had to kill these women "because of their obscenity" and "strangeness" and to "[make] the world sane and sage again." Quoted in Ibid., 10.

10 Ibid., 13–14.
11 Said, *Orientalism*, 59.
12 Ibid., 67.
13 Ibid., 59, 62–63, 66.
14 Ibid., 69.
15 Okihiro, *Margins and Mainstreams*, 13.
16 Ibid., 14.
17 Ibid., 15.
18 Ibid., 11.
19 Said, *Orientalism*, 67.
20 Ibid., 21.
21 This process was epitomized for Said in Napoleon's invasion of Egypt in 1798 after which contact between the East and West was primarily directed by the imperatives of Western imperialism. Ibid., 210.
22 Ibid., 121.
23 Ibid., 116.
24 Quoted in Okihiro, *Margins and Mainstreams*, 14.
25 Ibid., 23.
26 Vijay Prashad, *The Karma of Brown Folk* (Minneapolis: University of Minnesota Press, 2000), 2.
27 Okihiro, *Margins and Mainstreams*, 17.
28 John Tchen, *New York Before Chinatown: Orientalism and the Shaping of American Culture* (Baltimore: Johns Hopkins Press, 2001).
29 Prashad, *The Karma of Brown Folk*, 13.
30 Tchen, *New York Before Chinatown*, xv.
31 To be sure, Americans were of many different minds on the value of luxury commodities. There was debate about whether luxury goods were corrupting. This spoke to the danger that love of luxuries from China and the Indies represented the antithesis of Anglo–American virtue and bred addiction and corruption. English radical Catharine Macaulay as well as Benjamin Franklin had written about this fear of dependency and how it had ruined England. On the other hand, pro-commerce philosophers like David Hume disagreed, saying it was bad government, not bad things that people should worry about.
32 Ibid., 4.
33 Ibid., 14.
34 Ibid., 16–17.
35 Ibid., 17.
36 Ibid.
37 Ibid., 17, 21.
38 Ibid., 21.
39 Title is *A Journal of Captain Cook's Last Voyage to the Pacific Ocean, and in Quest of a North-West Passage between Asia and America, Performed in the Years 1776, 1777, 1778, and 1779*. Ibid., 26.
40 It was prohibitively expensive in China due to the imperial monopoly.
41 Ibid., 33.
42 Ibid., 46–47.
43 These included N.L. and G Griswold, Goodhue and Company, Grinnell, Minturn, and Company, Howland and Aspinall, Talbot Olyphant and Company, A.A. Low and Brothers.
44 Ibid., 56.
45 Ibid., 38.
46 Ibid., 25–26.
47 Ibid., 35.
48 Okihiro, *Margins and Mainstreams*, 24.
49 Ibid.
50 Tchen, *New York Before Chinatown*, 36.
51 Ibid.

52 Derek Chang, *Citizens of a Christian Nation: Evangelical Missions and the Problem of Race in the Nineteenth Century* (Philadelphia: University of Pennsylvania Press, 2010), 25–26.

53 Prashad, *The Karma of Brown Folk*, 14–15.

54 Joan Jensen, *Passage from India: Asian Indian Immigrants in North America* (New Haven: Yale University Press, 1988), 14.

55 Prashad, *The Karma of Brown Folk*, 11, 13.

56 Ibid., 13.

57 Ibid., 16.

58 Ibid., 20.

59 Jensen, *Passage from India*, 14.

60 Prashad, *The Karma of Brown Folk*, 27.

61 Ibid., 30.

62 Tchen, *New York Before Chinatown*, 64.

63 Quoted in Ibid., 67.

64 Ibid., 59.

65 Moon-Ho Jung, *Coolies and Cane: Race, Labor and Sugar in the Age of Emancipation* (Baltimore: Johns Hopkins Press, 2006), 5.

66 Tchen, *New York Before Chinatown*, 49.

67 Ibid., 50.

68 Ibid.

69 Jung, *Coolies and Cane*, 5.

70 Ibid., 34.

71 Ibid., 37.

72 Ibid.

73 Ibid., 143.

74 Quoted in Okihiro, *Margins and Mainstreams*, 28.

75 Ibid., 27.

76 Akira Iriye, *From Nationalism to Internationalism: U.S. Foreign Policy to 1914* (London: Routledge, 1977), 8.

77 Ibid., 8–9.

78 Ibid., 9.

79 Ibid., 13.

80 Ibid., 14.

81 Gordon Chang, "Whose 'Barbarism'? Whose 'Treachery'? Race and Civilization in the Unknown United States–Korea War of 1871," *Journal of American History*, Vol. 89 No. 4 (March 2003): 3.

82 Ibid., 5.

83 Ibid.

84 Ibid., 18.

85 Ibid., 16, 18.

86 Ibid., 19.

87 Rick Baldoz, *The Third Asiatic Invasion: Migration and Empire in Filipino America, 1898–1946* (New York: New York University Press, 2011), 22, 26.

88 Quoted in Ibid., 28.

89 Quoted in Ibid., 29.

90 Tchen, 42, 79.

91 Ibid., 79.

92 Jensen, *Passage from India*, 12.

93 Prashad, *The Karma of Brown Folk*, 14.

94 Lucy Cohen, *Chinese in the Post-Civil War South: A People Without a History* (Baton Rouge: Louisiana State University Press, 1984), 2.

95 Tchen, *New York Before Chinatown*, 103.

96 Ibid., 133.

97 Quoted in Tchen, 120.

98 On Chang and Eng, see Tchen, *New York Before Chinatown*, chapter 5 and Cynthia Wu, *Chang and Eng Reconnected: The Original Siamese Twins in American Culture* (Philadelphia: Temple University Press, 2012).

99 Jensen, *Passage from India*, 15.

100 Prashad, *The Karma of Brown Folk*, 35–36.

101 Tchen, *New York Before Chinatown*, 151.

102 Baldoz, *The Third Asiatic Invasion*, 40.

103 Ibid.

The Asian Diaspora in the Pre-Exclusion Years

2

In December 1906, five-year-old Mary Paik Lee arrived via ship with her parents in San Francisco, California. Having left their native Korea a few years earlier, the family had spent time in Hawaii, where Paik's father worked as a plantation laborer. Their first moments in San Francisco were memorable, but not in an exhilarating Ellis Island arrival sort of way. "As we walked down the gangplank," she recalled, "a group of young white men were standing around, waiting to see what kind of creatures were disembarking . . . They laughed at us and spit in our faces; one man kicked up Mother's skirt and called us names we couldn't understand."[1]

Around this time, Rufina Clemente Jenkins also arrived in California from the Philippines with her husband, an American soldier named Frank Jenkins, and their young daughter. Born in Naga, Nueva Caceres, Rufina was the daughter of a Spanish father and Filipina mother. Her parents planned to send her to school in Spain, but abandoned this idea due to the outbreak of the Spanish–American War. She met her future husband while he was stationed in Manila following the U.S. victory over Spain.[2] Shortly after the birth of their daughter in 1902 Jenkins was posted in California, so the couple moved to the United States. Five years later the family moved back to the Philippines, only to return to the United States again in 1909. Settling this time in Fort Lawton, Rufina would be one of first Filipinos in the Seattle, Washington area.

We begin this chapter with these stories because while they are atypical—few Asian women came to the United States at this time—they illustrate important points about Asian migration to the United States in the nineteenth and early twentieth centuries, the years of relatively open migration before U.S. laws effectively closed the gates. Lee's story highlights themes such as labor migration, American racism against Asians, and the pattern of serial migration in which immigrants rarely had a single destination. Clemente Jenkins' life, on the other hand, illustrates the impact not just of the world economy, but also of empire on migration, which were especially salient for Filipinos but also affected other Asian groups.

A global and diasporic approach to Asian migration to the United States in the nineteenth and early twentieth centuries illuminates how this movement was a phenomenon of developing international networks, the spread of capitalism, and the rise of economic and political imperialism. Among the developments setting the stage for this movement of people were the demise of African slavery by Western powers and persistent labor needs in their far-flung colonies; European incursions into Asia; and the modernization and capitalist transformation of two newcomers to empire, the United States and Japan. Moreover, the migrations precipitated by events like the discovery of gold in California, Alaska, Canada, and Australia generated their own momentum that sustained the flows of people across oceans and continents decades after the triggering events.

Asian migration in the nineteenth and early twentieth centuries, although unprecedented in scope and volume, did not mark a clean break with the past. In the communities from which many emigrants came, leaving home for opportunities abroad had long been a strategy for coping with uncertainty. Furthermore, those who arrived in the United States tended to be from places with histories of contact with Westerners and other foreigners. Although their reasons for leaving varied from education, business opportunities, political persecution, and other motivations, most Asian overseas migrants during this time were male laborers. They were generally not the most destitute members of their societies, instead coming from the ranks of fallen middle classes, displaced by external forces and willing to risk it all to better their lives. Most considered themselves temporary migrants, although not all would return home.

Figure 2.1   Photo of the Paik family in Korea: Shin Ku Paik, Kuang Do Song, Meung Sun and Kwang Son Paik, and five others, 1905. Kuang Son (also known as Mary Paik Lee) is the child seated in the front center. The Paiks were unusual in that few family units immigrated to Hawaii or the United States at this time. (Korean American Digital Archive, Korean Heritage Library, University of Southern California.)

This chapter explores the international context of migration, the influx of Asians to Hawaii and the United States during the nineteenth and early twentieth centuries, and their initial encounters in America, pointing out the ways that these movements were both new and continuations of existing traditions. It examines the varied motivations for emigration, and while discussing commonalities among Chinese, Japanese, Korean, Indian, and Filipino experiences, the chapter also explores distinct circumstances shaping each group's history. Building on the work of Edna Bonacich, Lucie Cheng, and others who have argued that capitalist development and imperialism "distorted the development of colonized territories" and created conditions that displaced people and made them available for emigration, the chapter centralizes economic and imperialistic dimensions of migration and sets the story of Asian immigration against a global backdrop, underscoring how it was not unidirectional and U.S.-centric, but rather diasporic.[3]

Most Asian immigrants crossed the Pacific Ocean, and in the early 1900s were processed at Angel Island in the San Francisco Bay, the less-storied counterpart to New York's Ellis Island. Most labor migrants rode in the steerage of large ships and endured month-long, sickness-filled journeys. Others entered the United States clandestinely, sneaking across the Canadian or Mexican borders to evade exclusion laws. Yet others never had any choices to make in how or whether to come, such as the hundreds, possibly thousands, of young women sold into prostitution or servitude. While journeying to America was, to be sure, a momentous event in the lives of individual immigrants—a leap of "extravagance," "overblown with hope," describes historian Ronald Takaki—it was also part of a broader movement embedded in a distinct global historical context. Asians were far from the only people migrating at the time, and the United States was just one of many destinations. Furthermore, as stated, most Asian immigrants to America came intending to stay temporarily. Although many did settle permanently, and, along with their children, came to identify themselves as American, their new lives did not begin with clearly laid paths, and none could know where they would lead.

Chinese Migration

The first Asians to come to the United States in significant numbers, Chinese immigrants were part of a diaspora stemming from changes triggered by Western incursions during the nineteenth century. This diaspora was diverse and expansive, encompassing free laborers and coerced "coolies," elite merchants and landless peasants, and sojourners and permanent settlers. Although conditions during the nineteenth century shaped the characteristics and scope of Chinese migration, emigration as a means of coping with change was not new, as people had engaged in maritime trade and labor emigration since the fourteenth century. In southern China, labor sojourning was a common response to population growth, reduced acreage per person, and other disruptive effects of economic commercialization. Migration initially stayed within China, but by the eighteenth century, overseas migration, mostly to Southeast Asia, became common.[4] This movement emanated chiefly from the southeastern provinces—Fujian, Guangdong, and Hainan Island—where residents, due to their coastal location and relative remoteness from the rest of China, had developed regular contact with foreigners, familiarity with seafaring, and knowledge of opportunities abroad.

Cantonese from Guangdong's Pearl River delta region would make up the primary group of Chinese immigrants to North America. In the Philippines, Java, Borneo, Siam, and elsewhere in Southeast Asia, Chinese worked as farmers, craftsmen, plantation laborers, and miners.[5] Also prominent among overseas Chinese were merchants who usually preceded the sojourner laborers and facilitated commerce between Southeast Asian countries and China.

From the sixteenth century, European colonization in Southeast Asia created new opportunities for emigrants and would-be emigrants, as colonial officials came to rely on Chinese for their services, labor, and connections to the China trade.[6] Beginning with the arrival of the Portuguese in the early 1500s, Chinese filled key middleman roles and economic niches in the colonies.[7] In the Philippines, after the Spanish seized Manila in 1571, Chinese carpenters and masons helped build the new capital city, and traders from Fujian traded silk and porcelain for silver that had been brought from Mexico.[8] Although Britain came to Southeast Asia relatively late, securing Penang, the first of the Straits Settlements, in 1786, its presence accelerated the pace of commerce and emigration.[9] Many of the Chinese in Southeast Asia, usually members of privileged classes, started second families by marrying local women. This led to the formation of hybrid creole communities in locations like Malacca, Penang, Singapore, and the Philippines.[10]

Maritime and international trade networks gave rise to cosmopolitan "contact zones" in port cities where Western and non-Western people regularly encountered one another. In these locations, which included Amoy, Canton, Hong Kong, Macao, Manila, and Batavia, Chinese people started to meet new strangers from the West, including Americans. The encounters had various outcomes, from the appearance of creolized communities to the walling off of foreigners.[11] They also facilitated the transmission of information about even more far-flung places and opportunities across the Pacific. From the late 1500s, Chinese craftsmen and servants went to Mexico aboard Manila galleons. And in the United States, shortly after the establishment of U.S.–China trade, Chinese people began appearing in eastern port cities.[12] In 1785, the ship *Pallas* arrived in Baltimore with a crew that included Chinese, Malays, Japanese, and Moors, and as mentioned in the previous chapter, there were Chinese domestic servants in New York in the 1790s. In turn, North American and Pacific cities such as New York, Boston, San Francisco, and Honolulu developed their own "contact zones" where "intermingling, integration, segregation, and exclusion," occurred.[13]

Several developments in the nineteenth century set the stage for the modern Chinese diaspora, starting with the "opening" of China by Britain following its victory in the Opium War of 1840 to 1842.[14] The Treaty of Nanking bolstered the West's power over China, forcing the vanquished country to open five of its ports—Canton, Amoy, Foochow, Ningpo, and Shanghai—to foreign commerce. Additional terms included limits on customs for Chinese goods, the cession of Hong Kong to Britain, a $21 million indemnity, and extraterritoriality for British persons in China.[15] Soon after, other Western nations wrested similar privileges and the interference of foreigners in China, via missionary work, political and military intervention, and commercial relations continued through the rest of the nineteenth century and into the twentieth.[16] A Second Opium War with Great Britain, from 1856 to 1860, resulted in further concessions from the Qing government, such as the opening of additional ports, legalization of opium, collection of further indemnities, and ceding of Kowloon.

After the first Opium War, southern China reeled from economic decline and civil conflict, which displaced large numbers of people from their land and jobs and enlarged the emigrant pool. China's accelerated integration into international commerce had also made the country vulnerable to cyclical depressions. Canton, which for eighty years had been China's dominant port, was especially hit hard by having to compete with the newly opened treaty ports.[17] Mounting desperation sometimes took the form of violent uprisings and feuds that brought chaos to southern China. Some people joined outlaw brotherhoods, whose expansion after the Opium War fueled the Red Turban Rebellion and unsettled the Pearl River delta in the mid-1850s.[18] Also adding to the disorder was the Taiping Rebellion of 1851 to 1864, which challenged Manchu rule and drew the support of discontented laborers.[19] Another major internal disruption that influenced emigration was the Hakka–bendi ethnic conflict of 1856 to 1868, which stemmed from long-time feuds between the Hakka, considered outsiders to southern China, and the *bendi* "natives." Tensions between the groups erupted violently over competition for land and resources, and in the Hakka–bendi wars, about two hundred thousand people died. The destruction directly impacted some of the chief emigrant areas, especially the district of Taishan.[20]

Between 1840 and 1900, about 2.5 million Chinese left for the Americas, the West Indies, Hawaii, Australia, New Zealand, Southeast Asia, and Africa.[21] Among the "pull factors" drawing them to these locations were Western colonial development and its attendant labor needs, the discovery of gold, and commercial opportunities. By the 1860s, the introduction of steamships transformed commerce and travel within Asia and across the Pacific.[22] In these years, Western firms and ships replaced the Chinese-dominated emigration networks of earlier periods, and Hong Kong, now under British rule, became the main international steamship port and point of departure.[23] As for the migrants themselves, Philip Kuhn delineates four categories, based on their means of departure: (1) those paying their way or relying on family resources; (2) those obtaining loans from merchants, brokers, shipping companies to be repaid through wages or profits from overseas work; (3) those whose indebtedness was certified by contracts of indenture which bound them to work for an employer for a set term; and (4) those who had been coerced or deceived into boarding a ship and signed a contract under duress.[24] The second and third groups comprised the bulk of Chinese overseas emigrants and most were young male labor sojourners.

A distinctive feature of nineteenth-century Chinese emigration was the predominance of Cantonese from Guangdong. A coastal province whose location exposed it to early commercialization, traditions of emigration, and contact with foreigners, Guangdong's proximity to Macao and Hong Kong also facilitated its status as the main emigrant province. In Guangdong, most emigrants came from the fertile, once economically robust Pearl River delta region, where by the eighteenth century population growth outstripped the land base. Compounding this were increasingly concentrated land holdings by clans and rising tenancy rates, which forced landless peasants to seek work as common laborers, handicraft makers, and personal servants. Elsewhere in Guangdong, such as the hilly and rocky district of Taishan, conditions were even worse. Taishan experienced 1440 percent population growth between 1657 and 1838, and residents had been leaving for Southeast Asia as early as the 1820s.[25] By mid-century an increasing number was journeying beyond Asia, and eventually Taishanese made up 40 to 50 percent of the Chinese immigrants in America and 70 percent in California.[26]

Although the Chinese government had long looked down on emigration, it was not effective at controlling it. Since the fifteenth century, after a brief period when Ming rulers embraced exploration, governments tried to proscribe both trade and emigration.[27] This opposition stemmed from worries about security and foreign plots, and rulers in turn viewed overseas Chinese as deserters and potential traitors. Imperial edicts, however, could not stop emigration and maritime trade, as coastal areas in the south depended on these activities for their wellbeing.[28] The Qing government, which took power in the mid-seventeenth century, not only forbade emigration and reentry, but also briefly banned coastal residence. As before, these policies were evaded.[29] By the late nineteenth century, faced with internal problems and pressure from Western countries to allow the importation of laborers to their colonies, the Chinese government began allowing its subjects to emigrate and return.[30]

As mentioned earlier, one subset of Chinese emigrants in the nineteenth century left under coercion and worked as indentured laborers in conditions resembling slavery. Under coolieism, contracts—sometimes sold in auction—substituted for purchase, giving it the appearance of free labor, but renewals were often compulsory and workers lived in conditions of captivity. The coolie trade, which also included Asian Indians, emerged as African slavery was on the decline and Asian "cheap labor" migration was on the rise, against the backdrop of Western colonization in places where wage labor was untenable and indigenous and white workers were unavailable. As early as the 1790s, British writers suggested that, were the slave trade to be abolished, Chinese "servants" could be substitutes, though in time the British Empire grew more reliant on Indians for this purpose.[31]

Two precursors of the coolie trade were the importation of 192 Chinese laborers to the British colony of Trinidad in 1806 to work on sugar plantations, and the 1810 arrival of about 400 Chinese contract laborers to grow tea in Brazil.[32] The experiments showed the viability of Chinese and other Asian labor in tropical areas and as a substitute for black slave labor. Finding a substitute was imperative after Britain abolished slavery throughout its empire in 1833, and other imperial powers faced pressure to follow suit. The following decade, an international coolie trade was underway, beginning with the shipment of Chinese indentured laborers to British Guiana in 1843 and Peru in 1847. The height of the trade—when it experienced its heaviest traffic—was the 1870s to 1890s, when most coolies from China were shipped out of Hong Kong, Canton, Amoy, Swatow, and Macao.[33] British, Spanish, Portuguese, Dutch, French, Peruvians, and Americans all participated in it, whether by transporting coolies, purchasing their contracts or employing them. Chinese coolies were found in Asia, the Americas, Africa, and Oceania, the largest numbers going to Peru and Cuba.[34] Coolies from India were most numerous in the British Empire. Javanese were also recruited as coolies, but on a smaller scale by the Dutch, who used them in South Africa.

The profitability of the coolie trade and its genesis as a substitute for African slavery made inevitable the system's cruelty. One reason why procurers used coercion and deception was because the destinations of coolie labor had terrible reputations. As one British agent reported, Chinese "would never come of their own accord to the emigration depot, because they hear of it only as a certain road to 'that bourne from whence no traveler returns.'"[35] The right of extraterritoriality provided by the Treaty of Nanking effectively allowed procurers to engage in kidnapping and fraud without fear of prosecution, and those wishing to completely escape Chinese jurisdiction could operate out of Macao.[36] In treaty ports, "press gangs" sought vulnerable targets—many were prisoners of war from the Hakka–bendi feuds—and conveyed them to "crimps" who sold the captives to foreign agencies for a few dollars per head. Once captured and sold, coolies were locked up in airless holdings on months-long voyages. The worst were to Peru, in which annual death rates in the early 1860s—from scurvy, dysentery, dehydration, suicide, and passenger mutinies—ranged from 22 to 41 percent.[37] Chinese officials' interviews with passengers of the *Maria Luz*, a storm-damaged ship bound for Peru that had been rescued by a British ship in 1872, revealed harrowing details. A 25-year-old farmer from Guangdong named Huang Muqing described being lured by a fellow villager to Macao with promises of finding work. "I lived there for two or three days and did not even go outside the building," he said, likely referring to his stay in a barracoon prior to being put on a ship. Describing time in terms of the lunar calendar, he continued:

> In the 19th day, 4th month, I was delivered by a small boat to a ship. Then I was pushed into the hold and locked up. The foreigners were supposed to give me eight foreign dollars. They wanted me to give them my fingerprints. They warned me that if I did not give them my fingerprints, they would hoist me up with a rope and beat me. So I had to give them my fingerprints. The boat left Macao, in the 22nd day, 4th month. We met with wind and the mast was broken. In the 4th day, 6th month, the ship arrived in Japan. Because of the unbearable suffering and starvation, on the 8th day, 6th month, I took a 'watches-beating drum,' and jumped in the water.[38]

The coolie trade, although profitable and deemed vital for colonial development as the African slave trade was phased out, raised serious moral and political issues. China was outraged by its abuses but could do little to regulate it.[39] Worried that the barbaric aspects of coolieism tarnished its reputation, Britain passed the Passengers Act of 1855, which imposed health and space standards on ships departing from Hong Kong. A few years later in 1858, it limited its participation in the trade to its colonies. Though coolieism did not take root in the United States, American ships participated in transporting coolies from 1843, mostly between China and Cuba. As discussed in the previous chapter, debates about its possibilities on southern plantations animated political discussions before and after the Civil War, but in 1862, responding to protests from China, diplomats, and abolitionists, the United States outlawed participation in the trade.[40]

Across the Pacific

Although it was not part of the United States until 1898, Hawaii holds an important place in Asian American history during the nineteenth century due to the large-scale recruitment of Asian laborers, initially from China. Migration to Hawaii, moreover, was a springboard to permanent settlement on the mainland for many Asians. After James Cook's "discovery" of the islands in 1778, white Americans grew interested in Hawaii, and they ingratiated themselves with its monarchy and eventually comprised a de facto ruling oligarchy. Also in the years after Cook's landing, Chinese people began to appear in the islands. Some of the earliest were guests who had been recruited by King Kamehameha to build a ship, while others came by way of their employment on Western trading vessels.[41] By 1850, on the eve of the arrival of the first group of Chinese labor recruits to its sugar plantations, Hawaii had fewer than four hundred Chinese residents. Most worked as merchants, sugar masters, and shopkeepers in Honolulu.[42]

As early as the 1830s, enterprising Americans who viewed the Pacific as the next frontier in the United States' westward march set their sights on developing Hawaii's commercial potential, to enrich themselves and augment national growth. Early on, Americans traded cotton and hardware with natives for sandalwood, the latter being coveted by Chinese for making incense, but the trade, which flourished from the 1790s to 1830s, depleted the forests that produced the resource. By the end of the century, the islands were effectively a U.S. economic colony, and in 1898 they were formally annexed. Hawaii's post-annexation development, however, maintained its colonial orientation with the mainland. In contrast to California, which attracted both independent producers and dependent capitalist industries, Hawaii was almost exclusively settled by those engaged in the latter.[43] The main mode of production on the islands was plantation agriculture, and the chief output was sugar for mainland consumption. This development, furthermore, relied heavily on imported Asian labor.

A turning point in Hawaii's transformation from a subsistence based to single-commodity market economy was 1835 when the Honolulu mercantile company, Ladd & Co., formed by three New Englanders, established the islands' first commercial sugar plantation on Kauai. Seeking laborers for the venture, partner William Hooper tried employing natives, but grew displeased with them, and then turned to Chinese, whom he had seen working in nearby sugar mills. In a letter to associates, Hooper wrote in 1836, "A colony of Chinese would, probably, put the plantation in order to be perpetuated sooner and with less trouble than any other class of husbandmen."[44] In 1850, investors and planters organized the Royal Hawaiian Agricultural Society to promote agricultural interests and explore Chinese labor. Explaining the society's preference for imported workers, its president said in 1852, "We shall find Coolie labor to be far more certain, systematic, and economic than that of the native. They are prompt at the call of the bell, steady in their work, quick to learn, and will accomplish more [than Hawaiian laborers.]"[45] The first shipment of 175 Chinese arrived in January 1852 from Fujian province, on five-year contracts that would pay $3 per month plus passage money, food, clothing, and lodging.[46]

The recruitment of Chinese laborers did not take off immediately; between 1853 and 1875, just 2,332 entered Hawaii.[47] Things changed in the mid-1860s when the American Civil War disrupted sugar production in the South, boosting the demand for Hawaiian sugar and renewing calls for Chinese labor. In 1865 the Hawaiian government, under King Kamehameha V, formed the Bureau of Immigration to wrest from private hands the responsibility for procuring foreign labor.[48] William Hillebrand, the Royal Commissioner of Immigration, investigated potential labor sources in Asia, and as the Royal Hawaiian Agricultural Society had concluded a decade and a half earlier, decided that Chinese were most ideal. Hong Kong was selected as the main recruiting port. Further shoring up the islands' sugar boom and sustaining labor demands was the 1875 Reciprocity Treaty between the United States and Hawaii, which allowed the latter to export sugar to the former duty-free.[49] With labor sources identified and commodity demands in place, sugar soon became Hawaii's chief export. Cane production expanded from 9,392 tons in 1870 to 32,792 tons in 1880 and then to nearly 300,000 in 1900, and in a similar time span the plantation workforce increased from about 3,800 to over 36,000.[50]

The recruitment of Chinese laborers was pivotal to this growth, and accordingly, Hawaii's Chinese population soared in the late nineteenth century. In 1884 they numbered 17,937, over 22 percent of the population, and made up about 40 percent of the sugar plantation workforce.[51] Whether some of these workers could be called "coolies" is not entirely clear, but by the late 1870s, the governor of Hong Kong had become alarmed at reports that emigrants in Hawaii were being held in virtual slavery, leading him to ban contract labor emigration from the port to the islands in 1878. Recruiters shifted their efforts to the Pearl River delta and the port of Whampoa, and another 24,126 labor migrants arrived between 1878 and 1885.[52] The importation of Chinese, while significant on its own, was also part of a larger transformation of Hawaii in which natives nearly disappeared from the population and over 400,000 newcomers, mostly laborers, arrived.

The 1890s were a turning point for Hawaii's Chinese. In this decade, sojourners were increasingly returning home or pursuing opportunities on the mainland and U.S. exclusion laws were applied to the islands. One effect of these developments was the decline of the islands' Chinese population. The shrinking numbers were also in part the design of planters who by the 1880s had come to fear they had grown overly dependent on Chinese laborers.[53] They, thus, turned to other groups, mainly Portuguese, Japanese, Koreans, and Filipinos. Chinese participation in Hawaii's plantation workforce dropped to less than four thousand in 1902 and less than three hundred in 1959.

At the same time they were landing in Hawaii, Chinese were also going to North America in increasing numbers. The first arrivals to California were merchants, and it was most likely they who brought word of the discovery of gold in the territory to their home districts. By spring 1849, the news had reached Canton, and a trickle of emigrants turned into an influx.[54] These gold-seekers, says Sucheng Chan, were the "true vanguard" of a major migration to North America that would comprise some two hundred thousand Chinese.[55] Miners comprised the largest class of Chinese emigrants, and the high point of their migration was 1852, when over twenty thousand entered the port of San Francisco. This migration was part of a larger historical and geographic phenomenon. As discussed earlier, going overseas to mine for precious metals was not a new practice among Chinese, as they had been traveling to Southeast Asia for this purpose for hundreds of years. And during the 1850s, California was just one of several destinations for gold miners. Australia also drew thousands of Chinese miners who nicknamed the country "New Mountain" (San Francisco was "Old Mountain").[56]

As before, overseas emigration during the gold rush emanated mainly from southern China. In 1855, the Reverend William Speer, a California missionary who had worked in the Pearl River Delta, said residents of Guangdong were "better acquainted with other countries than any other portion of the Chinese . . . They are . . . the richest people in the Empire. When the news of the discovery of gold . . . reached them, it was natural that they, above all other Chinese, should rush into California."[57] The news they received could be both encouraging and sobering. Appearing in the *China Mail* during the gold rush years was a "letter of Digger in California," which urged readers against "[imagining] some romantic nonsense about finding the gold lying on the surface of the ground and that they have nothing to do but pick it up."[58] Despite such warnings, the perception of California as "Gold Mountain" endured. Chinese people continued to arrive and became integral members of the dynamic, polyglot societies of gold rush country. They were a common sight in the foothills, especially along the Yuba River and its tributaries and in townships like Long Bar, Northeast Bar, and Foster Bar. One newspaper described groups of twenty to thirty Chinese "inhabiting close cabins, so small that, one. . .would not be of sufficient size to allow a couple of Americans to breathe in it.[59] In the mid-1850s, about twenty-four thousand Chinese—two thirds of the Chinese population in America—were working in California mines, the majority as independent prospectors.

To make the transpacific journey, some miners paid their own passage, although most used the credit-ticket system, also the means by which most voluntary Chinese immigrants came to America during the nineteenth century. Under this system, which emigrants also used to go to places such as Singapore and Australia, an individual received a ticket on credit from a broker, merchant, labor recruiter, or ship captain. Often, the brokers were former emigrants who recruited in their home villages. The emigrant signed a contract promising to pay back the fare plus interest (4 to 8 percent per month) out of future earnings. Chinese regional lodges in the United States often arranged to assume the passage debts and assured debtors that migrants would not return home without a document certifying payment of the debt. Such circumstances were not believed to constitute indentured servitude or contract labor because they did not bind individuals to a particular employer for a fixed period of labor. Nonetheless, they significantly restricted immigrants' freedom, something anti-Chinese groups highlighted as evidence of Chinese despotism.[60]

As for the journey itself, Chinese to North America in the 1850s and 1860s likely rode in the steerage of overcrowded ships. If they were like coolie ships, the mortality rate would have been high, anywhere from 5 to 10 percent.[61] The conditions on transpacific voyages improved somewhat from the late 1860s with the use of steamships, and after 1867, most Chinese traveling between Hong Kong and San Francisco rode on the vessels of the U.S.-based Pacific Mail Steamship Company.[62] Between 1867 and 1875 the company transported 124,800 Chinese in either direction and collected about $5.8 million in fees. Due to this profitability, the Pacific Mail Steamship Company later defended Chinese immigration during the exclusion movement.[63] Its ships could accommodate 250 people in the cabin and 1,200 in steerage. Steerage passengers paid between $50 and $55 for the Hong Kong to San Francisco trip and $40 for the reverse route. The journey, which was between 4,500 and 5,000 miles, took thirty-three or thirty-four days.[64]

Diplomatic agreements struck between the United States and China ensured an open channel of migration and at least a rhetorical commitment to the fair treatment of nationals abroad. The pivotal document in this regard was the 1868 Burlingame-Seward Treaty, under which the Chinese government finally sanctioned emigration. Other provisions included China's right to regulate commerce and appoint consuls in American ports, the protection of citizens of either nation from persecution on the basis of religion, the outlawing of the coolie trade, most favored nation status for each party, and the right of citizens of both countries to change their home and allegiance.[65] While these terms were an expression of mutual respect and interests between the nations, they also codified the second-class status of Chinese in America, as the treaty denied Chinese immigrants the right to U.S. naturalization.

Profits from gold mining declined around the mid-1860s, and Chinese immigrants started leaving the gold fields. By 1870, about sixteen thousand were still in the mines, but this was a significant drop from the 1850s, and many of these were wageworkers for mining companies. They nonetheless remained a major presence in California and the west, as economic development in the region generated new labor demands that they helped to fill. This phase also saw the transformation of Chinese in North America into a predominantly working-class population. Despite worries that Chinese labor in the United States would constitute coolieism, employers came to favor them as a cheap and amenable workforce, and labor shortages helped sustain their immigration into the 1870s.[66] Between 1867 and 1870, some forty thousand Chinese arrived in the United States, and by 1870, they numbered about sixty-three thousand. Of these, 77 percent lived in California, where they also represented 25 percent of the workforce.

To give a sense of the overall demographic picture, Chinese America in the second half of the nineteenth century was by and large a community of peasants from agrarian backgrounds. Members of China's gentry class were very few among immigrants, although a small number did go abroad for education. More visible were merchants and artisans, who often played important roles in their surrounding city or region's commercial and economic affairs. The immigrants tended to be accustomed to moving around, having undertaken internal migrations prior to going abroad, or coming from families long engaged in migratory patterns.[67] While most Chinese in North America were in California, this was a fairly dispersed population, and others, albeit in smaller numbers, were found elsewhere in the west, as well as the southwest, New England, and the south. New York, home to the largest Chinese community east of Sierra Nevadas, was a major center of manufacturing employment for Chinese. To be sure, its population was much smaller than San Francisco's; the 1880 Census reported 748 in Manhattan with another 143 in Brooklyn and Newark.[68] This population was drawn from mariners who had worked on coastal shipping routes who settled in New York in the 1860s and 1870s, as well as former employees of the transcontinental railroad.

This phase of Chinese immigration was also overwhelmingly young and male, a pattern that holds for all other Asian groups and whose consequences will be explored in the next few chapters. In a gendered and patriarchal world, economic opportunities abroad usually meant that men traveled alone or with other males to work and bring back or send money to their families and communities at home. The sojourner status of most migrants, high transportation costs, and inhospitable conditions in Hawaii and the American West during the nineteenth century were, furthermore, disincentives for females to accompany male relatives across the Pacific. Adding to these impediments were immigration laws such as the Page Act of 1875, which effectively excluded Asian women. Despite these barriers and disincentives, some women, mostly wives and other family members of migrants, did come. In Hawaii in 1884, about 5 percent of Chinese men had co-ethnic wives, and in 1900, this number had gone up 2 percent.[69] Women who accompanied their husbands to Hawaii usually worked, in fields and sugar mills as well as in household-based work such as sewing, growing vegetables, raising poultry, and working as domestics.[70] In San Francisco, in 1850, there were 7 Chinese women versus 4,018 men, and until the early 1900s, they made up about 5 percent of the total Chinese American population.[71]

Not only did the immigrants tend to be drawn from a subset of the population that was accustomed to migration, they were also risk-taking, intrigued by stories of America and convinced that it was worth a try. One man, who had a brother in Boston working in the tea trade wrote, "Good many Americans speak of California. Oh! Very rich country! I hear good many Americans and Europeans go there. Oh! They find gold very quickly, so I hear . . . I feel as if I should like to go there very much. I think I shall go to California next summer."[72] *Gam Saan* (gold mountain) promised not just gold but also employment. Labor brokers who advertised in Chinese port cities depicted America as a wealthy land that welcomed Chinese.[73] In the 1860s, a worker could earn $3 to $5 per month working in South China whereas in California he could make $30 per month working for a railroad company. Moreover, those returning home after working in Hawaii or the United States, with their money and stories of adventure, impressed family members and fellow villagers who might be inspired to emigrate as well. Immigrant Lee Chew recalled the homecoming of a returned emigrant, how he threw a grand party for fellow villagers and purchased land on which he had a "palace" built. For Lee, who was 16 at the time, this made a deep impression. "A popular saying of the time," remarks Ronald Takaki, "promised that if a sojourner could not save a thousand dollars, he would surely obtain at least eight hundred. But even with a saving of three hundred dollars he could return to China and become 'a big, very big gentleman.'"[74]

Japanese Immigration

Japanese immigration grew out of circumstances similar to and different from the Chinese experience. While patterns of and attitudes about emigration were shaped by Japan's unique history of modernization, they also stemmed from its incorporation into international networks of capitalist economies and shifting geo-politics in the Asia-Pacific region. Although Americans believed Japan had been isolated from the rest of the world until Commodore Perry's expedition in 1853, it had significant contact with foreigners prior to this encounter. Before the 1600s, Japan was China's main source of silver, and one of the consequences of these trade relations was the emergence of a Chinese merchant community in Nagasaki by the sixteenth century. The first Europeans to make contact with Japan were the Portuguese, who landed on a small island west of Kyushu in 1543. Christian proselytizing followed, with the arrival of Jesuit Francis Xavier in 1549, and Catholic missionaries eventually converted about three hundred thousand Japanese.[75] Contact with foreigners, however, came to an abrupt end in 1603, with the ascension of the Tokugawa shogunate, which sought to root out Western influences, although it continued to trade with other countries.[76] Foreigners were segregated; Chinese in Nagasaki had to stay in a walled off settlement, and Portuguese and Dutch were segregated on an artificial island.[77] Interaction with outsiders during the Tokugawa period was mostly limited to Chinese and Dutch traders, a handful of Koreans, and occasional shipwrecked sailors. Japanese were forbidden from leaving the country, and few traveled long distances, even within Japan.[78]

Commodore Perry's expedition, then, was significant for ending a long period of relative seclusion. It also placed Japan in a decidedly weakened position via the unequal Kanagawa Treaty of 1854. This and subsequent foreign incursions precipitated a political crisis in Japan and the downfall of the Tokugawa shogunate. Taking its place was a new set of leaders who heralded the Meiji Restoration of 1868. These included young samurai from Satsuma, Tosa, and Choshu, and they advocated learning Western ways to resist future foreign encroachments.[79] Meiji officials sought to overhaul the government, economy, and society, which entailed turning loosely connected feudal baronies into a cohesive nation, and reviving Shinto and the veneration of the emperor.[80] They disbanded han (fiefs) and pensioned off daimyo and samurai (knights of daimyo), turning members of once elevated castes into marginally privileged commoners. The economic program entailed the development of commercialized agriculture and industrial sectors.

In addition to effecting these internal changes, the Meiji government was also determined to reverse Japan's weak position against the West by making it an expansionist global power. Anxious to avoid China's fate after the Opium War, rulers believed that Japan's security depended on joining the international scramble, first by revising its unequal treaties with Western nations and then engaging in its own program of expansion. This process started with the colonization and settlement of Hokkaido in 1869, which had been modeled on the U.S. conquest of the North American frontier, and then Okinawa in 1879.[81] Japanese expansion in Asia continued in 1894 with the seizure of Taiwan after the Sino–Japanese War, and in 1905 with the acquisition of southern Sakhalin Island and Kwantung following the Russo–Japanese War. In 1910, Japan annexed Korea.

The beginning of Japanese trans-Pacific migration in the 1880s paralleled earlier population movements within Japan and Asia and blurred the lines between emigration, expansion, and nationalism. "When the state permitted the departure of common laborers in 1885 for Hawaii and later for the U.S. mainland," states Eiichiro Azuma, "many officials and educated Japanese viewed their migration in terms similar to the contemporaneous movement of surplus populations to Hokkaido and other new territories."[82] Although Japan was a modernizing nation, the dislocating effects of rapid transformation combined with its relative underdevelopment yielded a pool of potential labor migrants for the United States as well as Hawaii and European colonies in Latin America and Southeast Asia.[83] Meiji leaders said emigrants should "obey the call of nation" and support Japan's commercial, political, and territorial expansion.[84] Such ideas, framed as a "Japanese-style manifest destiny," projected Japanese hegemony extending to the western United States and Latin America. Although all emigrants would play a role, merchants would spearhead this mission by establishing "footholds of international trade" in the Americas and elsewhere.[85] Educator Fukuzawa Yukichi, a leading proponent of Western learning and Japanese entrepreneurial-ism, saw emigration as a means toward these ends and spread these ideas through his private academy Keio (later Keio University) and newspaper *Jiji Shimpo*. Viewing Britain as a model for national development via overseas emigration, he explained:

> the wealth that English traders abroad have garnered individually has become part of England's national assets. The land they reclaimed has turned into regional centers of English trade, if not its formal colonial territories. This is how Great Britain has become what she is today. In a similar vein, [a Japanese emigrant shall be regarded as a loyal subject. For while sacrificing himself at the time of national crisis is a direct way of showing loyalty, engaging in various enterprises abroad is an indirect way of discharging patriotism . . . When examining the example of Englishmen, no one would fail to see [that emigration] shall lead to the enrichment of Japan as well.[86]

Convinced that Japanese society could not absorb the growing number of young people coming out of the educational system, he urged them to pursue careers abroad, and touted the United States for its natural abundance and enterprising traditions. Emigrants would in turn "benefit Japan by expanding her contacts with foreign countries and generating a demand for Japanese goods abroad." [87]

With motivations from enhancing Japan's prestige, to expanding its commercial reach, to practicing Christian charity, to helping displaced farmers, enterprising Japanese started coming to America in the mid-1870s, seeking opportunities in urban and rural areas. [88] In 1887, Fukuzawa helped fund a venture organized by his former student, Inoue Kakugoro. As Inoue explained his view of the relationship between emigration and Japanese development:

> No reason exists for Japan to remain a small, isolated island in the Orient. Japanese should go to foreign lands without hesitation and select suitable places to live. They must not forget Japan, however in normal or other times. They should consume Japanese products for daily necessities, and they should start businesses, which will benefit the homeland. The more emigration flourishes, the further our national power will expand. [89]

After landing in San Francisco, the group of about thirty, which included Tsukamoto Matsunosuke, who became a leader in the San Francisco Japanese American community, went to Valley Springs in Calaveras County to start their settlement. Though short-lived, it paved the way for more successful colonies and inspired others to emigrate. For instance, having just failed his entrance exam to Tokyo Higher Commercial School, Ushijima Kinji, who would go by the name George Shima in the United States—and also became known as the "Potato King" for his extraordinary success in farming—read about the Valley Springs colony in *Jiji Shimpo* and in 1888 decided to try his luck in America. [90]

Students made up the largest category of Japanese immigrants to the continental United States before the twentieth century. Katayama Sen, a Christian socialist, was a prominent advocate of student emigration. He had attended high school in the San Francisco Bay Area while working as a houseboy, cook, and handyman before going on to Yale Divinity School. After returning to Japan, he was recruited to lead an American-sponsored settlement house in Tokyo where he spread his message of emigration as a solution for the lack of education and other opportunities. [91] By and large entering through San Francisco and settling in California, student migrants were categorized as either sponsored or private. [92] Sponsored students had been selected by the government to receive scholarships to attend school in Europe and the United States. Private students were a larger group, paying their own way, relying on assistance, or working while attending school. The latter were also known as student-laborers (*dekasegi-shosei*), and about 3,300 of these entered the United States in the 1880s and 1890s. [93] For aspiring student emigrants too indigent to travel abroad, an organization called Rikkokai was founded in 1897 to assist them. Many student emigrants ended up staying permanently in the United States and helped to lay the groundwork for Japanese American ethnic enterprises. These included Domoto Takanoshin, who came to San Francisco in 1884 and went on to become the proprietor of the North American Mercantile Company.

In addition to schools, newspapers, and lectures by returned students, published guides disseminated information about America to would-be emigrants. Usually written by former or current student-laborers, the guides began to appear in the 1880s and had titles like *Mysterious America; How to Go to America Alone;* and *Come, Japanese!* They generally painted a rosy portrait of the United States as a place where Japanese could easily work while studying and even achieve great fortune.[94] As *Come, Japanese! (Kitare, Nihonjin)* exhorted, "America is a veritable human paradise, the number one mine in the world. Gold, silver, and gems are scattered on her streets. If you can figure out a way of picking them up, you'll become rich instantly to the tune of ten million and be able to enjoy ultimate human pleasures."[95] Another key source was the newspaper *Tobei Shimpo,* established in 1907. Its publisher, Shimanuki Hyodau, also the founder of Rikkokai, had traveled to the United States in the 1890s and devoted the paper to disseminating information about America and advice on how to obtain passage across the Pacific.[96]

In addition to being drawn to the appealing descriptions of America, many student emigrants sought escape from unwelcome changes in Japan with the transition to Meiji rule. One of these changes was mandatory conscription. Beginning in 1873, all males between the ages of 17 to 40 were required to serve in the military, and among the only groups eligible for exemption were students abroad. Because they would face induction upon returning to Japan, many stayed in the United States until they were 32, the age of eligibility expiration.[97] Also departing Japan during the early Meiji period were political exiles who had participated in the People's Rights Movement. This movement, which emerged in the mid-1870s and drew from a broad spectrum of people disaffected with the new order—including former members of the samurai class, landowners, farmers, and dispossessed peasants—called for reforms such as a national assembly and greater local autonomy.[98] The movement culminated with the formation of the Liberal Party in 1881, but a few years later it collapsed, sending leaders fleeing the country for safety.[99]

By the second half of the 1880s, the emigration of laborers surpassed that of students, merchants, and political exiles. Their first destination was Hawaii, an independent monarchy until 1898. Responding to the demands of would-be emigrants as well as the urgings of the Hawaiian monarchy and plantation recruiters, Japan lifted its ban on labor emigration in 1885, and between 1885 and 1907, about 157,000 Japanese, mostly laborers, entered the islands. During this first phase of labor migration from 1885 to 1894, the Japanese government sponsored about 30,000 contract workers. From 1894 to 1899, private companies sponsored another 40,230.[100] Most of those who went to Hawaii and the U.S. mainland between 1885 and 1907 were rural residents who considered themselves *dekasegi,* or temporary migrants.[101]

Concerned about protecting its subjects abroad and maintaining a positive image of Japan, the government regulated labor migration. It required employers to cover transportation costs and basic living needs as well as deposit a percentage of the workers' wages with the Japanese consulate in Honolulu to prevent emigrants from wasting their earnings and ensure passage for their return home.[102] Labor contracts were limited to three-year terms, with men being paid $9 per month plus a $6 food allowance and women being paid $6 per month and $4 for food. The work month consisted of twenty-six days and a workday ten hours in the field or twelve in the sugar factories.[103]

The government-sponsored laborers—and ultimately most Japanese immigrants—came from a limited geographical area covering four southwestern prefectures—Hiroshima, Yamaguchi, Kumamoto, and Fukuoka. These accounted for about 96 percent of the emigrants.[104] The disproportionate representation of these prefectures was due to the concentration of recruitment efforts there by agents looking for laborers to send to Hawaii. The key recruiters during this period were Inoue Kaoru, the Japanese foreign minister who negotiated the preliminary agreement and Immigration Convention with Hawaii; Robert W. Irwin, special agent of the Hawaii Immigration Bureau and Hawaiian consul in Yokohama; and Masuda Takashi, the head of Mitsui Trading Company. Inoue urged Irwin to recruit from his home prefecture of Yamaguchi, and Irwin then sought the help of Masuda, who advised him to also focus on Hiroshima. Mitsui advertised opportunities in Hawaii and dispatched agents to the four prefectures.[105] For their part, planters thought the rural conditions of these prefectures made their residents better suited for agricultural labor.

Labor migrants were probably indifferent to the state's valorization of emigration and were motivated instead by their economic circumstances, made more precarious by the scope and speed of modernization and commercialization after 1868. Among those affected was the fishing community of Nihojima, whose livelihood were suddenly disrupted by the construction of Ujima Harbor in Hiroshima in 1884. Although hailed as a triumph of Japan's modern development, the project also displaced about one thousand fishermen, whose misfortunes compelled them to join the labor migrant pool.[106] Most contract laborers were landless or small landowners with farming backgrounds who had been casualties of the Meiji tax system, agricultural commercialization, and monetary policy. A new national tax system instituted in 1873 to finance Japan's modernization and nation building imposed a 3 percent tax on the assessed land value of all landed households, which did not reflect fluctuations in crop prices or currency values. Compounding these problems was inflation starting in the late 1870s, brought on by the state's issuing of 42 million yen of nonconvertible paper currency.[107] Attempts to stabilize the yen lowered the price of goods, but hurt farmers' revenue, undermining their ability to pay their taxes and sending many into default. Of those impacted by these conditions, young men were the likeliest to go abroad as contract workers to pay off debts or earn supplemental income. Some took their wives and children, although most did not. As Eiichiro Azuma points out, labor emigrants tended to have been better off before 1880 and were, thus, representative of a "fallen middle class," rather than the long-term poor.[108]

Hawaiian planters deemed the first wave of government contract laborers to the islands a success, and they found no shortage of willing recruits for subsequent shipments. Encouraging stories trickled to Japan via letters and return migrants, which in turn triggered "chain migrations" from the original sending areas and spawned emigration from new locations. Some people traveled back and forth from Japan to Hawaii, returning home in between work contracts.[109] Wages in Hawaii were attractive; a plantation worker there could, for instance, earn four to six times more than what a common laborer made in Hiroshima.[110] With their earnings, they helped their families and villages, and between 1885 and 1894 Japanese laborers in Hawaii remitted $2.6 million. When counting what emigrants carried back with them, the figure exceeded $3 million.[111] Whether it was the high wages, chance to explore other means of livelihood, illness and death, or the fact that they made new lives in Hawaii, less than half of the government sponsored contract laborers (13,861) returned to Japan.[112]

After government-sponsored emigration ended in 1894, private companies took over the business of transporting labor recruits. The first of these, the Nihon Yoshisa Emigration

Company, was established in 1891 with headquarters in Tokyo and a branch office in Hiroshima. It and other companies continued to focus recruitment on established emigrant prefectures. Although no longer directly involved with emigration, the government continued to regulate the companies, for instance limiting the kinds of jobs that subjects could hold, enforcing licensing and bond requirements on emigration companies (10,000 yen), prohibiting the transport of emigrants to countries where the companies did not have agents, and forbidding foreigners from participating in this business. In 1898, nine emigration companies were in operation, and in 1906 the number had grown to thirty, plus nine individual brokers. 1902 to 1907 were their peak years, when over ninety-eight thousand went abroad. Most of the passengers were contract laborers in private agreements with employers. In addition to Hawaii, companies shipped laborers to New Caledonia, Australia, Peru, Mexico, Fiji Islands, and Brazil.[113]

Private emigration companies also carried Japanese workers to the continental United States. In 1893 the company Hiroshima Kagai Toko struck an agreement with the San Francisco commercial firm Nichibei Yotatshusha, which had been formed by members of the Patriotic League. The emigration company agreed to direct laborers to the San Francisco firm, which in turn provided employment information, travel arrangements to work locations, and other assistance. As the exclusive agent of Hiroshima Kaigai Toko in the U.S., Canada, and Mexico, Nichibei Yotatshusha played a key role in facilitating early Japanese labor migration to North America. Two of the men involved with the San Francisco firm later returned to Japan and were elected to the Japanese Diet.[114]

The Japanese American population grew drastically between 1890 and 1910. In 1890 the U.S. Census reported just over 2,000 Japanese, most of them likely student-laborers in California.[115] In the subsequent decade, 27,440 Japanese entered the continental United States, and, then between 1901 and 1907 another 42,457 arrived. Adding to the mainland population were the approximately 38,000 who came via Hawaii between 1902 and 1907.[116] The migration from Hawaii accelerated in these years because, following U.S. annexation, laborers were "liberated" from their three-year contracts and, thus, free to explore opportunities elsewhere. Jobs on the continent paid more, so many decided to go there. 1897 was a turning point after which the number of Japanese immigrants entering the United States each year markedly increased. This was not merely because of the growth of emigration companies, but also due to the activities of Japanese labor contractors on the West Coast supplying railroad companies and later branching out into an array of industries (see Chapter 3).[117] Under this system, which flourished from 1891 to 1907 and covered all the western states and Alaska, the contractor would meet newly arrived immigrants at the port of entry and then channel them into agricultural, railroad, mining, lumber, or fishing jobs.

A persistent problem facing Japanese immigrants to the United States and post-annexation Hawaii was the issue of contract labor. In 1885 the United States had outlawed the impor-tation of contract laborers, defining such individuals as "person[s] who signed a contract to work at a job before he or she emigrated and whose passage was prepaid by someone else."[118] This prohibition built on anti-slavery and anti-coolie laws, as contract labor struck many as antithetical to the values of free immigration and labor. U.S. officials sometimes accused Japanese emigration companies of shipping contract laborers and denied many passengers admission because they mistook agreements with emigration companies for labor contracts.

For its part, the Japanese government took steps to ensure that its emigrants were complying with U.S. regulations. The Foreign Ministry instructed officials to screen passport applications and weed out contract laborers and members of other excluded classes, and also directed emigration companies to ship only "free emigrants" who had not signed employment agreements prior to leaving for the United States. To address the confusion about emigration company agreements being labor contracts, in 1898 the Ministry stopped requiring these written agreements, which had originally been intended to protect emigrants. Also that year, the Japanese government limited the number of Canada-bound passengers that companies could transport in order to curb the practice of emigration agents helping migrants evade the U.S. contract labor ban by routing them through Canada.[119] The lines between "free" and "unfree" with respect to immigration and labor were always blurrier than officials portrayed, for it was rare that any immigrant traveled completely on their own resources. Nonetheless, perhaps as a move to take greater control, from the late 1890s on, American vessels dominated Japanese passenger traffic to Hawaii and the mainland.[120]

With the rise of anti-Japanese agitation on West Coast, the Foreign Ministry ended the departure of Japanese laborers to the U.S. mainland in 1900, relaxing the restriction in 1902 only for those who had previously worked abroad and returned home[121] This was widely defied, however, with rural Japanese emigrants posing as businessmen, merchants and industrialists and others entering the U.S. by way of Mexico or Canada. Alarmed about these subjects it could not control and worried about the diplomatic repercussions of the anti-Japanese movement, particularly after a 1906 move by the San Francisco Board of Supervisors to segregate Japanese schoolchildren into the Oriental School, Japan enacted its most stringent ban on emigration under the terms of the Gentlemen's Agreement of 1907–08. Under this bilateral agreement with the United States, Japan limited the issuance of U.S.-bound passports to members of certain classes—international merchants, students for higher education, and spouses and minor children of legal U.S. residents—and the United States through executive order prohibited Japanese entry to the mainland via other countries and even U.S. territories, including Hawaii.[122] As a result, Japanese labor migration was greatly reduced, continuing mainly in the form of family chain migration.

As with the Chinese, women represented a small proportion of Japanese immigrants in the early years of migration. They were more numerous in Hawaii than on the U.S. continent prior to the 1910s, as planters and the Hawaiian government actively recruited them. In the government-sponsored phase of Japanese emigration from 1885 to 1894, some 20 percent of contract laborers were women, and in the next phase thousands more went to Hawaii under private contracts. Unlike in the U.S. mainland where women were largely viewed as a hindrance, employers saw them as potential workers who could serve as cooks, seam-stresses, and field laborers as well as a stabilizing force on male workers. After annexation, they were even more anxious to bring women for fear that men would leave the plantations for the mainland.[123] In turn, among immigrant women laborers, Japanese were the most numerous, accounting for about 80 percent of female workers in Hawaii.[124]

By contrast, in the continental U.S., there were very few Japanese women until after 1910. Between 1861 and 1900, only 1,195 females entered, and in 1900, about one thousand Japanese females were residing in the United States.[125] Yuji Ichioka believes the majority of these women were prostitutes who came by way of an organized traffic in which they were smuggled first to Hong Kong, Shanghai, or Singapore and then sold, sometimes to Chinese merchants who took them to America.[126] This probably explains why there were Japanese prostitutes in Butte, Montana as early as 1884. The largest inflow of Japanese women occurred after the peak years of male migration. They tended to come from the same prefectures and socioeconomic backgrounds as the men, but by and large came by way of family connections to immigrants in the United States, the vast majority under their status as "wives." The Gentlemen's Agreement left a loophole in which farmers and businessmen—although not laborers—could send for their wives from Japan, so between 1909 and 1923, 45,706 Japanese women were admitted, with 33,628 gaining entry as "wives."[127] Most of the wives were so-called picture brides, who were married by proxy and had not met their husbands until they arrived in America.[128] As will be discussed further in Chapters 3 and 4, the arrival of large numbers of women proved pivotal in the establishment of stable communities and economies among Japanese immigrants. Moreover, after 1908, the Japanese started to shed their *dekasegi* orientation, taking up farming and running small businesses, a transition facilitated by the presence of women as wives, mothers, and extra labor.

Korean Immigration

The circumstances of Korean immigration, which picked up on the heels of Japanese migration, had roots in contact with outside powers. Compared to the Chinese and Japanese, however, early emigration from Korea was limited in scale and scope. From the 1880s to 1902, a very small number of merchants and students traveled to the United States. The main migration took place between 1903 and 1920, when about eight thousand Koreans sailed to the United States, with most landing in Hawaii to work on plantations. The bulk of this migration, furthermore, occurred between 1903 and 1905. In terms of their backgrounds, Koreans were diverse; farmers, common laborers, miners, students, clerks, and monks were all among the arrivals. However, similar to other groups, the majority of entries were young, men; over 90 percent were between the ages of sixteen and forty-four.

Korea had effectively closed itself off from foreign powers until the mid-1860s, in part due to earlier traumas such as invasions by Japan in 1592 and 1597 and the Manchus in the 1630s. After that, it managed to keep outside forces at bay, but this changed in 1876, when Japan compelled Korea to sign the unequal Kanghwa Treaty, modeled on those imposed earlier by Western powers on China and Japan. China, once a protective power over Korea—stemming from their sadae relationship (serving the great) and cemented by tributes—was too weak by the 1860s to protect itself and its vassals.[129] Korea granted Japan the right to trade in three ports, giving it virtually complete control over the country's foreign trade. Japan also wrested the right to operate pawnshops and lend money as well as extra-territoriality. In 1882 the United States became the second nation to secure a treaty with Korea, and treaties with Britain, Germany, Russia, Italy, and France followed. As a result of these incursions, Korea by the end of the nineteenth century was weak, impoverished, and politically unstable.

As was occurring elsewhere in Asia, outside interventions led to intense power struggles, initially among internal factions in the Korean court and the yangban ruling class, and then involving foreign powers. The opening of trade undermined the economic self-sufficiency of many farming households as they were pulled into the market economy and grew dependent on foreign goods.[130] By the 1880s, Korea's cycle of debt and dependency on foreigners, mainly Japanese, was entrenched. Food shortages were compounded by persistently low agricultural output and exporting to Japan. Officials tried to stem the effects of famine by prohibiting food exports, but these measures could backfire. For instance, in 1889 the governor of the northeastern province of Hamgyong banned the export of food due to a severe famine. In response, the Japanese government sued the Korean government for damages, and the latter was forced to pay 110,000 yen, adding to an already spiraling debt on top of food shortages.[131]

Internal discontent and suffering also gave rise to social movements. Perhaps the most significant of these was the emergence of a syncretist religious group called Tonghak (eastern learning), which gained followers in the 1880s. In addition to impoverished and disgruntled farmers, the Tonghak movement drew members of the fallen yangban class.[132] Gaining momentum, it turned into a full-scale rebellion across the countryside but was eventually quelled with the help of Chinese troops. Japan reacted to the presence of Chinese soldiers by sending its own contingent to the peninsula, which escalated tensions and culminated in the Sino–Japanese War of 1894 to 1895, in which China was defeated. Outside rivalries over the Korean peninsula continued, however, and led to the Russo–Japanese War in 1904–05. After declaring victory over Russia, Japan made Korea a protectorate, and in 1910 formally annexed it and enacted measures to exploit the colony's resources and people. Amidst the political turmoil—and specifically following a failed coup during the Tonghak movement— the first three Koreans arrived in the United States in 1885. One of these was Philip Jaisohn, who would become the first Korean naturalized U.S. citizen and a leading voice of the Korean independence movement.[133]

A distinctive feature of Korean immigration was the preponderance of converted Christians; about 40 percent of Korean immigrants to the United States during the early years identified as such.[134] This phenomenon can largely be attributed to the American missionary presence. Although the French actually spearheaded Christian missionary work in Korea, they faced frequent persecution and never attained the influence that later American missionaries did. The small group of Koreans who went to the United States for education—about sixty-four from 1890 to 1905—were likewise influenced by missionaries, as they had been trained in mission schools in Korea. This group included Ahn Chang-ho and Syngman Rhee, who would become leaders of the independence movement against Japan.

Illustrating the connections between spreading religion and U.S. international expansion, American missionaries had a major impact on the Korean government and U.S.–Korea diplomacy after the 1880s. In addition to bringing religion, missionaries stimulated Koreans' interest in foreign goods, sometimes directly engaging in commerce.[135] The key figure in this regard was medical missionary Horace N. Allen, who arrived in Korea in 1884 and won King Kojong's confidence after saving the life of one of the queen's relatives.[136] After establishing a friendship with the royal couple, Allen opened the way for dozens of American Protestants, mostly Methodists and Presbyterians, to come to Korea and work with relative freedom. From 1890 to 1897 he served as the secretary of the American legation in Seoul, and from 1897 to 1905 was the American minister to Korea. In these capacities, Allen was an intermediary between the U.S. and Korean governments as well as between private American citizens and Korean authorities. Holding these positions also led to lucrative concessions and franchises for Allen's friends, including access to the Unsan gold mines.

Allen used his influence to promote Korean labor emigration to Hawaii. The HSPA, which had become interested in recruiting Koreans to counter the labor militancy of Japanese, who made up two-thirds of the plantation work force, requested a meeting with Allen in Honolulu in 1902. He returned to Korea to persuade the King to allow his subjects to emigrate. Kojong assented, in part because he thought it would relieve the suffering in the northern provinces caused by famine, and was further persuaded that emigration could benefit Korea's international standing.[137] Allen's friend, American businessman David Deshler, who already had enterprises in Japan and Korea, took charge of the emigration operation. He set up an office and opened a bank for which the HSPA was the sole depositor and whose purpose was to lend money for passage and to give emigrants "show money" to prove they would not become public charges.[138]

By 1900, thousands of Koreans were already living abroad, in places such as the Russian Maritime Provinces, Manchuria, China, and Japan, having sought escape from hardships caused by war, drought, and famine. As in China and Japan at the time, emigration was illegal but it could not be stopped. The northward migration to Russia—a relatively short trip across the border—began in the 1860s as word of the advantages in the country spread while conditions in Korea deteriorated. By 1868 about 2,000 Koreans could be found living near Vladivostok, and a famine in 1869 led an additional 4,500 to emigrate.[139] By 1900, the Korean population in the Maritime Provinces numbered about 23,000.[140] They tended to acculturate quickly, picking up the language, customs, and religion. Many also chose to stay within Korea, but moved to port cities such as Inchon and Wonsan, where they hoped jobs would be available. In time, these growing urban populations formed the pool from which emigrants to Hawaii and elsewhere across the Pacific would be drawn.

Hawaii emerged as an additional option for Koreans looking to go abroad, although it required a much longer journey than other destinations. American missionaries encouraged would-be emigrants to go there, telling them it was a Christian land. Koreans were intrigued by what they learned. In Hawaii, they could receive free housing and medical care and earn $16 per month, a small fortune for impoverished Koreans. The price of passage, about $100, would be covered by the bank Deshler had established, and the cost would later be deducted from paychecks over a three-year period.

Unlike the Chinese and Japanese who came from a handful of provinces or prefectures, Koreans came from all over the country, although chiefly seaports and where labor and transportation agents were active. As mentioned, the backgrounds of Korean immigrants were relatively diverse—including laborers, former soldiers, and artisans—and also, unlike early Chinese and Japanese immigration, the length of Korean immigration was very short.[141] In 1905 the Korean Foreign Office prohibited overseas migration, in part after hearing reports that about 1,000 Korean workers who had been recruited by an English contractor to work on plantations in Vera Cruz, Mexico were being held in virtual slavery. Although intended to be temporary, the ban was made indefinite under pressure from Japan, which had formalized its control over Korea later that year and was anxious to curb labor competition for its emigrants in Hawaii and undermine Korean independence movements abroad.[142] Korean migration then diminished to a trickle that included several hundred political activists who sought entry to the United States as well as Shanghai and Manchuria.[143]

As with other Asian immigrant groups, the proportion of Korean women in the United States and Hawaii was small. Of the approximately 7,000 who landed in Hawaii between 1903 and 1905, some 10 percent were women.[144] Many came as laborers, as employers had encouraged them—as they did with Japanese—to migrate as workers and stabilizing forces on men. Additionally, Korea's tenuous political status and uncertain future led many male migrants to bring their wives with them if they did not intend to return. Further boosting the female population were picture brides; in the decade and a half after 1905, 1,066 of them came to join their husbands.[145]

Hawaii's Korean population far outnumbered that of the mainland until the late twentieth century. In 1920, there were 4,950 in the territory and in 1940, 6,851.[146] On the mainland, meanwhile, the population in 1940 was just 1,711.[147] Nearly all settled in California, around Los Angeles, San Francisco, and the Central Valley. They were not always counted accurately, as prior to Korean independence the Census often identified Koreans as Japanese. Koreans, furthermore, had a lower return rate than Chinese and Japanese, likely stemming from their uncertain political status. One sixth of Koreans who went to Hawaii returned home while half of Chinese and more than half of Japanese returned home.[148]

Indian Immigration

Coming to the United States around the same time as Koreans and in similar numbers were Asian Indians. Unlike other Asians, they were not recruited to work in Hawaii, instead usually landing in North America via stops in Asia. Their migration to the United States was, furthermore, a small part of a diaspora that was millions strong and encompassed about one hundred years from the 1830s to 1930s. Nearly all of those who ended up in the United States were Punjabis of the Sikh faith. Initially, Asian Indians entered by way of Canada; in 1904, 258 did so via British Columbia, and their numbers increased until 1907 when some 2,000 were admitted.[149] This door was closed to many in 1908 as anti-foreigner sentiment in Canada led the government to start requiring Indians to carry $200 to enter the country, which led new migrants to instead seek passage directly to the United States. As a result, Asian Indian migration to the United States peaked in the years from 1907 to 1910, continuing until 1917 when Congress enacted exclusion legislation.

The dynamics of empire frame this period of Indian migration. Before the nineteenth century there was little organized emigration, but this would change with the establishment of British commercial and economic hegemony during the early 1800s and then formal colonial rule in 1857. The coolie trade, which proliferated with the growth of colonial industries such as sugarcane in Mauritius and the West Indies and railroad construction in East Africa, accounted for a major part of the Indian diaspora.[150] The term "coolie" may in fact originate in the word *kuli*, which means "bitter strength" in Chinese and "wages" in Tamil.[151] Most of the first Indian coolies came from Tamil in southern India, and although they were initially taken to places where they were to replace slaves, they were also used in locations such as Mauritius, Guyana, Trinidad, Surinam, Fiji, Natal, and Transvaal.[152] As with Chinese coolieism, the conditions were similar to slavery. The practice continued from

1840 to around 1900 when it was gradually replaced by contract labor emigration, although a small percentage of labor migrants secured their own passage and were not bound to labor agreements prior to leaving.[153] Most Punjabis to North America fell into this latter category.

The establishment of trade between the United States and India, beginning with the arrival of the first American trading ships to Calcutta in 1784, afforded opportunities for small numbers of Indians, probably all men, to come to the United States over a century before the larger wave of migrants to the West Coast. According to Joan Jensen, the first known Indian in the United States was a visitor from Madras who came to Massachusetts in 1790.[154] Additionally, records suggest that there may have been three Indians in California during the gold rush.[155] For those who settled permanently prior to the twentieth century, Indians held an ambiguous place in the racial and social order, either disappearing into surrounding communities or standing out as exotic curiosities. By 1900 there were about 500 Indian merchants in the Northeast and South who sold silks, linens, and other goods from India.[156] Others, especially working-class Indians, sometimes married African Americans and were absorbed into local black communities. The indeterminacy of Indians' racial status could have tragic consequences, as seen in the case of James Dunn, whose story came to light when he submitted a petition to the Pennsylvania Abolition Society in the 1790s. Dunn was an Indian from Calcutta, whose parents had indentured him when he was about eight to the mate of an English vessel. After a series of abandonments and misfortunes that befell his masters, he was sold to a man who took him to Georgia, still as an indentured servant. When this master died, the executors of his will, rather than free Dunn when his contract ended, sold him as a slave. It is not known if he ever achieved his freedom.[157]

Discontent against British colonialism, which turned increasingly violent after 1898, caused much disruption in India and triggered a new wave of emigration. Protest emanated from a cross-section of Indian society, including educated Indians, students, and farmers whose criticisms of British rule encompassed dislike for colonial trade policies, opposition to the partition of Bengal, and demands for a greater role for Indians in the administration.[158] The forceful repression of protestors furthermore bolstered sympathy for demonstrators and emboldened anti-colonialists.

Nationalists who sought support for their cause abroad joined the early trickle of Indians to the United States, a cause for concern for British authorities. Although there was little U.S. criticism of Indian colonialism, Britain nonetheless worried that U.S.–India contact—through trade, Christian proselytizing, or visits by Indians to America—could foment a rebellious anti-colonial spirit among its subjects. It, thus, placed restrictions on American merchant activities in India trade and kept a watchful eye on missionaries as well as Indians abroad.[159] British officials were especially concerned about people like Lala Lajpat Rai, who traveled to Boston in 1905 to speak about India's plight to the Boston Anti-Imperialist League, a group that spoke out against Philippine annexation.[160] He also coordinated the publication of an article titled, "India and Ireland Working Together," in the New York Irish American newspaper, the *Gaelic American*.[161]

Most Indians in the United States—99 percent of those who settled on the West Coast—in the first two decades of the twentieth century came from the state of Punjab and five districts in particular: Jullunder, Hoshiarpur, Gurdaspur, Amritsar, and Ludhiana.[162] Punjab, called the "land of the five rivers" and home to three million residents, is located in northwest India and was annexed by Britain in 1849 after a period of fierce resistance. While the region experienced economic growth in the second half of the nineteenth century with the commercialization of agriculture, it came at the cost of many residents' well-being, and land shortages were accompanied by population explosion, drought, famines, and epidemics.[163] Colonial policies, which included road, railroad, and canal projects and the opening of new lands for cultivation, resulted in large holdings falling under the control of hereditary owners, which was accompanied by increased absentee landlordism, rising cost of land, and general land shortages. They also instituted a system of collecting land taxes in cash that replaced payment in kind, which dramatically raised the amount of money collected but imposed an overwhelming burden on taxpayers. According to Joan Jensen, because Punjabi peasants of the Jat caste, "took great pride working with their hands, considered themselves good farmers, and looked down on debt," they preferred to pay taxes by mortgaging their land rather than selling it.[164] Despite such measures, transfers of land into the hands of moneylenders dramatically increased after 1900.

Other economic problems in Punjab included an underdeveloped manufacturing sector, which affected the well-being of laborers as well as independent artisans. Textile mills that had produced for the home market were displaced by competition from English mills in Lancashire and Manchester.[165] With regard to artisans, their already tenuous position, in which they depended on masters who owned and operated the workshops and held them in debt for their apprenticeship, worsened with the influx of foreign imports.[166]

Against this backdrop of economic and political turmoil, compounded by a 1907 plague in which half a million people died, many Punjabis turned to migration. The earliest emigrants from Punjab were mostly indentured laborers from the artisan class, and the largest volume took place in 1896 when about nineteen thousand Indians, mostly Punjabi, went to Uganda for work in railway construction. These jobs paid better than sugarcane work in Mauritius (30 shillings per month versus 11). Others went to Fiji, although employers preferred South Indian coolies, who were more accustomed to the weather.[167] Non-coolie emigrants motivated by economic hardship could stay closer to home, as there were opportunities within the region, such as in present-day Pakistan where Britain offered land to settlers who would help construct irrigation canals. There was also work available within India for railroad contractors and laborers. Since such labor migration was viewed as a temporary measure, it was made up of individual family members, especially younger sons, who would depart for their jobs and send money to their families and villages.

Economic woes in the region were also channeled into political unrest against Britain, as nationalists such as Lala Lajpat Rai and Agit Singh told peasants that petitions were useless and they must resist by withholding taxes and stopping cultivation.[168] At first, the suppression of protestors led to a small outmigration to various locations. The American consul general at Calcutta, William Michael, had briefly encouraged Indian students to go to the United States, writing letters of introduction to institutions on their behalf, and the first Asian Indian student arrived on the West Coast around 1901.[169] By mid-1907, as unrest spread through the Punjbai region, seen in rising student protests at Khalsa College in Amritsar and a general strike in the large military outpost of Rawalpindi, the volume of political emigration increased.

Joining the British army, which offered the chance to leave India, was another option for Punjabi men seeking to escape their hardships. The colonial army was, in fact, the largest employer of Punjabis outside their native area, as the British came to rely on them for security at home and abroad, using them, for instance, to quell the Revolt of 1857.[170] From there, they became a mainstay of the native army and made up about half of it by the late nineteenth century. Despite their prominence, Punjabi officers, like all other Indian officers, held a secondary status in terms of pay and responsibilities compared to officials from Britain. They were, for example, proscribed from commanding troops in India. Punjabis also served in such far-flung locations as the Sudan, the Mediterranean, and China, where they helped suppress the Boxer Rebellion.[171] After completing their service, some chose to stay abroad, especially in parts of Asia where Punjabi former soldiers, many of whom were Sikh and, thus, identifiable by their turbans and steel bangles, found jobs as cab drivers and municipal police.[172]

Overseas migration to North America was another alternative. While in China, many Punjabi soldiers learned about extensive Chinese migration to the West Coast, hearing that wages were relatively high and that they could go as free laborers instead of contract workers.[173] In Punjab, meanwhile, steamship companies and railroad contractors distributed leaflets encouraging migration and advertising job opportunities. Canadian railroad companies were especially active in this regard, as a $500 head tax on Chinese instituted in 1904 had curtailed their immigration and created new labor demands. The firm Mssrs. Gillanders and Arbuthnot, which recruited workers for the Canadian Pacific Railway, targeted Punjabi Sikhs through its branch in Calcutta, selling 1,200 tickets to them on the promise of railway jobs that would pay $2 to $3 a day. Agents in Hong Kong also helped bring Sikhs to help construct the railway. [174]

For the journey to North America, a trip to Vancouver from India cost at least 300 rupees, which was a very high sum. Veterans might have enough cash to pay, but it was beyond the means of most village men, so as many as 80 percent of North America-bound Indians mortgaged a share of family lands for passage money.[175] For those leaving Punjab, the journey usually entailed taking a train from Jullundur to Delhi and then another to Calcutta, followed by a boat to Hong Kong before taking a steamer to Vancouver.[176] Others went by way of Southeast Asia or China, which offered cheaper passages, and smaller numbers through Fiji or Australia. Punjabi Sikhs had particular advantages in travel due to the network of temples created by former army officers who had settled in different parts of the world. Thus, a Sikh trying to get to Vancouver who made it as far as Hong Kong would have places to stay en route while he earned the additional money to cover his fare.[177]

After railway jobs in Canada ended, Indians were usually able to find other work in British Columbia, in land clearing, sawmills, and other industries. Those who spoke English could work as foremen and earn up to $3 per day.[178] Eventually, however, many left Canada for the United States, and the first notable surge of Indians across the border was recorded in 1906, when six hundred Indians applied for admission.[179] That year, they appeared in logging camps and lumber mills in Oregon and Washington, and as far south as Chico, California. Also in 1906, a man from Chico made the first registered complaint about an Indian "influx" to the American consul at Vancouver, British Columbia. In response, the consul urged the State Department to be mindful of the porousness of the Canadian border, while noting the difficulty of excluding Indians because they came from the British Empire.[180]

The Punjabi immigrants who ended up in the North American West were rarely the most destitute from their societies. They were typically drawn from the small landowning peasant classes, although a small number of contract laborers also immigrated.[181] As mentioned, most were men in their early twenties who expected to rejoin their families after earning enough money to keep their land. A few were married and had left their wives and children with their father's families. They usually traveled in groups of five to ten with relatives and people from the same village or nearby villages, with the best English speaker acting as the leader.[182]

Filipino Immigration

Filipinos were the last major Asian group to immigrate to the United States prior to the mid-twentieth century. As was the case with the groups already discussed, dynamics of empire and global capitalism shaped Philippine migration. However, more so than with the earlier Asian immigrant groups, the forces of U.S. conquest and colonialism directly set the stage for this diaspora.

Philippine society represented diverse cultural influences and histories of movement, contact, and mixture by the time of the American conquest in 1898. The population included an array of racial and ethnic groups, such as the Negritos, who were indigenous to the archipelago, and Malays, who had entered by way of Indonesia some 4,500 years ago. Changes wrought by outsiders accelerated from the fourteenth century, beginning with Chinese who came to work as entrepreneurs and laborers. Spanish rule from the sixteenth century brought a new racialized social order to the Philippines, in which Spanish, or *peninsulares*, sat at the top, followed by creoles (*insulares*[183]), Spanish mestizos, Chinese mestizos, common people, and Chinese. Economic commercialization allowed for the rise of an urban merchant class, which included Spaniards, Chinese mestizos, Chinese, and natives. From the late sixteenth to early nineteenth centuries, the Manila–Acapulco galleon trade, which sailed each year between these nodes of the Spanish empire, facilitated and extended cross-cultural contacts between Europeans and Asians, as well as opportunities for Filipinos and Chinese crew members to travel to and settle in the Americas. In addition to crewmembers, it is possible that Filipina women were on the ships as prostitutes, serving men on ships and in Acapulco. As mentioned earlier, scholars have cited the settlement of Filipinos in Louisiana in 1763 as the first permanent Asian American community. In addition, during the 1700s a small number of Filipinos entered the U.S. east coast as servants of American ship captains.[184]

After the Spanish–American War of 1898, Spain surrendered control of the Philippines, but instead of ushering in an era of independence, the conflict ended with the United States taking the role of colonial power. This transition did not occur smoothly. In the decades prior to the war, resistance to Spanish rule had been growing among the mestizo population and, by the 1880s, a reform movement calling for Filipino representation in the government and clergy, freedom of speech and assembly, and lower taxes, led by the Western-educated Jose Rizal, had taken hold. After Rizal's execution in 1896, Emilio Aguinaldo, who led an organization called Katipunan, emerged as the new face of Philippine resistance, although he was forced into exile after being routed by Spain. During the Spanish–American War,

Aguinaldo agreed, at U.S. officials' request, to return to the Philippines, and committed Filipino forces to fight against Spain in return for American support for Philippine independence. After Spain's surrender, Aguinaldo declared Philippine independence, but the United States denied the existence of the earlier agreement, and shifted its military power to defeat him and his army. Aguinaldo was captured in 1901, but Philippine nationalists continued to resist U.S. rule until 1913.[185]

Although the Philippine insurrection against the United States went on for over a decade after the end of the Spanish–American War, Americans had moved ahead with their plans for colonization, annexing the territory in 1898. This action was part of a larger process of U.S. expansion that included trading with China and India, "opening" Japan and Korea, sending missionaries to Asia, and acquiring Hawaii. The colonization of the Philippines, however, marked the United States' formal entry into the worldwide race for empire, and in the wake of annexation, it established a civilian government and sent bureaucrats and teachers to the colony to bring "civilization" to the natives. Although U.S. officials claimed their mission in the Philippines was a benevolent one, their brutal suppression of the insurrectionists suggested otherwise. In the Philippine–American War, which occurred directly on the heels of the Spanish conflict, the countryside was devastated and the loss of life enormous; as many as six hundred thousand died in Luzon alone.[186] Furthermore, economic policies fostered Philippine dependence while leaving the colony underdeveloped. From 1900 to 1935, the Philippines relied on the United States for 65 percent of its imports and 83 percent of its exports, while just 1 percent of the U.S.'s foreign investments went to the Philippines. Foreign commodities displaced domestic production, manufacturing investment was virtually nil, and most large-scale production was in export-based agriculture. Until the 1910s, the main exports were sugar, abaca, copra, coconut oil, and tobacco, and by the following decade these were eclipsed by sugar.[187] These economic developments profited landed elites, but made many Filipinos poorer, as landholdings fell into a smaller and smaller set of hands.

Until 1946, the Philippines remained a U.S. territory, and emigration grew directly out of this relationship. H. Brett Melendy divides immigration in the early twentieth century into three chronologically overlapping groups: 1) young sojourners seeking education who migrated between 1903 and World War II; 2) workers to Hawaii who arrived between 1907 and the 1930s; and 3) West Coast migrants who came in the 1920s and early 1930s. In each phase, most of the arrivals were young men under the age of thirty.[188] With regard to students, Filipinos were similar to Japanese in that they sought modern, Western education in order to serve their home country, but the aims of the educational programs sponsoring Filipinos were distinct. The Pensionado Act of 1903, passed by the U.S. Congress, was the genesis of Filipino student emigration and established a program for government-sponsored Filipinos to study, mostly at the college level, in the United States. The first group of 100 pensionados was selected from a pool of 20,000 applicants, and all of them returned to the Philippines, where they secured high-status jobs in areas such as agriculture, business, education, engineering, and government. By 1907, 183 pensionados were enrolled in forty-seven schools across the United States, with the largest number at the University of Illinois.[189] Their achievements prompted further migration by independent students who hoped to duplicate their success, but because they were not sponsored and often had to find employment, they faced greater challenges in completing their education, and many never did. Between 1910 and 1938, some 14,000 Filipinos enrolled at various education institutions in the United States.[190] As with the pensionados, those who earned their degrees—some from institutions as prestigious as the University of California, Columbia, Harvard, and Stanford—went on to hold important posts in the Philippines.

As with earlier Asian immigrants, students and elites were later eclipsed by a larger wave of labor migrants. Filipino laborers first went to the territory of Hawaii and then the U.S. mainland. The demand for Filipino labor in the former stemmed from shortages of other Asians and planters' ongoing quest for the ideal worker. As early as 1901, the HSPA explored the possibility of importing Filipinos, although it was not until 1906 that the first group arrived, fifteen workers to Olaa Plantation in the big island. From there, recruitment was spotty, but resumed in earnest in 1909, due to the disruption of Japanese labor migration by the Gentlemen's Agreement of 1907–08. That year, there was a shipment of about eight hundred Filipinos recruited by HSPA officials in Manila and Cebu Island.[191] Emigrants first went to Hong Kong where their labor contracts were drawn up, food and clothing was distributed, and transportation was arranged.

The labor migration of Filipinos to Hawaii was, thus, largely an HSPA undertaking with government support, whose strategy was to recruit "cheap, not too intelligent, docile unmarried men."[192] As American nationals, Filipinos traveled with U.S. passports and were exempt from immigration restrictions, which made their importation convenient. Moreover, because the Organic Act was in effect, Filipinos did not come as indentured laborers, as previous waves of Asians had. These advantages led Hawaii's Territorial Board of Immigration to call them "the only hope of the future under the existing laws."[193] New legislation, furthermore, regulated the business and provided for the free return of laborers after the expiration of three-year contracts.[194]

During the main years of early Filipino migration, from 1909 to 1931, 112,828 entered Hawaii. The high point was 1925, when 11,621 arrived. By this time, moreover, the HSPA no longer had to recruit actively, as Filipinos, already with labor contracts or jobs promised by agents, were showing up voluntarily to depart for Hawaii. In 1920, 21,031 Filipinos were living in the islands and in 1930 the population grew to 63,052.[195] Emigration dropped off in the early 1930s due to the Great Depression and declining labor demands, and over that decade the number of Filipinos in Hawaii fell to 52,659. Most remained rural, with just 6,800 living in Honolulu.[196] Also in these years, 38,946 returned to the Philippines, while 18,607 went to the U.S. West Coast.[197]

The Philippines comprise a great deal of ethnic diversity, but before 1915, Tagalogs were the main ethnic group among Filipino immigrants, due to recruiters' focus on Manila, but afterward, Ilocanos would predominate, as recruitment shifted to the northwestern provinces in Luzon and elsewhere in the archipelago.[198] Unstable economic conditions in the northwest had produced a large potential pool of labor emigrants which was appealing to recruiters. In Luzon, because licensing fees had raised the cost of recruiting in Manila, labor agents increasingly turned to densely populated, mountainous provinces such as Ilocos Norte, Ilocos Sur, Pangasinan, La Union, Tarlac, and Abra. A recruiter could earn $3.50 for an unmarried worker from the provinces, compared to $2.50 for one from Manila.[199] They could get even more—about $10—if they recruited a worker who took his family with him. By the 1910s, Ilocanos from the northwestern provinces made up about 60 percent of Philippine recruits to Hawaii.[200] Plantation owners described them as "stalwart, mild mannered, energetic and saving," and "the best workers."[201] Recruitment also targeted the

Cebuano-speaking provinces of the Visayan Islands—Cebu, Bohol, Negros Oriental—which drew another 30 percent of Philippine immigrants after World War I. As central Luzon and the Visayan Islands were flourishing sugar production areas, the rates of emigration were lower there compared to the northwest. However, those who did leave these areas for Hawaii brought with them familiarity with sugar cultivation.[202]

Also by the 1910s, the United States' relationship with the Philippines moved toward "Philippinization," with the territorial government obtaining more control over labor recruitment and emigration. In addition to establishing a licensing system requiring recruiters to pay national and provincial fees, the government created a Bureau of Labor that supervised contracts and placed a resident commissioner in Hawaii. Before laborers left the Philippines, the HSPA in Manila had to provide each with a written contract, which was binding on the association, but not the laborer, and, thus, did not violate contract labor laws.[203] Under the contracts from 1915 on, workers received subsistence money, clothing, and transportation to a plantation. For signing a three-year contract, an unmarried worker received a bonus of 10 pesos while a married worker received 20. The worker and family received free housing, water, fuel, and medical care at the plantation. Field laborers worked ten-hour days, mill workers twelve, and the work month consisted of twenty-six days.[204] Men earned $20 per month, women $14, children's wages depended on how much work they did. When their contracts expired, they would get free transportation back to the Philippines. Workers who violated their contracts were not penalized but forfeited their benefits. The Philippine government also occasionally sent commissioners to Hawaii to investigate conditions, arranged for the return passage of pre-1915 immigrants, and appointed interpreters to work with immigrants still in Hawaii.[205]

As was the case among other Asian groups, going abroad to Hawaii and North America was a response to new conditions and an extension of ongoing practices. Labor sojourning had been a way of life for many Ilocanos from northwest Luzon. Because the region was dry and overpopulated, many of its residents would leave for other parts of the Philippines for temporary work. A common practice among people from Ilocos Norte, for instance, was to head south for the rice harvest and then return home. Others went east to Cagayan to earn money in fishing or trading cloth. The introduction of the cash economy made economic conditions more exploitative and precarious, leading people to consider traveling even farther distances. Filipinos from rural provinces faced especially acute poverty, shrinking land bases, and increasing rates of farm tenancy. One immigrant from Cebu recollected having to mortgage his share of the family's land in order to survive: "Though I worked hard daily, half of what I made I gave to my master as every tenant has to do. Therefore, my financial affairs were discouraging and most disappointing."[206] Another Cebu immigrant said in the late 1930s:

> My sole ambition was to save enough money to pay back the mortgage on my land. In the Philippines a man is considered independent and he is looked upon with respect by his neighbors if he possesses land. The amount of land possessed by a person determined his social status and wealth. My forefathers had always been wealthy and were respected citizens of the village. Therefore, I was anxious to uphold our family name and role in the community. To work there in the fields with common peasants was a great disgrace and disaster to my family.[207]

As for their journeys across the Pacific, these usually started in Manila, where most Filipinos headed for Hawaii would go to the HSPA office where they received physical examinations and bedding for the trip. As one traveler recounted:

> At four-o'clock the boat sailed from Manila Harbor carrying about two hundred or perhaps more Filipino emigrants to a new land which would mould and determine the lives of so many people. We were all ushered to the very bottom of the boat where several families slept on the floor on their mats in one big room. The smell of freight and oil together with Japanese food filled the air as we sat together like a pack of sardines in our room.

As the passengers anticipated their destination, "Some said that Hawaii had great big eagles which swept away children from the very cradles of their homes whenever they were hungry . . . Some said that women and maidens were often seized from their homes to be mates of bachelors who captured them. Others said that some men were going to be forced to join the army."[208] Upon disembarking, the arrivals were segregated by assignment to one of thirty HSPA-affiliated plantations on Maui, Oahu, Kauai, and Hawaii. As their numbers grew, the ethnic composition of islands changed greatly; in 1915 Filipinos represented about 19 percent of the workforce and Japanese were 54 percent, and by 1932 Japanese were 19 percent and Filipinos 70 percent.[209]

A large proportion of migrant laborers returned to their native barrios; by 1935, 58,281 had gone back to the Philippines while about 18,574 had gone on to the mainland.[210] When emigrants returned home, the stories they told and money they brought back with them made a strong impression on fellow villagers and triggered many to make their own plans to emigrate. "Hawaiiano" was a term for Ilocanos who had lived in Hawaii and returned with money, often used to purchase land.[211] Such displays of affluence made others want to go too. As one Ilocano immigrant recounted, "Those Hawaiianos who came back were very showy. They would walk around with white high-heeled shoes, even in the dust and wear those Amerikana suit [sic] and Stetson hats, even on hot days to blow on the outside."[212] Additionally, migration proved vital for the survival of many communities in the Philippines, as emigrant laborers would send money home while they were away, allowing families to buy land or save for later.

Filipino migration to the U.S. mainland, which had previously been limited to pensionados and a handful of people brought for events like the St. Louis world exposition in 1903, picked up in the 1920s. In 1910, just 406 Filipinos were counted outside of Hawaii and the largest group, about 100, was found around New Orleans. Ten years later, there were 5,603 Filipinos in Alaska and the U.S. mainland, with some 2,674 in California, 958 in Washington, and 1,844 in eastern states. The mainland influx continued into the 1920s, during which about 45,000 Filipinos arrived, with about 16,000 of these coming from Hawaii.[213] Most stayed on the West Coast, but sizeable numbers went to Chicago, Detroit, New York, and Philadelphia. In addition to the availability of agricultural and fishery jobs and the rosy portraits painted in letters home and by return emigrants, Filipinos were drawn to the United States due to being instilled in the "American Dream" by American educators working in the Philippines. Aggressive advertising by companies like Dollar steamship line also got the attention of would-be emigrants and sold them on trans-Pacific travel.

The Filipino newcomers to Hawaii and the mainland during the early twentieth century were predominantly young and male; 84 percent were under the age of 30 upon their arrival and 94 percent were men. They had little formal education and spoke neither English nor Spanish. In 1930, most Filipinos in Hawaii remained rural and were engaged in plantation agriculture. On the mainland, some 20,000 were employed in California agriculture, 11,000 worked as servants or in hotels and restaurants, and 4,200 in Alaskan canneries.[214] As discussed, the preponderance of young men was typical of broader patterns of Asian immigration and reflected social conventions—for instance the expectation that single women should stay home until married—and the priorities of the industries that hired them. A small number of Filipinas came to the United States during this period for reasons including education, employment, and to escape arranged marriage, but they were rare.[215]

Conclusion

Asian migrants to Hawaii and the United States began their new lives under an array of circumstances. The earliest Chinese who came to California in search of gold entered a male frontier society in flux where nearly everyone was a newcomer. They were sometimes met by a small number of their fellow countrymen who gave them a place to rest for a few days before outfitting them for the gold fields and sending them on their way.[216] Those headed to the southern mines walked, often alone and with only a vague sense of where they were headed, from San Francisco to San Jose and then eastward toward Stockton.

Asians arriving later could join family, friends, or fellow villagers who had preceded them and established burgeoning ethnic communities. Yet others, such as students of American missionaries, performers, and prostitutes, came at the urging or under the coercion of other people and lived much of their lives in America cut off from family and community networks of support. Despite the variations in migration experiences and circumstances, all Asian immigrants from the mid-nineteenth to early twentieth centuries encountered a land that was much different from where they had come, struggled to foster a sense of normalcy and familiarity, and tried to accomplish what they came for, whether that was serving out a contract, striking it rich, getting an education, or establishing permanent communities.

Notes

1 Mary Paik Lee, *Quiet Odyssey: A Pioneer Korean Woman in America* (Seattle: University of Washington Press, 1990), 12.

2 Dorothy B. Fujita-Rony, *American Workers, Colonial Power: Philippine Seattle and the Transpacific West* (Berkeley: University of California Press, 2003), 25–27.

3 Edna Bonacich and Lucie Cheng, "Introduction: A Theoretical Orientation to International Labor Migration," from *Labor Immigration Under Capitalism: Asian Workers in the United States Before World War II*, Lucie Cheng and Edna Bonacich, eds (Berkeley: University of California Press, 1984), 2.

4 Sojourners went to places like Taiwan, Guangxi, Sichuan and Yunan, Philip A. Kuhn, *Chinese Among Others: Emigration in Modern Times* (Lanham: Rowman and Littlefield, 2008), 15.

5 Sucheng Chan, *This Bittersweet Soil: Chinese in California Agriculture, 1860–1910* (Berkeley: University of California Press, 1986), 9. Also, according to Philip Kuhn, Chinese trade with Siam and sojourning can be traced to the thirteenth century. Merchants, craftsmen, and political

refugees all went there, with some going on to serve in the Siamese court, even becoming territorial governors. Kuhn, *Chinese Among Others*, 78.

6 Kuhn, *Chinese Among Others*, 103.

7 Madeline Y. Hsu, *Dreaming of Gold, Dreaming of Home: Transnationalism and Migration between the United States and South China, 1882–1943* (Stanford: Stanford University Press 2000), 20; Him Mark Lai, *Becoming Chinese American: A History of Communities and Institutions* (Walnut Creek: Alta Mira Press, 2004), 13.

8 Chan, *This Bittersweet Soil*, 13; Kuhn, *Chinese Among Others*, 62.

9 By the early 1800s, Chinese outnumbered all other groups in Singapore, part of the Straits Settlement. Kuhn, *Chinese Among Others*, 102.

10 Ibid., 71.

11 Japan did this in Nagasaki.

12 Roger Daniels, *Asian America: Chinese and Japanese in America Since 1850* (Seattle: University of Washington Press, 1988), 9.

13 John Kuo Wei Tchen, *New York Before Chinatown: Orientalism and the Shaping of American Culture* (Baltimore: Johns Hopkins University Press, 1999), xix, 79.

14 For three centuries China had been trading with Western powers, but the Westerners eventually desired greater access and control. Precipitating the war was China's attempt to suppress opium imports. In the years since Britain introduced it to the country, it bred addiction among residents and caused an unfavorable trade balance.

15 The right of extraterritoriality allowed them to be tried by their own consuls, effectively making them immune to Chinese law. Chan, *This Bittersweet Soil*, 22.

16 Although Christian missionaries had been there since the sixteenth century, after 1842 they were able to proselytize more freely.

17 This had numerous adverse effects, such as the unemployment of about one hundred thousand porters and boatmen and the displacement of native producers due to the influx of foreign goods. Kuhn, *Chinese Among Others*, 111.

18 Ibid.

19 After that rebellion was suppressed, its leaders and other participants fled China in fear of reprisal.

20 Chan, *This Bittersweet Soil*, 20; Hsu, *Dreaming of Gold*, 22, 27.

21 Chan, *This Bittersweet Soil*, 16.

22 Ibid., 11.

23 Kuhn, *Chinese Among Others*, 110.

24 Ibid., 113.

25 Hsu, *Dreaming of Gold*, 22.

26 Chan, *This Bittersweet Soil*, 17.

27 Daniels, *Asian America*, 11. Ming overturned the ban on maritime trade in 1567. Kuhn, *Chinese Among Others*, 9.

28 Daniels, *Asian America*, 11.

29 This was not helped by the Qing government's vacillations, which at various points imposed a death penalty on emigrants who sought to return, offered amnesty to returnees, and announced that those who did not return would be forever barred from reentry. Its policy on trade was also inconsistent, imposing sporadic bans until lifting them for good in 1727. Chan, *This Bittersweet Soil*, 15; Kuhn, *Chinese Among Others*, 9.

30 1868 marked end of the ban on emigration and in 1893 reentry was made legal.

31 Daniels, *Asian America*, 10.

32 Ibid., 10; also see Chan, *This Bittersweet Soil*, 21.

33 Chan, *This Bittersweet Soil*, 21.

34 Kuhn, *Chinese Among Others*, 114.

35 Kuhn, *Chinese Among Others*, 119.

36 They could offer their Chinese agents the same protection. In 1874 Portugal banned the coolie trade. Ibid., 127.

37 In the 1860s and 1870s brokers paid anywhere from $120 to $170 to secure a coolie and could sell him in Latin America for $350 to $400. Chan, *This Bittersweet Soil*, 20, 23; Kuhn, *Chinese Among Others*, 133.

38 Kuhn, *Chinese Among Others*, 131–32.

39 Because of extraterritoriality and the fact that emigration was illegal.

40 Some Americans continued to engage in the trade under foreign flags.

41 Tin-Yuke Char and Wai Jane Char, "The Chinese," *Ethnic Sources in Hawaii: Social Processes in Hawaii*, eds, Bernard L. Hormann and Andrew W. Lind (New York: McGraw-Hill, 1996), 37.

42 Adam McKeown, *Chinese Migrant Networks and Cultural Change: Peru, Chicago, Hawaii, 1900–1936* (Chicago: University of Chicago Press, 2001), 33.

43 Edna Bonacich, "Asian Labor in the Development of California and Hawaii," in Cheng and Bonacich, *Labor Immigration Under Capitalism*, 178.

44 Ronald Takaki, *Strangers from a Different Shore: A History of Asian Americans* (Boston: Little Brown, 1998), 22.

45 Ibid., 24.

46 McKeown, *Chinese Migrant Networks and Cultural Change*, 33.

47 Ibid., 34.

48 Char and Char, "The Chinese," 38.

49 Although a great boon for Hawaii, the well-being of its sugar industry became reliant on this arrangement, which the United States had the power to rescind or amend. It did this in 1887, when the treaty was up for renewal, compelling Hawaii to grant exclusive rights to maintain a naval station at Pearl Harbor. Duty-free sugar exports ended in 1891. However, annexation effectively restored and made permanent the protected status of Hawaiian sugar. Moon-Kie Jung, *Reworking Race: The Making of Hawaii's Interracial Labor Movement* (New York: Columbia University Press, 2006), 12.

50 Takaki, *Strangers from a Different Shore*, 24; Jung, *Reworking Race*, 12.

51 5,626 out of 14,539 workers. Char and Char, "The Chinese," 39.

52 McKeown, *Chinese Migrant Networks and Cultural Change*, 34.

53 Takaki, *Strangers from a Different Shore*, 25.

54 Yong Chen, *Chinese San Francisco, 1850–1943: A Transnational Community* (Stanford: Stanford University Press, 2000), 36.

55 Chan, *This Bittersweet Soil*, 37.

56 Ibid., 30.

57 Chen, *Chinese San Francisco*, 13.

58 Ibid., 36.

59 Takaki *Strangers from a Different Shore*, 83.

60 Depending on the destination country's contract labor laws, a contract would be signed at the point of embarkation or disembarkation. On the credit-ticket system, see Kuhn, *Chinese Among Others*, 123–126 and Chan, *This Bittersweet Soil*, 26.

61 Chan, *This Bittersweet Soil*, 26.

62 Ibid., 27.

63 Ibid., 28.

64 Ibid., 27.

65 Ibid., 38.

66 Ibid.

67 Ibid., 29.

68 Tchen, *New York Before Chinatown*, 225.

69 Ibid.

70 Ibid.

71 Judy Yung, *Unbound Feet: A Social History of Chinese Women in San Francisco* (Berkeley: University of California Press, 1995), 24.

72 Takaki, *Strangers from a Different Shore*, 34.

73 Ibid.

74 Ibid.
75 Sucheng Chan, *Asian Americans: An Interpretive History* (Boston: Twayne, 1991), 9.
76 Ibid.
77 Kuhn, *Chinese Among Others,* 82.
78 Paul Spickard, *Japanese Americans: The Formations and Transformations of an Ethnic Group* (New Brunswick: Rutgers University Press, 2009), 8.
79 Chan, *Asian Americans,* 9.
80 Spickard, *Japanese Americans,* 9.
81 Eiichiro Azuma: *Between Two Empires: Race, History and Transnationalism in Japanese America* (New York: Oxford University Press, 2005), 18, 19.
82 Ibid., 19.
83 Ibid.
84 Ibid., 19, 20.
85 Ibid., 23, 20.
86 Ibid., 21.
87 Yuji Ichioka, *The Issei: The World of the First Generation Japanese Immigrants, 1885–1924* (New York: Free Press, 1988), 10.
88 Ibid.
89 Azuma, *Between Two Empires,* 11.
90 Ibid.
91 Ibid., 24–25.
92 Ichioka, *The Issei,* 9.
93 Ibid., 7–9.
94 Ibid., 11.
95 Ibid.
96 Ibid., 13.
97 Azuma, *Between Two Empires,* 30.
98 Ichioka, *The Issei,* 14.
99 Ibid., 15.
100 Ibid., 3; Azuma, *Between Two Empires,* 27.
101 Prior to 1868 the term referred to internal migrants.
102 According to Azuma, at first it was 25 percent and it was later reduced to 15 percent. Also see Ichioka, 4.
103 Ichioka, *The Issei,* 40.
104 Ibid., 40; Azuma, *Between Two Empires,* 27.
105 Ichioka, *The Issei,* 41.
106 Ibid., 44–45.
107 Ibid., 27, 42.
108 Azuma, *Between Two Empires,* 28.
109 Ibid., 29.
110 Ibid.
111 Ichioka, *The Issei,* 46.
112 Ibid.
113 Ibid., 47–48.
114 Ibid., 50–51.
115 Ibid., 8–9.
116 Azuma, *Between Two Empires,* 29.
117 Ichioka, *The Issei,* 56.
118 Ibid., 53.
119 No more than thirty per month per emigration company. On the issue, see ibid., 54–55.
120 Chan, *Asian Americans,* 36.
121 Azuma, *Between Two Empires,* 30.
122 Ichioka, *The Issei,* 52.
123 Takaki, *Strangers from a Different Shore,* 50–51.

124 Ibid., 135.

125 Ichioka, *The Issei*, 28.

126 Ibid., 29–30.

127 Ibid., 5; Evelyn Nakano Glenn, *Issei, Nisei, War Bride: Three Generations of Japanese Women in Domestic Service* (Philadelphia: Temple University Press, 1986), 31.

128 Glenn, *Issei, Nisei, War Bride*, 27.

129 Linda Pomerantz, "The Background of Korean Emigration," from *Labor Immigration Under Capitalism*, 282.

130 Ibid., 283.

131 Ibid., 284.

132 Chan, *Asian Americans*, 13.

133 Brett Melendy, *Asians in America: Filipinos, Koreans, and East Indians* (Boston: Twayne, 1977), 121.

134 Takaki, *Strangers from a Different Shore*, 53, Chan, *Asian Americans*, 15.

135 Pomerantz, "The Background of Korean Emigration," 283–84.

136 Chan, *Asian Americans*, 13.

137 Ibid., 15.

138 Ibid.

139 Patterson, *Korean Frontier*, 1–2.

140 Ibid., 2.

141 Chan, *Asian Americans*, 15.

142 Melendy, *Asians in America*, 125; Chan, *Asian Americans*, 16.

143 Melendy, *Asians in America*, 129.

144 Takaki, *Strangers from a Different Shore*, 56.

145 Ibid., 56.

146 Ibid.

147 Melendy, *Asians in America*, 129.

148 Wayne Patterson, *The Ilse: First Generation Korean Immigrants in Hawai'i, 1903–1973* (Honolulu: University of Hawaii Press, 2000), 30.

149 Chan, *Asian Americans*, 23.

150 During the 1800s, about seven hundred thousand Indians were exported to the West Indies, British Guiana, and Mauritius as indentured laborers. Indian laborers also went to Southeast Asia. Sucheta Mazumdar, "Colonial Impact and Punjabi Emigration to the United States," from *Labor Immigration Under Capitalism*, 318.

151 Joan Jensen, *Passage from India: Asian Indian Immigrants in North America* (New Haven: Yale University Press, 1988), 9.

152 Ibid.

153 Mazumdar, "Colonial Impact and Punjabi Emigration to the United States," 319.

154 Jensen, *Passage from India*, 12.

155 Ibid., 14.

156 Ibid.

157 Ibid., 13.

158 Ibid., 4–6.

159 Ibid., 16–17.

160 Ibid., 19.

161 Ibid.

162 Mazumdar, "Colonial Impact and Punjabi Emigration to the United States," 316.

163 Jensen, *Passage from India*, 19.

164 Ibid.

165 Mazumdar, "Colonial Impact and Punjabi Emigration to the United States," 326.

166 Ibid., 327–28.

167 Ibid., 328.

168 Jensen, *Passage from India*, 20.

169 Ibid., 21.

170 Although Sikhs made up one percent of the Indian population, they represented one-fifth of the army in India. Ibid., 6; Mazumdar, "Colonial Impact and Punjabi Emigration to the United States," 328.
171 Jensen, *Passage from India*, 6–7.
172 Ibid., 25.
173 Ibid., 25.
174 Mazumdar, "Colonial Impact and Punjabi Emigration to the United States," 332.
175 Jensen, *Passage from India*, 25.
176 Ibid.
177 Ibid., 27.
178 Ibid.
179 Ibid., 15.
180 Ibid., 16.
181 Some of these people were turned away because of contract labor bans, but most were admitted, perhaps because contracts were verbal. Mazumdar, "Colonial Impact and Punjabi Emigration to the United States," 332.
182 Jensen, *Passage from India*, 26.
183 Spanish descent but born in the Philippines.
184 Melendy, *Asians in America*, 21; Fujita-Rony, *American Workers, Colonial Power*, 28–29.
185 For this paragraph, I used information from Chan, *Asian Americans*, 17; Melendy, *Asians in America*, 23–24.
186 Fujita Rony, *American Workers, Colonial Power*, 30.
187 Ibid., 33.
188 Melendy, *Asians in America*, 33.
189 Ibid., 32.
190 Ibid.
191 Melendy, *Asians in America*, 34.
192 Miriam Sharma, "Labor Migration and Class Formation Among the Filipinos in Hawaii, 1906–1946," from Cheng and Bonacich, *Labor Immigration Under Capitalism*, 583.
193 Chan, *Asian Americans*, 18. Also see Melendy, *Asians in America*, 33.
194 Sharma, "Labor Migration and Class Formation Among the Filipinos to Hawaii," 582.
195 Melendy, *Asians in America*, 37.
196 Ibid., 40.
197 Ibid., 37.
198 Chan, *Asian Americans*, 18.
199 Melendy, *Asians in America*, 36.
200 Ibid.
201 Ibid.
202 Chan, *Asian Americans*, 18; Fujita-Rony, *American Workers, Colonial Power*, 41-42.
203 Melendy, *Asians in America*, 35.
204 Chan, *Asian Americans*, 36.
205 Ibid., 37.
206 Quoted in Melendy, *Asians in America*, 37–8.
207 Quoted in Ibid., 38.
208 Quoted in Ibid., 39.
209 Sharma, "Labor Migration and Class Formation Among the Filipinos to Hawaii," 586.
210 Ibid.
211 Melendy, *Asians in America*, 39.
212 Quoted in ibid.
213 Demographic figures from ibid., 39–41.
214 Ibid., 43.
215 Linda Espana-Maram, *Creating Masculinity in Los Angeles's Little Manila: Working-Class Filipinos and Popular Culture, 1920s–1950s* (New York: Columbia University Press, 2006), 19.
216 Chan, *This Bittersweet Soil*, 32.

Making a Living:

3

The Politics and Economics of Work before the 1930s

In 1863, the Central Pacific Railroad began construction of the western side of the nation's first transcontinental line, building east from Sacramento, California. Before long, the company confronted a problem: its employees—native and foreign-born white men—had become "unsteady," "unreliable," and demanding, thus, threatening to drive up costs and halt the project's progress. Hoping to curtail the problem, in 1865, the Central Pacific hired fifty Chinese male laborers on an experimental basis.[1] The trial was a success, as the workers performed their tasks well and caused management few problems. The white workers who remained refused to work alongside the Chinese, however, and demanded the foreigners be let go. Charles Crocker, one of the company directors, was unsympathetic, and instead praised the Chinese employees' "reliability and steadiness, and their aptitude and capacity for hard work." He furthermore told the white workers, "If you can't get along with them . . . We'll let you go and hire nobody but them."[2] With the help of recruiters who advertised in West Coast immigrant communities as well as in China, the Central Pacific eventually hired about fifteen thousand Chinese laborers, four-fifths of its wage workforce.

Historians often cite the involvement of Chinese in the construction of the transcontinental railroad as emblematic of the integral role of Asian immigrant labor in U.S. history, but the episode also underscores some of the racialized and exploitative dimensions of industrial capitalism and economic development that likewise loom large in Asian American history. With regard to pay, a white employee of the Central Pacific received $35 per month and free board and lodging, while a Chinese, regardless of skills and tasks performed, earned between $26 and $35, without food and housing.[3] The work itself exposed laborers to great danger. For instance, in order to dig tunnels through large granite formations, workers lowered themselves in baskets over cliffs, chiseling holes in the rock surface and stuffing dynamite powder into them before getting hoisted up before the powder exploded. Suffice it to say, not everyone made it up in time. Laying track from California to Utah, the men labored in punishing conditions, from sweltering deserts to snow-covered mountains. Worried that the Union Pacific, which was building from the east, would outpace western construction and take up more land grants, the Central Pacific pushed its workers

Figure 3.1   Ceremony for the driving of the golden spike at Promontory Summit, Utah, May 10, 1869. This photo has become iconic as an illustration of both American ingenuity and technology during the nineteenth century as well as the erasure of Chinese laborers, who made up the majority of the workforce for the Central Pacific. (Records of the Office of the Secretary of Agriculture, National Archives at College Park.)

to power through the brutal winter of 1866, and the bodies of the Chinese men who perished in those conditions could not be recovered until spring.[4]

The completion and celebration of the railroad at Promontory, Utah, on May 10, 1869, has been heralded as a triumph of technology, capitalist vision, and national will. In Asian American history, the moment has come to symbolize the widespread disregard for and amnesia around the contributions of Asian immigrant labor. Chinese not only made up about 80 percent of the Central Pacific's workforce, but they were also present that day. As Wesley Griswold described the scene, "a slicked-up team of the Union Pacific's best Irish track-layers had already swung the west rail across the gap in the track and spiked it down, except on the missing tie. Now a gang of Chinese, in clean blue jackets, moved out to put the final, east rail in place."[5] Contrary to popular myth, Chinese workers appeared in some of the A.J. Russell photos of these moments and the celebration afterward. They were not, however, featured in what would become the most iconic image of the railroad's completion, taken at the joining of the rails ceremony.[6] Furthermore, in all of the speeches given at Promontory, none mentioned the Chinese. At a celebration in Sacramento, Charles Crocker did acknowledge his Chinese employees for their "fidelity and industry," but he also characterized them as a "poor, destitute class of laborers."[7] A century later, the transcontinental railroad's venerated place in the national memory was affirmed in celebrations that also perpetuated the erasure of Chinese in this history. At a 1969 commemoration of the centennial of the driving of the golden spike, Secretary of Treasury John Volpe paid tribute to the historic achievement but, in summarizing the contributions of the key players, left out any reference to the Chinese laborers.

This chapter examines the work lives of Asian immigrants in America from the mid-1800s through the 1920s. As discussed in the previous chapter, labor demands generated by imperialist expansion and global capitalism shaped and sustained large-scale Asian migration to America. Work was, thus, a critical facet of Asian American experience during these years. It was why thousands came to in Hawaii and the continental United States and how people survived and cared for their families and communities. Work, furthermore, was often the site of the formation and crystallization of people's individual and group identities and a crucial terrain on which social struggles were waged. Commenting on day-to-day aspects of work—their opportunities as well as abuses—the chapter situates these experiences against the larger structure of capitalism, labor politics, and the crystallization of a racialized class system in America that both differentiated among and lumped together Chinese, Japanese, Koreans, Indians, and Filipinos. Because the Asian American population in this period was predominantly foreign born, male, working class, wage earning, and concentrated in Hawaii and the American West, this subset will receive particular consideration. But the chapter also complicates early Asian American labor history and the meanings of work beyond the experiences of male wage earners in fields and factories. Work was diverse, encompassing wage earning and entrepreneurship, paid and unpaid labor, the working poor and elite merchants, the city and countryside, and men and women's participation. It was also dynamic, as people pursued and attained mobility, fought back against abuse, and engaged in activities that impacted local, national, and international economies. Furthermore, experiences varied greatly by region; work and labor systems in Hawaii were drastically different from those on the West Coast, and the experiences of Asian immigrant workers in the eastern United States were distinct from those in the West.

Early Forays in the Eastern United States and the Ideological Place of Asian Labor

The participation of Chinese workers in the construction of the transcontinental railroad cemented in the national consciousness the stereotype that they were cheap and exploitable laborers, an enduring perception that would be projected onto subsequent Asian immigrants. In an industrializing and expanding nation that was grappling with attendant ideological dilemmas about the meanings of personal independence and free labor, the mere specter of Chinese labor was very polarizing. Merchant Aaron H. Palmer was an early proponent of using Chinese labor to develop the American West. As he stated in 1848, "No people in all the East are so well adapted for clearing wild lands and raising every species of agricultural product . . . as the Chinese."[8] Opponents of such schemes, among them white labor groups, said Chinese laborers were capitalist pawns, and their willingness to work for low pay would undermine all workers' wages and throw many native-born Americans and free immigrants into poverty and unemployment.

In the 1860s and 1870s, reconstruction in the South and rapid industrialization in the North brought pressing questions about labor to the fore. Emancipation had created sudden labor shortages on southern plantations, and former slave owners searched desperately for a new workforce. Aware of Chinese "coolies" in the Caribbean, some started to consider the idea of employing Chinese laborers who could help resuscitate southern cotton and sugar, and hopefully discipline freedmen into being better workers. Planters were encouraged by promoters such as Cornelius Koopsmanschap, a Dutch immigrant and Chinese labor supplier. In 1869, the Memphis Chamber of Commerce held a convention to explore the feasibility of large-scale Chinese employment in the South, which was attended by about two hundred delegates. Koopsmanschap, who had supplied several thousand Chinese for the Central Pacific, spoke at the event and said the workers could be obtained from California for $20 a month, and from China for five-year contracts for just $8 a month. Also at the convention was Tye Kim Orr, a Chinese man from the Straits Settlements who had evangelized among Chinese in British Guiana. He assured attendees that, "The Chinese are a docile, patient, susceptible people and will follow . . . and love those who try to teach and benefit them."[9]

As early as 1867, the first group of Chinese plantation workers had come to Louisiana, entering through New Orleans via Cuba. About sixty-five of these went to cotton plantations in Natchitoches.[11] Optimistic about the future of Chinese laborers in the region, investors in different southern states established offices to ship and distribute the workers.[12] The *New Orleans Daily Picayune* said Chinese laborers had proven themselves "better railroad building labor than any other," and that this boded well for their prospects on plantations. They were, moreover, "good general servants" who compared favorably to the "sleek, fat, well fed and well clad lazy insolent niggers." Another advantage of employing Chinese, the paper noted, was that they would not demand citizenship, and thus not trouble the racial hierarchy.[10]

Despite this early enthusiasm, the large-scale employment of Chinese in the South never materialized. For one, the 1862 Coolie Act, discussed in Chapter 1, was a persistent legal obstacle. Concerned that the importation of Chinese laborers from Cuba violated coolie laws—although it was difficult to prove if the workers had been contracted under fraudulent or involuntary circumstances—the federal government tried to halt these shipments, leading planters to instead recruit in California.[13] Moreover, the post-emancipation valorization of "free labor" and repudiation of imported and involuntary labor as antithetical to American values made the widespread employment of a group associated with "coolie" labor highly problematic. African Americans and Radical Republicans couched their opposition to Chinese "coolies" in this way, arguing that a form of labor resembling slavery would imperil the newly won freedom of former slaves.[14] Other southerners, leery of these foreigners from Asia, preferred to hire white immigrants from Europe.[15]

Ultimately, the initial trials with Chinese laborers proved unsuccessful. The costs involved in recruiting, transporting, and employing them were unfeasible except for the very elite. Nor did Chinese turn out to be the docile workers employers expected them to be. At the Millaudon estate in Louisiana, for instance, 141 Chinese were brought from San Francisco in 1870 to cultivate sugar. Within a month, they were demanding changes, such as a shortened workday, and conflicts over the abuse of workers by an overseer escalated in an altercation in which the overseer fatally shot a Chinese employee. Conditions at the estate did not improve after the shooting, and a year after the arrival of the Chinese, just twenty-five remained.[16] Strikes, conflicts with supervisors, and desertions similarly beset other plantations, signaling that Chinese laborers would not, alas, be the salvation of the South.

Elsewhere, manufacturers also experimented with Chinese laborers. As early as 1853, William Kelly, one of the inventors of the Bessemer iron refining process, hired twenty to work at Suwanee Furnace and Union Forge in Eddyville, Kentucky, although their employment was short-lived.[17] In the Northeast, the factory system and proletarianization of the workforce had given rise to labor militancy in the 1860s and 1870s, leading some employers to turn to Chinese workers. In North Adams, Massachusetts from 1868 to 1870, employees of Calvin Sampson's boot and shoe factory—many of whom belonged to the local shoemakers' union, the Order of the Knights of St. Crispin—struck for higher wages and an eight-hour day. Sampson tried to break the strikes by hiring local, out of state, and Canadian workers, but they often ended up joining the strikers. With the help of San Francisco labor agency Kwong, Chong, Wing, and Company, he brought seventy-five Chinese on three-year contracts for less than half of what he had paid the striking workers.[18] Knights of St. Crispin leader Samuel P. Cummings urged the organization to reach out to the Chinese laborers, but the white members' rejection of the idea effectively sealed the union's fate and it was crushed.[19] Although a few other manufacturers in the Northeast hired Chinese, their employment did not become widespread in the region. At Sampson's, they remained part of the workforce until 1880 when their contracts were not renewed, due to the exclusion movement and availability of unemployed and unorganized craftsmen.[20] Most Chinese residents of North Adams had left by this time for cities like Boston and New York.

Japanese, Korean, Indian, and Filipino wageworkers before World War II tended to concentrate in similar geographic areas as Chinese immigrants, by and large working in the American West, but they also went to industrial areas and major cities in other regions. Pockets included Filipinos in Louisiana, who were in the New Orleans area since the 1760s. Forming the settlement of St. Malo, believed to be the first Asian American community, Louisiana Filipinos drew their livelihood from fishing and are credited with pioneering preparation methods that transformed the state's shrimping industry in the 1800s. Although most Asian agricultural workers were in Hawaii and the West, a small number also worked in the South, such as the Chinese plantation workers discussed above. Additionally, the presence of Filipino agricultural laborers in Florida was confirmed in newspaper accounts of their expulsion from West Palm Beach in 1932.[21] Regarding Asian Indians, by 1935, about one thousand had settled in the eastern United States.[22] Whereas the majority of Indians on the West Coast were Punjabi Sikhs, most of those in the East—who had entered via eastern ports—were Bengalese Muslim former sailors. Shortly after the turn of the century, many of them secured factory jobs in industrial cities like New York, Pittsburgh, Detroit, Milwaukee, Chicago, St. Louis, and New Orleans. About two hundred Indians, furthermore, worked in the Detroit auto industry.[23]

Hawaii Plantations and Asian Labor

As sociologist Edna Bonacich has explained, the economy and labor system that evolved in Hawaii by the end of the nineteenth century more closely resembled the antebellum

American South than the economies of other parts of the U.S. mainland. In both areas, monocultural agriculture reigned and race and labor aligned closely. Hawaii's plantation system relied on imported Asian labor, while the South's had depended on enslaved Africans.[24] Although California also drew many Asian workers, it—and the rest of the American West—was very different from Hawaii. Hawaii, says Bonacich, "demonstrates what would probably have happened in California had there been no white small producers and workers."[25] Specifically, the presence of small producers and workers in California checked capital and the development of monopoly power, while their relative absence in Hawaii allowed capitalism to function virtually without constraints. By 1909, over half of private lands in Hawaii were owned by haole corporations.[26] Large planters had also co-opted the state, which essentially acted as a labor recruitment agency.

Realizing that natives would be an insufficient source of labor due to their declining numbers and ability to sustain themselves by other means, planters turned to importing workers, which would in turn transform the islands' population. As described in the previous chapter, between 1876 and 1885 40,000 to 50,000 Chinese arrived to work on Hawaiian plantations. Following them were Japanese, of whom about 180,000 entered between 1886 and 1924, and the third major group of imported laborers came from the Philippines (120,000 from 1907 to 1931).[27] About 17,500 Portuguese, the largest non-Asian group, joined the islands' labor force, and smaller numbers of Koreans, Puerto Ricans, Germans, Russians, Norwegians, and other Pacific Islanders also came to work on the plantations.[28] Portuguese, Puerto Ricans, and other Caucasians never accounted for more than 15 percent of the sugar plantation workforce, and a large white settler population never took root.[29] Performing crucial tasks such as clearing virgin land, working in newly opened fields, and expanding old ones, planters nonetheless viewed their imported laborers as little more than commodities. As the president of the HSPA wrote about Filipino labor importation in 1930, "From a strictly ethical standpoint, I can see little difference between the importation of foreign laborers and the importation of jute bags from India."[30]

The organization of work on plantations not only aimed to maximize production, discipline workers, and keep down costs, but also shored up the racial and ethnic stratification of Hawaii society, which privileged whiteness and maintained planter elites' power. Managerial, supervisory, and skilled positions were generally reserved for whites, while Chinese, Japanese, Filipinos, Puerto Ricans, and Koreans dominated the ranks of common laborers. According to a 1902 survey of 55 plantations, 83 percent of plantation laborers were Japanese and Chinese, while members of these groups represented just 18 percent of superintendent jobs.[31] Portuguese and "other Caucasians" respectively comprised 6.3 and 1.4 percent of the workforce, but made up 24 and 44 percent of superintendents. In terms of wages, in 1902, a white American blacksmith earned $3.82 per day, a Portuguese $2.61, a Native Hawaiian $2.12, and a Japanese $1.63.[32] White overseers' wages were 57 percent higher than Portuguese and 100 percent higher than Japanese. Within the plantation workforce, Europeans were not only paid more than Asians, but they were also recruited as family groups or couples. This contrasted with how Asians were treated. To prevent their permanent settlement and the entry of unproductive individuals, recruiters discouraged the migration of laborers' wives and other family members. It was only when planters worried about labor shortages and other threats to the stability of the plantation workforce that they altered this practice, mainly with regard to Japanese.

While such approaches to managing labor helped foster the growth of commercial agriculture in Hawaii, they also reflected employers' constant worries about their control over workers, particularly as individual contracts expired and the Organic Act of 1900 brought an end to the contract system in the islands. Although Hawaii's ethnic diversity is often touted as a symbol of the social harmony that purportedly flourishes among its people, it was actually a vestige of a system of labor exploitation that sought to capitalize on racial and ethnic difference. As discussed in the previous chapter, it was planters' quest for a compliant imported labor force that compelled them to begin recruiting Chinese during the nineteenth century, and a few decades later, fearing that they had grown too dependent on Chinese laborers, they started hiring Japanese.[33] As one planter stated, "We lay great stress on the necessity of having our labor mixed. By employing different nationalities, there is less danger of collusion among laborers, and the employers [are able to] secure better discipline."[34] By the end of the first decade of the 1900s, Japanese dominance in the workforce as well as their involvement in labor agitation led employers to look to a new set of imported workers, this time Filipinos (and to a lesser degree Koreans). During a 1909 strike by Japanese plantation workers, a representative of the HSPA said: "It may be too soon to say that the Jap is to be supplanted, but it is certainly in order to take steps to clip his wings [and to give] encouragement to a new class [Filipinos]. . .to keep the more belligerent element in its proper place."[35]

This divide-and-control strategy had crystallized by the turn of the twentieth century, and included ethnically segregated living quarters and work gangs, which could strengthen intraethnic solidarities, but usually met their aim of precluding interethnic alliances.[36] Employers also exploited political conflicts in Asia. For instance, aware of anti-Japan feelings among Koreans in the wake of the Sino–Japanese War, they recruited Korean laborers to break Japanese strikes and keep their numbers in check. As an official from the William G. Irwin and Company once remarked, "The Korea immigration scheme which has been inaugurated will in due course give us an element which will . . . be of great service in countering the evil effects in the labor market caused by too great a preponderance of Japanese."[37]

Extracting the labor of workers while making sure they would not leave the plantations was a balancing act that required planters to make some accommodations to employees. Planters realized that paternalistic practices—"welfare" services like housing, hospitals, stores, and insurance—could be more effective than coercion in managing workers. And workers quickly found that these perks, as welcome as they might have been, were not "free." Planters sometimes took deductions from paychecks for services used, threatened to evict suspected troublemakers and labor agitators from their homes, and prohibited workers from receiving hospital treatment unless authorized by an overseer.[38] Concerns about keeping workers also led to arrangements that gave them a degree of on-the-job autonomy, especially from the 1880s on as penal contracts expired and the system faded. For instance, some employers modified the luna (overseer) system, in which lunas, who were usually of a different ethnicity than the workers they supervised, enforced the pace, quality, and quantity of production, under punishing conditions. To curb worker discontent and counter the negative images of the system, planters implemented changes that gave workers greater control over how they spent their workday, such as paying based on the amount of work performed (row, acre, etc.), and allowing them to determine their pace and earn more if they

wished.[39] Additionally, voluntary long and short-term contracts with groups, called hui, were increasingly utilized. These catered to workers' desire to stay together in groups and gave them the chance to select their own overseer or headman. Long-established huis could gain intimate knowledge about land, sometimes resulting in almost complete control over the areas they farmed.[40]

Asian Labor in the North American West

Because the majority of Asians who came to the United States in the nineteenth and early twentieth centuries were young men in the American West, it was in this region that Asian American laborers made their greatest impact on the mainland. They participated in a range of occupations in the developing region, from Chinese coal miners in Wyoming in the 1870s to Japanese stump clearers in the Hood River Valley around the turn of the twentieth century to Filipino apple pickers in Yakima Valley during the early 1930s. Subject to a racially stratified labor market, they earned less than whites, and employers often regarded them as cheap and disposable, but they were nonetheless critical and shaped the work cultures of key industries. It was seldom acknowledged, but Asian labor in the West helped to transform the region and enrich the country as a whole, connecting regions, facilitating commerce, and boosting industrial growth.

Chinese were the first major source of Asian labor in the continental West. Many were former miners who had entered California in the 1840s and 1850s, while others came via Hawaii or directly from China. The signing of the Burlingame Treaty of 1868 resulted in part from pressure from U.S. businessmen wishing to secure access to a plentiful supply of Chinese laborers. Labor groups blasted what they saw as a "cheap labor treaty" that would trigger a "coolie invasion," and the *New York Times* predicted that Chinese immigration would usher in "the negro question all over again."[41] After 1868, the profile of Chinese immigrants skewed increasingly toward the unskilled and semi-skilled, and the proportion of merchants, craftsmen, and professionals declined.[42] This "proletarianization" of Chinese immigration also resulted from changes in the economic landscape of the American West toward industrialization and large-scale production, and furthermore established patterns that would echo in the experiences of subsequent Asian immigrants to the continental West. Until their numbers began to decline due to exclusion in 1882, Chinese wageworkers were employed—sometimes as the predominant workforce—in nearly every major extractive and industrial enterprise in the region, starting with mining, which by the late 1850s, after surface deposits of gold and other minerals had been largely depleted, was dominated by large companies. In the late nineteenth century, Chinese miners worked all over the West, and in the 1870s miners represented one fifth to a third of the Chinese workforce in California.[43]

Mining, railroad, and lumber companies in the West hired Chinese early on and continued to employ other Asians into the early twentieth century. Having proven themselves effective railroad workers for the Central Pacific, Chinese were hired by other companies to perform similar work. For instance, in 1869, the Memphis, El Paso, and Pacific Railroad hired 500 Chinese rail hands to work on its line in northeast Texas.[44] However, after exclusion diminished the supply of Chinese laborers, companies began to turn to Japanese in the 1890s. Rail companies were among the first employers in North America use Issei labor contractors, who by the early twentieth century had supplied thousands of Japanese workers for companies like the Oregon Short Line, Great Northern, and Oregon Railway.[45] Asian Indians, Koreans, and Filipinos also worked for railroad companies in the early twentieth century. About 2,000 Indians worked for the Western Pacific in northern California, leveling land, replacing rails, and sawing ties, typically in all-Indian gangs.[46] Korean workers were usually too few in number to form their own gangs, so often had to work alongside Japanese. Filipinos' employment with rail companies also included construction work, but they additionally served as Pullman porters around the country.[47]

Asian participation in the West Coast salmon canning industry illustrated the dynamics of ethnic succession that characterized many of the industries in which they participated, as well as how the laborers were able to shape their internal cultures and hierarchies. The canned salmon industry flourished from Alaska to central California from the 1870s to 1930s, and during this time Asian and Asian American workers were the predominant labor force. Chinese were first hired in 1872 at George Hume's cannery in Oregon. Involved in each phase of production, from unloading fish to soldering cans, they numbered about three thousand across several dozen canneries along the Columbia River by 1880, and remained the dominant and generally preferred workers until the 1920s. After 1900, Japanese participation increased, along with Mexicans, Mexican Americans, Native Americans, and European Americans. By 1909, Columbia River, Puget Sound, and Alaska canneries employed 7,167 Chinese and Japanese out of total of 12,934 workers.[48] Filipinos entered the industry after 1910, and by 1936 outnumbered Chinese and Japanese.[49] Although all Asians enjoyed less pay and mobility than whites, they occupied different places in the workforce hierarchy. Because they entered the industry during its nascent years, Chinese were able to shape its labor market and retain a privileged position vis-à-vis Japanese and Filipinos, guarding the best jobs for themselves (e.g., can makers, fish butchers, can testers). When Japanese were new, they were limited to a narrow range of "line" jobs inside the plant, but by the 1910s, their ability to break into labor contracting brought them more power, higher wages, and dominance in certain canneries, although at an industry-wide level their access to skilled positions was still limited.[50] As the latest group to enter the canneries, Filipinos had the hardest time gaining leverage through contracting, so they instead pursued advancement by unionizing and challenging the contracting system.

The sector of the Western economy in which Asian laborers made their greatest impact was agriculture. Beginning with the cultivation and export of wheat in the 1860s and then the proliferation of intensive specialty crops such as nuts, fruits, and vegetables, the rise of commercial agriculture transformed the region. Between 1879 and 1909 the value of intensive agriculture crops rose from 4 to 50 percent of all crops grown in California.[51] Railroads and refrigerated cars facilitated access to distant markets, and a growing national population sustained demand for the products. As the scale and profitability of this type of agriculture expanded, farms grew larger, growers embraced big business models, and operators became reliant on large, cheap laborers.

Because they arrived prior to the development of large-scale agribusiness, Chinese were able to establish niches as gardeners and truck farmers supplying food to mining communities during the 1850s and emerging population centers across California in the 1860s and 1870s.[52] Others found steady employment as tenant farmers, as white landholders found this to be an easy way to make extra money from land they had not brought under cultivation. Chinese farmed in the Sacramento Valley, Sacramento-San Joaquin Delta, San Joaquin Valley, smaller coastal valleys, and southern California coastal plains. As tenant farmers leading plots as large as 100 acres, they played a major role in bringing new crops into commercial cultivation, such as berries in Santa Clara County, bitter melons and string beans in Marysville and potatoes in the Sacramento-San Joaquin Delta. Chinese immigrants were also responsible for agricultural innovations including the breeding of the Bing cherry by Ah Bing of Oregon and the development of the frost-resistant orange by Lue Gim Gong of Florida.

As large-scale agribusiness took hold in the last three decades of the nineteenth century, new immigrants found that their only point of entry into agriculture was at the bottom as laborers, and to some degree as tenant farmers for companies. Many truck farmers, moreover, experienced downward mobility into the ranks of laborers. As hired labor, Chinese were extensively involved in constructing the irrigation channels, levees, dikes, and ditches that transformed the Sacramento-San Joaquin Delta into arable land in the 1860s and 1870s. They made up about 18 percent of farm laborers in California in 1870, and on the eve of exclusion in 1882, were roughly half of the state's agricultural labor force. In 1880, they represented majorities of the labor force in several counties: 86 percent of the labor force in Sacramento, 85 percent in Yuba, 67 percent in Solano, and 55 percent in Santa Clara. In Yolo and Tehama Counties, they were 46 and 43 percent respectively.[53] During the 1880s, the largest concentrations of Chinese farm workers were in Los Angeles, with about two thousand, followed by Sacramento, Santa Clara, San Joaquin, and Colusa counties.[54] In locations such as the vineyards and orchards of Mendocino and Yolo, major settled populations of Chinese did not appear, but during harvest seasons their presence would suddenly surge.

After 1900, Chinese workers' role in farm labor dwindled due to exclusion and the aging of the population.[55] During the previous decade, they had been surpassed by Japanese in the agricultural workforce. The first group of Japanese farm laborers came to California's Vaca Valley as well as farms near Tacoma, Washington during the late 1880s, and between 1898 and 1908 agriculture became the leading area of Japanese immigrants' employment, eclipsing domestic service and railroad construction. Let go or frustrated with their limited prospects in these and other industries, many entered agriculture in the hopes that it would yield mobility and independence.[56] Demands for fresh produce remained high and the shift to intensive agriculture and fruit and vegetable cultivation kept up the demand for laborers, which only intensified in the wake of Chinese exclusion. As with the Chinese, farming was a respected occupation for Japanese and many brought with them farming backgrounds. By 1909, about half of Japanese in the United States and three quarters in California (about thirty thousand) worked in agriculture as laborers or tenant farmers, which they remained extensively involved in until World War II. Mastering various kinds of farming, Japanese helped to develop the commercial potential of rice and potatoes and dominated the vegetable and berry regions of the Sacramento, San Joaquin, and Imperial Valleys and Los Angeles and Orange Counties.[57] In the interior West, they were foundational in the development of the sugar beet industry. Hoping to build beet factories in southeastern Idaho just after the turn of the twentieth century, investors of the Utah and Idaho Sugar Company believed Japanese immigrants would be an ideal labor source, as many were already working on sugar beet fields in California and many former railroad crew workers were in the area looking for jobs.[58] Other sugar beet companies in Nebraska and Colorado soon followed suit.[59] Pleased at the productivity of the Japanese workers and eager to recruit and retain more, the companies offered free transportation and housing assistance to encourage the workers to stay.

Indian immigrants entered agriculture around the same time as Japanese. By 1913 about half of those in British Columbia worked as field laborers, truck gardeners, and stump clearers.[60] In the United States by the 1920s, most Indian agricultural workers were in California in the Sacramento, San Joaquin, and Imperial Valleys.[61] Many Punjabis were already familiar with irrigation and crop specialization and found California's agricultural lands and alluvial plains to be similar to those back home.[62] Making a particular impact on agriculture in the Imperial Valley, they entered this area around 1909 to pick cantaloupes and cotton. Water diversion projects from the Colorado River had recently made the valley arable, and this timing allowed them to establish niches as farmers. The dearth of available white labor in the Imperial Valley made landowners receptive to hiring Asians who, they argued, were better suited for the work than whites. E.E. Chandler, a ranch owner in Brawley and professor at Occidental College said, "I do not believe the Imperial Valley is a white man's country and I am willing to hand it over to the Hindus and Japanese."[63] Because Japanese farm workers outnumbered Indians, employers often turned to the latter to break the former's dominance and gain control over labor costs and worker intransigence. In 1908, for example, a Stockton rancher paid white laborers $1.65 per day plus board, Japanese $1.70 without board and Indians $1.10 without board.[64] In addition to accepting lower wages, Indians were also willing to perform work that others would not. The Bridge and Land Navigation Company in the San Joaquin Delta hired Indians to clean ditches because Japanese would not do it and Chinese were thought to be too old by then. At the same time, employers also complained about Indians' performance as laborers. Landowner H.A. Millis said, "Though they have commended themselves to some ranchers, they have generally been regarded as distinctly inferior to laborers of other races and not cheap labor at the wages which they have been paid."[65]

The majority of Koreans on the U.S. mainland worked in California agriculture as farm laborers, concentrating in and around Dinuba, Reedley, Sacramento and Delano. In a pattern that was typical among Asian immigrants, groups of Korean men relied on a co-ethnic contractor or gang leader and traveled from job to job. Like Indians, they were often hired as alternatives to Japanese laborers. Bong Youn Choy described how the Kongnip Hyo-hoe, a Korean mutual aid association, helped immigrants get jobs picking oranges in Riverside during the first few years of the 1900s. Because Japanese already formed the bulk of the labor force, the association tried to break this dominance by first sending a small group of the best and strongest Korean workers as a "sample labor force." By working hard and making few demands the employer would hopefully be impressed enough to hire more Koreans. The workers received the following guidelines from the association:

> Our only capital today in this land is nothing but honesty; therefore, work diligently without wasting time whether your employer watches you or not; then you will be working not only today but tomorrow and even the whole year round. If your employer has confidence in you, then your friends, Kim, Lee, or Park will also get jobs, because of your hard and honest work. In this way, eventually all Koreans will get jobs anywhere.[66]

Filipino laborers, whose migration to the continental United States accelerated in the second half of the 1920s, played a more extensive role in agriculture than Indians and Koreans.[67] By 1930, about 45,000 had entered the United States, and about 67 percent lived and worked in California.[68] Due to their numbers, as well as Chinese and Japanese exclusion, Filipinos succeeded the two groups to become the largest Asian agricultural workforce in California in the late 1920s and early 1930s.[69] Throughout the West Coast, approximately 20,000 held agricultural jobs, compared to 11,000 in service trades and 4,200 in salmon canneries.[70] Specialized crop growers in the San Joaquin, Imperial, and Salinas Valleys and the Santa Maria-Guadalupe coastal area were keen on hiring them because they were usually young and unattached and perceived as naturally suited for "stoop labor." One grower explained his preference for Filipinos over Mexicans, the other main immigrant labor source at the time, saying, "these Mexicans and Spaniards bring their families with them and I have to fix up houses; but I can put a hundred Filipinos in that barn [pointing to a large firetrap]."[71] In the lettuce fields of Salinas, in the 1920s and early 1930s, Filipinos could earn 15 cents an hour for eight- to ten-hour days.[72] Not only did they become the largest Asian group of farm laborers, but they also became the dominant workforce in a number of areas, including asparagus cutting, lettuce, strawberry, and sugar beet picking, and potato harvesting. Because of the seasonal and migratory nature of agricultural employment—80 percent of Filipinos were migratory workers—geographically stable communities generally did not emerge wherever Filipinos farm laborers worked.[73] An exception was Stockton, California, considered the "agricultural headquarters" for Filipino workers since the 1920s.[74] Additionally, because they entered at a time when enormous farms and large numbers of hired laborers were the norm, they had fewer opportunities to become tenant farmers or farm operators.

Urban Occupations and Ethnic Enterprises

Jobs for Asian immigrants could also be found in cities such as Honolulu, New York, San Francisco, Seattle, Portland, and Los Angeles. While most of the industries that employed Asian immigrants on a large-scale basis were concentrated in the countryside, urban areas also beckoned. Labor was needed in areas such as domestic labor, restaurants, hotels, gardens, and manufacturing, and burgeoning ethnic enclaves in turn generated their own demands for workers. Furthermore, after experiencing the rough conditions of rural or migratory labor, many immigrants preferred to relocate to and stay in cities where they could find wage work and pursue independent enterprises. Urban jobs for working-class Asians were different from, but not necessarily better than, what they could obtain elsewhere; they paid little and required few if any skills. A smaller number became entrepreneurs and ran businesses that served co-ethnic and interethnic clienteles and provided employment for their brethren.

As mentioned, domestic service was one of the most common urban occupations for working class Asian immigrants from the turn of the twentieth century until World War II. In California, population growth and the expansion of the middle and lower-middle classes created demand for household servants, which was largely filled by Asian men and women along with other immigrant women and single, Anglo women. The appearance of Chinese men in what was becoming a feminized occupation inspired stories such as "Poor Ah Toy," published in the *Californian* in 1882, which "reiterat[ed] the taboo on interclass and interracial intimacy" while also warning "female employers of Chinese servants."[75] Despite such concerns about hiring Asian men as domestic servants, the pattern continued with the participation of Japanese and Filipino men, most of whom were students supporting themselves while finishing their degrees. "Japanese schoolboys" appeared around the turn of the twentieth century, numbering about four thousand in San Francisco alone in 1907, but had all but disappeared by 1930.[76] Filipino "fountain-pen boys" were common during the 1920s and 1930s. Despite the low pay (Japanese schoolboys received $1 to $1.50 per week), irregular hours, and unregulated conditions, domestics often received free room and board and they could improve their English and learn about American culture on the job. For these reasons, schoolboys and fountain-pen boys preferred domestic service to migratory labor.

With regard to manufacturing, Asian employment—in and outside the West—was limited to a few industrial pockets. San Francisco was the main manufacturing hub in the American West, and here Chinese laborers were very visible, working both for non-Chinese and Chinese employers. During the 1860s and 1870s, they represented 46 percent of the labor force in the city's main manufacturing industries—boots and shoes, woolens, cigars and tobacco, and sewing.[77] It was also around this time that laborers eclipsed merchants, small producers, and professionals in San Francisco's Chinese population, paralleling the overall proletarianization of Chinese America. In New York, cigarmaking was a common vocation of Chinese. The first Chinese to enter the trade were skilled cigarmakers who had arrived via Cuba. During the 1870s, as the trade became mechanized, it demanded fewer skills and opened up to larger numbers of Chinese workers. From there the industry also divided into a hierarchy in which cigars made by Cuban Chinese were the best and most expensive, while factory-made cigars by Chinese laborers were cheaper and of lesser quality.[78] As Chinese were said to be good at this job because of their "natural quickness and deftness of finger," they earned more than other workers; in 1869 a skilled Chinese could earn $15 to $16 per thousand while Germans were paid $8 to $9.[79]

An urban vocation that was especially associated with Chinese across the country was laundering. They first entered the trade in San Francisco as employees of the Washerwoman's Lagoon in 1850. Because they worked for relatively low wages, the price for washing a dozen shirts dropped from $8 to $5, and laundries soon multiplied and appeared throughout the city. By 1882, there were 176 Chinese operated laundries in San Francisco.[80] Most establishments were small, employing about five men each. Laundries were a staple of Chinese workers in other cities as well, from St. Louis to Chicago to New York.[81] They were able to flourish in cities even with small Chinese populations because they served a non-Chinese clientele and were rarely confined to Chinatown borders. Laundries also represented the presence of an urban Chinese bourgeoisie, as most of those that employed Chinese laborers were Chinese-owned. Many of the owners had formerly been wageworkers who were able to move into entrepreneurship because of the relatively low start-up costs, gaps in laundry services in many communities, and existence of business associations that supported them and helped them to fight back against legal harassment. The owners, furthermore, often held a great deal of influence in the ethnic community, as they regularly served additional roles as court interpreters and other key middleman positions.

Indeed, one of the appeals of cities was the opportunity to pursue entrepreneurship, which offered greater autonomy compared to wage work, and Asian immigrants had engaged in it since the early years of migration. These included Ah Sue, a ship steward on a Hong Kong–New York route who landed in New York in 1847 and became the city's first known Chinese entrepreneur when he opened a tobacco and candy store and later a boardinghouse for Asian sailors.[82] Seeing further potential for Chinese in the city, Ko Lo Chee took over Ah Sue's boardinghouse in 1867 and recruited Chinese in California and China to move to New York. Meanwhile in San Francisco in 1878, Chinese ran 131 grocery stores and numerous other shops that sold items like medicine, tofu, and fruit, and over the decades the number and types of businesses only grew.[83] Such enterprises, which served Chinese and non-Chinese, laid the groundwork for smaller Chinatowns in cities from Logan, Utah to St. Louis, Missouri. In Butte, Montana, for instance, whose decreasing Chinese populations in the late nineteenth century mirrored their declining employment in mining, business owners were forced to shift to catering to non-Chinese customers.[84]

The success and scope of business enterprises—not just among Chinese but also other Asians—often relied on group resources, including startup capital acquired from rotating credit associations and the unpaid help of family members. Although they were small in number, Korean immigrants in the early twentieth century had high rates of entrepreneurship in urban pockets like Honolulu and Los Angeles. To illustrate the scope of their activities, by the 1930s in Los Angeles, they ran thirty-five fruit and vegetable stands, nine grocery stores, six trucking companies, five restaurants, one rooming house, three herb stores, two hat stores, and one employment agency.[85] With regard to Filipinos, this group's high rate of participation in migratory work during the 1920s and 1930s hindered their widespread entry into small business, although a handful of communities, such as Los Angeles and Stockton, developed sizeable year-round Filipino populations so that ethnic enterprises such as barbershops, restaurants, dance halls, and garages could flourish. Asian Indians during the early 1900s lived predominantly in rural areas, although pockets of merchants and business owners did appear in some cities. These included peddlers of Indian wares in cities across the East and even Honolulu, where the Hyderabad-born Watumull brothers, Jhamandas and Gobindram, who arrived in 1913 by way of Manila, established a merchandising firm.[86]

Among Asians in America, Japanese made the most pronounced move into business ownership, seen in the rapid rise of Nihonmachis over the first decade of the 1900s. In cities up and down the West Coast, networks of Japanese-owned hotels, boardinghouses, grocery stories, fruit and vegetable stands, restaurants, nurseries, barbershops, tailor shops, and pool halls had emerged and, according to the Immigration Commission, by 1909 there were between 3,000 and 3,500 Japanese-owned establishments in the western states, most of them concentrated in cities like San Francisco, Los Angeles, Seattle, and Sacramento. By 1939, 76 percent of Seattle's Japanese Americans engaged in small business, as owners or workers.[87] Although most Japanese-owned businesses were small, relied on the labor of unpaid family members, and served interracial clienteles, a handful grew very large and extensive. Furuya Masajiro, an Issei who arrived and settled in Seattle in 1890, became one of the most powerful Japanese American businessmen in the early twentieth century. He worked his way up running businesses including a tailoring shop and a grocery store, the latter of which he expanded into a department store that served Seattle's growing Japanese population. His operations grew to include branch stores in Portland and Tacoma, a post office, a labor supply agency, and a bank.[88]

Beyond the rewards for individual business owners, urban enterprises provided jobs for working-class residents and were the backbone of bustling ethnic enclaves. Furuya, for instance, was one of the largest employers of Seattle Japanese during the early twentieth century. Manufacturing units in San Francisco Chinatown—which numbered about 250 in 1885—provided employment for thousands of people.[89] This participation in manufacturing, however, was significantly undercut by white competition, anti-Chinese agitation, and the resumption of eastern manufacturing after the Civil War. By the turn of the twentieth century, less than one-quarter of Chinese in San Francisco worked in industrial manufacturing, mostly in the sewing trades.[90]

Women's Work

Our understanding of women's labor in this early phase of Asian American history has been obscured due to several factors. One is numbers; as discussed earlier, the vast majority of Asian immigrants to the United States prior to the mid-twentieth century were men. Another issue was the fact that women did not always have a primary occupation nor work outside the home, making them invisible to many observers as laborers. Numbers aside, however, Asian immigrant women not only participated, but were integral, in the world of work and production. Their labor—paid and unpaid—was critical to the stability and economic wellbeing of households and communities. In addition to holding jobs or working in family businesses, they also often had to attend to domestic chores, a phenomenon known as "double duty" that was particularly common among immigrant and working class women. As women were most numerous among Japanese Americans—Issei women represented a majority of Asian women in the workforce during the early twentieth century—they were especially crucial for this population's economic wellbeing. Asian women's experiences, furthermore, highlight both their agency and exploitation as economic actors, as well as how capitalistic imperatives reinforced gender and sexism.

While the labor demands of empire and capitalist development in the post-emancipation nineteenth and early twentieth centuries largely envisioned young, male imported workers for highly physical tasks, women also had distinct roles to play in this order in and outside the home. By and large these roles precluded women's migration. Catherine Ceniza Choy has described, for instance, how the export of U.S. medical practices to the Philippines—part of its mission to "civilize" the territory—entailed the training of Filipina nurses, starting with the opening of the first government nursing school in the Philippines in 1907.[91] This effort was also part of a larger professionalization and internationalization of nursing and indoctrinated Filipinas in gendered ideologies about "women's work." Although aimed at producing a domestic corps of medical professionals to work in the territory, the nursing programs also gave rise to opportunities for migration. After obtaining their primary education in the Philippines, nurses wishing to acquire post-secondary training—required for supervisory and faculty positions—went to the United States. One of these was Anastacia Giron-Tupas, who graduated from the Pennsylvania School of Social Work in 1917 and went on to become the first Filipina chief nurse and superintendent of the Philippine General

Hospital.[92] Although these students did not originally intend to, some ended up staying in the United States. Maria Abastilla Beltran came in the 1920s after an advisor she met while working at the Philippine chapter of the American Red Cross encouraged her to "improve yourself" and "be somebody else." After earning a bachelor's in public nursing in 1931, she married a Filipino immigrant and settled in Seattle, Washington.[93]

Turning to women immigrants, specifically working class immigrant wives and other family members, usually their chief duty was to perform domestic duties in the home, but financial exigencies often compelled them to take on paid work. In communities where wives were few in number, they commonly performed domestic chores for their families and for male boarders, neighbors, and husbands' co-workers.[94] Issei Tei Endow, who lived in Hood, Oregon during the 1920s, remembered her exhaustion from those days:

> For a woman in those days, there was no Sunday! Days were short, because there was so much to do. I made breakfast, cleaned the house, washed by hand, and still had to weed strawberries in the field. It was probably best that I had to work so hard, though. I was able to remain healthy and pour all my energy into my work—This may have been a good thing.[95]

Sometimes women earned extra money for these efforts. During her family's first few years in California, Korean Mary Paik Lee's mother, Song Kuang Do, did so by cooking for about thirty men.[96] Another common kind of home-based labor was piecework. For example, many Japanese women in San Francisco were paid to make oriental goods like embroidery and flowers in an arrangement in which contractors provided them with the materials and then picked up the finished products to sell in curio shops. When they worked outside the home, the types of jobs available were usually limited to "women's work," such as seamstressing, domestic service, and midwifery.[97] These were also generally low-paying, low-technology occupations that served co-ethnic clienteles or in which they did not have to compete with white women.

Women also worked alongside or in the same occupations as men. During the 1920s and 1930s about a third of Japanese women in the United States worked in agriculture, a high rate that roughly mirrored the overall Japanese American participation in the field.[98] In Hawaii, women agricultural workers were especially visible; in 1920, they made up 14 percent of the plantation workforce and the vast majority of these were Japanese, although other Asians were also represented.[99] Being female did not spare them from very physically onerous tasks, as they hoed, cut, and loaded cane, often beside male workers. In other types of businesses in Hawaii and the mainland, such as laundries and nurseries, husbands and wives were commonly hired together.[100] Working next to and in the same occupations as men did not mean they were treated equally, however. In Hawaii in 1915, for instance, Japanese women field hands were paid an average of 55 cents per day compared to the 78 cents men received.

Another common occupation for Asian women was domestic service, usually in the homes of middle class white families. It was a particularly common vocation among Japanese women, accounting for 50 percent of Issei women workers at the turn of the twentieth century and remaining one of the most common areas of employment for Nisei women.[101] The need for domestic servants stemmed from industrialization, which gave rise to an expanded urban middle class with affluent lifestyles and little time to do housework.[102] By 1870 domestic service had become a largely feminized occupation; nationally the field was 85 percent female, and was especially associated with marginalized women, such as European immigrants in the Midwest, Chicanas in the Southwest, and blacks in the South. In the American West, Asian men actually preceded women in the field, but it tended to be a temporary station for them (as well as white women), as they left once they finished school or other jobs became available.

As Asian men's participation in domestic service declined in the late nineteenth and early twentieth centuries, women's involvement grew. Many Japanese women entered the field as "schoolgirls" or day workers. The schoolgirls, usually young women, approached domestic work as an apprenticeship, in which they would do chores in exchange for nominal wages, housing, and training in American housekeeping and cooking methods. Those with responsibilities at home or in family businesses worked instead as day workers.[103] One of these, Mrs. Yoshida, arrived in the United States in 1909 as a picture bride to her husband who had come about twenty years earlier. The couple served as agents for day workers needed for cleaning, painting, and other jobs in the San Francisco Bay Area, but by 1912, after having two children, Mrs. Yoshida felt pressure to take on some of this work herself:

> I started to work because everyone went on vacation and the summer was very hard for us. The cleaning business declined during the summer . . . My husband disapproved of my doing day work. He said, "Stupid." . . . I worked half a day and was paid $1 . . . We didn't know the first thing about housework, but the ladies of the house didn't mind. They taught us how at the beginning: "This is a broom; this is a dustpan; when you finish that work bring it back here." So that's how we learned . . . At the time we were thinking of working three years in America and then going back to Japan to help our parents lead a comfortable life . . . But we had babies almost every year and so we had to give up that idea.[104]

As the quote illustrates, there were multiple pressures that wives working as domestic servants—and all working women for that matter—had to negotiate. Financial hardships in their own households and their home villages compelled them to join the workforce, but they also had to contend with male family members', husbands', and the larger culture's patriarchal biases against women's employment outside the home. Domestic work, thus, represented a paradox facing Asian immigrant women in the workforce; it afforded flexibility in some ways—for instance they did not have to speak English—but the tedious nature of the job, limited mobility, and low pay reflected and reinforced their subordinate status as women and minorities.

Perhaps no occupation reflected the oppressiveness of gender constraints facing Asian women in the nineteenth and early twentieth centuries—mainly Chinese and Japanese—more than prostitution. The circumstances that brought Asian prostitutes to America grew out of the same developments that set the stage for the systematic migration of male laborers. In China, for example, females were especially vulnerable during times of economic hardship because they were seen as unproductive workers who did not contribute meaningfully to the household. Prostitution represented one way for poor families to relieve themselves of the burdens of caring for a girl, whether through her earnings or by selling her. Those potential earnings, furthermore, were significant; as a Qing dynasty official report stated, for every prostitute in Canton, there were ten family members dependent for their sustenance on her earnings.[105] Japanese prostitutes in America likewise tended to be from poor families and had come under coerced or manipulative circumstances.

Prostitutes from Asia, Latin America, Europe, and North America were among the first women to go to California gold country in the 1850s, and were also an integral part of the economic landscape throughout rapidly industrializing areas of the American West. Sex workers helped to maintain a labor force of single young men and furthermore generated profits for the entrepreneurs who employed them. The relative scarcity of women in the region, and particularly among Asian immigrants, furthermore, sustained the demand for prostitutes. These conditions also shaped the early migration of Chinese and Japanese women, a large percentage of whom were prostitutes. Among Chinese during the nineteenth century, the majority of employed women were prostitutes, as much as 85 to 97 percent in San Francisco in 1860. Twenty years later, this decreased to 21 to 50 percent, due to the effective exclusion of Chinese women under the Page Act of 1875, mortality, and Protestant mission house "rescues."[106] Smaller proportions of Japanese women worked as prostitutes in the late 1800s and early 1900s. In 1890 the Japanese consul in California reported there were 161 in the state, and others were found elsewhere in the West, in states like Washington, Oregon, Idaho, Montana, and Utah.[107]

As for the lives of the women themselves, they could be harrowing and mundane, and the work tedious and exploitative, but also occasionally profitable. The circumstances under which they entered the occupation varied; some were free agents who came of their own accord, while others were indentured and enslaved, having been forced or manipulated by others. Many Chinese prostitutes, for example, had been kidnapped, lured, or purchased from poor parents by procurers for as little as $50. Some had been sold to Chinese merchants in Hong Kong and spent time there before coming to America. Once in America, they were placed in barracoons until they were turned over to their owners who, during the 1870s, might have paid as much as $1000 per woman.[108] Those who had not been purchased in advance were stripped, inspected, and sold to the highest bidder. Many could not read the contracts they entered and had signed them with their thumbprints while under duress. The contracts typically bound the women, usually between sixteen to twenty-one years old, to work for four to seven years for fixed wages, and once expired they could be extended indefinitely. Vulnerable to illness, many died before their contracts ended.

Living and working conditions depended on the wealth of clientele. A small number of Chinese prostitutes, considered the most privileged, were well cared for materially and served only their wealthy owners. The slightly less privileged were sold to parlor houses that catered to well-to-do clientele of Chinese and non-Chinese descent, and the least fortunate worked in cribs, small shacks facing dimly lit alleys where poor laborers, teenage boys, sailors, and drunkards paid them as little as 25 cents for their services.[109] The establishments where Japanese prostitutes worked varied; both Chinese and Japanese-owned brothels—with nondescript names like "Tokyo Hotel"—employed them, as well as bars where the women often doubled as bar maids. Their clientele was mostly white, Chinese, and Japanese men.[110]

As with other forms of labor in which women participated, prostitution was full of contradictions. It reinforced their gender and class subordination, but it could also be a source of economic agency for women to help themselves and their families with their earnings. One Chinese prostitute was able to send back as much as $200 to $300 after working seven months in San Francisco.[111] The work of prostitutes, furthermore, played a critical role in the growth of early ethnic economies, although it was never acknowledged as such. Profits generated through prostitution allowed for capital accumulation and the viability of urban Chinatowns, leading Lucie Cheng to characterize women sex workers as "sacrificial victims."[112] By virtue of their occupation and gender, women prostitutes always stood outside the boundaries of respectability in the ethnic community and larger society. Their very presence in America evidenced this; women traveling alone was taboo, and conditions in the American West were deemed particularly unsuitable for "decent women." More so than other workers, prostitutes lacked networks of support, so had little recourse against abuse and exploitation. White Protestant missionaries who advocated the "rescue" of prostitutes represented one escape, but they tended to treat them condescendingly, as "heathens" in need of civilization. With regard to occupational mobility, little was to be found in prostitution. Becoming a brothel owner was one path, but this was exceptionally rare.[113]

Another class of unfree Chinese women laborers was *mui tsai*. These were usually girls from China or daughters of prostitutes who worked as domestic servants in affluent Chinese homes or brothels.[114] This was a carryover from China, commonly seen as a form of charity for girls from indigent families. Some were freed for marriage, while others were forced to work as prostitutes when they reached a certain age. Quan Laan Fan immigrated as *mui tsai* in the 1880s after her parents sold her to a rich family. She worked for a woman who was the second wife of a "gold mountain man," whom she eventually decided to join in America, and Quan accompanied her as the couple's "errand girl." In the United States, she worked in the husband's store in San Francisco, fetched meals for her mistress, and took on extra tasks such as rolling cigarettes so that she could send money to her family. When she was 18 or 19, Quan married and was subsequently freed from service. She went on to have eight children and eventually got a job as a telephone operator in Chinatown.[115]

Hardship, Mobility, and Resistance

The world of work among working class Asian immigrants was diverse, but several themes emerge. As thousands arrived amid commercial development and capitalist expansion in a country with a racialized labor system, it is no surprise that the life of a wageworker was physically taxing, emotionally demoralizing, geographically isolated, and poorly compensated. As one early twentieth century Japanese sugar beet worker in the interior West recounted:

> Nothing [we had] heard in Japan prepared [us] for the Spartan life that awaited [us]. Sugar-beet thinning was the kind of work to break not only backs, but spirits, too. The rows were a mile long, and the beets were thinned by stooping with a short-handed hoe. By laboring at piece work for twelve hours a man earned $1.50 to $2 a day . . . At night [we] slept exhausted in a farmer's bunkhouse . . . [We] became badly malnourished on a diet of . . . flour doughball boiled in water . . . [and later] rice, shoyu, and a few other staples shipped in from . . . Seattle.[116]

The organization of work added to the punishing experience. If workers were paid by the piece, foremen—usually co-ethnics—often pushed them to produce faster.[117] Moreover, the seasonal nature of many jobs required them to adapt to abrupt changes in rhythm over extended periods of time. Indian lumber employees in the Pacific Northwest, for example, would have very little work for three months, but for the other nine, labored over grueling seven-day weeks from sunrise to sunset.[118] Others, particularly in agriculture and canneries, were simply let go during slack times.

The migratory labor circuit was especially trying and unpredictable. A male Korean immigrant who came to America via San Francisco in 1916 recalled meeting a co-ethnic labor contractor days after his arrival. With a group of about twenty other Koreans, he went to Stockton, where the contractor had arranged jobs for them on a bean farm. "We were hoeing the bean fields," he remembered, "and when we finished we went to another bean farm for hoeing. It was hard work. Then we went to Dinuba picking grapes. I was flocking with other Koreans, and I went where they went for available farm jobs."[119] Migrant workers actually represented the majority of Filipinos in the workforce during the 1920s and 1930s. With such a high level of participation in migratory labor, they devised strategies for coping with the challenges, such as pooling money with a group of co-ethnics to purchase a car to go from job to job.[120] Additionally, in Filipino America, labor migrants comprised a community unto itself with its own hierarchies. While they crisscrossed the American West for work in lumber mills, ranches, farms, canneries and homes, only the heartiest braved the Alaska canneries. Called Alaskeros, these men held an esteemed place in the Filipino labor community.

Living accommodations for laborers were spartan at best and reflected their lowly socioeconomic position. Railroad workers often lived in bug-infested boxcars that constantly changed location as they laid and repaired track. Moreover, the poor diets in remote workplaces caused malnutrition and night blindness.[121] To supplement unfamiliar or monotonous diets, workers sometimes kept small gardens or gathered food. Chinese cannery workers in the Northwest, for example, added seaweed, mussels, and clams from the Columbia River as well as wapato root to their diets, the latter of which had been introduced to them by Native Americans.[122] Agricultural and cannery workers usually lived in minimally appointed bunkhouses provided by employers or contractors, often sparse, barn-like structures with only a coal-burning stove for heating.[123] On Hawaii plantations, laborers were typically placed in ethnically segregated living quarters, whose conditions varied—from "splendid" to "rotten" according to a Bureau of Immigration official in 1899—but were usually overcrowded and dirty.[124] On Aiea plantation, a single "humble shed" housed about fifty bachelors along with several married couples, and families lived in rooms measuring six-by-eight feet. The camps at Paia plantation were even more crowded; male laborers lived in warehouse-like buildings with bunks stacked four or five high.[125]

The work itself was back-breaking. On sugar cane plantations, during workdays of ten to twelve hours, laborers hoed, planted, and weeded during cultivation, and cut, hauled, loaded, and flumed during harvest. "We worked like draft animals, cows, and horses in the plantation fields," recalled a Korean. Another said, "the plantation owners treated Korean workers no better than . . . animals rather than as human beings. Every worker was called by number, never by name."[126] They coped with their physical, spiritual, and material deprivations in different ways. "The most typical reaction to the first day of plantation work," says Miriam Sharma, "was to shed tears at night."[127] Other times, they sang to provide some release from their sorrows, and the songs themselves shed light on the onerous nature of their jobs. According to a Japanese work song sung on Hawaiian plantations:

> Hawaii, Hawaii
> But when I came
> What I saw
> Was hell
> The boss was Satan
> The lunas
> His helpers[128]

Filipino field laborers in California likewise sang about their exhaustion, from which there seemed to be no relief:

> Planting rice is never fun
> Bent from morn till the set of sun
> Cannot rest and cannot sit
> Cannot rest for a little bit[129]

Workers were also interested in longer term relief from punishing and exploitive jobs, and many simply left as they learned of better opportunities or completed their contracts. For example, many Korean sugar plantation laborers in Hawaii were unhappy as they had been unprepared for the physical demands of work, and left the plantations in droves after their peak involvement in 1905. Between 1903 and 1907, 1,100 left for the West Coast and slightly more than that returned to Korea.[130] By 1910, just 1,753 Koreans remained in the plantation labor force. Those who stayed in Hawaii agriculture moved to other industries for better-paying and less onerous jobs in pineapple, coffee, and tobacco production. Most former plantation workers, however, went to the city to start their own businesses. As early as 1907, Hyon Sun observed, "there are many peddlers, restaurateurs, cart-sellers, barbers, hot-tub keepers, grocery keepers and medicine sellers. The Koreans who can speak English work as shopkeepers in small American shops or translators in Plantations or courts to earn 30–70$ per month."[131]

Another strategy for Asian workers to better their circumstances was to seek advancement within their industries of employment, but for ordinary people without access to capital this was difficult due to racism in industrial unions and a tiered labor system in which non-white immigrants rarely rose above the level of unskilled or semi-skilled laborers. The main exception to these closed routes to mobility was in mainland agriculture, where thousands moved from the ranks of laborer to farmer, utilizing knowledge about farming that they brought with them. By 1919, Asians owned or leased two percent, or about 623,000 acres, of California's farmlands.[132] They also farmed in tenancy arrangements with individual or corporate landowners as well as share or contract agreements in which they grew crops in return for payment, either a set amount or percentage of the crop's profit. In these latter arrangements, because the landowner usually provided the capital, it was possible to farm without access to significant resources. As lessees, farmers had more autonomy over marketing and selling crops, but they also had to assume more of the costs. Here, they could obtain funds on credit from a bank or immigrant rotating credit associations formed with compatriots (*kae* for Koreans, *tanomoshi* for Japanese, and *hui* for Chinese).

Ethnic cooperation was vital for Asians' ability to move up the agricultural ladder, as they turned to co-ethnics not just for overhead and operating capital, but also for customers and markets. In turning their leased land into productive orchards, nurseries, and vineyards, Korean fruit and vegetable growers in the San Joaquin Valley depended on co-ethnics through arrangements that included forming cooperatives.[133] They furthermore shipped their products to wholesale markets run by Koreans in Los Angeles. Such cooperation facilitated the prominent role of Koreans in the rice production in the Sacramento Valley. In 1918 they grew 214,000 bushels, and one of their own, Kim Chong-nim, became known to locals as the "rice king."[134] Another success in Korean farming were the "Kim Brothers," whose story began when Kim Hyung Soon formed a partnership with fellow Korean Kim Ho (not actually brothers) in 1921 in Reedley. The men built Kim Brothers Company into an expansive operation of orchards, nurseries, and fruit packing sheds.[135]

Indians who climbed the ladder into farming had 88,450 acres under cultivation by 1919 in California, controlling 32,000 acres in the Imperial Valley alone, where they grew cotton, alfalfa, barley, corn, melons, and winter lettuce.[136] Like other Asians, they leased land by securing credit from banks and pooling resources with co-ethnics. One of the latter ventures was the Hindustani Farmers Company, which was established in the Imperial Valley in 1922 to support Punjbai cantaloupe growers in the area.[137] In the Sacramento Valley, Indians farmed in the fruit orchards of Folsom, Loomis, and Newcastle, as well as rice fields of Marysville, Colusa, Willows, Chico, Gridley, and Biggs. They helped to develop the land into fertile rice fields, and by 1919 leased over 35,000 acres and owned 1,218 acres of rice land.[138] The successful rice growers were called "Hindu rice kings."

Best known for their success climbing the agricultural ladder were Japanese, whose achievements did not escape the notice of white Americans. In 1921, Joseph P. Irish, the president of the California Delta Association said that Californians:

> had seen the Japanese convert the barren land like that at Florin and Livingston into productive and profitable fields, orchards, and vineyards, by the persistence and intelligence of their industry. They had seen the hardpan and goose lands in the Sacramento Valley, gray and black with our two destructive alkalis, cursed with barrenness like the fig tree of Bethany, and not worth paying taxes on, until [K.] Ikuta, the Japanese, decided that those lands would raise rice. After years of persistent toil, enduring heartbreaking losses and disappointments, he conquered that rebellious soil and raised the first commercial crop of rice in California.[139]

Along with Indians and Koreans, they entered farming at a time when agricultural profits and demands for specialty crops were rising and there was still room for small producers. They established niches all over the West, from rice fields in Texas to fruit orchards in Okanogan, with especially large concentrations in Gardena and Moneta near Los Angeles, Gresham near Portland, and Bainbridge Island near Seattle.[140]

Japanese farmers contributed to Western agriculture far out of proportion to their numbers. In California in 1900, they owned or leased 4,698 acres; twenty years later that number rose to 458,056.[141] In 1910, they were producing 70 percent of the state's strawberries, 67 percent of its tomatoes, 95 percent of its spring and summer celery, 44 percent of its onions, and 40 percent of fresh green peas.[142] By 1924, Japanese agricultural production was valued at $67 million, or 10 percent of the value of California's crops.[143] In Idaho, Issei grew between 35 and 40 percent of the state's entire sugar-beet crop in 1913, and in Arizona they grew more than half of the cantaloupes in 1917. They utilized many of the same strategies that other Asians did to move into farming and make their enterprises profitable, from rotating credit associations, agricultural cooperatives, and with marketing associations.[144]

From tenant farming, some Japanese made the leap into landownership, the ultimate objective of farmers and also hardest to attain, due to cost as well as the barrier of alien lands laws in western states, the first of which was passed in California in 1913. Nonetheless, by 1910 Japanese owned nearly 17,000 acres of farmland.[145] Other Asians also moved into landownership but in smaller numbers. George Shima was the best-known example of Issei farming success, and although the size of his fortune made his case exceptional, his path was common. Shima immigrated to the United States in 1887 and entered agriculture as a potato picker in the San Joaquin Valley. He took a major step toward mobility when he became a labor contractor supplying Japanese farm workers for white landowners. With the money from this venture, Shima leased and purchased land in the undeveloped swamps of the Sacramento-San Joaquin Delta near Stockton, which he converted and made fertile for potato cultivation. By 1912, he controlled 10,000 acres of land and his potato crop was valued at about $500,000. For transporting his potatoes from Stockton to San Francisco, Shima owned a fleet of steamboats, barges, and tugboats. When he died in 1926, his estate was worth $15 million.[146]

When such paths to mobility were unavailable or undesirable, Asian workers struggled in other ways to improve their lives. Whether it was Chinese workers in Koloa Plantation in 1866 confronting overbearing lunas with disobedience, or Indian farm workers in Holt, California pressing for higher wages with work slowdowns, Asian laborers engaged in resistance to assert themselves and demand better treatment, individually and collectively.[147] Although their demands were not always met, such actions nurtured a culture of resistance and reminded employers that their control over workers was incomplete.[148]

Hawaii has an especially rich and volatile history of Asian labor organizing, which stems from the islands' unique class structure. As Edna Bonacich has explained, the simple structure of class relations in the islands made very clear to laborers who the enemy was—white planters. Furthermore, because of the relative absence of middlemen and the almost exclusive non-whiteness of the workforce, the labor movement in Hawaii was not tainted by racism as it was on the mainland. "There were no double layers of oppression," explains Bonacich. "They were not caught in the middle of someone else's struggle."[149]

Plantation workers in Hawaii had been striking since 1841 but labor militancy surged around the turn of the twentieth century, by this time being especially associated with Japanese. In 1900 alone, Japanese plantation workers struck twenty times with as many as 1,350 workers in a single strike. By 1905 these activities had so alarmed authorities that the federal commissioner of labor spoke out against Japanese "blood unionism."[150] Japanese collective resistance culminated in 1909 when about 7,000 workers from all of Oahu's major plantations staged a strike lasting four months. It began after the Higher Wages Association, a Honolulu-based organization led by Japanese immigrant elites, was denied a meeting with the HSPA to discuss work conditions and wages. Demanding a raise from $18 to $22 per month for Japanese (which would still be 50 cents less than what Portuguese and Puerto Ricans earned) and an end to the stratified wage system, the Higher Wages Association helped orchestrate the strike.[151] Employers responded with repression and punitive actions, threatening to evict strikers from their living quarters if they did not return to work and also starting to hire Filipinos.[152] Although the strike ended without a decisive victory for the workers, results came through long-term changes. Months after the strike, the HSPA raised Japanese wages and abolished the wage differentiation system.[153]

Although initially used to break Japanese strikes, Filipinos in Hawaii forged a strong tradition of labor organizing. A prime mover among plantation workers was Pablo Manlapit, who had come to the islands as a laborer in 1910, and also dabbled in various trades in the city of Hilo. He had an awakening of sorts in 1916 after being beaten by a group of Filipinos for taking part in breaking a waterfront strike, and went on to form the Filipino Labor Union (FLU) in 1919 whose aim was organizing Filipino sugar workers. In January 1920, the FLU called a strike on five plantations after attempts to negotiate higher wages, a bonus system, and better working conditions with the HSPA fell through. Prices had been rising since World War I, but wages had stagnated. The FLU was joined by a Japanese union, and at the strike's height some 12,010 workers participated. However, it was marred by disorganization and internal squabbles and fizzled out.[154] In the 1930s, the suppression of labor leaders, including Manlapit's banishment to the Philippines in 1935, hobbled the movement, although the Great Depression and World War II would see a revival of Asian labor activism (see Chapters 5 and 6).[155]

Elites, Middlemen, and the Broker Class

The movement of Asian agricultural workers into landowning and tenancy underscored the existence of a class hierarchy among Asian Americans, a much-overlooked aspect of a history that tends to equate work with wage labor. Also exemplifying a class system and having a major impact on the labor market and work experiences were Asian American contractors, who were particularly important among Chinese and Japanese before the 1930s. Contractors, as well as the subcontractors and foremen who worked under them, played crucial middleman roles that brought them much power in immigrant communities. While these elite Asians were important advocates for their wage-earning brethren and provided services that enhanced immigrants' lives, they could also be exploitative. Yet as minorities whose power derived from relationships with others, namely their countrymen and the white Americans they linked them to, their positions were always tenuous.

The most powerful individuals that most Asian American wageworkers directly interacted with were not white employers, but co-ethnic labor contractors. The earliest Chinese contractors in America started out as emigration brokers who seized opportunities to expand their businesses by moving to the U.S. and servicing newly arrived immigrants. Labor contracting, depending on the size of the firm, could be a complex operation and include networks of subcontractors reaching wherever Asian laborers were hired in groups. Typically, the Chinese employees of a white employer would work under the supervision of a co-ethnic contractor or a foreman hired by the contractor. For example, in 1869, when the Houston & Texas Central Railroad faced a shortage of workers, its main labor contractor B.J. Dorsey worked with a Chinese subcontractor to arrange for the employment of several Chinese gangs. The subcontractor was responsible for recruiting the workers, bringing them to Texas, and supervising them.[156]

Japanese laborers also relied on co-ethnic contractors for employment in a variety of industries. Japanese labor contracting in the mainland began in railroad construction during the early 1890s by Tanaka Tadashichi, whose partner William Remington supplied workers for the Oregon Short line, and by the early twentieth century several major Japanese contractors were operating in the Pacific Northwest, California, and the Rocky Mountain states.[157] The largest contractor in California was the Japanese American Industrial Corporation of San Francisco, founded in 1902 by Abiko Kyutaro. The company supplied thousands of workers for sugar beet, mining, and railroad companies, sending workers as far as Wyoming and Utah.[158] The Japanese men who became contractors came from varied backgrounds. Ban Shinzaburo, who was based in Portland, Oregon and supplied workers in the Northwest, started out privileged, having served in the Foreign Ministry and as a secretary in the Honolulu consulate. Abiko Kyutaro, on the other hand, started out as a student laborer, worked in different kinds of occupations, and then later used his English skills, resources from previous ventures, knowledge of American labor practices, and networks with other former students to enter the contracting business.[159]

Due to Indians' and Koreans' smaller numbers and Filipinos' later entry into the labor market, members of these groups were not able to rely on such large contracting firms, although they did have co-ethnic contractors, bosses, and leaders with other titles who helped connect them to jobs and set them up in other ways. These contractors or their associates would often meet newly arrived immigrants at ports, promise to help them find work, and place them in a larger group of co-ethnic workers, which would then be sent to a job site. Among Indian immigrants, it was common for the best English speaker in a group to be appointed the "boss man," and this individual took responsibility for scouting jobs and negotiating the terms of employment. The boss man usually did not receive a commission from the crew's wages like contractors did, although they did get a higher hourly wage.[160] The Filipino padrone system was similar to the Chinese and Japanese contracting systems in that workers paid the padrone a fee for employment, and the padrone paid the workers and provided food and necessities, charging these costs against their wages.

The power of Asian American labor contractors and other middlemen grew as employers became more dependent on them. As larger workforces made it untenable for companies to deal with employees individually and the labor market became more stratified, the work of finding and managing workers fell on these ethnic middlemen who also negotiated wages and issued work orders. Sometimes contractors and subcontractors used their leverage to get concessions and extra accommodations from employers. For instance, in 1869 Chinese contractors working with the Houston & Texas Central Railroad negotiated side contracts that included the company's agreement to establish a Chinese store with $3,000 in stock, which the contractor supplied with work and living necessities and goods from China.[161]

Because they derived their income from taking a portion of their workers' wages, Asian American contractors who were responsible for very large workforces amassed considerable wealth. Moreover, the most powerful were usually involved in multiple business ventures that might include farms, stores, boardinghouses, and banks. Laborers for the Oregon Short Line during the 1890s, for instance, were paid $1.25 per day, but contractors Tanaka Tadashichi and William Remington took 10 cents each.[162] In another arrangement, Kuranaga Terusaburo supplied Japanese workers for the Southern Pacific Railroad, taking $1 a month out of each worker's $1 per day wage. Agents who supplied workers by the thousands could in turn make thousands of dollars per month from contracting services alone.[163] Their retail and other establishments generated additional income.

Contractors' power and involvement in many aspects of workers' lives could easily lead to exploitation. For instance, employers usually paid them, not the workers directly, leaving the contractor responsible for distributing payments. This created many opportunities for abuse. In 1894, Tanaka Tadashichi was ousted as a contractor for the Oregon Short Line when money he was supposed to have remitted to Japan on behalf of workers mysteriously disappeared.[164] In the West Coast canned salmon industry, if canners paid contractors by the number of cases packed, in times of large output the contractors' incomes soared while those of skilled and common laborers who were paid set monthly wages or a lump sum at the end of the season were unchanged. During the 1880s, as their services became more important, contractors' rates increased, but workers' wages did not advance in the same proportion.[165] Finally, contractors did not hesitate to withhold or take back wages for supplementary food, drugs, alcohol, and other services they provided. Gambling houses and stores run by contractors probably took up the greatest shares of workers' debts. For such reasons, Asian workers' discontent often focused on contractors as much as employers, and periodic strikes, work stoppages, and slowdowns were aimed at changing the behavior of contractors, such as delays in the disbursement of wages.[166] One of the main objectives, for instance, of Filipino organizing in the canned salmon industry was to reduce the power that Chinese and Japanese contractors held in the labor market.

Contractors, however, were not all-powerful and they had their vulnerabilities, particularly in the face of anti-Asian racism. For instance, the United States' ending of Japanese migration from Hawaii in 1907 threatened the wellbeing of Japanese contractors, who vocally protested the action. While their influence over the labor market grew with larger workforces and employers' dependence on immigrant labor, another aspect of modern industrialization, corporate mergers, undermined them. For example, in 1899 a handful of canneries merged and created the Columbia River Packers Association, or CRPA, with headquarters in Astoria, Oregon.[167] With fewer companies but the same number of contractors, intensified competition drove rates down and eventually put many Chinese contractors out of business. Such patterns took hold throughout the cannery industry, and from 1890 to 1900 the number of active Chinese contractors in the lower Columbia declined from a dozen or more to just six.[168] During the New Deal, the National Recovery Act (NRA) further chipped away at the power of contractors. As in other industries, canners agreed to minimum wages, which undercut contractors because they could no longer make promises of employment. Furthermore, the responsibilities of managing workers shifted from contractors and to cannery superintendants.[169] Their declining power, moreover, continued even after the NRA was declared unconstitutional.

Conclusion

As illustrated above, work was far from a monolithic experience in early Asian American history. While the dominant picture is that of male wage earners toiling outside in physically punishing conditions, this does not begin to capture the range of experiences with respect to how Asians and Asian Americans earned a living. As the chapter has described, wage work encompassed domestic and urban service occupations, and for most women, "work" defied simple categorization, as much of their labor was unpaid and occurred both inside and outside the home. Farmers, bosses, labor contractors, merchants, and business owners represented the small privileged classes of Asian Americans and their work was crucially intertwined with their working class brethren. While they could be generous and passionate advocates for their co-ethnics, they could also be abusive and become the targets of class-based resentments. Thus, labor politics and class conflict in Asian America were complex phenomena and broke down along multiple axes, at times shaped by the oppression of white employers, but just as often playing out in terms of intra-Asian and intraethnic tension.

Also significant about this facet of Asian American history is how racial formations and meanings were very much tied up in work and perceptions of Asian labor. Though there were exceptions, the American labor movement by and large drew a sharp line between white workers (of which Europeans were a part) and Asians. Organized labor made distinctions between servile and voluntary labor, with the former being the enemy of the latter, and while there was no evidence of Chinese coolieism in America, the association and specter stuck and influenced how other Asian laborers would be regarded. It was also a unifying force among diverse working class whites and an effective political vehicle in the West (see Chapter 6).

Despite how they were viewed by others, Asian and Asian American workers sought to defy the structures that limited their occupational roles and prospects. In addition to the strategies discussed in the chapter, at various points, they worked to overcome the divide-and-control strategies of employers and the interethnic antagonisms they themselves might have internalized. In 1903, for instance, five hundred Japanese and Mexican sugar beet workers in Oxnard, California joined together to form the Japanese Mexican Labor Association (JMLA), which successfully confronted the powerful Western Agricultural Contracting Company to take back some control over the labor market. In 1920 on Oahu, Japanese and Filipino unions coordinated an interethnic plantation strike that showed glimmers of the possibilities of a multiethnic labor strategy that would flower more fully after World War II under the leadership of the International Longshore and Warehouse Union.

Notes

1   Peter Kwong and Dušanka Miščević, *Chinese America: The Untold Story of America's Oldest New Community* (New York: New Press, 2005), 53.

2   Quoted in Andrew Gyory, *Closing the Gate: Race, Politics, and the Chinese Exclusion Act* (Chapel Hill: University of North Carolina Press, 1998), 7; quoted in Kwong and Miščević, *Chinese America*, 54.

3   Kwong and Miščević, *Chinese America*, 54; Sucheng Chan, *Asian Americans: An Interpretive History* (Boston: Twayne, 1991), 31.

4 Chan, *Asian Americans*, 31.

5 Wesley S. Griswold, *A Work of Giants: The First Transcontinental Railway* (New York: McGraw-Hill, 1962), 326.

6 They were said to have left by this time and were celebrating with James Strobridge.

7 Robert West Howard, *The Great Iron Trail: The Story of the First Transcontinental Railroad* (New York, 1962), 336–37.

8 Ronald Takaki, *Strangers from a Different Shore: A History of Asian Americans* (Boston: Little Brown, 1998), 22.

9 Quoted in Kwong and Miščević, *Chinese America*, 62.

10 Moon-Ho Jung, *Coolies and Cane: Race, Labor, and Sugar in the Age of Emancipation* (Baltimore: Johns Hopkins University Press, 2006), 98.

11 Fifteen went to cotton plantations in Natchitoches owned by Terence and Arthur Chaler, and another fifty worked for Jules Normand and Benjamin Bullitt, of in Natchitoches.

12 Benjamin Bullitt and Jules Normand established an office in New Orleans to take coolie shipment orders. Similarly, a group of investors created the Arkansas River Valley Immigration Company in 1869 for the purpose of bringing Chinese workers into the region. Cohen, *Chinese in the Post-Civil War South: A People Without a History* (Baton Rouge: Louisiana State University Press, 1984), 53–54.

13 Ibid., 58; Kwong and Miščević, *Chinese America*, 61.

14 Ibid., 108–09.

15 Jung, *Coolies and Cane,* 104.

16 Kwong and Miščević, *Chinese America*, 63.

17 This did not go well, as altercations with black workers led to the Chinese leaving the furnace. Cohen, *Chinese in the Post-Civil War South*, 17–18.

18 Kwong and Miščević, *Chinese America*, 65.

19 Ibid., 66.

20 Anthony W. Lee, *A Shoemaker's Story* (Princeton: Princeton University Press, 2008), 269.

21 Rick Baldoz, *The Third Asiatic Invasion: Empire and Migration in Asian America* (New York: New York University Press, 2011), 368.

22 H. Brett Melendy, *Asians in America: Koreans, Filipinos, and East Indians* (Boston: Twayne, 1977), 232.

23 Ibid.

24 Edna Bonacich, "Asian Labor in the Development of California and Hawaii," from Lucie Cheng and Edna Bonacich, eds., *Labor Immigration Under Capitalism: Asian Workers in the United States before World War II* (Berkeley: University of California Press, 1983), 179.

25 Ibid., 180.

26 Ibid., 192.

27 Evelyn Nakano Glenn, *Unequal Freedom: How Race and Gender Shaped American Citizenship and Labor* (Cambridge: Harvard University Press, 2002), 193.

28 Ibid.

29 John M. Liu, "Race, Ethnicity, and the Sugar Plantation System: Asian Labor in Hawaii, 1850 to 1900," from Cheng and Bonachich, eds., *Labor Immigration Under Capitalism*, 186.

30 Miriam Sharma, "Labor Migration and Class Formation among the Filipinos in Hawaii, 1906–1946," from Cheng and Bonacich, eds., *Labor Immigration Under Capitalism*, 582. Also see Liu, "Race, Ethnicity, and the Sugar Plantation System," 197.

31 Glenn, *Unequal Freedom*, 196.

32 Ibid.

33 Ibid.

34 Ibid.

35 Ibid., 27.

36 Liu, "Race, Ethnicity, and the Sugar Plantation System: Asian Labor in Hawaii, 1850 to 1900," 202.

37 Ibid.

38 Sharma, "Labor Migration and Class Formation among the Filipinos in Hawaii, 1906–1946," 587.

39 Liu, "Race, Ethnicity, and the Sugar Plantation System: Asian Labor in Hawaii, 1850 to 1900," 200.

40 Ibid., 201.

41 Kwong and Miščević, *Chinese America*, 56.

42 Ibid., 55, 80.

43 Daniels, *Asian America*, 19.

44 Edward J.M. Rhoads, "The Chinese in Texas," from Arif Dirlik and Malcolm Yeung, eds., *Chinese on the American Frontier* (New York: Rowman and Littlefield, 2001), 167.

45 Yuji Ichioka, *The Issei: The World of the First Generation Japanese Immigrants, 1885–1924* (New York: Free Press, 1988), 57–58.

46 Jensen, *Passage from India: Asian Indian Immigrants in North America* (New Haven: Yale University Press, 1988), 31.

47 Dorothy Fujita-Rony, *American Workers, Colonial Power: Philippine Seattle and the Transpacific West, 1919–1941* (Berkeley: University of California Press, 2003), 85.

48 Chris Friday, *Organizing Asian American Labor: The Pacific Coast Canned-Salmon Industry, 1870–1942* (Philadelphia: Temple University Press, 1994), 2.

49 652 Chinese, 1,179 Japanese, 3,730 Filipinos working in AK canneries, out of 15,023. Ibid., 3.

50 Ibid., 96.

51 Takaki, *Strangers from a Different Shore*, 189.

52 Sucheng Chan, *This Bittersweet Soil: The Chinese in California Agriculture* (Berkeley: University of California Press, 1989), 101.

53 Takaki, *Strangers from a Different Shore*, 91.

54 Chan, *This Bittersweet Soil*, 312.

55 Valerie Matsumoto, *Farming the Homeplace: A Japanese American Community in California, 1919–1982* (Ithaca: Cornell University Press, 1993), 20.

56 Ibid., 22.

57 Ibid., 23.

58 Eric Walz, "From Kumamoto to Idaho: The Influence of Japanese Immigrants on the Agricultural Development of the Interior West," *Agricultural History*, 74 no. 2 (Spring 2000): 408.

59 From 1904 to 1910, the Great Western Sugar Company in Nebraska employed about three hundred Japanese to work in the fields and processing factories. By 1909, three thousand Japanese worked in the beet fields north and east of Denver, making up a sixth of the beet labor force in Colorado. Ibid., 407.

60 Melendy, *Asians in America*, 226.

61 Ibid., 230.

62 Jensen, *Passage from India*, 33.

63 Quoted in ibid., 36.

64 Melendy, *Asians in America*, 229.

65 Ibid.

66 Bong Youn Choy, *Koreans in America* (Chicago: Nelson-Hall, 1979), 106.

67 Linda Espana Maram, *Creating Masculinity in Los Angeles's Little Manila: Working-Class Filipinos and Popular Culture, 1920s–1950s* (New York: Columbia University Press, 2006), 20.

68 Ibid.

69 Ibid., 21.

70 Melendy, *Asians in America*, 43.

71 Quoted in Maram, *Creating Masculinity in Los Angeles's Little Manila*, 21.

72 Ibid.

73 Ibid., 20.

74 Melendy, *Asians in America*, 75.

75 Robert G. Lee, *Orientals: Asian Americans in Popular Culture* (Philadelphia: Temple University Press, 1999), 98.

76 Maram, *Creating Masculinity in Los Angeles's Little Manila*, 22–23.

77 Takaki, *Strangers from a Different Shore*, 87.

78 John Kuo Wei Tchen, *New York Before Chinatown: Orientalism and the Shaping of American Culture, 1776–1882* (Baltimore: Johns Hopkins University Press), 228.

79 Ibid.

80 Yong Chen, *Chinese San Francisco, 1850–1943: A Transpacific Community* (Stanford: Stanford University Press, 2000), 65.

81 Huping Ling, *Chinese Chicago: Race, Transnational Migration, and Community Since 1870* (Stanford: Stanford University Press, 2012), 34.

82 In New York, confectionary and cigar manufacturers represented early vocation to cater to non-Chinese customers. Tchen, *New York Before Chinatown,* 81–82.

83 Chen, *Chinese San Francisco,* 64.

84 Daniels, *Asian America,* 78–79.

85 Melendy, *Asians in America,* 167.

86 Ibid., 233.

87 Spickard, *Japanese Americans,* 46.

88 Takaki, *Strangers from a Different Shore,* 196–97.

89 Chen, *Chinese San Francisco,* 66.

90 Mei, 378.

91 Choy, *Empire of Care: Nursing and Migration in Filipino American History* (Durham: Duke University Press, 2003), 25.

92 Ibid., 33.

93 Ibid., 40.

94 Ronald Takaki, *Pau Hana: Life and Labor in Hawaii, 1835–1920* (Honolulu: University of Hawaii Press, 1983), 79–80.

95 Ibid., 98.

96 Lee, *Quiet Odyssey: A Pioneer Korean Woman in America* (Seattle: Washington University Press, 1990), lvii.

97 Among Japanese Americans, 4.9 percent of women in San Francisco reported midwifery as their profession. Glenn, *Issei, Nisei, War Bride,* 74.

98 Linda Tamura, *The Hood River Issei: An Oral History of Japanese Settlers in Oregon's Hood River Valley* (Urbana: University of Illinois Press, 1993), 98.

99 Takaki, *Pau Hana,* 78.

100 Glenn, *Issei, Nisei, War Bride,* 69.

101 Tamura, *The Hood River Issei,* 101. According to Evelyn Nakano Glenn, domestic service was the most common kind of women's employment for Japanese, among first and second generations, outside of agriculture. See Glenn, *Issei, Nisei, War Bride,* 472.

102 Glenn, *Issei, Nisei, War Bride,* 100.

103 Ibid., 113.

104 Ibid., 109–110.

105 Cheng, 403.

106 Judy Yung, *Unbound Feet: A Social History of Chinese Women in San Francisco* (Berkeley: University of California Press, 1995), 29.

107 Ichioka, *The Issei,* 29.

108 Yung, *Unbound Feet,* 27.

109 Ibid., 29.

110 Ichioka, *The Issei,* 34, 45.

111 Lucie Cheng, "Free, Indentured, Enslaved: Chinese Prostitutes in Nineteenth-Century America," *Labor Immigration Under Capitalism: Asian Workers in the United States Before World War II,* Lucie Cheng and Edna Bonacich, eds. (Berkeley: University of California Press, 1984), 405.

112 Ibid., 403.

113 Yung, *Unbound Feet,* 34.

114 Ibid., 37.

115 Ibid., 38–39.

116 Quoted in Walz, 408.

117 Jensen, *Passage from India,* 35.

118 Ibid., 28.

119 Takaki, *Strangers from a Different Shore,* 174.

120 Melendy, *Asians in America,* 128.

121 Takaki, *Strangers from a Different Shore,* 183–84.

122 Friday, *Organizing Asian American Labor,* 54.

123 Ibid., 49.

124 Takaki, *Pau Hana,* 94.

125 Ibid., 95.

126 Wayne Patterson, *The Ilse: First Generation Korean Immigrants in Hawai'i, 1903–1973* (Honolulu: University of Hawaii Press, 2000), 25.

127 Sharma, "Labor Migration and Class Formation among the Filipinos in Hawaii, 1906–1946," 589.

128 Takaki, *Strangers from a Different Shore,* 136.

129 Ibid., 335.

130 In all, about one-sixth of Korean immigrants in the early period returned home. Patterson, *The Ilse,* 27.

131 Ibid., 73.

132 Melendy, *Asians in America,* 231.

133 For example in 1916 about sixty Korean beet farmers in Manteca formed a sugar beet cooperative. Ibid., 167.

134 Takaki, *Strangers from a Different Shore,* 276.

135 Ibid.

136 Melendy, *Asians in America,* 231, Karen Isaksen Leonard, *Making Ethnic Choices* (Philadelphia: Temple University Press, 1992), 50.

137 Leonard, *Making Ethnic Choices,* 51.

138 Melendy, *Asians in America,* 231.

139 Quoted in Takaki, *Strangers from a Different Shore,* 192.

140 Spickard, *Japanese Americans,* 43.

141 Takaki, *Strangers from a Different Shore,* 190.

142 Ibid., 189.

143 Ibid., 191.

144 Matsumoto, *Farming the Home Place,* 48.

145 Takaki, *Strangers from a Different Shore,* 188.

146 Ibid., 192.

147 Takaki, *Pau Hana,* 127; Jensen, *Passage from India,* 35.

148 Takaki, *Pau Hana,* 145–46.

149 Bonacich, "Asian Labor in the Development of California and Hawaii," 180.

150 Gary Okihiro, *Cane Fires: The Anti–Japanese Movement in Hawaii: 1865–1945* (Honolulu: University of Hawaii, 1991), 42–43.

151 Ibid., 47–48.

152 Takaki, *Pau Hana,* 162.

153 Ibid., 163.

154 Sharma, "Labor Migration and Class Formation among the Filipinos in Hawaii, 1906–1946," 591.

155 Epifanio Toak was jailed. Antonio Fagel took Filipino Labor Union underground under the name Vibora Luviminda and resurfaced in the 1936 strike in Maui. He did lead the HSPA to negotiate with the union for the first time and workers won a 15 percent pay increase. Ibid., 598–99.

156 Kwong and Miščević, *Chinese America,* 79.

157 Ichioka, *The Issei,* 57–58.

158 Ibid., 59.

159 Ibid.

160 Melendy, *Asians in America,* 230; Takaki, *Strangers from a Different Shore,* 273.

161 Kwong and Miščević, *Chinese America,* 79.

162 Ichioka, *The Issei*, 72.
163 Ibid., 73.
164 Ibid., 57.
165 Friday, *Organizing Asian American Labor,* 44.
166 Ibid., 39.
167 Ibid., 46.
168 Ibid., 71.
169 Ibid., 143.

Social Intimacy and Asian American Communities before World War II

4

During the 1800s and 1900s, outsiders' perceptions of Asian immigrant families and communities generally started and ended with deviance. A San Francisco health officer around the turn of the twentieth century described the city's Chinatown as a "laboratory of infection," explained and exacerbated by the preponderance of "bachelors" and prostitutes and the absence of Christian nuclear families.[1] Several decades later, the predominantly young and male Filipino American population in the West became targets of moral panics that cast them as predators who lusted after white women. Finally, in the 1910s, as Japanese established nuclear family-based communities, nativists decried the "immorality" of the picture bride system that had made possible this development. One complained, "In their pursuit of their intent to colonize this country . . . they seek to secure land and to found large families."[2]

Reflecting broader anxieties about domesticity, gender, and the nation's future, such claims overlooked external factors that constrained family and community formation in Asian America, not to mention the dynamic internal lives created beyond the sight or understanding of outside observers. As discussed previously, the labor demands of capitalism were key triggers of Asian trans-Pacific migration, and toward securing maximum profits, employers and government officials used a strategy of what Evelyn Nakano Glenn calls "family manipulation," which usually entailed excluding non-productive family members from migration.[3] This was used all over the world—in Western European guest worker programs, South African labor camps, and American agricultural companies. Recruiting prime-age laborers and excluding children, spouses, and old or sick family members not only separated workers from potential distractions, but also saved money by keeping amenities to a minimum. It also made it easier to expel workers when they were no longer needed. Family manipulation was used in Asian labor recruitment in Hawaii and the American West, initially by excluding spouses and other non-laborers, but later, some employers promoted family migration hoping it would stabilize the workforce and make laborers more docile, although generally they remained wary of the influence of kin in undermining their command over workers' time and loyalty.

In the United States, family manipulation in labor recruiting was used at a time when the meanings of citizenship, race, and sexuality were shifting yet increasingly salient and understood in relation to one another. Asian family units, family members, and permanent communities were undesirable not just from a labor standpoint; they were also anomalous in a nation where white, heterosexual nuclear families were the foundations of the citizenry and its social and cultural integrity. This outlook supported immigration restriction, miscegenation laws, alien land Acts, and other measures denying Asians full participation in American social and economic life (see Chapter 5), and these exclusionary vehicles, in turn, impeded the establishment or transplantation of families and communities. To be sure, family and community formation were not necessarily foremost goals during the early years of migration; male sojourners intended to return to Asia or preferred to leave family members at home while they traveled back and forth. But eventually, often due to longer than expected stays in America, many did wish to settle down and form or bring their families. While in some locations and among the larger Asian groups family and ethnic economy based communities flourished, many Asian immigrant men were confronted with long-term frustrations in finding social and emotional stability.

Discussions of social conditions in Asian America often lament these circumstances and how they forced immigrant men to choose between returning permanently to Asia or living out their lives in the United States as lonely "bachelors" or husbands separated from their families. Indeed, it is important to examine these and other impediments to family and community formation, as they underscore how systems of racial oppression and economic control extended into such arenas and how inhabiting "proper" family and other social roles has been a prerequisite for claiming citizenship. However, it is also important to explore how Asian immigrants were resilient and creative in their pursuit of social support and intimacy. For example, Chinese men utilized loopholes and extralegal strategies to keep their families intact, while, as mentioned, tens of thousands of Japanese men sent for "picture brides" from the home country to forge new households in America. Immigrants turned to family as a means of survival and resistance. "In a racist society where members were exploited as individual units of labor," explains Evelyn Nakano Glenn regarding Japanese Americans:

> the family was a necessary counterforce. It was the one institution that Japanese Americans could turn to for comfort, affection, and an affirmation of their individuality and self-worth. It was also in the family that ethnic culture was preserved and trans-mitted on a day-to-day basis: Japanese was spoken at home, ethnic foods were cooked and eaten, Shintoism and Buddhism were practiced, and folk wisdom passed on.[4]

Similar points apply to the importance that other Asian Americans attached to family with regard to the emotional, cultural, and practical needs it fulfilled.

At the same time, focusing only on nuclear families and co-ethnic communities—or their lack thereof—not only reproduces heteronormative and ethnocentric assumptions about what constitutes meaningful sociality, but also obscures the homosocial, interethnic, interracial, and translocal formations that were also part of the landscape of Asian America. Some single men, as well as married men wishing to establish households in America, responded to the lack of co-ethnic women by finding companionship across ethnic or racial lines. They also turned to community institutions for some of the practical and social functions of the traditional family. Men bonded with one another, in intraethnic and interethnic settings, to get their practical, social, and sexual needs met. Finally, for many

Asian Americans, communities and families were translocal entities not fixed to any one location. As Linda España-Maram discusses in regard to Filipinos in Los Angeles, whose migratory lives led observers to conclude that they lacked "real" communities:

> The assumption that Little Manila was unstable because it lacked permanent residents and buildings rests on an overly narrow definition of community as requiring a stationary population or a built environment. Because most Filipino laborers had to tailor a life in harmony with their migratory work patterns, they created a community that was versatile and, for them, functional. They took their communities with them.[5]

Also illustrating the translocalism of Asian American social lives were transnational families and communities, seen in split-household families and immigrant participation in homeland politics.

As this chapter will show, "family" and "community" were fluid yet meaningful aspects of Asian American history in the nineteenth and early twentieth centuries that belied exclusionists' attempts to pathologize this population. Expanding our conceptions of these categories and the meanings of intimacy and sociality can enrich our understanding of Asian immigrants' internal lives beyond the "sad and lonely bachelors" paradigm. As they settled in unfamiliar places, immigrants turned to one another, recreating and altering traditional practices and devising new strategies for their material, emotional, and spiritual sustenance. Additionally, family relationships and community formations, while vital, could also be oppressive and perpetuate their own forms of inequality. For instance, women lived under patriarchal gender norms that disempowered them and constrained their movements. Associations offered help and provided social cohesion, but they upheld the interests of merchant leaders and consular officials who sought control over the immigrant masses. Examining these facets of experience, typically beyond the purview of outsiders, tells us about the strategies immigrants employed to adapt to and build lives in America and how they found support and protection—but also negotiated conflict—in an often unfriendly society.

Community Organization and Infrastructures

From the beginnings of Chinese immigration to the United States, ethnic organizations provided critical material and social support for members. By the early twentieth century there were over eighty institutions in San Francisco alone that served Chinese men. Commenting on the importance of organizational networks among this population, Mary Coolidge noted in 1909, "Every Chinaman is enmeshed in a thousand other relations with his fellows."[6] In the United States, native place-based associations for Chinese immigrants, called huigan, first appeared in San Francisco in the early 1850s, and were the most important organizations among this population. Based on common regional or district affiliation and typically operating out of a store or lodging house, huigan provided assistance in housing and provisions, mail delivery, medical care, funeral arrangements, cemetery maintenance, and other needs. Reflecting their merchant leadership, they also arbitrated monetary disputes among members and provided credit and employment services. In 1883, to stabilize the community amidst association rivalries and coordinate a defense against the anti-Chinese movement, six district huigan in San Francisco formed the Chinese Consolidated Benevolent Association (CCBA), also known as the Chinese Six Companies. Other CCBA organizations emerged in Los Angeles, Sacramento, Portland, Seattle, and New York. Positioning itself as the ultimate arbiter of immigrant disputes and the voice of Chinese America to the larger society, the CCBA became the most visible political organ of the Chinese American community.

Huigan also held social control over members and reflected the class-based interests of their leaders. Membership was not voluntary; during the nineteenth century every Chinese male disembarking in San Francisco was automatically registered with an association, with dues being added to his debts. Additionally, immigrants could not purchase a return ticket to China without an association's certification. Although tongs—sworn brotherhoods, which during the nineteenth century challenged the power of associations—were commonly associated with violence, associations were also known to use force to compel members' obedience or exact punishment regarding matters such as debt, business turf, and control over operations (e.g., opium dens). The wide reach of these institutions meant that ordinary Chinese lived under the constant threat of coercion and violence. For example, in 1869, a $15 debt owed by one tong member to a member of another precipitated a fight between rival gangs of Chinese railroad workers near Camp Victor in Utah, requiring the intervention of the superintendent of the Central Pacific.[7]

Such organizations were nonetheless vital, providing needed services that immigrants could not get elsewhere, and cultivating a sense of community that bound merchants and ordinary migrants. Organizational networks furthermore influenced geographic patterns of settlement among Chinese immigrants. Smaller Chinatowns tended to be dominated by one or two clans—the Yees in Pittsburgh, the Moys in Chicago, and the Chins in Denver—which would then shape urban settlement patterns among Chinese in distinct ways. For instance, the Moy clan gained a foothold in Chicago by establishing one of the first Chinese associations in the city just prior to the turn of the twentieth century. When other Moys entered the United States, many went to Chicago, where they had fellow kin to welcome and help settle them in their new homes. Such "chain migrations" bolstered a clan's presence and shored up an association's power, while also locking individual newcomers into a cycle of mutual dependency with members of their clan and village.[8]

Scholars have noted the remarkable extent of institution building among Japanese immigrants, from the first labor firms established to help Issei find housing and jobs.[9] As the Japanese population in America grew and became settled, the array of farming and business associations, birthplace associations, newspapers, social clubs, and other institutions promoting economic success and bolstering ethnic solidarity proliferated. Throughout the late nineteenth and early twentieth centuries prefectural associations, or kenjinkai, played an especially large institutional role in immigrant men's social lives, in this way being similar to huigan.[10] In Japan, people's ken affiliation was not central to their identity, but in the United States it shaped everything from which customers businesses catered to, whom immigrants pooled money with for enterprises (in tanomoshi), whom labor contractors served, and which women Issei men would marry. It also influenced where immigrants settled. For instance, Okinawans made up a large portion of the Japanese population in Hawaii, but were comparatively few on the West Coast. In Southern California, people from

Hiroshima concentrated in Gardena, Little Tokyo, and Hawthorne, where they worked as vegetable farmers, while people from Wakayama clustered in San Pedro and worked in fishing trades.[11]

Kenjinkai promoted the material wellbeing and social enrichment of members, and did not seek control over members like huigan did over Chinese immigrants. Japanese associations, which were distinct from kenjinkai, did concern themselves with enforcing control and good behavior. Their reach was limited, however, and they never enrolled more than a third of the adult Japanese male population, but they claimed to be and were frequently regarded as representatives of Issei. With precursors appearing as early as 1891, the Japanese Association of America was formed in San Francisco in 1908, serving as a central body for local affiliates in California and several southwestern states. Three other central associations were established in cities with consulate offices: Seattle, Portland, and Los Angeles. The four central bodies occupied the middle of a three-tier hierarchy in which consulates were at the top and local associations were at the bottom. Locals generally emerged wherever significant numbers of Japanese lived, and by 1923, there were eighty-six locals affiliated with the central bodies.[12]

Because they derived their authority from the consulate, the associations were effectively arms of the Japanese state. They advocated on behalf of immigrants and promoted their positive image to non-Japanese. After 1907, they carried out the documentation requirements of the Gentlemen's Agreement, and sometimes wielded this authority to compel members' obedience by threatening to withhold residence certificates or leverage personal information.[13] Above all, associations were concerned about immigrants' behavior, and in addition to issuing and carrying out threats, they published guides on how Issei should conduct themselves. One guide targeted at women urged them not to reveal "domestic scandals" that might cause "embarrassment" to all Japanese.[14] Associations' approach to spousal desertion, identified as a problem in the mid-1910s, illustrates their methods of moral policing. To find and punish deserters, local and central associations would share information with each other. In one example from 1923, the Western Idaho Japanese Association received a letter from the North American Japanese Association of Seattle with details regarding an Issei woman named Araeda Asako who had abandoned her husband for another man, Amano Sanji, absconding with her paramour and child. Included with the letter were photographs of Araeda and Amano and instructions to the Idaho affiliate to refuse the couple any services, should they turn up, until they made proper restitution. Associations commonly treated deserters and absconding couples this way, and their organizational network was extensive enough that if these social pariahs wished to escape notice, they had little choice but to go where there were virtually no Japanese.[15]

While it was common for immigrants to feel strong ethnic attachments to their brethren while adapting to a new land, these ties were particularly intense among Koreans due to Japan's colonization of their homeland. Many Korean immigrants saw themselves as a people with "no homeland to return to," and so turned to one another.[16] In Hawaii, the earliest institutional bodies they formed included dong-hoi, or village councils, which emphasized co-ethnic solidarity, fellowship, and "love for fellow Korean immigrants."[17] Korean language schools, patriotic societies, and military training centers in Hawaii and the mainland also maintained immigrants' orientation toward homeland culture and politics. The Korean National Association (KNA), the main organization associated with Korean immigrants in the early 1900s, was formed in 1909 amid the crisis of Japan's annexation of Korea. Succeeding several organizations, it was launched in the wake of the 1908 assassination of the pro-Japanese U.S. diplomat Durham Stevens by two Koreans, Jang In-Whang of the Korean Restorative Association, and Jen Myeng-woon of the Korean Mutual Assistance Association.[18] Representatives from associations in Hawaii and the mainland met in San Francisco to plan the KNA, which they envisioned as the official voice of Koreans in the western hemisphere, champion of Korean independence, and advocate for the "intellectual and economic development" of immigrant communities.[19] Toward the latter, it organized social welfare services, set up schools, created textbooks, and published newsletters. Most Korean immigrants gave money to support the KNA, as anti-Japanese politics and mutual aid fostered powerful social bonds.[20]

As noted earlier, the religious persuasion of Koreans distinguished them from other Asian immigrants; the majority who arrived between 1903 and 1905 were Protestants, having been acquainted with American missionaries in Korea. As a result, Christian churches were the most important social institutions in this population. The first Korean church in Hawaii was established in 1903 on Wailua sugar plantation, and fifteen years later, there were thirty-nine Korean Protestant churches and about three thousand Korean Christians in the islands, with the bulk being Methodist and Episcopalian.[21] On the mainland, where Methodists and Presbyterians predominated, the first Korean church was established in 1904 in Los Angeles, and although the West Coast population was only around one thousand, they had about a dozen churches, with others scattered in cities such as Chicago and New York.[22] Besides providing worship services and spiritual support, churches served social, cultural, and political functions, such as running education programs for boys and girls and supporting independence activities.

Protestant churches were not as influential among other Asians, although missionaries in the United States had been reaching out to Asians since Chinese arrived in California during the gold rush. Although they were usually a distinct minority within their communities, Asian American Protestants, due to their beliefs as well as connections, often enjoyed more social capital and visibility in the mainstream society than their non-Christian counterparts. In the Japanese American community, such figures included Takie Okamura of Hawaii and Masasuke Kobayashi of California. For example, with the help the Dyes, a white missionary family, Filipino immigrant Sylvestre Morales, himself an evangelical Protestant, established the Filipino American Christian Fellowship in Los Angeles in 1928.[23] Despite the prominence of these Asian Protestants and the leadership status that non-Asians accorded them, such individuals remained exceptional, and white missionaries would not have widespread success in converting large numbers of Asian immigrants.[24] Those who did attend Protestant churches were most likely to do so for practical reasons, such as sanctuary from prostitution or the desire to take English classes.

For the most part, religious life among Asian Americans was characterized by transplanted practices from the homeland that informed individuals' outlooks and identities, strengthened ethnic ties, and often became tied up with political and economic matters. The majority of Filipino immigrants were Catholic, due to the legacy of Spanish colonialism. Because they were generally unwelcome in American Catholic churches, several parishes were set up for them, including Our Lady Queen of Martyrs Church in Seattle and St. Columban's Church in Los Angeles.[25] Throughout the early twentieth century the majority of Issei identified as

Buddhists, although, according to Paul Spickard, Buddhism was mainly a source of ethical ideals, and practicing consisted of little more than observing ceremonial rites during births, weddings, and funerals.[26] The first Japanese Buddhist temples, which were small and established with the help of missionaries from Japan, appeared in Hilo and San Francisco during the 1890s, and subsequently organizations such as the Young Men's Buddhist Association, North American Buddhist Mission, and Buddhist Women's Association provided further institutional support for the maintenance of Japanese Buddhism in the United States.[27]

With respect to Chinese immigrants, Sucheng Chan describes their religion as a "syncretist amalgamation of Confucian, Taoist, Buddhist, and animist beliefs."[28] Because churches and services were not required to practice, but rather just an altar with a deity and a metal pot with sticks of incense, shrines were found in association halls, shops, and hospitals. Temples devoted to one or several deities appeared in the landscapes of urban Chinatowns.[29] The deities that immigrants worshipped were familiar ones in South China, such as Mazu (Queen of Heaven), a tenth- and eleventh-century girl who was deified as a protector of sailors, and Guan Yu, a general from the second and third centuries who was deified as a god of war. Temples devoted to Guan Yu, as well as his images, were so pervasive in San Francisco Chinatown by the turn of the century that many outsiders thought he was the Chinese god.[30] Religion was also the basis of some of the largest community gatherings among Chinese immigrants, most notably the New Year parade, a tradition that started as early as 1855 in San Francisco, and in which firecrackers, drums, lanterns, torches, and bonfires were used to chase away evil spirits.[31]

The religious lives of Asian Indians, often mistakenly collapsed as "Hindus" or "Hindoos," were not as mystical as outsiders imagined them to be. During the early 1900s, Hinduism in the United States was mostly limited to several hundred Indian students and avid American followers, the latter of whom flocked to ashrams in cities throughout the country where visiting swamis taught lessons about Hinduism.[32] One Indian derisively remarked on this fad, saying, "Most of [the swamis] have taken up this profession for what they can get out of it. They have discovered that Americans, especially women, are curious creatures and will 'fall for' anything or anybody who looks odd or mysterious."[33]

As mentioned earlier, a majority of Asian Indians to the United States during the early twentieth century were Punjabi Sikhs who settled in the American West, and religious practice remained a central part of their lives. In 1912 Sikhs in Stockton formed the Pacific Coast Khalsa Diwan Society, and constructed a temple—or gurdwara—shortly thereafter, where men took turns serving as granthi, or priests.[34] The Society also arranged cremation services and coordinated festivals and religious observances, while also performing nonreligious functions like maintaining lodging accommodations and providing a meeting place for political discussions, and its presence eventually helped turn Stockton into one of the centers of the California Punjabi population.[35] Other Indian organizations were likewise formed along religious lines—the Pakistan House and Moslem Association, for example, provided recreational, burial, and other services for Punjabi Muslims in Sacramento and Imperial Valley during the early 1900s.[36] Oftentimes, however, these groups came to embrace all Indians regardless of affiliation and others were formed with explicitly non-sectarian purposes. In the Imperial Valley, Ram Chand, Asa Singh, Fazl Din, a Hindu, Sikh, and Muslim, established the Hindustani Welfare Reform Society in 1918 as a non-sectarian organization serving Indian immigrants that provided mutual aid and also helped mediate civil suits on behalf of members.[37] As was the case in other Asian American communities, Indian organizations shored up elites' power over their working class brethren, as prosperous and assimilated individuals usually provided the leadership and funds that sustained the operations and services.[38]

In addition to labor organizations, Filipino immigrants established an array of associations, and their activities, furthermore, belie the common contention that they lacked the resources and resourcefulness of other Asian immigrant groups. As Linda España-Maram explains, utang na loob referred to the Filipino philosophy of turning to one another for help, something Filipinos in America put into practice organizationally to attend to fellow immigrants' spiritual, educational, material, and other needs.[39] Filipino associations were mostly concentrated in the West Coast states, and these included the Filipino Patriotic Association of California, Philippine American Club, Philippine Catholic Club, Caballeros de Dimas-Alang, Legionarios del Trabajo, and the Gran Oriente Filipino. In Los Angeles alone during the 1930s, Filipinos formed at least twenty-four organizations. The Caballeros, one of the most important of these, was originally a fraternal organization founded in Manila in 1906 to promote Philippine liberation from the United States. The first U.S. branch was established in 1921 in San Francisco, and by the mid-1930s it grew to twenty-six lodges throughout California. Embracing all Filipinos, chapters conducted meetings in English after initially using Tagalog, and they supplied members with food, clothing, and money for medical and burial expenses, as well as enriching their social lives by hosting dances and banquets. Politically, Filipino American organizations were diverse; while some were radical and championed Philippine independence from the United States, others embraced more moderate and pro-American outlooks. The Filipino Federation of America, founded in 1925 in Los Angeles, sought to promote friendly relations between Filipinos and Americans, and its socially conservative leaders urged members to demonstrate high moral standards and loyalty to the U.S. Constitution and to oppose labor unions.

We can draw some generalizations about these institutions in Asian America. For many, they were sites of community and camaraderie among fellow countrymen, and because they were organized along the lines of national or regional affiliation or some other category from the homeland, they tended to reinforce ethnic solidarity and identity. Moreover, many of the organizations were crucial for immigrants' social welfare, as they usually did not look beyond ethnic and family resources for charity. At the same time, institutions maintained forms of inequality and sought social control over the populations they served. Most striking was the gender inequality they perpetuated. The institutional landscape in Asian America, practically without variation, was gender-segregated, with nearly all associations open to men only. Whether motivated by building power, promoting a positive image of countrymen, or fighting for causes in the homeland, institutions also tended to maintain the power of elite leaders whose acculturation, wealth, and/or contacts were also crucial for organizations' survival and integrity.

Co-Ethnic Nuclear Families

For those who created and maintained them, nuclear family households were vital for immigrants' survival and socialization in America. In the early years of immigration, such social units were rare, but as Asian immigrant communities took on a more settled or permanent orientation, nuclear family formation proceeded, albeit to varying degrees by group. Japanese Americans made the most marked transformation from male sojourner communities to family-based permanent ones, a shift facilitated in the first two decades of the 1900s by the picture bride migration. To illustrate the change, in 1900 there were 410 married Japanese women in America, ten years later there were 5,581, and by 1920 that number reached 22,193.[40] In 1930, the male to female ratio in Japanese America reached near parity at 1.65.[41]

Indeed, the picture bride migration had driven the rise of married Japanese couples in America. Relatively small numbers of Japanese women had been married prior to their husbands' emigration or met and married their grooms when the latter made a return trip to Japan. For most single Issei men, returning to Japan to find a bride was unfeasible due to the time and expenses involved, and so they turned to the picture bride system. In this adaptation of a traditional Japanese practice, an intermediary was consulted in the selection of a marriage partner.[42] The prospective bride and groom would exchange photographs and information, such as the man's occupation and other details about his life in America. A ceremony would be conducted in Japan without the groom present, but as long as the bride's name was entered into the groom's family registry, the marriage was recognized by Japan. Koreans were the only other Asian group that utilized the picture bride practice to a significant degree.[43] From 1910 to 1924, about 1,000 Korean picture brides went to Hawaii and another 115 to the West Coast. This migration allowed them to maintain a high rate of endogamy; as late as 1937, only 104 Koreans were married to non-Koreans.[44]

The picture bride migration was subject to rules enforced by Japanese and U.S. officials. The Japanese consulate required grooms to prove their means of support and a certain level of income and savings. Except in rare cases, laborers could not send for picture brides, although this restriction was relaxed in 1915 for those who could demonstrate having at least $800 in savings.[45] Prior to leaving for the United States, the brides had to have their names entered into their new husbands' family registries at least six months before submitting their passport applications, a measure meant to prevent fraud. After 1915 Japan imposed an age regulation in which a bride could not, with rare exceptions, be more than thirteen years younger than her husband.[46] The brides were subject to a physical examination at the point of embarkation, usually rode in third class steerage, and sometimes underwent a second examination when they disembarked. At the American port, the husbands had to appear at the immigration station with documents attesting to their identity, occupation, and savings. Before 1917 when the United States did not recognize picture bride marriages, couples had to be remarried, sometimes in mass ceremonies, at the immigration station or in nearby hotel lobbies or churches.[47]

Immigrant wives had their own expectations for life in America. Prospective picture brides were motivated by a range of factors to journey to the United States to join husbands they had never met, from filial obedience, to the chance to send money to their families, to a desire for escape from difficult circumstances. "Just as the men came to better their lot," says

Evelyn Nakano Glenn, "Issei women came with their own hopes—to further their education, to help their families economically, to seek a happier home life, and to experience new adventures. They expected to achieve their goals and then return to a better life in Japan."[48] Nonetheless, many women confronted disappointment, sometimes from the moment they met their husbands if the men were less attractive or older than they appeared in their photographs. As "Mrs. Yoshida" recalled, "Many times the picture was taken twenty years earlier and they had changed. Many of the husbands had gone to the country to work as farmers, so they had aged and become quite wrinkled. And very young girls came expecting more."[49] Other grooms exaggerated their success; one man said he was a hotel operator but in actuality ran a small boarding house, and another claimed to be a landowning farmer but was in reality a sharecropper.[50]

Although working-class wives' multiple roles in and outside the home, in paid and unpaid work, were critical for the survival of their households and the stabilization of ethnic communities, their lives were still constrained by gender norms in which husbands were the chief authority figures and wage earners and wives performed unpaid housework, depended on spouses for protection, and occupied a subordinate position. While they could leave the home to work, worship, and go shopping relatively freely, women rarely traveled far distances alone or mingled with men. Nor could they, as pointed out above, join associations, unless they were explicitly for women, or have much of a public role in community affairs.

The most isolated and cloistered women in Asian American communities tended to be the most socioeconomically privileged, perhaps none more so than the wives of elite Chinese merchants. Most of these women entered the United States after the passage of the Chinese Exclusion Act, which permitted only members of the merchant and other elite classes to bring wives and family members. They did not work, could not join associations, guilds, or tongs, and rarely went out in public. Their main interactions were with servants and they spent their hours doing activities like needlework designs. Around the turn of the twentieth century, Sui Sin Far described the lives of "genteel" Chinese women in the following way:

> The Chinese woman in America lives generally in the upstairs apartments of her husband's dwelling. He looks well after her comfort and provides all her little mind can wish . . . She seldom goes out, and does not receive visitors until she has been a wife for at least two years. Even then, if she has no child, she is supposed to hide herself. After a child has been born to her, her wall of reserve is lowered a little, and it is proper for cousins and friends of her husband to drop in occasionally and have a chat with "the family." Now and then the women visit one another . . . They laugh at the most commonplace remark and scream at the smallest trifle; they examine one another's dresses and hair, talk about their husbands, their babies, their food; squabble over little matters and make up again; they dine on bowls of rice, minced chicken, bamboo shoots and a dessert of candied fruits.[51]

While life in America for Asian immigrant couples had its share of struggles and challenges, their unions were also the foundation for the growth of stable, family-based communities. In Japanese America, Issei couples usually wasted little time in having children. At the turn of the twentieth century, there were just 269 U.S.-born Japanese, a number that rose to 4,501 by 1910 and then 29,672 in 1920.[52] The birth of children not only enabled immigrants to enjoy settled family lives, but also reinforced the economic foundations of permanent settlement. In studying the internal dynamics of immigrant families in America, scholars have suggested that life was in some ways less constraining compared to life in Asia. Judy Yung and Evelyn Nakano Glenn, for instance, have pointed out, regarding Chinese and Japanese, respectively, that the relative absence of in-laws and multi-generational households in the United States made a major difference. "Not only was the daughter-in-law freed from serving her in-laws," says Yung, "but she was also freed of competition for her husband's attention and loyalty and given full control over managing the household."[53] In communities where men greatly outnumbered women, wives were considered status symbols. They were essential in their households as helpmates and, thus, crucial for their families' survival, which could be a source of empowerment as well as oppression. Abused or unhappy wives had few options for escape; among them were seeking "rescue" by a mission home or absconding, either alone or with another man.[54]

Among Indians, Filipinos, and Chinese, the dearth of female immigrants as well as the burdens of daily life made nuclear families based on co-ethnic marriages very rare. Immigrant Zacarias Managan described the difficulties that Filipinos faced:

> So we were allowed to get our families if we would want to but the problem is some of us hesitated to get them because of the condition of living, you know. We don't earn enough money to support them and we have to support them so we thought . . . it would be better for us to be alone and if we have some money left . . . what we have to do is send [it] back home.[55]

Eligible Filipina women, along with women in other predominantly male immigrant communities, were often heavily courted, and the small number of nuclear households that

Figure 4.1   Created between 1898 and 1905 this picture, titled "A Chinese family," shows a Chinese immigrant woman with four children in California. At this time, women and children were rare in a population dominated by male sojourner laborers. (Library of Congress Prints and Photographs Division, LC-DIG-ppmsca-17886.)

did exist became the social centers for the local ethnic community. In these communities, moreover, the presence of a second generation (discussed in Chapter 7) was muted. Among Chinese Americans in 1860, there were 42 Chinese children in the United States and ten years later just 400.[56] In San Francisco, which probably had the largest concentration of children, they made up just 8 percent of the Chinese population.[57] As late as 1890, the male to female gender ratio was about 27 to 1, and children remained a minor part of this population until well into the twentieth century. As late as 1920 there were 695 Chinese men to every 100 women in the United States.[58]

Social Intimacy in the World of "Bachelors"

The term "bachelor society" has often been invoked to underscore the high ratio of Asian men over women in America during the nineteenth and early twentieth centuries. It calls to mind images such as gangs of male laborers surviving together by their wits and elderly men living out their twilight years alone. More to the point, Ronald Takaki has characterized these communities as men "trapped in a womanless world."[59] Japanese and Koreans transitioned to family-based communities most rapidly due to the migration of picture brides, and other Asians who were able to form nuclear units were considered lucky. Outsiders frequently cited the skewed gender ratios and relative absence of settled nuclear families to demonize and pathologize this population at a time when the white Victorian bourgeois family was the norm. During the late nineteenth and early twentieth centuries, the heterosexual family, explains Robert Lee, "was the principal background against which the ideology of citizenship was debated," and "oriental sexuality was constructed as ambiguous, inscrutable, and hermaphroditic."[60] With respect to Chinese immigrants, Lee says this group "represented a third sex—an alternative or imagined sexuality that was potentially subversive and disruptive to the emergent heterosexual orthodoxy."[61] Although the preponderance of men and lack of nuclear households stemmed from demographic, legal, and other structural factors, to xenophobes, these "bachelor communities" evidenced racial and moral deficiencies and unfitness for American belonging. Due to their skewed gender ratios, other Asian populations in America would be similarly regarded, especially in the early decades after arrival.

As common as these perceptions were, however, they failed to capture the internal dynamics of Asian American homosociality, a defining feature of many communities. Early Asian American history was in many quarters a male, working-class, and transient world. Men lived together in crowded bunkrooms, shared domestic duties, and provided companionship to one another. Most Indian immigrants, for instance, were in their early twenties when they left home, and virtually no women migrated. Thus, they relied on male blood relatives and other men for finding jobs, leasing land, and social interaction, largely keeping to themselves or occasionally joining nearby black and Mexican communities.[62] Although such conditions defied traditional gender and household norms, both in America and the home country, this did not mean the immigrants had no family life or relationships. In a critique of the "bachelor society model," Dorothy Fujita-Rony employs an expansive definition of "family." As she explains, among Filipino Americans, a population which before World War II was nearly all male and under the age of thirty, calling non-blood-related men "brothers" and "uncles" exemplified the importance of fictive kin. "Brother" often referred to ties among young laborers, and "uncle" to an older person from the same town or province who took a young immigrant under his wing.[63] Patron-client relations were likewise invested with familial significance and expressed in terms that gave otherwise formal or transactional relationships an emotional intimacy.[64]

Unsurprisingly, in the predominantly male immigrant communities that were shaped by labor markets, homosociality pervaded life and bonding outside of work. As described above, mutual aid organizations served and linked men, and living arrangements usually entailed men in close quarters, in bunkhouse and other communities. As Joan Jensen has explained regarding Indians in California, life was simple, but forged on cooperation. Immigrants in rural areas, "preferred to sleep in screened porches or outdoors in the summer and keeping few personal belongings. Floors often served as beds, fields as toilets . . . They took turns cooking or hired a cook to buy supplies and prepare meals."[65] The kinship ties or shared village and caste affiliation that formed the basis of work gangs were reinforced outside work hours as well, as the time people spent together deepened "ties of friendship, trust, and respect."[66]

Cities, especially those with Asian ethnic enclaves, offered a wide range of social options in which homosocial immigrant communities emerged and flourished. With regard to Chinatowns, while outsiders often fixated on so-called vice establishments like opium dens, brothels, and gambling halls, such businesses only represented a portion of the social and economic life of the Chinese American community. The variety of establishments and concentration of people made Chinatown a place where immigrants could meet with co-ethnics for tea and meals, purchase familiar groceries, visit Chinese doctors, and worship in temple. The cultural life was rich and varied. In addition to holiday celebrations like Chinese New Year and the Full Moon Festival, recreational activities like going to the theater were common features of Chinatown life.[67] Since the mid-1850s, professional troupes from China had toured the United States, and the first Chinese theater performance was given in San Francisco in 1852 at the American Theater. The following decade, there were three Chinese playhouses in the city that held nightly performances—the Chinese Royal being the most popular—and about thirty years later the number of theaters had doubled. The plays, which drew both Chinese and white audiences, portrayed traditional themes and historical events and employed conventions of popular Chinese popular theater, with productions about striving scholars, righteous officials, and the Confucian conflict of filial piety versus loyalty to throne.

In her examination of Filipino men in Los Angeles, Linda España-Maram has shown how, for the young immigrant men, entertainment spaces for dancing, gambling and other activities, located chiefly in nonwhite enclaves, became especially important sites for socializing. As Ray Corpus recalled about conditions for Filipinos in the 1920s and 1930s:

> we were all males at that time, from L.A. to Seattle . . . So what do we have to do? We were young so we go to Chinatown because there are a lot of, ah, things going on there. Taxi dances, prostitution, whatever, they were there. And of course young people like me at the time, I like to try everything to see what it looks like as opposed to, you know, [reading about] it in the books.[68]

The sporting culture of Filipino men, which revolved around boxing, was also a dynamic space for "creating masculinity." Fans sometimes drove hundreds of miles to watch matches at venues like Los Angeles' Olympic Auditorium, San Francisco's Dreamland Arena, and Stockton's Civic Auditorium where their idols Francisco "Pancho Villa" Guilledo, the American Flyweight Champion in 1922, Ceferino Garcia, Small Montana, Speedy Dado, and others appeared.[69] A Garcia fight on the West Coast, Maram notes, "[was] a signal for a cavalcade of motor cars of various vintages to converge on the scene of action."[70] When people were unable to attend events, ethnic newspapers provided them with recaps and thus helped sustain the ethnic sporting culture. This was also true for Chinese and Japanese immigrants, whose newspapers likewise covered sports. By reading about their sports heroes in publications like the *Philippines Review*, "Filipino workers codified their ideals of Filipino masculinity: Garcia, outnumbered fifty to one, relying only on his wits and raw muscle, fought undaunted, and emerged victorious."[71]

Worried about how their countrymen were perceived as well as the ill effects of some of the popular activities among male immigrants, particularly gambling and prostitution, ethnic leaders and organizations occasionally tried to reform the bachelor communities. Hermenegildo Cruz, the director of labor in the Philippines especially lamented the popularity of gambling among Filipino immigrants because they made so little money to begin with and it reduced how much they could send home.[72] In the Issei community, Japanese associations worked to eradicate gambling and other activities deemed unwholesome for the immigrant masses (see Chapter 6).

Interethnic Relations and New Social Units

Family and community life among Asian immigrants also crossed racial and ethnic boundaries, breaking taboos and giving rise to new kinds of social units and identities. From the mid-nineteenth century when Chinese came to mine for gold until nearly a century later, Asians in America made their way in predominantly male, multiethnic societies with few female co-ethnics. The social worlds they forged were rich and dynamic, reflecting the constraints against which they were created, the resourcefulness and diversity of the immigrants, and the importance of companionship and intimacy in daily life.

While co-ethnic homosocial communities (discussed above) were an important arena of socializing and intimacy, interethnic relations among men also flourished, particularly in locations in the West with large transient populations. Because Filipino immigrants, for instance, lacked the base of ethnic businesses that larger, longer-established Asian communities had during the early twentieth century, they often relied on Chinese and Japanese-owned grocery stores, restaurants, gambling houses, and other businesses for their living and social needs. Entering such spaces led to interethnic encounters that could reinforce both an overarching nascent Asian identity as well as a specific Filipino one.[73] Additionally bunkhouse communities in agricultural areas in California, where workers shared kitchens and housing and dining quarters, were frequently interethnic. Nor was it unusual for South Asian, Chinese, or Japanese contractors to manage Korean, Chinese, Filipino, Mexican, South Asian, Afghani, white American, and black workers. At the Tom Foon Ranch on Sherman Island, the community bunkhouse housed ten to twelve men who slept in very close quarters. In 1924, John Willis, a twenty-three-year-old Native American arrived there to work and shared a bunkroom with "a number of Mohammedans, either Hindus or Afghans."[74]

In these diverse and fluid areas—called "transit zones" by Nayan Shah—usually located in downtown sections of cities like Vancouver, British Columbia and Sacramento, California, "an ever changing assortment of men and boys moved through the city . . . but the frequency of encounters produced familiarity among the working men and boys."[75] The social encounters were especially facilitated by the presence of various commercial establishments like saloons, theaters, pool halls, restaurants, and cheap hotels. The case of Darrah Singh and Edward Bowen illustrates some of the social dynamics in the multiethnic, predominantly male societies of the early twentieth century American West, and especially how they could result in both physical intimacy and interpersonal misunderstanding. Bowen, a twenty-one-year-old English laborer met Singh and another South Asian man at the Fountain Saloon in downtown Vancouver. After inviting them to "drink and talk" about their lives in India and China, the men left for the Alexander Hotel, where a bartender noted how tall the "fine-looking" South Asian men were. Singh, a veteran of the British army in India, had been in the area for two years and was planning to immigrate to Washington. He eventually invited Bowen to his room in the Spokane Rooming House. In police records, Bowen claimed Singh tried to seduce him and, invoking male honor, claimed he had no choice but to shoot and kill him. A sympathetic judge sentenced Bowen to ten years in prison.[76]

Migrant men's activities drew the attention of authorities when they resulted in fatal violence, property damage, or riots, but cases like Singh's were suggestive of the existence of "subaltern counterpublics" that defied state regulation and bourgeois social conventions. "These experiments in social relations and intimacies," explains Shah, "were forged by challenges of migratory work and life. Through feeling and loving otherwise, migrant males' experimental intimacies were attempts to buffer the material challenges of survival and kept isolation, poverty, and death at bay."[77] The example above is also indicative of the presence of erotic desire and sexual relationships between men. Although such relationships are not well documented—sodomy cases in police records can provide one window, but a very partial one—these were a part of the social landscape of Asian America.[78] Other examples attest to the existence of same sex intimacy, such as the practice by labor contractors in the Pacific Northwest during the 1920s and 1930s of sending male as well as female prostitutes to cannery communities, and taking a percentage of the money they earned.[79]

In Hawaii, where interethnic mingling was not a transient phenomenon, but rather a fixture of plantation society, local cultures and practices were transformed by the presence and interaction of people of many different racial and ethnic backgrounds. One of the consequences was the development of a pidgin dialect and the emergence of a mixed-race population. With regard to the former, most laborers retained the language of their home countries, which was reinforced by the organization of gangs and plantations as well as establishment of language schools and other ethnic institutions. However, when working with members of other ethnic groups, they had to learn to communicate across boundaries, which led to the evolution of a plantation dialect called pidgin, which incorporated elements of Japanese, Chinese, Portuguese, and other languages. It was so developed and widespread by the early twentieth century that newly arrived workers thought pidgin was English.

Additionally, because it was associated with laborers, it facilitated the formation of a multiethnic working-class identity in Hawaii.[80]

During the early twentieth century, the most transgressive type of interethnic relationships—aside from same-sex relations—were those between white women and non-white men, and while legal, cultural, and other barriers impeded them considerably, they were nonetheless a notable part of Asian immigrants' social experience, among both working and elite classes. At taxi-dance halls, a popular working-class entertainment establishment that Filipino men were especially associated with, male customers would pay to dance with female employees for a set amount of time. Found all over the West Coast and in cities like New York and Chicago during the 1920s and 1930s, they brought together members of in-between and marginal groups, such as Italians, blacks, Chinese, Mexicans, and working-class white women.[81] Because of the populations taxi-dance halls catered to and interracial mingling they engendered, white moral crusaders and other officials denounced them as gathering places for "white trash" and "brown hordes," but for the patrons and employees, they had much different meanings. As Linda España-Maram explains, they "provided opportunities for poor immigrant men and working women to create identities that allowed them to be something other than what their ethnicity, class, or national origin dictated."[82] In addition to being outlets for interacting with women, the halls satisfied immigrant men's desire for respectability and social acceptance, something they were denied in their work lives. Encounters on the dance floor could, furthermore, lead to more intimate relationships.

Indeed, during the nineteenth and early twentieth centuries, Asian men seeking conjugal companionship with women were most likely to find it with non-Asians. The main exceptions to this were Japanese and Koreans who, due to the migration of picture brides, by and large took up with or married co-ethnic women. Miscegenation codes in various states and prevailing racism made marrying whites the most unlikely and dangerous option, although it did occur sporadically. Further, there were notable differences based on region and place. In New York City, for instance, interracial marriage was the dominant marriage pattern among Chinese during the mid-1800s and remained common into the exclusion period. Census records reveal that they were more common among laborers than merchants.[83] In 1870 eleven mixed-race couples were counted residing in New York's sixth ward, in effect over one-fourth of the ward's Chinese male population.[84] In 1900, there had been 133 new marriages in Chinatown, with 82 of these between Chinese men and non-Chinese women.[85] Most of the non-co-ethnic wives, furthermore, were white, both European and native-born, and a smaller number were black. These patterns continued into the twentieth century, albeit in a less pronounced fashion; between 1931 and 1938, 254 marriages occurred with a groom of Chinese descent, out of which about 26 percent were to non-Chinese women. Although outsiders' ingrained attitudes against race mixing and their depiction of the white women who entered relationships with Asian men as fallen women relegated these couples outside the bounds of respectability, these "transgressive" relationships were nonetheless a part of the daily fabric of Asian America.

Because of the barriers to white–non-white relationships and the preponderance of non-whites in working-class populations, Asian men frequently found companionship with non-white women. In Puget Sound and British Columbia, for instance, it was relatively common for Chinese men to live with or marry Native American women whom they had met in cannery communities.[86] Among Punjabi men in the Southwest and California, a pattern of intermarriage with Mexican women emerged as early as the 1910s.[87] Such marriages accounted for as much as 92 percent of Punjabi marriages in the Imperial Valley during the early 1900s.[88] As the possibility of going back to India diminished, they turned to women outside of their ethnic group to be their wives. Some Indian Muslims married black women, and East Indians who gained entry to American universities and elite social circles married white women.[89] According to the *San Francisco Chronicle*, by 1926 150 women had married "high caste" Hindus.[90] Although Indians were able to intermarry because most mis-cegenation laws did not apply to them, after the passage of the Cable Act in 1922, the American women who married them faced the loss of their citizenship.[91]

The Punjabi–Mexican communities of California did not draw the same level of scrutiny as Punjabi–white marriages, although they sometimes caused trouble with Mexican men.[92] The couples often met in agricultural fields where they were employed or where Mexican women worked for Punjabi farmers. A common pattern that gave rise to sizeable Punjabi–Mexican communities involved sisters and other female relatives from Mexican families marrying into groups of Punjabi relatives and associates. For example, members of the Alvarez family, immigrants from Mexico, picked cotton for Punjabi partners Sher Singh and Gopal Singh, who leased land on the Edwards ranch in Imperial Valley. In 1916, Sher Singh married Antonia Alvarez, and the following year, Gopal married her sister Anna Anita. A notable age difference separated the grooms and wives; Sher and Gopal were thirty-six and thirty-seven respectively, while Antonia and Anna Anita were twenty-one and eighteen at the time they married, and this was typical in other Punjabi–Mexican marriages. Another sister, Valentina, joined them, and one of her daughters, fourteen-year-old Alejandrina, married a Sikh friend of Sher and Gopal, Albert Joe.[93] The youngest Alvarez sister, Ester, also married a Sikh, Harnam Singh Sidhu, in 1919.

Such couples could be found in California, Arizona, New Mexico, Utah, Texas, and even Mexico and Canada, most settling in the Imperial Valley and vicinity.[94] For the Punjabi men, an incentive to marry Hispanic women (not all were Mexican) was that it was relatively easy to arrange similar marriages for their associates and relatives through the women's families. For the women, the marriages were a good idea because the men tended to be farmers, which promised some stability. One eighteen-year-old Mexican woman who had been deserted by her Mexican husband explained her desire to marry an Indian: "Through my sister and her husband, who was Hindu, I met my husband. I was thinking, now what am I going to do, left alone with two children and without being able to work. He was a nice person and single, so to get a father and home for my children, I married him."[95] As to other reasons why Asian Indians may have been inclined to marry Mexicans, Karen Leonard acknowledges but largely disputes the notion that these marriages were a strategy by Asian Indians to evade alien land laws and acquire land through their wives, as Indians could own land until 1923 and the women, after 1922 (Cable Act), would have lost their citizenship or eligibility for naturalization by marrying them.[96]

One of the most striking consequences of interracial and interethnic relationships among Asians in America was the rise of mixed-race children. The impact of this development varied based on how widespread it was. In Hawaii, a mixed-race population emerged fairly rapidly as a result of the great diversity in the working-class population, which had profound effects on the social organization and demographic characteristics of the islands. On the mainland, by contrast, the births of mixed-race children were relatively isolated events and usually did

Figure 4.2 Alvarez-Sher wedding photo, Imperial Valley, California, 1917. Relationships and marriages between Punjabi men and Mexican women were relatively common, especially in areas like the Imperial Valley during the early twentieth century. Such unions gave rise to Punjabi–Mexican families and communities that mixed cultural traditions. (Karen Leonard's Punjabi–Mexican American papers (M1808), Dept. of Special Collections and University Archives, Stanford University Libraries.)

not result in the emergence of mixed communities and identities. One case involved Teresa Ferrara ("Tessie"), the child of Italian immigrants, and Lee Young, a Chinese immigrant and carpenter, of New York. The couple married in 1904 when Ferrara was twenty-one and Lee was forty-six and, five years later, Teresa gave birth to a daughter, Edna Anna Filomena. Although of mixed parentage, Edna would be raised primarily according to her mother's traditions, reflected in her baptism and the family's residence in a building with mostly Italian American residents. This represents just one example, however, and there was no single pattern with respect to which community an interethnic family affiliated with. It is also important to note that interracial communities took forms other than marriages and nuclear families. They were also characterized by households with extended kin and boarders, for example. In one instance, recorded in the 1870 New York Census, a household included a young widow of Irish descent named Bridget Murphy who boarded with a Chinese named Ging Sak and his family.[97]

Translocal and Transnational Communities

An often-overlooked dimension of early community life in Asian America is its translocalism. The absence of ethnic enclaves in cities or towns or the migratory life of immigrants was not necessarily evidence of the lack of community. As Linda España-Maram, Nayan Shah, Dorothy Fujita-Rony, and others have pointed out, "community" for Asian Americans was a fluid entity and concept. Hotels, pool halls, barbershops, and other commercial establishments were not just stopping points for migratory workers, but also the nodes of ethnic communities. Newspapers also played a crucial role in connecting immigrants to one another and in keeping them informed of events in the homeland. The English-language paper, *Philippine Review*, which was published in Los Angeles in the 1930s by the fraternal order Caballeros de Dimas-Alang, conveyed information about developments in the Philippines regarding the emerging government, promises of liberation, and debates between leaders Manuel Quezon and Emilio Aguinaldo.[98] It also ran advertisements for businesses in anticipation of cannery and other work seasons, so migrant laborers relied on it for leads on where to stay and to find compatriots in different towns.[99]

Although Korean immigrants established geographically rooted communities in places like Los Angeles and Hawaii, due to their relatively small numbers they also relied on long-distance connections to maintain a sense of belonging and ethnic solidarity. For instance, in 1919, student organizations from New York to Honolulu formed the Korean Student Federation of North America, which was first housed in New York and then relocated to Chicago in 1923, communicating through media such as the *Korean Student Bulletin*.[100] The Korean independence movement, which was transnational in nature, also shaped immigrants' outlooks and created a feeling of unity among dispersed people who otherwise felt like exiles. The movement's leaders were drawn from around the Korean diaspora, including Siberia, the United States and Manchuria. Describing Koreans in America as a "community in exile," Richard Kim notes, "As diasporic migrants, the daily experiences of Korean immigrants in the United States extended beyond territorially bounded spaces or locales as they saw themselves inextricably linked to their compatriots geographically dispersed across national boundaries and borders."[101] Leaders of the Korean American community were, moreover, constantly on the move. Park Young-man had originally formed a Korean military association in Nebraska, but he also traveled to Hawaii and China to do similar work.[102] Syngman Rhee completed a Ph.D. at Princeton before returning to Korea in 1911 and working for the YMCA. He left Korea to attend a Methodist Mission conference in Minneapolis, but was unable to return to Korea due to his political activities. He then went to Hawaii to work at the Korean Methodist Compound, until a split over curriculum forced him out. After the Korean Provisional Government was formed and located to Shanghai in 1919, Rhee served as its president.

Other Asian political activists lived similarly peripatetic lives, both because of the dispersion of people they worked with and their surveillance by authorities. Indian anti-colonialist Taraknath Das fled his homeland for North America after a brief sojourn in Japan. He spent time on both sides of the U.S.–Canada border in the Pacific Northwest where he worked for wages and devoted his energies to anti-colonialism, traveling up and down the coast and visiting work camps to give lectures about British imperialism. He later relocated to Vermont where he attended Norwich University while continuing his anti-colonial work. While constantly on the move, Das was also being monitored by U.S. and British authorities who viewed him as a subversive.[103] To reach the places to which he could not travel, his publication *Free Hindustan*, which he started in Vancouver in 1908, spread the word among Indians throughout the diaspora.

Many of the Asian male immigrants arriving in the nineteenth and early twentieth centuries were neither bachelors nor unattached men, but husbands and sons who came to the United States as part of a family strategy to earn money, help others migrate, and eventually return home. Thus, families that were dispersed physically were not necessarily divided. Regarding Chinese immigrants and the sojourner–settler dichotomy, which he largely views as a false one, Yong Chen clarifies, "They did not have to make a choice between being settlers and sojourners or between China and America. Living in a trans-Pacific world, many traveled back and forth between Canton and San Francisco."[104] Similarly, among Indians, the lopsided gender ratio was not deemed a problem because most intended to return home. However, this would be cited by whites who charged that their women did not come because of "the peculiar reluctance of the Hindoos to expose their women to the shameless gaze of the western unbeliever."[105] Back and forth travel became increasingly unfeasible, particularly for working class men, after the passage of restrictive immigration laws. Furthermore, if wives wished to join their husbands in America, they had to contend with immigration restrictions and skeptical officials who assumed they were prostitutes or doubted the validity of their marriages. By 1900 the only Chinese women who could enter the United States were wives and daughters of merchants, diplomats and U.S. citizens.[106]

Due to these obstacles, most married Chinese immigrant men were part of so-called split-household families, in which production (e.g., wage earning) was carried out by the husband living far away while household functions such as reproduction, socialization, and consumption were performed by the wife and relatives in the home village. From 1890 to 1940, two-fifths of Chinese American men were married and living apart from their wives and children.[107] Some of them married their wives after emigrating, and it was not difficult to find wives in China, especially if they had earning power. Upon marrying, the wives would move to the husband's village to live with her in-laws. Although couples went for extended periods, sometimes decades, without seeing one another, for many of the wives, it was worth it because their material needs were taken care of, they enjoyed the authority of being the de facto household heads, and they had more control over how children were raised. Furthermore, few wished to go to America where they knew life would be more arduous.[108] After just ten months of marriage, Judy Ng became a "grass widow," as they were called, for nine years. She said she was relatively satisfied because "my husband loved me, and my father in law always mailed me the money."[109]

For Chinese, maintaining the integrity of split-household families was challenging and often a collective effort involving transnational publications and neighbors in the home village. One of the greatest challenges was having children in the face of husbands' long absences, which led some couples to adopt.[110] Villagers sometimes kept an eye on married women and used gossip to keep them in line. As Madeline Hsu explains, the key for the wives was to prove their virtue to their faraway husbands and the way to do so was to avoid becoming the subject of gossip. Husbands sometimes returned if they learned that their wives were behaving in a less than virtuous manner. For example, Chen Mingrui, who ran laundry in New York, returned to Taishan in 1934 after he found out that his wife was having an affair. When he learned that these rumors were not only true but she was also pregnant, he shot her.[111] For their part, immigrant husbands were expected to fulfill their responsibilities back home. While adultery was the worst offense a "grass widow" could commit, it was permissible if the gold mountain husband abandoned his marital responsibilities, by failing to send remittances and letters or establishing a new household abroad. In these instances, the women, with the husband's family's permission, could also remarry.[112]

Not only did transnational communications and remittances maintain social units and kin obligations across long distances, they were also vital for the material wellbeing of and improved standards of living for family members and other residents of the home villages. Such practices existed among all Asian groups. With regard to China, no district had become as dependent on overseas Chinese than Taishan by the 1890s. From 1900 to 1937, yearly remittances to Taishan exceeded the district's agricultural output.[113] With the money, recipients were able to build new homes and enjoy better lives, and in turn they became the objects of neighbors' envy, not to mention the targets of bandits.[114] Many of the gray brick homes with marble floors, stained glass windows, and Greek columns that were built during the 1920s in the Pearl River Delta were remnants of "gold mountain guests" who wanted to showcase their success.[115] In addition to creating a new class of upwardly mobile individuals, money from overseas altered the social configuration of village life, financing the construction of schools, textile factories, and even railroads.[116] Chen Yixi, an immigrant who became a successful merchant in Seattle, led an effort to build a railroad in Taishan in 1909, the second wholly Chinese-financed railroad in China.[117]

Various institutions helped to facilitate these transnational ties. Among Chinese, jinshanzhuang, or gold mountain firms, were crucial in connecting Chinese businesses in the United States to those in China. They were located in ports like Hong Kong and began operating in the 1850s by linking with Chinese merchants abroad, for whom jinshanzhuang managers took orders for Chinese goods and arranged their shipment. Their services extended to wherever there were Chinese emigrants, from Warren, Idaho to Lima, Peru and allowed overseas customers to buy an array of goods from the homeland, including traditional medicines, fruit, and meats.[118] By 1922, 116 of these firms in Hong Kong were doing business with North American companies, and by 1930 there were 290. They also provided mail services and handled monetary remittances, charging a fee of two percent for such transactions, and helped prospective emigrants with their paperwork and preparations to emigrate.[119]

Magazines for overseas Chinese, called qiaokan, also helped hold together transnational circles of community. Taishan was the first to produce such a magazine, *Xinning Magazine*, which was started in 1911 by the Ninyang Association amid revolutionary fervor in China. Its goal was to nurture connections and a sense of duty to Taishan among emigrants and their descendants. The printing press and postal service allowed county, village, and clan associations to maintain contacts with overseas members in locations as distant as Havana, Melbourne, Rangoon, New York, and Minneapolis.[120] Other qiaokan magazines raised money for schools and other community projects. In addition to strengthening transnational ties and reaching out to overseas brethren for monetary support, these also served as "village rags." With headlines such as "Is this Man this Woman's Previous Husband?" the publications reported on gossip and other events in the home village.[121]

Associations also played a role in maintaining immigrants' ties to their homelands. For instance, to gain credibility and respectability, huigan imported scholars from China to serve as their presidents. Moreover, among the most important social services they provided was shipping the bones of the deceased to China. In addition to providing services such as access to jobs, potential business partners, lodgings, and legal help, associations organized religious and other festivals that allowed immigrants to continue the customs of their native country. They also directly supported their home villages and districts, for example organizing fundraising drives for disaster relief in Taishan.

While Japanese associations promoted immigrants' welfare, ultimately their work was aimed at protecting Japan's national image and, in so doing, they bound overseas migrants to the home country. During the anti-Japanese movement and amidst negotiations of the Gentlemen's Agreement, Tokyo sought to organize and more closely manage its subjects abroad and agreed to implement a registration system for all Japanese immigrants. To elevate consuls' standing as the leaders of West Coast Japanese communities, the Foreign Ministry transferred the consul general of New York City, Koike Chozo, to San Francisco in late 1907 and changed the status of the San Francisco consulate to consulate general. Chozo and a group of Issei businessmen were the main leaders of the Japanese Association of America, whose duties included processing applications and issuing certificates as a proxy of the consulate (also called endorsement rights) per the registration requirements Japan agreed to in the Gentlemen's Agreement.[122] By distributing endorsement rights to local affiliates, which also brought revenue to the associations, Japanese diplomats could keep immigrant leaders under their command. Associations also used their power to suppress immigrant dissent against Japan. Japanese diplomats in the United States were particularly concerned about socialists and anarchists, especially after the establishment of the Socialist Revolutionary Party (SRP) in the California Bay Area in 1906, a group that was critical of Emperor Meiji and had made threats to assassinate him. To counter the group and its members, Chozo used the Japanese association network to secretly collect information about them.[123]

Conclusion

Before World War II, Asian immigrants created family and community lives in America that sometimes approximated conditions in the homeland and other times were dramatically different. Facing enormous barriers, they struggled to maintain connections to family members back home as well as to forge new families and communities in the United States, drawing on institutional resources, feelings of ethnic solidarity, and kin relationships. Eventually, a U.S.-born generation emerged, most quickly among Japanese Americans, and fundamentally reshaped the dynamics of life in Asian American communities (see Chapter 7). As the next two chapters will examine, community resources and family life, moreover, would become doubly important as shields against racist hostility that all Asians faced from the nineteenth through early twentieth centuries.

Notes

1 Nayan Shah, *Contagious Divides: Epidemics and Race in San Francisco's Chinatown* (Berkeley: University of California Press, 2001), 1.

2 V.S. McClatchy, U.S. Senate Japanese Immigration Hearings, 68th Cong., 1st sess. (Washington, D.C.: U.S. Government Printing Office, 1924), 5–6, quoted by Roger Daniels, *The Politics of Prejudice: The Anti-Japanese Movement in California and the Struggle for Japanese Exclusion* (Berkeley: University of California Press, 1962), 99.

3 Evelyn Nakano Glenn, *Issei, Nisei, War Bride: Three Generations of Japanese American Women in Domestic Service* (Philadelphia: Temple University Press, 1986), 194.

4 Ibid., 199.

5 Linda España-Maram, *Creating Masculinity in Los Angeles's Little Manila: Working-class Filipinos and Popular Culture, 1920s–1950s* (New York: Columbia University Press, 2006), 39.

6 Quoted in Peter Kwong and Dušanka Miščević, *Chinese America: The Untold Story of America's Oldest New Community* (New York: New Press, 2005), 87.

7 Ibid., 84, 87.

8 Kwong and Miščević, *Chinese America*, 136.

9 Paul Spickard, *Japanese Americans: The Formation and Transformations of an Ethnic Group*, rev. ed., (New Brunswick: Rutgers University Press, 2009), 55.

10 Ibid., 56.

11 Ibid., 55.

12 In Seattle the Northwest American Japanese Association which served the Pacific Northwest and Montana was formed in 1913; in Portland, the Japanese Association of Oregon, serving Oregon, Idaho, and Wyoming was formed in 1911; and in Los Angeles, the Central Japanese Association of Southern California which broke away from the Japanese Association of America and served Southern California, Arizona, and New Mexico was formed in 1915. Seattle had fifteen affiliated locals, Oregon ten, San Francisco forty, and Los Angeles twenty-one. Sucheng Chan, *Asian Americans: An Interpretive History* (Boston: Twayne Publishers, 1991), 69.

13 Yuji Ichioka, *Issei: The World of the First Generation Japanese Immigrants* (New York: Free Press, 1988), 163.

14 Ibid., 171.

15 Ichioka, *The Issei*, 171–72.

16 Won Moo Hurh and Kwang Chung Kim, *Korean Immigrants in America: A Structural Analysis of Ethnic Confinement and Adhesive Adaptation* (Rutherford: Fairleigh Dickinson University, 1984), 48.

17 Ronald Takaki, *Pau Hana: Plantation Life and Labor in Hawaii, 1835–1920* (Honolulu: University of Hawaii Press, 1983), 116.

18 The main ones being the Korean Consolidated Association, formed in Honolulu in 1907 and by 1908 had forty-seven affiliates in the islands; the Korean Mutual Assistance Association, which was established in San Francisco; and the Korean Restorative Association, formed in Pasadena in 1905. The Korean Restorative Association was founded in 1905 in Pasadena and moved to San Francisco in 1907. H. Brett Melendy, *Asians in America: Filipinos, Koreans, and East Indians* (Boston: Twayne Publishers, 1977), 148. In the Stevens assassination, Jang fired the shots that ultimately killed Stevens. Jen confronted Stevens but his revolver failed to fire. Ibid., 149.

19 Chan, *Asian Americans*, 74.

20 Mary Paik Lee, *Quiet Odyssey: A Pioneer Korean Woman in America* (Seattle: University of Washington Press, 1990), lv.

21 Melendy, *Asians in America*, 139; Chan, *Asian Americans*, 73.

22 Chan, *Asian Americans*, 73; Melendy, *Asians in America*, 144.

23 Chan, *Asian Americans*, 77.

24 Ibid., 73. According to Yong Chen, only about 300–400 Chinese Christians throughout CA in 1870s—missions weren't successful in converting. Yong Chen, *Chinese San Francisco, 1850–1943: A Trans-Pacific Community* (Stanford: Stanford University Press, 2000), 133; Spickard, *Japanese Americans*, 60.

25 Chan, *Asian Americans*, 77.

26 Spickard, *Japanese Americans*, 61.

27 Ibid., 59.

28 Chan, *Asian Americans*, 64.

29 Spickard, *Japanese Americans*, 59; Chen, *Chinese San Francisco*, 136.

30 Chen, *Chinese San Francisco*, 137.

31 Ibid., 138.

32 Melendy, *Asians in America*, 241.

33 Ibid.

34 Karen Leonard, *Making Ethnic Choices: California's Punjabi Mexican Americans* (Philadelphia: Temple University Press, 1992), 83. Also, according to H. Brett Melendy, the Khalsa Diwan constructed a temple in Stockton in 1909. Melendy, *Asians in America*, 243.

35 Joan Jensen, *Passage from India: Asian Indian Immigrants in North America* (New Haven: Yale University Press, 1988), 180; Leonard, *Making Ethnic Choices*, 83.

36 Melendy, *Asians in America*, 242.

37 Ibid., 59, 82.

38 The Hindustan Association started in Oregon in 1913 and was supported by funds from a prosperous lumber mill labor contractor in the Northwest. Chan, *Asian Americans*, 75.

39 España-Maram, *Creating Masculinity in Los Angeles's Little Manila*, 42.

40 Ichioka, *Issei*, 164.

41 Glenn, *Issei, Nisei, War Bride*, 197.

42 Ichioka, *Issei*, 164.

43 Melendy, *Asians in America*, 127.

44 Lee, *Quiet Odyssey*, lvi.

45 Ichioka, *Issei*, 165.

46 Ibid., 166.

47 Ibid., 167.

48 Glenn, *Issei, Nisei, War Bride*, 45.

49 Ibid., 46.

50 Ichioka, *Issei*, 168.

51 Ibid., 42.

52 Ichioka, *Issei*, 172.

53 Yung, *Unbound Feet*, 46.

54 Ibid., 47.

55 Dorothy Fujita-Rony, *American Workers, Colonial Power: Philippine Seattle and the Transpacific West, 1919–1941* (Berkeley: University of California Press, 2003), 135.

56 Chen, *Chinese San Francisco*, 56.

57 Ibid., 57.

58 Madeline Hsu, *Dreaming of Gold, Dreaming of Home: Transnationalism and Migration between the United States and South China, 1882–1943* (Stanford: Stanford University Press, 2000), 101.

59 Ronald Takaki, *Strangers from a Different Shore: A History of Asians Americans* (Boston: Little Brown, 1989), 125.

60 Robert Lee, *Orientals: Asian Americans in Popular Culture* (Philadelphia: Temple University Press, 1999), 85.

61 Takaki, *Strangers from a Different Shore*, 88.

62 Jensen, *Passage from India*, 40–41.

63 Fujita-Rony, *American Workers, Colonial Power*, 132.

64 Ibid.

65 Jensen, *Passage from India*, 41.

66 Nayan Shah, *Stranger Intimacy: Contesting Race, Sexuality and the Law in the North American West* (Berkeley: University of California Press, 2011), 102.

67 Kwong and Miščević, *Chinese America*, 147.

68 España-Maram, *Creating Masculinity in Los Angeles's Little Manila*, 54–55.

69 Ibid., 76, 79.

70 Ibid., 79.

71 Ibid., 81.

72 Ibid., 65.

73 España-Maram, *Creating Masculinity in Los Angeles's Little Manila*, 57.

74 Shah, *Stranger Intimacy*, 103.

75 Ibid.

76 Ibid., 33–35.

77 Ibid., 55.

78 Ibid., 103.

79 Friday, *Organizing Asian American Labor*, 55.

80 Takaki, *Pau Hana*, 118–19.

81 Kevin Mumford, *Interzones: Black/White Sex Districts in Chicago and New York in the Early Twentieth Century* (New York: Columbia University Press, 1997), 55.

82 Ibid., 106.

83 Mary Ting Yi Lui, *The Chinatown Trunk Mystery: Murder, Miscegenation, and Other Dangerous Encounters in Turn-of-the-Century New York City* (Princeton: Princeton University Press, 2005), 153.

84 Ibid., 154.

85 Ibid., 155.

86 Friday, *Organizing Asian American Labor*, 51.

87 Karen Leonard, *Making Ethnic Choices*, 64.

88 Jensen, *Passage from India*, 67.

89 Melendy, *Asians in America*, 240.

90 Ibid.

91 Ibid.

92 Leonard, *Making Ethnic Choices*, 63.

93 Ibid., 64.

94 Ibid., 69.

95 Ibid., 70.

96 Ibid., 70–71.

97 Lui, 155.

98 España-Maram, *Creating Masculinity in Los Angeles's Little Manila*, 38.

99 Ibid.

100 Melendy, *Asians in America*, 144.

101 Richard Kim, "Inaugurating the American Century: The 1919 Philadelphia Korean Congress, Korean Diasporic Nationalism, and American Protestant Missionaries," *Journal of American Ethnic History*, Vol. 26 No. 1 (Fall 2006): 52.

102 Melendy, *Asians in America*, 150.
103 Seema Sohi, "Race, Surveillance, and Indian Anticolonialism in the Transnational Western U.S.–Canadian Borderlands," *Journal of American History*, 98 no. 2 (September 2011): 428–29.
104 Chen, *Chinese San Francisco*, 57.
105 Melendy, *Asians in America*, 239.
106 Hsu, *Dreaming of Gold, Dreaming of Home*, 95.
107 Ibid., 99.
108 Ibid., 117.
109 Ibid., 104.
110 Ibid., 122.
111 Ibid., 108.
112 Ibid., 120.
113 Ibid., 42.
114 Ibid., 41, 44, 50–51.
115 Kwong and Miščević, *Chinese America*, 154.
116 Hsu, *Dreaming of Gold, Dreaming of Home*, 49.
117 Ibid., 47.
118 Ibid., 34.
119 Ibid., 38–39.
120 Ibid., 141.
121 Ibid., 137.
122 Attested to the bearers' status as bona fide residents of the United States, permitting them to journey to Japan and return to America with spouses, children, and/or parents if they wished, and travel to other countries. Ichioka, *Issei*, 160, 162.
123 Eiichiro Azuma, *Between Two Empires: Race, History, and Transnationalism in Japanese America* (New York: Oxford University Press, 2005), 45.

Racism and the Anti-Asian Movements

5

One of the unifying themes in Asian American history is racism. As targets of economic discrimination, legal disfranchisement, violence, ridicule, and segregation, Chinese, Japanese, Korean, Filipino, and Asian Indian immigrants in the nineteenth and early twentieth centuries were told repeatedly, and in myriad ways, that they were outsiders in American society. While anti-Asian xenophobia drew on long traditions of Orientalist thought, it intensified in times of social, economic, and moral crisis, during which Asian immigrants were scapegoated for an array of problems. All of the major Asian groups, moreover, became the targets of organized movements and eventually federal immigration exclusion, the ultimate symbol of their rejection from the American melting pot. Racism was not just a common thematic experience among Asians in America; the movements against Chinese, Japanese, Korean, Indian, and Filipino immigration that spanned over half a century were connected and successively built on one another. For instance, in 1892, the California anti-Chinese crusader Denis Kearney decried Japanese immigrants as "another breed of Asiatic slaves to fill up the gap made vacant by the Chinese," and unveiled the slogan "The Japs must go!" a modification of the phrase he popularized at anti-Chinese rallies in the 1870s.[1]

This chapter explores anti-Asian racism and organized campaigns to end Asian migration to the United States, beginning with the anti-Chinese movement and ending with the anti-Filipino movement. The chapter discusses how and why Asian immigrants experienced discrimination and also considers what exclusion meant to the excluders, for whom anti-Asian politics was a rational response to perceived threats and crises. Despite pervasive claims that Asiatic "hordes" would overtake the nation, anti-Asian discrimination was not about numbers; even in the continental states where they concentrated, they never approached more than a small fraction of the population. In the big picture of U.S. immigration, Europeans far surpassed Asians; between 1861 and 1924, more than thirty million people arrived from Europe, compared to about one million from Asia. In examining the subject of racism, the goal of the chapter is not to assess whether Asian immigrants were really a "threat," but rather to analyze aspects of their hostile treatment in order to understand the larger meanings of anti-Asian racism in American history. Indeed, the history of anti-Asian racism reveals much not only about the suffering that people of Asian ancestry endured, but also how the boundaries of U.S. citizenship and social belonging were redrawn in response to the immigration of racial "others." The chapter, thus, comments both on the centrality of racism in early Asian American history and the construction of whiteness as a privileged category.

The Legal Disfranchisement of Asians in America

Asian immigrants to the United States in the nineteenth century were entering a country already with enormous racial baggage. This baggage, combined with perceptions of the inherent foreignness and inferiority of "orientals," would inform and justify their subordinate legal status. Beginning with Chinese, Asians' legal disfranchisement hinged largely on the group's racial ineligibility for naturalized citizenship, a principle established in the Naturalization Act of 1790, which preserved the right of naturalization to "any alien, being a free white person." Having defined full citizenship as a white privilege, Americans would be loath to extend legal equality to newcomers who fell outside of this category. The classification of Chinese as "aliens ineligible to citizenship" not only underscored their inferior legal standing, but also proved a useful way for nativists to argue for their exclusion from other privileges, such as owning land, marrying American citizens, and immigrating.

Most Chinese immigrants to the United States in the mid-nineteenth century went to California, then still very much a frontier and, thus, relatively removed from the reach of federal power and dominant social and cultural norms. However, even in this society of newcomers, Chinese and other non-whites were singled out for discriminatory treatment. The fluid conditions in western mining communities, for instance, may have fostered a degree of equality in economic opportunities, but the courts that were established by Anglo-Americans to adjudicate conflicts were often corrupt and reinforced insider/outsider boundaries along racial and ethnic lines.[2] The subordinated legal standing of Chinese vis-à-vis their non-whiteness was affirmed in the 1854 California Supreme Court decision in *People v. Hall*. In this case, George Hall, a white man charged with murdering a Chinese man in Nevada County, successfully appealed his conviction, citing an 1850 state law providing that "no Black, or Mulatto person, or Indian shall be allowed to give evidence in favor of, or against a White man."[3] Through grasping logic, Hall's attorney argued that since American Indians originally came via Asia across the Bering Strait, Indians were in fact Asian, and therefore Chinese and other "Mongolians" should be subject to the ban on testifying against whites. The court agreed, stating, "Even if admitting the Indian of this Continent is not of the Mongolian type, the words 'Black Person' must be taken as contradistinguished from White, and necessarily excludes all races other than the Caucasian."[4] In 1863 the prohibition on Chinese testimony was formalized in the state's Civil Procedure Code, a ban that stood until 1872, when statutes had to be revised to conform to the Fourteenth Amendment of the U.S. Constitution. Even then, evidence from Chinese was rarely accepted except in cases involving other Chinese.[5]

People v. Hall solidified the link between Chinese immigrants' non-whiteness and their subordinate legal standing in California. At the federal level, their exclusion from naturalization followed a similar trajectory from implicit exclusion to explicit prohibition. Implicitly, Chinese were ineligible under the 1790 Naturalization Act, but by the 1860s anti-

Chinese officials repeatedly tried to explicitly block Chinese naturalization. They inserted language into the Burlingame Treaty of 1868, for instance, specifying that the treaty should not be construed as granting Chinese naturalization privileges. In congressional debates during Reconstruction to amend the 1790 Naturalization Act, the matter was raised again. Espousing a color-blind approach to citizenship, the Republican Senator Charles Sumner proposed to strike the word "white" from the new bill. Fellow Republicans, particularly from western states, warned that this would not only lead to Chinese becoming U.S. citizens, but also invite the further immigration of "coolies." Among their proposed alternatives was to replace the phrase "any alien, being a free white person," with "any aliens except natives of China and Japan." Ultimately, both options were rejected, and in 1870 Congress passed a new naturalization Act that simply added the words, "persons of African descent," still hoping to foreclose the possibility of Chinese naturalization without explicitly doing so.[6] Because this was not a clear ban and local courts decided on naturalization applications, a handful of Chinese immigrants became citizens.[7] However, in 1878, the issue was finally dealt with head-on when a U.S. circuit court ruled in the case *In re Ah Yup* that Chinese were ineligible. Further, in 1882, the Chinese Exclusion Act was passed with a provision explicitly denying Chinese the right to naturalization.

In the meantime, the right of other Asians to become naturalized citizens was unclear. With regard to Japanese, courts in different states had been granting applicants citizenship during the 1890s, albeit inconsistently and arbitrarily.[8] Conflicting views among officials in the Executive branch failed to clarify the issue. In 1906 U.S. Attorney General Charles Bonaparte said that Japanese were ineligible for naturalization but, around this time, President Theodore Roosevelt was urging Congress to pass legislation to permit Japanese naturalization as a quid pro quo for Japan restricting emigration to the United States.[9] Despite the absence of a guiding policy, the general interpretation of the federal naturalization statute was that Japanese (as well as Koreans) were ineligible, a position the Bureau of Immigration and Naturalization adopted in 1911. But until the matter was settled through Congress or the U.S. Supreme Court, Japanese immigrants continued to seek and argue for their right to naturalized citizenship, which by 1911 over four hundred had attained.[10]

The eligibility of Asian Indians was more vexing, as prevailing ethnological theories of race classified them as Aryan or Caucasian, which led them to claim status as whites. When the first Asian Indians applied for naturalization, courts were left to determine the issue of their whiteness, leading to unpredictable outcomes. When one clerk sought clarification, the Justice Department refused to give an opinion, but in August 1907 Attorney General Bonaparte weighed in, saying, "It seems clear to me that under no construction of the law can natives of British India be regarded as white persons."[11] Indian applicants as well as some American officials continued to insist on their racial eligibility, and in March 1908 in New Orleans the first two Indians were granted naturalization.[12]

The status of racially indeterminate groups like Asian Indians underscored the inadequacy of ethnological classifications and other categories as a guide on enforcing naturalization policy, and consequently, through much of the 1910s through early 1920s, courts struggled with the concept of race in naturalization cases. Trying to classify all persons as Caucasian, Mongolian, or Negro was untenable, and even if Indians were Caucasian according to anthropologists, few officials were ready to accord them the legal privileges of whiteness on that basis. Nor did the 1910 U.S. Census provide much help, as it classified Asian Indians (along with Koreans and Filipinos) in the category of "other."[13] Naturalization cases involving Syrians and Indians, who might be Caucasian by one measure despite being dark-skinned, caused the most confusion. In 1913, federal district court judge Henry A. Smith of South Carolina presided over the case of Syrian immigrant Faras Shahid and tried to clear up the matter. "To say that a very dark brown, almost black, inhabitant of India is entitled to rank as a white person," he said, "because of a possible or hypothetical infusion of white blood 30 or 40 centuries old, and to exclude a Chinese or Japanese, whose parent on one side was white, and who thus possesses manifestly at least one-half European blood, would seem highly inconsistent."[14] He concluded that "white" must be interpreted to refer only to people of European descent, but other cases elsewhere failed to establish a consensus.

After years of murkiness, arbitrary outcomes, clamors for clarity, and some twenty-five challenges to the racial prerequisites in federal courts, the matter of Japanese and Asian Indian eligibility for naturalized citizenship was addressed in the early 1920s.[15] This time the directive came not from Congress, but the U.S. Supreme Court. In November 1922 it ruled in the case of *Ozawa v. United States* that Japanese were ineligible for citizenship. The applicant, Takao Ozawa, was an Issei who had lived in the United States for twenty years and was originally denied citizenship in Hawaii in 1914. He pointed to his assimilation and good character as qualifications for citizenship. He spoke English, had attended the University of California, sent his children to American schools, and belonged to an American church. Ozawa's attorney said that the absence of a prohibition on Japanese in the existing naturalization law should mean that they were eligible. The Supreme Court rejected and turned this argument on its head, responding that the lack of specific *inclusion* of Japanese implied their ineligibility. The court also repudiated Ozawa's claim that his skin color made him white and asserted that the issue was not color, but whether or not he was Caucasian, which he clearly was not.[16] Treating "Caucasian" and "white" synonymously, the majority said that Ozawa's non-Caucasian status made him non-white and therefore ineligible for naturalized citizenship.

While the *Ozawa* case was being heard, Bhagat Singh Thind's naturalization case made its way to the Supreme Court. Thind, a graduate of Punjab University, immigrated to the United States in 1913 when he was twenty-one, served in the U.S. army during World War I, and applied for citizenship in 1920. His application was initially approved by an Oregon district court, but the Bureau of Naturalization appealed its decision. Thind's case cited anthropological theory and legal precedent; his counsel pointed out that not only did ethnologists and other authorities consider Indians to be Caucasian, but previous Indian applicants had also been granted citizenship.[17] Decided in 1923, the Court held in *United States v. Bhagat Singh Thind* that Asian Indians were ineligible for naturalization. This surprised Thind, as he expected the court to apply its own equation of "Caucasian" and "white" from the *Ozawa* decision. Acknowledging that Thind was Caucasian, it nonetheless sided with the government's case that "white" should be interpreted according to the usage of the "common man," in whose view Indians were *not* white. Further, the bar on Indian immigration enacted by the Immigration Act of 1917 (discussed below) implied that Americans did not want them to be citizens. After the ruling, the Justice Department and Bureau of Naturalization even took steps to denaturalize Indians believed to have obtained citizenship fraudulently, and by December 1924 forty-three Indian men had been stripped of their citizenship.[18] Thind spent his remaining years in the United States as part of the "circus of the transcendental," giving lectures with titles such as, "The Sacred Hum of the Universe," and "Can We Talk with the 'Dead.'"[19]

As Mae Ngai has explained, although the *Ozawa* and *Thind* decisions pertained to Japanese and Asian Indian applicants, "the court made a leap in racial logic to apply the rule of racial ineligibility to citizenship to Koreans, Thais, Vietnamese, Indonesians, and other people of Asian countries who represented discrete ethnic groups and, in contemporary anthropological terms, different racial groups."[20] The only Asians whose status remained unclear at this point were Filipinos, due to their status as U.S. nationals, conferred after the United States annexed the Philippines in 1898. This allowed them to travel with American passports and migrate between the Philippines and United States without restrictions, but the status was in other ways murky; it provided no guidance on the issue of naturalization. As with pre-*Ozawa* and *Thind*, this vagueness led to unpredictable outcomes on citizenship applications, but in general officials would reject Filipinos' petitions, citing the racial provisions of the 1870 Naturalization Act. By the 1930s, when anti-Asian exclusionists had turned their attention on Filipinos, calls for their explicit legal disfranchisement intensified. The main obstacle to this was the Philippines' status as a U.S. territory, but mounting anti-Filipino sentiment and the persistent ideological and moral contradictions of American empire eventually effected change in 1934 with the Tydings-McDuffie Act. In addition to establishing a ten-year timetable for Philippine independence, the law limited Filipino immigration to fifty persons a year and changed their status from nationals to aliens, throwing them with other Asians into the category "aliens eligible to citizenship."

A racial bar on Asian naturalization vis-à-vis their classification as "aliens ineligible to citizenship" asserted the yellow-white color line and for most immigrants represented an insurmountable obstacle to citizenship, but it was not impermeable. Small numbers of Asian immigrants continued to become citizens due to inconsistencies in the interpretation and enforcement of the law. Furthermore, because race was not the sole criterion of naturalization eligibility, select groups could attain citizenship via alternative routes, such as military service. In 1935 Congress passed a law according citizenship to veterans of the U.S. armed forces, which was how Bhagat Singh Thind, a World War I veteran, eventually became a citizen. Another crack in the system of Asian disfranchisement was widened when the U.S. Supreme Court affirmed the principle of birthright citizenship in 1898. The issue, which had been fiercely contested, assured the U.S. citizenship of the children of immigrants regardless of the parents' status. These exceptions notwithstanding, most Asians in America in the nineteenth and early twentieth centuries faced legal disfranchisement and subordination. The status "aliens ineligible to citizenship" not only denied them full participation in American democracy, no matter how loyal or American they considered themselves, but it would also validate and serve as the foundation of other forms of discrimination.

Creating Social Pariahs

In addition to being relegated to a secondary legal status, Asian immigrants were constantly reminded of their inferior social standing in America. Enforcing the yellow-white color line in daily life was especially imperative in cities and along the West Coast, where social and economic fluidity gave rise to encounters that transgressed and threatened to unsettle the dominant racial order. Whether subject to physical segregation, miscegenation laws, or mundane acts of harassment, Asians were ostracized and denied their dignity, not just as men, women, students, residents, and consumers, but also fundamentally as human beings. As the next chapter discusses, practices of segregation, subordination, and exclusion delimited Asians' lives and symbolized their inferior position in American society, but these did not strip them entirely of their agency and ability to challenge the racial order, even in the most virulent times.

The construction and enforcement of racialized spatial boundaries in urban areas across the country intensified as Asian immigrants laid down long-term or permanent roots and increasingly encountered non-Asians in daily life. The existence of xenophobic hostility and the clustering of immigrant businesses led most Asians to concentrate in or near their ethnic settlements, but the appearance of even a small number in predominantly white areas could ignite racial panic, and thus formalize segregation in the basic organization of urban space. Even when they were isolated from the larger cities, Asian districts were still vulnerable to harassment.

Since the nineteenth century in San Francisco, for instance, municipal officials sought to reform residents' behavior and organize space in the name of environmental and public health, early on singling out Chinatown, which they deemed in 1854 an "unmitigated and wholesome nuisance."[21] Although courts usually blocked attempts to invoke nuisance law to racially discriminate against Chinatown residents, the perception of the quarter as a blight on the city set the stage for its surveillance and harassment during major health scares. One infamous case involved a quarantine of Chinatown (and neighboring Japanese areas) in March 1900, ordered after the body of a Chinese man believed to have succumbed to bubonic plague was found in a hotel basement. Quarantining people in their homes during epidemics was not unprecedented, but sequestering an entire district was. After ordering all white people to leave the area, officials disinfected Chinatown and inoculated its residents. The quarantine was lifted after sixty hours due to complaints about the draconian and discriminatory way it was carried out as well as doctors' determination that there was no plague.[22] Chinatowns elsewhere were similarly targeted, and perhaps none fared worse than Honolulu's. In early 1900, following a bubonic plague-related quarantine of the quarter, home to about 10,000 Chinese and Japanese, new cases of the disease were discovered.[23] Instead of calling a new quarantine and round of disinfection, officials ordered the burning of several buildings, which eventually consumed all of Chinatown and left 4,500 people homeless.[24] After the fire, the epidemic reemerged in other parts of Honolulu and other islands, revealing the fallacy of the notion that disease could be contained by controlling racialized bodies and spaces.

While the ineffectiveness of quarantines showed that contagion, race, and space were not as tightly linked as people presumed, racial segregation remained a fixture of urban geographies well into the twentieth century. Asians who immigrated after the Chinese usually ended up settling in or near Chinatowns because they were the only areas where they could live and get services. Racial segregation was reinforced and maintained through the use of restrictive covenants, zoning laws, white flight, and outright intimidation. Asian sections, usually in or near other marginal areas where working class people and other minorities converged, tended to also be racially transgressive spaces, or what Kevin Mumford calls "interzones."[25] The location of "taboo" establishments such as integrated dance halls, brothels, and Chinese opium dens in these neighborhoods, furthermore, simultaneously fascinated and repulsed "respectable" whites. For Asians, living and socializing in constrained and segregated conditions was not merely a survival strategy or preference to be near people like them; it was also a reality imposed upon them. In turn, the emergence of distinctive Chinatowns, Japantowns, and other Asian enclaves, while crucial to immigrants' daily life and survival, solidified outsiders' assumption that racialized spaces and bodies were connected. Their imagination about life in Asian spaces was vivid; public health reports and popular writings about San Francisco's Chinatown (with titles like *Horrors of a Mongolian Settlement*) dwelt on "dens, density, and the labyrinth" of the area and "cast Chinatown as a deviant transplantation of the traditional East in the modern Western city. This contrast emphasized the uneasy coexistence of growing, progressive San Francisco and decaying, regressive Chinatown. Chinatown was impervious to progress and instead liable to rot and regress like the enervated Chinese empire across the Pacific."[26]

While controlling and containing Asian spaces was critical to enforcing racial boundaries, the incidence and prospect of interracial mingling, in and outside those spaces, represented the most alarming threats to racial order. One illustrative episode from New York in 1909 followed the discovery of the body of a young white woman named Elsie Sigel in the trunk of a Chinese man, Leon Ling. Ling had gone missing prior to the grisly discovery and a set of love letters addressed to him from Sigel made him a suspect of her murder. Details of their relationship and the ensuing manhunt, which captivated New York and much of the nation, were spun by journalists into a cautionary tale about the dangers of modern life, Chinese men, and interracial relationships. Sigel had met Ling while teaching at a Chinese Sunday School, a job she held against her parents' wishes, and was described as a "girl missionary" whose biggest mistake was treating a Chinese as a social equal, or "white man," as one newspaper said.[27] The incident also raised concerns about the work of Chinese missions, leading to the closing of some and the expulsion of white women workers from others.[28] Stories about New York's Chinese were not new, but they took on a sinister cast around the figure of Leon Ling, who was portrayed as stereotypically inscrutable and foreign, yet acculturated and charming enough to draw the affections of Sigel. The fruitless search for Ling did lead to a string of arrests of Asian men—several of whom were Japanese—mistaken for the suspect based on descriptions and photographs. Chinese residents complained of intrusive searches, which went on for months, extended throughout the country, and included police, reporters, and ordinary citizens invading the homes, workplaces, and neighborhoods of Chinese immigrants.[29]

Its sensationalistic nature notwithstanding, the Sigel–Ling episode gave expression to underlying anxieties about relations between Asian men and white women. Although revelations about the relationship and the search for Ling suggested that a degree of elusiveness would always accompany efforts to control and contain racialized bodies, calls to prevent such unions only grew more urgent. As Mary Lui has explained, coverage of the Sigel murder and other stories of interracial liaisons "worked to construct categories of sexual and moral deviance and helped in the absence of anti-miscegenation laws to support other institutional forms of policing these relationships."[30] Chiefly a symbolic expression of racial separation, as most Asian immigrants were not inclined to seek to marry whites anyway, the first anti-Asian miscegenation law was enacted in 1880 when California added to its Civil Code "Mongolians" to the list of groups prohibited from intermarrying with whites.

Interracial marriage was not a real "threat" in the sense that it would not have been wide-spread in the absence of legal proscriptions, but this did not stop alarmists from painting lurid pictures of Asian men lusting after white women—in ways reminiscent of stereotypes of black men—as the ultimate stake in continued immigration, and eventually most western states passed prohibitions on Asian–white intermarriage.[31]

Discussions about Asian intermarriage and other forms of interracial intimacy betrayed nativists' multiple and intertwined concerns about racial order, the family, and white women's sexuality. Chinese men, furthermore, were not the only targets of this anxiety. In the North American West, relationships between South Asian men and white women ignited local panics.[32] And despite Japanese immigrants' high rate of endogamy, sexual panic was nonetheless woven into arguments for their exclusion. In 1907, the *Grizzly Bear*, the paper of the Native Sons of the Golden West (NSGW), a leading voice of the anti-Japanese and anti-Filipino movements in California, warned of the "Asiatic Peril" of Japanese immigration by asking, "Would you like your daughter to marry a Japanese?"[33] In 1920, the *Los Angeles Times* put it more explicitly, saying, "Japanese boys are taught by their elders to look upon . . . American girls with a view to future sex relations . . . What answer will the fathers and mothers of America make? . . . The proposed assimilation of the two races is unthinkable. It is morally indefensible and biologically impossible. American womanhood is by far too sacred to be subjected to such degeneracy."[34] Belying the motive of sexual control over women, in 1922 Congress passed the Cable Act, which stripped American women of their citizenship if they married aliens ineligible for citizenship, a category which at the time applied chiefly to Asians.

During the early 1900s, the most notorious cases involved young Filipinos, whom nativists complained engaged in interracial relations more openly than had Chinese and Japanese. As Judge D.W. Rohrback of Watsonville, a prominent voice during the anti-Filipino movement, stated, "the American people will find in [the Filipinos] a problem they did not find with the negro, who usually understood how to act, but these Filipinos feel they have the perfect right to mingle with white people and even to intermarry and feel resentful if they are denied that right."[35] Prominent California philanthropist and eugenics advocate, C.M. Goethe, added to the landscape of opinions, itself a powerful influence on social norms, by proclaiming, "Filipinos are vain, unreliable and of a rather low mentality . . . These men are primitive jungle folk and their primitive moral code accentuates the race problem . . . The Filipino tends to interbreed with near moron white girls."[36] Taxi-dance halls on the West Coast and in major cities were singled out as particularly problematic spaces in need of policing due to the physically intimate dancing between Filipino (and other non-white) men and white women that occurred in them.[37] Sensationalized news stories also drove home the urgency of keeping white women on the right side of the racial boundary. The arrest and trial of twenty-five-year-old Filipino immigrant Perfecto Bandalan in Watsonville in 1929 encap-sulated many of these fears. Bandalan was charged with contributing to the delinquency of minors after he was caught one evening with two partially dressed white girls, aged eleven and sixteen. In the wake of the discovery, the district attorney assured outraged citizens that Bandalan would be punished to the full extent of the law, but the details about the events leading to his apprehension were vague; the story offered by the girls' father that Bandalan had kidnapped them unraveled, and news outlets only alluded to things that were "unprintable but revolting."[38] It also emerged that Bandalan was engaged to one of the sisters, sixteen-year-old Esther, for which he had received her mother's blessing. The perplexed media described the couple as a "strange case" and spun it into a cautionary tale about a white family gone awry due to the dangerously seductive power of Filipinos.

The deployment of the stereotype of lascivious Asian men chasing white women and measures to prevent contact between the two were part of a larger effort to enforce racial and sexual propriety in a rapidly changing nation. However, Asians found that they were seen as deviant regardless of how they behaved. As discussed, Chinatown's purported impenetrability—its "dens of degraded bestiality"—made it and its residents dangerous.[39] To outsiders, it was an immoral bachelor society of men frequenting opium dens, gambling houses, and brothels. And Chinese women were summarily painted as prostitutes or persons of low moral standing. On the other hand, although many Japanese by the mid-1910s had formed co-ethnic households, these were also cited as evidence of their deviance. A popular target in this regard was the picture bride system. Cora M. Woodbridge of the Native Daughters of the Golden West, who also served in the California legislature, railed against the practice as a "beast of burden up to the time of the birth of her child," who "within a day or two at most, resumes her task and continues it from twelve to sixteen hours a day."[40] Local and state officials also claimed that high Issei birthrates—usually exaggerated or distorted—made them a threat.[41] Officials in Los Angeles, for instance, said that Japanese wives' childbearing and labor contributions on farms constituted a "double-threat," and the journal *Southern California Practitioner* urged white women to have more children, warning that if they did not "bear sufficient children the Japanese and other foreign women [would] keep up the needful production, just as the Japs and foreigners [would] meet the farming needs of the country when American men fail or refuse to do it."[42]

By stigmatizing Asians for their purportedly diseased bodies, filthy living conditions, hyper-fertility, and immoral habits, white nativists cast them as social inferiors and used these arguments to push for racial segregation. However, because interracial contact could not be eliminated altogether, local governments, school boards, and private businesses tried to place limits on these encounters however they could. With respect to education, in the late 1800s, where nonwhites had access to public schools, segregated facilities were the rule. In 1885 San Francisco established an Oriental School after years of inadequate to nonexistent public education for Chinese, and communities elsewhere in California generally followed suit with separate Chinese or Asian schools.[43] Elsewhere in the country, where there were no separate "Oriental" schools, Chinese attended the local black or white schools, although in the latter, they could be thrown out if their presence came to the attention of authorities.[44] In Rosedale, Mississippi, Martha Lum, a Chinese student and merchant's daughter, quietly attended the white school, but was expelled after the superintendent learned about her. Lum's father hired attorneys to contest the decision, and in 1924 the case reached the U.S. Supreme Court. It upheld the lower court's ruling that white schools were for Caucasians only, and that by placing Lum in the black school (a separate but equal institution), the child's rights under the Fourteenth Amendment were not violated.[45]

Initially, Japanese, Filipino, Korean, and Indian students fared better, especially if their numbers were small and they had come to the United States on scholarships. In San Francisco, however, as the presence of Japanese students grew around the turn of the century, officials took action by ordering them into the city's Oriental School, so "our children should not be placed in any position where their youthful impressions may be affected by association with pupils of the Mongolian race."[46] The order, which also targeted Koreans, was handed down on October 11, 1906. While the local press cheered, an international crisis between the United States and Japan (see below) ensued and the order was eventually rescinded. If carried out, the segregation of Japanese students in San Francisco would have been largely symbolic, as there were just ninety-three of them across twenty-three public schools at the time. It was a powerful issue, nonetheless, and indicative of the public will to separate people based on race.

When Asians could not be forced into separate schools, agitators played up the specter of racial pollution within classrooms. In 1909, for instance, Grove Johnson, a leading anti-Japanese orator and father of Hiram Johnson, said, "I am responsible to the mothers and fathers of Sacramento County who have their little daughters sitting side by side in the school rooms with matured Japs, with their base minds, their lascivious thoughts, multiplied by their race and strengthened by their mode of life."[47] And in colleges and universities, as well as integrated secondary schools, Asians were often subject to segregated conditions. At the University of California at Berkeley, where there were about thirty Indian students in 1910, a group of them formed an Indian fraternity, but were refused admission to the inter-fraternity council.[48]

Asians were singled out and excluded in other ways that reinforced their second-class status. Hotels, boardinghouses, restaurants, and recreation establishments on the West Coast routinely turned away Asian customers or forced them into non-white sections. Sometimes their exclusion was literally written on the landscape. During the 1920s and 1930s signs in public places and in businesses in San Francisco, Stockton, and Los Angeles read, "Positively No Filipinos," and "No Dogs or Filipinos Allowed," and one neighborhood association member in Hollywood unfurled a sign on her porch reading "Japs Keep Moving—This is a White Man's Neighborhood."[49] Asians were also mocked and persecuted for their appearance. Starting with Chinese men, whom outsiders found both fascinating and offensive for their "peculiar" physical features and dress, one of the starkest symbols of difference was the queue, a part of immigrants' heritage, as men were required to wear these braided ponytails by their Manchu rulers. Not only was the queue continually a point of mockery in anti-Chinese cartoons, in 1870 the San Francisco board of supervisors authorized prison wardens to cut them off, although this was later vetoed by the mayor. Also frequently ridiculed for their appearance were Punjabis, many of whom stopped wearing turbans and cut their hair in order to lessen the racial antipathy directed at them.[50]

While there were regional variations and changes over time in the fluidity of racial boundaries, anti-Asian sentiment and practices tended to be less pronounced where they were less visible as a group. With regard to Asian Indians in the Northeast during the early twentieth century, Joan Jensen says that the turban, which on the West Coast was a symbol of their outsider status that made them vulnerable to attack, was considered a "passport to high society."[51] In nineteenth century St. Louis, Missouri, Chinese immigrants were one of several groups of newcomers, and did not appear to have been singled out for particular mistreatment. A pioneer of this community was twenty-four-year-old Alla Lee, who settled in St. Louis in 1857 after stops in the East Coast. He opened a tea and coffee shop on North Tenth Street in a neighborhood known as Hop Alley, which would become synonymous with Chinatown. By 1869 about 250 Chinese came to St. Louis for jobs in mines and factories. The city drew other newcomers, mostly from Ireland, Germany, Eastern Europe, and the

American South. Lee interacted mostly with Irish immigrants and ended up marrying one, Sarah Graham, with whom he had several children.[52]

Economic Exclusion

Going hand in hand with political and social disfranchisement was economic discrimination. Americans took for granted that Asians were not entitled to the same economic freedoms as others, with a host of reasons being offered to justify this position, from Asians' unfair physical advantages at performing "stoop" labor, to their funneling resources out of the country, to their being tools of greedy capitalists. Just after the Civil War, Henry George claimed that there were "60,000 or 100,000 Mongolians" on the West Coast and that this was "the thin edge of the wedge which has for its base the 500,000,000 of Eastern Asia . . . The Chinaman can live where stronger than he would starve. Give him fair play and this quality enables him to drive out the stronger races."[53] Subsequently, toward each successive Asian immigrant group, perhaps no argument was made more than the charge that their "cheap labor" threatened the well being of white workers and the integrity of the U.S. economy.

Ironically, while Asians were often blamed for white unemployment during economic downturns, it was the former that experienced widespread economic inequality since the early years of migration, as they were systematically relegated to low-paying, low-skill jobs and denied paths to mobility. Even in the gold mining frontier of California in the mid-1800s, where nearly everyone was a newcomer, Chinese were quickly deemed among the most unwelcome foreigners. While among Europeans, Frenchmen were occasionally targeted for mistreatment and English, Scotch, German and Irish miners gained acceptance as "insiders" Latinos—native Californians (Californios), Sonorans, Chileans and other Latin Americas— and Chinese were routinely driven off claims if they failed to pay miners' taxes, or sometimes without any cause.[54] Chinese who did stay in mining districts were allowed to do so only if they performed such secondary roles as cooks and food peddlers. And those who mined only had access to diggings that had already been worked over. By the early 1850s, Western politicians and miners began expressing concern about and calling for the expulsion of Chinese, a year that saw a significant rise in Chinese migration with some twenty-five thousand entering. Supporting calls to "check this tide" was governor John Bigler, who denounced Chinese as servile contract laborers who threatened the wellbeing of mining districts and the entire state.[55] He supported a new foreign miners license tax in 1852, which by exempting foreigners who intended to become naturalized, clearly favored whites. The law mandated a monthly fee of $3 per miner. Before it was voided in 1870 by the Civil Rights Act, it extracted $5 million from Chinese miners, or 25 to 50 percent of the state's revenue.[56]

Anti-Asian groups also coordinated economic boycotts to discourage the employment of Asians. As early as 1859, cigar maker guilds in San Francisco were calling for boycotts of companies that hired Chinese workers. To displace these companies, the Cigar Makers Association of the Pacific Coast began putting labels on cigars that said, "The cigars herein contained are made by WHITE MEN." Boot and shoemakers associations followed suit with similar tactics, while anti-coolie clubs distributed placards to businesses so that they could signal their opposition to Chinese-made goods and their employment.[57] Similar strategies were used against other Asians. The Japanese and Korean Exclusion League, for instance, undertook campaigns urging customers to boycott produce that had been handled by Asian laborers, which invoked both the wellbeing of white workers and the health menace of Asians.[58] In a similar vein, in the early 1900s, public health workers in Los Angeles raised the specter of food-borne disease, especially intestinal ailments like typhoid, in produce that had been touched by Japanese.

Boycotts were also used to undermine and harass Asian business owners. In June 1906, the Japanese and Korean Exclusion League urged affiliated unions to enforce penalties if their members patronized Japanese or Chinese restaurants.[59] During one three-week boycott in October, Japanese restaurants were picketed, windows were smashed, a few proprietors were beaten, and prospective customers were handed matchboxes that said "white men and women, patronize your own race[60] The boycott ended when Japanese restaurant owners agreed to pay the local police $350 for protection. Around the same time, the Anti-Jap League organized boycotts of Japanese-owned laundries.[61] Such campaigns were usually short-lived and ultimately ineffective at driving Asians out of business, but they sent a strong message and caused their targets considerable distress.

Municipal codes targeted Asian business niches, often in the name of public health. Chinese laundries, whose visibility was enhanced by their dispersion rather than concentration in Chinatowns, were the first widespread targets in this regard. They tended to be different from white-owned establishments, the latter of which were larger and mechanized. Citing public health concerns, the San Francisco Board of Supervisors passed ordinances mandating an array of certifications and rules for laundries, which required approval by the health officer, fire warden, and other authorities. These regulations included proscriptions on laundries operating at night and on Sundays, as well as the use of scaffoldings as drying racks, a practice most common in Chinese-owned laundries. It was primarily the unevenness of the enforcement of these regulations that revealed their discriminatory nature, but they were also occasionally discriminatory in design. Meanwhile, in Los Angeles, zoning laws, originating with a 1908 Residence District Ordinance, were also used against Chinese laundries in a discriminatory manner. The ordinance designated three sections of the city as residential areas from which certain types of businesses, including laundries, were prohibited. Many Chinese laundries, which the *Labor Press* had decried as a "disgrace to the city and a positive menace to the health of the community," were located in these zones.[62] While it was possible for affected businesses to seek extensions from the city to continue operating their establishments, Chinese businesses had a much harder time securing these than whites.[63] In one case, a white woman named Nellie Snodgrass, who operated a laundry in Hollywood in a residential zone, sought and was granted a three-year extension that allowed her to keep her business open. To support her case, she provided signatures from neighbors who vouched for her good standing and the sanitary condition of her business. On the same block, Quong Long ran a laundry and also sought an extension, collecting signatures from his mostly white neighbors who vouched for him and his "industrious and unobtrusive" character.[64] Despite the similarities in their cases, the city council denied Quong's petition. Even in cases where the Chinese operators successfully challenged ordinances (see Chapter 6), the resources that these fights required could result in them going out of business.

Produce vending, a field in which Asians established footholds throughout the West, also came under scrutiny. By the 1910s in Los Angeles, Chinese produce vendors already faced unequal conditions. They were not allowed to sell their goods in the city's two main city markets, which gave them little choice but to sell door to door and on the street. While market vendors could store their merchandise in the city's facilities, the Chinese wagon vendors had no such options, so often stored their goods in wooden corrals where they also lived or even boarded their horses. To monitor and curb such practices, which officials deemed unsanitary, the city appointed in 1912 a fruit and vegetable commissioner, and the following year created a municipal market department, which allowed for the penalizing of the Chinese vendors. In 1914 eighteen Chinese produce peddlers were arrested for "carelessness in the handling of fruit."[65] Those storing produce where they boarded their horses were charged with violations and forced to rebuild new corrals in Chinatown, leading to the displacement of many.[66]

Perhaps the most punitive and widespread form of economic discrimination that Asians faced were proscriptions from owning land, which started in California in 1913 and eventually spread throughout the West as well as Louisiana and Kansas. By the 1910s with the increased presence of Japanese in western agriculture, land became the focus of nativists. Although it would be several years before the *Ozawa* decision, it was generally accepted that Japanese were racially ineligible for citizenship, and it was this status that Californians used to restrict Japanese immigrants' access to land. Framing the law in this way would purportedly be less insulting to Japan and also allow it to withstand Fourteenth Amendment challenges.[67] On May 19, 1913, Governor Hiram Johnson of California signed the Alien Land Act, which limited leases of agricultural land to three years and barred further land purchases by aliens ineligible to citizenship. Although under pressure by Secretary of State William Jennings Bryan to veto it, Johnson justified his support, saying it did not cause any racial offense against the Japanese or violate treaty law.[68] As to its effect on Japanese landholding, it was easily evaded and did not have a significant impact on Japanese farming. Nor did the law appease anti-Japanese groups in the state who felt it did not go far enough. Outside California, the Japanese government registered its offense and protested to Washington, and the eastern press largely opposed the law.[69]

When it was apparent that the Alien Land Act did not achieve its intended effects—by the end of World War I Issei were drawing 10 percent of agricultural profits in California— prominent organizations demanded more stringent legislation to close the loopholes of the 1913 law.[70] The Farm Bureau and State Grange called for taking away the right of Japanese to lease or rent land and in November 1919 the Native Sons of the Golden West urged, the "only thing that will save California is . . . a state law that will make it impossible for Japanese to get possession of the soil."[71] The Native Sons of the Golden West and American Legion collected signatures for a new law that appeared on the 1920 state ballot as an initiative measure. The 1920 law, which passed with voters, prohibited transfers of land to Japanese nationals, the leasing of land, and acquisition by lease or purchase of land by any corporation with majority Japanese stock.[72] Its enactment, however, was deemed an empty gesture, as it did not significantly affect land tenure in California. Nonetheless, other states continued to enact their own land laws, and in 1923, the U.S. Supreme Court upheld their constitutionality in *Terrace v. Thompson*, which ruled that alien land laws were within states' powers to protect the public interest. Furthermore, in the wake of the *Thind* decision, district attorneys in several California counties began proceedings to revoke Indian land purchases, and the state's attorney general, U.S. Webb, urged district attorneys to enforce the land law against Indians.[73]

Racial Violence: The First and Last Resort

When laws were absent or fell short of their demands, anti-Asian individuals and groups regularly resorted to violence, both spontaneous and organized. The first known anti-Chinese riot occurred in 1849 in Tuolomne County in California, when a group of white miners drove off Chinese employees of a British company.[74] Violence continued as their numbers grew and targeted both urban and rural Chinese. In the winter of 1867 Chinese workers on the Potrero Street railway were chased out of San Francisco by a crowd of four

Figure 5.1 Wood engraving of an anti-Chinese riot in Denver, Colorado. This illustration, which originally appeared in *Frank Leslie's Illustrated*, shows Chinese being beaten by a mob during a riot on October 31, 1880. Although California was ground zero for the anti-Chinese movement, some of the most vicious rioting occurred in the intermountain West, where many Chinese immigrants were employed for mining, railroad, and other companies. (Library of Congress, Prints and Photographs Division, LC-USZC2-760.)

hundred people who threw rocks at them, destroyed their barracks, and roamed the city terrorizing other Chinese.[75] In this case, ten participants served just two months out of their eleven-month sentences, and in general, lenient treatment of white assailants involved in such attacks was the rule, not the exception.[76] One of the most chilling instances of anti-Chinese violence was the Chico Massacre of March 13, 1877, in which a group of armed white men stormed a cabin where Chinese men were sleeping, and without provocation opened fire, threw oil on their bodies and set their cabins ablaze.[77] The single most deadly known riot occurred in 1885 in Rock Springs, Wyoming, during a period when organized anti-Chinese outbreaks spiked throughout the American West. The attack occurred after about six hundred Chinese coal mine employees refused to join with white co-workers in a planned strike. Seeking retaliation, a mob of white workers gathered upon the Chinese on September 2, firing on them, chasing them, and burning down their living quarters. In the end, twenty-eight Chinese were killed, fifteen wounded, and losses suffered totaled over $147,000.[78]

For other Asian immigrants, racial violence was also a fact of life. Generally, wherever a discrete group of Asians resided or worked, local white labor groups and citizens' committees organized expulsions to drive them out of town. In fall 1907, Asian Indians in Bellingham, Washington found themselves the targets of white mill workers. After notices were circulated for a meeting to "drive out the Hindus," a mob of several hundred people gathered. Two boys were arrested for stoning a group of Indians and the crowd surrounded police, demanding their release. From there, the agitators descended on the waterfront barracks where Indians lived. They battered down the doors, threw their belongings into the street, took their money and jewelry, and dragged out and beat them.[79] As a result of the disturbance, most of the Indians fled the area.

Japanese were also regular victims of assault. One of these, who provided a statement for a special investigation ordered by President Theodore Roosevelt, described his ordeal:

> I am proprietor of Sunset City Laundry. Soon after the earthquake the persecutions became intolerable. My drivers were constantly attacked on the highway, my place of business defiled by rotten eggs and fruit; windows were smashed several times . . . The miscreants are generally young men, 17 or 18 years old. Whenever newspapers attack the Japanese these roughs renew their misdeeds with redoubled energy[80]

Anti-Japanese expulsions were also organized in rural areas, the most well known incident occurring in Turlock, California during the summer of 1921. Similar to the anti-Indian Bellingham riot, it started with the circulation of a petition. This one was produced by labor organizers and business people and read:

> We the undersigned merchants and businessmen of Turlock, protest against the annual influx of Japanese into this community and, believing that it is the birthright of American citizens to fill available jobs, we call upon the growers and farmers of this district to employ white labor exclusively. We call upon the packers and distributors to handle only such fruits and produce as has been produced by American labor exclusively. As evidence of our good faith, we pledge our hearty and unqualified support to the accomplishment of this purpose.[81]

An armed mob of fifty to sixty whites rousted eighteen sleeping Japanese cantaloupe pickers, who were put on trucks and driven to a Stockton railroad line with instructions not to return lest they be lynched. No one was convicted of any crime.

The last group to undergo a cycle of violence was Filipinos. The first known anti-Filipino riot occurred in Yakima in 1927. As with other anti-Asian outbreaks, anger over their employment was usually a factor, but outrage over interracial sexual transgressions also played a role. The most famous anti-Filipino riot took place in Watsonville in 1930, just on the heels of the Perfecto Bandalan episode and the opening of a new Filipino dance hall nearby. Newspapers and community leaders such as Judge Rohrback railed more generally against Filipino immigration. On January 19, 1930, a group of local whites tried to enter the Monterey Bay Filipino Club in neighboring Palm Beach after hearing rumors that white girls were employed there. After being turned away, carloads of white men who had formed "Filipino hunting parties" arrived and roamed the streets, randomly attacking Filipinos, and over the next five days, "terror and violence reigned throughout the region."[82] Amid the chaos, one Filipino, Fermin Tobera, was shot and killed at a ranch three miles outside of Watsonville. As in earlier anti-Asian riots, the vigilantes had the support of the community, and in the end eight men were charged in connection with Tobera's killing. However, the two-year sentences they received were suspended and they spent no time in jail.[83]

Closing the Gates

For many Americans, and eventually the nation's highest officials, the "Asiatic invasion" called for the draconian step of cutting off immigration, the ultimate rejection of Asians from the American body politic. Whereas riots, land Acts, miscegenation laws, and naturalization policies enforced the yellow–white color line and signaled Asians' subordinate status as non-whites and non-citizens, singling them out for immigration restriction was particularly harsh. Beginning with Chinese exclusion, the United States reversed its long-standing policy of relatively open immigration, and in the decades that followed, general immigration laws transformed the country into a "gatekeeping nation" that carefully guarded its doors and imposed stringent requirements for entry. To be sure, other groups faced heightened restrictions, such as political radicals, southern and eastern Europeans, prostitutes, the infirm, and contract laborers, but from the late nineteenth to early twentieth centuries, Asians were continually targeted, and by 1934 with the passage of the Tydings-McDuffie Act, which affected Philippine migration, Asian immigration was virtually eliminated.

The Chinese Exclusion Act was a turning point after which the United States increasingly restricted its borders. Prior to the late 1800s, there were few requirements for entry at the federal level, and, thus, a minimal bureaucracy of enforcement. A short-lived Alien Act in 1789 allowed the deportation of aliens at the discretion of the president, and the Act of March 2, 1819 provided for the enumeration of immigrants at ports of entry. A legal watershed in several respects—it was, for instance, the first federal immigration law to single out a group for exclusion on the basis of race and ethnicity—the Chinese Exclusion Act of 1882 was preceded by piecemeal measures that were vetoed or invalidated by the courts. At the state level, the California legislature sought to restrict Chinese immigration, but encountered obstacles. An 1855 tax of $50 on transporters of any person "incompetent by the laws and constitution of California or the United States to become citizens," and an 1858 prohibition on the entry of any Chinese or "Mongolian" were invalidated, as only the U.S. Congress could regulate immigration or impose taxes on immigrants, a principle established by the Passenger Cases of 1849.

By the late 1860s, immigration exclusionists faced an additional hurdle, the Burlingame Treaty of 1868, which established reciprocal privileges for Chinese and American citizens abroad and recognized the right of voluntary Chinese immigration. Furthermore, it voided the collection of indemnity bonds, such as those that the California legislature had imposed. Realizing they would have to prevail over the federal government to achieve exclusion, western representatives did successfully help to prevent the amendment to the Naturalization Act that would have opened the way to Chinese naturalization. They then set their sights on abrogating the Burlingame Treaty and persuading national legislators of the evils of Chinese immigration.

Some of the piecemeal measures on the road to Chinese exclusion were the anti-coolie law of 1862, the Page Act of 1875, and the Fifteen Passenger Act of 1879. The prohibition on coolie importation was, as discussed earlier, framed as an anti-slavery measure and did not cut down on Chinese immigration, although by defining "coolies" as Chinese, it cemented an association of Chinese as degraded labor that would prove central to the Chinese Exclusion Act. The Page Act of 1875, sponsored by Horace Page of California, was the first significant federal measure to deal with Chinese immigration. Although on the surface it was a general law that asserted the ban on contract labor and the entry of women for prostitution, it was a thinly veiled anti-Chinese Act that carefully stayed within the provisions of the Burlingame Treaty. Its intent was laid bare before and after passage, however. When introducing the bill in a speech in February 1875, Page said that that 90 percent of the Chinese female population in America were prostitutes and that restricting further entry was necessary to safeguard the nation's moral health. He also emphasized that the law was an interim measure that should lead to a more comprehensive restriction. The selective enforcement of the law also revealed its intent to target Chinese women.

Californians continued to lead the campaign for federal exclusion by sending delegates across the country, holding anti-Chinese rallies, and giving speeches to Congress. On April 5, 1876 a day of rallies was held in San Francisco with about twenty-five thousand people in attendance. From April to June, the state senate conducted an investigation in which sixty witnesses were interviewed. Its final report, which was sent to Washington, D.C., called for repealing the Burlingame Treaty and limiting Chinese immigration to ten persons per ship. In the meantime, prominent anti-Chinese leaders from California toured the country to raise national support for their cause. One of these, state senator and newspaper editor Philip Roach, gave a lecture in Chicago in which he said that Chinese were not only cheap laborers who drove out their competition in every trade, but were also moral degenerates who introduced a host of vices in California. Similar arguments were echoed in Washington, D.C., such as one speech by Republican Senator Aaron Sargeant in May 1876. The former forty-niner said, "The emigration of Chinese is not like that of Europeans who seek our shores voluntarily to become citizens. They are quasi slaves" and will turn San Francisco into "a purely Asiatic city."[84] By this time, both national parties either endorsed exclusion or the need to investigate it. This growing consensus was signaled in a Congressional report on Chinese immigration issued in February 1877. The investigation encompassed 17 sessions held in San Francisco in late 1876 and included testimony from 128 manufacturers, ministers, public officials, and workers—none of whom was Chinese.[85] The report, authored by Aaron Sargeant, stated, "Chinese immigration involves sordid wages, no public schools, and the absence of the family."[86] It continued, "they are cruel and indifferent to their sick . . . have no knowledge or appreciation for our institutions," and lacked "sufficient brain capacity . . . for self-government."[87] The report recommended a modification of the Burlingame Treaty and new restrictive legislation.

With this national momentum in place, other hurdles were cleared toward Chinese exclusion. In 1879, Congress passed the Fifteen Passenger Bill. As Republican Senator James Blaine said in support of it, "We have this day to choose . . . whether our legislation shall be in the interest of the American free laborer or for the servile laborer from China . . . You cannot work a man who must have beef and bread, and would prefer beer, alongside of a man who can live on rice. It cannot be done."[88] Although President Hayes vetoed the law, he did so due to timing rather than a principled opposition to exclusion. As Andrew Gyory explains, Secretary of State William Evarts was about to open formal negotiations with China to modify the Burlingame Treaty when the Fifteen Passenger Bill was passed, so the president worried that signing the bill would be seen as a breach of faith.[89] The final obstacle was cleared when the United States and China signed the Angell Treaty in 1880. Under its provisions, the United States could regulate, limit, or suspend Chinese immigration if it were deemed harmful to national interests, but it could not absolutely prohibit it.[90] Congress got to work in drafting a Chinese exclusion bill, which was vetoed by President Chester Arthur because he thought the twenty-year ban it called for was overly harsh and feared China would retaliate by closing off trade.[91] An identical bill with a ban of ten years that also substituted the word "certificate" for "passport" was submitted and passed by the House 201 to 37 (53 abstaining) with solid support from all regions and parties.[92] Explaining the threat of Chinese immigration to his region, Alabama Democrat John Tyler Morgan said if exclusion were not enacted, Chinese would descend into the South and cause "the utter destruction of the last vestige of civilization we have there."[93]

Signed by President Arthur on May 6, 1882, the Chinese Exclusion Act was anticlimactic given the long struggle that preceded it, but it was highly significant nonetheless. Although it targeted Chinese laborers, its passage was the first step in a general transformation of immigration in the United States. Enforcing the Act's provisions called for the creation of a new federal bureaucracy of trained officials and interpreters, which only expanded with the passage of additional restrictions against Chinese and other groups. These officials worked within the Customs Office until 1891 when the first federal agency on immigration was created. The criminalization of and penalties for illegal entry and its abetting set forth by the Chinese Exclusion Act would also be codified in a general immigration law passed in 1891.[94] Another significant aspect of Chinese exclusion was that it provided a framework and language for the racialization of other threatening and undesirable aliens. For instance, as nativist hostility mounted against them, Southern and Eastern Europeans were likewise denounced as "coolies, serfs, and slaves."[95]

While its effects would be far-reaching, the Chinese Exclusion Act and subsequent laws extending it and tightening its restrictions placed the greatest burdens on Chinese people.

Going further than restricting immigration, the 1882 Act also explicitly denied Chinese the right of naturalization. With respect to the process of immigration, it required verification of admissibility prior to leaving China, shifting the burden to the Chinese government, although starting in 1884 American diplomats would share this responsibility. Additionally, Section 4 of the Act required certificates of registration for departing laborers that they would need to present upon returning to the United States. Until 1924, Chinese were the only group subject to such a requirement. The Scott Act of 1888 bolstered exclusion in several ways. It changed the terms of exclusion by targeting all Chinese except for "teachers, students, merchants, or travelers for pleasure or curiosity" instead of explicitly prohibiting only Chinese laborers.[96] It also prohibited any Chinese laborer from returning unless he had a wife, child or parent in the United States or had property or debts due to him worth at least $1,000. Most punitive was its nullification of about twenty thousand return certificates that had already been issued. The Geary Act of 1892, which extended the ban on Chinese immigration for ten more years, imposed additional burdens, such as a requirement for all Chinese residents of the United States to possess certificates of residence and identity as proof of their legal entry and right to remain in the United States. Beginning in 1909, members of the exempt classes were also required to have these certificates of identity, which contained personal data, occupational information, and photographs. This regime of processing and certification in effect subjected Chinese in America to an elaborate tracking system that extended well beyond the border. No other groups were subjected to these documentary requirements until 1928, when immigrant identification cards—precursors of "green cards"—were issued to immigrants coming to live in the United States permanently.[97] In 1898 Chinese exclusion was extended to Hawaii and in 1902 another extension was passed, covering all insular possessions, including the Philippines. Finally in 1904 it was extended without a time limit.

Chinese exclusion achieved its objective of curbing immigration. Just prior to the law taking effect, nearly forty thousand rushed in, but in 1887 Chinese immigration hit an all-time low when just ten gained entry.[98] In the fourteen months after the Act's passage, over eleven thousand Chinese left the United States, a trend that continued through the 1880s. The restrictive policies did not, however, completely seal off the border, as Chinese proved resourceful at challenging and defying the laws, through the courts and fraud (see Chapter 6), to the great frustration of immigration officials. Chinese exclusion, moreover, also sanctioned racism at the highest levels of government. For instance, in arguing for the documentation requirements of the 1892 extension of the Chinese Exclusion Act, California Congressman Thomas Geary said they were necessary because it was impossible to tell one Chinese from the other.[99] Chinese exclusion, thus, not only validated racism in policymaking but also provided a model of success for movements against Japanese, Indians, and Filipinos. Nativists sought passage of similar laws while dredging up the same arguments, such as their inability to assimilate, immorality, and tendency to be disease carriers. After the 1882 Act's passage, the *Chicago Times* expressed its hope for future policy, saying, "Hereafter we are to keep our hand on the door-knob, and admit only those whose presence we desire."[100]

Indeed, during debates to extend Chinese exclusion in 1892 and 1902, anti-Japanese rhetoric entered these discussions and gradually built into a full-scale movement to stop Japanese immigration. In 1892, the San Francisco *Call*, an anti-Chinese mouthpiece, began warning of this latest Asian menace, charging that Japanese immigrants were "taking work away from our boys and girls [and] men and women," and hyperbolically predicting that they would enter the United States at a rate of 120,000 per year by the turn of century.[101] San Francisco Mayor James Phelan, who emerged as an early anti-Japanese political figure, stated in 1900, "The Japanese are starting the same tide of immigration which we thought we had checked twenty years ago . . . The Chinese and Japanese are not . . . the stuff of which American citizens can be made . . . Personally we have nothing against Japanese, but as they will not assimilate with us and their social life is so different from ours, let them keep at a respectful distance."[102] Chester Harvey Rowell, the editor of the Fresno *Republican*, added to the early anti-Japanese chorus by calling them "coolie[s]" and "the most undesirable class possible." He lambasted the "cowardice and apathy of the rest of the country" for failing to act on this threat and hoped that "the country [would] be aroused to the necessity of doing something in regard to immigration in general."[103] The Japanese and Korean Exclusion League, formed in San Francisco in May 1905, supported the anti-Japanese cause through economic boycotts, legislative lobbying, and propaganda. It understood the Japanese "threat" through the lens of Chinese immigration, but made the additional claim that if Japanese immigration were not stopped, then Chinese immigration would also resume.[104]

An important step toward exclusion occurred in March 1905 when the California legislature passed a resolution officially stating its opposition to Japanese immigration and calling on Congress to take action. In a manner that had become typical in the ranks of anti-Asianists, the resolution displayed astounding ignorance; in describing conditions in California, it stated that Japanese did not buy land nor add to the state's wealth, although their extensive participation in farming at the time showed the opposite.[105] Pleas from California eventually found a receptive audience with some legislators in Washington, D.C., and between 1905 and 1909 anti-Japanese bills were introduced in every session of Congress.[106]

More so than for other groups, diplomacy shaped the timing and methods of Japanese exclusion, as Japan's military victories over China and Russia accorded it more respect from western powers than other Asian countries enjoyed. Against intensifying clamors about the "Orientalization" of the Pacific coast, Japan and the United States worked out a diplomatic solution to limit migration. The precipitating event was the San Francisco Board of Education's decision to send Japanese and Koreans to the city's Oriental School in 1906. Seeking to preserve good relations while responding to exclusionists' concerns, President Theodore Roosevelt urged Californians hold off on passing discriminatory laws so he could pursue a diplomatic resolution of the immigration issue. In the meantime, he assured Japan that the United States was treating the school board matter seriously and that the rights of Japanese in the country would be protected. As Roger Daniels explains, Roosevelt "wanted the Japanese treated courteously and with the respect that he felt their military prowess demanded. But he also felt very strongly that the Japanese, and all colored peoples generally, should be willing to take fatherly advice."[107] Under Roosevelt's pressure, San Francisco rescinded the segregation order, which made Japan amenable to a bilateral agreement on immigration. In February 1907, Congress passed a bill forbidding holders of passports issued by foreign governments to go anywhere besides the United States and its possessions from using them to enter the United States. The following month Roosevelt issued an executive order barring mainland immigration from Hawaii, Mexico, and Canada, which cut off a major stream of Japanese to the continental U.S. The next step was Japan's halting of the direct immigration of skilled and unskilled laborers, which it agreed to in the Gentlemen's Agreement, the substance of which was found in six notes exchanged between late 1907 and early 1908.[108] After the agreement took effect, Roosevelt continued to pressure the governor of California to veto anti-Japanese laws, as these would have been viewed as a breach of faith.

Although the Gentlemen's Agreement has been described as effectively a Japanese exclusion measure, to exclusionists in the West it did not do nearly enough. For one, Japan continued to issue passports to laborers who had already been in America as well as the parents, wives, and children of those already there. Furthermore, the migration of picture brides picked up in the years after the agreement. Anti-Japanese agitators felt betrayed by diplomats and accused them of being dupes of Japan.[109] The picture bride migration was eventually halted, again through a diplomatic agreement in 1920, so exclusionists continued to demand federal legislation.

While Indian exclusion was informed by the legacy of the anti-Chinese movement and simultaneous campaign against Japanese, pressures from Canada and Great Britain played additional roles. To be sure, the exclusion of all major Asian groups was for much of the late nineteenth and early twentieth centuries one of the issues around which U.S. and Canadian interests converged. A coordinated effort between the countries was necessary because of the migratory patterns of immigrants, who often crossed and re-crossed the international border. Anti-Indian sentiment was, furthermore, animated by anti-radicalism. After 1910, British concerns about immigrant activists advocating Indian independence led the Canadian government to monitor the activities of Indian nationalists in Canada.[110] Furthermore, due to the peripatetic ways of immigrant leaders such as Teja Singh and Har Dayal, U.S. officials also cooperated in the surveillance of Indians.[111]

American anti-Asian activists helped their Canadian counterparts in other ways. At the height of the anti-Japanese and anti-Indian movements in British Columbia, Vancouver exclusionists asked Olaf Tveitmoe of the San Francisco Japanese and Korean Exclusion League to help them create their own chapter.[112] Under the slogan "White Canada Forever," Canadians effectively curbed immigration from China, Japan, and India through head taxes, diplomatic agreements, literacy tests, and political disfranchisement.

Responding to pressure from Britain and Canada as well as incidents such as the 1907 riot in Bellingham, Washington, Americans began calling for Indian exclusion. The San Francisco *Call*, building on its record of anti-Asian agitation, printed a series of pictures with the caption, "The Hindu Invasion," as well as articles that exaggerated the number of Indians in California, and before long, national politicians and publications joined the chorus against Indian immigration.[113] In March 1910 *Collier's Weekly* ran an article on the "Hindu Invasion" featuring pictures of turbaned immigrants, which claimed, "They are as a whole inferior workmen" and "manifest no interest in the country or its customs; and they differ from the unobtrusive Chinaman by being sullen and uncompromising."[114] The Japanese and Korean Exclusion League changed its name to the Asiatic Exclusion League (AEL) in 1907 as it took on Indian immigrants as a target. As a leading anti-Indian voice, it accused members of this group of being carriers of exotic Oriental diseases and reported on each arriving ship carrying Indians into San Francisco.[115] The AEL also publicly exposed and called for the ouster of U.S. immigration officials believed to be sympathetic to Indians. Its biggest target in this regard was Hart Hyatt North, whom the AEL and San Francisco newspapers nicknamed "Sahib North."[116]

After officials like North were removed from their positions, the exclusion of Indians was partially achieved through an informal system in which existing proscriptions—usually the ban on immigrants likely to become public charges—were used to deny them entry. At Angel Island station, for instance, the month after North was removed in late 1910, 181 out of 184 South Asians were rejected, whereas the month prior to his ouster, 46 percent were denied entry, and throughout the immigration station's history from 1910 to 1941, South Asians had the highest rate of rejection.[117] At the port of Seattle, an immigration inspector said that the charge of polygamy was frequently used to reject Indians whom he claimed were "Muhammadans," and an Indian interpreter for the Bureau of Immigration said that "virtual exclusion" was the practice against Indians.[118]

Despite this reduction of Indian immigration, exclusionists continued to call for federal legislation. In response to demands for further action, the Immigration Commission issued a report in 1910 concluding that Indians were "universally regarded as the least desirable race of immigrants thus far admitted to the United States." It called for congressional exclusion, a gentlemen's agreement with Britain to stop the migration of Indian laborers, and a literacy test to prohibit the entry of all unwanted immigrants.[119] California Senator Anthony Caminetti, who went on to serve as the commissioner general of immigration from 1913 to 1921, stated:

> I have come from the Pacific Coast, where we have had two race problems which we have had to fight, and a third one about to be thrown upon us out there, and I have known practically and personally the patience of our people in waiting for diplomatic negotiations upon the Chinese immigration question . . . The people of California waited very patiently for diplomatic arrangements upon the Japanese immigration problem what that was under consideration, and I do not think they are anxious now for diplomatic arrangements upon the Hindu problem.[120]

To support their case, Caminetti and others misrepresented and exaggerated the size of the Asian Indian population in the United States. For instance, even though between 1907 and 1913 6,656 entered the United States and 811 left, the Bureau of Immigration claimed that 6,656 was the size of the total population, adding that many more had probably entered illegally.[121] Elsewhere, the Bureau claimed that there were over 6,000 in San Joaquin Valley alone and between 20,000 and 30,000 in California, Oregon, and Washington.[122] This question of the true scope of the "problem" of Indian immigration plagued congressional debates. Augustus Gardner of Massachusetts said that just 154 entered in the second half of 1913 and did not think this warranted drastic action. On the other hand John Raker of California claimed there were at least 150,000 Indians in the state and Anthony Caminetti predicted that after World War I a heightened influx from western Asia would flood the United States.[123]

A potential stumbling block to legislation, British objection to the exclusion of its subjects, proved to be a non-issue. In contrast to Japan, Britain did not make appeals on behalf of Indian immigrants, instead offering its unofficial support to exclusionists in Canada and the United States out of concern about anti-colonial nationalists. In 1915, the British government of India had imposed a regulation that criminalized embarking on a journey from any British India port without a passport.[124] During congressional debates, the Labor Department proposed adding a "barred zone" provision to a pending general immigration bill that would accomplish Indian exclusion. Despite some objections—Senator James Reed asked, "Why exclude citizens of India, whom you say are of white blood and permit inhabitants of most of Africa to enter?"—Congress passed the Immigration Act of 1917 with the new provision.[125] Fearing diplomatic repercussions for a literacy clause that tested all adult immigrants in their native language, President Woodrow Wilson vetoed the law, only to be overridden by Congress. The Act also tightened restrictions on suspected radicals, and the barred zone provision effectively excluded immigrants from India, Burma, Siam, Malay States, Arabia, Afghanistan, part of Russia, and most of the Polynesian Islands, with exemptions for travelers, students, teachers, merchants, and professionals. Given who was immigrating at the time, South Asians were the main group affected, although informal policies practiced by immigration officials had already reduced their entries. By 1940 the South Asian population in the United States was just 2,400.[126]

After World War I, anti-Asian groups continued to demand a statutory ban on Japanese immigration and a bar on all categories of Chinese. One of the organizations at the forefront of this effort was the Japanese Exclusion League of California, which had been formed in September 1920 in San Francisco, with state senator Inman serving as its president and other offices held by members of the Native Sons, American Legion, California State Federation of Labor, California Federation of Women's Clubs, California State Grange, Farm Bureau, and Loyal Order of the Moose. Figures from the pre-Gentlemen's Agreement era reemerged, such as Chester Rowell, V.S. McClatchy, and now U.S. Senators James Phelan and Hiram Johnson. A propaganda campaign magnifying unease about Japan's international rise and the presence of Japanese in America helped build support for this cause. In 1922 and 1923, for instance, McClatchy coordinated a "Swat the Jap" campaign that involved the distribution of anti-Japanese leaflets and books such as Montaville Flowers' *The Japanese Conquest of American Public Opinion*, Peter B. Kyne's *Pride of Palomar*, and Wallace Irwin's *Seed of the Sun*, which stoked fears about continued Japanese migration. James Phelan, who sent copies of the Flowers book to friends, called for a stricter land law in California, the abrogation of the Gentlemen's Agreement, a Japanese exclusion law, and strengthened defenses on the West Coast.[127]

Although Asian immigration by the early 1920s had been drastically reduced, the patchwork means by which this was achieved, exceptions for certain groups, and notable growth of the U.S.-born Asian population (especially among Japanese Americans) kept alive the perceived urgency to enact even more stringent and sweeping measures. The rhetoric turned particularly ugly at this time. During his reelection campaign for the Senate in 1920, Phelan, under the slogan "Keep California White," said the growth of a native-born Japanese population and Japanese landholdings were proof of their perfidy, and he called for a constitutional amendment that no child born in the U.S. would be a citizen unless both parents were eligible.[128] Exclusionists also targeted Americans who supported Japanese immigrants, calling them "white-Japs who masquerade as Americans, but in fact, are servants of the mikado."[129]

The Japanese problem, by and large viewed as a regional issue and reluctantly addressed by federal legislators, gained national attention by the early 1920s. After the passage of the 1920 alien land law in California, exclusionists hoped this would lead to a federal Japanese exclusion Act. Indeed, statutory Japanese exclusion was finally achieved, but through a general immigration law passed amid a nativist movement in which southern and eastern Europeans were actually the main targets. In December 1923, Congressman Albert Johnson introduced a bill designed to dramatically reduce immigration from southern and eastern European countries through discriminatory quotas based on "national origins," but added to it was a provision barring the immigration of "aliens ineligible to citizenship." The latter piece was a blunt instrument aimed at achieving statutory Japanese exclusion, but effectively excluded half of the world's population.[130] Californians celebrated the passage of the 1924 Johnson-Reed Act, and although his demand to strip Nisei of their citizenship was not met, Phelan proclaimed, "The Japs are routed."[131]

The alteration of Filipinos' status from nationals to aliens in order to decisively exclude them from naturalization has been discussed earlier, but this action also impacted immigration, and, thus, marked the final act in the long campaign to close the gates to immigrants from Asia. By the 1920s, Filipinos were the only Asian group still entering the United States in large numbers, but this was ended by the Tydings-McDuffie Act of 1934, which reduced Filipino immigration to 50 per year and changed their status to *aliens*. Exclusionists celebrated. U.S. Representative from California, Richard Welch, sent a congratulatory letter to Paul Scharrenberg of the California State Federation of Labor for their success in the hard fought battle to exclude Filipinos. The Act was, Welch said, "an accomplishment of which we can both be proud." Welch then connected the Tydings-McDuffie Act to his hopes for long term Asian exclusion, saying, "the very fact that the Filipinos, who were practically wards of ours, have been placed on a quota of fifty annually is assuring that the bars will not be let down for other Asiatics."[132]

A Greater Good? Mobilizing the Marginalized

As is usually the case in nativist movements, exclusionists' complaints about Asians in America were provoked by anxieties stemming from external factors such as economic depression, worker discontent, and social and cultural change. Accordingly, anti-Asian leaders often linked Asian immigration to corporate power, public health, racial purity, and other concerns. In this way, anti-Asian politics and activities in the late nineteenth to early twentieth century can be viewed through the lens of what historian Robert Wiebe has called a "search for order," an impulse that captured many of the reform movements of that era.[133] While xenophobia and racial antipathy surely informed anti-Asian nativism, its proponents claimed, and likely believed, that exclusion was necessary for a greater good. Believing in the moral uprightness of their cause, participants of anti-Asian movements also saw a way to advance their personal and group interests—and overcome their own marginalization—through working for the subjugation of another group.

It should not be a surprise, then, that some of the most vocal proponents of exclusion were immigrants and leaders of the "workingman." To the degree that anti-Asian politics mobilized the white working class, no group exemplified this more than the Workingmen's Party of California (WPC), formed in the fall of 1877 and led by president Denis Kearney. Taking its name from a socialist group in the East, the California party was decidedly unsocialist and rather hostile to trade unions. Kearney was less a workingman than a middling entrepreneur who ran a draying business, and most of the party's affiliates were not labor organizations but rather language and neighborhood associations and anti-coolie clubs.[134] Yet this did not stop the organization from claiming to be the voice of the workingman, and Kearney's sandlot speeches in which he singled out targets like the Central Pacific, "capitalist bondholders," the two-party system, and the Chinese made him a working class hero. A charismatic speaker, he used confrontational and violent rhetoric, which enthralled audiences and led to his being arrested several times. At one meeting in San Francisco's Nob Hill he said, "I will give the Central Pacific just three months to discharge their Chinamen, and if that is not done, Stanford and his crowd will have to take the consequences."[135] Workingmen's Party meetings began and ended with Kearney exhorting, the "Chinese Must Go!" Not only did the WPC help to make Chinese exclusion a major issue in the state elections of 1878, but it also swept local offices in San Francisco and won thirty seats throughout the state. Workingmen also made up one-third of the delegates at the 1879 state Constitutional Convention, and their influence was evident in pro-labor and anti-Chinese provisions in the new state constitution.[136] The latter included a prohibition on the employment of Chinese by corporations and on public works, authorization for the legislature to relocate Chinese beyond city and town lines, and the discouragement of immigration, all of which were later invalidated.[137]

In explaining the success of an organization like the Workingmen's Party in channeling working class discontent into Chinese exclusion, its bona fides as a worker organization can be disputed and, to be sure, many in Kearney's audiences were put off by his antiunionism. Key to the group's appeal was growing discontent due to the flagging economy. In 1877, the United States was in its fourth year of depression. High unemployment and rising discontent had led to a labor uprising touched off by a railroad strike.[138] Amidst this suffering and uncertainty, politicians, from regional figures like Denis Kearney to members of Congress in Washington, D.C., seized the issue of immigration and framed it as the answer to people's problems. As Andrew Gyory explains:

> Chinese exclusion served as a panacea for a complex web of problems, with politicians striving to turn a regional, cross-class issue into a national, working class demand. Although immigration restriction offered scant relief and appealed to few wage earners, politicians seized it, amid the clamor for government retrenchment, as an easy solution with which they could pose as defenders of working people everywhere. As a result of the national railroad strike, Chinese exclusion would find new champions in the highest echelons of government.[139]

In California, labor politics and the anti-Chinese movement evolved closely and reinvigorated one another. At sandlot meetings where unemployed workers gathered to air their grievances and hear orators like Kearney rail against monopolies and the Chinese, worker identity and solidarity were forged upon anti-Chinese xenophobia. In the East, intellectuals and politicians took the lead in tying immigration to economic decline, and among workers the reception was mixed. For instance, in the New York cigar industry, whose diverse labor force went on strike in 1877, European immigrants, women, Latinos, and even Chinese took part. The *New York Labor Standard* praised Chinese for asserting "their manhood in this strike and [rising] to the dignity of the American trade unionists."[140] However, the anti-Chinese issue was used as a wedge when rumors surfaced that a San Francisco firm was going to bring Chinese to break strikes.[141] As other Asians migrated to the United States, worker organizations remained at the forefront of calling for their exclusion. The American Federation of Labor was among the first to sound the alarm about Japanese immigration and the leaders of the Asiatic Exclusion League—men such as Patrick Henry McCarthy, Andrew Furuseth, and Walter MacArthur—were drawn from various segments of the labor movement.[142]

In a state like California during the nineteenth century, where many people were newcomers and grappled with a sense of displacement, non-Chineseness united workingmen and became a basis of commonality and solidarity. It was certainly notable that many of the most prominent anti-Asian agitators were themselves foreign-born. In California, by 1870, about a quarter of the state's wageworkers were Chinese, and excluding this group, about 28 percent of the state's residents were foreign born. Thus, the working-class population had a high proportion of foreign born, and among Europeans, Irish, Germans, and British were especially prominent.[143] Denis Kearney was an Irish orphan who had come to San Francisco as a chief mate on a ship and became naturalized in 1876. Another key anti-Chinese figure was politician Philip Roach, also an Irish immigrant. He came to the United States with his family in 1822 when he was two, lived in New York, and came to California during the gold rush.[144] From there, he entered politics, took part in framing the state constitution, became a judge and mayor of Monterey, and established himself as one of California's early anti-Chinese politicians. Asiatic Exclusion League leaders Olaf Tveitmoe, Andrew Furuseth, and A.E. Yoell were also immigrants.

European immigrants, especially Irish, but others as well, had been targets of virulent nativism during the nineteenth century. As historians have described elsewhere, embracing not just anti-Chinese, but also anti-black politics, conferred upon them a "wage" of whiteness that not only identified an "enemy" to work against, but also in some ways compensated for their social and economic marginalization, a dynamic that similarly played out among the white working class more generally. Martha Mabie Gardner has shown how white women similarly gained from anti-Chinese politics. Anna Smith was a popular sandlot orator in the late 1870s who usually framed her remarks on behalf of white women. "Every white woman should be allowed to earn her own living," she said, and blamed Chinese for getting in the way of this.[145]

Conclusion

The history of anti-Asian racism in the United States in the nineteenth and early twentieth centuries was varied, targeted successive groups, and saw the employment of a range of strategies. Eventually, all Asian immigrants were racialized as "aliens ineligible to citizenship," a categorization that signaled their unique outsider status and underlay numerous forms of legal discrimination. As oppressive as the hostility that they faced was, leading many to leave the United States, the landscape was not monolithically anti-Asian, and, moreover, Asian Americans and their allies fought back against discrimination, the focus of the following chapter.

Notes

1   Roger Daniels, *The Politics of Prejudice: The Anti-Japanese Movement in California and the Struggle for Japanese Exclusion* (Berkeley: University of California Press, 1962), 19–20.

2   Alexander Saxton, *The Indispensable Enemy: Labor and the Anti-Chinese Movement* (Berkeley: University of California Press, 1971), 52.

3   Quoted in Peter Kwong and Dušanka Miščević, *Chinese America: The Untold Story of America's Oldest New Community* (New York: New Press, 2005), 46.

4   Ibid., 46.

5   Sucheng Chan, *Asian Americans: An Interpretive History* (Boston: Twayne Publishers, 1991), 48.

6   Andrew Gyory, *Closing the Gate: Race, Politics, and the Chinese Exclusion Act* (Chapel Hill: University of North Carolina Press, 1998), 52.

7   Chan, *Asian Americans*, 47.

8   Joan Jensen, *Passage from India: Asian Indian Immigrants in North America* (New Haven: Yale University Press, 1988), 247.

9   The latter did not come to pass and Japanese emigration restriction was attained through the Gentlemen's Agreement, negotiated in the wake of the San Francisco school board crisis. The Act of 1906 standardized naturalization requirements and procedures. In conjunction with the law, the Attorney General ordered federal courts to cease issuing naturalization papers to Japanese applicants. However, this did not have the same weight of a judicial ruling. After October 1906 when the San Francisco School Board resolved to segregate Japanese school children into the Oriental School, President Roosevelt denounced the decision in a message to Congress in December in which he recommended legislation to grant Japanese naturalization rights, thus throwing the status of eligibility for citizenship into question again. Yuji Ichioka, *Issei: The World of the First Generation Japanese Immigrants* (New York: Free Press, 1988), 211–12.

10   According to the 1910 Census, over 420 Japanese had been naturalized. Ichioka, 211. Also see Jensen, *Passage from India*, 257.

11   Ibid., 248.

12   Ibid., 249.

13   The non "other" categories were white, Negro, American Indian, Chinese, and Japanese. Ibid., 252.

14   Ibid., 253.

15   According to Mae Ngai, there were 25 cases heard by federal courts between 1887 and 1923. Mae Ngai, "The Architecture of Race in American Immigration Law: A Reexamination of the Immigration Act of 1924," *Journal of American History*, Vol. 86 No. 1 (June 1999): 81.

16   Ian Haney Lopez, *White by Law: The Legal Construction of Race* (New York: New York University Press, 1996), 57–8.

17   He also cited the fact that some Indian men were being given licenses to marry white women. Jensen, *Passage from India*, 255.

18   Ibid., 264.

19   Vijay Prashad, *The Karma of Brown Folk* (Minneapolis: University of Minnesota Press, 2000), 36.

20   Ngai, "The Architecture of Race in American Immigration Law," 85.

21   Nayan Shah, *Contagious Divides: Epidemics and Race in San Francisco's Chinatown* (Berkeley: University of California Press, 2001), 51.

22   Ibid., 132.

23   Ibid., 127.

24   Ibid., 128.

25   Kevin Mumford, *Interzones: Black/White Sex Districts in Chicago and New York in the Early Twentieth Century* (New York: Columbia University Press, 1997).

26   Shah, *Contagious Divides*, 43.

27   Mary Lui, *The Chinatown Trunk Mystery: Murder, Miscegenation, and Other Dangerous Encounters in Turn-of-the-Century New York City* (Princeton: Princeton University Press, 2005), 8.

28   Ibid., 15.

29 Ibid., 13.
30 Ibid., 11.
31 In California, the proscription on "Mongolians" marrying whites did not clearly apply to Filipinos. This led to an amendment of the state's miscegenation laws in 1933, to reverse an appellate court's ruling in that the law did not apply to Filipinos, who were considered "Malay." The revised code simply added "Malays" to the list of proscribed groups.
32 Nayan Shah, *Stranger Intimacy: Contesting Race, Sexuality, and the Law in the North American West* (Berkeley: University of California Press, 2011).
33 Daniels, *The Politics of Prejudice*, 85.
34 Paul Spickard, *Japanese Americans: The Formation and Transformations of an Ethnic Group*, rev. ed., (New Brunswick: Rutgers University Press, 2009), 64.
35 Rick Baldoz, *The Third Asiatic Invasion: Empire and Migration in Filipino America, 1898–1946* (New York: New York University Press, 2011), 122.
36 Ibid., 130.
37 Ibid., 134.
38 Ibid., 124–125.
39 Shah, *Contagious Divides*, 30.
40 Daniels, *The Politics of Prejudice*, 86.
41 Though the rate was higher, the profile of the Japanese female population, mostly child-bearing age and wives, was much different from the white female population, aged fifteen to forty-five (usually child-bearing age and wives), thus making such comparisons dubious. Ibid., 89.
42 Natalia Molina, *Fit to be Citizens?: Public Health and Race in Los Angeles, 1879–1939* (Berkeley: University of California, 2006), 56, 57.
43 Chan, *Asian Americans*, 57.
44 Ibid., 58.
45 Ibid.
46 Daniels, *The Politics of Prejudice*, 32.
47 Ibid., 47.
48 Jensen, *Passage from India*, 172.
49 Scott Kurashige, *The Shifting Grounds of Race: Black and Japanese Americans in the Making of Multiethnic Los Angeles* (Princeton: Princeton University Press, 2008), 23.
50 Jensen, *Passage from India*, 171.
51 Ibid.
52 Huping Ling, *Chinese St. Louis: From Enclave to Cultural Community* (Philadelphia: Temple University Press, 2004), 25–6.
53 Quoted in Daniels, *The Politics of Prejudice*, 69.
54 Saxton, *The Indispensable Enemy*, 52.
55 Kwong and Miščević, *Chinese America*, 45.
56 Ibid.
57 Saxton, *The Indispensable Enemy*, 74.
58 Daniels, *The Politics of Prejudice*, 33.
59 Ibid.
60 Ibid.
61 Ibid., 28.
62 Molina, *Fit to Be Citizens?*, 36.
63 Ibid., 39.
64 Ibid., 40.
65 Ibid., 34.
66 Ibid., 35.
67 Daniels, *The Politics of Prejudice*, 51.
68 Ibid., 62.
69 Ibid., 64.
70 Ibid., 87.

71 Ibid., 87–8.
72 Ibid., 88.
73 Jensen, *Passage from India*, 258.
74 Kwong and Miščević, *Chinese America*, 45.
75 Saxton, *The Indispensable Enemy*, 72.
76 Ibid.
77 Gyory, *Closing the Gate*, 94.
78 Chan, *Asian Americans*, 49.
79 Jensen, *Passage from India*, 47.
80 Daniels, *The Politics of Prejudice*, 34.
81 Spickard, *Japanese Americans*, 66–7.
82 Baldoz, *The Third Asiatic Invasion*, 140.
83 Ibid., 142.
84 Gyory, *Closing the Gate*, 82.
85 Ibid., 84–5.
86 Ibid., 93.
87 Ibid.
88 Quoted in ibid., 3.
89 Ibid., 166.
90 Ibid., 216.
91 Ibid., 244.
92 Ibid., 250.
93 Ibid., 251.
94 Defining illegal immigration as a criminal offense, the Chinese Exclusion Act held that any person who falsified their identity or secured their certificates fraudulently was guilty of a misdemeanor and would face a $1,000 fine and prison sentence of up to five years. Additionally, anyone who abetted illegal landing could be charged with misdemeanor, fined, and imprisoned. Erika Lee, *At America's Gates: Chinese Immigration During the Exclusion Era, 1882–1943* (Chapel Hill: University of North Carolina Press, 2003), 43.
95 Ibid., 30.
96 Ibid., 45.
97 Ibid., 42.
98 Lee, 44.
99 Lee, 42.
100 Gyory, *Closing the Gate*, 254.
101 Daniels, *The Politics of Prejudice*, 20.
102 Ibid., 21.
103 Ibid., 24.
104 Ibid., 28.
105 Ibid., 27.
106 Ibid., 29.
107 Ibid., 36.
108 Ibid., 44.
109 Ibid., 45.
110 Ibid., 170.
111 Ibid., 174.
112 Jensen, *Passage from India*, 66.
113 Ibid., 101.
114 Ibid., 107.
115 Ibid., 101, 105.
116 Ibid., 104.
117 Erika Lee and Judy Yung, *Angel Island: Immigrant Gateway to America* (New York: Oxford University Press, 2010), 151.

118 Ibid, 158; Jensen, *Passage from India*, 111.
119 Jensen, *Passage from India*, 141.
120 Ibid., 155.
121 Ibid., 156.
122 Ibid.
123 Ibid., 157, 160.
124 Ibid., 158; Shah, *Stranger Intimacy*, 194.
125 Jensen, *Passage from India*, 160.
126 Lee and Yung, *Angel Island*, 170.
127 Daniels, *The Politics of Prejudice*, 91–2.
128 Ibid., 85.
129 Ibid., 86.
130 Ngai, "The Architecture of Race in American Immigration Law," 80.
131 Daniels, *The Politics of Prejudice*, 104.
132 Baldoz, *The Third Asiatic Invasion*, 181.
133 Robert Wiebe, *The Search for Order, 1877–1920* (New York: Macmillan, 1966).
134 Saxton, *The Indispensable Enemy*, 119.
135 Ibid., 118.
136 Gyory, *Closing the Gate*, 169.
137 Ibid., 170.
138 Ibid., 94–5.
139 Ibid., 96.
140 Ibid., 98.
141 Ibid., 99.
142 Patrick Henry McCarthy, head of Building Trades Council of San Francisco, Andrew Furuseth and Walter MacArthur of Sailor's Union. See ibid., 28; Daniels, *The Politics of Prejudice*, 22.
143 Saxton, *The Indispensable Enemy*, 11.
144 Gyory, *Closing the Gate*, 79.
145 Martha Gardner, "Working on White Womanhood: White Working Women in the San Francisco Anti-Chinese Movement, 1877–1890," *Journal of Social History* 33, no. 1 (Fall 1999): 73.

Response and Resistance 6

In June 1885, immigrant and San Francisco laundryman, Yick Wo, applied for a license for his business to comply with an 1880 city ordinance, which required that business owners obtain licenses for washhouses in wooden buildings or face a $1,000 fine or six months in jail. The ordinance was the most recent in over a dozen codes targeting laundries that the Board of Supervisors had enacted since 1873. Furthermore, though their language was neutral, and intentions were apparently to increase public and occupational safety, they were thinly veiled attempts to harass and disenfranchise Chinese laundry owners and employees. As discussed earlier, Chinese laundries became ubiquitous in several major U.S. cities by the turn of the twentieth century. In the 1880s in San Francisco, Chinese ran about three hundred laundries—the majority of such businesses in the city—and employed approximately three thousand workers. All of them, furthermore, were in wooden buildings. The enforcement of the ordinance revealed its discriminatory intent; in 1885, the board rejected all applications from Chinese, while granting all but one of eighty from non-Chinese. One of the rejected applicants was Yick Wo and, two months after his denial, he was arrested and imprisoned.

As the previous chapter has described, the face of anti-Asian racism was manifold, responding to a variety of perceived threats, and taking shape at the local, state, and national levels. What has not yet been addressed is how Asians fought back to protect themselves and demand their rights. In Yick Wo's case, he joined about two hundred other Chinese laundrymen in a class-action suit organized by the laundry guild Tung Hing Tong. A white lawyer was hired to defend the laundrymen, and the suit got underway after Yick filed a writ of habeas corpus. Although he was released from imprisonment, the city appealed, and the case eventually went to the U.S. Supreme Court. Yick's lawyer argued that the ordinance discriminated against him. In particular, he pointed out that dividing laundries arbitrarily into two classes and then enforcing the ordinance in a discriminatory manner amounted to a denial of equal protection and due process as guaranteed by the Fourteenth Amendment of the U.S. Constitution. This protection, furthermore, extended to all persons, including Chinese aliens (Yick had arrived in 1861 and as a Chinese was ineligible for citizenship).[1] In a landmark decision having ramifications for the interpretation and application of the Fourteenth Amendment, the court ruled in the case of *Yick Wo v. Hopkins* (1886) in favor of the plaintiff.

Yick Wo v. Hopkins is among the most well-known litigation cases in Asian American history; not only was it a victory for the underdog, but it also impacted American jurisprudence for decades to come. For those reasons alone, the case is a fitting start to a chapter about Asian American resistance and responses to white racism, but it also exemplifies other underappreciated but equally important aspects of the subject. Many accounts give the impression that Yick Wo was a lone crusader who heroically took on and prevailed over powers that be. While individual courage certainly played a role in his and other cases, resistance was also a function of coordinated and disciplined action by plaintiffs, ethnic associations, diplomatic representatives, and co-ethnic legal brokers, as well as white lawyers and other allies.

Furthermore, stepping back from legal activism in cases like Yick Wo's to consider a larger picture of how Asian immigrants resisted and responded to racism, both their articulations and actions were anything but uniform. Tactics like litigation were intrinsically confrontational and critical of the existing structures of power, and brought Asians into direct engagement with American institutions and authorities. In other cases, immigrants, with the assistance of an elaborate network, opted to evade discriminatory laws rather than launch full-scale assaults on them. They also responded to racism by turning inward and working on building ethnic resources and strengthening homeland ties. Yet others placed the onus on themselves and took actions that betrayed their own internalized prejudices. In the 1890s, for example, Japanese consular officials urged immigrant leaders on the West Coast to "clean up" their communities of "immoral, criminal, irresponsible, and alcoholic" elements, believing that the targets of anti-Japanese racism had brought it upon themselves.[2] The presence of Japanese prostitutes was an especially "deplorable situation" and "cause of public scandals" that in turned resulted in "unnecessary hardship in our endeavor to maintain the reputation of the Japanese as a whole."[3]

The point here is not just that Asians' efforts to overcome racism in America reflected different approaches and philosophies, but also that the history anti-Asian racism cannot be reduced to simply what whites did to Asian people. It is critical to understand how Asians and other targets responded to racism, as it underscores the agency of people on the receiving end of oppressive systems and, perhaps more importantly, how those systems are shored up or subverted. Historian Gary Okihiro has pointed out that, in their pursuit of equality, Asian Americans and others have regularly faced rejection, but this pursuit, in and of itself and regardless of the outcomes along the way, is profoundly significant. As he states, "racial minorities, in their struggles for inclusion and equality, helped to preserve and advance the very privileges that were denied to them, and thereby democratized the nation for the benefit of all Americans."[4] In other words, their fight against discrimination, while demonstrating agency and bringing change into their own lives, also had repercussions for society writ large, transforming its institutions and values, as well as the meanings of American identity.

This chapter examines Asian Americans' responses to racism from the nineteenth through early twentieth centuries. It takes up Okihiro's point that the struggles of people on the "margins" impact the "mainstream" by exploring how Asian Americans' pursuit of equality challenged and clarified interpretations of the law and insisted on a more inclusive democracy. The chapter considers a range of strategies that Asians employed to combat racism, and how approaches differed based on class, ethnicity, place, national origin, and ideological persuasion. What constitutes an act of resistance can be diced in many ways and encompasses everything from suing the state to mouthing off at a supervisor. Furthermore, white racism was just one form of discrimination that Asian immigrants faced. As discussed earlier, class and gender-based oppression within ethnic communities was also salient, but for the purposes of this chapter, I will focus on the responses to racism.

Breaking the Law

Racially discriminatory laws sent a powerful message to Asians about their undesirability while greatly hampering their daily lives. With immigration restrictions, many would-be emigrants in Asia were forced to abandon their plans to come to the United States and go elsewhere or stay home. Proscriptions on landholding and other policies pushed people out of their chosen areas of employment or made it impossible to enter them. Miscegenation statutes, moreover, foreclosed marital prospects based on race. In numerous cases, however, people broke or evaded these laws rather than submit to or let their lives be dictated by them. Asian immigration, for instance, did not end during the exclusion years; people still came via exempt categories, but larger numbers simply entered or stayed illegally. In these and other kinds of cases, disobeying the letter and spirit of legislation that discriminated on the basis of race was, to many Asians in America, a justifiable response to fundamentally unjust treatment.

Its aims notwithstanding, Chinese exclusion failed to close the gates completely; between 1882 and 1943, 300,955 were admitted to the United States.[5] Although this number represents Chinese who gained entry by passing their interrogations, immigration officials believed that a large proportion of these—as many as 90 percent, according to one commissioner—had done so fraudulently.[6] Indeed, one of the unsurprising consequences of federal exclusion was the rise of "illegal" immigration, and because they were the targets of the most restrictive laws, Chinese were singled out as the main problem during much of the late nineteenth and early twentieth centuries. To be sure, those who sought entry at this time were continuing decades-long practices, but the legal regime they encountered across the Pacific had changed greatly, turning once mundane border crossings into criminal acts.

Nonetheless, during the exclusion period, the exigency of migration—whether for jobs or family—and the belief in the unjustness of the laws overrode the legal proscriptions. Many of those who had entered through Angel Island in San Francisco acknowledged the common use of fake papers and identities to gain admission. In addition to presenting documents to pass as a member of an exempt class (e.g., a merchant or child of a U.S. citizen), applicants had to pass rigorous interrogations, and toward this end, people sometimes acquired "coaching books" from agents that contained details about their "paper families" and advice on how to answer questions. Additionally, interpreters employed by steamship companies sometimes took bribes to relay to applicants and witnesses what the interrogation questions would be.[7] In this way, Chinese illegal immigration was a function of highly organized, transnational networks of documents, immigration slots, and information, held together by complicit friends, family, agents, smugglers, and government officials. In turn, the federal government worked to break up these networks by confiscating the fake documents and prosecuting their purveyors. In one case from 1885, the chief clerk of the San Francisco Chinese Bureau's registration office was caught and charged for selling over two hundred certificates of residence to brokers in Hong Kong.[8]

With the proliferation of networks to help otherwise inadmissible Chinese negotiate the border crossing process, illegal immigration became a "normalized" part of life in Chinese American communities and families.[9] As immigrant Arthur Lem explained in an interview, if a person in China at this time expressed his or her intention to go to the United States, a typical response was, "Whose papers are you using?"[10] This reliance on fake identities gave rise to an entire subset of "paper" relatives in the Chinese American population. To describe the experience of one "paper son," Lee Fong You came to the United States in 1922. Prior to leaving China, his father called on the help of a family friend, Fong Norm, who was a U.S. citizen and arranged for Lee to immigrate as Fong Norm's son. Lee took on the name Fong Yoy, memorized the Fong family history, and successfully gained admission to the United States. Although Lee and Fong Norm were not blood relatives, Fong Norm took in his "paper son" and gave him a place to live for a year in Stockton. When another "paper son" arrived a few years later, Lee acted as a witness to his "brother."[11]

The post-earthquake fire of 1906 in San Francisco, in which all of the city's birth records were destroyed, suddenly opened new opportunities for migration that thousands of Chinese took advantage of. Claiming to be a U.S. citizen was the preferred method of seeking entry because it required fewer witnesses than was required for other exempt classes, and with the loss of the city's birth records, it was impossible for officials to verify all individuals' claims of being born in the United States. By the 1930s, returning U.S. citizens were the largest single class of Chinese admitted to the country. The numbers, however, did not line up with Census figures from the years they claimed to have been born in the United States, leading one official to state that there would have to have been "at least ten times as many Chinese women in the country . . . as actually ever have been in this country since the first Chinaman landed on its shore."[12] Once admitted, these individuals could pave the way for others in China to enter as paper relatives. As one official explained, whether a Chinese entered lawfully or fraudulently, "the groundwork is provided for the subsequent coming of another generation . . . and so the process grows by accretion and is never ending."[13]

The success of many Chinese in eluding the exclusionary state and inspectors' scrutiny should not downplay the harshness of immigration restriction. The interrogations and detentions could be agonizing, and thousands, even those representing themselves truthfully, were turned away. Initially, the Chinese Six warned would-be immigrants in China to seek entry through American ports other than San Francisco, which was known to be the toughest port through which to gain admission, but increasingly they also used the "backdoors" of Mexico and Canada. Until the 1920s, when these countries enacted restrictive immigration laws of their own, they were easier to enter. Once within Mexican or Canadian borders, Chinese could seek entry into the United States, whether by claiming to be a member of an exempt class, relying on professional smugglers, or simply walking across an unguarded part of the northern or southern border.[14] At the southern border, reports also surfaced of Chinese trying to pass as Mexican in order to escape immigration inspectors' suspicion. As officials complained of the "open secret" of Chinese clandestine entry from Mexico and Canada, the land borders were tightened, but resourceful immigrants would find other routes. These included Chinese hiding in vessels or pretending to be seamen when landing in Jamaica and then going on to Florida, Louisiana and Mississippi.[15] While such clandestine methods of entry allowed people to avoid the scrutiny of immigration inspectors and their possible detention and rejection, they also meant they would have to live their lives in America in the shadows, always fearful of being caught in a raid, arrested, and deported.

Asian Indians, who were subject to "virtual exclusion" at the port of San Francisco, increasingly sought admission via eastern and southern ports in the United States. Additionally, after the passage of the Immigration Act of 1917, a growing number entered through Central America via the Atlantic and also smuggled themselves across the Mexican border.[16] In 1914 the Bureau of Immigration reported that there were many Indians in Cuba and Panama, "ready to invade the Southern States through the Gulf ports of entry should it appear at all likely that they could gain admission."[17] Another option for Asian Indians was to come by way of Hawaii and the Philippines where examinations were relatively lax. Additionally, a loophole in a 1907 immigration law allowed immigrants entering the United States through its possessions to go onto the mainland without a second examination.[18] Alarmed at the use of these "side doors," immigration officials in Manila warned that 6,000–7,000 South Asians in the Philippines were planning to enter the United States through San Francisco. In response, in December 1911 the Immigration Bureau started requiring all aliens seeking admission to the United States by way of the Philippines to provide proof of examination and admission to the territory. Despite such efforts, the migration of Indians via the Philippines continued. The Philippines side door was eventually closed in 1913 when the exemption from a second examination was lifted and steamship companies agreed to stop selling tickets to South Asian laborers there.[19]

Asian immigrants and white exclusionists viewed illegal immigration very differently. For the former who broke or evaded the laws, such actions were justified because the laws themselves were so unfair. As one Seattle Chinese merchant said to the assistant commissioner of immigration, "It is not wrong, under the Chinese moral law for a Chinaman to swear falsely in support of an application made by a fellow clansman to gain admission into the United States."[20] Immigrants interviewed by the Chinese American sociologist Wen-hsien Chen in 1940 explained that because Chinese people did not enjoy "the same protection and privileges as other races or nationalities," they had little choice but to break the law in order to "keep life going" in the United States.[21] For exclusionists, on the other hand, knowledge of illegal Chinese immigration only affirmed the stereotypes that they were a treacherous and immoral people. Immigration service officials largely worked under the assumption that Chinese applicants were lying and ineligible to enter. Although illegal entry was a general problem arising from the passage of many different immigration laws, other groups were not subject to the same level of suspicion.

Well into the twentieth century, Chinese remained the primary illegal immigrant "problem," but other Asians also turned to evasive and unlawful methods to enter the United States. After the passage of the Johnson-Reed Act of 1924, Japanese illegal immigration increasingly came to the attention of officers, who used similarly invasive interrogation tactics that they had on Chinese to detect fraud. In San Francisco, if an inspector suspected an applicant was lying, the applicant would be held at Angel Island while the claims were verified through interviews with family members and other witnesses.[22] Due to the intense climate of suspicion, people with legal claims to entry, such as the *kibei*, were occasionally denied. Like the Chinese, Japanese frequently turned to lawyers, brokers, or ethnic associations to help them appeal unfavorable decisions, but not always with success. In one case, a Japanese woman named Miyono Nojima, who had originally come to the United States in 1912 as the picture bride of laundry operator Fukujiro Nojima, and settled in Elko, Nevada, sought to reenter in 1931. The couple had gone to Japan in 1915 and, while there, Miyono bore two children. Fukujiro returned to America in 1916 and after two more visits to Japan, made arrangements in 1930 for his wife to join him. However, the length of Miyono's stay in Japan disqualified her status as a "returning" immigrant. With the help of a broker, she obtained a fake visa and was told to say that she departed from Seattle and had been in Japan for less than a year. During the interrogation, she broke down and was subsequently denied admission in October 1931, on the grounds that she was neither a returning resident nor a non-quota immigrant, and by lying she was guilty of a crime of moral turpitude.[23] Despite the intervention of powerful attorney Mark Coleman of Thomas, Beedy, Presley, and Paramore, the decision was unchanged.

Another response to exclusion was to test the restrictive laws with the goal of overturning them or at least bringing attention to their unfairness. A case involving Asian Indians that occurred in western Canada in 1914 illustrates immigrant activism and the transnational and cross-border networks that they forged and relied on to build their struggle. Gurdit Singh, a Sikh immigrant who became a wealthy contractor in British Columbia, chartered a Japanese vessel called the *Komagata Maru* to challenge Canada's "continuous journey" law. Enacted in 1908, the law aimed to curb Indian immigration by barring the entry of persons who did not arrive from their country of birth or citizenship by a "continuous journey." The long distance between India and Canada required ships traveling between these points to make stops at places like Japan and Hawaii. In May, the *Komagata Maru*, carrying several hundred Indians from Punjab, arrived in Vancouver harbor. Because the ship originated in Hong Kong and had other stops in Asia prior to reaching Vancouver, none of the Indian passengers met the continuous journey requirement. A small number of returning residents were permitted to land, but the rest remained on the ship, which faced food shortages and remained in the harbor. Members of the Vancouver Sikh community protested, but British and Canadian authorities were unsympathetic, and in July, the *Komagata Maru* set sail back to Hong Kong with most of its original passengers. Although it ended in defeat, the incident had a powerful impact on Indians on the West Coast, galvanizing some to fight discrimination in North America and inspiring others to return to India to work for its independence.

In other cases, Asian immigrants did not have to resort to breaking or testing exclusion laws; instead they simply utilized loopholes in them. One group that did so with notable success was Japanese farmers in western states with alien land laws. In California, after the passage of the first of such Acts in 1913, Issei continued to farm under arrangements such as leasing or placing land in the name of U.S.-born children. Although such actions did not violate the letter of the law, they certainly went against its spirit, as alien land laws were designed to push Japanese out of farming, so legislators responded by tightening the laws. This simply resulted in Issei adapting and finding new loopholes. These included so-called middlemen agreements in which an adult U.S. citizen (the "middleman") would lease farmland on which a Japanese, under the title "manager" or "foreman," took charge of all the farming duties and financial burdens.[24] Such arrangements were risky for the Issei, as they were based entirely on mutual trust. Until the 1930s, there were few adult Nisei who had been born on the continent, so as a result, many of the middlemen agreements were between Issei farmers and non-Japanese or Hawaiian-born Nisei whom they did not know very well. Because of these relatively weak ties, it was not uncommon for the middlemen to blackmail the farmers for higher fees. Another adaptation by Issei was to farm on land leased by companies. In 1926, there were 415 such companies involved with Japanese farmers, mostly in northern and central California. One of these was the Lodi Corporation, which had been established in the California town of the same name in 1926. The local Japanese Association managed its 1,026 acres of land and some 29 Issei farmed under the corporation's auspices.[25]

Strengthening Ourselves and the Homeland

Faced with the sobering fact that racism was simply a part of the fabric of American life, Asian immigrants understood that attaining full rights and belonging would be elusive at best. Whether acting on demoralization, indignation, or strategy, many responded to incidents of racial hostility by turning inward to seek strength and sustenance in family relationships, community resources, and homeland politics. Such actions did not necessarily underscore disengagement with American society, but rather a critique of it and its racial customs. They also revealed immigrants' belief that bettering their futures in America depended at least in part on developing internal resources and maintaining connections with their countries of origin.

During the movements against them, Chinese and Japanese immigrants often looked to their homeland governments and diplomatic representatives to advocate for them. Perceiving an intrinsic link between international diplomacy and domestic race relations, they believed a stronger China or Japan would command the respect of American officials, and in turn result in better treatment of immigrants in the United States. In 1876, huigan presidents in San Francisco wrote to a Chinese official in Washington, D.C. to ask for his help in dealing with racial hostility. In his response, which appeared in *The Oriental*, the official said the absence of a consulate office in the city explained "why the Chinese were bullied," and recommended that San Francisco's Chinese request the establishment of one.[26] Immigrants' hopes for diplomatic action on their behalf, especially during the years of Qing rule, were often disappointed, however, due to China's weak place in the international community.[27] For many this was illustrated in April 1886, when the Chinese minister to America, Zhang Yinhuan, tried to enter the United States through San Francisco and immigration officials initially blocked him.[28]

Although the Chinese government lacked the diplomatic muscle to prevent the passage of anti-Chinese laws and other forms of discrimination against its subjects in the United States, diplomats worked to protect immigrants in other ways. In 1875, two ministers to America were appointed in Washington, D.C. in 1875 and, six years later, a consul general was installed in San Francisco.[29] Accepting the reality of Chinese exclusion, they lobbied instead for the fair enforcement of laws and treatment of immigrants. In 1900, for instance, minister Wu Ting-fang wrote to the U.S. Secretary of State to complain that Chinese immigrants at Angel Island were "entirely at the mercy of inquisitors, who . . . are generally unfriendly, if not positively hostile, to them."[30] China representatives also worked to secure justice for victims of racial violence. After the infamous anti-Chinese riot in Rock Springs, Wyoming in 1885, minister Zheng Zhaoru sent a delegation that included the New York consul Huang Sih Chuen and American lawyer Frederick Bee to investigate and collect eyewitness accounts about the incident. Their findings were included in a report to Congress, but when authorities failed to punish any of the rioters, Zheng asserted constitutional and treaty obligations to demand indemnity, and eventually the United States agreed to pay $150,000 to cover property losses from the riot.[31] Throughout his tenure from 1881 to 1885, Zheng and other ministers took seriously the job of defending the rights of Chinese immigrants, and in addition to working to improve the treatment of Chinese by immigration inspectors and seeking compensation for victims of violence, they were active in fighting discrimination against laundry workers and trying to stop the trafficking of Chinese women. Although Zheng was successful in many of his cases, he was demoralized by the lawlessness and violence against Chinese and eventually requested a transfer.

Meanwhile, by the turn of the twentieth century, China's humiliations in the international arena had fueled a nationalist movement to modernize and strengthen the country, which struck a chord with Chinese Americans who believed that a strong China could more effectively champion the rights of immigrants. A boycott of American goods led by Chinese merchants in 1905 solidified ties between nationalist reformers in China and their brethren in the United States, and affirmed Chinese Americans' understanding of the links between homeland politics, international relations, and U.S. race relations.[32] The boycott was forged against the backdrop of mounting tensions over exclusion and discrimination against Chinese of all classes, and a breaking point came just after the turn of the twentieth century. One issue was the renewal of the 1894 Sino–American treaty, which anti-Qing reformers strongly opposed, as it sanctioned the exclusion of Chinese laborers and acknowledged right of the United States to deny naturalization to Chinese. Another key development was the disgraceful treatment of Chinese performers and exhibitors at the St. Louis World's Fair of 1904, which surprised those who had assumed anti-Chinese discrimination was directed only at laborers.[33] Legal setbacks also intensified calls to protest the actions of U.S. officials against the Chinese, and the Supreme Court's ruling in *Ju Toy v. United States* (1905) proved pivotal. In this case, the court stated that federal district courts could not hear Chinese admission cases, effectively closing off one of the main channels for successfully appealing applicant rejections.

The idea for an economic boycott emerged from the realization that China lacked the diplomatic pull to compel the United States to repeal exclusion. Shortly after the St. Louis World's Fair, Wong Kai Kah, the vice commissioner of the Chinese exhibition, issued a statement to Americans in the *North American Times* warning of a possible retaliation by China to "the businessmen and statesmen of the West and of the Pacific Coast, whose growth and prosperity will be measured by the extent of American trade with the Orient."[34] Although merchants in China led the boycott, which was hampered by poor coordination and internal division, and ultimately had little effect on trade or policies, the movement did draw wide support from reform-minded Chinese living abroad. Among Chinese in the United States, supporting the boycott strengthened their homeland nationalism and belief that conditions in America would not improve unless China's international standing did. Notably, the boycott did result in some concessions around the enforcement of exclusion. Acknowledging, "grave injustices and wrongs have been done to this nation and to the people of China," President Theodore Roosevelt directed officials to refrain from unduly harsh treatment of Chinese applicants.[35] Immigration authorities also discontinued the Bertillion system of identification, a humiliating body measurement system originally used in the control of prisoners that was also used on Chinese at Angel Island.[36]

Japanese Americans, especially during the 1930s, also held the view that a strong home-land would mitigate racism and lead to their acceptance in America. For its part, Japan, although sensitive to how outsiders perceived its subjects, was inconsistent in responding to anti-Japanese racism. To be sure, diplomatic intervention in the 1906 San Francisco School Board controversy had been decisive, and officials in Japan vocally protested the Johnson-Reed Act, but in these and other cases Japan was not motivated so much by outrage over the unjust treatment of its subjects as its desire to maintain its standing in the international community. It was quiet on the issue of Japanese ineligibility for U.S. naturalization and failed to press the matter during the negotiations leading to the Gentlemen's Agreement and 1911 U.S.–Japan Treaty of Commerce and Navigation. Nonetheless, as Japan embarked on its militaristic course over the 1930s, many Issei felt a surge of homeland patriotism and organized fundraising and care package drives for Japanese soldiers, which they had also done during the Sino–Japanese and Russo–Japanese wars.[37] Through such demonstrations of nationalism, immigrants solidified their attachments to their homeland and participated in Asian geopolitics, but they also shored up intraethnic ties and leadership positions within Japanese America. For example, many Nisei as well as Americanized Issei capitalized on Japan's rise and the changing dynamics of U.S.–Japan relations by positioning themselves as cultural and political "translators" with intimate knowledge about both Japan and America. They hoped the understanding they could foster would, in turn, diminish Americans' anti-Japanese prejudice. In this sense, explains Eiichiro Azuma, "helping Japan thus became tantamount to helping themselves."[38]

The situation was different for Koreans, Indians, and Filipinos, who could not look to their homeland governments and diplomatic relations to improve their lives in America, as their countries of origin were under colonial control. Filipinos' circumstances were especially complicated because their homeland was a U.S. territory. The life of intellectual Carlos Romulo illustrates the difficult and ambivalent negotiations that faced Filipinos who sought to reconcile their U.S. loyalty—or colonial mentality—and Philippine nationalism.[39] Born in 1899 in Camiling, Tarlac, Romulo was educated in the Philippine system that extolled American values while reserving admiration for "acceptable" Filipino leaders. He attended Columbia University on a government scholarship from 1918 to 1921, and during these years experienced both anti-black and anti-Filipino racism and strongly embraced the cause of Philippine independence, for instance organizing a rally to memorialize Jose Rizal. After completing his education, he returned to the Philippines to serve in the political machine of Senate President Manuel Quezon, who would be elected President of the Commonwealth in 1935. Although a champion of Philippine nationalism, Romulo maintained his admiration for the United States, which led critics to accuse him of being an "architect of subservience" with a "fawning attitude toward Americans." This awkward mix of allegiances manifested in statements such as the following, made by Romulo in 1923: "We stand at the crossroads, uncertain but unafraid, the future imaged forth in our one supreme aspiration to freedom, the present a recessional that our faith in America shall not die."[40]

Regarding Asian Indians, the British government was silent during congressional hearings in the United States to restrict South Asian migration, although it tacitly supported exclusion due to its concern about the Indian nationalist movement spreading to North America.[41] While this meant that Indian immigrants could not turn to a homeland government to fight against their mistreatment, for many individuals as well as diasporic organizations, this circumstance only strengthened their commitment to anti-colonialism and determination to eventually return to an independent India. After the Bellingham riot, for example, Saint Nihal Singh, a New York-based Indian journalist, wrote an article appearing in a Calcutta-based journal in which he called on Indian migrants to take up "the brown man's burden" to assert their self-determination and liberate themselves from both colonialism at home and racism abroad.[42] Additionally, the Ghadar Party theorized, through its publication *Ghadar*, which circulated out of San Francisco and reached readers in Asia, Europe, Africa, and Latin America, that the racial exclusion of Indians—in the United States as well as settler colonies across the Pacific—was linked to colonial subjugation.[43] Taraknath Das articulated similar ideas in his journal *Free Hindustan*. Speaking to the situation in Canada in 1908, he urged Indians to resist exclusion and warned the British imperial government that continued injustice would lead to "an upheaval which will rend the Empire to pieces."[44] In 1911 representatives from organizations including the United League of India and Khalsa Diwan Society expressed to the Ottawa government that racial violence in Canada "was not local" but "in their very nature Empire question[s]" would be a "strong weapon in the hands" of those demanding self-rule.[45] Aside from addressing fellow Indians in the diaspora or protesting to the Canadian and U.S. governments, activists took more direct action. From 1914 to 1918, 500 to 900 Indians from the United States and Canada joined about 8,000 Indians from Panama, the Philippines, Hong Kong, Shanghai, and elsewhere in returning to India to help overthrow British rule.[46] This movement aroused enough concern among British authorities that in 1914 they passed an ordinance restricting the entry of foreigners—including Indians who had been living abroad—to India. The following year India was placed under martial law and its government was given special powers to deal with revolutionary threats.

Korean immigrants' critique of colonialism was somewhat narrower; they condemned Japan's actions and, like Asian Indians, threw much energy and resources into the struggle to liberate their homeland, but the leaders of this community did not draw the same links between American racism and colonialism. The situation in Korea was distinct from colonialism in India because the imperial power was another Asian nation. Encounters with domestic racism strengthened the resolve of many immigrants to free Korea so that they could return to their homeland. One of the major priorities for Koreans throughout the diaspora was to supplant Japanese authorities by organizing their own bodies to represent their interests.

Toward these ends, Koreans worked mainly through the Korean National Association (KNA). Established in 1909, the KNA also provided critical assistance for immigrants in various locations. It had, for instance, helped about one thousand Korean former contract laborers in Yucatan, Mexico who sought escape from the country due to the Mexican Revolution. KNA representatives went to Mexico to assist the Koreans and they eventually arranged with the HSPA to have them sent to Hawaii to work on plantations.[47] The KNA's work also had a strong nationalist orientation. In the United States, the organization came to wide attention in 1913 following an incident in which Korean fruit pickers were driven out of the town of Hemet, California by a group of whites. Because of Korea's colonial status, Japanese consular officials from Los Angeles tried to represent the Koreans, a gesture that the KNA rejected. In a telegram to Secretary of State William Jennings Bryan, President David Lee said, "Please regard us not as Japanese in time of peace and war. We Koreans came to America before Japan's annexation of Korea and will never submit to her so long as the sun remains in heaven."[48] Bryan responded that any matter dealing with Koreans in the United States should be addressed to the KNA.[49] With the establishment of the Korean Provisional Government in Shanghai in 1919 by political exiles, diasporic Koreans in North America and elsewhere were further wedded to nationalism and united by the struggles for independence from Japan and survival of the Korean people.

The Logistics of Resistance and the Role of Brokers and Allies

Fighting against discrimination was often a struggle waged from below, but it also relied on people in the middle, that is members of relatively privileged classes who sympathized with or were otherwise motivated to challenge the dominant structures of power. These included elite Asians, or members of the broker class, whose personal interests were often at odds with those of the immigrant masses, but nonetheless had the networks that were instrumental to challenging the system. Others were white Americans. Indeed, the help of others was critical for any group denied the full privileges and rights of citizenship and treated as social outcasts. Although the white Americans who opposed anti-Asian policies sometimes viewed Asian people condescendingly and were not always motivated by a belief in racial equality, their voices were nonetheless important because they commanded more respect and attention than ordinary Asians could. However, some were moved by a principle of fairness and basic human dignity. For example, during Congressional debates about restricting Chinese immigration, Senator George Frisbie Hoar, a Republican from Massachusetts, objected to legislative exclusion on the basis that it was a "violation of the ancient policy of the American Republic" and "of the rights of human nature itself."[50]

Asians turned to co-ethnic brokers, lawyers, and other middlemen to help them negotiate or evade the maze of legal hoops and obstacles they faced. For instance, after entering Seattle by way of Japan in 1906, Indian activist Taraknath Das got a job with the U.S. immigration service in Vancouver, and through his post was able to coach other immigrants on how to pass interrogations and help detained Indians initiate habeas corpus proceedings.[51] In Canada, Chinese legal brokers provided interpretation and other services for immigrants, and although they were limited in what they could do—they faced racial bars to serving as lawyers and sitting on juries, for example—their work was crucial. One of these brokers, David Lew, was commonly referred to in his community as a "Chinese lawyer," even though he was not actually a lawyer. His clients included Lee Ghia, who went to Lew in 1908 because he feared being deported for using another man's documents. Assuring Lee that "everything has followed as planned, and all will be okay," Lew collected information, wrote briefs, and made arrangements with Anglo attorneys.[52] Brokers and middlemen like David Lew held a critical place in Asian communities in Canada as well as the United States, as they represented crucial links between immigrants and dominant structures. According to Lisa Mar, Chinese legal interpreters in Canada "helped to offset Anglo power in the legal system . . . that increased their Chinese clients' chances of effective representation."[53]

Helping immigrants navigate the legal system created opportunities for these middlemen—Asian and non-Asian—to profit and amass power, sometimes through fraud and graft. Clarkson Dye had become acquainted with San Francisco's Chinese community by selling insurance in Chinatown and, with the passage of exclusion laws, was able to expand his business into immigration broker services.[54] Moreover, the passage of anti-Chinese immigration laws in Canada and the United States created opportunities for individuals to increase their power by helping people evade or break the law. In Canada, for instance, interpreter Yip On helped thousands of Chinese gain entry using false papers and defraud the government of $1 million in head taxes between 1906 and 1910.[55]

With regard to non-Asians, attorneys were perhaps the most important resources for immigrants seeking to navigate or challenge the law. Prior to exclusion, the Chinese Six Companies, the consulate, and individual Chinese immigrants of all class backgrounds relied on American lawyers to help them with the entry process and to contest laws.[56] On immigration cases, especially in appealing rejections, a lawyer's assistance could be vital, as they could point out the flaws in an official judgment and get unfavorable decisions reversed. Thomas Riordan, whom the Chinese consulate retained for high profile cases, represented many Chinese seeking to enter through San Francisco during the 1880s and 1890s. Also prominent in this regard in the early 1900s were George McGowan and Alfred Worley.[57] These and other attorneys had notable success in overturning individual denials through the federal courts. Their extensive experience working on Asian immigration cases gave them a unique understanding of exclusion legislation, and many in turn became outspoken opponents of anti-Asian policies. These included Oliver Stidger, a lawyer who had worked on many Chinese cases and later published a pamphlet criticizing the Johnson-Reed Act of 1924.

Attorney Frederick Bee was active in helping Chinese secure justice for racial violence during the late 1800s. His first major case involved filing suit on behalf of the Chinese residents driven out of Placer County in 1877 to recover losses in property. A former forty-niner and merchant, Bee was one of the few attorneys who represented Chinese in the San Francisco congressional hearings in 1877, and was appointed to a three-year term as Chinese consul at San Francisco in 1879.[58] In addition to representing victims in the incidents at Placer County and Rock Springs, he investigated, in his capacity as an attorney and consul, outbreaks in Denver, Rocklin, and Truckee, often appealing to government officials. Demanding the protection of Chinese immigrants, he wrote to Governor William Irwin in the wake of a purge in Rocklin, California in September 1877, "I have no desire to point out your plain duty. You have abundant precedent . . . whereby the state and national authorities have put down mob violence. The Chinaman who has come under here under solemn treaty obligations has a right to demand that his life and his property shall be protected the same as that of citizens of the most favored nation."[59]

Christian organizations and spokesmen were among the most consistent defenders of Asian immigrants over the years. In the early 1900s in San Francisco the YMCA had a full-time immigration secretary to assist Asians with their applications, and the Presbyterian Mission Home regularly intervened on behalf of Chinese immigrants and returnees. Donaldina Cameron, the director of the Mission Home, who also gained fame for her work "rescuing" Chinese prostitutes, was especially active, often meeting with immigrants who were waiting on their decisions, serving as a witness on their behalf, and sending appeals to officials for speedy decisions. Moreover, those who had helped Chinese immigrants often continued their work with other Asians. Otis Gibson, who helped Japanese immigrants found the Gospel Society, had previously been an active opponent of the anti-Chinese movement.

Other prominent friends of Japanese immigrants included Sidney Gulick, a member of the Commission on Relations with Japan of the Federal Council of Churches of Christ, Herbert Johnson, superintendent of Japanese Methodist Episcopal Mission, Ernest Sturge, super-intendent of Japanese Presbyterian Mission, and Harvey Guy, professor at Pacific School of Religion. In addition to helping Asian immigrants through various forms of aid, religious figures would defend them against racist accusations, for instance disputing charges that they were unassimilable. Speaking up for Japanese in the midst of the anti-Japanese movement, Sidney Gulick said, "whoever will consider the efforts put forth by Japanese leaders and also by the rank and file to adapt themselves to the conditions of life here, to learn our ways, and conform to our standards will surely realize that much has already been done and that the prospects for the future are hopeful."[60]

White Christian leaders were important allies because they not only helped to coordinate services, but as religious figures, they brought a moral loftiness to their work with Asian immigrants. Women missionaries such as Donaldina Cameron, Rose Livingston of New York, and Katherine Maurer, who worked on Angel Island, drew on their female moral authority in their efforts to assist Asians. For their work helping and "rescuing" immigrants, Livingston and Maurer were known, respectively, as the "angel of Chinatown" and the "angel of Angel Island."[61]

Korean Americans' struggle for the independence of their homeland from Japan gained attention and sympathy from Americans in part due to the support they drew from American missionaries. As described in earlier chapters, Christian missionaries in Korea had been influential among Korean immigrants to Hawaii and the United States, and the U.S.-based leaders of the independence movement, such as Syngman Rhee, were by and large western educated and devout Christians. As leaders of the Korean Congress, a body formed in Philadelphia in 1916 to mobilize support for the Korean independence movement and new government, they lobbied U.S. officials, often while invoking American ideals and comparing Korea's plight to that of the thirteen colonies during the Revolution.[62] Doing so, as well as constantly invoking Christianity in their speeches and writings, was designed to give Koreans the moral upper hand while aligning them with Americans. An organization that worked closely with the Congress was the League of the Friends of Korea, formed in June 1919. This group had strong ties to American missionaries in Korea and worked to raise U.S. support for democracy and Christianity in East Asia.[63] These missionaries, however, shied away from trying to directly influence U.S. policy toward Korean inde-pendence, focusing instead on bringing attention to Korea's plight under Japanese rule. Influential sources included the report, *The Korean Situation: Authentic Accounts of Recent Events by Eye Witnesses* (1919), by William Haven and Sidney Gulick, which was written under the auspices of the Commission on Relations with the Orient for the Federal Council of Churches of Christ in America.[64]

Though they defended Asians in America, white Christians could also be also very condescending toward them. Reverend Henry Ward Beecher, for instance, said that Americans should welcome Chinese immigrants because they did the "underwork" of society.[65] In 1877, Otis Gibson wrote a book titled, *The Chinese in America*, which, while a defense of Chinese, said that they were heathens who could only be elevated through learning English and Christianity. He stated, "A door has been opened into the shady chambers of his mind and soul," and they will "be aroused to intellectual activity, to a higher and better culture, and to a new spiritual life."[66] It was on this basis, furthermore, that Gibson argued against Chinese exclusion, as permitting them to enter the country would be beneficial for their enlightenment and give American Christians a chance to bring "paganism in actual contact with the best form of Christian civilization."[67] Further, the reliance of some Asians on Christian representatives to speak on their behalf undermined their own agency. Although it was a central part of their strategy, Koreans' dependence on American missionaries to champion their cause of homeland independence often resulted in the marginalization of Koreans' own voices. This was illustrated, for example, in the lack of Korean figures participating in U.S. Congressional hearings after the Korean Congress.[68]

Going with the Flow

Some Asians sought improved treatment through strategies that fell short of challenging or even criticizing racist laws and practices. With the growing realization that Chinese exclusion would not be overturned, Chinese merchants, citizens, and other members of exempt groups tended to focus protesting on their own behalf instead of all Chinese, and frequently invoked their class and citizenship distinctions to support their applications. In 1899, for example, Lee Fook's attorney appealed his case to the secretary of the treasury and said he was a "gentleman of elegant leisure," whom the exclusion laws were not intended to restrict.[69]

Tacitly accepting the inferiority of lower class Chinese and often taking exception to being called "coolies," people and organizations would invoke their more "honorable" status that purportedly entitled them to better treatment.[70] In 1911 the Down Town Association of San Francisco, a group representing Chinese businessmen, sent a ten-page memorial to President William Howard Taft in which they decried the treatment of merchants on Angel Island and warned that U.S.–China relations and trade were at stake if conditions did not improve.[71] In 1910, the Chinese American citizens group, the Native Sons of the Golden State, sent a letter to the secretary of commerce and labor, in which it protested "oppressive and unjust" immigration laws, but reserved its outrage on behalf of "the native born citizen of Chinese parentage."[72] These limited tactics were often effective, as the Bureau of Immigration responded to such complaints with new procedures that simplified the examination process for members of exempt classes.[73]

In Japanese American communities, elite Issei leaders, Japanese associations, and religious figures, often with input from officials in Japan, advocated accommodation and assimilation to deal with discrimination. Rather than condemn American racism against Japanese people, the Japanese Association sought, as early as 1911, to reach out to whites through education campaigns, as it believed racial prejudice was the result of ignorance that could be easily corrected. Moreover, rather than fight and resist, Japanese were encouraged to gain acceptance and be inconspicuous by acting respectably, learning English, dressing in Western clothing, making homes look American, and eliminating vices such as gambling and prostitution from the community. Also as part of their acculturation, wives were instructed to walk next to their husbands, not behind them, workers were advised to observe the Sabbath as a day of rest, and all were told to celebrate American national holidays.[74] Eager to stamp out activities that reflected poorly on the ethnic community, Japanese leaders organized their own anti-vice campaigns while also cooperating with local police. Framing their work as moral crusades, Japanese associations and immigrant units within the Salvation Army led anti-gambling drives in nearly every Japanese settlement in the early 1900s, which included circulating literature about the harmful effects of gambling and shaming individuals whose lives were destroyed by it. Through its Committee for the Eradication of Gambling, formed in 1912, the Japanese Association of America required local chapters to compile blacklists of gamblers, publish their names in the vernacular press, and notify family members in Japan about behavior.[75]

As part of the anti-gambling campaigns carried out by the Japanese Association, Issei were particularly urged not to visit Chinese gambling houses, which was also part of a larger strategy to disassociate Japanese from Chinese.[76] Not being mistaken for Chinese was a central preoccupation for many Issei, starting with the first student laborers, and this sometimes led them to accommodate anti-Chinese racism. "From the student-laborers' point of view," explains Yuji Ichioka, "Americans had excluded the Chinese, understandably and justifiably, because the Chinese were lower class laborers who had not adapted themselves to American society."[77] As one student laborer in 1892 commented about San Francisco Chinatown, "a world of beasts in which, behind its outward façade, exists every imaginable depravity, crime, and vice known to the human world."[78] Disassociation from Chinese stemmed from Japan as well. In 1885 Yukichi Fukuzawa wrote an essay in *Jiji Shimpo* that called on Japan to divorce itself from China and Korea. He saw those two countries as "mired hopelessly in a conservative tradition and therefore doomed to perpetual backwardness."[79] Many Americans did not care, however, and saw Japanese as just as bad, if not worse, than Chinese. Community leaders and diplomats would describe Japanese immigrant laborers as "Sinified," a "degenerated class," "dirt peasants," and "ignorant fools."[80] "From a Japanese perspective," explains Yuji Ichioka, "Americans perceived Chinese immigrants as unassimilable aliens, in part, because the Chinese had refused to adopt American clothing."[81] Labor contractors like Tanaka Tadashichi insisted that railroad workers wear American work clothes and eat American food to differentiate themselves from the Chinese.[82]

Issei spokesmen tried to project through example their ideal of respectability and assimilation. These included men like Kiyoshi Kawakami and Yamato Ichihashi. Kawakami was born in 1879 and came to the United States in 1901 as a student, earned a master's in political science at the University of Iowa, and then worked in the United States as a journalist and writer. From 1914 to 1920 he directed the Pacific Press Bureau, a news agency controlled by the Japanese government, and in this capacity was an unofficial publicist for the Japanese Foreign Ministry. Kawakami often made his case for Japanese assimilability by comparing them to Chinese, arguing that Issei "were not plagued by so-called hatchet men whose deeds strike 'terror in the hearts of all denizens . . . of Chinatown.'"[83] He insisted, "Issei especially impressed upon American-born children to show good Americanism," and that the U.S.-born "caught the Yankee spirit" and "disdainfully call the newcomers from Japan 'Japs.'"[84] Yamato Ichihashi came to the United States in 1894 at 16, attended public school in San Francisco and earned bachelor's and master's degrees from Stanford in 1907 and 1908. In 1913, he completed a Ph.D. at Harvard and taught at Stanford until 1943. A scholar who did research about Japanese immigrants in the West and an active figure in the campaign to eradicate racism by educating Americans, Ichihashi was commissioned by the Japanese Association of America to write a pamphlet called *Japanese Immigration: Its Status in California*

(1913 and expanded in 1915). In it, he said that Japanese were not "coolies," but young men and women with much capital and eagerness to become American.[85]

Issei leaders' belief that education and understanding could defeat racism partly explains why the Johnson-Reed Act of 1924 was so crushing for Japanese Americans and deeply offensive to the Japanese government. Prior to 1924, Japanese immigration was regulated mainly by diplomatic agreements, and many categories of people could still enter the United States. With the 1924 Act, however, all Japanese immigration was abruptly terminated by a unilateral action of the United States. Reaction from Japan was very emotional, with mass rallies held throughout the country.[86] Immigrant newspapers in the United States also expressed their shock, particularly their indignation that the Act effectively lumped Japan with other Asian countries whom they deemed inferior. As Yuji Ichioka has pointed out, during the Japanese exclusion movement, Issei leaders repeatedly said, "We are afraid that we will be excluded as the Chinese have been."[87] With the Johnson-Reed Act their fears materialized.

Confronting the Law, Expanding Democracy

When racism endangered their livelihoods and principles, Asian immigrants sometimes chose the path of greatest resistance, that is, protesting and challenging laws and practices they believed were unjust. This was not merely a way of protecting individual and group interests; these struggles, especially those that couched their protests in terms of the Fourteenth Amendment, clarified and expanded constitutional protections available to all persons, and, thus, had broad and lasting consequences.

As discussed earlier, many Asians in America recognized the fundamental injustice of laws that singled them out for discrimination. While some focused their protests to how the laws were enforced, others criticized the laws themselves. In 1892 Yung Hen, a Chinese poultry dealer in San Francisco asked a newspaper reporter: "Why do they not legislate against Swedes, Germans, Italians, Turks and others? There are no strings on these people . . . For some reason, you people persist in pestering the Chinamen."[88] Chinese protested the overcrowded and poorly ventilated conditions in which immigrants were detained in the Pacific Mail Steamship Company shed in Pier 40, where they were kept while their applications were reviewed. One called Americans "barbarians" for subjecting humans to such deplorable conditions.[89] The outrage eventually led to the opening of Angel Island immigration station in 1910. However, immigration officials were generally unsympathetic to Chinese criticisms and often responded by criticizing the Chinese in kind. As Frank Sargent, the Commissioner-General of Immigration, once said, any mistreatment of Chinese in the screening process was due to the "failure of the Chinese themselves to comply with the provisions of the law."[90]

Chinese immigrants have a storied legacy with regard to Constitutional challenges to racially discriminatory laws. Their numerous victories against local, state, and federal authorities had far-reaching significance not just for Chinese American communities, but also for the interpretation and enforcement of the Constitution itself. One of the most significant challenges dealt with the issue of birthright citizenship. The Chinese Exclusion Act affirmed the ineligibility of Chinese immigrants for U.S. citizenship, but the status of those born in the United States remained unclear. Politicians wanted to extend the denial of naturalization to this group, using the charge that, regardless of where they were born, they were incapable of assimilating. *Look Tin Sing*, a habeus corpus case involving an American-born Chinese who was denied reentry in 1884 after a period of studying in China, was the first to weigh in on birthright citizenship. The immigration official who rejected Look Tin Sing did so on the grounds that the exclusion Act did not list U.S.-born Chinese as an exempt class. The decision was appealed to the U.S. District Court for the Northern District of California, which reversed the original ruling and said Section 1 the Fourteenth Amendment provided that "all persons born or naturalized in the United States" are citizens.

Exclusionists hoped to overturn this ruling, and saw an opportunity with the case of Wong Kim Ark. Born in San Francisco in 1873, Wong sought reentry after a visit to China in 1895, something he had done successfully before. The collector, who happened to be anti-Chinese, refused him admission based on his belief that Wong, as the child of parents ineligible for citizenship, was also not a citizen. Wong hired attorney Thomas Riordan and filed a writ of habeas corpus in federal district court, saying he had been unlawfully confined and that he was a citizen under the Fourteenth Amendment. The question before the court was whether U.S.-born Chinese were citizens even if their parents were ineligible for citizenship. The attorney arguing against Wong said that his citizenship was an accident of birth, and that he could not be considered American because he had been "at all times, by reason of his race, language, color, and dress, a Chinese person."[91] The attorney also warned that to accept Wong as an American would imperil "the existence of our Country."[92] The U.S. District Court of the Northern District of California refuted this argument and ruled in favor of Wong, and in 1898 the U.S. Supreme Court upheld the lower court's decision. Stating that all persons born in the United States regardless of race were native-born citizens, the Court upheld the principle of birthright citizenship as a guarantee of the Fourteenth Amendment.

Meanwhile, for Japanese immigrants, until the 1910s, naturalization was not a major preoccupation. Yuji Ichioka explains that Issei leaders felt torn on the issue, as some believed that pursuing American citizenship would reflect a lack of Japanese allegiance.[93] Things changed after 1913, however, after California passed its first alien land law. Because this law heightened the material stakes of being excluded from citizenship and threatened the economic livelihoods of thousands of Issei farmers, Japanese Americans took action, and over the 1910s the Japanese Association of America and its affiliates came to embrace the goal of citizenship. They did not always have the support of the Japanese government or diplomats in this struggle, however. In 1913, the Japanese ambassador in Washington, D.C., Chinda Sutemi, appealed to American officials (at the urging of an Issei delegation from California), but after being rebuffed and assured that naturalization and land tenure were domestic matters outside of the realm of diplomacy, he dropped the matter.[94] Seeing the writing on the wall, the *Nichibei Shimbun* called on Japanese Americans to mobilize and solve their own problems, stating in 1916, "We. . .must reorient ourselves. We must become independent and self-reliant. We must resolve to solve all problems which lie in our path by ourselves. With such a resolution, we must exert ourselves and struggle on to share our own future."[95]

Through much of the 1910s and 1920s Japanese Americans embarked on a crusade to secure naturalization rights and challenge the alien land laws, with much of the coordination provided by Japanese associations. In 1914, association leaders on the West Coast formed the Japanese Association Deliberative Council. In 1916, the naturalization case of Takao

Ozawa, which by that time was in appeal, came to the Deliberative Council's attention. Seen as a paragon of assimilation and thus an ideal test case on naturalization, his suit was closely followed by the immigrant press from the summer of 1917, after the Ninth Circuit Court of Appeals in San Francisco referred the case to the U.S. Supreme Court. Despite the discouragement of the Japanese government, which refused to support Ozawa, the Deliberative Council pushed ahead by forming a naturalization committee. It worked with Ozawa's attorney and retained George Wickersham, a former U.S. Attorney General, as the primary counsel. The case was delayed twice due to diplomatic concerns during World War I, and even some Japanese American newspapers recommended delaying a naturalization test case, as a negative outcome would be a major setback.[96] Two companion cases from Washington State were added and were decided in accordance with *Ozawa*. As discussed in the previous chapter, the U.S. Supreme Court ruled that Japanese were ineligible for citizenship. When the Court rendered its decision, reaction from the immigrant press ranged from anger to resignation. The *Shin Sekai* commented, "The slim hope that we had entertained . . . has been shattered completely," while the *Nichibei Shimbun* stated, "the expected decision has been handed down," and urged there was no need for "pessimism."[97] At the very least, the decision clarified the matter of naturalization eligibility.

Litigation committees formed by Japanese Association central bodies were extensively involved in challenging alien land laws in the western states during the 1920s. The urgency to do so intensified after voters in California passed a more stringent law in 1920 and other western states passed similar Acts. The Japanese Agricultural Association estimated that of 300,000 acres leased as of November 1921, 90,000 were due to expire.[98] The Northwest American Japanese Association of Seattle acted first, challenging the Washington anti-alien land law in a case involving a lease between two parties, the Terraces (Frank and Elizabeth) and N. Nakatsuka. After being denied in the lower court, the case was immediately appealed to the Supreme Court, which in 1923 affirmed the prior ruling and upheld the constitutionality of Washington's alien land law. The *Terrace v. Thompson* ruling set the stage for similar decisions upholding California's land law in *Porterfield v. Webb*, *Webb v. O'Brien*, and *Frick v. Webb*. All decided in 1923, these decisions, which found that the laws were neither unconstitutional nor violations of the 1911 U.S.–Japan Treaty of Commerce, were devastating because they effectively prohibited the major loopholes that would have allowed Japanese to continue farming through leases, landholding companies, and cropping contracts.[99]

If exclusionists did not get the decisions that they wanted from the courts, they could simply resort to changing the law. For example, in 1922, in a case involving Hayao Yano, an Issei who had purchased land in Butte County, California, and placed it in the name of his minor daughter, the State Supreme Court said that the state could deny a petition of guardianship only on the basis of proven incompetency, effectively invalidating the section of the 1920 Alien Land Law prohibiting the appointment of aliens as guardians of minors who have title to agricultural land. The legislature responded to the court ruling by adding a new section to the Code of Civil Procedure making it illegal to appoint aliens ineligible to citizenship or companies in which majority shareholders are such aliens from acting as guardians of estate that includes real property.[100] In other areas, legislators similarly amended the law to counter unfavorable enforcement or court decisions. In 1933, for example, the California legislature added to the state's miscegenation code "Malays" to the list of groups prohibited from marrying whites, after a court decision that ruled Filipinos—who were widely considered Malay rather than Mongolian—were not subject to the intermarriage statutes.

With regard to Japanese Americans and their campaign against alien land laws, their failed efforts left them greatly demoralized. As the *Rafu Shimpo* described Japanese in southern California, "The extreme dejected spirits of the Japanese . . . cannot be concealed. Some people are thinking of returning to Japan. Some are seeking safe havens outside the state or country. Some are planning to change occupations despite lack of experience."[101] Describing the mood in the Northwest, the *Taihoku Nippo* said:

> People believed that even if anti-Japanese land laws were enacted they would be probably unconstitutional; if they were taken to the Supreme Court, we would be permitted to lease land at least; barring that we would surely be able to farm under cropping contracts . . . The Supreme Court decisions—our last ray of hope—have determined unequivocally that we do not have the right to purchase, lease, or transfer agricultural land, that we cannot enter into cropping contracts, and that we cannot own stocks in landholding companies.[102]

In turn, Japanese participation in farming did decline over the 1920s, although this was due to a combination of factors—such as the desire of Nisei to pursue other occupations and declining profits in agriculture—rather than the alien land laws alone. Japanese acreage in California—whether owned, leased, or contracted—peaked in 1920 at 458,056 acres, went down to 330,653 in 1922, and then 307,966 in 1925.[103]

In the face of these setbacks, many Japanese considered leaving California and some the United States altogether. In 1920, the New York consul recommended that the Foreign Ministry consider scattering Japanese throughout the United States, believing they were too concentrated on the West Coast. In fall 1924, the Japanese Association of America sent a representative to investigate the American south as a possible destination for farmers and concluded that Georgia and Florida looked most promising. The *Rafu Shimpo* editorialized about Mexico as another possible destination, calling it a "pro-Japanese nation" where Japanese would be treated well, and the Central Japanese Association of Southern California sent its head of Agricultural Section to conduct a survey there. Others looked to South American countries like Brazil, and the head of Rikkokai, the organization that helped indigent student laborers, proposed putting together a Japanese colony there. Despite all the talk of alternative destinations for Japanese on the West Coast, most did not leave where they were. Some spokesmen argued in the pages of the *Nichibei Shimbun* that it was better to stay on the Coast and make the best of the situation.[104]

Conclusion

As shown in the preceding chapter, Asian Americans had a mixed record of success in their responses to racism, but regardless of the strategies they pursued, they demonstrated their determination to change their lives for the better and make American society more inclusive for all. In addition to taking action, Asian immigrants often reflected and commented upon their hopes for life in America and the contradictions they perceived between the promise of equality and acceptance and the reality of racism and exclusion. A handful of them took to the pen to assert a political and social identity that exclusionists had sought to strip from them.

Wong Chin Foo, one of the most prolific Chinese immigrant writers in the English-language press, was among those who called on Americans, and white Christians in particular, to live up to their values. He came to the United States in 1868 at age seventeen under the sponsorship of Christian missionaries. He returned to China, became a political activist, and then returned to the United States in 1873, where he spent most of his life in the East and Midwest. Wong started a weekly newspaper called *Chinese America* in 1883, and formed the Chinese Equal Rights League in 1892, through which he often expressed his criticisms of Chinese exclusion and American racism. One of his most famous essays, "Why Am I a Heathen?" appeared in the *North American Review* in 1887. Employing a sarcastic tone, he addressed the charge of Chinese heathenism. "Though we may differ from the Christian

May 26, 1877.]   HARPER'S WEEKLY.

WONG CHING FOO.

Great interest was excited in this country some weeks ago by the announcement that a missionary from China had come among us for the purpose of preaching the religion of Buddha. This was partly a mistake. Mr. Wong Ching Foo disclaims the character of a missionary, and says he has come only for the purpose of explaining away certain misapprehensions concerning his country and people which prevail among Americans. He is an intelligent, cultured gentleman, speaks English with ease and vivacity, and has the power of interesting his audiences.

His first lecture in New York was delivered in Steinway Hall before a rather small audience. The greater part of his discourse was devoted to an exposition of the religious system known as Buddhism, and its effects on the character of the Chinese; but he also referred to other matters. In enumerating the wrong impressions the Americans have of the Chinese, he said they thought nothing was raised in China but rice, and that the Chinese lived exclusively on rice and rats and puppies. "Why," said he, "I never knew rats and dogs were good to eat till I learned it from Americans." If Mr. Wong Ching Foo had taken the pains to inquire a little into the real condition of American ideas respecting China and the Chinese, he would have discovered that he has no occasion to be quite so smart and flippant in his criticisms. But some of his points were well made, and deserving of consideration.

THE GREAT BENCH SHOW.

On the opposite page will be found the portraits of some of the most interesting and valuable of the aspirants for honors at the first annual New York Bench Show of Dogs. The show was a great success. It was held in the Hippodrome, which had been fitted up expressly for the purpose. Stalls were erected around the capacious arena for the accommodation of the dogs; but the entries were so much in excess of the calculations that extra stalls were built, at the last moment, inside the arena. There were also two rings into which the several classes of dogs were taken to be judged.

The show opened Tuesday, May 8. As early as ten o'clock Monday the dogs began to arrive. They came by all sorts of conveyances. Some were packed in huge coops marked "with care," others were led by stout iron chains, and still others were carried in baskets or in the arms of

WONG CHING FOO.—[Photographed by Rockwood.]

Figure 6.1 Wong Chin Foo. Wong Chin Foo was a Chinese immigrant, journalist, and outspoken critic of the anti-Chinese movement. He wrote prolifically about Chinese immigration, authoring such biting pieces as his 1887 essay, "Why am I a Heathen?" (Illustration from *Harper's Weekly*, May 26, 1877.)

in appearance, manners, and general ideas of civilization," he said, "we do not organize into cowardly mobs under the guise of social or political reform, to plunder and murder with impunity; and we are so far advanced in our heathenism as to no longer tolerate popular feeling or religious prejudice to defeat justice or cause injustice . . ."[105] Wong criticized Western powers for betraying their Christian values by behaving in a self-interested fashion. "Love men for the good they do you is a practical Christian idea, not for the good you should do them as a matter of human duty. So Christians love the heathen; yes, the heathen's possessions; and in proportion to these the Christian's love grows in intensity."[106] Toward the end he wrote, "'Do unto others as you wish they would do unto you,' or 'Love your neighbor as yourself,' is the great Divine law which Christians and heathen alike hold, but which the Christians ignore."[107]

Several decades later, on the eve of the Watsonville Riots of 1930, a Filipino organization published a pamphlet called *The Torch*, of which ten thousand copies were distributed in Watsonville and surrounding towns. The pamphlet responded to growing anti-Filipino allegations trumpeted by leading citizens such as Judge Rohrback. Author David DeTagle's central message was to defend Filipino immigrants' freedom to interact with whom they wished, in his view a fundamental American right. He furthermore asserted that Filipinos did not wish to be "treated as slaves," and that, like Americans, they were instilled in egalitarian values and raised in "the Christian principle that God created all men equal . . . so that we do not believe in racial superiority."[108] All they wanted, he urged, were the rights that other Americans enjoyed.

The writings of people like Wong Chin Foo and David De Tagle did not generate the responses they might have hoped for from white society, as anti-Asian sentiment did not show signs of lessening until all Asians had effectively been excluded from immigrating. Nonetheless, their observations, the legal challenges that immigrants and their lawyers mounted against laws they believed to be unfair, and the everyday strategies and acts of resistance that Asians employed to survive in a harsh land all demonstrated an individual and group resolve to not just make life more liveable for themselves but to make America a more open society for all.

Notes

1 Sucheng Chan, *Asian Americans: An Interpretive History* (Boston: Twayne Publishers, 1991), 94–5.
2 Andrea Geiger, *Subverting Exclusion: Transpacific Encounters with Race, Caste, and Borders, 1885–1928* (New Haven: Yale University Press, 2011), 82–3.
3 Ibid., 83.
4 Gary Okihiro, *Margins and Mainstreams: Asians in American History and Culture* (Seattle: University of Washington Press, 1994), 151.
5 Erika Lee, *At America's Gates: Chinese Immigration During the Exclusion Era, 1882–1943* (Chapel Hill: University of North Carolina Press, 2003), 111.
6 It is impossible to know just how many, but in 1909 San Francisco immigration-commissioner Hart Hyatt North surmised that nearly 90 percent had gained entry fraudulently. Ibid., 190.
7 Ibid., 196.
8 Ibid., 199.
9 Ibid., 216.
10 Ibid., 191.

11 Ibid., 195.

12 Ibid., 202.

13 Ibid., 203.

14 Ibid., 153–59.

15 Ibid., 156, 162, 194.

16 Sucheta Mazumdar, "Colonial Impact and Punjabi Emigration to the United States," Lucie Cheng and Edna Bonacich, eds., *Labor Immigration Under Capitalism: Asian Workers in the United States Before World War II* (Berkeley: University of California Press, 1984), 328.

17 Erika Lee and Judy Yung, *Angel Island: Immigrant Gateway to America* (Oxford: Oxford University Press, 2010), 159.

18 Ibid.

19 Ibid., 160.

20 Ibid., 192–93.

21 Ibid., 193.

22 Lee and Yung, *Angel Island*, 136.

23 Ibid., 138.

24 Yuji Ichioka, *Issei: The World of the First Generation Japanese Immigrants* (New York: Free Press, 1988), 237.

25 Ibid., 239–40.

26 Yong Chen, *Chinese San Francisco, 1850 to 1943: A Transnational Community* (Stanford: Stanford University Press, 2000), 111.

27 Ibid., 110.

28 Ibid., 111.

29 Judy Yung, Gordon Chang, and Him Mark Lai, editors, *Chinese American Voices: From the Gold Rush to the Present* (Berkeley: University of California Press, 2006), 43.

30 Lee, *At America's Gates*, 124.

31 Chen, *Chinese San Francisco*, 112; Yung, Chang, and Lai, *Chinese American Voices*, 48.

32 Chen, *Chinese San Francisco*, 148.

33 Ibid., 152.

34 Ibid.

35 Lee, *At America's Gates*, 126.

36 Ibid.

37 Eiichiro Azuma, *Between Two Empires: Race, History, and Transnationalism in Japanese America* (New York: Oxford University Press, 2005), 165.

38 Ibid.

39 Augusto Espiritu, *Five Faces of Exile: The Nation and Filipino American Intellectuals* (Stanford: Stanford University Press, 2005), 11.

40 Ibid., 14.

41 Lee and Yung, *Angel Island*, 161.

42 Seema Sohi, "Race, Surveillance, and Indian Anticolonialism in the Transnational Western U.S.–Canadian Borderlands," *Journal of American History*, 98 no. 2 (2011): 426.

43 Ibid., 428.

44 Ibid.

45 Ibid.

46 Ibid., 433–34.

47 Lee and Yung, *Angel Island*, 183–84.

48 H. Brett Melendy, *Asians in America: Filipinos, Koreans, and East Indians* (Boston: Twayne Publishers, 1977), 135.

49 Ibid.

50 Andrew Gyory, *Closing the Gate: Race, Politics, and the Chinese Exclusion Act* (Chapel Hill: University of North Carolina Press, 1998), 251.

51 Sohi, "Race, Surveillance, and Indian Anticolonialism in the Transnational Western U.S.–Canadian Borderlands," 428.

52 Lisa Rose Mar, *Brokering Belonging: Chinese in Canada's Exclusion Era, 1885–1945* (New York: Oxford University Press, 2010), 51.
53 Ibid., 52.
54 Lee, *At America's Gates*, 140.
55 Mar, *Brokering Belonging*, 25.
56 Lee, *At America's Gates*, 139.
57 Ibid.
58 Jean Pfaelzer, *Driven Out: The Forgotten War Against Chinese Americans* (New York: Random House, 2007), 81–2.
59 Ibid., 85.
60 Ichioka, *Issei*, 189.
61 Timothy Gilfoyle, *City of Eros: New York City, Prostitution, and the Commercialization of Sex, 1790–1920* (New York: Norton, 1992), 305; Lee and Yung, *Angel Island*, 4.
62 Richard Kim, "Inaugurating the American Century: The 1919 Philadelphia Korean Congress, Korean Diasporic Nationalism, and American Protestant Missionaries," *Journal of American Ethnic History*, Vol. 26 No. 1 (Fall 2006): 53.
63 Ibid., 63.
64 Ibid., 65.
65 Gyory, *Closing the Gate*, 248.
66 Ichioka, *The Issei*, 188.
67 Ibid.
68 Kim, "Inaugurating the American Century," 70.
69 Lee, *At America's Gates*, 133.
70 Ibid., 130.
71 Ibid.
72 Ibid.
73 Merchants and officials with Section 6 certificates and pre-investigated returning citizens with return certificates could be examined on boat and bypass the island.
74 Ichioka, *Issei*, 185–86.
75 Ibid., 178.
76 Ibid., 177.
77 Ibid., 191.
78 Ibid.
79 Ibid.
80 Azuma, *Between Two Empires*, 38–9.
81 Ichioka, *The Issei*, 185.
82 Ibid.
83 Ibid, 190.
84 Ibid., 192.
85 Ibid., 194. Also on Ichihashi, See Gordon H. Chang, *Morning Glory, Evening Shadow: Yamato Ichihashi and His Internment Writings* (Stanford: Stanford University Press, 1999).
86 Ichioka, *The Issei*, 247.
87 Ibid., 249.
88 Lee, *At America's Gates*, 123.
89 Ibid., 124–25.
90 Ibid., 125.
91 Ibid., 105.
92 Ibid.
93 Ichioka, *Issei*, 214.
94 Ibid., 217.
95 Ibid., 214–15.
96 Ibid., 224–25.
97 Ibid., 226.

98 Ibid., 227.

99 Prior to the Supreme Court decision, California had plugged the contracting loophole to restrict the use of contracts. Ibid., 231–32.

100 Ibid., 231.

101 Ibid., 233.

102 Ibid., 233–34.

103 Ibid., 235.

104 Ibid., 241–43.

105 Yung, Chang, and Lai, *Chinese American Voices*, 76.

106 Ibid.

107 Ibid., 78.

108 Rick Baldoz, *The Third Asiatic Invasion: Empire and Migration in Filipino America, 1898–1946* (New York: New York University Press, 2011), 140.

Americanization, Modernity, and the Second Generation through the 1930s

7

In 1926, the journal *Survey Graphic* featured the autobiography of Kazuo Kawai, a young Japanese American who had immigrated to the United States at the age of six. Although not native-born, he was presented as an exemplar of the second-generation experience. Kawai said that life as an Americanized person of Japanese ancestry had been difficult and confusing. During his high school years, he identified with American culture and did not connect with classmates whom he viewed as overly "Japanesy." In college, however, where he was no longer surrounded by other Japanese Americans, he grew increasingly self-conscious about his racial "otherness." "[For] the first time," said Kawai:

> I felt myself becoming identified with Japan, and began to realize that I was Japanese . . . What would I be able to do in Japan? . . . I couldn't speak the language except for a silly baby-talk . . . I didn't know any of the customs or traditions of Japan."[1] He continued, "Where did I belong? . . . in language, in thought, in ideals, in custom, in everything, I was American. But America wouldn't have me . . . Once I was American, but America made a foreigner out of me—Not a Japanese, but a foreigner—a foreigner to any country, for I am just as much a foreigner to Japan as to America.[2]

Such sentiments were common among young Asian Americans—both U.S. and foreign born—during the early twentieth century. For the most part, they considered themselves American, but in the course of their lives, came to realize that their ethnic backgrounds and "Oriental" faces impeded their full belonging in American society.

This chapter examines the lives of Asian Americans against the backdrop of modernity in the early twentieth century, with a focus on issues such as education, work, politics, racism, popular culture, and generational relations. It pays particular attention to young Asian Americans, mainly second-generation Japanese Americans (Nisei) and Chinese Americans, whose experiences have been the most widely documented, although the lives of U.S.-born and/or young Filipinos, Koreans, South Asians, and Asian Americans of mixed parentage will also be considered. The chapter will discuss the pressures and challenges that young Asian Americans faced, whether from their own families and ethnic communities or the larger society, and how their responses ranged from accommodation to rebellion. While their lives can be understood as part of a larger second generation experience bearing similarities to European and other immigrant communities in America, Asian Americans' lives were also shaped by race, and specifically the perception that they, regardless of nativity and citizenship, were "Orientals," and hence fundamentally foreign. Finally, the chapter considers Asian America against the backdrop of the "Roaring Twenties" and the Great Depression, demonstrating how Chinese, Japanese, Koreans, Filipinos, and Asian Indians in the United States were affected by and participated in the major developments of these eras.

The Emergence of the Second Generation

Among Chinese Americans, children were present since the mid-1800s, but the second generation, as a sizeable and discrete cohort, did not really emerge until the 1920s, as its growth was most dramatic after the turn of the century.[3] The small number of American-born Chinese before the 1900s was a consequence of exclusion, highly skewed gender ratios, and the sojourner orientation of most male immigrants. The birth of a child in Chinese America during the late 1800s and early 1900s, then, was a rare and joyous occasion, and

Figure 7.1   Chinese American baseball team from Hawaii, 1914. This photograph shows a Chinese American baseball team from Hawaii that came to the United States to play against university teams. Sports and recreation were an important part of life among many young Asian Americans growing up during the early 1900s, providing an outlet for socializing and engaging with mainstream American culture. (Library of Congress Prints and Photographs Division, LC-B2-3075-13.)

often the mark of a family's elite status.[4] Things would change gradually; between 1870 and 1900, the American-born went from one to 11 percent of the U.S. Chinese population, and by 1930, that number shot up to 41 percent. Ten years later, they represented a majority at 52 percent.[5]

In Japanese America, the Nisei were an increasingly visible element of the population after 1910. As discussed previously, most Issei men had come to Hawaii and North America between 1890 and 1908, and the entry of Japanese picture brides facilitated nuclear family formation and the rise of a second generation. Between 1900 and 1910, the number of Nisei in the continental United States rose from 269 to 4,502.[6] Significant as this was, this paled in comparison to the growth of subsequent decades. From 1920 to 1930, Nisei went from nearly 30,000 to 60,000, and on the eve of Pearl Harbor in December 1941 they numbered nearly 80,000, outnumbering Issei two to one. Because most of their births occurred between 1910 and 1940, the Nisei—and to a degree other second-generation Asian Americans—developed a strong cohort identity based on a shared historical life cycle that included eras such as the Roaring Twenties, the Great Depression, and World War II.

The second-generation presence among Koreans and Filipinos was more pronounced in Hawaii than on the mainland, as a larger number of women went to the islands than the continent during the early years of these groups' migrations. The arrival of picture brides to Hawaii was pivotal in driving the growth of the female population among Koreans; from 1910 to 1920, they went from 13 to 30 percent of the islands' Korean population. In turn, this led to the rise of the second generation. Over these same years, Filipinos in Hawaii likewise saw dramatic growth in the second-generation population; by 1920, the Hawaiian-born represented 29 percent of the islands' Filipino population.[7]

On the whole, Asian immigrants leaned toward endogamy, but a significant portion of the second generation was of mixed parentage. Mixed-race children of various backgrounds were especially visible and numerous in Hawaii by the early 1900s, but they also appeared on the continent. For example, prior to 1946, 80 percent of the approximately four hundred Asian Indian families in California included Indian husbands and Mexican wives. The families were concentrated in the Imperial Valley, but were also found in smaller numbers throughout the state as well as in Arizona, New Mexico, Texas, Utah, and Canada. As a result of these intermarriages, which can be traced to the 1910s, most second-generation Asian Indians, until the late 1960s, were racially mixed. In the biethnic households in which they grew up, cultural traditions were melded: tortillas were substituted for roti and chapattis and jalapenos for Punjabi chili peppers, and children had names such as Oscar Bupara and Anna Luisa Bupara.[8]

Negotiating the Generational Divide

The emergence of a second generation dramatically altered the dynamics of daily life in Asian American communities. The rising number of U.S. births meant that parents and community leaders would have to grapple with the matter of education and other issues concerning how to raise children in a new land. Around 1908, Issei leaders began addressing the second-generation problem, or "dai Nisei mondai." In an editorial published that year, a writer for the *Shin Sekai* opined that the issue of dual nationality would grow pressing as children got older, particularly around matters like military service. Parents, thus, needed to decide if their families' futures were in Japan or America.[9] This also demanded a thoughtful and deliberate approach to Nisei education, and in 1909 the Japanese Association of America in San Francisco convened a group called the Thursday Club to discuss the issue. One of the assumptions the group worked from was that Nisei, because of their nativity and American acculturation, would have a different national identity from their parents, and, should, thus, be exposed to curricula that reflected and developed their Japanese and American sides.

While recognizing that their children would grow up in a much different environment than they had, many Asian parents nonetheless sought to ensure that their children knew the language and culture of their homeland. While some hoped to stem the Americanization of their children, others sought to bridge potential cultural gaps between them. In Chinese American communities, for instance, parents, usually from the merchant class and with the assistance of family associations, sent their children to tutors, language schools, and even to China.[10] As early as 1880, San Francisco Chinese Americans had established at least twelve language schools, open on weekends and weekday afternoons, that offered courses in Chinese classics, music, history, geography, and math.[11]

Japanese and Koreans likewise formed language schools, which children usually attended in the afternoon. These were less prevalent among Filipinos and Asian Indians. As the Japanese Association explained, the purpose of Japanese schools was to strengthen Nisei connections to the homeland and supplement U.S. education without impeding the goal of preparing the second generation to be permanent residents of the United States.[12] Preschool children learned English as preparation for American school, and those enrolled in American schools would receive supplemental instruction in Japanese ethics, history, geography, and language. The Issei did not always agree on the curricula, debating, for instance, whether moral education based on the Imperial Rescript on Education should be stressed or if this was too parochial. Sensitive to anti-Japanese proponents' charges that these schools resisted children's Americanization, the Pacific Coast Japanese Deliberative Council and Northwest American Japanese Association emphasized their supplementary purpose and even said that Nisei, if they so wished, should be able to renounce their Japanese citizenship.[13]

Parents with the resources and connections to do so sent their U.S.-born children to Asia to study. Many Issei embraced this after the passage of the Johnson-Reed Act of 1924, as the law confirmed American anti-Japanese racism and impressed upon them the urgency to prepare their children to be cultural mediators in order to improve race relations. Educator Abiko Kyutaro advocated the idea that the Nisei should be "bridges of understanding" between the United States and Japan, but to play this role effectively, they had to spend time in Japan. After a group of four girls from Seattle returned from a trip there in 1924, they traveled to the Pacific Northwest and California to share their experience with other Japanese Americans, inspiring Abiko to underwrite Nisei tours of Japan through his newspaper *Nichibei Shimbun* and with the cooperation of Japan financier Shibusawa Eiichi. In 1925, the paper said about these tours:

> After the young Nisei boys and girls see and understand Japan, they will become conscious of their own ethnicity and gain confidence in themselves. Individually, they

will be blessed with self-assurance; they will become essential links in fostering Japanese–American amity, each in their own personal way; and they will naturally realize what they must do as Americans for America . . .[14]

Coordinating his first group in 1925, Abiko selected applicants based on their leadership potential, and eventually assembled eleven males and females for a three-month trip.[15] Miya Sannomiya, who went with the second group in 1926, said the tour "changed my life." The trip also had its intended effect of molding her into a "bridge of understanding," as she went on to become the English secretary of the Kokusai Bunka Shinkokai (International Society for Cultural Relations), a Japanese education society that disseminated information about Japan in western languages.[16] Other newspapers and organizations followed suit with similar Nisei education tours.

Nisei who were sent to Japan for extended periods (usually to live with grandparents or other relatives) as part of their education were known as the *kibei*. While education and being properly "Japanized" were major factors behind the kibei phenomenon, it also freed up parents' time to work more. It is difficult to know just how many there were in the pre-war years, but about 9 percent of the internment camp population during World War II identified themselves as kibei. By the time they returned to the United States, they were usually teenagers or young adults, and the extended time they had spent in Japan made them less Americanized than their Nisei counterparts. As a result, Nisei who had never left the United States tended to view them as much different from themselves and did not socialize with them extensively. The relative lack of acculturation among kibei, furthermore, proved to be a long-term disadvantage to this group, as they were generally less socioeconomically successful than the Nisei.[17]

Concerns about language retention notwithstanding, most evidence indicates that Asian parents did not actively resist the Americanization of their children, and in daily life they continued some customs while adopting new ones, so children grew up entrenched in multiple cultural traditions. In Chinese families, for instance, many parents carried over the practice of ceremonially bathing a newborn and confining the mother and child to the home for one month after birth.[18] Some also maintained superstitions aimed at protecting children from soul-stealing devils and other malevolent forces. Boys might be dressed in girls' clothes to confuse demons, and images of tigers were secured to keep harmful spirits at bay.[19] Class and religious background often factored into how and to what extent families adopted American and western customs. Chinese Protestant families, for instance, were more likely to baptize their children in churches to celebrate a birth rather than follow Chinese folk practices, although many families attended church on Sundays while continuing to worship Chinese gods at home. Such examples of retention and borrowing meant that members of the second generation usually grew up with knowledge of multiple cultural practices. For example, U.S.-born Chinese children learned about and participated in American culture, but they were also familiar with Chinese herbs and remedies, special dishes for ancestral holidays, ghost stories, and other traditions.

Middle class and elite Asian American families tended to pursue Americanization more intentionally and enthusiastically than their less affluent counterparts did, as facility in English and American culture was often a requisite for their roles as businessmen, social elites, or brokers. In turn, this shaped how they raised their children. Chinese American

Pardee Lowe, for example, was named after George Pardee, a former governor of California, and his parents named their other sons after Woodrow Wilson and Thomas Riley Marshall. He also had a sister named Alice Roosevelt.[20] Seid Gain Back Jr. and Moy Bow Hing, the sons of two of Portland's wealthiest Chinese merchants, were also raised in a Western style. After attending the Baptist Chinese Mission School, both went to the mostly white and private Bishop Scott Grammar School. Their fathers believed the environment of these institutions would best facilitate the sons' assimilation and future success.[21]

After 1911, Chinese American middle class families' embrace of Westernization and modernity also increasingly stemmed from the influence of the Chinese Revolution. It shaped, for example, some parents' decision to adopt more liberal approaches to raising daughters. Florence Chinn Kwan's parents were nationalistic and modern in their outlook and lifestyle; her father, for instance, had cut his queue and her mother unbound her feet. Kwan played tennis, wore Western clothes and, along with her sisters, was allowed to serve as princesses in a parade celebrating the Chinese republic. Her parents also encouraged her to go to college, which was still unusual for Chinese daughters, and she attended Mills College before going on to earn a Masters in Sociology from the University of Chicago.

At the same time, tension between members of the first and second generations was common, often playing out as cultural conflicts and parent–child disagreements. To many in the older generation, young Asians did not show proper respect for their elders, and they blamed this on the influence of American culture. In 1924, George Lem, who had emigrated from China to California in 1875, observed:

> [the] children here have no respect for the old people. It is not so in China, there they respect the old people. But here, if you are old, they think you ought to die. When the boy is twenty-one, he says, 'I am twenty-one, I will do as I please.' And when the girl is eighteen, she says, 'I am eighteen and I can do as I please.' . . . There is too much liberty. I believe in liberty, but I think in some ways there is too much among the young people.[22]

These dynamics also appeared in other Asian communities. In 1930, the Korean immigrant Young Kang, who lived in Honolulu, said that young people were not interested in their heritage or studying Korean and were too wrapped up in American culture.[23] He was especially concerned about the moral wellbeing of young Koreans who left the church. For their part, the second generation did not always understand why the first generation so strenuously emphasized the importance of respect and knowing one's heritage, and often bemoaned parents' and elders' sternness and high expectations. One young Korean American said in 1927, "So far I have read very little about my parents' native land. I have never felt a sense of pride in knowing about my parents' native land but I have pity and sympathy for them."[24] Bernice Kim, another second generation Korean American, thought generational conflicts were rooted in misunderstanding. Young Koreans, she said, wanted freedom, but parents mistook this for disrespect.

When children and parents clashed over gender roles, the situation could be especially complicated. For some traditional parents, male–female equality was a novel concept, but modernized daughters came to expect this and resented what they perceived as sexist parental pressures. Recalling how her father favored her brother over her and her sisters, Chinese American Esther Wong stated:

> When I was 13 my brother was born and then [my father] lost interest in us girls, did not care to bother teaching girls, and seemed to forget what we were like. When we were small he used to work at a machine next to ours, and when we were all busy he would tell us stories as we worked; but later he became very stern and cold and did not try to understand us at all.[25]

Another Chinese American, Alice Sue Fun, who grew up in San Francisco in the early 1900s, focused her angst on her mother. She recalled how each day after school—she attended the Oriental Public School and then the True Sunshine Chinese School—she did chores at home and took care of her siblings. Lamenting these burdens and lack of freedom, Fun remembered:

> Mother watched us like a hawk. We couldn't move without telling her. When we were growing up, we never allowed to go out unless accompanied by an older brother, sister, or anybody else . . . If you wanted to go shopping, you might as well forget it because, one thing, you didn't have the money. Secondly, you knew your mother wouldn't let you go, so what's the use of asking, right?[26]

Her yearning for freedom from parental authority led her to get a job at Canton Bazaar and then marry her Chinese teacher, with whom she moved to New York. She eventually divorced her husband, and traveled the world as a maid and companion to the actress Lola Fisher.[27] Fun looked back with satisfaction on the independent life she forged, but regretted that similar freedoms eluded her mother in her lifetime. "My mother lived a very sheltered life," she said. "Even up to her old age, she never trusted herself to go out alone. She was afraid that she'll get lost . . . I would go out anytime I want and anywhere I want. Even in foreign countries, I wasn't afraid to go out alone . . . I like to be independent. I don't like to always be accompanied by people. I guess I had enough of that when I was a young girl."[28]

In families that embraced some aspects of modernity, parents' gendered expectations and hypocrisies confused daughters and led to clashes. Jade Snow Wong, the fifth of seven daughters in a prominent San Francisco Chinatown family, recalled how her parents were very progressive in their support for educating daughters, but were also traditional and strict, for instance, in their expectation of obedience and use of physical punishment. Her father, the owner of a garment factory, was a Christian and Chinese nationalist and had impressed upon her the importance of girls' education for the sake of strong families and a strong China. Wong, however, clashed frequently with her parents over her ambitions and desire to be a part of mainstream American culture. Her father would not let her go to college because he felt it was more important for her brother to go. She eventually struck out on her own and worked as a live-in housekeeper, using her contacts and money earned to go to Mills College.[29]

Although patriarchal conventions from the homeland and in American society meant that sons were frequently prioritized over daughters, the former nonetheless often chafed at the pressures and responsibilities that came with being boys. Examples of favoritism included limiting property inheritance to male children, and prioritizing college education for sons if resources were scarce. For instance, in Punjabi families in California in which fathers owned agricultural land, the norm was that only sons inherited property. However, with these privileges came greater expectations, which could foster resentment. Sons were expected to follow their fathers into agriculture and work in the fields from their teenage years alongside other Punjabi men. Remembering how his father pushed him into agriculture and in other areas of his life, Pritham Sandhu came to believe that pressure and dogged persistence were traits of all Punjabi patriarchs, something he lamented: "They were out to win, they didn't care how they played the game; they wanted to be the best. When I was growing up, I thought this was an isolated thing with my father, but later on, I saw it was a Sikh thing, a Punjabi thing. They never quit, and they wouldn't let us either."[30] Such pressure could lead to sons rebelling against their parents. Chinese American Edwin Wong, who helped at his family's laundry and worked as a domestic, resented his father's order that he spend many hours working and send the money he earned to family members in China. Unwilling to continue living under this authority, he ran away from home to live in Berkeley and continue his high school education.[31]

The generational divide in Asian American families also led to explosive conflicts over dating and marriage, especially between daughters and parents.[32] In 1917, when she was just fifteen-years-old, Chinese American Elsie Chan of Oakland resisted her parents' attempt to place her in an arranged marriage, a still-common practice among Chinese in the early twentieth century. In her distress, she tried to commit suicide and, before doing so, wrote a note to her true love, William, which said, "Sorry to say that I could get no chance to see you before I died, as my mother forces me to marry, but I didn't obey her about it. I really intended to marry you, and I will follow you any time if I can. I am just worrying about my mother forcing me to marry, and that makes me die."[33] Daughters also turned to other less drastic solutions, such as seeking the intervention of a third party. A Chinese American named Bessie Jeong vowed, after seeing her older sister enter an arranged marriage, to avoid the same fate. Fearing that her father was going to take her to China to marry her off, she sought the protection of Donaldina Cameron of the San Francisco Presbyterian Mission Home and later married the man of her choice, Dr. Ying Wing Chan, the Chinese consul in San Francisco.[34] In Punjabi–Mexican families, when fathers tried to set their daughters up with Punjabis or Punjabi–Mexicans, the daughters sometimes turned to their mothers for help. "Dad wanted me to marry a well-established man eighteen (or twenty-eight?) years older than I," recalled one daughter. "He tried three times to get me married, but mother said, 'No way!' It bothered him a lot that I made my own decision."[35]

As suggested in the suicide letter by Elsie Chan, second-generation Asian Americans tended to prefer companionate marriages and relationships. In Japanese American families, parents often forbade dating, but many Nisei, especially those in cities who had opportunities to meet potential partners at various community events, embraced the idea of marriage based on choice and emotional connections. They found support for these wishes from Nisei writer Mary Oyama, who wrote an advice column in the *Nichibei Shimbun* and *Shin Sekai Asahi*, under the pseudonym "Dierdre" for the latter. Although she addressed men and women, Oyama's advice to young women was radical for its time, as she encouraged them to chart their own course, and opined that it was fine for a woman in her twenties to be unmarried. "Here in America where living standards are so high it takes a longer time for a young Nisei man to arrive at an age and station where he can adequately support a wife."[36] Oyama urged Nisei women to know themselves, especially in terms of how Americanized they were, and to select husbands who were good matches for them, rather than giving in to the wishes of others. While such advice was scandalous to some parents and community elders, Oyama's writing fell short of advocating gender equality or challenging the wisdom that women should eventually marry. Further, Nisei couples generally maintained the tradition of seeking parental consent to marry, and parents continued to employ go-betweens to investigate a prospective partner's background.[37]

Another source of tension, particularly in endogamous families and communities, was interracial and interethnic relationships. Interracial dating, while not a widespread phenomenon among Asian Americans in the early 1900s, grew out of day-to-day encounters in integrated school and neighborhoods. Although among Nisei, for instance, out-marriage rates were low in the prewar years—just over 2 percent for women and 3 percent for men— Japanese American newspapers regularly printed stories warning of the shame and tragedy that interracial and interethnic relationships would bring upon a family.[38] None were warned against more than those with Filipinos. Because Filipinos often encountered Nisei as laborers on Japanese-owned farms, a class bias as well as ethnocentrism colored these tales. Issei warned that Filipino blood would dilute Japanese racial superiority and portrayed Filipinos as lascivious toward young Japanese women.[39] The story of Alice Kaneko of Newcastle, California, which the *Shin Sekai* published in January 1934, illustrated Issei fears about Filipino–Japanese relationships. Kaneko, the twenty-three-year-old daughter of a Japanese farmer, had planned to marry Shizuo Haramoto, which greatly upset a Filipino agricultural employee, whose relationship with Kaneko was unclear, although he had once proposed to her. The day before Kaneko's wedding, the lovestruck Filipino appeared at the family's home and declared that if he could not have her, then nobody could. He shot Kaneko (who was hospitalized but did survive) and then turned the gun on himself, committing suicide.[40]

Community leaders responded more mildly to relationships between Japanese and whites, although they still depicted them as risky and potentially tragic affairs. Throughout the nineteenth and much of the twentieth century, such relationships were not only socially taboo, but marriages between whites and Asians were against the law. One of these involved twenty-four-year-old Nisei farmer Sam Kurihara and his white girlfriend Jennie Jean Salsan, both of the Dinuba, California area. In January 1938, Salsan's father, who had opposed the couple's relationship, shot Kurihara one evening as he approached the Salsan home to meet Jennie. Although Kurihara recovered from his wounds, a distraught Jennie Salsan killed herself by consuming poison.[41] Not only did such relationships put Asian Americans at risk of being attacked by disapproving whites, but the mixed couples also faced ostracism from both Asian and white communities. In one case, Chinese American Tye Leung ran away to the San Francisco Presbyterian Mission Home to avoid an arranged marriage. While working as an assistant to matrons at Angel Island, she fell in love with a white immigration inspector named Charles Schulze, and the two got married in Washington State, where there were no miscegenation laws. Due to the disapproval of their communities, both resigned from their civil service jobs and lived close to Chinatown, where their children were taunted by such insults as "foreign devil child."[42]

The dynamics of parent–child relations were different in mixed families because mothers and fathers were unlikely to put up a united cultural front and often disagreed with each other on child-rearing methods and objectives. In Punjabi–Mexican families, for example, the Mexican wives often insisted on raising children to speak Spanish and practice Catholicism. Because husbands spent less time at home and Indians were usually greatly outnumbered by Mexicans in the surrounding community, children would grow up with distant relationships with their fathers and knew little about their Indian heritage.[43] As highlighted earlier, it was common, for instance, for daughters to enlist the support of their mothers or Hispanic godmothers if they disagreed with their father's rules or decisions. One daughter remembered a fight between her parents over her father's objection to a prospective groom based on his caste background. Her mother exclaimed, "What is this caste thing, we're all Americans here!"[44] Such patterns of turning to mothers and other relatives for support against fathers sometimes reinforced children's negative perceptions of their fathers as hot-tempered men incapable of giving affection. As one Punjabi–Mexican recalled about his father, "He was hard, he didn't talk a lot to me . . . he was a strict authoritarian and didn't show his feelings."[45]

Such tension and conflicts notwithstanding, parents and children, first and second generations, were not always at odds with each other, and, moreover, the dynamics of intergenerational relations in Asian American families were not much different from those of other immigrant and non-immigrant households and communities. As noted above, parents did not regard the Americanization of their children as something to resist and did what they could to assist their children's assimilation. Many Issei, for instance, helped form Boy Scout troops, youth organizations, and athletic leagues, and supported white teachers who worked with their children. The larger point here is that for the second generation, relationships with parents and elders were an important part of the terrain on which their experiences and identities were forged. Children were raised by them, looked up to them, and relied on them for support but also chafed and rebelled against them and ultimately had to figure out on their own how to negotiate their unique position.

Growing Up Asian American in the Early 1900s

Misunderstandings with parents stemmed in part from very different life experiences separating the immigrant and American-born generations. On the one hand, the latter group was bound by traditional expectations, but as assimilated Americans with citizenship and greater contact with people outside their ethnic communities, they were also less constrained by them. To be sure, there was no singular "second generation experience," as it could vary considerably from one ethnic group to another, family to family, class position, and place. For instance, in the early twentieth century, the social lives of Chinese Americans in dense, urban Chinatowns tended to be more ethnically circumscribed than in communities without large Chinese populations. Generally speaking, though, members of the second generation grew up instilled in the "American Dream," something that seemed more within reach than it had been for their parents. However, the realization that they, like their parents, were not immune to racial discrimination and would thus face limitations could be a bitter pill to swallow.

Outside the home, through their engagement with various institutions and people, young Asian Americans' lives were immersed in American culture. Public schools were especially important in this regard. Here, during the late nineteenth and early twentieth centuries, teachers instilled in pupils values of individuality, equality, and freedom. Also influential, especially in cities, were municipal agencies and organizations such as the YMCA and YWCA, which also reached out to the younger generation and exposed them to American ideas, recreation activities, and daily habits. In San Francisco Chinatown, for example, the city's playground commission and YMCA built facilities in the neighborhood—in 1911 and 1927, respectively—to promote wholesome play and the Americanization of its youngest residents.[46] The YWCA, moreover, taught girls and women that they should participate in civic affairs and take on public roles, ideas that clashed with what many were taught at home. From peers whom they encountered in school and after school, they learned about fashion, dating, sports, and entertainment.

As important as public schools could be as sites of socialization for Asian Americans, access to them was elusive through much of the nineteenth century, and into the twentieth century, many attended segregated institutions. The history of Asian Americans and public education, thus, illustrates their struggle for belonging via entry into mainstream institutions, a pervasive theme in the second-generation experience. In California until the 1880s, the public education of Chinese children was tenuous, as there were no explicit provisions for their schooling. As a result, most of those who did attend school went to private and missionary institutions.[47] Access to public education, albeit usually in segregated settings, opened up after the California Supreme Court decision in *Tape v. Hurley* (1885). In 1884, the Spring Valley Primary School in San Francisco had refused to admit eight-year-old Mamie Tape, the daughter of middle-class couple Mary and Joseph Tape, because she was Chinese. The Tapes sued the San Francisco School District, and the case eventually reached the state supreme court. Their lawyer William Gibson argued that in the absence of legislation prohibiting Chinese from going to school with whites, they had a right to public education, and to deny them entry into public schools violated both California law and Fourteenth Amendment protections.[48] In a decision that secured young Mamie's place as a "civil rights pioneer," the court ruled in Tape's favor."[49]

Rather than lay the groundwork for integrated schools and equal access for Asians in San Francisco, however, the *Tape v. Hurley* decision led to the opening of the city's racially segregated Chinese Primary School, later called the Oriental School.[50] Although its curriculum—emphasizing language, geography, history, and reverence of American heroes—was similar to other schools' in the district, the Oriental School always had to make do with fewer resources. It had become so overcrowded by the mid-1920s that all-white schools elsewhere in the district had to admit a handful of Asian students. Nonetheless, until 1947, the public education experience of Chinese up to the high school level was largely a segregated one.[51] After graduating from the Oriental School, those wishing to continue their education had to apply to local public high schools, but most would be rejected. In 1908, just eleven Chinese Americans attended high school in San Francisco.[52]

Japanese Americans in the city had greater success in resisting school segregation than the Chinese, largely because of Japan's diplomatic standing. As discussed in previous chapters, in 1907, in response to pressure from the Japanese government and President Theodore Roosevelt, the Board of Supervisors exempted Japanese students from having to attend the

Oriental School. Japanese American leaders placed a high priority on adequate public education for the children in their community, and in California Nisei made up about 3 percent of the state's student population and attended school at higher rates than the overall population. A large percentage—some 35 percent of Nisei students—were in Los Angeles County alone.[53]

To be sure, there was much diversity across Asian Americans' experiences in public schools. For instance, many rural, poor, or working-class Asian Americans could not attend school for long periods due to other demands on their time.[54] To illustrate, the 1924 yearbook for Seattle's Garfield High School showed that students had formed a Filipino Club. The accompanying text indicated that the club had suffered due to its fluctuating membership, caused by the departure of Filipino students who worked during the year as migrant laborers.[55] With regard to the racial and ethnic makeup of the schools Asian Americans attended, they generally went to segregated institutions or "integrated" schools in minority neighborhoods, but this varied too, especially when it came to a family's class status and geographic location. Although segregated schools (de jure and de facto) were symbols of inequality and struggled with inferior resources, strong minority concentrations insulated students from the isolation and taunts that they might otherwise be subjected to if they were the only or one of few Asians. At Bailey Gatzert Elementary School in Seattle, which had an enrollment that approached 99 percent Chinese and Japanese in the early 1920s, Shigeko Sese Uno, who attended the school around this time, remembered, "I think we were very fortunate . . . I remember just a few Chinese, no black person, no Filipino. We were all Japanese."[56]

For those who spent a major portion of their lives in school, these were foundational years in which they learned much about race and being Asian in America. Large concentrations of co-ethnics and other Asians existed mainly in elementary and junior high schools, and furthermore, into the twentieth century, attending integrated schools increasingly became the norm. If they had not already been acquainted with the notion that they were racial "others," Asian American students were unlikely to escape this by high school. For example, in San Francisco during the 1910s, school officials noted that the recent entry of Chinese students into several schools had sparked numerous fights with Italian classmates.[57] The content of school curricula, furthermore, underscored to Asian students that they belonged to a subordinate group. They learned from textbooks that portrayed China as a weak, arrogant, and antiquated nation and argued that Chinese were excluded from immigration because "[they] fail to become Americanized, fail to adopt as their own the interests and customs of this country."[58] Finally, in addition to enduring teasing from fellow students and insensitivity from teachers, they were often placed on vocational tracks that reflected the dim prospects projected on them.

The limited job and career options of the second generation were also shaped by family and community needs. In working-class as well as many middle-class families, parents generally expected children to contribute to the household and their own support, and many started doing so by their early teens. In rural Japanese American communities, where family members were a crucial source of labor on farms and at home, most Nisei had to cut short their schooling and forgo completing high school. Urban Nisei were also expected to work, but they were usually able to stay in school, working in their spare time as babysitters, store assistants, or employees in family businesses. Punjabi–Mexican sons in the Imperial Valley who were expected to follow their fathers' vocational footsteps had more options than the previous generation, although they tended to be limited to jobs in the lower tiers of the economy. For example, while Punjabi immigrants worked primarily as laborers, farmers, and ranchers, their U.S.-born sons were able to find work as truck drivers, gas heating installers, freight agents, money exchangers, tractor drivers, and mix men.[59] They also entered these fields because by the time they joined the labor market in the 1930s and 1940s, the trend toward larger farms made landowning exceedingly difficult. Others left the Imperial Valley for opportunities in cities.

Women were doubly limited in the jobs available to them as well as their freedom to enter and exit the labor market. They usually found that the fields open to them had not changed a great deal from the first generation's experience. For example the 1900 and 1910 censuses found that prostitutes and seamstresses were the most common occupations reported among U.S.-born Chinese women in San Francisco.[60] Also like the first generation, second-generation Asian American women had to contend with the traditional taboo in many communities against women having roles outside the home. This diminished somewhat into the twentieth century, but remained significant nonetheless. And among those who did work, especially women from merchant and middle class families, jobs rarely turned into long-term careers, due to the limitations of the jobs themselves and the expectation that marriage and motherhood would eventually consume their lives.[61] On the other hand, working-class Asian American women often had to enter the labor force at a young age and stay in it longer than they would have preferred. When she was in sixth grade, Nisei "Mrs. Fujitani," the eldest of six children, had to drop out of school to work on her family's strawberry farm. When she was in her late teens, she got a job as a live-in housekeeper, staying in this position for fourteen years. While she had to forego plans to continue her education, her wages allowed her younger siblings to finish high school and get white-collar occupations. When she was in her mid-thirties, she entered an arranged marriage to a divorced Issei and finally left domestic service.[62]

The general picture of second-generation employment until the 1940s, then, is of concentration in ethnic economies or niches, a tendency to stay within the same fields as the first generation, and limited mobility or movement into the mainstream economy. To illustrate through the example of Japanese Americans in California, although few Nisei from farm families actually grew up wanting to be farmers, in 1940 about 40 percent of those in the workforce were employed in agriculture. Of the 60 percent in nonagricultural fields, clerical and sales positions predominated, with domestic and unskilled jobs also being highly represented.[63] In San Francisco and Los Angeles, the vast majority of Nisei—some 90 percent or higher—worked in the ethnic economy, either in family businesses or for co-ethnic employers. Although by the 1920s Nisei and other U.S.-born Asian Americans were increasingly finding work outside traditional low-status immigrant niches, entering clerical and sales jobs as well as professional occupations such as teacher, doctors, nurses, dentists, bank managers, tellers, and beauty parlor owners, these positions were usually confined to ethnic economies, usually located in urban enclaves or serving a mainly co-ethnic clientele.

Those who did obtain professional or white-collar jobs in the mainstream economy were the exception and often relied on family and other connections to get their positions.[64] Seid Back, Jr., the son of a prominent Portland Chinese merchant, worked as an interpreter for a U.S. district court and the Bureau of Immigration during the early 1900s. He was able to secure the position because of his father's standing and connections with white Americans in Portland. When he applied to work as an interpreter in San Francisco for the Immigration Service, former Oregon governor of George Chamberlain wrote a letter of support on his behalf.[65] Such advantages opened doors for a few, but they did not always protect them from discrimination on the job. In the 1920s, Alice Fong Yu was hired by the San Francisco School District as a teacher, but was not allowed to work in the classroom and was assigned other tasks.[66]

Handfuls of professionals notwithstanding, in the early twentieth century, most young and educated Asian Americans were unable to secure employment commensurate with their backgrounds or ambitions, a deeply frustrating predicament for people who had grown up expecting more. In Japanese America, the underemployed included Nisei who had completed commercial courses for office jobs or who held engineering and science degrees, only to be relegated to laundry and restaurant work.[67] Some parents, like Chinese American Pardee Lowe's, tried to protect their children from the rejection they feared awaited them by dissuading them from certain pursuits. Lowe remembered how, at the age of thirteen, he told his father of his desire to leave school and get a job as an office boy at an American law firm, to which the elder Lowe told his son that he would never be hired because he was Chinese. Discouraged, he stayed in school. [68] Ultimately, however, the greatest barrier facing the second generation with regard to mainstream employment and fulfilling careers was racism and structural discrimination in hiring and education. As a personnel officer at Stanford University explained in the 1920s:

> Many firms have general regulations against employing [Chinese]; others object to them on the ground that the other men employed by the firms do not care to work with them. Just recently, a Chinese graduate of Stanford University, who was brought up on the Stanford campus with the children of professors, who speaks English perfectly, and who is thoroughly Americanized, was refused consideration by a prominent California corporation because they do not employ Orientals in their offices.[69]

Mickey Fong was rejected from Stanford's nursing school around this time because it did not accept Asians. She eventually enrolled at the San Francisco Hospital School of Nursing, but there she was discouraged from taking the public health nurse's exam because, as she was told, she would not be able to work with white patients.[70] When she later attempted to take the civil service exam to become a nurse supervisor, she was similarly discouraged from taking it. As she recalled, "They didn't seem very friendly or encouraging. One of them said, 'How do you think that you could supervise American nurses!'"[71]

Whither the American Dream?

As noted above, Asian Americans' encounters with racial discrimination and limited job prospects caused disillusionment and frustration. As a second–generation Chinese American woman lamented in the *Chinese Times*, sometime in the 1920s:

So far as the occupational opportunities are concerned, the American-born Chinese is a most unfortunate group of human beings ... The Americans will not accept us as citizens ... We cannot get occupational status in the American community, not because we are not worthy, but because we have yellow skin over our faces. If we turn back to the Chinese community there are not many places which can employ us ... There is a barrier between us and the old Chinese who are hosts of the Chinese community. We cannot get occupational status there either. The Americans discriminate against us, and we cannot get along in the Chinese community very well; what opportunities do we have in the country?[72]

Japanese Americans expressed similar disappointments. A Los Angeles Nisei said, "I am a fruit stand worker ... It is not a very attractive or distinguished occupation ... I would much rather it were a doctor or lawyer but my aspiration of developing into such [was] frustrated long ago ... I am only what I am, a professional carrot washer."[73] The newspaper *Sei Fujii* warned readers of college-educated Nisei working as janitors and gardeners and concluded that higher education for Nisei was pointless. As Nisei Joseph Shinoda affirmed, "They go to college, learn a heterogeneous body of facts relating to anything from art to architecture and end their days in a fruit stand."[74]

Many second generation Asian Americans, thus, entered adulthood full of pessimism about their occupational prospects and if they would ever belong in America. Bitter from being barred from social activities and establishments due to his race, L. Toyama, a Nisei from Southern California, held very critical views of white Americans. They "are the narrowest-minded people in the world," he said. "They think only about and for themselves and exclude all others."[75] Others, while less angry, were confused and bewildered about how to reconcile their Asian and American identities. When asked if growing up in the United States made him wish he were white, Chinese American Edward L.C. replied, "[It] is a very hard question to answer yet my conscience seems to say to me—why is it necessary to say anything—you have nothing to regret being a Chinese and member of the Mandarin race. My conscience says so but my heart seems to say—I am American. If you were me, what would you say?"[76]

The question of where the second generation belonged was a common preoccupation. People grappled with it in essay and oratorical contests sponsored by community organizations as well as speeches and newspaper editorials. Nisei women mulled over how they were supposed to negotiate conflicting standards for women's behavior in which American culture expected them to be spirited and boisterous while Japanese norms dictated they be modest and demure.[77] In New York in 1936, the Chinese American group the Ging Hawk Club of New York sponsored an essay contest on the question, "Does my future lie in China or America?" It drew a variety of responses that illustrated the collective ambivalence of young Chinese Americans, as many wholeheartedly cast their lot in the United States, while others, disillusioned with American racism and felt obligations to help China, saw their futures in the ancestral homeland. Winner Robert Dunn, a student at Harvard University embodied both perspectives, expressing great pride in his Chinese ancestry and attachment to China while also having a strong loyalty to America.[78]

Forging their Own Path

The elusiveness of mainstream belonging and the belief among many second generation and other young Asian Americans that their concerns and identities were distinct led them to forge their own social and organizational path, by both turning to one another and building bridges with others. In the process, they created vibrant subcultures that gave them alternatives to immigrant-led or all-white organizations, and that allowed them to nurture identities and skills that reflected their distinct positions. In describing Nisei in California, David Yoo says their subculture was a "vital, alternative space between immigrant and native contexts."[79]

As early as the 1890s, as a small cohort of second generation Chinese Americans came of age and realized that they had unique concerns that immigrant associations did not always address, they formed organizations that catered to their particular interests as U.S. citizens of Chinese ancestry. In San Francisco in 1895, they formed the Chinese American Citizens Alliance, and shortly thereafter, Portland Chinese Americans established the American-Born Chinese Association (ABC). Usually led by the children of elite immigrants, these organizations emphasized U.S. loyalty, acculturation, and good citizenship and, until the 1920s, were very small or short-lived due to the limited size of the second-generation cohort. For example, the ABC in Portland, which engaged in activities such as patriotic demonstrations for its Chinese American members, was active for just twelve years.[80]

In the 1920s and 1930s, as the number of adult second-generation Asian Americans grew, their organizational activities proliferated. On college campuses, where student associations often excluded them, they formed their own groups. After Chinese students at Stanford University were expelled from their dormitory by whites, they formed the Chinese Club House, which became one of few places on campus where they could live.[81] Elsewhere, other Chinese student groups included the Chinese Students' Alliance and Sigma Omicron Pi Chinese Society, the latter of which was founded in 1930 by Chinese women at San Francisco State Teachers' College. As Shirley Jennifer Lim has described, Asian American fraternities, sororities, and alumni organizations formed in the 1920s and 1930s helped foster a sense of belonging in otherwise alienating environments and gave members the opportunity to exercise their "cultural citizenship."[82] In 1928, Japanese Americans at UCLA founded the Chi Alpha Delta sorority, serving as a haven against racism, a place to help students apply for scholarships, and a source of housing and social prestige.[83]

These organizations also developed and reflected Asian Americans' dual identities and their ties to Asia and America. The Chinese Students Association, for instance, which had about three thousand members, held a strong anti-imperialist stance and took a strong interest in Chinese politics.[84] The Square and Circle Club of San Francisco, formed in 1924 as a service organization for second-generation Chinese American women, similarly intertwined China affairs with ethnic politics and gave the U.S.-born a place to express their bicultural identity. Reaching a membership of about eighty, it appealed mainly to middle-class, educated, and professional women. As member Alice Fong explained the group's origins, "Usually the Chinese Chamber of Commerce or the Six Companies are in charge of these charitable and public affairs . . . But we wanted to help too. American girls can do these things. Why shouldn't we?"[85] The organization emerged from meetings of the seven founding members at the Chinese Congregational Church, with a key impetus being their concern for flooding and famine victims in Guangdong. It was named for the shape of Chinese coins and the Chinese motto, "In needs be square, in knowledge be all-around." The group's fundraising drives, which incorporated jazz dances, variety shows, chest raffles, and fashion shows, bridged Chinese American and Chinese concerns, supporting Sun Yat-sen, war and famine victims after the 1911 Revolution, and Chinese orphanages, as well as Chinese American hospitals and youth programs in San Francisco.[86] Members saw their U.S. patriotism and Chinese nationalism as compatible, and during World War II, they volunteered for the Red Cross and raised money for the war effort through the YWCA.[87] Despite this work, the club was denied admission to the local Federation of Women's Clubs in 1937.

Much of the early institution building among Asian Americans also promoted their autonomy as a generational cohort and aimed to combat racism. In 1922, at a time when the number of adult Nisei was still relatively small, a handful formed the Seattle Progressive Citizens League, and the following year, Nisei in California established the American Loyalty League. From there, Nisei organizing proliferated. The Young Buddhist Association (YBA) and Young People's Christian Conference (YPCC) gave Nisei the space to take charge of their religious lives on their terms.[88] Additionally, in English language newspapers or sections in immigrant newspapers, Nisei writers expressed themselves on a range of issues. In terms of political organizations, the Japanese American Citizens League (JACL), formed in 1930, was the most prominent, drawing the support of Japanese Americans along the West Coast and growing to thirty-eight chapters in six years.[89] Patrick Okura, a Los Angeles Nisei, found a sense of purpose working in the JACL. He described once being an angry young man due to his inability to find employment commensurate with his master's degree in psychology. As a member of the JACL, to which he was appointed executive director in 1936, Okura worked to improve conditions in Little Tokyo and strengthened relationships with local politicians and non-Japanese businessmen. This experience helped him to become one of the first Japanese American civil servants in Los Angeles.[90]

Beyond having their own space free of the interference of the first generation, second-generation political organizations sought to initiate change, promote full citizenship, and assume leadership in the ethnic community. Although the Square and Circle Club was mainly a service organization, it occasionally branched into politics by registering voters, protesting racist legislation, and supporting the war against Japan in China. Additionally, the *Chinese Digest*, founded in 1935 by Thomas Chinn and Chingwah Lee, positioned itself as a voice of the second generation.[91] In print for five years, it encouraged Chinese Americans to improve their communities and be politically engaged, and also promoted tourism as the economic base of Chinatown. It featured columns by and for second-generation women, such as articles by Clara Chan about fashion and sociological pieces by Ethel Lum. Through their annual Nisei Week festival in Los Angeles, which began in 1934, Japanese Americans demonstrated their civic virtue and political allegiance as Americans. As John Maeno, a USC-educated lawyer and president of the JACL, explained, "Through the medium of this festival . . . the JACL hopes to present, acquaint, and contact you directly with the young Japanese American citizen, his life and environment."[92] Such activities also aimed to strengthen the electoral power of the Nisei, and by the 1930s, in major West Coast cities, white office seekers started to court their vote by showing up to events such as Nisei Week.

Through their organizational activities, young Asian Americans sought to turn their in-between status into a resource and then use it to improve their lives and communities. For all the anguish that members of the second generation expressed about their liminality, they also recognized their unique advantages. In many households, for example, immigrant parents depended on their U.S.-born children, who had stronger facility with the English language and American culture, to handle day-to-day transactions. As this generation grew older and more conscious of itself as a group, it sought to formalize this power through organizations like the Chinese American Citizens' Alliance (CACA) and the JACL. The CACA fought negative perceptions of Chinese in America and the JACL promoted the notion, originally touted by Issei educators like Abiko Kyutaro, that Nisei should be "bridges of understanding" by using their bicultural abilities to overcome misunderstanding and foster friendship in both domestic race relations and international affairs.

Other second generation Asian Americans saw their futures in Asia. Chinese American Rose Hum Lee found a niche and sense of purpose in China. Having grown up in Butte, Montana, she had never before been surrounded by other Chinese people. She, furthermore, believed that the second generation had a mission there:

> The men could effect more rapid social and occupational mobility in China as teachers, professors, foreign firm representatives, minor consular officials, junior executives of foreign branch offices, engineers, doctors, dentists, salesmen, business men, manufacturers, chemists, physicists, etc. The girls could find work in foreign and Chinese firms, government offices, educational institutions, and churches. They lived in better residential areas, often peopled entirely by American-born Chinese and sojourners, and could maintain a lifestyle and a standard of living far above that of the local population.[93]

Lee would have stayed in China had World War II not broken out, but upon her return to America, she went on to become the first Chinese American to earn a Ph.D. in sociology (University of Chicago) and lead a sociology department (Roosevelt University). Florence Chinn Kwan moved to China after marrying a medical student from there, eventually finding work as an English teacher and board member of the YWCA.[94] After studying journalism at the University of Chicago and marrying a Chinese graduate student, Flora Belle Jan also went to China with her husband and worked as a journalist for English language publications. Her experience differed greatly from Lee's and others who found a renewed sense of purpose while living abroad. Jan's adjustment was difficult and being in China made her more conscious of and attached to her American identity. She insisted on dressing her children in Western styles and made them speak English at home, and eventually returned to the United States in 1949.[95]

In carving out a distinct identity and mission, second-generation Asian Americans did not always critically rethink ideas about citizenship and inequality and sometimes reproduced the classism and sexism of the larger society. Although the JACL purported to speak for all Nisei, it represented a distinctly male, Christian, and professional point of view. Its leadership was drawn from the older wing of the Nisei cohort (born in the early 1910s) and the very elite echelon of Japanese America, with many lawyers, doctors, dentists, and entrepreneurs serving as officers.[96] JACL and other Nisei leaders often criticized fellow members of their cohort who did not live up to their ideals of proper decorum. For example, they dismissed Nisei gang members, or "rowdies," as the dirty laundry of the Los Angeles community.[97]

Masao Satow, who worked with the YMCA, lamented that his generation was "shallow" and lacked "culture" and refinement," saying, "We are so one-sided . . . we naively wonder why Americans won't accept us as equals!"[98] Joseph Shinoda, on the other hand, targeted his criticism at female Nisei. In particular, he said that women students at Berkeley were "deficient," as demonstrated by their poor academic performance. He pressed that Nisei women in college made a mockery of higher education, that they viewed college only as a marriage market, and blamed their parents for sending them.[99]

Orientalism and Modernity in the 1920s and 1930s

As discussed earlier, many Asian immigrants believed that anti-Asian prejudice would subside with the rise of the second generation. Discrimination, they thought, stemmed from cultural intolerance and a fear of foreigners, and the younger generation's nativity and Americanization would undercut xenophobes' arguments about Asians' inability to assimilate and, thus, lead to mainstream incorporation. To many white American observers, second-generation Asian Americans were fascinating, as they illustrated the consequences of migration, human adaptability, and other modern phenomena, and their presence compelled them to rethink the roots of racial difference. The heightened attention that this generational cohort, as well as "Americanized Asians," received in the 1920s and 1930s signaled a distinct phase in Asian racial formation in the United States in which people revised earlier assumptions about Asians. To be sure, their conclusions were still orientalist, but they were adapted to modern conditions and concerns.

Earlier complaints about and efforts to reach out to Asian American children were functions of broader national anxieties as well as anti-Asian prejudice. In the late nineteenth and early twentieth centuries, a wave of reformers invoked the need to provide children with structure, protection, and discipline in the face of a rapidly changing society. Against this backdrop, in certain locations, Asians—parents and children—were singled out as a peculiar menace. Writers not only depicted Chinese mothers as callous and neglectful, but they also ridiculed and demonized their children. In 1896, for example, a reporter for the *Wave* wrote, "There is very little in a Chinese child's life that a 'Christian kid' need envy unless it's having a queue to jump rope with."[100] Such descriptions added to the construction of Chinatowns as fascinating tourist destinations, but in casting the youngest residents as well as women as the most pathetic residents, they also prompted efforts by reformers to "rescue" and Americanize them.[101] As early as the 1870s, Christian missionaries went to urban Chinatowns to conduct home visits to teach mothers about things like proper hygiene, and they later opened mission homes and schools for children.[102] In California, the state's role in Americanizing immigrant children through Progressive curricula was boosted in 1913 with the formation of the California State Commission of Immigration and Housing.

By the 1920s, the plight of second generation Asian Americans had drawn the interest of researchers affiliated with the Sociology Department at the University of Chicago and one of its eminent professors Robert Ezra Park. In studying the experiences of U.S.-born Asians, they sought to answer larger questions about assimilation and race relations in modern America. Asians in America stood out because their experience seemed to deviate from that of European immigrants, in which mainstream incorporation was usually achieved within a generation. They identified this issue as the "Oriental Problem" and set out to understand why integration for Asians proceeded in a halting manner.[103] Joining the sociologists were Protestant social reformers also interested in Asians in America, and they combined their efforts in the *Survey of Race Relations*, a research project funded by the Rockefeller Foundation based on the West Coast devoted to understanding the adjustment and assimilation problems of "Orientals" in America. The researchers produced and disseminated new information about Asians in America, but because they largely took for granted prevailing assumptions about East–West difference, their work tended to fetishize their subjects and perpetuate the view that American and Asian cultures were incompatible. Acculturated Asian Americans were often portrayed as people stuck between two worlds, a "lost generation" that belonged to neither the immigrant community nor mainstream society.[104] Some concluded that this marginality doomed Asian Americans to a state of perpetual maladjustment, while others, like Robert Park, believed it freed them from stifling customs to be able to move among different cultures with relative ease.[105]

One of the unique aspects of this early twentieth century strain of orientalism was the involvement of dozens of Asian people, not just as objects and informants on the "Oriental Problem," but also as researchers. These included Kazuo Kawai, Flora Belle Jan, Caroline Chew, S. Frank Miyamoto, and Ching Chao Wu. Recruited through missionary networks and university classes, they were initially seen as "interpreters" by white American sociologists—Emory Bogardus, William Carlson Smith, and Roderick McKenzie and others—who hoped their language and cultural knowledge as well as insider positions could be tapped to gain access to Asian communities. The researchers especially valued those who were highly Americanized yet versed in ethnic customs, as they could most effectively "translate" the ways of Asians to an American audience. Flora Belle Jan, described by Robert Park as "the most emancipated girl I have ever met," was regarded as an ideal informant due to her "Clever, sophisticated, Americanized" character.[106] Asian and Asian American sociology students at the University of Chicago and elsewhere proved particularly useful, with both their disciplinary training and ethnic capital. Sociologist Ernest Burgess summarized about Chinese students, "As one of the cultural groups most deviant from the typical native American culture it provided sharp contrasts which clarified theoretical issues which otherwise might be vague. Also, the attendance of Chinese graduate students provided an opportunity for insightful research."[107]

For the Asian American informants and researchers, participating in the study of the "Oriental Problem" allowed them to use their marginal status for personal and group advancement. Rose Hum Lee and S. Frank Miyamoto went on to become accomplished sociologists in their own right. For Miyamoto, a Nisei from Seattle, pursuing graduate studies in sociology was part of a deeply personal path. He grew up away from the Japanese American community because his father had moved the family out of Nihonmachi, and, thus, felt very self-conscious as a racial and ethnic minority. "I felt a step removed from both and no strong subjective attachment to either," he wrote. "In this way I was developing the attitude of detachment fundamental to the sociologist—I was becoming, in a sense, a 'marginal man.'"[108] As a sociologist, he could explore how to overcome race prejudice and better understand the tightly knit ethnic community to which he felt like an outsider. Similarly, Kazuo Kawai hoped that sharing his life story would enable him to make productive contributions to American race relations. "If I can learn Oriental history and become able to teach Oriental history to Americans," he said, "I would be rendering a service as an interpreter of the East to the West."[109] Others developed more critical attitudes about American society and its treatment of Asians. Caroline Chew, daughter of Ng Poon Chew, used her platform to criticize writers and film producers who "have thrown a bizarre light on it, giving the general impression that it is a round of trap doors, secret passages, opium dens, and the like."[110]

Ironically, white researchers desired the participation of people like Miyamoto for researching the "Oriental Problem" because they believed these Asian Americans had unique access to and knowledge of the communities they were studying. However, like Miyamoto, most of the Chinese and Japanese American student researchers were U.S.-born and grew up away from the "ethnic ghettos" they wrote about. Others were recently arrived Asian nationals who spoke little English and were also disconnected from ethnic communities, having come to the United States on scholarships and through missionary networks.[111] Ching Chao Wu, for instance, regarded himself as more Chinese than Chinese American, and did not identify with the immigrant community he studied, even though he thought his ancestry made him an apt informant. He did not conduct personal interviews, rather using already-compiled life histories in the *Survey of Race Relations*. As such cases show, the Asian American researchers were often no better informants and translators of the "Oriental" in America than the white sociologists they worked under, but their racial background nonetheless accorded them credibility, which may have helped them in their careers, but also boxed them in.

Frank Miyamoto had originally aspired to be a writer, but was discouraged at the lack of opportunities for Asian novelists in America. Indeed, Asian American participation and visibility in the American arts scene during the 1920s and 1930s was nascent, but nonetheless significant and bears comment. Asian America during the early twentieth century produced numerous creative minds that were influenced by the racialized boundaries of American society as well as the larger cultural dynamism that characterized this period. Notable figures included the Nisei artist and landscape architect Isamu Noguchi, Korean American novelist Younghill Kang, and Indian writer Dhan Gopal Mukerji. Although their work was frequently informed by their lives as Asians or immigrants—and this was often key to their appeal—these artists, especially after they attained a measure of success, led unconventional, cosmopolitan lives and usually had little connection to co-ethnics. Mukerji, for instance, lived among New York's literary elite and both he and Kang were married to white women. Noguchi was primarily raised by his white mother and spent his life in locations all over the world, never explicitly identifying as a Nisei artist until World War II. Noguchi's father, Yone, was an established writer who had mixed with the bohemians of San Francisco and carried on a passionate correspondence with Charles Stoddard.[112] As Asians, these artists sometimes struggled for the kind of recognition they wanted and to be seen as something other than mysterious "Orientals" or cultural translators. Isamu Noguchi, for instance, was once dismissed in 1935 by a critic as "wily." The same critic impugned his talents by saying, "once an Oriental, always an Oriental."[113]

Asian Americans and the Roaring Twenties

The scholarly research on Asians described above was part of a larger grappling with modernity, of which mass consumerism and leisure culture were also parts. A rich subculture embracing modernity, American identity and popular culture built on motion pictures, consumerism, and advertising flourished among second-generation and other young Asian Americans during the 1920s and 1930s. America in the 1920s was undergoing revolutionary social and cultural change, which included postwar prosperity, rebellion, and consumerism. Additionally, this was the era of the "new woman," who was individualistic, independent, and sought self-fulfillment. While race and class and other structural constraints limited who could participate in the new culture of modernity, young Asian Americans drew from the landscape to carve out distinct identities and exercise their cultural citizenship.[114]

Many young Asian Americans embraced the "new woman." Among Chinese Americans, it was not just a construct of American culture, but also of the Chinese Revolution. Ideals of women's emancipation were embedded in the Chinese nationalist movement, which encouraged parents to educate daughters and allow them to work outside the home. Janie Chu said that the Chinese American woman:

> gets her knowledge of social America from the 'movies,' from the street, from what she hears from the girls at service in homes. She wants to be American and she has always a struggle in her mind as to what is right and what is not right in respect to Occidental thinking. She teems with the life that urges on this new generation of Americans. She wants excitement and thrills. She wants to live.[115]

Chinese American actress Anna May Wong gained notice as a flapper who reveled in rebellion, flirtatiousness, and sexual frankness. While she embodied the sultry and provocative side of the "New Woman," as an actress she also exemplified female accomplishment and independence. Flora Belle Jan also typified the new Chinese American woman. Born in Fresno, California in 1906, and the third child in a family of seven, she was a regular contributor to publications such as the *Fresno Bee*, *San Francisco Examiner*, and *Chinese Students' Monthly*, in which she shared her ideas on being a young Chinese in America. In 1925 she moved to the San Francisco Bay Area, where she attended college and held a number of jobs, including a check girl at the Mandarin Café.[116]

Young Asian American women who embraced modern culture and flouted social convention often did so at the risk of alienating their families and communities. Because Flora Belle Jan advocated young women's freedom and often wrote critically about generational relations, she irked elders in the Chinese American community. Additionally, Asian American women professionals like physicians Margaret Chung, Bessie Jeong, and Rose Goong were trailblazers, but were also subjected to discouraging treatment because they were seen as such oddities.[117] Bessie Jeong, the first Chinese American woman to graduate from Stanford University in 1927 before going on to earn a medical degree from the Women's Medical College of Pennsylvania, often withheld her first name in her professional listings in order to attract more patients.[118] And Margaret Chung moved to San

Francisco from Los Angeles to escape the discrimination she had experienced as a single woman.[119]

The rise of Asian American beauty contests captured some of the contradictions of women's status in the 1920s and 1930s, which were mirrored in the larger society. On the one hand, the pageants were vehicles of modernity and a break from Asian traditions. The first San Francisco Chinatown beauty contest was held in 1915 and organized by the Chinese Six Companies. The winner was crowned at a lavish ball held at the Fairmont Hotel and presided over Chinatown celebrations during the Panama Pacific Exposition. At the coronation, which featured lion dancing and Western music, the queen and her court dressed in Chinese clothing while guests wore Western clothing.[120] Los Angeles Japanese Americans crowned a Nisei Week Queen during their annual festival. Their contest, like the one in the San Francisco Chinatown, was aimed at fundraising, but also reflected the bicultural identity of Nisei. It offered a chance for young Japanese American women to perform their cultural citizenship in ways that affirmed their American identities and Japanese ethnic solidarity. In 1938, the JACL president said that the ideal candidate for Nisei Week Queen blended "the quiet charm of the Japanese wom[a]n with the more lively personality of the American girl."[121] The pageants, in both Chinese and Japanese communities, also were clearly predicated on a commodified and orientalized image of Asian women. For instance, during Nisei Week, in trying to attract tourists, Little Tokyo merchants hired hostesses to wear kimonos and hand out guidebooks with orientalized script.

During the 1920s and 1930s, Asian American businesses increasingly engaged the consumer culture and economy via tourism and spectacles like beauty pageants. In San Francisco, a "New Chinatown" emerged from the rubble of the 1906 earthquake after a merchant named Look Tin Eli rebuilt his store to reflect the Orientalized tastes of tourists and other entrepreneurs followed his lead. The most popular Chinese American establishment in San Francisco, patronized by white Americans and middle class Chinese Americans, was Forbidden City, a cocktail bar on the outskirts of Chinatown that had its heyday in the 1930s and 1940s. Owner Charlie Low wanted the business to be an Orient-themed club that appealed to modern patrons, and central to his strategy was gender and the sexual objectification of women. Forbidden City, Low said, would present the Chinese American woman as modern, because "We can't be backwards all the time; we've got to show the world that we're on an equal basis. Why, Chinese have limbs just as pretty as anyone else!"[122] In cabaret style routines, Chinese Americans performed tap, ballroom, and other kinds of dances. The club drew 100,000 customers per year, including Hollywood actors and politicians.[123]

A range of occupations opened up for Asians in entertainment as Americans became interested in them as performers. Although community elders looked down on Forbidden City and similar establishments such as Chinese Village and Twin Dragon, also in San Francisco, and the young women employees were represented as exotic showpieces, these businesses provided them with well-paid employment unavailable elsewhere. As Bertha Hing, who worked at Forbidden City, explained, "Chinatown mothers wouldn't let their daughters do anything like that. But what they didn't realize was that we all just loved to dance. And we didn't particularly care for drinking or smoking or anything like that. It was just another way of earning a living."[124] Chung and Rosie Moy were a husband and wife team (Rose and Joe Moy) who performed at Ziegfield Follies and other venues across the country with Jack Benny, Will Rogers, and the Marx Brothers.[125] At their height, they earned $200 to $300 per week.

For young Asian Americans, especially in urban areas, following popular trends and fashion allowed them to express their identities and exercise citizenship in a society that denied their full belonging. Women mimicked what they read about fashion and dating in magazines to embody middle class modern femininity and break from their parents' generation, and youths, most notably Filipinos and Nisei, took part in the automobile culture also to participate in the modern. As discussed in previous chapters, Filipino men were visible in the taxi dance hall scene, where they were noted for their flashy clothing and charm with women. Dance halls, gambling halls, boxing matches, and other recreation venues were part of a subculture in which Filipino Americans drew on popular culture to form identities and communities. "[These] leisure centers," explains Linda España-Maram, "provided opportunities for poor immigrant men and working women to create identities that allowed them to be something other than what their ethnicity, class, or national origin dictated."[126]

Figure 7.2 Filipino American boxers in Los Angeles. The photo shows (left to right) Felix Santiago, 1931 Pacific Coast bantamweight and flyweight champion Speedy Dado, manager Jess Cortez, and future American middleweight champion, Ceferino Garcia. (Reproduced from the original held by the Department of Special Collections of the Hesburgh Libraries of the University of Notre Dame.)

While engaging popular culture allowed Asian Americans to prove their modernity and claim cultural citizenship, in light of the anti-Asian sentiment and scientific racism of the era, it was also a way to disprove stereotypes. In this regard, Asian Americans who achieved visibility in the popular media were significant, but they also faced tensions between how they wished to be portrayed and public expectations. The career of actress Anna May Wong illustrates this bind. Wong was born in Los Angeles Chinatown in 1905 to U.S.-born parents and got her start in 1919 as an extra in *The Red Lantern*. On the one hand, she symbolized modern Asian femininity in America, a woman both proud of her heritage and loyal to America. She starred in several Chinese American themed films such as *King of Chinatown* (1939) in which she played surgeon Dr. Mary Ling, a character based on the Chinese American physician Margaret Chung.[127] She enjoyed the heyday of her career in the 1920s and 1930s, and in 1938 *People* magazine called her "The World's Most Beautiful Chinese Girl."[128] Wong was typecast for much of her career, however; her most famous roles were as a Mongol slave in *Thief of Baghdad* (1924) and the character Lotus Flower who commits suicide in *Toll of the Sea* (1922). The themes of the films she appeared in were often predicated on East–West difference and her characters were non-modern, colonized, and/or sinister. After making *The Daughter of the Dragon* (1931), her last role as a villain, critics praised Wong's performance, but she nonetheless criticized the film and continued to speak out against what she deemed inappropriate representations of Chinese people.[129]

Anna May Wong and other modern performers were transcendent yet limited. Another famous actor from the early 1900s was Sessue Hayakawa, a Japan-born performer whose masculine image led to frequent comparisons to Rudolph Valentino. Although such individuals broke boundaries, they could not cross borders at will. To travel, Wong had to file papers upon leaving the United States as proof of her citizenship so she could reenter. Moreover, their popularity owed greatly to the public's appetite for the exotic. "Modernity factored into orientalism," says Shirley Jennifer Lim, "and was heightened by the need to manage the 'yellow peril' and 'Asian menace,' which manifested itself in movies of the 1920s such as *Old San Francisco* and the *Fu Manchu* films."[130]

The Great Depression and Eve of War

With the close of the 1920s, like other economically marginalized populations already at or near the bottom, Asian Americans had little ground to lose during the Great Depression, and in many ways were better equipped to weather the economic downturn than the general population. Women who worked outside the home, for instance, continued to find jobs in female-dominated areas of employment such as sewing, domestic service, sales, and clerical work. Also, because the communities in urban Chinatowns and Little Tokyos had developed segregated ethnic economies and relied on internal resources and networks, they were insulated from the larger economy's downward spiral. Additionally, those who did lose their jobs had assistance they could readily turn to. The CCBA was a crucial source of assistance for Chinese Americans. In San Francisco it expanded its services with free medical care at the Chinese Hospital as well as a shelter.[131]

On the mainland, Filipinos were active in labor organizing—mostly in the agricultural and salmon canning sectors—in part because their later entry into the workforce compared to other Asians denied them the same paths to mobility.[132] They also lacked the support of co-ethnic contractors that helped, protected, and negotiated on behalf of Japanese and Chinese. The Filipino Labor Union (FLU), established in 1933 during a strike of seven hundred lettuce pickers in Salinas Valley, is known as the first successful Filipino labor organization. The FLU's membership grew to two thousand by 1934 and that year its members joined the Vegetable Packers Association, an AFL affiliate, during a strike in Monterey.[133] Also in 1933, Northwest Filipino salmon cannery workers entered the AFL as the Cannery Workers and Farm Laborers Union (CWFLU), Local 18257, which challenged the power of contractors, called for shorter hours, and emphasized the need for Filipinos to attain more skills that would lead to greater mobility. It also enacted social welfare programs and engaged the wider Filipino community, paying a Filipino-owned café in Seattle to serve meals to indigent members and providing financial support for Filipino American newspapers. In Washington during the 1930s, the CWFLU was also a political voice for Filipino Americans, appearing at NRA code hearings, protesting the state's alien land law, and fighting the passage of miscegenation bills. Envisioning a multiethnic class-based coalition, CWFLU members also reached out with some success to Chinese and Japanese, and in 1938 it joined the CIO due to its more inclusive vision compared to the AFL.[134]

The activities of Filipinos and other Asian Americans in interethnic organizing highlight a little-known history of Asian American labor radicalism. Filipinos were instrumental in the formation of the Cannery and Agricultural Workers Industrial Union (CAWIU) in 1930, which brought together white leftists and immigrant workers and urged for working class unity against contractors and ethnic middlemen. In 1935, the exploitative practices of San Francisco-based contractors led to the formation of the Alaska Cannery Workers Union (ACWU), an AFL local. Although it did not appeal broadly to Chinese Americans and Japanese Americans, it did draw leftists from these communities, such as Karl Yoneda and Willie Fong. The ACWU, moreover, achieved notable success, gaining the recognition of canners in San Francisco and negotiating a wage scale that was higher than the industry minimum of $50 per month established by the National Recovery Act. Its membership peaked in the late 1930s and early 1940s at about four hundred, and in 1937 it became a CIO affiliate.[135]

Although union activity could be an effective and empowering vehicle for laborers to change their work cultures and develop a class-based solidarity, it was also accompanied by setbacks and frustration. For instance, despite its efforts to combat the ethnic-based contracting system in salmon canning, the CWFLU was never quite able to break the power of Chinese and Japanese contractors, nor did it gain the recognition of companies. At times class solidarity conflicted with interethnic cooperation. In 1930 in Seattle, the Filipino Laborers' Association was formed for agricultural workers in the Northwest but represented the interests of Filipinos against Japanese growers. Moreover, efforts to build interethnic class solidarity were disrupted by groups that favored nationalistic strategies. For instance, second-generation leader and Seattle resident Clarence Arai urged Nisei to support all-Japanese organizations instead of unions such as the CWFLU, which tried to counter this by recruiting more progressive Nisei such as George Taki and Dyke Miyagawa. Some organizations were also beset by ideological disagreements among members, such as when Filipino leftists in the CWFLU broke away and created a rival organization called the Fishermen and Cannery Workers' Industrial Union (FCWIU).[136]

While utilizing services offered by ethnic associations bound Chinese Americans more tightly to the institutions, the Depression also offered opportunities to break away from ethnic networks and look to other avenues for relief and empowerment, such as the labor movement and the government. Workers in Chinese-owned garment factories, where some employers exploited the predominantly female and immigrant labor force, mobilized for better conditions. At Joe Shoong's factories, worker abuse prompted the organization of strikes under the leadership of Chinese Ladies Garment Workers, an affiliate of the International Ladies Garment Workers Union formed in 1937. In 1931, Chinese Marxists in San Francisco formed the Huaren Shiyi Hui (Chinese Unemployed Alliance) to organize the working class and unemployed, and later joined the Communist Party-organized Unemployed Council of the U.S.A., which called for racial and class unity on unemployment and government relief. The 1930s also marked a new era in labor relations. The Wagner Act of 1935 gave organized labor the right to collective bargaining, which strengthened the position of all workers across a number of industries. During this period, the CIO and the Communist Party were instrumental in bringing minorities and women into the fold. Chinese and blacks had been historically excluded from the labor movement, but they joined picket lines in the San Francisco strikes of 1934 and were welcomed into the International Longshoremen and Warehousemen's Union, Culinary and Miscellaneous Workers' Union, and Apartment and Hotel Union.[137]

For many Asians in America, obtaining government relief through New Deal programs like the Federal Emergency Relief Act (FERA) and the Works Progress Administration (WPA) was a major step. It reflected both the desperateness of the economic downturn and the New Deal's unprecedented openness to previously marginalized communities. By 1935, about 18 percent of the Chinese population in San Francisco—about 2,300 people—were on government assistance. The opportunities the programs offered, however, were limited; most racial minorities who obtained WPA jobs were placed in semiskilled and unskilled occupations, with a small number getting white-collar jobs such as social workers, recreation aides, teachers, and clerks.[138] The federal programs, moreover, made starker the divide between first and second generations, as U.S. citizenship was usually a requirement.

Asian Americans also responded to the challenges of the Depression by finding new ways to boost their communities. San Francisco's Chinatown recovered before the rest of the country due to the organizing of businessmen, recovery of the Chinese import trade, as well as heightened promotion of tourism, leading the *Chinese Digest* to declare in 1936 that the community had "passed its winter." By 1938, Chinatown tourism was bringing in $5 million per year.[139] The Golden Gate International Exposition of 1939, furthermore, drew tourists and created new jobs, both at the fair and in Chinatown. The Nisei Week festival in Los Angeles, which started in 1934, likewise emerged from the hope that boosting Little Tokyo's appeal to outsiders would help the community weather hard times. The economic downturn, as well as the numerical rise of the Nisei, made immigrants realize that they needed to look to clientele they had traditionally ignored, namely whites and young Japanese Americans.[140] It was immediately successful and spurred business and improved public relations.

Others left for Asia during the Depression, voluntarily and under pressure. Between 1930 and 1934, about 7,000 Chinese returned to China via San Francisco, while 2,300 entered.[141]

Filipinos, along with Mexicans, faced pressure from the federal government to go back to their homelands. In 1935, the Repatriation Act offered Filipinos free transportation to the Philippines on condition that they not return. Some 2,190, or about 7 percent of the Filipino population, took up the offer.[142]

Conclusion

Until the 1930s, Asian Americans found ways to reconcile being Asian and American, creating fluid identities and multiple allegiances that complemented one another. Portland Chinese Americans Back and Hing, discussed earlier, grew up identifying as Americans while still proud of being Chinese. Just after the Spanish–American War, they formed patriotic organizations for other Chinese American youths, including a pro-U.S. paramilitary organization called the Chinese Brigade.[143] Likewise, Nisei across the country embraced a bicultural outlook in which they maintained identities as Japanese and Americans and regarded themselves as "bridges of understanding." All of this would change abruptly and dramatically with the outbreak of World War II.

Notes

1 Henry Yu, *Thinking Orientals: Migration, Contact, and Exoticism in Modern America* (New York: Oxford University Press, 2001), 98.

2 Ibid., 98–99.

3 Between 1900 and 1940 the foreign-born Chinese population in the city was reduced by half while the native born quadrupled. While a significant number were probably "paper sons" and "paper daughters," many were also born in the United States. See Judy Yung, *Unbound Feet: A Social History of Chinese Women in San Francisco* (Berkeley: University of California Press, 1995), 106.

4 Wendy Rouse Jorae, *The Children of Chinatown: Growing up Chinese American in San Francisco, 1850–1920* (Chapel Hill: University of North Carolina Press, 2009), 55.

5 K. Scott Wong, *Americans First: Chinese Americans and the Second World War* (Cambridge, MA: Harvard University Press, 2005), 189; Ronald Takaki, *Strangers From a Different Shore: A History of Asian Americans* (Boston: Little Brown, 1988), 255.

6 Yuji Ichioka, *Issei: The World of the First Generation Japanese Immigrants, 1885–1924* (New York: Free Press, 1988), 10.

7 Ronald Takaki, *Pau Hana: Plantation Life and Labor in Hawaii, 1835–1920* (Honolulu: University of Hawaii Press, 1983), 122–24.

8 Karen Isaksen Leonard, *Making Ethnic Choices: California's Punjabi Mexicans* (Philadelphia: Temple University Press, 1992), 66; Takaki, *Strangers from a Different Shore*, 311.

9 Yuji Ichioka, "Dai Nisei Mondai." Yuji Ichioka, *Before Internment: Essays in Prewar Japanese American History*, edited by Gordon H. Chang and Eiichiro Azuma (Stanford: Stanford University Press, 2006), 11, 12.

10 Jorae, *The Children of Chinatown*, 130.

11 Ibid., 13.

12 Ichioka, *Issei*, 15.

13 The Japanese Diet amended the Japanese Nationality Act in 1916, allowing parents or guardians of Nisei aged fourteen or younger to renounce Japanese citizenship and for Nisei aged fifteen or older to renounce. Male Nisei aged seventeen or older could forswear only if they fulfilled

Japanese military obligation. The 1924 Japanese Nationality Act amended again and allowed Nisei to renounce Japanese citizenship with no precondition. It abolished automatic Japanese nationality based on paternal descent. Ibid., 17, 19.

14 Ibid., 57–8.

15 Ibid., 26.

16 Ibid., 26.

17 Evelyn Nakano Glenn, *Issei, Nisei, War Bride: Three generations of Japanese American Women in Domestic Service* (Philadelphia: Temple University Press, 1986), 53.

18 Jorae, *The Children of Chinatown*, 56.

19 Ibid., 67.

20 Ibid., 57.

21 Marie Rose Wong, *Sweet Cakes, Long Journey: The Chinatowns of Portland, Oregon* (Seattle: University of Washington, 2004), 185.

22 Jorae, *The Children of Chinatown*, 208.

23 H. Brett Melendy, *Asians in America: Filipinos, Koreans, and East Indians* (Boston: Twayne Publishers, 1977), 145.

24 Ibid., 144–45.

25 Jorae, *The Children of Chinatown*, 59.

26 Yung, *Unbound Feet*, 110–11.

27 Ibid., 111.

28 Ibid., 112.

29 Ibid., 121.

30 Leonard, *Making Ethnic Choices*, 151.

31 Jorae, *The Children of Chinatown*, 209.

32 Yung, *Unbound Feet*, 116.

33 Jorae, *The Children of Chinatown*, 210.

34 Yung, *Unbound Feet*, 166.

35 Leonard, *Making Ethnic Choices*, 157.

36 David Yoo, *Growing Up Nisei: Race, Generation, and Culture among Japanese Americans of California, 1924–49* (Urbana: University of Illinois Press, 2000), 82.

37 Glenn, *Issei, Nisei, War Bride*, 57.

38 Yoo, *Growing Up Nisei*, 83.

39 Ibid., 84.

40 Ibid., 84–5.

41 Ibid., 86.

42 Yung, *Unbound Feet*, 170.

43 Leonard, *Making Ethnic Choices*, 149.

44 Ibid., 157.

45 Ibid., 146–47.

46 Jorae, *The Children of Chinatown*, 64.

47 In 1854 San Francisco first established a separate school for black children (the first in the state)—in 1855 the legislature passed a law saying that state education funds could only be used for white children.

48 Ibid., 115. Also for more on the case and the Tape family, see Mae Ngai, *The Lucky Ones: One Family and the Extraordinary Invention of Chinese America* (New York: Houghton Mifflin, 2010). Chapter 4 focuses on the *Tape* case.

49 Ngai, *The Lucky Ones*, ix.

50 There were other Chinese schools prior to 1885. In 1859 the first Chinese Public School opened in San Francisco and the following year the legislature passed a law prohibiting blacks, Indians, and Mongolians from attending school with whites. This law was gradually liberalized in 1860s and children could attend school with whites if the district couldn't provide for their education in any other way. In 1870 a new segregation law provided for the creation of separate schools

but did not mention Chinese, leading to the shutdown of the Chinese School in 1871. Between 1871 and 1885, Chinese effectively had no access to public education. See Jorae, *The Children of Chinatown*, 113.

51 Ibid., 117.

52 Ibid., 127.

53 Yoo, *Growing Up Nisei*, 19.

54 In 1900 about a third of Chinese children in San Francisco were attending school. Christian institutions were the first to address education for Chinese girls and women, and in 1903 a Baptist mission started a girls' school in San Francisco Chinatown to teach Chinese, English, and fine arts. Yung, *Unbound Feet*, 126.

55 Shelley Sang-Hee Lee, *Claiming the Oriental Gateway: Prewar Seattle and Japanese America* (Philadelphia: Temple University Press, 2011), 41.

56 Ibid., 113.

57 Ibid., 129.

58 The quote comes from a civics textbook used at the Oriental school in the 1910s. Jorae, *The Children of Chinatown*, 126, 127.

59 Leonard, *Making Ethnic Choices*, 159.

60 Yung, *Unbound Feet*, 135.

61 Jorae, *The Children of Chinatown*, 211; Glenn, *Issei, Nisei, War Bride*, 125–26.

62 Glenn, *Issei, Nisei, War Bride*, 128.

63 Yoo, *Growing Up Nisei*, 3–4.

64 Ibid., 138–39.

65 Kevin Scott Wong, *Americans First: Chinese Americans and the Second World War* (Cambridge: Harvard University Press, 2005), 196.

66 Yung, *Unbound Feet*, 141.

67 Glenn, *Issei, Nisei, War Bride*, 56, 57.

68 Jorae, *The Children of Chinatown*, 211.

69 Yung, *Unbound Feet*, 135.

70 Ibid., 141.

71 Ibid., 142.

72 Ibid., 134.

73 Lon Kurashige, *Japanese American Celebration and Conflict: A History of Ethnic Identity and Festival, 1934–1990* (Berkeley: University of California Press, 2003), 27.

74 Ibid.

75 Yoo, *Growing Up Nisei*, 27.

76 Jorae, *The Children of Chinatown*, 212.

77 Glenn, *Issei, Nisei, War Bride*, 52.

78 Yung, *Unbound Feet*, 159.

79 Yoo, *Growing Up Nisei*, 2.

80 Wong, *Americans First*, 190.

81 Yung, *Unbound Feet*, 128.

82 Shirley Jennifer Lim, *A Feeling of Belonging: Asian American Women's Public Culture, 1930–1960* (New York: New York University Press, 2005), 31.

83 Ibid., 16.

84 Yung, *Unbound Feet*, 207.

85 Ibid., 153–54.

86 Ibid., 155.

87 Ibid., 157.

88 Yoo, *Growing Up Nisei*, 8.

89 Kurashige, *Japanese American Celebration and Conflict*, 29.

90 Ibid., 32.

91 Yung, *Unbound Feet*, 206.

92 Kurashige, *Japanese American Celebration and Conflict*, 63.

93 Ibid., 145.

94 Yung, *Unbound Feet*, 113–15.

95 Ibid., 143.

96 Kurashige, *Japanese American Celebration and Conflict*, 30.

97 Ibid., 39.

98 Ibid., 37.

99 Ibid., 27.

100 Jorae, *The Children of Chinatown*, 58.

101 Ibid., 71.

102 Ibid.

103 Yoo, *Growing Up Nisei*, 24.

104 Yu, *Thinking Orientals*, 100.

105 Ibid., 109.

106 Henry Yu, "The Oriental Problem in America," *Claiming America*, 196.

107 Ibid.

108 Yu, "The Oriental Problem," 201.

109 Yu, *Thinking Orientals*, 107.

110 Jorae, *The Children of Chinatown*, 206–07.

111 Yu, *Thinking Orientals*, 115.

112 Amy Sueyoshi, *Queer Compulsions: Race, Nation, and Sexuality in the Affairs of Yone Noguchi* (Honolulu: University of Hawaii Press, 2012).

113 Gordon H. Chang, "Emerging from the Shadows: The Visual Arts and Asian American History," Gordon H. Chang, Mark Johnson, Paul Karlstrom, eds., *Asian American Art: A History, 1850–1970* (Stanford: Stanford University Press, 2008), x.

114 Yung, *Unbound Feet*, 148.

115 Ibid., 147.

116 Ibid., 123.

117 Ibid., 142.

118 Ibid., 132–33.

119 For a full biographical treatment of Margaret Chung, see Judy Tzu-Chun Wu, *Doctor Mom Chung of the Fair-Haired Bastards: The Life of a Wartime Celebrity* (Berkeley: University of California Press, 2005).

120 Yung, *Unbound Feet*, 148–49.

121 Kurashige, *Japanese American Celebration and Conflict*, 56.

122 Yung, *Unbound Feet*, 202.

123 Ibid., 203.

124 Ibid., 202.

125 Ibid., 138.

126 Linda Espana-Maram, *Creating Masculinity in Los Angeles's Little Manila: Working-Class Filipinos and Popular Culture, 1920s–1950s* (New York: Columbia University Press, 2006), 106.

127 Lim, *A Feeling of Belonging*, 47.

128 Ibid., 48.

129 Ibid., 58.

130 Ibid., 54.

131 Yung, *Unbound Feet*, 183.

132 Maram, *Creating Masculinity*, 47.

133 Ibid., 44–5.

134 Friday, *Organizing Asian American Labor*, 136, 145, 161.

135 Ibid., 135, 155.

136 Ibid., 138, 140, 161–62.

137 Ibid., 187.

138 Ibid., 185.
139 Ibid., 187, 204.
140 Kurashige, *Japanese American Celebration and Conflict*, 24.
141 Yung, *Unbound Feet*, 186.
142 Ibid.
143 Wong, *Americans First*, 185.

Asian Americans and the Crucible of World War II

8

From June to August 1943, the daily newspaper version of the popular *Superman* comic strip featured a storyline centering on Superman's heroics against an evil foe referred to as "The Leer, dreaded Jap saboteur." It began with the hero's visit to a Japanese internment camp where he subdued a group of disloyal internees ("enraged enemy Japs") who tried to escape with smuggled firearms. Afterward, as Clark Kent, he and Lois Lane wrote a series of articles for the *Daily Planet* calling on Americans to strengthen their resolve against Japanese. The articles drew the attention of "Chinese citizens of this city" and "Lum Wong, the mayor of Chinatown," who invited Clark and Lois to ride in a float in a bond-selling parade through Chinatown. Sinister henchmen of Japanese ancestry (and ambiguous nationality) tried to sabotage the parade by bombing Chinatown. Not only did Superman foil the "Japs" once again, but he also went on to deliver needed war supplies to the Allied Powers. The last frame showed the hero speaking to readers with a message wildly out of sync with the storyline, but consistent with recent rhetoric about Japanese in America: "It should be remembered that most Japanese–Americans are loyal citizens. Many are in combat units of our armed forces, and others are working in war factories. According to government statements, not one act of sabotage was perpetrated in Hawaii or territorial U.S. by a Japanese–American."[1]

This comic strip was indicative of how much the fortunes of Asian Americans were shaped by wartime politics and exigencies. Chinese and Japanese were not lumped together, but separated, the former depicted as friends and good Americans and the latter as treacherous and demonic, through "stereotypic Orientalia, dialogue, and slurs." Aside from the striking juxtaposing of Japanese villains and Superman's declaration of Japanese Americans' loyalty, an interesting back story that played out around the strip's publication shed light on the fluid, but contentious, state of wartime racial politics. Upon learning about the internment-focused storyline, officials at the Office of War Information became alarmed. Although they condoned anti-Japanese propaganda earlier in the war, they had come to believe that fanning the flames of racial hatred would undermine U.S. morale.

Terms like "crucible" and "watershed" are often used to describe America during World War II, and these aptly capture the Asian American experience. The Superman comic discussed above evoked changing ideas about and popular depictions of Asian Americans.

Additionally, wartime economic expansion generated new opportunities for people of Asian ancestry, along with white women and other minorities, who had traditionally been marginalized and excluded. Although long-regarded as undesirable foreigners incapable of becoming American, Asians in the United States nonetheless caught the patriotic spirit during this war, giving their time, money, and lives to support the country. They were also able to push the boundaries of belonging and citizenship because the war against fascism, the loyal service of minorities, and the imperative of strong international alliances had undercut the ideological and moral justifications for racism in American life, and with it the regime of Asian exclusion, whose dismantling began with the repeal of the Chinese Exclusion Act in 1943. Meanwhile, as they cheered the United States and pressed to expand their rights, Chinese, Koreans, Filipinos, and Indians in America also turned their attention to Asia and hoped that the war would also hasten the liberation of their homelands from colonial control and new threats.

On the other hand, this was a traumatic time when wartime anxiety and hyper-nationalism brought out people's darker natures. Perhaps no group in America had a more bewildering experience than Japanese Americans. Even though the Nisei—who by the 1940s made up a majority of this population—proclaimed their loyalty to the United States, all persons of Japanese ancestry were regarded as enemies, and the entire West Coast Japanese population was removed and placed in concentration camps, enduring what historian Greg Robinson has called a "tragedy of democracy."[2] The reactions of other Asians to internment varied. Some distanced themselves from Japanese Americans through acts of "ethnic disidentification," and added their voices to the anti-Japanese chorus. On the other hand, many Chinese, Koreans, Filipinos, and Asian Indians were deeply troubled by the anti-Japanese racism of the war, particularly when its targets were their friends and neighbors.

Focusing on the critical World War II years (1941–1945), this chapter describes the experiences of Chinese, Japanese, Koreans, Asian Indians, and Filipinos in the United States, as well as how major wartime developments impacting Asian Americans were part of a broader transformation in domestic race relations and racial ideologies. As internment looms large in this history, a major portion of the chapter is devoted to Japanese Americans from the West Coast, although it will also consider the experiences of those who lived elsewhere in North America as well as in Hawaii, Canada, and Latin America. In describing the lives of Chinese, Koreans, Filipinos, and Asian Indians, the chapter looks at how wartime developments both deepened Asian Americans' transnational orientation vis-à-vis homeland politics and bolstered their resolve to claim rights and belonging in America, starting with the dismantling of Asian exclusion. Finally, the chapter seeks to underscore how these years were a turning point, for Asian Americans and U.S. history writ large. The start of the war, for example, saw the vilification of Japanese Americans, but by its end, they were being hailed for their loyalty and sacrifices. This turnaround was in part an outcome of shifting geopolitical relationships whereby the United States and Japan went from being wartime enemies to postwar allies. Additionally, however, the changing rhetoric about Japanese Americans was part of a coming sea change in domestic racial ideology in which the hegemony of white supremacy was displaced by a new orthodoxy of America as a multi-cultural and multiracial democracy.

The Road to War

Although the attack on the U.S. naval station at Pearl Harbor on December 7, 1941 was a surprise, U.S. officials had for years been preparing for a conflict with Japan. Since the end of World War I in 1919, military and civilian agencies monitored and made plans for the possible detention of Japanese in America who were deemed security threats. In Hawaii, these efforts intensified after the 1920 Oahu strike, which many officials blamed Japanese agitators for fomenting. After Japan's invasion of Manchuria in 1931, the Federal Bureau of Investigation (FBI) and Office of Naval Intelligence (ONI) began gathering information on mainland Japanese, particularly those with business and political connections to Japan, leadership positions in the ethnic community, and jobs through which security breaches or other calamities could be instigated (such as fishermen and produce distributors). Just before Pearl Harbor, the federal government had files on over 2,000 mainland Japanese, placed in one of three categories of suspicion (A, B, or C). Over the 1930s, as conflicts around the world spread and escalated, the United States officially maintained its neutrality but provided non-military assistance to Allied powers. Japan, meanwhile, forged ties with the Axis powers and continued its campaign of aggression in Asia, bringing its relationship with the United States to a tipping point.[3]

Also in these years, Japanese Americans increasingly found themselves the targets of suspicion, and incidents that would have drawn little notice before became cause for alarm. Upon receiving an intelligence report about Japanese naval ships visiting Hawaiian ports and the entertainment of sailors by local Japanese, President Franklin D. Roosevelt recommended the close monitoring of the Hawaii Japanese population and preparations for their possible removal, stating in a letter to the military's Joint Board chief in Washington:

> One obvious thought occurs to me—that every Japanese citizen or non-citizen on the Island of Oahu who meets these Japanese ships or has any connection with their officers or men should be secretly but definitely indentified and his or her name placed on a special list of those who would be the first to be placed in a concentration camp in the event of trouble.[4]

Local, state, and national officials also made accusations that dialed up people's worries and increased suspicion about Japanese Americans' loyalty. Former FBI agent Blayney F. Matthews said that West Coast Issei truck farmers were spraying arsenic on their crops to poison Americans, and a council member from West Adams in Los Angeles County opposed a housing development for Japanese Americans because Nisei would "stab America in the back."[5] Such rhetoric found a national platform as members of Congress trumpeted these and other charges. The Texas congressman Martin Dies alleged that Japan was conscripting Japanese American dual citizens, and Richard Welch of California called for the removal of Japanese fishermen and their families from Terminal Island and other military facilities. Welch made his recommendation in response to the unsubstantiated but widely circulated rumor that Japanese American fishermen were assisting Japanese naval officers off the Pacific Coast.[6]

Japanese Americans—both Issei and Nisei—felt the strains of the deepening rifts between the United States and Japan and rising anti-Japanese sentiment. To assuage immigrants' worries, in October 1941 the Central California Japanese Association president Gongoro Nakamura and journalist Togo Tanaka went to Washington, D.C. to meet with Justice Department officials who gave their assurance that Issei would not be placed in concentration camps in the event of war.[7] Describing the besieged mindset of Nisei, James Omura wrote in the San Francisco Nisei monthly *Current Life*, "WE ARE AT WAR." Fearful that Japanese in America would be persecuted in a fashion similar to what German Americans endured during World War I, he advised Nisei to lay low and foster the goodwill of the surrounding community:

> We are all under suspicion. We are all being observed. . .We know we have nothing to conceal, but this does not preclude the fact that people living around us may not know it. And we cannot produce convincing enough evidence to acquit ourselves of suspicion. Our course, then, is to remain inconspicuous.[8]

Nisei found that their "bicultural" identity, in which they embraced their Japanese and American sides, celebrated U.S.–Japan relations, and served as "bridges of understanding," was now untenable. The Japanese American Citizens League (JACL), once a supporter of Japan's actions in China, adopted a rigid pro-America stance, raising money for the Red Cross and encouraging Nisei to enlist in the army. Fred Makino of Hawaii went as far as advocating denationalization, or the disavowal of all ties to Japan, proposing the prohibition of dual citizens from public employment.[9]

Other Asian Americans were also drawn into international events before the United States entered World War II, but for different reasons. For China and Chinese Americans, the war actually began when Japan invaded Manchuria in 1931, a turn of events that brought an anti-Japan tenor to Chinese American homeland politics. The Chinese American newspaper *Chung Sai Yat Po* urged the United States to go to war with Japan, and in 1937, the *Chinese Digest* said, "being a patriotic Chinese means also that one must hate the Japanese."[10] In the 1930s, Chinese Americans organized boycotts of Japanese goods and picketed docks where Japan-bound ships were moored. Overall, however, helping China and building unity among Chinese Americans were the aims of homeland activism, and much of this was accomplished through fundraising by organizations such as the Chinese War Relief Association (CWRA) and the CCBA.[11] In 1940, the *Chinese News* reported that since 1937 overseas Chinese had raised $54,000,000 for China relief. Popular "Rice Bowl" parties and marches held in various cities, often in partnership with white pro-China organizations, raised a great deal of money, such as San Francisco's 1940 Rice Bowl, which netted about $87,000.[12]

As discussed earlier, Koreans in America had been deeply engaged with events in their homeland since Japan asserted its dominance in Korea in 1905, but over the 1930s they became particularly vocal in anti-Japan politics. On April 1941, the United Korean Committee, a U.S.-based Korean nationalist organization, called on Koreans in America to unite and support the Allied Powers "until they bring a final victory of the present war against the Axis Powers."[13] Immigrants who saw themselves as exiles from their homeland hoped a war would hasten Korea's liberation. Kilsoo Haan, the head of the Sino–Korean People's League, was a prominent anti-Japan advocate before and during the war. One of the League's purposes, he explained, was to spy on Hawaii Japanese, and in early 1941 he claimed there were 35,000 to 50,000 Japanese in the islands who were ready to assist Japan in a war against the United States.

Asian Indians and Filipinos were less preoccupied with the activities of Japan at this time, but they did pay close attention to international developments as they pertained to their countries of origin and potentially impacted their standing in the United States. The promulgation of the Atlantic Charter in August 1941, in which FDR and Churchill committed the U.S. and Britain to a common set of principles, including the right of people to choose their own government, struck hope among many Indians in America. Through organizations such as the India Welfare League and the India League of America, they intensified their activism for both Indian independence and their rights in the United States.[14] Filipino leaders also became more vocal, especially in highlighting the contradiction of Americans' condemnation of fascism abroad and condoning of racism at home. In an open letter to U.S. leaders in 1940, Filipino organizer Trinidad Rojo stated:

> We, Filipinos, owe allegiance to the United States. In case of war, we are duty bound to lay down our lives for the STARS AND STRIPES. If the American flag imposes upon us the duty to die for it, if necessary; in all fairness, it must also give us the right to live as American citizens . . . [We] are victims of a Philippine–American relationship which started before most of us were born. Certainly we are not responsible for that relationship . . . we are here because America is in the Philippines.[15]

Thus, on the eve of the United States' entry into World War II, Asian Americans were highly attuned to the myriad ways—politically, socially, ideologically—that the international conflict might usher in a new world. Many, furthermore, were determined to participate in bringing about those changes.

On December 7, 1941 Japanese forces launched a bombing raid on Pearl Harbor, the chief base of the U.S. navy's Pacific fleet, and other military bases on Oahu. The U.S. fleet was destroyed and 2,390 American soldiers and civilians were killed. The next day, President Roosevelt secured from Congress a declaration of war against Japan, which passed both houses with one dissenting vote.[16] After the attack, Japan went on to invade territories in Asia, conquering Burma, Siam, and Indonesia and occupying the Philippines, Guam, and other Pacific Islands by early 1942.

The impact of Pearl Harbor and the United States' entry into World War II was jarring and profound. Initially, politicians such as California Governor Culbert Olson and Los Angeles mayor Fletcher Bowron, as well as many newspapers, urged for calm and that people not lash out at Japanese Americans. The *Los Angeles Times* told readers, "Let's Not Get Rattled," and the *Seattle Post-Intelligencer* affirmed, "Japanese in America are as loyal as any white Americans."[17] At the same time, however, the events of December 1941 reignited the anti-Japanese agendas of groups like the Native Sons of the Golden West, the Western Grower's Protective Association, and the American Federation of Labor. As calls for the removal of West Coast Japanese intensified, an official from the California Joint Immigration Committee stated, "This is our time to get things done that we have been trying to get done for a quarter of a century."[18] Similarly, in May 1942 Austin Antin of the California Grower–Shipper Vegetable Association revealed how his support for internment drew from a well of anti-Japanese sentiment among farmers. "If all the Japs were removed tomorrow," he said, "we'd never miss them . . . because the white farmers can take over and produce everything the Jap grows. And we don't want them back when the war ends, either."[19]

By declaring war against Japan, the United States solidified its alliances with other Asian countries, and Asian American leaders, in turn, pledged their support for the Allies while they worked to advance their homeland causes.[20] Syngman Rhee, who was based in Washington, D.C. when the U.S. entered the war, called on Koreans everywhere to sacrifice for Japan's defeat. "Every armed Japanese is your enemy and you visit upon them the fury of an unconquerable people," he said. "To fight for America is to fight for Korea."[21] Rhee, as well as Kilsoo Haan and other diasporic Korean leaders, also seized the moment to secure the Allied Powers' recognition of the Korean Provisional Government. With regard to the Philippines, hours after the Pearl Harbor attack, Japan invaded the archipelago, becoming its third colonial power in less than fifty years.[22] Although Philippine leaders wanted independence, most supported U.S. forces because they believe an Allied victory was the surest path to national self-determination. Many Filipinos in America agreed and also supported the Allies, participating in letter-writing campaigns and issuing statements of support for the United States.[23]

Japanese Americans were stunned at the news of Pearl Harbor and then filled with trepidation about what might follow. Even those who had been following events in Asia could not believe an attack on American soil had occurred. One Nisei fruit stand worker said, "I was shocked . . . I still continued to think that it was impossible for such a thing to happen," and a Nisei woman typist recalled, "we thought that maybe it might be a mistake or some kind of play."[24] The shock soon turned into despair and panic as an anti-Japanese backlash set in. In the weeks after Pearl Harbor, a handful of Japanese people were murdered in Los Angeles, Stockton, Imperial Valley, and Chicago, and reports of assaults and vandalism also surfaced.[25] In the western states, farmers cut their ties with Japanese Americans by releasing them from their leases, and in California and the city and county of Los Angeles, Japanese civil servants were dismissed from their jobs. In San Francisco, the local Red Cross branch even stopped taking aid to or donations from Japanese. Most Nisei who were in the U.S. military at the time were discharged, although a small number was retained for intelligence work.[26]

For their part, Japanese Americans were torn on how to respond to the circumstances. From some quarters came a barrage of loyalty statements. The JACL, which positioned itself as the voice of the population, pledged its obedience to the U.S. government. The artist Isamu Noguchi started the Nisei Writers and Artists Mobilization for Democracy in 1942, which vowed to be "useful to our American homeland" by educating the public on "a clear and accurate picture of the American citizen of Japanese extraction."[27] Others responded critically toward the United States, such as the *Shin Sekai* of northern California, which blamed it for precipitating the war. Additionally, over the war years, thousands of Japanese Americans applied to renounce their U.S. citizenship and be repatriated to Japan.[28] The impact of such disagreements on intracommunity relations could be devastating. Tamotsu Shibutani despaired that his fellow Nikkei were engaging in witch hunts against each other, and ensuing developments showed that his fears were warranted. In the months after Pearl Harbor, some Nisei assisted the government's surveillance of Japanese Americans, and Northern California JACL chapters provided federal authorities with information from a survey of kibei. Vicious cycles of accusations then followed, with those who cooperated with the government being

Figure 8.1   Syngman Rhee, 1939. Rhee was a diplomat, activist, leader among diasporic Koreans and played a key role in keeping Korean independence at the center of Korean American politics. (Library of Congress Prints and Photographs Division, LC-DIG-hec-26756.)

condemned as squealers, and critics of the United States being labeled treacherous. In declaring his allegiance to the United States, Tokutaro Nishimura Slocum also took the opportunity to bring down "nefarious" elements from the Japanese American community:

> [the] Central Japanese Association is a nefarious, spying organization, and I am proud to say to you here that, on December 7 [1941] night, I went over the top again, leading

my buddies of the Federal Bureau of Investigation and the Naval Intelligence to arrest the Central Japanese Association leaders, everyone from that lecherous Gongoro Nakamura down.[29]

Japanese Internment: The Decision to Remove and Imprison

The road to mass Japanese removal was swift yet haphazard. After the United States entered the war, all Japanese, German, and Italian nationals were classified as enemy aliens. As such, they had to register with the federal government, could not sue it for any action against them, and faced travel restrictions. Within hours of Pearl Harbor, FBI agents were on the ground arresting individuals from the lists that had been compiled by federal authorities.[30] Hawaii was placed under martial law and the U.S.–Mexico border was closed. By 1943, 14,738 Japanese "enemy aliens" had been arrested. Most were eventually paroled after their hearings, but over 5,000 were interned in camps in New Mexico, Montana, South Dakota, Los Angeles, and the Bay Area.[31] Compared to German and Italian nationals, Japanese were detained in smaller numbers, but in far greater proportions. A Western Defense Command officer even admitted that Japanese Americans were interned on slimmer evidence than German Americans had been.[32]

In the weeks after Pearl Harbor, military and government officials were divided on what to do about the Japanese in Hawaii and the West Coast, whether they had been complicit in the attack, and if they posed an ongoing threat. An army board of inquiry investigation of conditions in Hawaii concluded there had been no sabotage by the islands' Japanese. Despite this finding, Navy Secretary Frank Knox held to the claim that fifth columnists had orchestrated Pearl Harbor. Treasury Secretary Henry Morgantheau wanted to remove Japanese from strategic coastal areas, but Hawaii commander Walter Short and FBI director J. Edgar Hoover thought this was unnecessary.[33] Kenneth Ringle of the ONI also disagreed with internment and proposed enlisting loyal Nisei, with the government's help, to take charge of the property and safety of Japanese aliens. General John DeWitt of the Western Defense Command emerged as the leading advocate of Japanese removal. Convinced that Japan was planning to invade the West Coast with the aid of Japanese Americans, he requested federal authority to designate the Coast a military area from which people could be removed. U.S. Attorney General Francis Biddle, who had consented to warrantless raids on the homes and businesses of enemy aliens, tried to draw the line at mass removal and arbitrary actions against U.S. citizens, as he preferred to proceed through individual investigations and arrests. He cited reports from J. Edgar Hoover and Kenneth Ringle affirming the loyalty of the vast majority of Japanese Americans and lack of any sabotage since Pearl Harbor. Over several months, Biddle argued with DeWitt, Assistant Secretary of War John McCloy, and military attorney Karl Bendetson over issues like the size of proposed military areas, the extension of military power that removal would entail, and the constitutionality of incarcerating U.S. citizens. To the latter concern, McCloy responded, "The Constitution is just a scrap of paper to me."[34]

By January 1942, American morale was shaky; the United States was losing the war, and people were at a loss to explain Japan's successes in Pearl Harbor, Guam, and the Philippines. According to Greg Robinson, a turning point was the release of the Roberts Commission report on January 24. The Commission, composed of military officers and tasked with inquiring into the Pearl Harbor disaster, said that Tokyo had relied on spies for information and used the Hawaii consulate as a recruitment center. It specified neither who the recruits were nor if they were Japanese, but anti-Japan militants took the statement as evidence of the treachery of all Japanese.[35] "Yellow peril" newspapers published by William Randolph Hearst and James McClatchy fanned the flames with sensationalized articles about what the FBI raids allegedly uncovered and other evidence of purported Japanese disloyalty. Officials who initially defended Japanese Americans backtracked. Culbert Olson said the Roberts report made him feel unsafe and endorsed the State Personnel Board's suspension of Japanese civil servants. And although Earl Warren acknowledged to a House committee in early 1942 that no concrete evidence of espionage or fifth column activity by Japanese Americans had been found, he said this should be taken as implicit proof that they were planning an attack.[36]

Many scholars have written on the subject of Japanese internment, detailing its injustices, debating the policy's merits, and offering explanations on why it occurred, from public pressure fueled by racism to military strategies for ensuring Japan's humane handling of American prisoners. Racism certainly underlay the conflation of ethnicity with national loyalty that rationalized the imprisonment of about 110,000 Japanese Americans, of whom over 70,000 were U.S. citizens. Moreover, although the United States was also at war with Germany and Italy, the government did not intern Germans and Italians in America en masse, instead investigating them individually. As Earl Warren offered as an explanation for the differing approaches, "We believe that when we are dealing with the Caucasian race we have methods that will test the loyalty of them . . . But when we deal with the Japanese we are in an entirely different field and cannot form any opinion that we believe to be sound."[37] Internment was also a consequence of lapses in executive leadership. Worried about the threat Japanese Americans posed to national security, yet mindful of the impossibly complex operation that mass removal would be, Secretary of War Henry Stimson ultimately deferred to his military commanders. For FDR's part, as Japanese removal was being debated in December 1941, he delayed weighing in and eventually decided that violating the rights of a few Japanese Americans was an acceptable cost for winning the war. On February 19, 1942, he signed Executive Order 9066, conferring upon the Secretary of War the authority to designate military zones "from which any or all persons may be excluded" and for which the right of any person to "enter, remain in, or leave" was left to the discretion of military authorities.[38] Although its language was neutral, the order's intent was to clear the way for Japanese mass removal. The day after its signing, Stimson authorized DeWitt to create the West Coast defense zone he had requested and to remove civilians as he saw fit.

Following the issuance of EO 9066, Japanese Americans were encouraged to leave the West Coast voluntarily, but very few did due to logistical obstacles and fear of the unknown. Subsequently, on March 2, the voluntary evacuation phase ended, and all Japanese living in Military Zone 1—covering southern Arizona and half of the states of Washington, Oregon, California—were told to register with authorities and report to temporary assembly centers, where they would stay until being taken to permanent relocation centers, or "concentration camps". These and other orders were given teeth by Public Law 503, passed by Congress on March 21, which made it a federal offense to disobey military exclusion. The army handled the initial evacuation, and then the main responsibility for relocation and camp admini-stration fell into the hands of the War Relocation Authority (WRA), a civilian agency directed by Milton Eisenhower.[39] The ten relocation centers were in California, Arizona, Idaho, Wyoming, Utah, and Arkansas, the sites being selected based on expediency and availability of resources, with little consideration for the impact on locals.[40]

Critics of internment emerged in the wake of the executive order, but they were few in number and ultimately drowned out. Prominent among them were academics, employers of Japanese, the Quakers and other Christian organizations, civil rights groups, and black press organizations. During the House Select Committee Investigating National Defense Migration hearings in February and March 1942, also known as the Tolan Committee hearings, opponents of internment—including Japanese Americans—had a chance to express their concerns. Witnesses included Farm Security Administration official Richard Neustadt, University of Washington professors Jesse Steiner and Robert O'Brien, and CIO Secretary Louis Goldblatt, who condemned evacuation as a racist and agenda-driven policy.[41] These examples aside, the left as a whole was not united on the issue of Japanese internment.[42] Most Jewish and Mexican American organizations were silent or supportive of the policy, and lefitst organizations like the American Civil Liberties Union, CPUSA, and Common Council for American University twisted themselves into ideological pretzels, endorsing evacuation as a "regrettable but necessary" policy.[43] An editorial by the activist and scholar Carey McWilliams appearing in *Common Ground*, the publication of the Common Council for American Unity, captured the limits of wartime liberalism. McWilliams denounced

Figure 8.2 This photo from April 1942 shows a Japanese American mother and her three children on a train from Los Angeles to Manzanar internment camp. (Library of Congress Prints and Photographs Division, LC-USZ62-43695.)

overtly racist anti-Japanese expressions, but accepted the legitimacy of internment, offering that Japanese had to be removed "not because they are suspect en masse" but "to allay popular uneasiness created by their presence on the West Coast in large numbers and in strategic areas."[44] He largely avoided the issue of constitutionality, merely stating some "due compensation" might be paid down the road.

For the most part, Japanese Americans followed orders and cooperated with evacuation. On why internment did not provoke a mass resistance, it is important to consider the context. With the arrests and detentions of community leaders, freezing of Issei assets, imposition of curfews, and other restrictions, Japanese America was effectively paralyzed, and stepping into the vacuum was the JACL, which pledged Japanese Americans' loyalty and obedience. A handful of Nisei did challenge internment in the courts and, of these, four cases—filed by Minoru Yasui, Gordon Hirabayashi, Fred Korematsu, and Mitsuye Endo—reached the U.S. Supreme Court. The first three cases originated in Spring 1942; Yasui and Hirabayashi, of Portland and Seattle, respectively, intentionally violated the military curfew to test the legality of removal, and Korematsu, who had failed to report to an assembly center, was picked up by police in San Leandro, California.[45] All three cases, moreover, were unsuccessful, the first two cases being decided in June 1943 and Korematsu's in December 1944 (the *Endo* case is discussed below). The court said that the curfew and removal policies were legal and that Yasui, Hirabayashi, and Korematsu's constitutional rights had not been violated. In its 6–3 decision against Korematsu, the court stated that military necessity, not race, was the reason behind removal, and that the "urgency of the situation" justified internment. Legal scholar Peter Irons has shown that the government's cases were compromised by the concealment of reports establishing the absence of Japanese American espionage, a revelation that undercut the military necessity argument, but details of this deception did not come to light for several decades.[46]

Removal and Life Behind Barbed Wire

From the attack on Pearl Harbor, Japanese America was plunged into crisis. The arrests of Issei from the ABC list paralyzed communities along the coast and in Hawaii by depriving them of their leaders. As enemy aliens, Japanese immigrants were ordered to turn in their short-wave radios, cameras, and other equipment considered to be contraband, and many destroyed personal and other items for fear of incrimination. Japanese consulates, press agencies, and the vernacular press were closed down. The ethnic economy, furthermore, was hobbled by government orders to freeze the bank accounts of all Japanese aliens, a directive eased only with the intervention of Eleanor Roosevelt.[47] On the West Coast, Japanese fishing boats were grounded and produce markets shuttered. The first removal actually took place five days prior to EO 9066, when the approximately five hundred families that made up the Japanese fishing community in Terminal Island were told to leave.[48] It was a preview of things to come.

Orders for the remaining Japanese residents on the Coast were posted, with the alert, "Instructions to All Persons of Japanese Ancestry," and removal was in full swing by the end of March. People had about a week to pack their essential belongings and appear at specified locations from which they rode buses to one of fifteen temporary assembly centers along the West Coast. The rush to prepare for removal was chaotic and desperate. In Los Angeles, where Japanese Americans owned about 1,100 homes, less than 10 percent were able to sell their property. A few made arrangements to protect their assets, such as the Nakatas of Palo Alto, who put their money in an account under the name of their friend and employer Alice Sinclair Dodge.[49] The Los Angeles JACL helped forty people establish a trust company with a white American appointed power of attorney. Once removed, however, they had little control over what happened to their property, and in some cases friends who agreed to collect rent or assume other responsibilities betrayed their trust and robbed them.[50]

Japanese Americans did their best to carry on and create a sense of normalcy amid these circumstances. The army's Wartime Civil Control Administration (WCCA) managed the assembly centers, which were usually located at racetracks and fairgrounds. At Tanforan, where about eight thousand Bay Area Japanese lived under the watch of armed military guards, the accommodations included horse stalls as sleeping quarters. Individuals and families lost the power to make decisions over basic living arrangements and activities, which were now under the purview of WCCA authorities. To make conditions in the assembly camps livable, Japanese Americans set up schools and church services, planted gardens and plants, and arranged for friends to visit and send goods. Members of the Nakata family, for instance, made arrangements with white American friends to continue receiving copies of *Reader's Digest* and other items that helped sustain them during their stay at the Santa Anita assembly center.[51]

After several months in the assembly centers, Japanese Americans were taken by train inland to one of ten "concentration camps."[52] Families were crowded into stark one-room apartments, which were usually hastily constructed barracks made of tar-paper, and their autonomy and privacy continued to be encroached upon by communal dining and other living arrangements. The food quality left much to be desired and medical services were inadequate.[53] Despite the reality that about 110,000 Japanese Americans had been imprisoned and forced to live behind barbed wire, the WRA (as well as JACL) portrayed the camps as an "experiment in democracy." They were run as though they were small towns, complete with schools, dances, movies, sports teams, fire departments, newspapers, and elected councils. Dillon Meyer, who replaced Milton Eisenhower as WRA director in June 1942, insisted that Japanese Americans were better off because of internment, and that in the camps, "probably at least half [of the Issei] never had it so good."[54]

Public relations claims notwithstanding, the internment camps were barbed-wire prisons where democracy was an illusion. While Japanese Christians were free to worship, Shintoists could not practice their religion and Buddhists were also subject to discriminatory treatment. For much of the time, only Nisei could participate in camp elections, and those in elected positions held power over such low-stakes matters as when to schedule recreation events. All decisions were furthermore subject to WRA veto. The only roles inmates held that came with any significant power were as block managers, but these were WRA appointees.[55] Internees could work, but for very low wages; unskilled workers were paid about $12 a month and professionals about $19. Private enterprise was forbidden, although Japanese Americans could form agricultural collectives and other cooperative enterprises, within which individuals were allowed to open barbershops and other personal service operations.

Camp life brought jarring changes into Japanese American families and communities. The WRA's preferential treatment of Nisei solidified that generation's ascension to the reins of leadership in Japanese America. Camp officials generally distrusted the Issei, and so gave Nisei more responsibilities and better paying jobs, as teachers, firefighters, nurses, cooks, and other positions. The changes were evident in family life. As mentioned above, the communal eating arrangements of the camps took away an important source of family cohesion and parental authority, as mothers and fathers were no longer responsible for providing and preparing food. The power of Issei men as breadwinners and authority figures was especially diminished, as the WRA usurped these roles. Wives and children spent more time with peers and pursued opportunities (e.g., work, social events, craft classes) that took them away from their nuclear families.[56] Recalling his father's struggles at Tanforan assembly center, Charles Kikuchi said that the conditions:

> Made me feel sorry for Pop . . . He has his three electric clippers hung up on the wall and . . . a barrel chair for the barber seat. It's a bit pathetic when he so tenderly cleans off the clippers after using them . . . He probably realized that he no longer controls the family group and rarely exerts himself . . . What a difference from . . . when I was a kid. He used to be a perfect terror and dictator.[57]

Although internees were portrayed as and urged to be loyal and peaceful, conflict and protest occurred regularly. During an uprising in November 1942 in Poston, internees went on strike in response to the arrests of two men connected to the beating of a kibei, which had occurred against a growing rift in the camp over suspicions that some internees were WRA and FBI informers. The strike also tapped into a well of resentment over inmates' treatment. After supporters of the arrested men were rebuffed in demanding their release, the entire camp, save essential staff, went on strike and called for meaningful self-government. Camp administrators relented, releasing one prisoner, arranging for the trial of the other by an inmate court, and recognizing the Emergency Executive Council formed by strikers as the legitimate representative of the camp population.[58] The following month at Manzanar, a riot that also grew out of suspicions about WRA collaborators resulted in the deaths of two inmates and the imposition of martial law in the camp for two weeks. In the wake of the riot, sixteen men who were suspected of inciting unrest—they were also critics of the JACL and WRA—were removed to a high security camp in Moab, Utah, despite not being charged with any crimes or given a trial.[59]

Another flashpoint came in early 1943 when camp officials distributed a loyalty questionnaire to internees aged eighteen and older. Its goals were to weed out the loyal from the disloyal in order to start the process of inducting Nisei into the army (discussed below), and to help the WRA determine whom it should grant early leave permits. Respondents were asked a series of questions, but two in particular generated much controversy. They asked respondents if they would serve in the U.S. armed forces and swear unqualified allegiance to the United States (questions 27 and 28). Issei were especially disturbed at being asked to commit their allegiance to a country that prohibited them from citizenship. Some twelve thousand respondents, or about 20 percent of the camp population, most of whom were Issei, kibei, and/or rural Japanese, answered "no" to question 28, and in October 1943 they were taken to Tule Lake in northern California, where the most "troublesome" internees were segregated.[60]

The Tule Lake segregation did not quell internees' spirit of resistance, which reared its head again in 1944 when the military introduced the draft for Japanese Americans after voluntary enlistment yielded disappointing numbers. An anti-draft movement led by Kiyoshi Okamoto and Frank Emi of the Fair Play Committee (FPC) emerged at Heart Mountain, Wyoming. Members of the Committee asserted their loyalty, but objected to the expectation that they serve after their constitutional rights of due process had been violated. Attacked viciously by JACL leaders, the 85 Heart Mountain draft resisters, along with about 230 from other camps, were indicted for draft evasion by a federal grand jury. The U.S. Court of Appeals for the Tenth Circuit upheld their convictions and sentenced them to federal prison.[61]

Outside the Coast

The mass removal and imprisonment of Japanese Americans from the West Coast is often treated as the sum total of Japanese American history during the war. To be sure, it captures what most Japanese in America endured and raises larger issues about the rights of U.S. residents and citizens during war, but it does not represent the full scope of the wartime Japanese American experience. As discussed, those arrested by the FBI received hearings and were held in separate detention centers. Japanese outside the West Coast were not subject to mass internment, and, thus, had a very different experience from those in camps. Finally, as World War II was a global conflict, Japanese in other Allied countries were targeted, with many being transferred to U.S. custody. Australia was actually the first nation to implement a large-scale confinement of Japanese when, after Pearl Harbor, 1,141 Japanese men, women, and children—about 97 percent of the country's Japanese population—were taken into custody and housed in a camp in Southern Australia.[62] In the French colony of New Caledonia, all Japanese were removed from the countryside and placed in a prison camp.

Elsewhere in the Americas, Japanese people experienced persecution and disruption. Like the United States, Canada had declared war on Japan on December 8, 1941, and Japanese in British Columbia, like their counterparts on the U.S. West Coast, faced vandalism and violence, the grounding of their fishing boats, curfews, restrictions on purchases, and confiscation of contraband.[63] Japanese newspapers and schools on the Coast also shut down.[64] Mass arrests and raids did not occur, but 38 Japanese Canadians considered to be dangerous were arrested and sent to a POW camp in Ontario. In February 1942, the Canadian government, in consultation with U.S. officials, created protected zones from which 1,500 to 4,000 able-bodied, male Japanese were removed to inland provinces to work in sugar beet fields, road construction, and domestic service.[65] This disrupted Japanese Canadian families and communities, as family members who were ill or lacked sufficient funds could not accompany the men, nor did the government offer assistance to those left behind.[66] Eventually, most of Canada's West Coast Japanese, about 22,000 in all, were forced into "interior housing" in former mining communities in eastern British Columbia's Slocan Valley. The British Columbia Security Commission (BCSC) selected this location due to its availability of abandoned housing and the hope that moving Japanese there would bring an economic boost to the area. The BSCS had fewer resources than the WRA, so most Japanese

Canadians neither lived behind barbed wire nor were watched by guards, but their movements were tracked and the rugged mountain terrain of eastern British Columbia limited their movement.[67]

In Latin America, the treatment of Japanese varied widely. In Mexico, they were excluded from Baja California, and about 80 percent of the country's Japanese population—much of it rural—was uprooted. Many ended up in cities like Mexico City and Guadalajara, where conditions were safer and help was available.[68] Additionally, twelve Latin American countries received help from the United States to deport German and Japanese enemy aliens. In the name of hemispheric security, the U.S. State Department agreed to take those who were considered dangerous and placed them in an internment center in Crystal City, Texas. About 2,100 of these, mostly from Peru, were used in prisoner exchanges for the release of American POWs.[69]

One might wonder why Japanese in Hawaii were not removed. Following Pearl Harbor, Governor Joseph Poindexter declared martial law in the islands and the military regulated all aspects of civilian life, setting curfews, fixing wages and prices of goods, rationing gas and other supplies, censoring the mail, and banning any speech or action critical of the government. Although these rules applied to all residents, it was commonly understood that they were meant to control the Japanese. In other ways, they were explicitly singled out, such as the sudden discharge of Japanese in the Hawaiian National Guard after Pearl Harbor.[70] Additionally, people from the ABC list were taken into custody and sent to an internment camp at Sand Island, Japanese schools were closed, Japanese-owned buildings seized, and the main vernacular newspapers shut down for several weeks. Japanese farmers living near Pearl Harbor were told to leave their homes, and about 1,500 residents were ordered out of the Iwilei district without advance notice.[71] There was no mass incarceration, however, and had a large-scale removal of Japanese been carried out, the territory's economy would likely have collapsed.[72]

Mainland Japanese outside the excluded area also escaped mass imprisonment. Many of the "free zone Nikkei," as they were called, had relocated from the West Coast during the voluntary evacuation, settling mainly in intermountain states like Colorado and Utah. Although they were not required to evacuate their homes, the free zone Nikkei faced anti-Japanese hostility, FBI arrests, and police raids. In fall 1942, when internment camps started granting short-term leaves for inmates to work as agricultural laborers, internees and free zone Nikkei had a chance to interact with one another, often in employer–employee arrangements. Mr. Kasai, a longtime Idaho Falls farmer, was unimpressed with the Japanese Americans from the camps, saying there "had been some hard feelings between the evacuee beet workers and our local fellows. The evacuee boys do not measure up to our standards and so the local farmers feel they are not receiving their money's worth. Most of the evacuees are more satisfied to work for Caucasians than for the Japanese."[73] Other free zone Nikkei used their positions outside the camps to support internees. Jimmie Omura had moved to Denver from California in March 1942. As a journalist based near four internment camps, he publicized the plight of the Heart Mountain draft resisters, becoming a crucial lifeline to the camp population.[74]

Koreans, Chinese, Filipinos, and Asian Indians during the War

By the end of 1941, the United States, China, Korea, and the Philippines had all come under attack by Japan, creating a bond among these countries and reorienting Americans' perceptions of Asia. The United States' relationship with India evolved a little differently. It was mediated on the one hand by its alliance with Great Britain, which still held colonial control there, but the Allies' avowed commitment to self-determination compelled Americans to support Indian independence. U.S. officials' investment in India deepened as they came to fear that Japan might try to expand into the subcontinent. Whereas Japanese Americans felt pressure to disavow their ties and loyalties to Japan, the war strengthened the transnational outlooks of other Asians, as supporting homeland liberation went hand in hand with rooting for the United States and the Allies. For instance, Asian Indian activists organized the National Committee for India's Freedom in 1944 to keep Americans apprised of the independence movement.[75] As the English-language *Chinese Press* stated: "Bound by the ties of race to the people of that Republic across the Pacific, [they] can do no less than to bend their every effort in helping China emerge victorious from her present war with Japan, and later aid her in the gigantic task of reconstruction."[76]

At home, one outcome of wartime international realignments was the sudden embrace of Chinese, Filipinos, Koreans, and Asian Indians living within the nation's borders, whether as America's "friends," or as good Americans. For their part, non-Japanese Asian Americans took advantage of the opportunities this presented, even if it meant exacerbating Japanese Americans' misfortune. Along the West Coast, where Japanese had for decades lived in close proximity to other Asians, the wartime fissures in Asian America were particularly stark. In describing a pre-internment sale at her family's Los Angeles home, a Nisei woman said, "[The] people in the neighborhood went right through our house like vultures after we left."[77] In San Francisco, Chinese business owners found that Japanese removal had eliminated a major source of competition in Chinatown, and while existing establishments thrived, people were also able to start new ventures in formerly Japanese-occupied properties.[78] As Jane Kwong Lee observed of the Chinese buyouts of Japanese properties on Grant Avenue, "There was a spirit of revenge everywhere."[79] Also in the wake of removal, many Filipinos bought previously Japanese-controlled farms in the Imperial and San Fernando Valleys as well as homes in more desirable neighborhoods.

Many Chinese, Koreans, Filipinos, and Asian Indians in the United States, moreover, accommodated the patriotic and anti-Japanese fervor of the war years. Initially this entailed taking steps to avoid being mistaken for the enemy.[80] The *Chinese Press*, for instance, told readers to carry identification to prove they were not Japanese. "Scores of Chinese have been stopped on bridges and highways . . . Many are reported to have been refused street-car services."[81] Chinese across the country wore buttons declaring "I Am Chinese" and shopkeepers displayed signs announcing, "This is a Chinese shop."[82] Filipinos and Koreans also wore buttons or displayed signs signaling they were not Japanese. Koreans' efforts to disidentify from Japanese were particularly frustrating. Long-lumped with Japan due to Korea's colonial status, Korean immigrants were classified by the 1940 Alien Registration Act as Japanese subjects and were considered "enemy aliens" after the U.S. declared war on Japan, something Koreans in America protested vehemently. The *Korean National Herald-Pacific* insisted, "Korea is an enemy of Japan . . . Since December 7, the Korean is here between the devil and the deep sea for the reason that the United States considers him a subject of Japan, which the Korean resents as an injustice to his true status."[83] In January 1942 the Department of Justice determined that Koreans would not have to register as enemy aliens, and in March Hawaii Governor Poindexter said Koreans there were no longer considered Japanese nationals for economic matters.[84]

Some went beyond just distancing themselves from Japanese and cheering for the United States, perpetuating rumors of fifth column activities and endorsing internment. Exhibiting little sympathy for their fellow Asian Americans, the *Chinese Press* mocked the JACL and called Japanese Americans the "enemy of China and the United States."[85] Korean American Kilsoo Haan said, "It is our conviction that the best way to prepare against the Japanese is

Figure 8.3 *San Francisco Examiner* issues in Oakland from February 27, 1942 with the headline, "Ouster of all Japs in California Near!" On February 19, President Roosevelt issued Executive Order 9066, which began to lay the groundwork for the evacuation of Japanese Americans from the West Coast. (Franklin D. Roosevelt Presidential Library.)

to let the American people know the Japanese plans and what the Japs and Japanese Americans are doing in this country."[86] Finally, Filipino American Manuel Buaken suggested that Japanese Americans' banks, schools, and businesses bound their loyalties and interests to Japan, whereas Filipinos had always been good Americans and shopped at American stores, "not stores devoted to the selling of products from across the seas."[87]

As anti-Japanese sentiments intensified, federal officials and the mainstream media portrayed other Asians more positively. After Japanese forces invaded the Philippines, tales of the natives' gallantry—as well as the U.S.'s reliance on them to fight against Japan—seemed to change many Americans' perceptions of Filipinos.[88] FDR spoke of an interracial brotherhood uniting white Americans and Filipinos against Japanese aggression, a striking turnaround from the descriptions of savagery and immorality that marked earlier characterizations of the Philippines and its people. "No longer on the streetcar do I feel myself in the presence of my enemies," said Manuel Buaken. "We Filipinos are the same—it is Americans that have changed in their recognition of us."[89] Regarding Chinese in America, a U.S. Congressman said that after Pearl Harbor, "we discovered the saintly qualities of the Chinese people. If it had not been for December 7, I do not know if we would have ever

Figure 8.4 Dr. Seuss cartoon, "Waiting for the signal from home...," February 1942. Anti-Japanese sentiment was pervasive during World War II. In this cartoon, the children's illustrator depicts Japanese Americans as agents of Japan. (Dr. Seuss Collection, MSS 230, Mandeville Special Collections Library, UC San Diego.)

found out how good they were."[90] As Chinese American sociologist Rose Hum Lee observed about the change in tone, "as violently as the Chinese were once attacked, they are now glorified and mounted on a pedestal."[91]

As they could no longer be indiscriminately lumped as "Asiatics" or "Orientals," Asians were also depicted very differently in the media during the war. Spreads like *Time* magazine's feature from December 22, 1941, "How to Tell Your Friends from the Japs," impressed upon readers the need to distinguish their Chinese "friends" from Japanese "enemies." The piece included illustrated instructions on how to read physical features such as the "placid" expression of Chinese and "arrogant" demeanor of the Japanese.[92] The visibility of Chinese and Chinese American wartime celebrities also signaled a new status for a people who, until very recently, were regarded as undesirable foreigners. Named *Time*'s "Man and Wife of the Year" in 1938, Chinese Nationalist leader Chiang Kai-shek and his wife, May-Ling Soong, were popular symbols of the country's modernization and U.S.–China friendship during the war years. A Wellesley-educated Christian, Soong was admired by Americans for her beauty and Westernization and was met with admiring crowds during a tour of the United States in 1943.[93] A more homegrown celebrity was the Chinese American medical doctor, Margaret Chung, whose brief notoriety stemmed from her association with American soldiers, sailors, and flyboys, earning her the nickname, "Mom Chung of the Fair-Haired Bastards."[94] In the movie industry, filmmakers, often in cooperation with the federal government, portrayed Asian allies positively. *Flying Tigers* (1942), *Dragon Seed* (1944), *Lady from Chungking* (1942), and other wartime movies showed China and its people as valiant, and the Chinese installment of Frank Capra's wartime series, *Why We Fight*, praised the country's "indestructible spirit."[95] These years also saw the release of at least eight war-themed films about the Philippines, among the most notable being *Manila Calling* (1942) and *Bataan* (1943).[96] At the insistence of the Office of War Information (OWI), the producers of *Bataan* included Filipino characters who evinced "an invincible determination to drive out the invader."[97] In addition to the positive portrayals of Asian allies the films offered, they also provided Asian American actors with welcome job opportunities in Hollywood.

The Quest for Rights and Belonging

Asian Americans were driven to contribute to the United States' war effort in order to prove their good citizenship and pursue the mainstream acceptance that long eluded them. These contributions took many forms. Between 1942 and 1943, Koreans in Hawaii purchased more than $239,000 worth of bonds, an enormous sum for such a small population, and Filipino Americans oversubscribed by nearly 100 percent above their $1 million goal of war-bond purchases.[98] Chinese Americans formed patriotic organizations, such as the Chinese Young Women's Society in Oakland in 1944, which provided a welcoming space for Chinese American servicemen passing through the area. Others put their unique skills and knowledge to use against the enemy. Korean Americans who knew Japanese worked as propaganda broadcasters in the Pacific front, agents for underground activities in Japanese-occupied parts of Asia, and for the U.S. government as teachers and translators of secret documents. Bong-youn Choy, an instructor of Oriental Languages at UC Berkeley, taught Japanese-language courses in Oakland and San Francisco while also working for the OWI.[99] Older and female volunteers ineligible for military service were channeled into civilian support roles, such as working for the Red Cross and serving as emergency fire and air-raid wardens. The Chinese American actress Anna May Wong, for instance, signed up to be an air-raid warden in Santa Monica, and Filipino veterans of World War I were recruited by the Civilian Defense Corps in California to provide logistical support for emergency preparedness on the West Coast.[100] Supporting the war could also bring families together. In a prizewinning essay for the *Oakland Post-Enquirer's* "I Am an American" contest, Florence Gee of Berkeley, California, detailed how she joined an American citizenship club, one uncle joined the army, another worked in a shipyard, her sisters worked in the civilian defense, and her mother took first aid classes.[101]

Perhaps the most powerful demonstration of one's allegiance to the United States was joining the army, and despite decades of being treated as unassimilable foreigners, Asian Americans, especially Filipino nationals and U.S.-born Chinese, served in impressive numbers. Asian Indians and Koreans were less prominent as uniformed soldiers due to the small size of their communities, but they made significant contributions in their own right. For instance, the United Korean Committee organized a military brigade, nicknamed the Tiger Brigade, which was incorporated into the California National Guard and began training in Los Angeles in late December 1941. Composed completely of immigrants, many of whom were past the age of military duty, it was separate from the regular National Guard and attached to the civilian militia.[102] Nonetheless, the brigade had important symbolic meaning for Korean Americans and drew the appreciation of non-Koreans. In August 1943, during a Korean National Flag Day celebration in Los Angeles in which the Tiger Brigade led a procession, local Koreans wore badges with the flags of U.S. and Korea crossed and the motto, "Korea for Victory with America." Mayor Fletcher Bowron made an appearance at the event to raise the Korean flag.[103]

Chinese Americans had been interested in helping to build China's military power, especially after the invasion of Manchuria, forming aviation clubs and schools with money raised in local communities. Located along the West Coast as well as cities such as Chicago, Pittsburgh, Phoenix, Honolulu, and Boston, they accepted male and female trainees and influenced many Chinese American volunteers in the U.S. army to pursue aviation.[104] After the passage of the Selective Training and Service Act of 1940, Chan Chong Yuen of New York went to register on the day that the law took effect, and his number was the first to be drawn.[105] Overall, between 12,000 and 15,000 Chinese Americans, or about 20 percent of the U.S. adult Chinese male population, enlisted in the armed forces, serving in both integrated and all-Chinese units. The most visible Chinese American contribution to the military during World War II was the Fourteenth Air Service Group (ASG), which consisted of nine units and accounted for about 10 percent of Chinese Americans in military. The ASG grew out of successful joint U.S.–China efforts in the China-Burma-India Theater and was deployed in China in 1944.[106]

Eager to help defeat the Axis powers, free their homeland from Japanese aggression, and gain belonging in America, Filipinos also joined the military. Their bid to serve with "American boys" was initially impeded by their political status, because while the Tydings-McDuffie Act classified them as "aliens" for immigration purposes, they were still regarded as "nationals" in other contexts, a category whose meaning was unclear.[107] In the absence of guidelines on how to treat them, Filipinos were routinely turned away at recruiting offices, but in response to their protests, Congress modified the Selective Service Act to allow them to register for military service.[108] In February 1942 Secretary of War Henry Stimson announced the formation of the First Filipino Infantry Regiment, organized under the California National Guard.[109] "This new unit is formed in recognition of the intense loyalty and patriotism of those Filipinos who are now residing in the United States," Stimson stated, "and the eventual opportunity of fighting on the soil of their homeland."[110] In California, about sixteen thousand, or about 40 percent of the state's Filipino population, registered for the draft.[111] Praising the Filipino Regiment, which served in the Philippines to help liberate the country from Japanese forces, its commander Colonel Robert Offley said, "The minute he gets a rifle he wants to get on a boat. He can't understand why we don't ship him out right away, so he can start shooting Japs."[112] Andy Flores, a Filipino veteran of World War I expressed his desire to fight again, telling the *Washington Post*, "I am ready to die . . . I only ask to kill two Japs for my one life."[113]

Military service gave Asian Americans the chance to travel to new places, which, in turn, impacted their identities as Asians and Americans. Training usually took them to other regions in the country, which could be a culture shock, as well as an education in the broader racial landscape and different social customs. This was certainly the case for Hawaiian Asian Americans in the Jim Crow South. While attending officer candidate school in Miami, Florida, Hawaii Chinese American William Lum had his first run-ins with blatant racism.[114] Serving in their countries of origin was powerful in a different way. For some Chinese Americans, going to China heightened their sense of their Americanness, while others immediately felt at ease and even met their spouses there.[115] When members of the First and Second Filipino Regiments entered the Japan-occupied Philippines, they were hailed as liberators of their country of ancestry and earned a storied place in their homeland's struggle for freedom, a marked contrast from the "defeated expatriates" of repatriation during the Great Depression.[116]

Asian American women also contributed to the U.S. war effort by serving in military auxiliary units such as the Women's Airforce Service Pilots (WASP) and the Women Army Corps (WAC). Emily Shek, the first Chinese American woman to join WAC, and Maggie Gee and Hazel Ah Ying Lee, both of WASP, were among those celebrated by their communities for their service. Gee was a student at UC Berkeley when the war began and worked as draftswoman at Mare Island Shipyard. She later attended flight school and joined the very selective WASP, whose purpose was to train pilots for the Air Transport Command and transport airplanes from one base to another in order to train men who were to be sent overseas for combat. She flew a variety of aircraft, trained male pilots, and ferried military aircraft. Hazel Ah Ying Lee was a graduate of Portland's Chinese Aeronautical School and was part of the WASP first class.[117] She hoped to eventually ferry aircraft that would be used in combat against Japanese in China, but died in late 1944 when her plane collided with another plane in Montana. Although the military service of women in these auxiliaries was a crucial part of the war effort, they never received the glory that men did, and since the women's auxiliaries were not formally militarized, they did not qualify for the GI Bill or other veterans' benefits until after 1977.[118]

Asian Americans were inspired by international events as well as the participation of members of their community in the U.S. military, and service brought the elusive goal of citizenship to many. In early 1942, Congress passed the Second War Powers Act, which provided expedited naturalization for aliens or nationals serving in the U.S. military.[119] The

GI Bill also provided benefits, allowing people like Celestino Gloria to obtain a bachelor's degree and then a master's in education.[120] As Harold Liu recalled:

> all of a sudden, we became part of an American dream. We had heroes with Chiang Kai-shek and Madame Chiang Kai-shek . . . It was just a whole different era and in the community we began to feel very good about ourselves . . . My own brother went into the service. We were so proud that they were in uniform.[121]

Charlie Leong of San Francisco echoed the optimism, saying, "World War II was the most important historic event of our times. For the first time we felt we could make it in American society."[122]

Mobility and the War

The industrial demands of the war, combined with the enlistment of millions of young men created acute domestic labor shortages, which, for many women and minorities, were opportunities for economic mobility. Under pressure from labor and civil rights leaders, government officials and patriotic organizations such as the American Legion came around to supporting the hiring of minorities for defense jobs.[123] A key turning point was FDR's signing of Executive Order 8802, issued in the face of public pressure escalated by A. Philip Randolph's planned March on Washington to protest discrimination against minorities in defense jobs. The order prohibited racial discrimination in employment and created the Fair Employment Practices Commission.

Defense industry employment was another way for Asian Americans to contribute to the war effort and prove their loyalty while pursuing socioeconomic mobility. Not only did the jobs pay well compared to what they earned in agriculture or the ethnic economy, but they also sometimes came with government-subsidized housing, so offered the chance to move out of ethnic enclaves. For many educated and skilled Asian Americans, defense employment also meant they could finally obtain work commensurate with their training in fields such as architecture and engineering. During the war years, Asian American employment in service occupations remained high, but declined slightly while employment in craft and technical occupations increased. Such patterns also created worker shortages in ethnic economies and caused the shuttering of Chinese restaurants, laundries, and other niche establishments.[124]

Along the West Coast, Asian Americans became a visible part of the industrial workforce in shipyards and airplane factories. The U.S.–China alliance made employers receptive to hiring Chinese Americans. At the Kaiser shipyards in Richmond, recruiters announced they would hire them regardless of their citizenship status or English skills, and Marinship president Kenneth Bechtel praised his 300 Chinese employees as the "finest workmen" who "know that every blow they strike in building these ships is a blow for freedom."[125] By 1943, about five thousand Chinese were employed throughout Bay Area defense industries, making up about 15 percent of shipyard workers.[126] Additionally, outside California, they worked in shipbuilding firms in Washington State, Delaware, and Mississippi and in airplane factories in Long Island.

Filipino Americans also found employment in West Coast defense plants, while pursuing new opportunities in farming. They filled slots at airplane manufacturers such as Lockheed, Douglas, Vultee, and Boeing, and naval shipyards including Kaiser, Wilmington, San Pedro, Bremerton, and Todd Pacific. They worked in a variety of positions, including welders, technicians, assembly and office workers, and engineers.[127] Their entry into industrial jobs, however, worried officials who feared western agriculture would suffer from an exodus of Filipino farm laborers. As incentives, Filipino farmers were allowed and even encouraged to purchase or lease lands seized from Japanese Americans and to cultivate crops, and the California attorney general issued a directive in 1943 to suspend alien land laws against Filipinos in part because of the "heroism and loyalty" demonstrated by the citizens of the Philippines.[128] Thus, while many Filipinos left agriculture for industrial jobs during the war, others chose to pursue mobility within farming. In Los Angeles, they made inroads into truck farming, a field previously dominated by Japanese Americans, and also purchased farmland in San Fernando Valley and Torrance-Gardena in areas once controlled by Japanese that had been appropriated by the government. After working for years as a migratory laborer, Toribio Castillo purchased 25 acres of land in Gardena, where he grew a variety of vegetables and branched into truck farming, establishing a lucrative business.[129]

The expanded job opportunities of World War II were especially significant for women, whose employment prospects were the most limited due to community norms, family needs, and employer sexism. As discussed in the previous chapter, these constraints were especially difficult for the second generation, which tended to hold higher expectations regarding mainstream belonging than their parents had. In the San Francisco Bay Area, 500 to 600 Chinese American women held defense jobs.[130] Among them was Jade Snow Wong, who worked as a typist-clerk in a shipyard in Marin County, and Helen Young, Lucy Young, and Hilda Lee who worked at aircraft manufacturers in San Diego. Chinese American newspapers celebrated these women as "alert, young Chinese American girls" who were "part of the millions who stand behind the man behind the gun."[131] Although most defense jobs were temporary or women were let go as men returned from the war, some of the changes were long-lasting. According to Xiaojian Zhao, most Chinese American women who were employed during the war continued to work in the postwar years. After Ah Yoke Gee's shipyard shut down, for instance, she found a job at a post office in Berkeley. Additionally, many Asian American women realized from their wartime experiences that greater gender equality was possible. Jade Snow Wong said that working in a shipyard was transformative, and she later decided to open a business so she could make a living in a way she could "call her soul her own."[132]

Another important area of change for Asian Americans, benefiting some more than others, was in housing. Through the nineteenth and much of the early twentieth centuries, Asians were among the most segregated groups on the West Coast, denied access to most residential neighborhoods and neglected in public housing programs. This began to change during the war as housing authorities, neighborhood associations, and others started to treat the matter as an extension of international relations. These years also saw the beginning of a large-scale movement of middle class and educated Asian Americans out of urban enclaves, a pattern that would accelerate during the Cold War years. With regard to public housing, the case of Ping Yuen illustrated important changes. In early 1941 the Ping Yuen housing development in San Francisco Chinatown was approved for extra funding by the city and county's board of supervisors. Although it was not completed until after the war due to rising steel prices and residents had to be U.S. citizens, the project was still a watershed and consistently discussed in terms of foreign relations. Charles Palmer, the housing coordinator for the Office of Emergency Management, said, "the building of this project has real importance from the standpoint of our international relations with China."[133]

Ambivalence and the Stubbornness of Racism

The opportunities that Asian Americans enjoyed as well as positive wartime rhetoric about Chinese, Koreans, Filipinos, and Indians were suggestive of the dawning of a new era in U.S. race relations. As important as these were, it was also apparent that racial prejudice would not simply disappear from the landscape. The Filipino immigrant writer and activist Carlos Bulosan expressed the hopes for and limits of racial progress during World War II. Selected to write an essay titled "Freedom from Want" for the *Saturday Evening Post*'s "Four Freedoms" feature, he celebrated the virtues of U.S. democracy and the Allied campaign against fascism, while also pointing out that minorities' faith in America had "been shaken many times" by racial discrimination. He said that America's "march to freedom [was] not complete" and would be unrealized until it extended full social and political citizenship to all those within the nation's borders.[134]

The war also brought the contradictory status of Asian Americans and other minorities into focus. On the one hand, they were being asked to demonstrate their loyalty to the United States, but on the other, they continued to experience racial discrimination. In a 1942 essay in *Survey Graphic*, Rose Hum Lee criticized American employers who would not hire Chinese for defense jobs, especially in light of the war. "Surely racial discrimination should not be directed against those who are America's Allies in the Far East and are helping her in every way to win the war," she said. "To be fighting for freedom and democracy in the Far East, at the cost of seven million lives in five years of hard, long, bitter warfare, and to be denied equal opportunity in the greatest of democracies, seems the height of irony."[135] Even when they were hired, Chinese Americans often faced discriminatory treatment and were judged based on stereotypes. At Moore Dry Dock in Oakland, the company placed most of its Chinese employees in an all-Chinese electrical unit. Managers claimed that this was necessary due to language difficulties, even though at the time 80 percent of the Chinese American employees spoke English.[136] Other employers placed Chinese Americans in segregated crews and rarely promoted them to supervisory positions. In defense jobs, they were often assigned electrical work because employers thought they were better suited for light, detail-oriented tasks.[137]

Asian Americans in the military found that serving in uniform did not protect them from racism. Members of the First Filipino Regiment stationed at Camp Beale quickly learned this. In early 1943 a small group went to nearby Marysville, California for a weekend respite, but when they tried to get service at a restaurant, they were told by the proprietor, "We don't serve Filipinos here."[138] On other occasions, Filipino American GIs reported being turned away from movie theaters or forced to sit in segregated sections and being denied hotel rooms when their wives came to visit. Due to the state's miscegenation laws, Filipino–white couples could not marry, and, thus, were ineligible for family allowances and other military family benefits such as life insurance. Such discrimination led Manuel Buaken, who served in the regiment, to call wartime expressions of freedom and equality, "another mirage of democracy."[139] The regiment's commander Robert Offley and its chaplain Eugene Noury protested to local and state officials on the Filipinos' behalf. In an open letter to the governor of California, Noury argued to repeal the miscegenation laws and said, "I am sure you will agree with us that in this time of war there should be no place for racial discrimination anywhere in the country."[140] In the meantime, to circumvent the proscription on intermarriage, Offley and Noury granted furloughs to Filipino soldiers and caravanned them to New Mexico where they could legally marry their white fiancées.[141]

Although U.S. citizenship had been an elusive goal for many Asians in America, some expressed ambivalence about suddenly acquiring it under wartime circumstances. Mariano Angeles, who belonged to the First Filipino Infantry, resented that citizenship was offered only to soldiers preparing to be shipped off to war. "Why now?" he asked. "When we were . . . private citizens [and] we ask[ed] . . . and they don't like us. In fact they brand us. Why now . . . are [citizenship rights] given . . . when we are soldiers? And at the same time why do they have to give [them] only to the soldiers rather than to all [Filipinos]?"[142] Rosario Macabebo, one of the first Filipinos inducted into the U.S. Army, held similarly bitter feelings, saying in a letter in the *San Francisco Chronicle*, "I consider it a privilege to make this sacrifice. I have no intention of avoiding this highest of duties, but I do protest against the glaring denials directed at me!"[143]

The wartime image of some Asian nations as "friends" changed perceptions of Asian Americans and led to improvements in their lives, but this did not equal their full acceptance in American society. For one, many of the new rights and privileges were limited to U.S. citizens. Because their improved status stemmed from international relations, the perception of Asians in America as foreigners persisted, only now they were welcome ones. In praising Chinese American defense workers in the Bay Area, reporter Marie Carey said they "go about their war work with the same patient, and enduring spirit that built the China wall, the Burma road, and the courageous defense of the last seven years."[144] The dissonance between China's favorable status and the treatment of Chinese Americans was especially glaring during a housing controversy in 1945 in San Francisco. That May, a judge upheld a restrictive covenant in the Nob Hill neighborhood, leading to the eviction of a Chinese American woman named Mabel Tseng. Ironically, as the suit was being heard, delegates from China were in the city to discuss the formation of the United Nations.[145] This contradiction led Chinese American reporter Gilbert Woo to exclaim, "San Francisco . . . I am ashamed of you."[146] As Charlotte Brooks comments, wartime "[transnationalism] gave many Chinese Americans a sense of personal empowerment, but it offered little more than high self-esteem when they had to compete for scarce wartime resources."[147]

The most telling evidence of the persistence of racism against Asians during the war was, of course, the anti-Japanese hysteria that followed the attack on Pearl Harbor. As noted, many non-Japanese Asian Americans helped fan the flames of wartime prejudice, but others were markedly distressed about it. For instance, although Korean leaders in the United States were among the most vociferous advocates of internment, members of the second generation tended to be less so. As one U.S.-born Korean in Hawaii said regarding Pearl Harbor, "It didn't make me feel any differently toward the Japanese . . . We lived with them all along and know them well and it didn't occur to me that they were responsible."[148] Korean American Jean

Park, from Reedley, California, reacted not with indignation, but empathy toward Japanese Americans when a group of whites shouted at her family, "Japs, go home!" as it reminded her of the cruel treatment Japanese Americans had to endure.[149]

Another reason for some Asian Americans' opposition to internment was it directly affected them and their families. An overlooked aspect of removal was the ordeal of Japanese Americans who belonged to interethnic families. About a dozen Filipino American soldiers were married to Japanese American women on the West Coast, and after Executive Order 9066 was issued, they faced the prospect of being separated from their wives and children. In Los Angeles, Reverend Felix Pascua and his congregation at the Filipino Christian church tried unsuccessfully to convince authorities to release a Filipina–Japanese–American daughter of a church member from the camps.[150] It was the imperative to keep these and other mixed families together that led to the first court challenges to internment. One of these, coordinated by Filipino American leaders in Seattle and San Francisco working with the ACLU, was a test case involving a Seattle couple named Mamerto Ventura and Mary Asaba Ventura. The attorneys representing the Venturas argued that the government had not proven that Mrs. Ventura, a Japanese American, held an allegiance to any nation other than the United States. The case was dismissed by federal district judge Harold Black, who asserted the "blood loyalty" of Japanese to Japan.[151]

Leaving the Camps and the End of War

As early as 1942, the WRA began releasing Japanese Americans from the internment camps, and by the end of 1944, nearly 36,000—mostly Nisei—had left and about 75,000 remained in custody. Anti-Japanese hysteria had dissipated since its fever pitch in the weeks after Pearl Harbor. As mentioned, no evidence of sabotage had been uncovered, and the camp loyalty questionnaire had confirmed the loyalty of the overwhelming majority of Japanese Americans. Several factors raised the pressure to release inmates, including concerns about Japan's use of the camps in its race propaganda, the effects of prolonged incarceration on internee morale, and the protests of religious and progressive organizations. Initially, internees were released for short-term leaves, or "furloughs." Local governments could hire them if they paid prevailing wages and provided transportation and security. In spring 1942, 1,500 workers were recruited from the camps, and that fall, after sugar beet companies became interested in hiring Japanese, about 10,000 signed up for the beet harvest in Rocky Mountain states.[152]

College students were also released early. When the war broke out, about 2,500 Nisei were enrolled in college, and their fate had come to the attention of West Coast educators like Lee Paul Seig of the University of Washington, Remsen Bird of Occidental College, and Robert Gordon Sproul of the University of California. In March 1942 these and other educators met to explore the problem and discuss how to help interned students continue their education. Their work, which involved reaching out to college and university officials outside the Coast, resulted in the formation of the National Student Relocation Council (NSRC), a nongovernmental organization that coordinated the relocation of Nisei students. Eligible students had to be U.S. citizens who had never lived or attended school in Japan, and receiving institutions had to be cleared by the military. From summer 1942 through the end of the war, over 5,500 students were placed in colleges and universities in the East and Midwest. NSRC officials told the students to show exemplary behavior, as if they were ambassadors of Japanese America. They were also advised not to associate in groups, so as to avoid unwelcome attention.[153] Kiyo Sato, who was placed at Hillsdale College in Michigan, had a challenging adjustment to life in the Midwest, but remained grateful to the NSRC, saying in 1943, "I realize the responsibility I have . . . Most of the people here in Hillsdale have not seen a Japanese face before and also many of them have not heard of evacuation . . . I don't know how I can ever thank you for this opportunity."[154] Because the schools to which Nisei students were relocated were in locations with few or no Japanese, students became accustomed to standing out and often sought out their Nisei peers from nearby institutions (against the NSRC's advice). Despite these issues of isolation and dependence, the relocated students reported generally positive experiences. Agnes Kawate, who attended college at St. Mary's, said that race relations in the Midwest were more open because people there were not as conscious of Japanese as a discrete group.[155]

With an eye on closing the camps and scattering the inmate population, the WRA also issued early leave permits to U.S. citizens whose loyalty had been confirmed, who had jobs promised, and whose proposed settlement did not attract opposition.[156] In 1943 and 1944, about thirty-four thousand received permits, along with $25 allowances and train tickets to their destinations. Like the college students, they were told to assimilate, abandon their ethnic characteristics, and avoid congregating with other Japanese Americans.[157] Because the West Coast was still closed, most went to urban areas in the intermountain West, Midwest, and East. Florence Sakada and her family relocated to Denver, Colorado, where her parents opened a restaurant.[158] Chicago's Japanese American population, which numbered about twenty-two thousand by the end of the war, experienced especially dramatic growth.[159] As they settled in these unfamiliar places, they encountered their share of resistance and discrimination. Most were unable to get jobs in defense plants and lacked the resources to start businesses, so found themselves limited to fields such as domestic labor.

The adjustment was tumultuous, but it also marked a new era in Japanese American history. During the war years, Chicago, whose Japanese population grew by about twenty thousand (compared to four hundred before), replaced the West Coast as the center of Japanese America. This was followed by Salt Lake City.[160] In these and other places, resettlers learned that race relations were different than on the West Coast. For instance, when they encountered racism, it was less because of their ethnicity than their non-whiteness. At the same time, they had to learn to navigate being "in the twilight zone between blacks and whites," as historian Charlotte Brooks has described. While still subordinate to whites, they were able to get jobs in factories and offices in the mainstream economy, as many employers preferred to hire them over blacks. As a Nisei manufacturing worker said, "more doors are open to Nisei than ever have been open to Negroes."[161] Some Japanese even adopted anti-black attitudes and parroted employers' complaints that they were "lazy." Brooks explains, "As members of a racial minority, Japanese Americans in the city enjoyed only limited social, residential, and employment opportunities. Whites would work with them but not live beside them. But because they were not black, the Nisei escaped the worst of Chicago racism. They quickly learned that being in between was far better than being on the bottom."[162]

Another group of internees released served in the Army. Throughout the war, the JACL had been lobbying for the right of Nisei to join the military, and WRA director Dillon Meyer looked for ways to show the public that most Japanese Americans were loyal. Despite objections from John DeWitt and others that inducting Nisei would undercut the rationale for internment, most top officials eventually agreed that the propaganda value of Japanese in American uniforms could give the United States an upper hand against Japan. By the end of 1942, the U.S. Army decided to create an all-Nisei combat unit to serve in Europe. FDR supported the action as a blow against racial bigotry in America, stating in February 1943: "No loyal citizen of the United States should be denied the democratic right to exercise his citizenship, regardless of his ancestry . . . Americanism is a matter of the mind and the heart; Americanism is not, and never was, a matter of race or ancestry."[163] After Army officials' initial attempt to secure recruits from the camps resulted in just 1,700 volunteers—compared to about 10,000 from Hawaii—they announced in January 1944 that the draft would be opened to Nisei. Most ended up working for the Military Intelligence Service (MIS) or joining the all-Nisei 442nd Regimental Combat Team. The 442nd was the successor to the 100th Infantry Battalion, which had been organized in summer 1942 with Nisei from Hawaii. It fought in Europe and went on to become the most decorated unit of its size during the war. This distinction, however, came at great cost, as the unit suffered a casualty rate six times higher than that of the U.S. military at large.[164]

The recognition and celebration of the 442nd—it was even the focus of a major Hollywood film released by MGM in 1951 called *Go For Broke*—signaled a turning point, not just in perceptions of Japanese Americans during World War II, but also in the discourse on race relations. The soldiers' sacrifices and their positive media coverage made a strong impression on U.S. officials and the public. After Kazuo Masuda died while fighting in Italy, Gen. Joseph Stilwell presented his family with a distinguished service cross and praised Masuda and other Nisei for their service. Stilwell also added that racial tolerance was now a necessity. "Now the war is over, but the responsibility of our nation is not finished . . . We must build a true democracy here in our land [and] the peaceful world." Additionally, in October 1945, the Los Angeles Area Council for the American Veterans Committee passed a resolution calling for an end to anti-Japanese hate crimes, which they called "un-American persecution."[165]

The early releases, induction of Nisei into the Army, and developments in the Pacific War signaled that the urgency of imprisoning Japanese Americans was weakening and the end game of internment approaching. Another critical development toward the closing of this chapter was the U.S. Supreme Court decision in *Ex parte Endo*. Mitsuye Endo was a California state employee who had been dismissed from her job in early 1942. After reporting to Tanforan assembly center, she was approached by attorney James Purcell of the ACLU and agreed to be part of a challenge to the dismissal of state employees and detention of U.S. citizens. In its ruling, handed down in December 1944, the Supreme Court affirmed that the government could not detain loyal citizens. The decision came, however, as the release of internees was already well underway and one day after the government announced the West Coast would be reopened, so it flowed with the ongoing direction of events. However, it was highly significant in striking a decisive blow against the general principle of incarcerating U.S. citizens.

The Army announced the end of Japanese exclusion from the West Coast on December 17, 1944, to be effective January 2, 1945. Japan surrendered that August, and the camps were gradually shut down, Tule Lake being the last to close in March 1946.[166] The WRA hoped to steer former internees away from the West Coast, but by 1946 about half had returned. They faced a daunting process of rebuilding their lives, however, as about 75 percent of internees lost all of their property. Before Mary Yogawa Saito's family was evacuated from Tacoma, Washington, her parents sold their dry cleaning business under an agreement that they would reclaim it after the war, only to find upon their return that the buyers had sold it and left the city.[167] Some Japanese Americans came back to their old neighborhoods to discover new residents inhabiting them, such as Los Angeles's Little Tokyo, which, in the course of the war, transformed into a predominantly African American area known as Bronzeville. Such circumstances led to the emergence of new Japanese population centers like Gardena in Southern California. Rebuilding their livelihoods was also difficult, due to resistance and changes in the regional economy. In February 1945, Howard Otamura returned to the flower market in Los Angeles, where he endured harassment and required police protection. Some were able to return to agriculture, but not at their prewar levels, as alien land laws were still in effect and opportunities for small farmers had diminished due to mechanization. In Southern California, the ubiquitous roadside produce stands run by Japanese all but vanished. In a dramatic change from prewar patterns, most Japanese Americans were neither self-employed nor working in the ethnic economy by 1948, instead working for white employers as gardeners, domestic workers, busboys, and dishwashers. Increasing numbers also got jobs in light industries such as garment work.[168]

Acknowledging that Japanese in America had not been guilty of subversion and suffered financially during internment, Congress passed the Japanese American Claims Act of 1948 after a major lobbying effort by the JACL. Although it did not apologize or take a position on the lawfulness of internment, the Act provided up to $25 million to help former internees recover some of their losses of real or personal property. This amount would turn out to be woefully inadequate, as about twenty-three thousand claims totaling $131 million were filed, a mere fraction of official loss estimates.[169] The process, furthermore, was slow and inefficient, and each year just hundreds of claims were processed, with some people waiting up to twenty years to be paid.

It was not just that Japanese Americans could not restore their prewar lives; many wanted to get as far from them as they could by capitalizing on the positive wartime rhetoric, and there were indications of a turning tide. In November 1946, the Los Angeles JACL sponsored a banquet attended by Mayor Fletcher Bowron, who apologized for supporting internment.[170] Also that month, California voters defeated Proposition 15, which called for strengthening the state's alien land laws. Other signs of change included Mike Masaoka's invitation to join Harry Truman's civil rights committee. Beneath the surface, however, former internees remained divided. For many, the reputation of the JACL was damaged as a result of its cooperation with internment and persecution of individuals under suspicion, and the organization had shrunk considerably by war's end. While the new public face of Japanese America emerging from the war was decidedly middle class, assimilationist, and non-radical, this approach was criticized by members of the community who disagreed with its politics or simply did not match the image. Their voices and lives, however, would be increasingly pushed into obscurity.[171]

A New Day for Race Relations?

Out of World War II, the legal, ideological, and cultural landscape of America was dramatically transformed. Before, the notion of Asians assimilating, achieving mainstream acceptance, and being an integral part of the fabric of American society was nearly inconceivable. While on the ground, conditions showed that obstacles remained, it was significant nonetheless that these ideas were no longer outlandish ones. Americans' understanding of the United States changed from a white nation to a multicultural one. This shift was compelled by wartime developments in which new windows of possibilities opened up for Asian Americans and other minorities, to not just hope for equality and belonging, but to expect and demand it.

Racism was not eradicated, but over the course of the war there were signs that traditional nativism was on its way out. Americans were eager to counter Axis propaganda that brought attention to U.S. racism in order to weaken its credibility, and were also greatly disturbed by the horrors of Hitler's genocidal war. Ground-up momentum generated by the heroism of minorities in the Army as well as domestic protests for civil rights and racial equality pushed Americans to embrace a more open attitude about race. This was seen, for instance, in war posters that showed black and white workers united and proclaimed, "Americanism is not, and never was, a matter of race or ancestry."[172] At a Town Hall forum in Los Angeles in November 1943, the author and pro-China advocate Pearl Buck spoke and told the audience that race relations were at a crossroads and the era of unquestioned white dominance was coming to an end. Leading the world in this new era of human relations would be the United States and Asia, as the center of geopolitical power had shifted to the Pacific. This made places like California especially crucial, according to Buck. "[Because] you in California face the Pacific and Asia," she said, "you among us have the crux in your hands. You can, by what you decide, be a barrier—or you can be a gateway to a new and better world, for us and for all peoples."[173]

Movements to repeal anti-Asian immigration and naturalization laws signaled a coming sea change in Asian America. To some, repeal would be a step toward creating an equal society, while to others it was a necessary gesture for maintaining the United States' standing with its allies or its upper hand over its rivals. Chinese exclusion was the first to go. Pressure to repeal came from outside figures such as Madam Chiang Kai-shek and domestic lobby groups like the Citizens Committee to Repeal Chinese Exclusion (CCRCE). Formed in 1943 and led by publisher—and husband of Pearl Buck—Donald Dunham, the CCRCE was made up of scholars and other liberals who said that Chinese exclusion violated American principles of equality and was an unacceptable affront to a wartime ally.[174] Meanwhile, Asian Americans mobilized to repeal Chinese exclusion. Representatives from the CCBA and Chinese American organizations across the country called for the end of exclusion, and spokespersons from other Asian American communities, including Kilsoo Haan and Taraknath Das, also weighed in at congressional hearings. As Das, by then a professor at the City University of New York, testified to a congressional committee, "As long as Anglo–American powers would continue to practice racial discrimination against the peoples of the Orient, a vast majority of the orientals will not have any genuine confidence in the professions of promotion of world democracy and world brotherhood."[175]

By 1943, repealing Chinese exclusion had drawn broad support, with even old foes of the Chinese—such as the San Francisco Board of Supervisors and the *San Francisco Chronicle*—endorsing the cause. After considering several bills, the House of Representatives focused on a measure introduced by Democrat Warren Magnuson of Washington. Republican Congressman Walter Judd of Minnesota, also a supporter of repeal, urged the law's passage, saying, "The Chinese are good enough to die by the millions in a war against Axis tyranny—but a Chinese who is not born in the United States is not good enough, so the law implies, to become an American citizen by naturalization. A man of German descent may be so naturalized, and so may an Italian. But a Chinese alien is not so fortunate. He is beyond the pale." California Democrat Thomas Ford expressed his confidence that Chinese would make a "distinct and tremendously valuable contribution to freedom."[176] The proposed legislation did encounter opposition from labor organizations, patriotic societies, and nativist groups. Compton White of Idaho pressed the old claim that Chinese could not assimilate and furthermore predicted that if they were granted immigration and naturalization rights, "you will still have race riots and other racial problems confronting you."[177] The momentum, however, was with the advocates of repeal, and in November 1943, the Magnuson Act was passed. It repealed all or part of fifteen statutes passed between 1882 and 1915 which had effected Chinese exclusion, instituted a quota of 105 Chinese per year (people of Chinese descent or from China), and made Chinese persons or persons of Chinese descent eligible for naturalization on the same terms as other immigrants.

The status of Filipinos had long been unclear and unfixed, a problem the war brought into relief. Sometimes treated as "aliens," and other times "nationals" and "citizens," they were subject to the provisions of the Alien Registration Act of 1940, yet were classed as nationals and citizens with respect to the Neutrality Act and Selective Service Act. According to Rick Baldoz, the underlying logic was to confer Filipinos citizenship when it came to their martial sacrifice, but to assign them alien status when it came to rights.[178] Bolstered by the passage of the Magnuson Act and widespread praise for Philippine fighters, Filipino Americans pushed to expand their rights in the United States. Figures such as Diosdado Yap, the publisher of *Bataan* magazine, and Manuel Adeva of the Philippine resident commissioner's office highlighted Filipinos' wartime service and emphasized that racist laws undermined America's standing. Six different bills proposing immigration and naturalization rights for Filipinos were introduced in 1944. In predictable fashion, opponents warned that an unwanted Filipino influx would result from such reforms. Rep. A. Leonard Allen of Louisiana, who had also been against Chinese naturalization, dredged up old stereotypes of Filipino criminality and also tried to boost his claims of their treachery by charging that they had fraternized with Japanese on the West Coast.[179]

As in the campaign to repeal Chinese exclusion, American officials' desire to reform the laws affecting Filipinos and Indians stemmed from their desire to shore up wartime morale. Regarding the latter, they worried that Japan would exploit Indian disaffection with British rule and undermine Allied solidarity. Additionally, the war and issuing of the Atlantic Charter created new pressures on the United States to support the principle of Indian independence. Asian Indians had been praised for their contributions to the war, mainly via British military service, which in turn raised the expectations of Indians in America. As S. Chandrasekhar of the University of Pennsylvania wrote in the *Far Eastern Survey*, "If the United States is successfully to combat [Nazism], it can ill afford to practice racial discrimination in its relations with Asiatic countries. The immigration policy of this country now excludes nearly a quarter of the human race. America cannot afford to say that she wants the people of India to fight on her side and at the same time maintain that she will not have them among her immigrant groups."[180] In March 1944, Emmanuel Celler of New York introduced to Congress a bill that would grant Indians immigration and naturalization rights and, he claimed, help the United States' position in the war by "[dulling] the edge of Jap propaganda."[181] This was combined with a separate naturalization bill for Filipinos to become the Luce-Celler Act of 1946. On July 4, two days after its passage, President Harry Truman proclaimed Philippine independence and relinquished U.S. sovereignty, framing this action as a reward for Filipinos who had proven during the war that they were ready for self-rule. The Luce-Celler Act made "persons of races indigenous to India, and the Philippine Islands" eligible for citizenship.[182] In removing the status "aliens ineligible to citizenship," it allowed Indians to immigrate to the United States, but set the cap at one hundred per year. After the Philippines became independent, its quota was raised from fifty to one hundred.

Reform for Koreans and Japanese would wait until 1952. Several Korean immigration and naturalization bills were considered during and just after the war, but none passed.[183] The Korean War of 1950–52, however, brought a new urgency to expanding the rights of Koreans in America and, by this time, Japan was now a U.S. ally. The McCarran-Walter Act of 1952 established that citizenship would "not be abridged or denied on the basis of race, sex, or marriage" and opened the doors to all other Asians while granting Korea and Japan annual immigration quotas of one hundred.[184]

Conclusion

The World War II years illustrated how much international relations could shape Asian American experience, and the onset of the postwar era witnessed another set of dramatic realignments and reformulations in Asian Americans' relationships with their countries of ancestry. Korea's liberation from Japan in 1945 and Philippine and Indian independence in 1946 and 1947, respectively, radically altered the consciousness of those immigrants who had long considered themselves exiles. Syngman Rhee returned to Korea in 1945 and became the president of the Republic of Korea (South Korea) in 1948. The United States occupied Japan with about two million personnel for nearly seven years, and Japan took on a new interest in showing that it was a friend capable of Western-style democracy. With Japanese commerce growing in importance, especially to the Pacific Coast, it was no longer dangerous or suspicious for Japanese Americans to identify with Japan. On the other hand, China, the United States' closest Asian ally during the war, became Communist in 1949, having numerous repercussions for the lives of Chinese Americans in the postwar years.

While symbolically significant, the repeal of Asian exclusion did not usher in immediate or sweeping change. In the first ten years of the Magnuson Act's operation, an annual average of just 59 Chinese came to the United States, and between 1944 and 1952, only 1,428 Chinese were naturalized.[185] Furthermore, while the war years brought significant moments of promise and progress in American race relations, it was clear, once the dust had settled, that there was still a long way to go. Blacks in the South still lacked basic rights to vote and participate in civic life. Segregation in all regions of the country and affecting all minority groups remained widespread. These contradictions and shortcomings were not lost on nonwhite observers. Regarding immigration reform, Chinese American journalist Gilbert Woo warned members of his community not to be taken in by the U.S.–China friendship propaganda and mocked the Magnuson Act for its quota of 107, dismissing it as a "cheap political gesture."[186] Asian Americans, along with other minorities, would, thus, enter the 1950s with raised hopes and improved circumstances, but also new and old concerns as the nation grappled with both Cold War fears and postwar prosperity.

Notes

1 Gordon H. Chang, "'Superman is About to Visit the Relocation Centers' and the Limits of Wartime Liberalism," *Amerasia Journal* 19, no. 1 (1993): 55.
2 Gregory Robinson, *A Tragedy of Democracy: Japanese Confinement in North America* (New York: Columbia University Press, 2009).
3 In response to Japan's occupation of Indochina in 1940, the United States imposed a trade embargo on fuel, munitions, and scrap metal.
4 Gary Y. Okihiro, *Storied Lives: Japanese American Students and World War II* (Seattle: University of Washington Press, 1999), 19.
5 Charlotte Brooks, *Alien Neighbors, Foreign Friends: Asian Americans, Housing, and the Transformation of Urban California* (Chicago: University of Chicago Press, 2009), 121.
6 Evidence of Japanese spy networks was uncovered through raids and information-gathering expeditions by the Office of Naval Intelligence, but no evidence of Japanese American complicity. After one raid in 1941 of the Japanese consulate office in Los Angeles, Kenneth Ringle of the ONI asserted that Japanese American communities were loyal and if anything Japanese agents did not trust them. Furthermore, the Munson Report, commissioned in early 1941 by FDR to investigate Japanese American communities in Hawaii and the West Coast, also affirmed no threat of JA subversion. Aside from the odd fanatic, it said the majority of Issei and Nisei constitute no threat. Nisei in face are "pathetically eager to show this loyalty." Robinson, *A Tragedy of Democracy*, 54–6.
7 Ibid., 50–1.
8 Ibid., 52.
9 Ibid., 51.
10 Ibid., 35.
11 K. Scott Wong, *Americans First: Chinese Americans and the Second World War* (Cambridge: Harvard University Press, 2005), 34.
12 Ibid., 39.
13 Ronald Takaki, *Strangers from a Different Shore: A History of Asian Americans* (Boston: Little Brown, 1988), 364.
14 H. Brett Melendy, *Asians in America: Filipinos, Koreans, and East Indians* (Boston: Twayne, 1977), 214; Takaki, *Strangers from a Different Shore*, 368.
15 Rick Baldoz, *The Third Asiatic Invasion: Empire and Migration in Filipino America, 1898–1946* (New York: New York University Press, 2011), 196.
16 Jeanette Rankin was the sole dissenting vote.
17 Robinson, *A Tragedy of Democracy*, 62.
18 Ibid., 72.
19 Okihiro, *Storied Lives*, 25.
20 Shortly after Pearl Harbor, China declared war on Japan, making it an ally of the United States.
21 David Yoo, *Contentious Spirits: Religion in Korean American History, 1903–1945* (Stanford: Stanford University Press, 2010), 119.
22 It had been no secret that Japan had designs on the Philippines as part of its vision of imperial hegemony in the Pacific. Filipino and American fighters were overwhelmed by better-equipped Japanese army. Baldoz, *The Third Asiatic Invasion*, 195.

23 Ibid., 205.

24 Brooks, *Alien Neighbors, Foreign Friends*, 126.

25 Brian Hayashi, *Democratizing the Enemy: The Japanese American Internment* (Princeton: Princeton University Press, 2004), 70.

26 Paul Spickard, *Japanese Americans: The Formation and Transformations of an Ethnic Group* (New Brunswick: Rutgers University Press, 2009), 132.

27 Hayashi, *Democratizing the Enemy*, 74.

28 Chan, *Asian Americans*, 131.

29 Hayashi, *Democratizing the Enemy*, 74–5.

30 This did not apply to the small handful that had been naturalized by way of their service in World War I or other special circumstances.

31 Ibid., 76.

32 Ibid., 77.

33 Okihiro, *Storied Lives*, 25

34 The Western Defense Command had been organized in March 1941 to coordinate the defense of the Pacific Coast states. DeWitt spread unfounded rumors such as allegations that Japanese in Washington were setting fires as signals. He did not hide his distrust of all Japanese people but initially confined his recommendation to removing aliens (Japanese, Germans, and Italians). For detailed background on the decision, see Robinson, *A Tragedy of Democracy*, 63–87.

35   Ibid., 80.

36 Ibid., 107.

37 Mae Ngai, *Impossible Subjects: Illegal Aliens and the Making of Modern America* (Princeton: Princeton University Press, 2004), 176.

38 Ibid., 92.

39 The office of Indian Affairs oversaw the camps in Arizona, and WRA administered the rest.

40 In California, these were located in Manzanar and Tule Lake. The ones in Arizona were in Poston and Gila; Minidoka, Idaho; Heart Mountain, Wyoming; Granada, Colorado; Topaz, Utah; Rohwer and Jerome, Arkansas.

41 Robinson, *A Tragedy of American Democracy*, 107–08.

42 The Socialist Party was the only national political organization that opposed removal. Leader Normal Thomas denounced the government for totalitarianism and other party members organized lobbying and aid efforts. A petition called for immediate recission of the president's order. Blacks were supportive of Japanese Americans—newspapers like *Pittsburgh Courier* and *Los Angeles Tribune* came out against evacuation. Ibid., 109.

43 Ibid., 108; Chang, "Superman is About to Visit the Internment Camps," 47.

44 Chang, "Superman is About to Visit the Internment Camps," 47.

45 Yasui was in Portland and Hirabayashi in Seattle.

46 Peter Irons, *Justice at War* (New York: Oxford University Press, 1983).

47 Robinson, *A Tragedy of Democracy*, 61.

48 Brooks, *Alien Neighbors, Foreign Friends*, 130.

49 Okihiro, *Storied Lives*, 5.

50 Brooks, *Alien Neighbors, Foreign Friends*, 129.

51 Okihiro, *Storied Lives*, 6.

52 Manzanar and Poston were assembly centers and concentration camps. Yoo, *Growing Up Nisei*, 96.

53 Robinson, *A Tragedy of American Democracy*, 157–58.

54 Scott Kurashige, *The Shifting grounds of Race: Black and Japanese Americans in the Making of Multiethnic Los Angeles* (Princeton: Princeton University Press, 2008), 192.

55 Spickard, *Japanese Americans*, 124.

56 Yoo, *Growing Up Nisei*, 100.

57 Spickard, *Japanese Americans*, 119.

58 Ibid., 126.

59 Ibid.

60 Robinson, *A Tragedy of American Democracy*, 186.
61 Spickard, *Japanese Americans*, 134. Eric Muller, *Free to Die for Their Country: The Story of the Japanese American Draft Resisters in World War II* (Chicago: University of Chicago Press, 2001).
62 Robinson, *A Tragedy of Democracy*, 67.
63 Ibid., 77.
64 Ibid., 64.
65 Ibid., 65.
66 Ibid., 78.
67 Ibid., 133, 172.
68 Ibid., 147–48.
69 Ibid., 150.
70 Men from Oahu were on the 298th and from other islands on the 299th. See Wong, *Americans First*, 150.
71 Ibid., 66.
72 Okihiro, *Storied Lives*, 25.
73 Robert C. Sims, "The 'Free Zone' Nikkei: Japanese Americans in Idaho and Eastern Oregon in World War II," Gail Nomura and Louis Fiset, eds., *Nikkei in the Pacific Northwest: Japanese Americans and Japanese Canadians in the Twentieth Century* (Seattle: University of Washington Press, 2005), 248.
74 Arthur A. Hansen, "Peculiar Odyssey: Newsman Jimmie Omura's Removal from and Regeneration within Nikkei Society," Nomura and Fiset, *Nikkei in the Pacific Northwest*, 287.
75 Ibid.
76 Brooks, *Alien Neighbors, Foreign Friends*, 139.
77 Ibid., 129.
78 Ibid., 137; Wong, *Americans First*, 83.
79 Brooks, *Alien Neighbors, Foreign Friends*, 138.
80 China, Korea, and the Philippines from Japan, and India from Britain. Indians were not as susceptible to being mistaken for Japanese.
81 Ibid., 137.
82 Takaki, *Strangers from a Different Shore*, 371.
83 Ibid., 365.
84 Melendy, *Asians in America*, 157–58.
85 Brooks, *Alien Neighbors, Foreign Friends*, 138.
86 Takaki, *Strangers from a Different Shore*, 366.
87 Ibid., 362.
88 Ibid., 359.
89 Ibid., 359.
90 Ibid., 370.
91 Brooks, *Alien Neighbors, Foreign Friends*, 135.
92 *Life* magazine printed a similar article the same day.
93 Brooks, *Alien Neighbors, Foreign Friends*, 148. Also see Karen Leong, *The China Mystique: Pearl S. Buck, Anna May Wong, Mayling Soong, and the Transformation of American Orientalism* (Berkeley: University of California Press, 2005).
94 Judy Tzu-Chun Wu, *Doctor Mom Chung of the Fair-Haired Bastards: The Life of a Wartime Celebrity* (Berkeley: University of California Press, 2005).
95 Brooks, *Alien Neighbors, Foreign Friends*, 148.
96 Linda España-Maram, *Creating Masculinity in Los Angeles's Little Manila: Working-Class Filipinos and Popular Culture, 1920s–1950s* (New York: Columbia University Press, 2006), 157.
97 Ibid., 158.
98 Takaki, *Strangers from a Different Shore*, 367; Baldoz, *The Third Asiatic Invasion*, 209.
99 Takaki, *Strangers from a Different Shore*, 366.
100 España-Maram, *Creating Masculinity in Los Angeles's Little Manila*, 140; Baldoz, *The Third Asiatic Invasion*, 209.

101 Wong, *Americans First*, 70.

102 A similar unit formed in San Francisco. Melendy, *Asians in America*, 157; Bong-youn Choy, *Koreans in America* (Chicago: Nelson-Hall, 1979), 174.

103 Ibid.; Melendy, *Asians in America*, 157.

104 Xiaojian Zhao, *Remaking Chinese America: Immigration, Family, and Community, 1940–1965* (New Brunswick: Rutgers University Press, 2002), 60.

105 Wong, *Americans First*, 43.

106 Ibid., 164.

107 Under the Tydings-McDuffie, Filipinos were reclassified as aliens, but only for immigration purposes.

108 Their service in World War I was under the auspices of the colonial government. Baldoz, *The Third Asiatic Invasion*, 196, 205; Takaki, *Strangers from a Different Shore*, 359.

109 Public Law 360 modified the Selective Service Act of 1941. The provision allowed "every other male person residing in the United States" between the ages of eighteen and sixty-five to register with the Selective Act. Before only aliens and citizens could explicitly apply (aliens had to declare intention to become citizens). With the broader language, Filipinos, as nationals, could register. More than seven thousand served in the First Filipino Infantry Regiment and Second Filipino Infantry Regiment. A third regiment was formed, made up of Filipino National Guard members from Hawaii, but was prevented from joining the war due to the intervention of the HSPA, which invoked martial law to keep them on the plantations for food production. See Baldoz, *The Third Asiatic Invasion*, 212–13.

110 Takaki, *Strangers from a Different Shore*, 359.

111 España-Maram, *Creating Masculinity in Los Angeles's Little Manila*, 152.

112 Takaki, *Strangers from a Different Shore*, 359.

113 Baldoz, *The Third Asiatic Invasion*, 212.

114 Wong, *Americans First*, 147, 151–52.

115 Ibid., 65–6.

116 España-Maram, *Creating Masculinity in Los Angeles's Little Manila*, 156.

117 Zhao, *Remaking Chinese America*, 61.

118 Wong, *Americans First*, 56.

119 Waived the declaration of internment, five year residency, and English language requirements of the previous requirements. Baldoz, *The Third Asiatic Invasion*, 213.

120 España-Maram, *Creating Masculinity in Los Angeles's Little Manila*, 161.

121 Takaki, *Strangers from a Different Shore*, 373.

122 Ibid.

123 In early 1942 the American Legion called for hiring of Filipinos and blacks. Baldoz, *The Third Asiatic Invasion*, 209.

124 Takaki, *Strangers from a Different Shore*, 374.

125 Wong, *Americans First*, 52; Zhao, *Remaking Chinese America*, 55.

126 Zhao, *Remaking Chinese America*, 56.

127 Baldoz, *The Third Asiatic Invasion*, 210.

128 España-Maram, *Creating Masculinity in Los Angeles's Little Manila*, 151.

129 Ibid., 152.

130 Zhao, *Remaking Chinese America*, 56.

131 Wong, *Americans First*, 46–7, 51; Takaki, *Strangers from a Different Shore*, 375.

132 Zhao, *Remaking Chinese America*, 76.

133 Brooks, *Alien Neighbors, Foreign Friends*, 140.

134 Baldoz, *The Third Asiatic Invasion*, 207.

135 Takaki, *Strangers from a Different Shore*, 375–76.

136 Brooks, *Alien Neighbors, Foreign Friends*, 145.

137 Ibid., 146.

138 Takaki, *Strangers from a Different Shore*, 361.

139 Baldoz, *The Third Asiatic Invasion*, 214.

140 Ibid., 215.

141 Ibid., 216.

142 España-Maram, *Creating Masculinity in Los Angeles's Little Manila*, 153.

143 Baldoz, *The Third Asiatic Invasion*, 207.

144 Brooks, *Alien Neighbors, Foreign Friends*, 138.

145 Ibid., 155.

146 Ibid.

147 Ibid., 139.

148 Takaki, *Strangers from a Different Shore*, 366.

149 Ibid., 365.

150 España-Maram, *Creating Masculinity in Los Angeles's Little Manila*, 146.

151 Baldoz, *The Third Asiatic Invasion*, 216.

152 Robinson, *A Tragedy of Democracy*, 182.

153 Schools engaged in classified research or located near power installations, defense factories, or terminal facilities were ineligible. Okihiro, *Storied Lives*, 9, 31, 38, 108.

154 Ibid., 72.

155 Ibid., 109.

156 Robinson, *A Tragedy of Democracy*, 184.

157 Ibid., 187.

158 Spickard, *Japanese Americans*, 130.

159 Robinson, *A Tragedy of Democracy*, 187; Charlotte Brooks, "In the Twilight Zone between Black and White: Japanese American Resettlement and Community in Chicago, 1942–1945," *The Journal of American History* (2000) 86(4): 1655–687.

160 Brooks, 1655.

161 Ibid., 1669.

162 Ibid., 1686.

163 Robinson, *A Tragedy of Democracy*, 184.

164 The regiment was sent on a rescue mission to find a white unit from Texas that had been caught behind enemy lines in France. Two thousand Nisei were wounded and over 200 died in order to save 211 members of the battalion. A Japanese American chaplain complained that when the 442nd was ordered to rescue the battalion, the soldiers were sent straight into "machine gun nests and well-prepared defense," and whites were not forced to take the same responsibility. Scott Kurashige, *The Shifting grounds of Race: Black and Japanese Americans in the Making of Multiethnic Los Angeles* (Princeton: Princeton University Press, 2008), 190, 194.

165 Ibid., 190.

166 Robinson, *A Tragedy of Democracy*, 255.

167 Ibid., 257.

168 Kurashige, *The Shifting Grounds of Race*, 197.

169 Robinson, *A Tragedy of Democracy*, 282; Spickard, *Japanese Americans*, 141. The U.S. Commission on Wartime Relocation and Internment of Civilians estimated that prisoners' losses totaled about $370 million in property losses.

170 Kurashige, *The Shifting Grounds of Race*, 191.

171 Ibid., 194.

172 Brooks, *Alien Neighbors, Foreign Friends*, 150.

173 Kurashige, *The Shifting Grounds of Race*, 199.

174 Brooks, *Alien Neighbors, Foreign Friends*, 152; Wong, *Americans First*, 110.

175 Takaki, *Strangers from a Different Shore*, 377.

176 Ibid.

177 Ibid., 116.

178 Baldoz, *The Third Asiatic Invasion*, 200–01.

179 Ibid., 225–26.

180 Takaki, *Strangers from a Different Shore*, 368–69.

181 Ibid., 368.

182 Baldoz, *The Third Asiatic Invasion*, 227.
183 Melendy, *Asians in America*, 137.
184 Ibid., 138.
185 Takaki, *Strangers from a Different Shore*, 378.
186 Brooks, *Alien Neighbors, Foreign Friends*, 152.

Asian America in the Early Cold War Years

9

Born in South Korea and adopted by American families, Thomas Park Clement and Mark Hagland were part of a modest but significant revival of Asian immigration during the early Cold War years, which differed markedly from the immigration of previous eras. Far removed from the young, working-class, adult men of the nineteenth and early twentieth centuries, Korean adoptees came as children and generally lived away from the traditional centers of the Asian American population. Clement, who knows little about his early years, believes he was born around the start of the Korean War (1950–53). Abandoned by his parents when he was four or five, he was eventually found by a missionary who took him to an orphanage. He stayed there until 1959, when the Clement family of North Carolina adopted him and brought him to the United States. Hagland was adopted as an infant along with his twin by a German–Norwegian family in Wisconsin. Standing out because of his adoptee status and Korean ancestry, he said of his early years in America, "Growing up in Milwaukee [it felt like] I was a Martian who landed in a spaceship."[1]

Thousands of Korean adoptees like Clement and Hagland came to America at a time of dramatic change in the nation and the world in the 1950s and 1960s. The United States had fought in the Korean War to contain the global spread of Communism, and in its aftermath Americans felt captivated by—and obligated toward—war orphans and children of GIs in need of homes. The incorporation of Korean children into white middle-class families and the positive coverage these adoptions received, moreover, signaled more accepting attitudes about the place of Asians in America and by extension the possibilities of pluralism. When framed as compassionate acts of rescue, Korean adoptions also projected American moral authority and U.S.–Asia bonds. Finally, the migration of Korean adoptees underscored general features of Asian migration during the 1950s and 1960s. From the end of World War II to the 1965 Immigration Act, new Asian immigrants differed greatly from their pre-exclusion counterparts. Whereas uneducated and unskilled people primarily valued for their physical labor once dominated the immigrant stream, they would be eclipsed by adoptees, military brides, students, and skilled workers during the 1950s and 1960s as Asian immigration, and the immigration system in general, were reoriented around political and economic exigencies shaped by the Cold War.

This chapter discusses Asian America during the early Cold War years, with a focus on the period from the end of World War II to the passage of the Immigration Act of 1965. In American history, this time is associated with economic prosperity, the baby boom, and a return to domesticity. It was also a conservative era whose politics were shaped by Cold War worries. Asian Americans were deeply affected by these developments. For instance, after China "fell" to Mao's forces in 1949, the United States devoted much of its attention to resisting Communism's spread elsewhere in Asia, an extension of which was to persuade the American public both of the menace of Communism and the importance of Asia and its people to U.S. interests. On the one hand, fears of international Communism resulted in the singling out of Chinese and other Asian American leftists for persecution, but on the other, as Americans grew sensitive to charges of racism lest it be wielded against them in Communist propaganda, and realized the imperative of forging friendships with countries they hoped to "save" from Communism, they came to espouse liberal ideologies, including the notion that Asians could be part of the American melting pot. The early Cold War period was also a turning point for Asian immigration, during which exclusionary practices were gradually reversed and a significant rise in new migration occurred, setting the stage for sweeping legislative reform in the mid-1960s. This new immigration and the context of the Cold War opened the way for Asians to attain unprecedented visibility and success in mainstream life, although some of this success was a function of the skills and privilege with which they entered the United States. Connected to the heightened attention to Asian success and Americanism were constructions of the Asian American "model minority." Although touted as a positive development for Asian Americans and a larger symbol of racial progress, this stereotype implicitly disparaged other minorities, especially African Americans, and only exalted Asian Americans who embodied an anti-radical, middle-class, conformist position.

Caring about Asia and Asians during the Cold War

The Cold War atmosphere of competition and the specter of nuclear war generated much domestic anxiety and paranoia, prompting campaigns to find enemies at home, such as those led by the House Un-American Activities Committee (HUAC). The dominant political culture of the 1950s and 1960s was characterized not just by anticommunism, but also conformity and anti-radicalism, putting leftists and outsiders of various stripes on the defensive. Yet the exigencies of winning the Cold War also called on Americans to embrace new priorities such as rejecting racism and reaching out to the nonaligned word, two pillars of Cold War liberalism.[2]

As mentioned, the United States' relationship with Asia had changed dramatically with the onset of the Cold War. It occupied Japan, its one-time foe, for nearly seven years after its surrender, funneling resources to transform the country into a Western-style democracy and buttress against Communism in East Asia. China had been "lost" in 1949 and the United States committed military and other resources toward the containment of Communism in Korea. Additionally, after anti-colonial forces under Communist leader Ho Chi Minh defeated the French in 1954, the United States played a larger role in Southeast Asia with the aim of preventing the unification of North and South Vietnam under Communist rule. U.S.

officials also intervened in nearby Laos, supporting various right wing and anti-communist governments against the Communist Pathet Lao.

Against these developments, Americans were exposed to new writings, films, and other productions about Asia, much of it aimed at educating the public on the importance of this part of the world in the fight against global Communism and for their own wellbeing. Notable popular works about Southeast Asia and Americans' obligations there included the novel, *The Ugly American* (1958) by Eugene Burdick and William Lederer, as well as Norman Cousins' writings about Americans in Laos for the *Reader's Digest* in the early 1960s.[3] The postwar years also saw a boom in travel writings by Asian and white authors which enhanced middlebrow readers' interest in and familiarity with Asia. In the 1940s and 1950s, the Indian intellectual Santha Rana Rau gained fame for her writings about Asia and, among white Americans, James Michener became perhaps the most prolific and well-known writer of this period.[4]

The most resonant writings about Asia and Asian people were those that appealed to readers' emotions and invited them to take action. So-called "virtual adoptions," promoted by organizations such as the Christian Children's Fund (CCF), enabled Americans to participate in the "rescue" of Asian children simply by making small monetary donations and participating in letter exchanges. Founded in 1938 by Presbyterian minister Dr. J. Calvitt Clarke to help Chinese children orphaned by the Sino–Japanese war, by 1955, the CCF had expanded into 15 countries. It reached out to people through advertisements in national magazines, often with graphic photographs of maimed children.

Another notable outreach campaign that sought to cement emotional ties between Americans and Asians was the Hiroshima Maidens Project. Launched and publicized by Norman Cousins in the *Saturday Review* in 1953, it brought twenty-five young women disfigured by the atomic bomb to the United States to receive plastic surgery.[5] Because the project raised funds from the public, Cousins presented it as a way for ordinary Americans to participate in world events.[6] Depicted as innocent virgins and victims, the "Hiroshima maidens" fit into the larger construction of Japan as feminized and wounded dependents to the United States' masculine and benevolent shield. At the same time, helping the Japanese women heal from their scars healed Americans' own psychological scars about the suffering they had inflicted on them in the first place.

Immigration during the Cold War: Adoptees, War Brides, and the "Brain Drain"

Paralleling the changing relationships with and perceptions of Asia and Asian people were piecemeal adjustments in immigration and refugee policy that resulted in significant new migration. As discussed in the previous chapter, proscriptions on Asian immigration and naturalization were repealed in 1943, 1946, and 1952, but because the annual quotas for Asian nations remained small, the reforms had a negligible effect on new immigration. Most of the Asian migration from the late 1940s to mid-1960s, then, took place via non-quota categories established by laws such as the War Brides Act of 1945, Displaced Persons Act of 1948, and Refugee Act of 1953. The smaller Asian subgroups were especially transformed by this postwar migration.[7] For instance, in 1940 the American Korean population was about

1,700 in the mainland, and 6,850 in Hawaii, and in the 1950s to early 1960s, these numbers would be augmented by the entry of about 14,000 students, military brides, war orphans, and professional workers.[8] Asian Indians, who numbered about 1,500 in 1946, added nearly 6,500 to their population between 1948 and 1965.[9] Filipino immigration also increased dramatically; in the 1950s, about 1,000 Filipinas entered each year as U.S. dependents and this rose to 1,500 per year in the 1960s.[10] The Chinese American population, which stagnated during exclusion, also grew in the postwar years due to new immigration. Between 1940 and 1960, the mainland population increased from about 77,000 to nearly 200,000. Rapid economic growth in postwar Japan absorbed much of the potential emigrant pool in that country, but about 4,500 newcomers, mostly war brides, entered the United States each year during the 1950s and 1960s. In all, postwar Japanese immigration until 1980 amounted to a little more than half of the number of Issei who arrived between 1900 and 1924.[11]

Asian immigrants in the twenty years after World War II were very different from their nineteenth and early twentieth-century predecessors. The newcomers included a larger proportion of women, children, and elites compared to the first wave. Nor did they come from the traditional sending regions within the countries of origin. A large number of Chinese science students, for instance, were from Taiwan and Hong Kong, as opposed to the old sending regions in Guangdong and other southern provinces. Also, while the majority of the first wave of Indian immigrants spoke Punjabi and came from the Punjab region in the northern Indian subcontinent, the arrivals during the postwar years were more likely to come from cities like Bombay and Calcutta and speak Gujarati.[12]

One of the most striking features of Asian immigration during this period, across all groups, was the preponderance of women, a marked turnaround from earlier decades. Between 1947 and 1964, about 72,700 Asian women entered, most of whom came as non-quota immigrants under the sponsorship of family members in the United States. Of these, about 45,853 were Japanese, 14,435 Filipina, about 7,000 Chinese, and 6,500 Korean. Among Koreans entering between 1951 and 1964, women outnumbered men 3.5 to 1, and in 1965, about 82 percent of entering Koreans were female.[13] Women's migration helped balance the skewed gender ratios in Asian American communities. For example, by 1960, the sex ratio in Chinese America was 1.3 to 1.[14]

So-called "war brides" constituted the majority of Asian women migrants in the fifteen years after World War II, also representing about 20 percent of the Asian American population's growth in this period.[15] Beginning with the Magnuson Act, which permitted the entry of Chinese family members, military spouses from Asia came to the United States through a variety of legislative reforms. The War Brides Act, passed in December 1945, allowed the "admission of alien spouses and alien minor children of citizen members of the United States armed forces," as non-quota immigrants. Between 1945 and 1948, over five thousand Chinese women entered under its provisions.[16] In 1952 the Act was amended to allow for the entry of military brides from Korea and Japan, but most of these women were sponsored as non-quota dependents of U.S. citizens under the McCarran-Walter Act.[17] Japanese were the largest group of military brides, making up 80 percent of Japanese immigrants in the 1950s and entering at an annual rate of two thousand to five thousand in the 1950s and 1960s.[18]

In cases where military spouses married co-ethnics, usually the case among Chinese and to a significant but lesser degree among Filipinas, this migration greatly changed the

Figure 9.1   Public Law 717, passed in 1950, was one of several laws facilitating the entry of Asian military brides married to American G.I.s into the United States after World War II. This photograph from 1951 shows the last couple to be married under that law, a Japanese woman and white American G.I. (Library of Congress Prints and Photographs Division, LC-USZ62-85807.)

dynamics of Asian American communities. In the three years that the War Brides Act was in effect, 5,132 Chinese women entered the country. Thousands of other Chinese wives, not necessarily married to servicemen, came under the Chinese Alien Wives of American Citizens Act (1946) between 1947 and 1950, further boosting female migration. Most of the couples settled in metropolitan areas on the East or West Coasts, where their husbands were already settled. According to Xiaojian Zhao, most Chinese military brides had actually been married for at least ten years prior to joining their husbands, having previously maintained transnational marriages and homes.[19] Yee Wing, for instance, had been separated from her husband for fifteen years before coming to the United States under the War Brides Act.[20]

Chinese also tended to be older than other war brides, with most between thirty- and forty-years-old at the time of their arrival. Regarding long-term consequences, the migration of military and other wives allowed communities to transition from "bachelor" to "family communities." In Chinese America, it hastened a postwar baby boom; this population experienced a 286.5 percent increase in the birth rate between 1946 and 1947.[21]

The picture was different for Korean and Japanese military brides, most of whom married white American servicemen.[22] As Japan and Korea were reeling from the destruction of World War II and the Korean War, many young women in these countries had to go out and earn a living, sometimes far from home on military bases where the U.S. occupation of the two countries had created jobs in sales service, clerical work, bars, and restaurants. Their reasons for marrying American men and leaving their countries varied, but frequently centered on their need for emotional or material support. Korean women who worked as entertainers and waitresses in "camptowns," where U.S. soldiers were stationed, often found conditions there to be abusive, so looked to marriage as a way out of that life. Others, like Japanese military bride Reiko Simeone, believed that an American husband would treat her better than a Japanese one. "In Japan, when I was young," she said, "I never thought I'm going to marry . . . men do what they want even if they're married. A couple of years later, he'd be fooling around."[23]

In the United States, Asian military brides found familiar and new challenges. Those who had entered interracial marriages often faced isolation from both co-ethnics and the mainstream society. That they had intermarried at all was transgressive—marrying blacks was especially taboo in many families—so they often embarked on married life estranged from kin and social networks of support.[24] The brides usually settled in the husbands' hometowns, where they were likely to be the only Asians, and had to quickly learn English and adapt to American life. Military wives in the Bay Area and other cities with Asian American communities were generally more socially independent because they could find support outside the home, compared to their counterparts in remote places. This support usually came through friendships with other military brides, as the wider ethnic community could be ambivalent toward them. Korean military brides, for instance, were often discriminated against by other Korean Americans due to their backgrounds as entertainers, waitresses, or prostitutes.[25]

For much of American society, Asian military brides were fascinating objects of curiosity. Their lives in America represented "fish out of water" stories that the public consumed with much interest. Furthermore, intermarriages between Asian women and white American servicemen affirmed principles of Cold War liberalism, symbolizing U.S. benevolence toward Asia and the transcending of social taboos in a multiracial America. Films like *Japanese War Bride* (1952) and *Sayonara* (1957), which depicted interracial intimacy between white American men and Japanese women, criticized Japanese and U.S. attitudes against intermarriage and celebrated colorblind love. In February 1955 *Life* magazine featured an article titled, "Pursuit of Happiness by a GI and a Japanese." Written by James Michener, a well-known Asia expert who also authored the book on which *Sayonara* was based, the piece centered on Sachiko Pfeiffer, a "tiny girl" from Japan, who came to the United States in 1948 after marrying Frank Pfeiffer of Chicago, a "soft-spoken slaughterhouse butcher."[26] Describing their courtship, Michener wrote, "After four speechless dates they knew they were in love." Although he described Sachiko's struggles to adjust to America and the couple's travails against the racism of Frank's family and the surrounding community, Michener ultimately presented a story of love conquering all, including the socioeconomic ladder into the middle class.

Also adding to the U.S. Asian population and holding a similar place in the American Cold War imagination were Asian adoptees, especially those from South Korea. American inter-country adoptions from Asia were an extension of practices originating in Europe during World War II, when the U.S. Committee for the Care of European Children facilitated the adoption of 4,177 European children from war-torn countries between 1940 and 1952.[27] By the 1950s, Asian adoption became a phenomenon in itself and helped propel the Asian population in the United States in the Cold War years. Between 1953 and 1963 Americans adopted 8,812 Asian children. As far as the legal channels through which they entered, early adoptees gained admission to the United States through ad hoc measures, usually special military or congressional clearance as well as provisions in refugee laws.[28] In 1957 amend-ments to the Immigration and Nationality Act authorized unlimited orphan visas still subject to national quotas, and a subsequent Act in 1961 made non-quota visas permanently available for foreign-born adopted children.[29]

Interest in Asian children especially focused on Koreans. The Korean War had resulted in the separation of ten million families, widowing of half a million wives, and abandonment of tens of thousands of children. Many of the latter were, moreover, the mixed race offspring of American GIs and Korean women. National publications ran articles about the orphans and the humanitarian work being done on their behalf (with names like "Operation Kiddy Car," and "Operation Winter").[30] Especially pivotal in bringing the attention of Korean and other Asian orphans to Americans' attention were Henry and Bertha Holt, an Oregon couple who adopted eight Korean children after the Korean War. They also arranged a baby lift mission that flew ninety-one Korean children to the United States and established the Holt Adoption Program in 1956, which expanded into the Holt International Children's Services, the first U.S. agency to handle international adoptions.[31] In her 1956 memoir, *The Seed from the East*, Bertha Holt described her odyssey to Korea and larger mission in the following way:

> Korea . . . 1954 . . . Thousands of children suffered in crowded, understaffed and poorly supplied orphanages—children, it seemed, that no one wanted. But God gave one couple a heart to love these children. This most ordinary family—a lumberman with a heart condition, a farming wife and six children—changed the world when they adopted eight Korean–Amerasian children.[32]

By the mid-1950s, the attention brought to Korean children by the Holts and other writers as well as the institutional and legal mechanisms put in place to facilitate adoptions resulted in a dramatic rise in the entry of Korean children to join American families. From 1955 to 1961, Americans adopted 4,190 mixed-race and full-blooded Korean children.[33] Each year during the 1960s, Korean children were adopted by the hundreds, and the following decade by the thousands.

For prospective adoptive parents, a variety of factors drew them to Korean children. Reaching out to black prospective adoptive parents, *Ebony* magazine featured an article in September 1955, titled "How to Adopt Korean Babies." Appealing to their sense of racial justice, it emphasized the bleakness of mixed-race children's lives because in Korea "racial purity is deeply entrenched in social fetish."[34] Amid the baby boom, adoption also appealed to infertile couples and families wishing to add more children to their households.[35] Although the image of Asian children being raised by non-Asian parents disrupted the ideal of mono-racial (read white) American families, their coming together in nuclear, heterosexual units normalized both the Asian child and otherwise childless parents. As Arissa Oh has stated, "[the adopted child] verified her adoptive parents' worthiness for inclusion in the nation at a time when status as a parent was equated with citizenship."[36]

The adoption rhetoric simultaneously appealed to Americans' yearning to be parents and good cold warriors. The agency *World Vision* ran an ad in 1956, which read, "A Korean Orphan for You: Many Inquire, 'How can I help Korean Orphans?' Although few can bring them to this country, YOU can be a Mother or Daddy to your own child in a Christian orphanage in Korea . . . Yours for the asking!"[37] Additionally, by reaching out to Korean orphans, Americans could gain a better understanding of Korea and overcome their own prejudices. An article appearing in the *Christian Science Monitor* in 1953 titled, "GIs Clothe South American Waifs," said:

> American soldiers—who once called all Koreans "gooks"—now are engaged in a number of projects which indicate that affection and respect have largely replaced their earlier skepticism. Many GIs who find Korean customs confusing and Korean politics unsavory are putting their efforts into the most promising of many unofficial relief activities: aid for South Korea's ragged, appealing children. For these soldiers, the tattered waifs with the beguiling faces are the most understandable feature of the Korean scene.[38]

The adoption of children from other Asian nations was likewise framed as acts of compassion against the backdrop of U.S. global leadership during the Cold War. Pearl Buck's Welcome House, the first transracial adoption agency, brought to America Asian and part-Asian children as part of its liberal, antiracist, anticommunist project. Buck, herself an adoptive parent of Amerasian children, was distressed at the spread of Communism in China and saw international and transracial adoption as a way to facilitate friendship between the United States and Asia.[39] Initially focusing on children born in the United States, by the late 1950s Welcome House coordinated international adoptions for children from Japan, Korea, Hong Kong, and Taiwan.

Adoption programs and efforts to reform immigration laws to allow adoptees' entry, furthermore, drew little opposition, as potential criticism was blunted by GI babies' presumptive American paternity, and as well as the powerful image of "innocent, imperiled children" and the "self-evident" imperative to save them.[40] Furthermore, as children they did not pose the same kind of economic and political threat ascribed to adult immigrants. Like the rhetoric around war brides, adoptees solidified the narrative that "love conquers all," including divisions of race and nationality, while glossing over histories of imperialism, racism, patriarchy, and exploitation in the adoption market.

In contrast to military brides and adoptees, the other main groups of immigrants in the early Cold War years—students, scholars, and skilled professionals—were drawn from the elite strata of Asian societies. This migration, which expanded after legislative reform in 1965, was driven by Cold War internationalism as well as U.S. economic demands for educated and technically skilled human labor. Until the 1940s, the United States was primarily interested in importing poorly educated laborers, but having emerged from the war as a mature, industrial nation locked in a competition for global influence with the Soviet Union, its needs changed. Policy adjustments included reserving 30 percent of the slots under the Displaced Persons Act of 1948 for scientists and skilled professionals and 50 percent of the quotas under the McCarran-Walter Act of 1952 for skilled immigrants, specifying "college professors, chemists, meteorologists, physicians and surgeons, dentists, nurses, veterinarians, engineers, tool designers, draftsmen."[41] The latter legislation also allowed foreign exchange students in the United States to apply for permanent status and naturalization as quota immigrants after earning their degrees and securing sponsorship by an American firm, a provision utilized by thousands of students from East, South, and Southeast Asia.[42] The Cold War imperative to spread U.S. influence around the world gave rise to additional pull factors, such as a program set up by the National Science Foundation in 1957, which awarded scholarships to international students undertaking graduate work in science and engineering at American universities.

The earliest Chinese students and professionals who immigrated to the United States during the Cold War years had actually come during World War II when the Nationalist government was in power and encouraged study and training in America as part of its push for modernization. With China's transition to Communism in 1949, however, these individuals, who were in the United States on temporary visas, now sought status as political refugees so they could stay permanently.[43] These included five thousand so-called "stranded students" and some of China's most illustrious and talented professionals, such as Chen Ning Yang and Tsung-tao Lee, the joint winners of the Nobel Prize for Physics in 1957, An Wang of Wang Laboratories, and architect I.M. Pei.[44] According to Madeline Hsu, 3,645 Chinese residents—students, officials, sailors, other temporary visa holders—were able to adjust their status, and 3,517 students and 119 scholars from China received congressional funding for living expenses, tuition, and medical care.[45] The latter was part of a State Department Committee on Educational Interchange Policy that supported "humanitarian and national interests," but also clearly favored people with desirable skills and training.

Other Asian governments cooperated with American agencies to encourage student and professional migration, with the intention that emigrants would return to their home countries and apply their skills and expertise there. In the 1950s, the Korean government started organizing programs to send doctors and nurses abroad to gain experience, through which a large number of Yonsei University medical school graduates, for instance, were able to work in the United States. In the Philippines, a large number of women nurses joined the professional migration. Their entries were facilitated by the Exchange Visitor Program (EVP), which was launched by the U.S. government in 1948 to draw international students and workers, and thereby foster better understandings of the United States in other countries. Participants worked or studied in sponsoring U.S. institutions, receiving a monthly stipend, and after up to two years, would return to their countries. Filipino nurses, sponsored by the American Nurses Association and individual hospitals, were one of many groups to take part in the EVP, but by the late 1960s, they dominated the program, and between 1956 and 1969, over eleven thousand participated.[46] By the mid-1960s the use of Filipino exchange nurses in the United States had become so commonplace that the Philippine Department of

Labor described the EVP as a "loophole for the circumvention of the United States immigration law."[47]

The Filipino nurses in the EVP came to America with high expectations, but their experiences were mixed. They were drawn to the prestige of living in America and believed that working conditions would be better than in the Philippines, where many complained of long hours, sexism, low wages, and little respect. Lourdes Velasco said, "We heard that here [in the United States] you're off two days a week . . . We were off [in the Philippines] only two days a month. In 1963 after graduation, one of my close relatives was getting married. I could not attend the wedding because I did not have that day off."[48] Luz Alerta, who worked at the University of Texas Galveston in the late 1960s, was pleased with her experience, especially the chance to gain valuable training and learn about life in America.[49] The nurses enjoyed a higher standard of living and were able to purchase items unavailable in the Philippines, such as appliances and cosmetics. For the reasons described above, upon their return to the Philippines, they experienced an elevation in social status, which, in turn, inspired others to become nurses and go to America. On the other hand, Filipino exchange nurses experienced exploitation, often because hospitals viewed them as inexpensive solutions for a domestic nurse shortage. Their stipends were smaller than American nurses' incomes, and they were often assigned to the least desirable work shifts. Although they had few avenues of recourse—their visas only allowed them to work at their sponsoring hospitals—the nurses were not helpless, as they organized, petitioned, and formed branches of the Philippine Nurses Association.[50] Additionally, Philippine representatives sometimes protested on their behalf, such as congressman Epifano Castillejos, who criticized the EVP for subjecting Filipino nurses to discrimination, overwork, and insufficient training.[51]

Despite its problems, the EVP was popular for several decades, and had the unintended effect of many exchange nurses deciding to stay in the United States, whether for more training, better wages, or the perception that Philippine nursing was inferior. As Catherine Ceniza Choy explains, the nurses "fulfilled American nurses' expectations by publicizing the achievements of American nursing in the Philippines. However, their belief in the superiority of American nursing also led to the development of a common prejudice among Filipino exchange nurses against Philippine nursing."[52] To avoid returning to the Philippines, they employed a number of strategies, including marrying American citizens, going to Canada and re-entering, and appealing INS rulings to change their status.

Cold War Politics and Asian America

The shifts in U.S.–Asia relations and immigration policies were also reflected in changes in domestic racial ideologies and attitudes toward Asians in America. By the early 1950s, Asia's importance to U.S. global interests reshaped states like California, with its increasing trans-Pacific trade, expanding military facilities, and growing presence of defense contractors. With regard to social relations, Americans seemed more mindful about the consequences of anti-Asian racism than they had before, and according to Charlotte Brooks, they "showed a real willingness to make the racial 'sacrifices' they now deemed necessary to win the cold war."[53] A December 1950 editorial in the *San Francisco Chronicle* illustrated some of these changes with regard to Chinese:

Chinese in Chinatown are predominantly anti-Communist . . . To show resentment of them merely plays the Communist game of setting races against each other . . . Most Chinese are Americans, too, and anyone who display[s] a prejudice toward them . . . is displaying a lack of respect for American citizenship itself.[54]

In Los Angeles, which emerged after the war as a major Pacific Rim hub, the new U.S.–Japan relationship reshaped the social and economic landscape. In October 1951, at the invitation of Japanese commerce officials, Mayor Fletcher Bowron visited Japan with a delegation of local business leaders, and by the end of the decade the port of Los Angeles was receiving more tonnage from Japan than anywhere else in the world.[55] After a period of distancing themselves from Japan, Southern California Japanese American leaders, including many Nisei and Sansei, found it once again advantageous to identify with Japan and present themselves as bridges of understanding. JACL leader Mike Masaoka, for instance, worked as a consultant for Japanese corporations that sought to establish business connections in the United States.[56]

U.S. government agencies also enlisted Asian Americans in their bid to spread goodwill in Asia. The Voice of America, the State Department-run international radio broadcasting operation, hired second-generation Chinese American Betty Lee Sung to produce a program called *Chinese Activities*, which consisted of six-minute segments and was broadcast in different dialects throughout the Asia Pacific region. The contents focused on topics of Sung's choice about Chinese living in America. In 1952, she highlighted architect IM Pei, saying, "It always makes us Chinese in America experience great pride when we see that another Chinese has attained success or has accomplished something outstanding."[57] Although the program was not explicitly anti-communist, as Sung believed she was merely "reporting on the events in the Chinese American community," its contents and messages nonetheless consistently extolled America.[58]

Government sponsored tours by Asian American writers and artists also sought to cement understanding between the United States and Asia. During the 1950s, Chinese Americans Jade Snow Wong and Dong Kingman traveled to Asia as personal ambassadors under the auspices of the Leaders' and Specialists' Exchange program. The State Department had recommended the translation and overseas distribution of Wong's 1950 memoir, *Fifth Chinese Daughter*, because it painted a "favorable picture of American institutions," and then sent her on a goodwill mission tour of Asia in 1952, during which she gave speeches about liberal democracy, East–West understanding, and cultural pluralism.[59] In talking with Asians about America, Wong also downplayed racism and played up self-reliance as a core American value. "I learned that my background as a Chinese was my particular asset, a point of distinction not to be rejected," she said, "I learned never to count on the false comfort of racial discrimination to excuse personal failure."[60] Artist Dong Kingman's travels to East and Southeast Asia in 1954 were covered by national media, which said of him, "We cannot think of a better U.S. Ambassador to the people of the East . . . He likes people and with his outgoing spirit, he invites confidence and trust. He has sown the seed for a great harvest of friendship for the U.S."[61] These visits were significant because they brought an unprecedented level of visibility to people of Asian ancestry and legitimized the citizenship of Chinese Americans, but they were not revolutionary. That they were selected to be ambassadors because of their achievements and Chinese ancestry underscored that Wong and Kingman were "not quite" American. Furthermore, by framing them as exemplars of Chinese achievement in America, the tours did nothing to bring light to or efface the realities of racial discrimination.

Also signaling change during the Cold War was how people responded to anti-Asian outbreaks. Once part of the fabric of daily life, they were increasingly a source of embarrassment in communities. Most embarrassing were incidents that involved Asian American veterans of World War II. One of these occurred in late 1952, when Sam Yoshihara, a disabled Nisei veteran of the 442nd, sought to purchase a house in San Jose, California, a growing community with defense and military industries in northern California. Several residents of the street where the house was located circulated a petition to reject Yoshihara. This action, however, was eclipsed by an outcry by other residents and a local civic unity group in defense of Yoshihara.[62] Supporting him based on his military service and fear of negative publicity, Yoshihara's backers argued that contemporary exigencies made it necessary to accept Japanese and other Asians because, as one resident said, "my property values aren't as important as my principles."[63] As the *San Jose Mercury News* stated, people were especially worried that the neighborhood would become associated with "Communist propaganda" and "prove that Americans are intolerant toward the Orientals whose friendship is so important."[64] Sufficiently shamed, the residents apologized for the petition and welcomed Yoshihara. Similar incidents occurred elsewhere in California and, according to Charlotte Brooks, "a growing number of white community leaders and businesspeople had come to fear the kind of publicity that anti-Asian housing incidents could generate."[65] Picking up on this, JACL legal counsel Frank Chuman pressed to quietly resolve disputes involving Nisei in the Los Angeles area.[66] By the mid-to-late 1950s a discernible shift had occurred with respect to the housing market in California. A San Francisco real estate broker stated, "Japanese and Chinese are often accepted almost like whites."[67] This did not mean Asians faced no discrimination, as obtaining FHA or VA financing remained difficult for many, but brokers were increasingly willing to sell to Asian Americans especially if they had financing.

At the same time, the Cold War atmosphere promoted suspicion of radicals and placed a premium on conformity, and leftists and progressives were singled out for persecution while organizations like the JACL and Chinese Six, which embraced anticommunism, were protected and elevated. Anticommunist politics could be devastating in Chinese American communities. In terms of the ethnic economy, a U.S. embargo on the People's Republic of China (PRC) impacted Chinatown economies, forcing the closure of dry goods, grocery stores, pharmacies, and other businesses. To survive, some curio and souvenir shops started carrying Japanese goods.

The persecution of Chinese American leftists was another consequence of Cold War developments. The FBI had compiled a list of suspect Chinese American organizations to investigate, such as the Chinese Hand Laundry Association, the *China Daily News*, and Chinese Workers' Mutual Aid Association, and director J. Edgar Hoover claimed, "Red China has been flooding the country with its propaganda and there are over 300,000 Chinese in the United States, some of whom could be susceptible to recruitment either through ethnic ties or hostage situations because of relatives in Communist China."[68] Officials in the FBI and Immigration and Naturalization Service (INS) cracked down on Chinese leftists, suspected Communists, and critics of Chiang Kai-shek. Among their targets was the Oasis Bookstore in San Francisco, whose supply sources they blocked due to suspicion of its progressive Chinese American owners. The *China Daily News*, along with other investigated organizations, had to turn over its subscriber list. Found guilty of violating the Trading with the Enemy Act, the newspaper's editor Eugene Moy served two years in jail.[69]

Such forms of government surveillance as well as the conflict between the Nationalist government and the People's Liberation Army divided Chinese America. While leftist groups such as the Chinese Workers' Mutual Aid Association celebrated Mao's victory and the establishment of the PRC, bourgeois and merchant Chinese Americans who supported the Nationalists formed anti-Communist organizations and waged campaigns against Communists in their midst.[70] As noted, the CCBA was especially hostile toward critics of the Guomindang, calling them Communist agents, imperiling their businesses with threats to remove advertisements in their newspapers, and colluding with federal authorities to harass them.[71] While these schisms were usually limited to wars of words, they occasionally erupted violently. In one incident in San Francisco in 1949, news had circulated that leftists were planning a new paper called *China Weekly*. The San Francisco branch of the Guomindang responded by threatening to destroy any printer that published the newspaper. After its first issue appeared in May with the headline, "The Liberation Army Ready for Its Final Attack on Shanghai," "hoodlums" from the Guomindang-controlled Bing Kung Cong association intimidated the newspapers' employees and removed copies from private mailboxes and dormitories. Several months later, also in San Francisco, about four hundred Chinese Americans, joined by several non-Chinese activists, gathered at the Chinese American Citizens Alliance auditorium to celebrate the founding of the PRC. Forty men armed with pipes, eggs, and blue dye, believed to have been sent by the Guomindang, broke up the event, tearing down decorations and breaking chairs.[72]

The Chinese Confession Program

During this period, anticommunist paranoia merged with latent xenophobia, leading officials to turn their attention to immigration and beef up federal power to exclude and deport subversives. The McCarran Act (Internal Security Act) of 1950 permitted the president to declare internal security emergencies, during which the attorney general could suspend habeas corpus and apprehend and detain suspects. The McCarran-Walter Act of 1952, although liberalizing some aspects of immigration and naturalization policy, added to the list excludable classes, eliminated the statute of limitations for nearly all deportable offenses, and reenacted provisions of the Internal Security Act to expel aliens deemed "prejudicial to the public interest."[73] It also closed a loophole in the Nationality Act of 1940 that allowed immigration petitioners to seek temporary residency through the courts if their applications were denied.

In this context, Chinese students and experts came under heightened scrutiny for fear that they would return to China and use their knowledge against the United States. The federal government, for instance, barred Tsien Hsue-shen, one of the founders of the Jet Propulsion Laboratory, from leaving the country in August 1950.[74] Chinese seamen were also singled out for surveillance and deportation following the FBI's release of a report in October 1951, called "Movement of Communist Chinese." The report, which was forwarded to the INS, alleged that the Seamen's Union of Hong Kong was controlled by Communists and expediting the entry of Chinese to the United States.[75]

These fears of Communist subterfuge merged with longstanding worries about Chinese illegal entry in the so-called "Chinese Confession Program." This link was initially made in a December 1955 report to the State Department by the American consul general in Hong Kong, Everett F. Drumright. In it, he alleged rampant immigration fraud in Hong Kong and "a criminal conspiracy" by the People's Republic of China "to evade the laws of the United States through networks in Hong Kong, New York, and San Francisco.[76] He furthermore elaborated that a "fantastic system of passport and visa fraud" was in place and characterized Chinese people as "[lacking] a concept equivalent to the western concept of an oath."[77] Drumright's office was overwhelmed with about 117,000 applications from Chinese seeking entry to the U.S. through derivative citizenship, most of which, he believed, were fraudulent. He also argued that this system was being perpetrated by Communists to send spies to the United States.[78] FBI director J. Edgar Hoover validated these allegations in 1955, saying, "The large number of Chinese entering this country as immigrants provides Red China with a channel to dispatch to the United States undercover agents on intelligence assignments."[79]

The INS, which was not originally alarmed about Communist infiltration, saw the consul's warnings as an opening to aggressively break up fraudulent Chinese immigration networks. In the 1950s it was still overwhelmed with reviewing applications that claimed family connections in the United States. Denied applicants could turn to the courts, out of whose proceedings—which were costly to the government—many emerged with discharge papers that constituted documentation of native birth citizenship, which were in turn used to sponsor others as "relatives."[80]

Toward stopping this practice, the INS announced the Chinese Confession Program, to be carried out with the cooperation of several government agencies.[81] This was an informal program with neither official policies nor guidelines. Reaching out through advertisements and civic leaders, officials asked Chinese Americans who had fraudulently established their U.S. citizenship or had otherwise entered the country illegally to come forward. They were told if they confessed and provided full disclosure on every relative and friend who had also entered illegally, they could regularize their status. By the time the program ended in 1966 13,895 people confessed, leading to the exposure of 22,083 others and the closure of 11,294 potential paper son slots. Considering the Chinese American population on the mainland at the time was about 118,000, this program had a very deep impact. Most of the confessors were able to stay, but a few, usually those engaged in "subversive" political activities, were deported.

Because the program was never official, the potential for abuse was widespread. Agents entered Chinatowns and randomly stopped people on the streets to see their documents. As Maurice Chuck of San Francisco explained, "They would stop you on the street. Harassed you and asked you all sorts of questions, push you around. It became a daily part of our lives in Chinatown during that time."[82] Furthermore, although government officials claimed they were not interested in entrapment and that confessors would benefit, no formal provisions were made for the amnesty of confessors, and other details remained vague. Confessors had to surrender documents of citizenship to the INS and sign papers stating they were amenable to deportation if their confessions were denied.[83] Participating in the program also divided families, as confessing always entailed implicating others. Furthermore, because the United States had no relationship with China, it could not deport people there, so instead sent them to Hong Kong.

The ordeals of Lew Bok Yin and Lee Ying illustrate the devastation the Confession Program wreaked on people's lives. On paper, Lew had been a naturalized U.S. citizen since 1902. According to INS records, seventeen people had gained entry as his sons and grandsons and their wives, and authorities suspected that some of these were not really his descendants. They approached several of them, threatening deportation if they did not make full confessions about their true status. After admitting their fraud, some faced deportation hearings, and all were barred from sponsoring the future immigration of family members. In the case of Lee Ying, the co-owner of a theater in San Francisco, the FBI targeted him after learning the theater showed films imported from Russia and China and sponsored events for Communists and pro-Communists. As Lee had entered the United States as a paper son of Hui Suey, the FBI interrogated Hui, and after extracting his confession of fraudulent sponsorship, Lee was deported.[84]

Asian American Integration and the Origins of the Model Minority

While the backdrop of Cold War ideology and economic expansion had varying effects on the lives of Asians in America, by the late 1950s outside observers were noting their remarkable strides toward achieving mainstream integration and middle class respectability. This period saw a number of Asian American "firsts" in various fields, and many of the vestiges of structural discrimination were on their way out. In addition to the immigration policy already discussed, in 1946 California voters rejected Proposition 15, which proposed to make the state's alien land law part of its constitution. The *Pacific Citizen* said this represented the "final repudiation for the native fascists on the 'Japanese Issue.'"[85] Two years later, the U.S. Supreme Court dealt two decisive blows against institutional racism, by striking down California's alien land law and racially restrictive covenants.

The most striking areas of Asian American progress in the years after World War II were residential and economic mobility. With regard to housing, Asian Americans were moving in unprecedented numbers into previously all-white neighborhoods, indicating that cases like Sam Yoshihara's were not simply Cold War-driven public relations gestures. In San Francisco, as Chinatown expanded beyond its borders and old and new residents sought alternative residential options, Chinese started to move into neighborhoods such as the Richmond and Sunset. In turn, living in these residential and suburban areas meant their children attended better schools, which then facilitated their social and economic mobility. The movement of Japanese Americans into the mainstream economy and white-collar occupations was especially pronounced. In Los Angeles as early as 1948, just 30 percent of workers were employed by co-ethnics. Other changes from prewar patterns included business owners increasingly drawing their incomes from outside Little Tokyo, the entry of educated Nisei into professional and technical fields, and an overall decline in Japanese participation in farming.[86]

New immigration also played a role in driving up the socioeconomic profile of Asian Americans, especially with the entry of students and skilled workers in the 1950s and 1960s. For example, from 1940 and 1970, the percentage of Chinese Americans in professional and technical fields grew from 2.8 percent to 26.5 percent, and a quarter of Chinese had completed four or more years of college, compared to 11.6 percent of whites.[87] In Chinese America, the recent skilled and educated immigrants, called "uptown Chinese", tended to set themselves apart from and look down on longtime Chinese Americans, called "downtown Chinese." As sociologist Rose Hum Lee explained in 1960, "On the whole, American Chinese who have little occasion to interact with the students and intellectuals from China exhibit little interest in them, and vice versa."[88]

An unprecedented degree of mainstream recognition accompanied Asian Americans' changing socioeconomic position. A handful achieved important "firsts" in electoral politics. Especially notable in this regard was Dalip Singh Saund, a Punjabi Sikh who had immigrated in 1919 and in 1956 became the first Asian American elected to Congress. A former farmer in the Imperial Valley who had gone on to earn a Ph.D. in Mathematics from UC Berkeley, Saund had been politically active in the campaign for Indian naturalization, and became a citizen in 1949. He held the seat representing the 29th District in Los Angeles County in the U.S. House of Representatives, and went on to serve three terms.[89] Also during this period, Hawaii produced the first two Asian Americans to serve in the U.S. Senate. In 1959, Chinese American Hiram Fong became the first elected, and he was followed by Nisei Daniel Inouye in 1963. In 1965 Patsy Mink, also of Hawaii, became the first woman of color elected to Congress. At the local and statewide levels, major strides were achieved in these years as well. In 1962, Chinese American Wing Luke became the first elected official in the Pacific Northwest when he won a seat on the Seattle City Council. Alfred Song, a Hawaiian Korean, became the first Asian American elected to the California Assembly in 1961 and then to the state senate in 1966.[90]

Asian American writers also broke new ground in the late 1940s and 1950s as readers developed a newfound interest in their lives against the unfolding postwar multicultural orthodoxy. Particularly prominent were Filipino immigrant Carlos Bulosan, Nisei John Okada, and Chinese Americans Pardee Lowe and Jade Snow Wong whose autobiographical or semiautobiographical accounts about being Asian in America were published by major East Coast publishing houses and enjoyed glowing reviews and national success. Jade Snow Wong's book, *Fifth Chinese Daughter*, was selected by the Book of the Month Club and Christian Herald Family Book Shelf for November 1950, and was described by the *New York Times* as a "gravely charming and deeply understanding self-portrait by a brilliant young woman who grew up midway between two cultures."[91]

C.Y. Lee was another Chinese American writer who gained notice for his work about Asian Americans. Lee came to the United States in 1942 to complete an M.F.A. at Yale University, and planned to return to China afterward, but after Mao's victory decided to stay and settled in San Francisco. Launching his literary fame was his 1957 book, *Flower Drum Song*, which explored the dilemmas of Americanized Chinese negotiating the pressures of traditional parents and their own personal, modern sensibilities.[92] Because Lee's intention was to explain to Americans the world of Americanized Chinese, the book had a touristic quality, which was also key to its mainstream appeal and eventual adaptation into a Broadway musical and motion picture. A "spectacle of assimilation," according to scholar Christina Klein, *Flower Drum Song* embraced the "mixed-up quality" of American life to convey a liberal message about race relations. In presenting Chinese as "ethnic Americans, and not as an alien 'yellow peril' threat," *Flower Drum Song* broke new ground.[93] Richard Rodgers, one of the musical's creators, was aware of this, stating, "We show that East and West can go together with a little adjustment."[94]

For their part, Asian Americans responded to the changing atmosphere—with its opportunities and dangers—to claim Americanness, align themselves with pluralism, and advance their own interests. To distance themselves from the PRC and revive the Chinatown economy, prominent Chinese Americans in San Francisco initiated the modern Chinese New Year's festival in February 1953. The event promoted Chinese as good Americans committed to anticommunism and contented with the existing social order.[95] Along with dragon dances and firecrackers, Chinese American veterans and sports teams were prominently featured. Moreover, the mainstream media and non-Chinese figures took an interest in the event. Government officials and celebrities regularly sent greetings for the occasion. California governor Goodwin Knight in 1954: "It is a splendid thing that such groups as our Chinese–American neighbors can in this country keep alive their ancestral traditions and at the same time contribute so much to the preservation of the American heritage of freedom and individual dignity through responsible citizenship."[96]

Japanese Americans forged similar traditions that cemented their image as acculturated, patriotic, and nonthreatening citizens. In Los Angeles they revived the Nisei Week festival in 1949, whose postwar incarnation celebrated a new era in U.S.–Japan relations and reached out to non-Japanese officials and media. It also reflected a new Japanese America in Los Angeles, which was more geographically dispersed, less oriented around Little Tokyo, and no longer led by the Issei. Whereas supporting Little Tokyo businesses and promoting Nisei obligations were once its primary goals, promoting "integration" was now the main objective. According to the *Pacific Citizen*, the event also symbolized a chance to heal from, and curiously forget, the ordeal of wartime internment. "[The] big story of Nisei Week," it stated, "is its reflection of the economic and social health of the displaced Americans who have returned home. The race-baiters have been routed and the songs and dances of Nisei Week serve to wipe out the memory of bitterness and frustration of the mass evacuation experience."[97] Ethnic solidarity was still an important component of the festival, particularly as the population became more dispersed. Moreover, politicians and business leaders from Japan were invited to play prominent roles, for instance showcasing products and sponsoring floats, as strengthening ties with the country was now in line with Los Angeles' civic mission. In 1968, the largest contributors to Nisei Week included Toyota, Honda, Mitsubishi Bank, Japan Airlines, and Sumitomo Bank.[98]

The involvement of women in such community events captured contradictions of Asian American representation. Although they originated before the 1950s, Asian American beauty pageants became more like their mainstream counterparts. In Nisei Week, for example, contestants, who were increasingly drawn from areas outside of Little Tokyo, began wearing swimsuits in 1950. Winners were often picked based on having Western features such as big eyes and curly hair.[99] This was part of an overall effort to present an Americanized image of Nisei womanhood. No longer were the contestants described as symbols of the blending of East and West, but rather of unqualified Americanism. Some were ambivalent, however, about embracing Western standards of beauty in Japanese American beauty pageants. For instance, in 1947 Bill Hosokawa lamented the trend among some women who were surgically enlarging their eyes and bleaching their hair in order to appear more white.[100]

The San Francisco Miss Chinatown pageant, which was held as part of the Chinese New Year celebration from 1953 to 1957, differed slightly in emphasizing the bicultural identity of Chinese American women. On the one hand, contestants were described as all-American, but their Chinese background was presented in an exotic and sexualized manner. According to Chiou-Ling Yeh, the pageants and use of Chinese women in other capacities at Chinatown festivals "indicat[ed] a desire to cater to the sexualized Orientalist fantasy among white America."[101] In the pageant's postwar incarnation, contestants wore cheongsams (Suzy Wong style dress), whereas before the war, they donned only Western garb. "[This] choice indicated an intention to cater to the mainstream China doll stereotype," explains Yeh.[102] The use of physically and sexually attractive women as ethnic ambassadors to white Americans was further signaled at the 1956 New Year's celebration when Mayor George Christopher kissed Miss Chinatown in a gesture hailed as a symbol of harmony between the community and City Hall.[103] The pageant also sought to bind contestants to the ethnic community, as winners would be praised for being family-oriented and responsible community members. Bernice Wong, Miss Chinatown 1954, said that serving her reign strengthened her interest in community affairs. "Before I was not concerned about the community at all," she said, "Now, after meeting many people from various classes, I realize that every public affair in the Chinese American community directly or indirectly influences the lives and business of Chinese Americans."[104] In their pursuit of authenticity and ethnic integrity, pageant organizers showed a preference for contestants who spoke a Chinese dialect and only those who had a Chinese father could compete, which left the door open to a number of interracial contenders over the years. The pageant's simultaneous striving for white middle-class acceptance was revealed, however, in its exclusion of contestants of African descent.[105]

The Cold War Origins Of The Model Minority

In line with the growing mainstream visibility and participation of middle-class Asian Americans—mainly Chinese and Japanese—national publications celebrated their postwar achievements as illustrations of their tenacity and good citizenship, not to mention the greatness of America. An early example of this appeared in 1948, in a series in the *Saturday Evening Post* called "How Our People Live." Highlighting and celebrating America's multicultural character, the series included an installment about the family of Jade Snow Wong, whose members were presented as exemplary Asian Americans who represented the possibilities of hard work and good citizenship. After immigrating in 1903 father Wong Hong learned English, converted to Christianity, built a business, and raised several children, who for their own part were assimilated and productive members of society. Acknowledging that the Wongs were unusually accomplished, author George Sessions Perry nonetheless said they were models to which other immigrant families should strive to be.[106] Seven years later, the *Saturday Evening Post* ran another article about accomplished and exemplary Asians, this time about Japanese. Titled, "California's Amazing Japanese," it highlighted the achievements of Los Angeles Nisei and expressed amazement that they were able to thrive after their bitter wartime experience.[107] Similar articles that appeared over the next few years in national publications like the *New York Times* and *U.S. News and World Report* uniformly praised Japanese Americans for their achievements despite being "almost totally unaided," and like the Perry piece on the Wongs, helped to establish the "model minority" stereotype of Asian Americans.

Understood in context, the model minority was very much a construction of the 1950s and early 1960s. An often-overlooked aspect of it was its implicit critique of other minorities, especially African Americans, who did not enjoy the postwar mobility and media adulation that Asian Americans did. They were, for instance, unable to match Asian Americans' movement into formerly all-white neighborhoods and were actually more segregated than they had been before the war. In 1955, sociology students at UC Berkeley found that twice as many brokers would sell to "Orientals" than they would to blacks in neighborhoods where members of neither group lived.[108] By the mid-1950s, real estate brokers and insurance firms openly acknowledged that while they were willing to work with Asians, they refused to do business with blacks. One broker in San Francisco stated, "generally the feeling is against non-Caucasians, but most people will qualify this by saying they mind Orientals less than Negroes."[109] Illustrating this dynamic was an incident in San Francisco, in which a black doctor offered to pay $24,000 for a home, but was turned down by the owner because of his race. The same house was sold a week later to a Chinese American family offering $22,000.[110] Nor was it unusual for white homeowners to react violently to the arrival of black neighbors, showing none of the same trepidation that they did about the repercussions of discriminating against Asians. In March 1952, vigilantes firebombed the home of black teachers who had purchased a house in the west side of Los Angeles.[111] Frustrated by the lack of progress for blacks in housing, the African American state assemblymen William Rumford and Augustus Hawkin sponsored a bill prohibiting racial discrimination in the sale or rental of private dwellings with more than four units. Although it passed in 1963, the California Real Estate Association and conservative groups launched a successful drive to repeal the Act the following year.

As Asian Americans—again mainly Japanese and Chinese—were increasingly lauded in the mainstream media from the mid-1950s, other minorities, especially blacks, were criticized for their purported alarming militancy and lack of good values. Indeed, much of the Asian American model minority rhetoric was shaped in reaction to the rising momentum and militancy of the black freedom struggle. A white resident of Gardena, California named Irene Dalrymple said that Japanese "have earned their position because they are industrious, clean, considerate and reliable; and because they do not go around with a 'built-in' ship on the shoulder."[112] Adding to this, a Los Angeles officials was quoted in a *U.S. News and World Report* story that "Japanese Americans want to solve their problems in their own way—through hard work, education, and high moral standards, more than by court actions or publicity," while "a contrasting attitude of militancy and suspicion . . . often turns up among top Negroes."[113]

Conclusion

Wary of the model minority construction and the increasingly negative rhetoric about African Americans, journalist Gilbert Woo urged his fellow Chinese Americans not to be fooled. "Now that [white reactionaries] have made blacks their sworn enemies," he wrote, "they have no time to deal with us and even go so far as to be a little polite to us . . . But this isn't their real intention. If they had a day, white Southerners and the North's ultra-rightist factions would form a huge front, take blacks and settle scores with them, and Chinese would also receive the same treatment. Our future in America is closely bound to the future of other minority groups."[114]

While Woo worked to keep attention on the common struggles of Chinese and blacks, conditions throughout Asian America also demonstrated the myth of the model minority stereotype. In the Los Angeles Japanese American community, for example, the problem of juvenile delinquency, something kept under wraps from the media, revealed the limits of integration. The JACL and Japanese Chamber of Commerce started seriously tackling the issue after the murder of a Sansei in 1958, and the *Kashu Mainichi* blamed it on residential dispersion, especially interaction with working-class and poor blacks and Chicanos.[115] On the other hand, a youth organization called Japanese American Youth, Inc. (JAY) blamed the high expectations and material striving of Nisei parents. Sansei columnist Ellen Endo concurred, saying that neglectful and misguided parenting was turning the Sansei into a lost generation. "Children too often see their parents strive not only to keep up with the Joneses," she wrote, "but trying to keep one step ahead. It is natural for young people, in view of this fact, to question their parents' motives when status symbols, such as a fancy college or car, are involved."[116]

As Chapter 11 will show, by the late 1960s and 1970s increasing numbers of Asian Americans had grown disaffected with the status quo, both within their own families and communities and American society at large. Many channeled their feelings of discontent into political organizing for a variety of objectives, from redress for Japanese internment to ethnic studies curriculum in higher education. During this tumultuous and dynamic period, Asian America also grew larger and more diverse than ever before due to further reforms in immigration policy, unfolding another new chapter in Asian American history.

Another source of renewed growth was the migration of refugees from Southeast Asia, the focus of the next chapter. Although people fleeing Vietnam, Cambodia, and Laos—eventually numbering about one million—began arriving in the United States during the mid-1970s, the conflict that this migration grew out of had origins in the 1950s when the United States first became involved in Vietnam, where it hoped to help the French regain control over their former colony and thereby contain Communism's spread in that part of the world. In the following decade, as the United States committed troops and took on a direct role in fighting off the North Vietnamese, Americans were plunged into crisis over the Vietnam War—over the war's toll on people's lives as well as confidence in U.S. influence and power abroad. However, few could have anticipated during the 1960s that another consequence of this war would be a dramatic revival of Asian migration, which would have profound repercussions for how Americans understood refugees and human rights and the demographics of Asian America.

Notes

1 Eleana Kim, *Adopted Territory: Transnational Korean Adoptees and the Politics of Belonging* (Durham: Duke University Press, 2010), 96.

2 Thomas Borstelmann, *The Cold War and the Color Line: American Race Relations in the Global Arena* (Cambridge: Harvard University Press, 2001).

3 Christina Klein, *Cold War Orientalism: Asia in the Middlebrow Imagination, 1945–1961* (Berkeley: University of California Press, 2003), 86.

4 Ibid., 102.

5 Ibid., 149.

6 Ibid.

7 There were a variety of laws in addition to these. The Chinese Alien Wives of American Citizens Act (not war brides but U.S. citizens) admitted an additional 2,317 between 1947 and 1950. Xiaojian Zhao, *Remaking Chinese America: Immigration, Family, and Community, 1940–1965* (New Brunswick: Rutgers University Press, 2002), 80.

8 H. Brett Melendy, *Asians in America: Filipinos, Koreans, and East Indians* (Boston: Twayne, 1977), 129–30.

9 Ronald Takaki, *Strangers from a Different Shore: A History of Asian Americans* (Boston: Little Brown, 1988), 445; Melendy, *Asians in America*, 207.

10 Sucheng Chan, *Asian Americans: An Interpretive History* (Boston: Twayne, 1991), 140.

11 Lon Kurashige, *Japanese American Celebration and Conflict: A History of Ethnic Identity and Festival in Los Angeles, 1934–1990* (Berkeley: University of California Press, 2002), 190.

12 Melendy, *Asians in America*, 207.

13 Won Moo Hurh, *Korean Immigrants in America: A Structural Analysis of Ethnic Confinement and Adhesive Adaptation* (Rutherford, N.J.: Fairleigh Dickinson University Press, 1984), 39; Nancy Abelmann and John Lie, *Blue Dreams: Korean Americans and the Los Angeles Riots* (Cambridge: Harvard University Press, 1997), 58.

14 Chan, *Asian Americans*, 140.

15 Zhao, *Remaking Chinese America*, 78.

16 This 1945 law, however, excluded members of "racially ineligible races"—which at the time excluded Japanese and Koreans, and it was not until 1947, when an amended version did away with the racial requirements, that all Asians could enter through the War Brides Act.

17 About 6,400 Korean military brides came to the United States between 1951 and 1964. Abelmann and Lie, *Blue Dreams*, 58; Hurh, *Korean Immigrants in America*, 33; 39; Ji-Yeon Yuh, *Beyond the Shadow of Camptown: Korean Military Brides in America* (New York: New York University Press, 2002), 2. According to Ji Yeon Yuh, by 1989 nearly 100,000 had entered.

18 Chan, *Asian Americans*, 140.

19 Zhao, *Remaking Chinese America*, 81; K. Scott Wong, *Americans First: Chinese Americans and the Second World War* (Cambridge: Harvard University Press, 2005), 195.

20 Wong, *Americans First*, 195.

21 Ibid., 196.

22 Among Japanese war brides, 75 percent married Caucasians. Many came under the McCarran-Walter Act.

23 Evelyn Nakano Glenn, *Issei, Nisei, War Bride: Three Generations of Japanese American Women in Domestic Service* (Philadelphia: Temple University Press, 1986), 62.

24 Ibid. Also see Ji-Yeon Yuh, *Beyond the Shadow of Camptown: Korean Military Brides in America* (New York: New York University Press, 2004).

25 Ibid.

26 Michener himself married a Japanese American woman. Caroline Chung Simpson, "Out of an obscure place: Japanese War Brides and Cultural Pluralism in the 1950s," *differences: A Journal of Feminist Cultural Studies* 10.3 (1998): 70.

27 Kim, *Adopted Territory*, 46.

28 Ibid., 51.

29 Klein, *Cold War Orientalism*, 175; Arissa H. Oh, "From War Waif to Ideal Immigrant: The Cold War Transformation of the Korean Orphan," *Journal of American Ethnic History*, 31 no. 4 (Summer 2012): 40.

30 Kim, *Adopted Territory*, 62.

31 Klein, *Cold War Orientalism*, 175; Oh, 35.

32 Kim, *Adopted Territory*, 44.

33 From 1952 to 1975 more than two thousand children from Japan were adopted by servicemen or foreigners in Japan and overseas. The Refugee Relief Act of 1953 allowed for four thousand orphans younger than ten from any country with oversubscribed quotas to be adopted in the U.S. by citizens. This expired in 1956. Subsequent legislation extended availability of non-quota visas and raised the age limit from ten to fourteen until a permanent law for eligible orphans was passed in 1962. Kim, *Adopted Territory*, 46, 56. Also see Klein, *Cold War Orientalism*, 175 and Oh, "From War Waif to Ideal Immigrant," 41.

34 Kim, *Adopted Territory*, 55.

35 Ibid., 45.

36 Oh, "From War Waif to Ideal Immigrant," 45.

37 Klein, *Cold War Orientalism*, 55.

38 Ibid., 50.

39 Klein, *Cold War Orientalism*, 144.

40 Oh, "From War Waif to Ideal Immigrant," 41.

41 Peter Kwong and Dusanka Miscevic, *Chinese America: The Untold Story of America's Oldest New Community* (New York: New Press, 2005), 230; Madeline Hsu, "The Disappearance of America's Cold War Chinese Refugees," *Journal of American Ethnic History*, 31, no. 4 (Summer 2012): 17.

42 Ibid., 231.

43 About 4,000 applied for asylum shortly after the 1949 revolution. The Displaced Persons Act was the first legislation that directly benefited political refugees and stranded scholars. It was adopted to help victims of Nazism and fascism in Europe and to rectify America's failure to help them but added new categories to reflect anticommunist orientation. 3,465 refugees of Chinese descent were given permission to settle. Ibid., 228–29.

44 Ibid., 228.

45 Hsu, "The Disappearance of America's Cold War Chinese Refugees," 16.

46 By the late 1960s about 80 percent exchange participants in the U.S. were from the Philippines, with nurses comprising the majority. Other countries turned to Filipino nurses too—Holland, Germany, Brunei, Laos, Turkey, Middle East, other parts of North America. Catherine Ceniza Choy, *Empire of Care: Nursing and Migration in Filipino American History* (Durham: Duke University Press, 2003), 65.

47 Ibid., 80.

48 Ibid., 68.

49 Ibid., 69.

50 Ibid., 78.

51 Ibid., 81.

52 Ibid., 87.

53 Charlotte Brooks, *Alien Neighbors, Foreign Friends: Asian Americans, Housing, and the Transformation of Urban California* (Chicago: University of Chicago Press, 2009), 205.

54 Chiou-ling Yeh, *Making an American Festival: Chinese New Year in San Francisco's Chinatown* (Berkeley: University of California Press, 2008), 26.

55 Lon Kurashige, *Japanese American Celebration and Conflict: A History of Ethnic Identity and Festival, 1934–1990* (Berkeley: University of California Press, 2003), 138.

56 Scott Kurashige, *The Shifting Grounds of Race: Black and Japanese Americans in the Making of Multiethnic Los Angeles* (Princeton: Princeton University Press, 2008), 201.

57 Ellen Wu, "'America's Chinese': Anti-Communism, Citizenship, and Cultural Diplomacy during the Cold War," *Pacific Historical Review*, 77, no. 3 (August 2008): 399.

58 Ibid.
59 Ibid., 409.
60 Ibid., 410.
61 Ibid., 418.
62 Brooks, *Alien Neighbors, Foreign Friends*, 206.
63 Ibid.
64 Ibid.
65 Ibid., 209.
66 Ibid., 210.
67 Ibid.
68 Kwong and Miščević, *Chinese America*, 221.
69 The paper allegedly accepted money from the People's Republic of China. Ibid., 223.
70 These included the Committee for Free China, All-American Overseas Chinese Anti-Communist League.
71 Zhao, *Remaking Chinese America*, 115.
72 Ibid., 120.
73 Ngai, *Impossible Subjects: Illegal Aliens and the Making of Modern America* (Princeton: Princeton University Press, 2004), 239.
74 Kwong and Miščević, *Chinese America*, 221.
75 Ibid., 222.
76 Ibid., 221.
77 Ibid., 224.
78 Ibid.
79 Ibid., 224.
80 Ngai, *Impossible Subjects*, 206.
81 These included U.S. district attorney's offices, the Criminal Division of the Justice Department, the FBI, the Passport Office, and the State Department. Zhao, *Remaking Chinese America*, 163.
82 Yeh, *Making an American Festival*, 23.
83 Kwong and Miščević, *Chinese America*, 225.
84 Roger Daniels, *Guarding the Golden Door: American Immigration Policy and Immigrants Since 1982* (New York: Hill and Wang, 2005) 156.
85 Kurashige, *Japanese American Celebration and Conflict*, 123.
86 Ibid., 127–28.
87 Hsu, "The Disappearance of America's Cold War Chinese Refugees," 20.
88 Ibid., 22.
89 Takaki, *Strangers from a Different Shore*, 370.
90 Melendy, *Asians in America*, 169.
91 Wu, "America's Chinese," 406.
92 Klein, *Cold War Orientalism*, 227.
93 Ibid., 233.
94 Ibid., 231.
95 Ibid.
96 Ibid., 35.
97 Kurashige, *Japanese American Celebration and Conflict*, 119–20.
98 Ibid., 141.
99 Ibid., 146.
100 Ibid., 148.
101 Yeh, *Making an American Festival*, 41.
102 The pageant became a national competition in 1958. Ibid., 43.
103 Ibid., 47.
104 Ibid., 49.
105 Ibid., 71.
106 Wu, "America's Chinese," 404.

107 Lon Kurashige, *Japanese American Celebration and Conflict*, 125.
108 Brooks, *Alien Neighbors, Foreign Friends*, 210.
109 Ibid., 212.
110 Ibid.
111 Ibid., 203.
112 Ibid., 223.
113 Ibid., 224.
114 Ibid., 235.
115 Kurashige, *Japanese American Celebration and Conflict*, 148.
116 Ibid.,149.

10

The Vietnam War, Southeast Asians, and the Transformation of Asian America

In 1979, Kao Kalia Yang's family, members of the Hmong minority group, left their native Laos to escape life under the Communist Pathet Lao. They crossed the Mekong River into Thailand and were met by UN workers who eventually placed them at Ban Vinai Refugee Camp, the largest camp for Hmong people. Yang was born in 1980 at Ban Vinai, a place she described as dirty and dusty, where "kids kept secrets and adults stayed inside themselves."[1] Once it was announced sometime in the mid-1980s that the camp would be closed, residents scrambled to make plans to go elsewhere. Among their options were to go to Australia, France, or the United States, where people were offering to take in Hmong refugees. In 1987, Yang and her immediate family members arrived in Minnesota, where an uncle was already living and a family friend who had also been at Ban Vinai was able to sponsor them. Having come without any resources, they settled in a low-income housing unit in St. Paul and relied on welfare. To help support the family, Yang's father took classes at a technical college to learn how to operate heavy machinery.

Yang's descriptions of her early years in America are punctuated by memories of poverty and disorientation, but also of close family and community bonds, both in Minnesota and across long distances. She also illustrates a generational divide that separated older members of the community and young people like herself, rooted in their varied distances from traumatic events in Laos. The adults, she said, "continued having nightmares. They cried out in their sleep. In the mornings, they sat at the table and talked to us about their bad dreams: the war was around them, the land was falling to pieces, Pathet Lao and North Vietnamese soldiers were coming . . ."[2] Although the adults often reminded her and other children of how lucky they were, "I wasn't convinced," she said. "I saw them walking in the snow drifts, their backs bent, their hands curled to their sides. I felt the humiliation of not knowing English, and the bubble of hurt began."[3]

Adult refugees' memories of war and trauma and the younger generation's struggle to find themselves amidst challenges of poverty, dependency, social instability, and racial discrimination are common themes in the histories of post-Vietnam War Southeast Asians in the United States in the 1970s and 1980s. Theirs is among the very recent chapters in Asian

American history and, as Yang's story underscores, it diverges markedly from earlier eras of migration. To be sure, persecution and political instability are not new themes, but the depth of the desperation and horror endured by large numbers of people in these waves does seem to distinguish the Southeast Asian refugee experience. That so many entered as refugees and parolees underscores the abrupt circumstances of their migration, their distinct relationship to the U.S. state, and direct links between U.S. foreign policy objectives and Asian migration. Furthermore, these migrants came from different countries compared to earlier eras; prior to the mid-1970s, there were no Cambodian, Vietnamese, or Hmong communities in America.

This chapter examines the experiences of Southeast Asians who settled in America in the 1970s to 1990s, discussing how the war engendered a "refugee crisis" that prompted far-reaching changes in U.S. policy, and describing early experiences of refugees as they settled in the United States. The chapter also explores how the post-Vietnam refugee migration added to and diversified Asian America, ethnically, culturally, politically, geographically, and otherwise. Along with the effects of the 1965 Immigration Act (see Chapter 12), the presence and growth of this population gave rise to new opportunities and challenges in the development of an "Asian American" community, identity, and history. Attentive to how U.S.-born Asian Americans became cognizant and critical of the racist aspects of the Vietnam War, the chapter also considers the war's impact on domestic racial politics broadly and Asian American racial and ethnic politics particularly. In this regard, as well as its attention to the lives of refugees in America, the chapter goes beyond standard histories of the Vietnam War that focus on foreign policy and the anti-war movement to shed light on its impact on immigration, race, and the evolution of "Asian America." Its focus on Southeast Asian migration to America, furthermore, underscores the Vietnam War's impact on the lives of Southeast Asian people, something often elided in diplomatic and political histories of the conflict.

French Colonialism in Indochina

With regard to the history of refugees, the terms "Southeast Asian" and "Indochinese" are most often employed to describe the people who fled Vietnam, Laos, and Cambodia. Both have their problems. "Indochinese" is a relic of French colonialism, and "Southeast Asian" also encompasses Thailand, Burma, Malaysia, Singapore, Philippines, Indonesia, and Brunei. The populations of Vietnam, Cambodia, and Laos, furthermore, represent centuries of intermixture, conquest, and exchange. The Vietnamese, for instance, draw from a number of origins and ethnic groups, including Vietnamese, Mongolian, Chinese, Thai, Austro-Asian, Melanesian, and Negrito.[4] Cambodia likewise consists of many ethnicities and languages, with Khmer being the dominant group.[5] In Laos, the Lao people represent the largest ethnicity, but the Hmong, a minority group concentrated in the hill country and also found in Vietnam and Thailand, would be a major part of the refugee exodus. Acknowledging these inexactitudes of terminology, I will use "Southeast Asian" and "Indochinese" to refer to people from Vietnam, Cambodia, and Laos who fled their countries due to war and political turbulence stemming from the United States' involvement in the region.

After about two and a half centuries as an informal presence in Southeast Asia, France colonized southern Vietnam (Cochinchina) in 1862, Cambodia in 1863, and central and northern Vietnam (Annam and Tonkin) in 1883. In 1887 it amalgamated these areas as the Indochinese Union, adding to it Laos in 1893. French rule transformed the region, albeit unevenly and differentially. In Vietnam, which was made into a major rice-exporting area, the colonial system elevated to power a small class of French officials, settler colonists, and indigenous Vietnamese landlords. In Indochina, the preferential treatment that Vietnamese received over Laotians and Cambodians was evident in the kinds of educational opportunities and administrative appointments distributed among the colonized populations. Laos, considered the least important colony, also experienced the least amount of change compared to other parts of Indochina.[6]

Indigenous resistance against the French surfaced with the onset of colonial rule. In Vietnam by the 1920s and 1930s, a modern anti-colonial nationalism had emerged, and encompassed many political parties and organizations.[7] Among the leaders was Ho Chi Minh, the scion of a scholar-gentry family from central Vietnam who had been deeply influenced by the late nineteenth and early twentieth century intellectual and critic of French rule Phan Boi Chau. Traveling the world while on a French ship working as a cook's assistant, Ho eventually moved to Paris in 1917 where he participated in anti-colonial political activities. As such, he was the first Vietnamese to join the Young Socialists in France and he later applied his Marxist-Leninist learnings to conditions in Vietnam.[8] In the early 1930s, he went to Moscow, where he met with other anti-colonial intellectuals and nationalists from around the world and found support for his cause.

Ho returned to Vietnam with the outbreak of World War II to lead the Communist wing of the anti-colonial movement. In May 1941 the Indochinese Communist Party (ICP) established the Viet Minh, or Vietnamese Independence League, which soon fell under Ho's leadership. In mid-1943 the Viet Minh struck and made a bid for power, and two years later a critical opportunity surfaced with Japan's coup d'état and subsequent surrender in Indochina. The Viet Minh captured Hanoi in August 1945 and went on to control Hue, Danang, and Saigon. With the abdication of Emperor Dao, Ho Chi Minh proclaimed Vietnam's independence and established the Democratic Republic of Vietnam (DRV).

After the war's end, however, France wished to re-colonize Indochina and reasserted its control in Cambodia and Laos. Vietnamese resistance, bolstered by assistance from the Soviet Union and the People's Republic of China, led to the First Indochina War of 1945–54.[9] After nine years of fighting, France surrendered to the DRV, an outcome that shocked the world. At China's and the Soviet Union's urging, the country was divided at the 17th parallel, with the DRV ruling in the North and the newly named Republic of Vietnam controlling the South. A general election scheduled for July 1956 was to determine the country's future.

U.S. Involvement in Southeast Asia

The United States was involved in Vietnam during the first Indochina War, when it paid nearly 80 percent of France's war cost.[10] U.S. officials viewed France as a bulwark against Communism in Southeast Asia, but its defeat in 1954 led to increased American involvement, initially by supporting anti-Communist regimes in the South. However, Americans' relationship with Ngo Dinh Diem, the first president of South Vietnam, quickly soured. They were dismayed at his intransigence regarding the coming 1956 elections, such as his refusal to consult with officials in the North. Additionally, the brutality with which he suppressed his enemies was shocking; among the most chilling images, seen throughout the world, from the Diem era was the self-immolation of a Buddhist monk during a protest in June 1963.[11] Frustrated with Diem, the United States covertly supported a plan by South Vietnamese generals to murder him and topple his government. Nonetheless, following Diem's assassination in November 1963, South Vietnam endured one short-lived government after another.

After the death of President John F. Kennedy, also in November 1963, America's involvement in Vietnam deepened even further. Kennedy had been reluctant to send combat troops to Vietnam, preferring instead to use advisors and Green Berets (US Army Special Forces) to train and support the Army of the Republic of Vietnam (ARVN). But under successor Lyndon Johnson, the U.S. began conducting missions—including surveillance and bombing raids—aimed at destroying the North's transportation and communication infrastructure. Over 1964, the United States' involvement intensified, particularly after the Gulf of Tonkin incident, but Johnson initially focused on an air war; a massive one, to be sure, which hit targets in North Vietnam, South Vietnam, Cambodia and Laos, and dropped more tonnage than was used on Germany during World War II.[12] In March 1965, Johnson deployed combat troops, who within three years numbered about 540,000.[13] This marked the beginning of the Second Indochina War, which has been detailed in numerous studies. It ended in January 1973 when the United States and North Vietnam signed a ceasefire, after which the former dismantled its bases, exchanged prisoners of war, and left South Vietnam. Civil war then ensued between the North and South, and on April 30, 1975, the capital of South Vietnam, Saigon, fell.

Americans' campaign to prevent the spread of Communism in Vietnam also led to its interfering in neighboring countries. As U.S. officials had in South Vietnam, they had meddled in the national elections of Laos. Moreover, in 1961, the CIA established a military aid program to disrupt Lao Communists' (Pathet Lao) and North Vietnamese penetration of soldiers and supplies through Lao territory along the Ho Chi Minh Trail. Highland ethnic minorities were recruited, armed, trained, and organized into special guerrilla units (SGUs) that served under Vang Pao, the Hmong anti-Communist leader of the Royal Lao Army.[14] The so-called "secret war" was for all intents and purposes directed by the U.S. embassy in Laos and the CIA. Although by 1969 the army numbered forty thousand, U.S. officials insisted their only involvement in Laos was humanitarian, pointing to the hospitals and schools whose construction they oversaw. In 1970, the "secret war" was exposed, but public outrage was contained by the fact that no American soldiers had been used.[15] Shortly after the ceasefire between the United States and North Vietnam in January 1973, representatives of the Royal Lao Government and Pathet Lao agreed to end their civil war, but in the wake of this agreement, the latter waged a brutal purge of former American collaborators.

Meanwhile, Cambodia was also undergoing political turmoil after independence from France in 1954. Prince Sihanouk had dominated the country's political life, but he was deposed in March 1970 in a military coup led by General Lon Nol. Lon declared himself president of the newly created Khmer Republic, an action supported by the United States, but he soon faced opposition from the Communist Khmer Rouge, which had backing from North Vietnam. From 1970 to 1975 a civil war ravaged the country from which the Khmer Rouge emerged victorious after capturing Phnom Penh in April 1975.

Population Movements and the Refugee Crisis

The displacement of people in Southeast Asia, which did not really come to the U.S. media's attention until the late 1970s, had been decades in the making and was breathtaking in scope. In the early years of the First Indochina War, about 55,000 ethnic Vietnamese in Cambodia and Laos, whose ancestral homes were in North Vietnam, fled to nearby Thailand. Those with political sympathies to the Viet Minh were eventually repatriated to North Vietnam. The end of the conflict in 1955 and division of Vietnam triggered a larger flood.[16] More than 900,000 people left the North for the South, the majority being Catholics and well-to-do people who did not wish to live under Communist rule. Meanwhile, between 130,000 and 140,000 Communist cadres, military personnel, and their dependents moved from the South to the North while 10,000 to 15,000 Communists stayed in the South. As result of the Second Indochina War, which saw ground fighting and bombing raids as well as the use of napalm and defoliants, about twelve million South Vietnamese, or about half of the country's population, was displaced.[17] It is unknown how many were displaced in the North, but estimates suggest it was a much larger percentage than in the South.

The Civil War in Cambodia had also created a massive displaced population. In that war, about five hundred thousand people died and at least three million were uprooted from their homes.[18] After the fall of Phnom Penh, Americans and several hundred Cambodian elites were immediately flown out as the rest of the city was evacuated.[19] The scene was grisly, especially as patients from Phnom Penh's largest hospital appeared on the streets. As the French missionary Francois Ponchaud described the evacuation:

> A few moments later a hallucinatory spectacle began. Thousands of the sick and wounded were abandoning the city. The strongest dragged pitifully along, others were carried by friends, and some were lying on beds pushed by their families with their plasma and IV bumping along. I shall never forget one cripple who had neither hands nor feet, writhing along the ground like a severed worm, or a weeping father carrying his ten-year-old daughter wrapped in a sheet tied around his neck like a sling, or the man with his foot dangling at the end of a leg to which it was attached by nothing but the skin.[20]

By March 1975, the United States started to make plans at home, with international agencies, and other governments, to evacuate Americans, their dependents, and at-risk Vietnamese, Cambodians, and Hmong from Indochina. The United Nations High Commission for Refugees (UNHCR) and the Intergovernmental Committee for European Migration (ICEM) also began work to find countries that would take refugees. On April 14 the U.S. attorney general authorized the admission of Vietnamese and Cambodian dependents of American citizens, and around this time President Gerald Ford created an Interagency Task Force with officials from various federal agencies to plan for the reception of refugees in the United States. In a rather arbitrary fashion, the State Department decided to admit 130,000 evacuees, with 125,000 slots reserved for Vietnamese and the rest for Cambodians. The Indochina Migration and Refugee Assistance Act of May 1975 furthermore established a program for the domestic settlement of Vietnamese and Cambodian refugees.[21]

Figure 10.1 This ink and graphite drawing by political cartoonist Herb Block ("Herblock") shows President Gerald Ford and Henry Kissinger, who is carrying an empty brief case labeled "U.S. Policy", among a throng of Vietnamese refugees just weeks before the fall of Saigon, April 2, 1975. (© The Herb Block Foundation.)

The 130,000 slots were filled by the "first wave" of Vietnamese and Cambodian refugees, most of whom were educated, Westernized, urban, and had ties to the U.S. government or American officials. Air evacuations in Vietnam began on April 1 in Saigon and proceeded through April 29, the day before the North Vietnamese takeover.[22] The process was chaotic, and many people who were not actually "at risk" were able to bribe their way onto the lifts, while others who should have been evacuated were left out. Tens of thousands of others, meanwhile, escaped by sea.[23] Those selected for settlement in the United States were placed in four processing camps located at Fort Pendleton in California, Fort Chafee in Arkansas, Fort Indiantown Gap in Pennsylvania, and Eglin Airforce Base in Florida. There, refugees received medical examinations, learned English, and were socialized for their new lives. Federally assisted non-governmental agencies run by charities and religious organizations coordinated the resettlement and finding of sponsors (often private individuals), and the sponsors, in turn, took responsibility for helping the refugees secure jobs and living necessities. The Interagency Task Force set October 31, 1975 as a deadline for moving the refugees out of the system, and the resettlement centers were closed gradually over the year. The task force itself disbanded on December 31.

A smaller group of people from Laos also made up part of the first wave. The Pathet Lao purges, ending of food supplies from U.S. airdrops, and the disruption of subsistence agriculture heightened uncertainty for Laotians, especially those who had worked with the United States in the secret war. In mid-May 1975, word spread of an American airlift for military personnel and family out of Long Cheng, prompting the arrival of thousands of people who hoped to escape.[24] About 2,500 were airlifted out, and over the course of the year, tens of thousands of others left by land routes.[25] Those who were airlifted were taken to a military base in Thailand called Ban Namphong, which by the end of 1975 held 10,000 residents, the majority of whom were Hmong. Of these, a small number was paroled to enter the United States beginning in early 1976, and others were dispersed elsewhere in North America as well as in South America, Europe, and Oceania.[26]

After these early resettlement efforts, however, refuge seekers continued to leave Cambodia, Laos, and Vietnam, and in the second half of the 1970s, the United States was taking in an additional 1,800 refugees per month. The "second wave" was poorer, less educated, and less urbanized, and unlike their first wave counterparts had experienced life under Communist rule. It furthermore far eclipsed the first wave in numbers. These included "boat people" as well as overland refugees who had spent time in refugee camps in Thailand, Malaysia, Singapore, Hong Kong, and elsewhere in Southeast Asia.[27]

In Vietnam, conditions had worsened for many people after July 1976 when the country was reunified as the Socialist Republic of Vietnam. Former elected officials, police, military officers, teachers, and religious leaders—anyone who would have politically opposed the Communist regime—were shipped to camps where they were indoctrinated and forced into hard labor. Anti-capitalist measures included the confiscation of businesses and the transport of merchants to remote "New Economic Zones" where they performed physical labor.[28] Such policies took a particular toll on ethnic Chinese, and by 1978 about 160,000 had fled to China's southern provinces, leading the country to seek UNHCR aid.

Cambodians, meanwhile, reeled from the traumas of Khmer Rouge rule and the uncertainties of life after its ouster. In power from 1975 to 1979, the Khmer Rouge was dominated by a hyper-Cambodian nationalist wing. It was also highly ethnocentric, removing and executing any non-ethnic Khmer from leadership positions. Seeking a return to a pre-modern agrarian age, its policies included uprooting urban populations to the countryside and destroying bedrocks of Cambodian culture like religion and family. Toward undoing the latter, young people were encouraged to spy on their parents.[29] Some three million people in a country of about seven million perished while the Khmer Rouge was in power. An invasion by Vietnam precipitated its fall, after which scores of Cambodians fled across the Thai border, and in 1979 about six hundred thousand Cambodians, or 15 percent of the country's remaining population, were living in Thai refugee camps.

As the 1970s came to a close, the continued and growing exodus of refugees from Southeast Asian countries turned into a global crisis. Receiving particular attention was the plight of the "boat people" of Vietnam, who by Spring 1978 were fleeing the country at a rate of 1,500 per month. Countries of first arrival, such as Thailand, Singapore, and Malaysia, had become overburdened or unwilling to assist newcomers. In an attempt to manage and contain the problem, the UN held conferences in Geneva in 1979 and 1989. After the first meeting, Vietnam agreed to place a moratorium on illegal departures and help facilitate the legal departure of refugees through the Orderly Departure Program (ODP). Countries of first asylum agreed to stop turning people away and grant temporary asylum, while countries of second asylum increased their intake and contributed to UNHCR expenses.[30] New processing centers were, moreover, built in the Philippines, Indonesia, and Thailand. For its part, the United States delineated three categories of people who could enter its borders under the ODP: close family members of Vietnamese and ethnic Chinese from Vietnam already in the United States; former employees of U.S. government agencies; and other individuals closely connected to U.S. activities in Vietnam before 1975.[31] The second Geneva Conference came up with a Comprehensive Plan of Action (CPA), which stipulated cutoff dates (1988 and 1989) for the ODP, after which arrivals from Laos and Vietnam would be subjected to refugee status determination or screening. About 500,000 Vietnamese entered the U.S. under the ODP between 1979 and 1989.[32]

These actions by the UN brought a modicum of order to the refugee crisis, but it did not capture its full scope. The conventions, for instance, did not address Cambodian refugees. Additionally, while people fleeing Cambodia during the years of Khmer Rouge rule from 1975 to 1979 were bona fide refugees, the status of those who left afterward was unclear.[33] In limbo as "illegals" in countries of first asylum, about 360,000 Cambodians who were unable to gain entry into UNHCR holding centers were repatriated by the UN between 1982 and 1992. Those who were selected for resettlement in the United States were drawn from the holding center population and, thus, represented a very small portion of Cambodian refugees.

After the 1979 Geneva Conference, the United States, the largest country of second asylum, implemented sweeping changes in its own refugee policy, which had previously been ad hoc and reliant on the attorney general's parole power. For instance, in spring 1976 Congress authorized the attorney general to parole eleven thousand people to the United States under the Expanded Parole Program. Then in fall 1977 another fifteen thousand parolees entered under a new Indochinese Parole Program, which allowed for the admission of boat people scattered in Southeast Asia as well as refugees in Thai camps. The following January an additional seven thousand people were authorized to enter as parolees. In all of these cases, the highest priority was for individuals with family members already in the

United States or who had worked for the U.S. government or American companies. In February 1979, President Jimmy Carter created a U.S. Coordinator for Refugee Affairs post to facilitate cooperation among federal departments that dealt with refugees, and over the course of the year continued to raise the U.S. intake.[34]

On March 17, 1980, Congress passed the Refugee Act, the first law to explicitly deal with refugees apart from other immigration policies. Upon signing it, President Carter stated, "it is the historical policy of the United States to respond to the urgent needs of persons subject to persecution in their homelands."[35] The law brought the U.S. definition of refugee in line with the UN's from 1951, which defined them as people with a "well-founded fear of persecution from their own governments due to their political ideologies or activities, religious affiliation, or membership in certain groups that the government in question has chosen to persecute."[36] Although it removed earlier ideological and geographic biases and spelled out procedures for dealing with asylum seekers already on U.S. soil, foreign policy continued to dominate considerations of who was admitted. The law also removed the executive branch's parole authority to admit large groups of people, and placed responsibility for determining ceilings in the executive and Congress.

The State Department laid out six priorities for accepting refugees for resettlement, the top three being for persons in immediate danger of loss of life and for whom there is no alternative to resettlement in the United States; people who had worked for U.S. government agencies; and family members of people in the United States. The new system slowed the refugee flow in part because it narrowed the paths of entry. Prior to mid-1981 applicants did not have to prove that they had been or were likely targets of persecution but, following an INS ruling on the Refugee Act, officers were required to review claims on a case-by-case basis.[37] The ruling came on the heels of a rising number of cases in which officials suspected that economic migrants were falsely claiming to be fleeing political persecution. This led to rising rejection rates, and the second wave of Southeast refugee migration would crest in 1981.

Refugees and the American Conscience

The arrival of Southeast Asian refugees was unprecedented in Asian American and U.S. immigration histories. With regard to refugees in America, until 1948, with the passage of the Displaced Persons Act, the United States did not recognize refugees as a distinct legal category of persons. Before that, many groups of immigrants would have fit the modern definition of refugee, but the differentiation did not exist in the law. As immigration was more tightly regulated from the late nineteenth century, however, refugees faced greater difficulty gaining admission, particularly when it came to passing the proscription against likely public charges.

Things changed after World War II as U.S. officials increasingly championed America's need to help and receive refugees, their ability to assimilate, and bonds they represented to other nations. However, even after the passage of the Displaced Persons Act, refugee policy was piecemeal and shaped by diplomatic considerations. With the onset of the Cold War, the United States largely limited admission to people from Communist regimes and withheld protection from those fleeing dictatorships with which it was friendly. Policies implemented during the 1950s, moreover, required the vetting of applicants' economic backgrounds and their securing of employment. With regard to Asians, the largest group admitted before the 1970s came from the People's Republic of China. Between 1948 and 1966 about thirty-two thousand entered or gained permanent residency through refugee legislation and procedures, a large portion of these being students and skilled professionals.[38]

In the face of the intensifying Southeast Asian crisis in the late 1970s, Americans grappled with how they should respond. On the one hand, many wished to distance themselves from the Vietnam War, which had been deeply demoralizing, and were reluctant to open the gates to a new wave of Asian migrants, especially ones who were so desperate. In 1977, the *New York Times* reported that many members of Congress were expressing opposition to the admission of more refugees and, as the *Economist* explained, Americans disliked that "the Vietnam War should come back, in the persons of its victims, to haunt [them] on their own ground."[39] On the other hand, because the refugees were fleeing Communist governments, others felt obligated to help them. Harrowing stories about the boat people being preyed upon by pirates, the poor conditions of refugee camps, and the legacy of Khmer Rouge leader Pol Pot further tugged at people's heartstrings and consciences.

Perhaps no groups captured the mainstream imagination as much as children and Amerasians from Vietnam. The "Operation Babylift" campaign, which airlifted about two thousand Vietnamese orphans (a tiny fraction of the total number of orphans in the country) out of Saigon to be adopted by American families, generated interest in helping war refugees while casting the United States once again as global savior. Amerasians were also highly sentimentalized, sometimes described as "vets" and "hostages" as if to underscore the idea that they were basically Americans trapped in a foreign country, waiting to be brought "home."[40] Media coverage about Amerasians often highlighted their physical features to heighten readers' sympathy and sense of kinship toward them. For instance, in a 1985 profile about Amerasian teenager Le Van Minh, the *Long Island Newsday* emphasized his physical disabilities, impoverishment, and mixed-race appearance. Minh's well-being, the publication stressed, depended on whether "a foreigner would be moved by his American face and broken body."[41] The attention his case generated resulted in lobbying by UN and U.S. representatives and his expedited entry into the United States. Another account of Amerasians in Vietnam detailed a trip by actress Julie Andrews to Ho Chi Minh City in 1982 in her role as an advocate for the relief agency Operation California. Andrews was struck by the "beautiful looking" Amerasian children she encountered. "My God they are simply lovely. It's a real jerk to the soul—and to the senses. You think you know the face. Some of them look very Caucasian. They come running up to you and say, 'Are you an American? I'm one too.'"[42] Such coverage helped launch the plight of Amerasians as a cause celebre and, eventually, about 4,500 Vietnamese Amerasians, known as bui doi or con lai, were admitted via the UNHCR's Orderly Departure Program as well as U.S. laws passed in 1982 and 1987.[43]

Highlighting the patriarchal and imperialistic dimensions of the discourse about Amerasians, Jana Lipman has shown how the settlement of this group not only elevated the United States as a benevolent global power, but also valorized American (usually white) fathers and minimized the role of Vietnamese mothers. In lobbying for their admission, legislators often pressed the importance of reuniting fathers with their long lost children and intimated that the mothers were giving up their children.[44] This perception was inscribed into policy in the 1982 Amerasian Amendment, which excluded mothers and required them to revoke their custody rights if their Amerasian child applied to come to the United States, a policy that was not changed until 1988. This binary of the male, paternal, responsible, white American versus the female, sexualized, all-sacrificing Vietnamese was echoed in the popular musical, *Miss Saigon* (debuted in London in 1989 and on Broadway in 1991), whose plot involved a Vietnamese prostitute (Kim) who bore a child by a white American GI (Chris). Despite falling in love in Vietnam, the couple's future was doomed; for one, Chris had a white American wife at home. At the end of the story, Chris took on the responsibility of raising the child in America while Kim committed suicide, as an expression of her despair and sacrifice for her child.

American Lives

All told, Southeast Asia was the largest source of refugees to the United States stemming from foreign policy interests during the twentieth century. By March 1980, 350,000 Vietnamese (many ethnic Chinese), 35,000 Laotians, 30,000 Lao minorities, and 20,000 Cambodians gained admission, and by the end of the century the number of Southeast Asians who entered as refugees reached about one million.[45] They tended to be young; nearly 46 percent of the first wave was under eighteen, and 35.6 percent was between eighteen and thirty-four.[46] Most came as family units, often with extended members. As refugees (and in some cases asylees and parolees), they were eligible to adjust their status to become U.S. citizens or permanent residents after one year of continuous residence, and by 1992 close to 70 percent of Vietnamese, 66 percent of Cambodians, and 92 percent of Laotians had received their green cards.[47] By the late 1980s and early 1990s the refugee flow to the United States had largely ended as refugee admission programs were terminated. After settling about 500,000 Vietnamese in the United States, the Orderly Departure Program ended in 1989, and other U.S. refugee programs for Vietnamese were ended in 1997. The Cambodian refugee resettlement program, which since 1975 had helped settle nearly 160,000 people, ended in 1994. The Laotian program also ended in 1994.[48] The timing of the termination of these programs also reflected thawing relations between the United States and Southeast Asia as well as the onset of what one scholar has called "compassion fatigue" after three decades of welcoming refugees.[49] Despite this, Southeast Asian migration continues, but through channels such as family reunification provisions in the general immigration system or humanitarian parolee status.[50]

The adjustment to life in America was a difficult one, as it could be for all newcomers, but the circumstances that brought Southeast Asian refugees to the United States suggested this was a particularly burdened and disadvantaged group. Many, especially in the second wave, were not only unfamiliar with American culture but also with modern life. Most Hmong refugees, for instance, were rural people and had never been exposed to city life until arriving in the United States. Because so many Southeast Asian refugees had experienced the horrors of war, starvation, and desperate flight, by the early 1980s, they had been identified as a case study for understanding the condition of post-traumatic stress disorder (PTSD). Cambodians who had lived under the Khmer Rouge were especially susceptible to mental disorders stemming from trauma, or what some Cambodians called

"Khmer illness."[51] At a clinic for Indochinese refugees in Portland, Oregon, a 1990 survey found that 70 percent of all patients suffered from PTSD.

Also distinctive about the adjustment of Southeast Asians was the highly orchestrated nature of their settlement by the federal government and voluntary agencies, which aimed to disperse them geographically to avoid large concentrations of new refugees. During the settlement of the first wave of Vietnamese out of the four U.S. camps, the government contracted voluntary agencies such as the United States Catholic Conference, the International Rescue Committee, and the Lutheran Immigration and Refugee Service to find sponsors. The sponsors could be any person, group, or organization willing to take responsibility for the refugees' housing, clothing, and other expenses until they became self-supporting. They were also to help them find employment, learn English, and train for jobs, for which they received grants of $500 per refugee.[52] By December 1975, about 27,000 refugees, mostly Vietnamese, were in California, 9,100 in Texas, and 7,100 in Pennsylvania, with smaller numbers found in other states. The geographic settlement patterns were generally limited by the locations of the U.S. holding centers and voluntary agencies' contacts. The latter, for instance, explains why many refugees assisted by the Lutheran Immigration and Refugee Service ended up scattered in the Midwest.[53] Corporate sponsors also shaped where refugees were initially settled; a large number of Vietnamese, for instance, went to Florida, Texas, and Louisiana, where they were employed by chicken processing firms, nursing homes, and agricultural companies that needed workers.

Before long, a pattern of secondary migration took hold as many refugees left the places of their original settlement to be closer to friends, family, jobs, and assistance. In some cases, sponsors could no longer provide for them, and the refugees had no choice but to seek better fortunes elsewhere. The poor state of the labor market during a recession in the late 1970s compelled others to move, particularly those who had been settled in rural areas. This secondary migration led to even more heightened concentrations of Southeast Asians in certain locations, precisely what the government had hoped to avoid; by 1978, for example, a third of Vietnamese were in California and another 10 percent could be found in Texas. The arrival of the second wave refugees further contributed to the population clusters. By the 1980s, the leading centers of the Hmong population were St. Paul–Minneapolis, Minnesota and Fresno, California.[54] Among Cambodians, Long Beach, California, which emerged as a major enclave as early as the 1970s, became known as the "Cambodian Capital of America." Lowell, Massachusetts was another major center of this population. Finally, the largest Vietnamese concentrations emerged in Orange County and San Jose, California and Houston, Texas.

While the socioeconomic backgrounds of Southeast Asians were diverse, as refugees many experienced downward mobility in the United States, skewing the entire population in the lower sectors of the economy. Among Vietnamese, for instance, a large portion of the first wave was well educated, with about 38 percent having secondary school training and 20 percent university training.[55] A significant percentage, furthermore, came from the technical, managerial, and military elite; over 7 percent had worked as doctors, nurses, or dentists and 24 percent as lawyers, technicians, managers, or university teachers. Despite this profile, few had language ability to transfer their skills to the American economy. In March 1976, nearly 65 percent of first wave Vietnamese spoke no English and only about 14 percent could communicate effectively in it.[56] Moreover, professionals faced licensing and other bureaucratic obstacles that made it impossible to pursue their professions or maintain the status they held in their countries of origin.

These obstacles did not just take their toll personally, but also impacted the well-being of their communities. Cambodian G. Chan was fortunate in that he was able to continue working as a medical doctor in the United States.[57] The struggle to maintain his profession, however, was bitter and sobering. After Chan was resettled in the Bronx he tried to obtain a residency to practice in America, with much bureaucratic hassling. This was particularly concerning because his services were very much needed. As he explained in 1991, "[There] are six thousand Cambodian refugees in the New York area and not one Cambodian medical doctor . . . It is as if the U.S. officials opened the gates in this country and let you into the courtyard. But nobody will now open the front door."[58] Sarout Suon Seng received her medical degree in Phnom Penh in 1982, and soon after escaped to Thailand before being settled in the United States. For her, becoming a practicing physician was out of the realm of possibilities. "I do not know how to get into medical school because of my English. I have to go through everything again. Probably take me ten years . . . before I get my M.D."[59] She wished to work in the medical profession, so earned a physician assistant degree from UC Davis. Though she held a lower status than doctors, she found the work fulfilling. As she said in 1989: "I see a lot of Cambodian patients . . . You know, American hospitals are very frightening . . . because they can't tell everything they want to tell or need to tell . . . It's not only Cambodian[s]. Even Lao, Hmong or Vietnamese . . . it is easier to reach them because I understand."[60]

In the larger picture, however, the experiences of these professionals are atypical, and second-wave Vietnamese, as well as refugees from Laos and Cambodia, were less skilled and educated than their first-wave counterparts and, as noted, those from elite backgrounds in their countries of origin found it difficult to retain this status in the United States. The majority of refugees from Laos, for instance, were not only illiterate, but had few skills beyond those acquired from slash and burn agriculture. In 1980, 75 percent of Lao ethnic minorities (Lowland Lao) in the United States lived below the poverty line. By 1989, this had improved somewhat, to about 63 percent, but they remained the most impoverished Asian American group. Cambodians were not far behind. In 1980, more than half of Cambodians in the United States were unemployed and over 60 percent lived in poverty.[61] Of those gainfully employed, just over 2 percent worked in managerial or administrative positions and the largest segment, about 34 percent, worked as common laborers or machine operators. Nearly 78 percent would be characterized as blue collar.

The overall socioeconomic status of Southeast Asians in America has improved since 1980. As mentioned above, between 1980 and 1989, the percentage of Hmong living below the poverty line decreased, albeit modestly. Among Cambodians, a small elite middle class comprising about 5 percent of the population emerged, with professionals and business people, although the lower middle class and blue collar was much larger at about 40 percent.[62] More than half of the population remained unemployed.

In recent decades, many Southeast Asians have become successful entrepreneurs, in areas serving co-ethnic and general clienteles. These have usually been former members of the elite who brought with them some business experience, and reflecting the merchant populations of Southeast Asia, a large percentage is ethnic Chinese. For instance, Sino–Cambodians run about two-thirds of Cambodian businesses in the United States, even though this group is far outnumbered by Khmer and other ethnic groups. Some of the niches that now transcend co-ethnic clienteles include Vietnamese nail salons and Cambodian doughnut shops. With regard to the latter, by the end of the twentieth century, Cambodians owned or operated 80 percent of doughnut shops in California.[63]

The path toward establishing a niche in the doughnut industry in California was broken by Ted Ngoy, a Sino–Cambodian who arrived in the United States in 1975. Along with seven family members, Ngoy was sponsored by a Lutheran church in Tustin, California. He worked as a janitor at the church as well as at a gas station. During this time, he tasted a doughnut for the first time and decided to learn how to make them, becoming a trainee at a Winchell's in Newport Beach. In 1977 he had saved enough to buy a doughnut shop in La Habra, California, and by the mid-1980s owned more than fifty doughnut shops throughout the state and expanded his empire into taco and hamburger shops. This success launched Ngoy as the first Cambodian American millionaire.[64] As other Cambodians followed Ngoy into the dough-nut business, it developed into an ethnic niche in California. They not only opened shops, but also became involved in other levels of the industry. Bun H. Tao, Ngoy's nephew, established B&H Distributors, which provides credit and coffee-making machines to shop owners and would-be shop owners. Additionally, although men dominate the upper echelons of the industry, women's participation has been critical, as they often run the doughnut shops.[65]

Another important area of the economy in which Southeast Asians have been crucial, as both laborers and entrepreneurs, is the seafood industry around the Gulf of Mexico.[66] After voluntary agency staff learned about the fishing backgrounds of many refugees, especially Cambodians and Vietnamese, they worked to match them with Gulf Coast seafood com-panies that agreed to be their sponsors. Located in states like Florida, Texas, and Louisiana, some of the companies organized programs to train the refugees in American fishing methods and then employed them in a range of tasks from fishing to dockside processing and packing.[67] In Bayou Le Batre, Louisiana in the 1990s, 70 percent of the workers in the crab industry were Southeast Asian and 62 percent were women.[68] Vietnamese women workers were especially visible in oyster shucking and crab picking in Mississippi, Louisiana, and Texas. In describing their preference in hiring these workers, employers' remarks echoed sentiments heard earlier regarding Asian laborers. As one stated, "Asians are the best workers, they listen to you and they do what you tell them. After Asians I'd rather hire blacks; they aren't necessarily good workers, but they'll do what you tell them. Whites on the other hand don't want to work all that hard and won't do what you tell them to do."[69]

Working in the seafood industry via company sponsors was a springboard for a number of Southeast Asians to enter more independent forms of employment. Most Vietnamese eventually left their original employers to fish on their own or do business with smaller firms in arrangements more beneficial to them.[70] They were able to take these steps toward greater autonomy and play a more extensive role in fishing in the area by purchasing and rigging second hand boats or entering partnerships with fellow fishermen to acquire larger boats. In West Florida as early as 1980, Vietnamese fishermen controlled sixty vessels. This often meant taking on considerable financial risk through bank loans, but as one Vietnamese fisherman stated about his $50,000 loan, "What do I have to lose? . . . Even if I lose everything I started with nothing three years ago and will still be much better off than those people who couldn't get out of Vietnam."[71] Resourceful as they were, their refugee immigration status limited the scope of their fishing activities, as they were not allowed to go beyond a three-mile territorial limit. Because of this, they tended to limit their activities near urban areas.

With the growth of Southeast Asian participation in the seafood industry, Gulf Coast states became common areas of secondary settlement, particularly for Vietnamese and Cambodians. As these communities were far away from the historical centers of Asian America, many of the longtime white and black locals had never before directly interacted with Asian people. As a result, the arrival of Southeast Asians did not occur without skirmishes and misunderstandings, as illustrated in several high profile incidents involving white and Vietnamese fishermen in the Gulf Coast.

Historically, new immigrants in the region who entered the area's fishing industry encountered some resistance from old-timers, but the late 1970s were a particularly tense time due to the economic recession. This, in addition to racial intolerance and cultural misunderstandings, exacerbated conflicts between white and Vietnamese fishers. Sometimes the clashes stemmed from Vietnamese fishermens' unfamiliarity with the norms and rules of Gulf Coast fishing. In Vietnam, fishing was relatively unregulated and governed by different rules of etiquette. Furthermore, the jerry-rigged recreational craft and old fishing boats that they operated in the Gulf Coast often lacked required safety equipment such as fire extinguishers, life preservers, and running lights. Thus, they learned the rules of fishing in the United States by inadvertently breaking them and being accused of "poor seamanship" by locals. Common complaints about Vietnamese fishermen included their cutting in line for fuel and unloading catch, consuming seagulls and pelicans in violation of federal law, and catching undersize shrimp.[72]

The misunderstandings among fishermen could become combative and even violent. Not only did locals make complaints such as those described above, but some also spread pernicious—and historically familiar—rumors that Vietnamese were spreading cholera through their fish and eating dogs and cats. In retaliation for what they deemed poor seamanship, Americans targeted Vietnamese fishers, crabbers, and shrimpers by cutting or stealing their gill nets, removing their floats, sideswiping their boats, and refusing to sell them fuel and ice. Some Vietnamese even received death threats or had their boats burned.[73] The harassment also rose to the level of legal discrimination. In Santa Rosa and Escambia counties in Florida, complaints that Vietnamese used longer nets and were, thus, "raping the waters," resulted in prohibitions on nets longer than 2,000 feet. The state legislature eventually passed a law proscribing the use of these long nets and the governor defended it, claiming it was not discriminatory.[74]

In one incident in 1979, two Vietnamese crabbers were accused of murdering a white American man in a dispute in Seadrift, Texas. Within hours of the man's death, three Vietnamese boats were burned, one of their dwellings was firebombed, and an attempt was made to bomb a local crab-packing house that employed Vietnamese. Two-thirds of the refugees living in the community fled to another town.[75] The accused were eventually acquitted. Having drawn national attention, the incident inspired the 1985 film *Alamo Bay*, whose plot centered on a demoralized American veteran of the Vietnam War who lashes out against Vietnamese arrivals in his small fishing town in Texas.

Ethnic Identity and Solidarity

Along with the challenges described above, Southeast Asians in America have struggled to maintain their traditions and ethnic solidarities while adopting new practices and identities. In locations where sizeable and visible populations have taken root, vibrant communities have flourished and drawn co-ethnics from far and wide. In the Hmong American community in Minnesota, for example, New Year's celebrations, which grew from a small affair to an elaborate event that includes beauty pageants and attracts Hmong from across the country, have become a crucial site for the maintenance of traditions and solidifying of ethnic identity.

In some cases, preserving tradition has gone beyond creating a sense of belonging or continuity in a new land. For Cambodians, cultural maintenance or revival has taken on a particularly urgent meaning after so many people were wiped out under the Khmer Rouge. This has informed the practice of Buddhism and the arts in Cambodian communities, as the Khmer Rouge tried to uproot Buddhism and an estimated 90 percent of classical dancers and musicians were killed. The Khmer Classical Dance Troupe was made up of individuals who had been part of the prestigious Cambodian Royal Ballet and escaped to the Khao I Dang holding center in Thailand. Eventually the dancers were settled in Wheaton, Maryland, and in 1981 the troupe gave its first public performance at the National Folk Festival outside of Washington, DC.[76]

For many Cambodians, Theravada Buddhism is fundamental to the homeland culture and identity, and one of the first things refugees did after being settled was to set up temples. Further, many Cambodians who adopted Christianity because of their relationship with sponsors continued to practice Buddhism and did not see the two as mutually exclusive.[77] While maintaining Buddhist identity has been an important way to preserve a sense of Cambodian-ness, the practices themselves have changed. For instance, in America, monks have been unable to continue their custom from Southeast Asia of going door to door for their meals, and instead often have to prepare their meals themselves. Additionally, many have adapted their apparel to better fit some of the cold areas in which they live, for instance, abandoning traditional wardrobes and open-toed sandals for more winter-appropriate gear. Another major change among monks has been their taking up driving and handling money, even though they are traditionally not supposed to do these things.[78]

Participating in homeland politics has likewise reinforced ethnic cohesion while additionally sustaining a transnational orientation among Southeast Asians in America. Vang Pao, the former commander of the Royal Lao Army and Cold War ally of the United States practiced what Chia Youyee Vang calls "long distance nationalism," along with other Hmong ex-military leaders, when they formed the United Lao National Liberation Front in 1981. The group's purposes were to support resistance fighters against the Lao People's Democratic Republic, which it believed was controlled by Vietnam and, thus, an illegitimate government, and to advocate for the normalization of U.S.–Laos relations.[79] Cambodian Americans have also taken part in long distance nationalism through activities that allow them to play a role in the reconstruction of their country of origin. The United Nations Transitional Authority in Cambodia's (UNTAC) preparations for elections in 1993 represented an opportunity for Cambodians abroad to get involved, as they were eligible to vote, albeit under many restrictions (e.g., in the United States the only polling place was in

New York, and yet voters would have to register in Cambodia). Some even launched their own political parties, and eight of the twenty-one parties that vied for votes in the election had been formed by Cambodian Americans, among them Ted Ngoy, who led the Free Development Republican Party. Two Cambodian Americans—Por Bun Sroeu and Ahmad Yhya—actually won seats in the National Assembly.[80]

The establishment of the new government in Cambodia gave rise to further opportunities for Cambodian Americans to reconnect or create new connections with their country of origin. Professionals who had worked in mutual aid associations returned to Cambodia to serve as consultants or take up executive or staff positions in the new government. Formed in 1988 in Chicago, and later based in Texas and Washington, D.C., the Cambodian Network Council (CNC) coordinated—with aid from the Office of Refugee Resettlement—mutual aid associations in the United States and also encouraged young people to go to Cambodia to aid in the country's reconstruction through the Cambodian–American National Development Organization (CANDO). CANDO had been founded in 1993 by Thida Khus and was modeled after the Peace Corps. Between 1993 and 1997, the year it disbanded, it sent eighty-seven volunteers from the United States, a handful of them white Americans, to work with NGOs and units of the Cambodian government as well as teach English.

As with the example of Buddhism, Southeast Asians' efforts to maintain tradition have had to accommodate some degree of change. This has been especially evident in family life with regard to gender and intergenerational relations. Among Cambodians, for instance, women's domesticity is greatly valued and the virginity of daughters is highly prized. According to Sucheng Chan, it is not uncommon for them to be physically punished by parents if they are caught with boys or have boyfriends. In the economy and socio-cultural milieu of 1970s and 1980s America, family dynamics with regard to gender relations underwent substantial change in Cambodian and other Southeast Asian communities. The difficulties that men faced in the economy meant that women often had to enter the labor force, bringing much change into household dynamics. As Chan has found, while some men reported that the growing role of women as economic contributors undermined their self-esteem, others said that they welcomed it. This heightened importance of women in and outside the home has also led to their greater assertiveness in finding and drawing on resources. For instance, wives in unhappy or abusive marriages have been able to turn to the Aid to Families with Dependent Children program (AFDC) for monetary support as well as pursue the option of divorce, and the divorce rate among Cambodian couples has risen after their arrival in the United States. Such changes should not, however, be taken to suggest that greater equality is the result of Americanization, as there are feminists in Cambodia and women are influential there too.[81]

The arena of parent–child relations underwent considerable strain due to the power that children have been able to draw from their higher degree of assimilation and social resources outside the household. Some Cambodian children, for instance, have admitted to lying to parents in order to do what they want in their social lives. As one young woman explained, "[Parents] don't trust us because we lie to them. We tell them we have to go to a meeting but instead we go to meet boys. If you lie too much they don't want to believe you anymore."[82] Research on Cambodians in 1991 showed a drop in the marriage age among young women from 21 to 16, which has been interpreted as an expression of their desire for freedom from parental constraints. Children have also been able to exercise greater power over parents due to their superior knowledge of English and American culture. It is common, for instance, for them to help pay bills, translate documents, answer the phone, and the like. Sometimes children would use this power to outwit their parents. As Cambodian American Sambath Rim related:

> The kids are smarter than the parents. Let me tell you a story. One of the kids told me he never went to school. The school sent a letter to the parents saying, "What happened to this kid? Why isn't he coming to school? Why is he absent?" The parents told the kid, "You know, I got a letter from I don't know where; can you translate it?" The kid says, "Oh, it's a letter from school saying that I'm a very, very good kid doing a really good job in school." . . . the parents are very excited, until the police calls . . . "This kid is locked up; he was shot." . . . So you have to be smarter than the kids in order to control them. Otherwise, they just do whatever they want.[83]

While the local and national media have been attentive to the adjustment problems of refugees and their children, reporting on issues such as mental health, gangs, and poverty, Southeast Asians have also engaged in numerous efforts, such as those described above, to forge strong and productive ethnic communities, take part in homeland politics, and stake their own claims to American society and identity. Younger generations have recently focused their activities on domestic matters such as combating racism. In Minnesota in 1998, a group called Community Action against Racism was formed in the aftermath of insensitive comments made by a St. Paul radio host against Hmong people.[84] The host ridiculed Hmong families, clans, and their diet of boiled chicken after childbirth, and furthermore demonized them as a people who practice infanticide after an incident in which a Hmong girl gave birth to a baby in a YMCA bathroom. Hmong Americans also mobilized in the wake of a racial backlash following the 2004 killing of six white hunters in northern Wisconsin by a Hmong American named Chai Soua Vang, who was found guilty and sentenced to life in prison without parole. There were conflicting accounts of what occurred that day and whether or not Vang had intended to kill the hunters. The racial backlash against Hmong appeared locally, for instance, on bumper stickers reading "Save a Deer. Shoot a Mung." Additionally, the killing of a Hmong hunter named Cha Vang by white hunter James Nichols in 2007 was regarded by many as retaliation.[85] Concerns about racism and negative stereotypes also led to protests against movies like *Rambo* (2008) and efforts to raise awareness about the casualties suffered by Southeast Asians in the Vietnam War.

The rapid and striking growth of the Southeast Asian population has also had important ramifications for Asian America at large, expanding notions of who is Asian American and in some quarters heightening awareness about the poverty and other struggles that many refugees have faced. For example, in Philadelphia, whose Asian American population grew dramatically in the 1980s due to the secondary resettlement of Southeast Asians, Asian American activists of Chinese and Japanese descent altered their approaches to community outreach and activism in response to the newly visible refugee population. Following the arrests of several Southeast Asian youths for the 1991 murder of a white teenager, a vicious racial backlash against the defendants and Asian people in general resulted, in turn motivating members of the organization Asian Americans United (AAU) to organize on behalf of the defendants and other Southeast Asians in Philadelphia. In particular, AAU worked to bring attention to the structural disadvantages faced by many poor, urban refugees while building panethnic bridges with these relatively new Asian Americans.[86]

Conclusion

For many Southeast Asians, constructing a new identity in America had involved incorporating the legacy of war and being a refugee into their personal and collective narratives. Some turned to artistic expression to work through this process. Tou Ger Xiong, a Hmong American, was born in 1973 and left a Thai refugee camp in 1979 to settle in Minnesota. He became a rapper and used this medium to tell his story. "My family was moving from place to place / Running from the guns at a very fast pace. / My people was dying, there and there. / Dead women, children, everywhere. / When I think about these tragedies / I thank God for my life and family."[87]

The presence and struggles of Southeast Asians in America have discredited the model minority stereotype of Asian Americans and called on long-time Asian Americans and their organizations to be more mindful of issues like war, poverty, and psychological well-being. On the other hand, the refugee newcomers have found they have much in common with other Asian Americans, often stemming from their experiences with racism in the United States. As one Hmong American reflected about learning to adjust to the racial customs of his adopted home, being called epithets such as "gook" and "chink," "I wondered what was wrong with me—I didn't like being Hmong for a long time."[88] They have also faced similar kinds of complaints that other Asians historically faced. Vietnamese Andy Anh of the Economic and Development Council in Los Angeles said, "If we are successful in jobs . . . other minorities complain that we take the jobs away from them. But if we aren't successful, they say we rely too much on government assistance."[89]

The shared experience of American racism has become a common basis of identity that has led some Southeast Asians to organize with other Asian Americans and even explicitly identify as "Asian American." And for many Asian Americans with longtime roots in the United States, the war that triggered the arrival of Southeast Asian refugees, with its highly racialized dimensions, reverberated powerfully. The use of the epithet "gook" to describe the North Vietnamese or Viet Cong enemy was extremely disconcerting, and the employment of brutal tactics (use of napalm and killing of civilians) exposed the disregard and dehumanization of Vietnamese people by U.S. authorities. The casualty rate was also staggering, with latest estimates at about four million Vietnamese civilians and about one million military personnel dead compared to the U.S. death toll of about fifty-eight thousand. Asian Americans, particularly those turning to radical politics, felt both a racial and ideological affinity with the supposed enemy, as they identified with Vietnamese as fellow Asians, supported the goals of Ho Chi Minh's Communist party, and saw the U.S. as an outside Western power seeking to impose its will on the Third World. "Asian Americans," says Daryl Maeda, "were uniquely positioned by the war in Viet Nam, for unlike every other racial group, they were conflated with the enemy because they bore faces that looked like those of the enemy."[90] As one Japanese American veteran remembered, "I saw how Whites were treating the Vietnamese, calling them Gooks, running them over with their trucks. I figured I am a Gook also."[91]

The next chapter, which examines Asian American political activism during the 1960s and 1970s, further explores—in the context of the "Asian American Movement"—how the Vietnam War critically informed the outlooks and criticisms of U.S. policies and domestic racism among young Asian American activists during this period. Placing anti-war protest within a larger spectrum of activist work in these tumultuous decades in American history, it will consider how Asian Americans participated in some of the historic movements of the 1960s and 1970s and helped create lasting social and political change.

Notes

1   Kao Kalia Yang, *The Late Homecomer: A Hmong Family Memoir* (Minneapolis: Coffeehouse Press, 2008), 55
2   Ibid., 178.
3   Ibid.
4   The Lac were one of many ethnic groups who lived the area and comprised the Vietnamese people. Sucheng Chan, ed., *The Vietnamese American 1.5 Generation: Stories of War, Revolution, Flight, and New Beginnings* (Philadelphia: Temple University Press, 2006), 3.
5   Sucheng Chan, *Survivors: Cambodian Refugees in the United States* (Urbana: University of Illinois Press, 2004), xxv.
6   Chan, *The Vietnamese American 1.5 Generation*, 16.
7   Ibid., 16–7.
8   Ibid., 21.
9   Ibid., 35.
10 Ibid., 44.
11 Ibid., 47.
12 The *Maddox* sailed from Japan to the Gulf of Tonkin in July 1964 to collect surveillance data off coast of North Vietnam. It encountered three North Vietnamese boats that fired torpedoes at it but missed. The *Maddox* returned fire and chased the boats away. On August 4, the *Maddox* claimed that it and the Ticonderoga were under attack so they fired guns for hours into darkness. There is no agreement today on whether the attacks ever occurred, but Johnson ordered a retaliatory attack against North Vietnam. The Gulf of Tonkin Resolution allowed the U.S. to fight an undeclared war. Ibid., 50.
13 Ibid., 52.
14 Chia Youyee Vang, *Hmong America: Reconstructing Community in Diaspora* (Urbana: University of Illinois Press, 2010), 24.
15 Ibid., 20.
16 Chan, *The Vietnamese American 1.5 Generation*, 42.
17 Ibid., 56.
18 Chan, *Survivors*, 3.
19 Ibid., 12.
20 Ibid., 16.
21 Amended in 1977 to include people from Laos.
22 Chan, *The Vietnamese American 1.5 Generation*, 63.
23 Ibid.
24 Vang, *Hmong America*, 35.
25 Ibid., 41.
26 Ibid.
27 Ibid.
28 Chan, *The Vietnamese American 1.5 Generation*, 67.
29 Chan, *Survivors*, 19.

30 Ibid., 81.

31 Chan, *Survivors*, 45.

32 Jana Lipman, "'The Face is the Roadmap': Vietnamese Americans in U.S. Political and Popular Culture, 1980–1988," *Journal of Asian American Studies* 14 no. 1 (February 2011): 38.

33 Chan, *Survivors*, 63.

34 53,000 to 84,000. In June, it was announced the U.S. would increase its intake to 168,000 per year, or 14,000 per month. Chan, *The Vietnamese American 1.5 Generation*, 83.

35 Ibid.

36 Chan, *Survivors*, xxiv.

37 Ibid., 70.

38 Madeline Hsu, "The Disappearance of America's Cold War Chinese Refugees," *Journal of American Ethnic History* 31, no. 4 (Summer 2012): 13.

39 Lipman, "The Face is the Roadmap," 39.

40 Ibid., 46.

41 Ibid., 43.

42 Ibid., 55.

43 Chan, *The Vietnamese American 1.5 Generation*, 93.

44 Lipman, "The Face is the Roadmap," 49.

45 Gail Kelly, "Coping with America: Refugees from Vietnam, Cambodia, and Laos in the 1970s and 1980s," *The Annals of the American Academy of Political Science*, Vol. 486 No. 1 (September 1986): 139.

46 Ibid., 142.

47 "A refugee is a person outside his or her country of nationality who is unable or unwilling to return to that country because of persecution or well-founded fear of persecution. An asylee is an alien living in the United States or at a port of entry who is unable or unwilling to return to his or her country of nationality ... because of persecution or a well-founded fear of persecution. A parolee is an alien, appearing to be inadmissible to the inspecting officer, allowed to enter the United States under emergency (humanitarian) conditions or if that entry is determined to be in the public interest." Philip Q. Yang, *Asian Immigration to the United States* (Cambridge: Polity Press, 2011), 127–28.

48 Chan, *The Vietnamese American 1.5 Generation*, 87.

49 Ibid., 88.

50 From 1975 to 1994 when the Cambodian refugee resettlement program ended 157,518 had entered the United States. Ibid, 128; Chan, *Survivors*, 79.

51 Chan, *Survivors*, 239.

52 Kelly, "Coping with America," 143.

53 Ibid.

54 By the mid-1990s, Hmong numbered about sixty thousand in Minnesota and this population was exceeded only by Fresno's.

55 Ibid., 141.

56 Kelly, "Coping with America," 142.

57 Chan, *Survivors*, 139.

58 Ibid., 141.

59 Ibid., 140.

60 Chan, *Survivors*, 141.

61 Ibid., 133.

62 Ibid., 137.

63 Ibid., 148.

64 Ibid., 147.

65 Ibid., 149.

66 Kelly, 142.

67 Paul D. Starr, "Troubled Waters: Vietnamese Fisherfolk on America's Gulf Coast," *International Migration Review*, Vol. 15 No. 1/2 (Spring–Summer 1981): 227.

68 Chan, *Survivors*, 109.

69 Ibid.

70 Starr, "Troubled Waters," 228.

71 Ibid., 299.

72 Ibid., 231.

73 Ibid., 235.

74 Ibid., 236.

75 Ibid., 235–36.

76 Chan, *Survivors*, 261.

77 Ibid., 171.

78 Ibid., 177.

79 Vang, *Hmong America*, 137.

80 Chan, *Survivors*, 244.

81 Ibid., 201.

82 Ibid., 207.

83 Ibid., 211.

84 Vang, *Hmong America*, 145.

85 Ibid., 147.

86 Scott Kurashige, "Pan-ethnicity and Community Organizing: Asian American United's Campaign Against Anti-Asian Violence," *Journal of Asian American Studies* 3 no. 2 (June 2000): 163–90.

87 Helen Zia, *Asian American Dreams: The Emergence of an American People* (New York : Farrar, Straus, and Giroux, 2000), 255.

88 Ibid.

89 Chan, *Survivors*, 131.

90 Daryl J. Maeda, *Chains of Babylon: The Rise of Asian America* (Minneapolis: University of Minnesota Press, 2009), 99.

91 Ibid.

Politics and Activism in Asian America in the 1960s and 1970s

11

In 1968, a new student organization at San Francisco State University, the Philippine American Collegiate Endeavor (PACE), released its statement of goals and principles, which read:

> We seek . . . simply to function as human beings, to control our own lives. Initially, following the myth of the American Dream, we worked to attend predominantly white colleges, but we have learned through direct analysis that it is impossible for our people, so-called minorities to function as human beings, in a racist society in which white always comes first . . . So we have decided to fuse ourselves with the masses of Third World people, which are the majority of the world's people, to create, through struggle, a new humanity, a new humanism, a New World Consciousness, and within that context collectively control our own destinies.[1]

Made up of students of Filipino ancestry, PACE reflected the burgeoning radical consciousness among Asian Americans and other minorities who, during the late 1960s, embraced a "Third World" identity. This signaled solidarity with people around the world struggling against colonialism and was rooted in the belief that minority communities in America were themselves "internal colonies." Along with other student groups, PACE joined the Third World Liberation Front (TWLF), a new coalition organization at SF State, which led an historic five-month strike at the campus that demanded, among other things, an autonomous College of Ethnic Studies.

Organizations like PACE are often discussed in terms of the "Asian American movement," a period of heightened political organizing during the 1960s and 1970s by progressive and radical Americans of Asian ancestry who aimed to dismantle racism, imperialism, and other forms of structural oppression, while promoting Asian American empowerment, often under an explicitly pan-Asian umbrella. Asian American activism during this period can be situated within a larger moment of grassroots organizing that also included anti-war activists, students, African Americans, Latinos, women, and homosexuals, but it was also distinct. Asian Americans grappled with a unique set of historical experiences and challenges. Long subject to stereotypes of passivity and docility, young radicals rejected assimilationism and the "model minority," while other activists, across the generations, sought justice for past wrongs and ongoing threats within a broader agenda of demanding dignities long denied to them and their forebears. While much of the organizing that this chapter covers was framed by critiques of American society and history, it was also driven by claims to American belonging and a desire to overcome the historical foreignization of Asians in America.

This chapter explores Asian American political activism during the 1960s and 1970s, with the aim of integrating this subject within a larger understanding of American social movements during a period of political ferment and social transformation. It should be noted, however, that as revolutionary as this era has been proclaimed to be, the 1960s and 1970s were not the first time that Asian Americans became politically engaged and resisted oppression, as earlier chapters in this book have described legal and other forms of activism by Asian Americans to challenge discrimination and exclusion. What was distinct about these years was the dynamism and visibility of political action, as well as its militancy and confrontational tactics. Moreover, activists of varied backgrounds self-consciously organized under a common identification as "Asian Americans," and the expression and consolidation of a pan-ethnic Asian American sensibility has been perhaps one of the most profound and lasting legacies of the Asian American movement.

Political Awakenings and Connections

Black political activism and thought played a pivotal role in inspiring and awakening Asian Americans as well as other minorities to the possibilities of grassroots organizing. The modern black freedom struggle unfolded against a backdrop of postwar prosperity, ideological transition, and social change. Furthermore, Americans had come out of a war against fascism and started to embrace, on a much wider level than before, an ideology of antidiscrimination, in part due to the honorable service of minorities. As economic change sent people in motion from region to region, country to city, city to suburb, their frames of reference expanded and their expectations heightened. With regard to race relations and civil rights in black America, important legal victories such as the Supreme Court's decision in *Brown v. Board* in 1954 were attained, but progress on the ground was frustratingly slow. The recognition that meaningful change would not come from the top down but required bottom-up awareness and action fueled grassroots movements in the South and elsewhere. Images of black protestors, such as students in lunch counter sit-ins or children in bus boycotts—often met by violence or state suppression—awoke and stirred many people to take action. Many northern white college students, for instance, went to the South to participate in black voter registration drives, while others were moved to organize locally, in their own schools and communities.

Young Asian Americans were inspired by the writings of black intellectuals as well as their exposure to black political organizing. Movement veteran Steve Louie credited Stokely Carmichael, Malcolm X, and Huey Newton for "[laying] the groundwork that really brought . . . the Asian American movement out," and Gary Okihiro remarked that Asian Americans "found our identity by reading Franz Fanon and Malcolm X, Cheikh Anta Diop and W.E.B. DuBois . . . "[2] Moreover, in their recollections of the process by which they became politicized, a number of Asian Americans pointed to their involvement in the civil rights movement or encounters with black radicals as defining experiences that led to their own transformations as activists. Sansei Ray Tasaki was born in 1936 and had moved to Los Angeles with his family after World War II. As a wayward youth, he ended up in prison, and it was during this time that he encountered Black Muslims and became "fascinated by their sense of pride, their discipline to their beliefs, and how they identified very clearly who they felt was their enemy."[3] This led to his development of critical perspectives about:

> how the system created conditions with individuals seeking refuge and escape by using alcohol, drugs, religion, gangbanging, fantasy or whatever and getting all into the hippy culture. It began to fall into place especially how the system was exploiting all the poorer Third World countries and how all this affected conditions in our communities, particularly in L.A.'s Little Tokyo.[4]

Another Sansei, Pat Sumi experienced a personal and political transformation during a visit to the South while she was a college student at Occidental College during the mid-1960s. She had gone there with friends who belonged to the Congress of Racial Equality (CORE), and worked for a Headstart Agency in Mississippi and Georgia, attended numerous demonstrations, and helped people register to vote. Reflecting on the impact that these experiences had on her, Sumi noted, "the courage of even the youngest of the black community who were willing to face the Klan." From this, "I learned a little bit about what racism really means."[5] Steve Louie recalled witnessing the civil rights movement and nonviolent protests, but found himself drawn to the militant elements of black politics. "When the Black Panther Party marched into California's legislative chambers in Sacramento with unloaded shotguns," he said, "I sure liked that attitude . . . I thought the Panthers were right to defend [themselves against police brutality]. In my first year of college, I began volunteering in a storefront in Watts . . ."[6]

As these examples show, some Asian Americans were inspired from a distance by black activism, while others became directly involved in civil rights and black power politics. Diverse areas like Los Angeles and San Francisco Bay Area, moreover, were fertile ground on which Asians and blacks could interact and establish intellectual and political camaraderie in social movement organizing. While some Asian Americans took away inspiration from their exposure to civil rights and other political work to serve their own communities, others dedicated much of their activist lives to black politics and serving black communities. These included some of the most celebrated Asian American figures of recent decades, such as Grace Lee Boggs and Yuri Kochiyama.

The Chinese American organization, the Red Guard Party, one of the first radical groups to emerge from Asian American communities during this period, illustrates the central influence of black politics in Asian American organizing. Formed in San Francisco in 1969, it grew out of a youth organization called the Leways (Legitimate Ways). Its name, moreover, came from the Chinese Communist student organization, the Red Guards, and had been suggested by local Black Panthers. According to Daryl Maeda, a key feature of Red Guard politics was members' performance of black nationalism. In particular, they borrowed from the Black Panther Party, for instance, issuing their own ten-point statement, wearing berets and armbands, and engaging in speech that denounced the "colonialist presence" in

Chinatown. In doing so, they put forth an empowering Asian American identity that rejected passivity and dominant white norms. Beyond this performativity, the Red Guard also responded to the poverty and disfranchisement of urban Asian Americans through community service such as a free breakfast program for Chinatown residents, and initiatives to help workers and improve living conditions.[7] The organization, however, was not without its problems. According to Warren Mar, it was falling apart by the early 1970s because members were "undisciplined and semi-lumpen. They couldn't shake the street scene."[8] Furthermore, by this time, in 1971, it merged with the New York based radical group I Wor Kuen (IWK) to become the National IWK, making it the largest Asian American revolutionary organization.

Despite the observation above about the Red Guard's disorganization, Mar was positively impacted by his association with the group. He had grown up in the 1950s and early 1960s in San Francisco Chinatown, which he remembered being overcome by segregation and poverty. Once an aimless youth who "spent more time in poolrooms than in school or at home," he said that the radicals he met gave him a sense of focus and mission in his life. After Mar got into trouble with the law, it was a member of the Red Guard Party who helped him obtain a lawyer for his court date.[9] Although admitting that he was "too undisciplined" for theoretical trappings of the Red Guard, he nonetheless came to see himself as a revolutionary nationalist and became a youth activist. In 1969, as a junior in high school, Mar was elected chair of the Chinatown North Beach Youth Council, a government program for at-risk youth consisting of nearly fifty groups. In his role, he tried to make the organization radical and street-oriented, remembering, "We reprioritized services to meet the needs of young people who were poor. We legitimized the hangouts. We geared services toward the young who were in the pool halls rather than at the YMCA or in the churches."[10]

Vietnam

Reflecting his radicalized anti-colonial consciousness, Mar also found himself rooting against the United States in Vietnam during the late 1960s. Indeed, for many Asian Americans, the Vietnam War and accompanying anti-war movement was another pivotal moment in their political awakening. In the nation at large, a variety of reasons led people to protest the war, from opposition to the draft, the government's secretiveness, U.S. arrogance, and the toll of the war on American soldiers and families. Chinese American Bob Hsiang grew up in a middle-class, staunchly anti-communist household and initially supported the war and the goal of containment. While attending college in Buffalo, New York, however, he was exposed to the politics of anti-war groups like Students for a Democratic Society (SDS), but was especially affected by seeing television footage of the war, leading him to become skeptical of U.S. intervention abroad in general.[11]

Asian American anti-war activists, who organized their own contingents to rallies such as an April 24, 1971 mobilization in San Francisco and the Inaugural Day demonstrations in Washington, D.C. on January 20, 1973, were additionally motivated by racial and class critiques of the war that played little, if any, role in the mainstream movement. Working-class activists of color tended to be more cognizant and critical of how poor and minority soldiers were bearing the disproportionate brunt of combat, as well as the war's imperialist and racist dimensions. Civil rights and Black Power leader Stokely Carmichael, for instance, characterized the draft as "white people sending black people to make war on yellow people in order to defend the land they stole from red people."[12] Additionally, as *La Causa*, the newspaper of the Brown Berets said, "The Vietnam War is the ultimate weapon of genocide of non-white people."[13]

Pat Sumi's critique of the war likewise came to center around race. While in the South, she met college students from the North and West who were involved in the anti-war

Figure 11.1
Pat Sumi before an anti-Vietnam War demonstration calling attention to Japan's collaborative role through the U.S.–Japan Security Treaty, Little Tokyo, Los Angeles, 1971. (© Mary Uyematsu Kao, 1971.)

movement, but as she explained, "I left their circle because of the issue of violence/ nonviolence, which is actually a debate about tactics."[14] To her, the war had more to do with endemic racism—evident for instance in the fact that the majority of front-line infantry were "black and brown"—and she found herself more interested in what critics like Malcolm X, the Black Panthers, and American soldiers themselves had to say about the conflict. However, in working with soldiers in order to "understand the war from the inside," Sumi grew troubled that even those who opposed the war "came back with a hatred of Vietnamese," which further reoriented her anti-war activism and outreach with soldiers.[15] At Camp Pendleton, for instance, she helped create a newsletter called "Attitude Check," intended to educate and enlighten soldiers that was distributed at bus stops and barracks doorsteps.[16]

Against this milieu of protest, Asian Americans also developed critical perspectives about their unique position in America and the world. Many had come to see U.S. involvement in Vietnam as inherently racist and felt a kinship with the Vietnamese people based on shared histories of imperialism and military incursion in Asia. Such sentiments found expression in the Bay Area Coalition Against the War (BAACAW), which was formed in May 1972. Drawing from student leaders and radical organizations, the BAACAW coordinated protests, study groups, fundraising drives, and teach-ins, and in critiquing racist aspects of the war, called attention to the killing of Asian people in Vietnam. In the area of cultural production, Filipino American Melvyn Escueta's play *Honey Bucket* articulated a pan-Asian sensibility, which for him was solidified by the Vietnam War. The first play written by an Asian American to deal with the war, *Honey Bucket* centered on a Filipino American veteran named Andy Bonifacio who becomes deeply tormented after killing Asians in Vietnam. "Although he had joined the Marines as a gung-ho cold warrior," explains Daryl Maeda, "Andy has come to identify with the Vietnamese people as subjects of the same U.S. imperialism that colonized the Philippines and oppresses and exploits Asians in the United States."[17]

International Imaginations

Taking an interest in Asia and expressing solidarity with Asian people against the forces of imperialism and Western domination was part of a larger Third World identity and perspective that took hold among many Asian Americans and other people of color. U.S.-based activists followed international developments and drew inspiration from anti-imperialist wars in Asia, Africa, and Latin America, as well as the writings of Third World intellectuals such as Frantz Fanon, Amilcar Cabral, Che Guevara, and Mao Zedong. Asian Americans drew connections between their positions as racial minorities in America and anti-colonialism abroad, and they also perceived many commonalities between themselves and colonized and oppressed peoples around the world, leading some to think of their own communities as "internal colonies." Such politics was also a fruitful site of interracial solidarity and coalition building, especially in multiethnic and multiracial cities like Oakland and San Francisco. Members of the Black Panthers, for instance, introduced Steve Louie to Mao's *Little Red Book*, which subsequently inspired him to organize workers of color on truck docks and elsewhere.[18]

Others tried to make concrete their imagined global ties to Asia through travel and strengthen their identification with an internationalist left. In summer 1970 on an invitation from the International Journalists Conference, a leftist organization, Pat Sumi went with a delegation to North Vietnam, North Korea, and the People's Republic of China as part of her anti-colonial work as well as efforts to bridge Asians around the world. The delegation included black activists such as Eldridge Cleaver and Elaine Brown as well as fellow Asian American activist Alex Hing of the Red Guard Party. Sumi went in her capacity as a GI activist, and said of the experience, "It was fantastic . . . We saw places and saw things that no Americans had ever seen. It was a chance to see what socialist societies were like."[19] Visiting Asian countries impressed on her the need for other Asian Americans to be better informed about what was going on in this part of the world. For one, lessons about being revolutionary could be obtained, and for her part, Sumi learned in Vietnam that "you can win with superior thinking and not necessarily superior technology."[20]

Overall, the war, anti-colonial movements abroad, and domestic social movements proved to be a fertile backdrop not just for Asian American radicalization, but specifically for Asian–black solidarities and mutual understandings. This occurred not just in local settings, but also through international travel and meetings with delegations from Asia. In an expression of international racial solidarity, the black radical David Hilliard appeared in front of National Liberation Front representatives in Vietnam and said, "You're Yellow Panthers, we're Black Panthers."[21] Pat Sumi had traveled to Africa during the mid-1960s, which impacted her consciousness with regard to her identification as a Third World radical. Observing peasant farmers on the continent, Sumi noted their similarities with her relatives in Japan. "Seeing the rich culture of Africa," summarized Daryl Maeda, "made her realize that segregation and discrimination in the United States could not be justified by the claim of black cultural inferiority."[22]

At the same time, however, many Asian American radicals felt estranged from white liberal activists and organizations. As mentioned above, Pat Sumi had become disaffected with the mainstream anti-war movement's inattention to racism. In 1970, she attended a women's conference in Vancouver with other women from the Asian American Movement in Los Angeles, where she met with women from Indochina. She recalled being embarrassed about the North American women who represented the old left—CPUSA and SDS feminists for their disunity. "We couldn't even agree on an agenda, much less anything else . . . and these poor women from Indochina were forced to see how dis-unified we were."[23]

Meanwhile, there were other international developments besides the Vietnam War that politicized Asian Americans. For many Filipino Americans, this came through learning about colonialism as well as being exposed to the Marcos regime and the anti-Martial Law movement in the Philippines. Prosy Abarquez-Delacruz's father had made arrangements for her to come to the United States in 1972, shortly after the declaration of Martial Law. These circumstances of her immigration gave her a sense of mission, and she joined the National Committee for the Restoration of Civil Liberties in the Philippines. Carol Ojeda-Kimbrough also came to the United States in 1972 due to Martial Law and became active in various Philippines-oriented Los Angeles organizations. She also joined the U.S.-based Katipunan ng mga Demokratikong Pilipino (KDP), and planned to return to the Philippines after the struggle.[24] After her husband, who was targeted for his activism, was killed in the Philippines, Ojeda-Kimbrough lived under fear of being deported due to her own political activities. Her Philippines-based activism also led her to ponder her immigrant and Asian American identity, asking, "Am I a Filipino first or a Filipino–American?"[25]

"Yellow Power" and Asian American Identity

Influenced by struggles against oppression at home and abroad, many Asian Americans and other Third World radicals came to see different forms of oppression—race, gender, class—as interlinked. In other words, the Vietnam War and domestic racial and class issues all emanated from the forces of white supremacy and imperialism. At the same time, newly radicalized Asian Americans wanted to delve into their unique histories and identities. "B.I." worked in the fields of Fairfield and "knew what they were saying about the low wages, and the twelve- to fourteen-hour day . . . I learned later on that Pilipinos were involved in organizing the first farmworkers' strike. And that made me very proud. . ."[26] Young Filipino Americans also unearthed Carlos Bulosan's *America is in the Heart*, using the book to connect with their roots in America. "Through Bulosan," remembered Estella Habal, "we learned that the elderly and the young people shared internationalist perspectives, common experiences, and a rediscovery of the Philippines."[27] Originally published in 1946, *America is in the Heart* was reissued in 1973 and achieved a wider circulation than it ever had before. The recovery of old texts and study of these histories—especially working-class histories—also represented for many young Asian Americans a rejection of the middle class and assimilationist strivings of their parents' generation as well as their own aspirations for whiteness. As "J.M.," an Asian American woman, said, "I was going with a white man whom I met at Berkeley, whom I eventually married. And so I don't know how to explain this to you, it seems very disorganized and very chaotic, but at the same time I was aspiring to be White, wanting a white child, wanting to marry a white man, I was simultaneously being impacted by all these events that were challenging me as an Asian woman."[28]

In addition to excavating buried histories and grappling with internalized racism, Asian American activists also turned to cultural production to develop and articulate empowered identities. Creative works produced during this period helped to construct a new Asian American identity premised on "Yellow Power." Janice Mirikitani was a member of the Third World Liberation Front and found her involvement in it to be generative for her work. With other women activist–writers, she co-founded the Third World Communications Collective (TWC), which published the journal *Aion*. This process of creating could be exhilarating, but also highly fraught, exposing fissures in the population, often along gendered lines. In this way, writer Frank Chin holds a place as a groundbreaking and controversial figure. His play, *Chickencoop Chinaman*, won a 1971 playwrighting contest sponsored by the East West Players of Los Angeles and became the first Asian American play produced off-Broadway. The play and Chin's other works emphatically rejected assimilation as an antidote to racism and condemned the model minority image.[29] Chin also cofounded the Asian American Theater Workshop in San Francisco and co-edited *AIIEEEEE!*, a seminal anthology of Asian American literature.

While Chin's role in the history of Asian American activism is certainly that of a path breaker, he was also, and remains, a controversial figure. Staking Asian American identity politics tightly around the recuperation of heterosexual masculinity, Chin has been accused of perpetuating misogynistic ideas. These charges were amplified in a high-profile dustup with novelist Maxine Hong Kingston, the author of *Woman Warrior*, whom he accused of peddling "fake" depictions of Asians for white consumption.

In the arena of music, the folk trio, Grain of Sand, consisting of Joanne Miyamoto, Chris Ijima, and William "Charlie" Chin traveled the country in the early 1970s, performing their brand of "radical culture." Their lyrics encapsulated a broad range of ideas associated with the Asian American movement: multiethnic unity among Asians, interethnic solidarity with other minorities, and Third World identity. They also invoked forgotten histories from America's past to highlight the presence of Asian people and thereby affirm their claims to U.S. belonging. Their song, "We Are the Children" inserted Asian American history into American history while asserting an empowered position and identity:

> We are the children of the migrant worker
> We are the offspring of the concentration camp.
> Sons and daughters of the railroad builder
> Who leave their stamp on Amerika.
> Sing a song for ourselves.
> What have we got to lose?
> Sing a song for ourselves.
> We got the right to choose.
> . . .
> We are the children of the Chinese waiter,
> Born and raised in the laundry room.
> We are the offspring of the Japanese gardner,
> Who leave their stamp on Amerika.
> Foster children of the Pepsi Generation,
> Cowboys and Indians—ride, red-man, ride!
> Watching war movies with the nextdoor neighbor,
> Secretly rooting for the other side.
> We are the cousins of the freedom fighter,
> Brothers and sisters all around the world.
> We are a part of the Third World people
> Who will leave their stamp on Amerika.
> Who will leave our stamp on Amerika.[30]

As artistic production proliferated along with political organizations among Asian Americans, the 1960s and 1970s also saw the emergence of a flurry of community-based arts organizations in several major cities. These included the Kearny Street Workshop (KSW) in San Francisco, Basement Workshop in New York, and Asian Media Collective, which used a do-it-yourself approach to create slides and Super-8 films "to present an alternative view of the events concerning Asian Americans."[31] A number of professional and community theater groups were also formed, such as the East West Players in Los Angeles, Pan-Asian Repertory Theater in New York, and the TEA/Asian Exclusion Act in Seattle.[32] Many of the arts organizations established during the Asian American movement remain active today, and they also leave behind a rich legacy of creative works, found in murals, music, publications, and other media.

Sexism and Homophobia

Like many other radical and other social movement organizations during the 1960s, Asian American movement leaders had a tendency to prioritize some critiques over others and, as seen in the example of Frank Chin, issues of gender equality often took a backseat in the Asian American movement. Merilynne Hamano Quon, a Sansei from Los Angeles, recalled a general disregard among men for the input of women organizers, saying, "Some men did not take a woman's input in a meeting seriously or would simply shout her down."[33] In turn, she and many other Asian American women decided to form their own organizations to focus on issues of particular concern to them. With other Sansei from working class families, Quon established Asian Sisters, which she described as a "serve the people" group that offered crisis intervention and counseling. It received funding from Nisei women's organizations and in 1972 received federal money that members used as seed money for the Asian Women's Center. At its height, Asian Sisters grew to two hundred people, with Japanese, Chinese, and Filipina members. Also finding themselves marginalized or neglected in the Asian American movement were gay activists. During his involvement with an IWK study group in Sacramento, Chinese American Steve Lew realized that the group viewed homosexuality as deviant. Its position, he explained, was that gays "couldn't be good revolutionaries, that it was a bourgeois and psychological aberration one had to 'struggle' against."[34] As Russell Leong explains, "Asian American activists who were lesbian or gay did not reveal their sexual preferences," because activists feared revealing their homosexuality would "jeopardize" their organizing efforts.[35] At the same time, the burgeoning gay rights movement was not the most welcoming place for Asian Americans. Hong Kong-born Daniel Tsang recalled having much difficulty joining his identities as an Asian American and gay person. Having come to the United States in 1967 to attend college at the University of Michigan, he was active in the school's Gay Liberation Front chapter and helped found East Wind as the university's main Asian American activist group. However, he felt isolated in both as if he did not fully belong to either the gay or Asian American community. According to Russell Leong, "In the 1970s there were few gay organizations that were not dominated by white males. For Asian and Pacific lesbians and gays, politicization involved confronting white racism, whether in heterosexual mainstream or gay and lesbian institutions."[36]

For his part, Daniel Tsang gravitated toward writing about Asian American gay identity and politics.[37] He wrote an essay in 1975 for the Asian American movement magazine *Bridge* titled, "Gay Awareness," which he believes was the first gay Asian male manifesto. In it he described revealing his sexuality at a meeting in February 1974 of the Third World People's Solidarity Conference in Ann Arbor as part of a group that collectively came out to express their anger about anti-gay sentiments on podium, such as Angela Davis' remark about George Washington's "sissy" shoes. Critiquing homophobia in the Third World movement, he said for "too long, gays have refused, or strategically delayed, confronting Asian American straights about their homophobia. This conspiracy of silence . . . occurred under the mistaken notion that by not rocking the boat we could gain the respect of the dominant culture."[38]

Other Asian American gay activists were drawn to gay people of color circles or leftist groups that embraced them. In these areas, they were able to carve a niche for themselves. An early example of organizing among gay Asian Americans was at the first National Third

World Lesbian and Gay Conference at Howard University in 1979, where a group of Asian American attendees formed the Lesbian and Gay Asian Collective. Although they did not issue a statement of principles, it was a significant moment of nascent organizing and visibility, and the following year *Gay Insurgent* magazine featured a photograph of nine Asian Americans at this meeting raising their arms behind a banner reading, "WE'RE ASIANS, GAY AND PROUD."[39]

Action: The Movement for Asian American and Ethnic Studies

One of the signature achievements of the Asian American left in the late 1960s occurred on the campus of San Francisco State University. Here, student activists joined the coalition organization the Third World Liberation Front (TWLF) and played an integral role in an historic strike that led to the establishment of a college of ethnic studies and touched off movements at other colleges and universities across the country to institute Asian American and ethnic studies curricula. Formed in 1968, the TWLF reflected a growing militancy among young people of color as well as the broader student movement in America. It brought together black, Latino, Asian American, and Native American student organizations as well as predominantly white groups such as Students for a Democratic Society (SDS), and was formed amidst disagreements between students and administration over minority recruitment and control of Black Studies.

Prior to the TWLF's formation, students at San Francisco State had been engaged in activism to bridge their campus with local communities. By the mid-1960s, using aid from student groups, they developed "counterhegemonic" programs that addressed racial and other issues. Programs like the Fillmore Tutorial, Community Involvement Program, Experimental College, and Work Study brought students into contact with urban youth, rural farm workers, and other constituencies traditionally cut off from higher education resources. Through the Experimental College, students took courses with titles such as "Perspective on Revolution" and "Urban Action," which instilled in them a commitment to social change and the outlook that education should be relevant to the needs of local communities, equip people to control their lives, and disseminate knowledge that comes out of the community.

Asian American students and campus organizations that became involved in the Experimental College and tutorial programs were profoundly affected by their experiences. The Intercollegiate Chinese for Social Action (ICSA) was formed in 1967 primarily as a social, cultural, and community group. However, as its members worked at Chinatown social service agencies, taught English to immigrant teenagers, and worked with existing Chinatown organizations for a senior center, youth center, low-cost housing, and an investigation of the Chinatown-North Beach Equal Opportunity Commission, it took on an activist orientation. These experiences were particularly transformative for students from middle class families who had not spent much time in Chinatown. One example of ICSA members' growing militancy was their establishment of the confrontationally named Free University for Chinatown Kids, Unincorporated (FUCKU), which was dedicated to finding ways to bring together college students and "street kids" in Chinatown.

The more ICSA members worked in Chinatown, the more they came to desire ethnic studies and were convinced it could be a key to improving conditions in local communities.

It joined the TWLF and issued a position paper deploring Chinatown as a segregated and neglected "GHETTO." In calling for ethnic studies, specifically Chinese American Studies, the paper read, "There are not adequate courses in any department of school at San Francisco State that even begin to deal with problems of the Chinese people in this exclusionary and racist environment."[40] Members found inspiration in Chinese historical figures such as Sun Tzu, and applied this knowledge to crafting a new identity that held pride in being Chinese American. "We came together, I think, a little more comfortable with who we were," recalled one member. "We found issues we felt were lacking in our lives . . . I think the one thing you can't do when you are trying to melt into the white world is to complain about it. But if you join with others of your own kind, you have the opportunity to trade stories . . . and to articulate your hostility."[41]

PACE, which was discussed at the beginning of the chapter, was another Asian American organization that joined the TWLF and supported the strike. Its Filipino American members had been engaged in programs similar to those of ICSA, organizing counseling programs, tutorial programs, tutor training, study centers, and newsletters. Outside of the college community, members worked to recruit and retain low-income Filipino American residents of the Mission in San Francisco in the college, established channels of communication with Bay Area youth organizations, researched socioeconomic problems and their solutions, and served as a referral agency for employment, medical, housing, recreation, and counseling. Despite the similarities in their activities, PACE and ICSA were quite different in their memberships, reflecting the diversity of the pan-Asian coalition that was coming together at this moment. Whereas ICSA members were by and large middle class and U.S.-born, most PACE members were from the Philippines and a significant number came from working class military or farm families. Like other members of the TWLF coalition, PACE developed a critique of inequality as rooted in racism and advanced the objectives of self-determination and "power to the people".

Another key Asian American organization that supported the movement for ethnic studies and the TWLF strike was the Asian American Political Alliance (AAPA), formed in summer 1968. Preceded by a chapter at UC Berkeley, most of the AAPA leaders at SF State were Japanese American women, although the group explicitly presented itself as a vehicle for pan-Asian politics. Members had become politicized through exposure to the Experimental College and campus activism. One of the founders, "P.N.," said, "I felt a lot of need to do something about racism. Also, there was a need to do something about the lack of political involvement of Asians . . . [There] was also this amorphous sense of wanting to build a sense of Asian American identity and . . . overcome what I saw as nationalistic kinds of trends. I wanted to see Asians from different ethnic backgrounds working together."[42] In 1968 AAPA stated in its fall newsletter: "We believe that the American society is historically racist and is one which has systematically employed social discrimination and economic imperialism both domestically and internationally to exploit all people, but especially nonwhites."[43]

ICSA, PACE, AAPA, and other student and labor organizations at SF State and campuses across California set their sights on the state's Master Plan of 1960, which aimed to restructure its higher education system in order to better meet the needs of industry, defense, and the growing student population. It divided the state's institutions of higher learning into three tiers, with each targeting particular sectors of the population and performing specialized functions. The University of California (UC) system would serve the most select and elite students and focus on professional training and Ph.D.s; the state colleges would emphasize liberal arts and science, applied fields, and teacher education; and junior colleges would provide vocational and general liberal arts training.[44] As the plan was put into effect, the increasingly selective admissions procedures implemented at the UC and state campuses had a negative impact on minority enrollments.[45] African American student enrollment at San Francisco State dropped from 11 percent of the student body in 1960 to 3.6 percent in 1968. The Master Plan also centralized major decision-making power into the hands of twenty-one business and political figures on the Board of Trustees. Furthermore, a chancellor who presided over the entire system held absolute power over all academic programs, distribution of funds, and major personnel decisions.

Student organizations especially objected to the centralized decision-making structure and partnerships with the defense industry formalized in the Strategic Plan. Students of color at San Francisco State were additionally concerned about the accessibility of higher education for working class and poor residents in the state. The TWLF, which had been formed with the encouragement of key faculty members, was to be the main vehicle of protest. Made up of six organizations, it stated the following as its philosophy and goals:

> The TWLF . . . has its purpose to aid in further developing politically, economically, and culturally the revolutionary Third World consciousness of racist oppressed peoples both on and off campus. As Third World students, as Third World people, as so-called minorities, we are being exploited to the fullest extent in this racist white America. And we are therefore preparing ourselves and our people for a prolonged struggle for freedom from this yoke of oppression.[46]

After winning some concessions from the administration around minority enrollment and faculty hiring, but frustrated with delays, it decided to call for a strike. The triggering event was the administration's suspension of George Murray, a member of the Black Student Union central committee and teacher in the English department. Murray had also served as the minister of education for the Black Panther Party and been an outspoken critic of the university. He was suspended due to his rhetoric, which included advocating political power "through the barrel of a gun."[47] The strike commenced on November 6, 1968, and participants made a set of demands that included the establishment of an autonomous Ethnic Studies college, open admissions, "self-determination," and the reinstatement of George Murray. Students were joined by the American Federation of Teachers, although the union was motivated by its own interests regarding a labor dispute with the university. On the first day of the strike, students engaged in actions intended to disrupt campus operations, such as entering buildings and dismissing classes and setting garbage cans on fire. As the days passed, the size of the crowds grew and class attendance continued to drop, but as the strike's momentum grew, so did repression by campus authorities, including arrests and beatings by police. The arrests of hundreds of student leaders created voids in the movement, but this also politicized participants even more.

To focus on the rationale behind the TWLF's demand for ethnic studies, it was trying to change institutions and enact broad social change. Closely connected to the push for ethnic studies curricula was advocating for the right of minorities, or "Third World people," to obtain a higher education. Their access was limited by what protectors deemed institutional racism in standardized tests and admissions processes. The TWLF also challenged the purpose and ideological work of education. Ethnic studies would be involved in confronting "racism, poverty and misrepresentation imposed on minority peoples by the formally recognized institutions and organizations operating in the State of California."[48] Such an education would be relevant to minority students in ways that existing curricula was not; it would fulfill their desire to learn about their own backgrounds and histories, and also connect them to the communities from which they came or wished to serve, such as Chinatown. In their call for "self-determination" and academic autonomy, strikers said that classes should be taught by "Third World" people and that students should be able to make decisions about curriculum and the hiring of faculty. As the TWLF stated:

> As assurance against the reoccurrence of education's traditional distortion and misrepresentation of Third World people's cultures and histories, the School of Ethnic Area Studies is to be developed, implemented, and controlled by Third World people. Whether on area study is at a developmental or a departmental level within the school, the people, of an area study will have sole responsibility and control for the staffing and curriculum of their ethnic area study.[49]

As mentioned, the TWLF was a coalition organization, and the major political Asian American student groups—PACE, ICSA, AAPA—all joined. Initially, some ICSA members were reluctant to do so and support the strike because they preferred to work on their own. However, once they availed themselves to working within a coalition, the experience added another layer to their politicization. ICSA member, "A.W." recalled about his conversation with a Black Student Union leader:

> And I said, "Okay fine, you Blacks need to go to school, so you guys fight it, and I won't go against it. But I'm not for it because what am I getting out of this?" And he said, "What about all your Chinese who can't get into school?" . . . And I said, "Okay you convince me what you can give me and my people" . . . And he said, "We've got counseling, tutoring service, we have special admission." . . . So I said, "All right, I'm in." That was the first time in my life that somebody, not Asian, was willing to share with me their pot of gold. So I had nothing to lose, and all to gain, and then I got involved.[50]

Although it is usually identified with young student radicals, the strike at San Francisco State drew the support of a wide cross-section of the Bay Area Asian American population. Members of the ICSA, for example, both challenged and reached out to elder power brokers in Chinatown. Initially the Equal Opportunity Council (EOC) board in Chinatown, while sympathetic to the issue of educational access, did not think a strike was necessary. Activist "G.W." recalled a conversation with a board member, in which the latter said, "How dare you people make such a racket! My grandson's trying to apply for the university and couldn't get in!" "G.W." replied, "Read our demand carefully. We're doing this for your grandson. It is precisely people like your grandson who feel that they have been kept out . . . and we want to get him in." Somewhat improbably, "G.W." says that the board member then embraced the strike. "And he said, 'Oh, is that right? I'm for it!' . . . So we had EOC in Chinatown voting to support this San Francisco State Third World Strike."[51]

Figure 11.2 Third World Liberation strike at Sather Gate, UC Berkeley, 1969. Students at UC Berkeley supported the strike that started at San Francisco State, across the Bay. Asian American students on both campuses played a crucial and visible role in the strikes, which culminated with the establishment of an ethnic studies college at SF State. (© Douglas Wachter, 1969.)

Japanese Americans, young and old, who supported the strike, were forced to break free of entrenched patterns in which they generally opted to pursue legal strategies and not "rock the boat." As the Director of the YMCA in Japantown reflected, "[It could] be that we were far more interested in civil liberties, and in the question of freedom of speech, the freedom of assemblage . . . It could also be that we really didn't feel that restrained to rock the boat, to challenge the status quo." The campus uprising and radical spirit of late 1960s activism, however, awoke the Director to new ways of thinking about social injustice, past and present. "I think it might have been the lessons learned from the evacuation," said the Director, regarding many Japanese Americans' complacent approach to racism. "If there is a wrong, you don't keep quiet about it . . . I think the evacuation was wrong. And this was one way to say so many years later."[52] Others in the Japanese American community were likewise moved to rethink their historical positions and support the young activists at San Francisco State. For example, at a meeting at the Christ United Presbyterian Church, one hundred Japanese American members formally gave their support to the strike.

As challenging as it was to build broad-based support among Asian Americans for the strikers, the movement and call for intraminority solidarity was complicated by the fact that the most visible face of the opposition was an administrator of Japanese ancestry. This signaled both the political diversity of Asian America and a broader ideological landscape against which the battle for ethnic studies was waged. S.I. Hayakawa, a Canadian-born Japanese academic in the United States and future U.S. Senator, became the president of San Francisco State after the previous president Robert Smith resigned on November 26.

Hayakawa seemed to relish his role as a critic of the strike and entire student movement. He denounced the strikers for disrupting the university for a frivolous political agenda, calling them a "gang of goons, gangsters, con men, neo-Nazis, and common thieves."[53] In terms of his actions against the strike, he banned campus rallies and authorized using police force on the protestors. Hayakawa even took matters into his own hands at one point, jumping on top of a sound truck and ripping off the speaker cords during one rally.

The strike eventually came to an end in mid-March, 1969, but before that it rocked the SF State campus and received national media coverage. It would turn out to be the longest student strike in American history. The student arrests and AFT's decision to return to work cost the movement precious momentum and precipitated its end. Although the strikers did not receive all of their demands, they did win their largest: the establishment of the first School of Ethnic Studies in the nation. In the decades since, other ethnic studies and Asian American studies curricula and departments have been instituted at colleges and universities across the country. And as historic as the strike at SF State was, it was part of a broader upsurge of Asian American student activism that also overtook UC Berkeley, the University of Hawaii at Manoa, Seattle Central Community College and other campuses.[54]

For Asian Americans who took part in the strike, the experience was profound, both personally and collectively. As "G.C." reflected, "I think it changed my life in terms of providing some focus to the extent that my career wasn't that important to me . . . Take a look at the decisions people made back then. It was what the community needed first; and what you could contribute emanated from that."[55] Some decided to commit themselves to careers in law or community activism. As Karen Umemoto has explained, "a less tangible, but equally significant, outcome of the strike was the emergence of a new generation of fighters who either remained on campus or entered their communities. Many took the concept of self-determination or establish self-help programs to continue political education and promote self-reliance."[56]

The Fight for the I-Hotel

As mentioned earlier, Asian American movement organizations emerged to address problems facing the urban poor and working class, such as juvenile delinquency, unemployment, and the encroachment of urban renewal projects on Asian immigrant neighborhoods. With regard to the latter, activists organized to maintain community integrity and preserve historic sites in places such as the International District in Seattle, Philadelphia Chinatown, and Los Angeles Little Tokyo. Another pressing matter that emerged by the late 1960s was that of renters' rights and affordable housing. These were formative issues for Corky Lee while growing up in New York. Lee was the son of a laundryman and had worked as a welder during World War II and was inspired by witnessing the Civil Rights movement. By 1970 he was organizing within the Two Bridges Neighborhood Council which, among other things, worked to open apartment buildings that had been taken over by the New York Telephone Company.[57]

In San Francisco, around the same time as the TWLF strike, activists were also mobilizing against the forces of urban renewal, which threatened many of the city's long-time Filipino and Chinese residents. Here, the fight to save the International Hotel ("I-Hotel") was another critical flashpoint in the history of Asian American political activism during the 1960s and 1970s. After a period of deindustrialization and urban decline, in the late 1950s San Francisco entered a phase of renewal, which has also been called the "Manhattanization" of the city. Led by the city government, planning commissions, and corporate investors, urban renewal saw the upward expansion of San Francisco, with new high-rise office buildings, and outward development in adjacent areas. By the 1960s, Manilatown was one of the historical neighborhoods standing in the way, until only the I-Hotel remained. Vulnerable because it sat at the heart of the new financial district, the I-Hotel and the struggle of its tenants became a rallying issue for Asian American activists. In addition to being a site for protest and engagement, it also exposed the activists to the politics of housing rights and neighborhood, working-class, and urban policies, increasingly pressing issues in post-war, post-industrial America.

The conflict over the I-Hotel began in 1968 when its owner, Milton Meyer Company, applied to demolish the building so that a parking lot could take its place. The company proceeded to send eviction notices to tenants, most of whom were middle-aged to elderly men. After the eviction notices were issued, a third of the residents left immediately, but the action also mobilized protestors from the community and nearby universities who organized demonstrations against Milton Meyer Company. San Francisco mayor Joseph Alioto, who embraced a pro-growth program for the city, especially around making it a hub for Pacific Rim finance, expressed little sympathy for the tenants. As he and city developers saw it, parking lots and towers would be more profitable than low-rent hotels. At the same time, however, Alioto wished to avoid negative publicity, so met with tenants' representatives and

Figure 11.3 "The Struggle for Low Income Housing" by Jim Dong and Nancy Hom, 1976. This "portable mural" expressed San Francisco community activists' opposition to the demolition of the International Hotel. The mural foregrounds an older Filipino resident and depicts him a defiant, heroic figure. (© Jim Dong.)

Figure 11.4 A large group of protestors and onlookers prepares for the International Hotel eviction, August 1977. Although this decade-long movement ultimately ended with the hotel's demolition and eviction of its elderly Asian American residents, the protest galvanized many Asian Americans as well as the movement for affordable housing. (Photograph by residential hotel tenant from across the street of I-Hotel, used by permission from Steve Louie. Reproduced from Louie and Omatsu, *Asian Americans: The Movement and the Moment*, 117.)

reached a series of agreements to keep the remaining tenants in the hotel. In 1969, a three-year lease was negotiated, but by this time, just 65 out of 184 rooms were occupied.

While keeping Asian tenants in their homes was the imperative that drew activists to the I-Hotel, as the number of residents dwindled, the cause took on a symbolic importance and also became part of a larger struggle to stem the march of urban development. Regarding the major groups that became involved, Filipino American individuals and organizations emerged early on as vocal representatives and supporters of the tenants. According to Beverly Kordziel, Filipino Americans who had not wanted to be involved in the Third World Strike did, nonetheless, wish to be involved with the I-Hotel because many of the residents were Filipino. Filipino American organizations that lent their support included the United Filipino Association, a Manilatown community organization led by local residents, business leaders, longtime activists, and union members, and the Katipunan ng mga Demokratikong Pilipino, or KDP, a radical organization of primarily young activists.[58] The movement, thus, fostered intergenerational bonds between old timers and college-age activists, among Filipinos as well as other Asian Americans.

The I-Hotel itself, while a symbol of resistance, also became a venue for organizing, as various offices and projects associated with the Asian American left set up shop in its storefronts. These included a community arts center; the Leways; the Filipino American newspaper *Kalayaan*; a radical bookstore; the Asian Community Center (ACC); Chinese Progressive Association (CPA); and the International Hotel Tenants Associations. The latter was made up of tenants and some students and its goal was to keep the hotel afloat while pursuing the issue of low cost housing for elderly Filipinos and Chinese.[59]

Although Asian Americans were the heart of the anti-eviction movement at the I-Hotel, the struggle, which went on for a decade, eventually drew support from a broad range of constituencies in San Francisco and the greater Bay Area. Labor unions, civil rights groups, religious leaders, the antiwar movement, students from nearby San Francisco State, and the gay community all expressed solidarity with the tenants, and the demonstrations outside the hotel grew to thousands of people. The movement withstood the I-Hotel's change of ownership when the Four Seas Investment Company, a Thailand-based corporation, purchased it from Milton Meyer and picked up the effort to evict the tenants.

The eviction finally occurred on August 3–4, 1977. While this was considered a major setback to anti-corporate activists and those working to preserve the working-class character of the city, the long duration of the strike and the solidarity it forged among Asian Americans and across racial and other boundaries was inspiring and deeply impactful for the activists involved. After the remaining tenants were evicted and the building demolished, a hole remained in the ground where the hotel was located, which remained for decades. Development was delayed as Filipino and Chinese American activists put pressure on the city to ensure that anything built at the site would include a significant low-income housing component. Finally in 2005, a victory of sorts was achieved when a new hotel was completed, with units for low-income residents and a Manilatown Center located on the ground floor.

The long and hard fought battle to save the I-Hotel stands out as a seminal struggle of the Asian American movement. As mentioned above, it became about much more than the hotel itself. Activists like Harvey Dong expanded their activism beyond the hotel by organizing tenants in other buildings, holding rent strikes and demanding repairs, and building broader political awareness in the Chinatown-Manilatown community.[60] The I-Hotel episode, furthermore, raised a larger awareness among those involved as well as many outside observers about community conditions and the plight of elderly, poor Asian Americans.

Justice for Japanese American Internees

While the struggles for ethnic studies at SF State and the I-Hotel are associated with, and to a significant degree did, emanate from the Asian American radical left, the scope of Asian American political activism in the 1960s and 1970s is much broader than these examples suggest. To discuss one final example, the movement for Japanese American redress certainly reflected a heightened politicized consciousness among this historically moderate community, but grew out of a tradition of legal activism that stretched back to the early twentieth century.

The years after the war were characterized by Japanese American silence around the ordeal of internment. As noted earlier in the book, the mainstream media praised Japanese Americans for their obedience and peacefulness during and after the war, despite having been subjected to government incarceration. To be sure, there had always been voices that were critical of internment, but these viewpoints tended to be marginalized or silenced. The Japanese American Citizens League, whose official stance was to comply with the government's orders and demonstrate U.S. patriotism, had by and large been accepted as the dominant outlook of Japanese Americans during the war.

Things had changed by the early 1970s. By this time, third- and fourth-generation Japanese Americans were coming of age and many, perhaps politicized by the events of the 1960s, rejected the older generations' stoicism around the unjust internment to which they had been subjected during World War II. One turning point occurred in 1970 when the Seattle Museum of History and Industry and National Endowment for the Humanities held an exhibit on local Japanese American history, which for the first time made the history of internment visible to a general public. On display from July to September 1970, the exhibit was seen by about thirty-four thousand people and was positively received. This reception emboldened Japanese Americans to continue talking about their experiences after years of suppressing their feelings about them.

The heightened public awareness of the internment led to the politicization of many Japanese Americans across the generations who had been silent for so long. In the mid-1970s, Henry Miyake, who had been interned when he was twelve, decided to look into legal redress after reading the book, *Prejudice, War, and the Constitution*, which an attorney friend had recommended to him.[61] His politicization was gradual, stemming in part from his employment as an engineer at Boeing, where he encountered his fair share of racial discrimination and insensitive comments. He went on to co-found the Seattle Evacuation Redress Committee (SERC), which pushed Japanese American organizations, including JACL chapters, to make the redress issue a more prominent one. The Committee also had to overcome the national JACL's hesitancy about championing a redress bill as well as its historical pattern of not speaking out about internment.

Through much of the 1970s, SERC worked to build support in the JACL, chapter by chapter, as well as grassroots support for redress. Much of this work entailed urging Japanese Americans to come to terms with their silence. It sent out an information packet to JACL chapters, government representatives, and other Japanese American organizations, called, "An Appeal for Action to Obtain Redress for the World War II Evacuation and Imprisonment of Japanese Americans."[62] In it, the authors did not just emphasize the injustice of internment, but also criticized Japanese Americans for being "brainwashed" into thinking that "they had been born of an unworthy race and that they had to submit meekly to practically any governmental trampling of their human rights."[63] The fact that no real attempt, thirty years later, had been made to obtain redress was further proof that "the older Nisei at least, have been psychologically crippled by their pre-war and wartime experience."[64] The committee then recommended that each former internee receive $5,000 plus $10 per day incarcerated. The response to the committee's work was encouraging and indicated an awakening in Japanese America; it received monetary support from local Japanese churches and a strong majority of respondents said they favored pursuing some form of redress.

Meanwhile, SERC also had its detractors. S.I. Hayakawa, now a U.S. Senator, attacked the Seattle JACL members who joined SERC as "third-generation Japanese Americans eagerly conforming to the radical-chic fads of their non-Japanese college contemporaries."[65] Hayakawa's attempt to dismiss redress activists as young radical flunkies, however, did not hold up. SERC leader Shosuke Sasaki responded to the attacks in the *Seattle Times* by pointing out that the "Appeal for Action" was actually written by a sixty-three-year-old Issei, in collaboration with a fifty-eight-year-old Nisei and a forty-six-year-old Nisei, all of whom were professionals or retired professionals.

In terms of how to engage national politics, redress activists decided to focus on getting Executive Order 9066 revoked, which they hoped would then become an opening to push for monetary payments. SERC leaders worked with Washington governor Dan Evans, who happened to be a friend of Vice President Nelson Rockefeller. These ties allowed for a swift path to rescission in 1976, and in President Ford's rescission statement, he said, "evacuation was wrong, but Japanese–Americans were and are loyal Americans."[66]

This achievement added momentum to the redress campaign, and JACL chapters entered the fold more quickly. Mike Masaoka even expressed his support for the campaign in the *Pacific Citizen*, although he favored the establishment of a public trust rather than individual payments. In Spring 1976, the JACL formed a National Reparations Committee and explored various plans.[67] At its first convention, held in 1978, it proposed redress legislation that would award $25,000 to each individual and set up a community trust fund. It also produced a widely distributed booklet laying out its case, *Japanese American Incarceration: A Case for Redress*.

As the redress movement became national in scope, it garnered broad support in and outside of the Japanese American community. In 1980, the National Coalition for Redress Reparations (NCRR) was established in Los Angeles as an umbrella organization for diverse groups to join the campaign.[68] The NCRR attracted progressive and working class Japanese Americans as well as members of the radical Communist organization, the League of Revolutionary Struggle. It worked in a variety of areas, from launching community education campaigns to get people to testify and attend the Commission on Wartime Relocation and Internment of Civilians (CWRIC) hearings to arranging for translation assistance for Issei.

A key ally to the movement from outside the ethnic community was Frank Chin, who had come to Seattle during the 1970s to research and write a story about redress. While there, he was impressed by the growing redress activism he witnessed, saying, "I thought Japanese America had recovered its conscience and was at last making a stand for Japanese American integrity and reclaiming its history."[69] Chin met with Henry Miyake, Shosuke Sasaki, and other SERC officers and brainstormed the idea of a homecoming at Puyallup fairgrounds, a former assembly center, to bring wider attention to the issue of redress. The event, called Day of Remembrance, was scheduled for November 25, 1978. Widely advertised and supported by JACL chapters, churches, students, and others, the Day of Remembrance was seen as a "major cultural shift in our community" with regard to the history of internment and Japanese Americans' willingness to use the media to bring attention to their cause.[70] The turnout was better than expected, with over two thousand people caravanning from Sick Stadium in Seattle to Puyallup. Among the attendees were writer Monica Sone, actor Pat Morita, and activist Gordon Hirabayashi. People were able to see arts and crafts that had been made in camp, watch odori performances, view a slide show on Minidoka, and take in a performance of the Japanese American play *Lady is Dying*. In the wake of the event's success, Day of Remembrance commemorations were planned in other cities.

Washington representative Mike Lowry, an ally of Japanese Americans and the redress cause, introduced a bill in November 1979, which was subsequently passed and signed by President Jimmy Carter on July 31, 1980. The bill established a commission on Wartime Relocation and Internment of Civilians to review the circumstances and facts around EO 9066 and its impact on Japanese immigrants and the U.S.-born, the U.S. military directives that led to relocation, and to recommend appropriate remedies. The commission went to work gathering testimony in nine cities for a total of twenty-one days of hearings, and in December

1982 it published its findings. The report offered detailed documentation of evacuation and concluded that, "the record does not permit the conclusion that military necessity warranted the exclusion of ethnic Japanese from the West Coast."[71] The committee later recommended that the federal government apologize for the grave injustice of internment and that those individuals who had been convicted of violating the curfew be pardoned. It also stated that Congress should direct executive agencies to which Japanese Americans could apply for restitution, establish an education and humanitarian foundation to address injustices, and appropriate $1.5 billion to pay each survivor $20,000. With the work of the committee completed, congressional redress bills were introduced. In June 1983, Mike Lowry presented the first of these, HR 3387, the World War II Civil Liberties Violation Redress Act. The bill that Congress did pass, HR 442, the Civil Liberties Act, was introduced by Tom Foley, another Democrat from Washington, in 1987. Although it was signed by President Ronald Reagan on August 10, 1988, payments were not made until 1991. Former internees, starting with the oldest, received $20,000 checks and an apology from the president.

The decades long struggle for redress transformed Japanese America. According to Robert Sadamu Shimabukuro, it "played an important role in unifying a community whose generations had been torn apart by World War II. It enabled Nikkei to talk not only to legislative bodies, the media, and the greater American community but, just as important to other Nikkei generations as well."[72] As SERC leader Henry Miyake characterized it:

> I dare say that Nihonjin [people of Japanese ancestry] came out of the closet. That's the result of redress, the Day of Remembrance, and all those events. I think these guys were able to come out of the closet and tell the stories to their kids, their grandchildren. The commission . . . was a lot of good, because of the exposure of information that created a wealth of ideas that were generated by these people. [They were able to say] 'Okay, I'm willing to speak about it,' but until then, they were reticent.[73]

Conclusion

In recalling the I-Hotel struggle, historian and activist Estella Habal noted that one of the challenges that anti-eviction protestors confronted was how to relate to and incorporate new immigrants from Asia. During the late 1960s and 1970s, a renewed influx of Filipino immigration was underway, and it was much larger than during previous periods. These newcomers were also different economically and politically from previous immigrants, representing a greater proportion of professionals and urban migrants than earlier waves had seen. Describing the new immigrants from the Philippines, Habel said, "Those from urban areas tended to be more influenced by American consumerist cultural values that had continued to proliferate in Philippine culture since the end of American colonization. Moreover, many of them had no knowledge of a previous Filipino community, nor did they look for one when they arrived in the United States."[74] Rather than coming to San Francisco's Manilatown, the new Filipinos settled in neighborhoods like SOMA and Bernal Heights or moved to the suburbs, to places like Daly City and Union City. The KDP tried to reach out to them by selling its bimonthly newspapers in these burgeoning Filipino neighborhoods, and did outreach with recent immigrants, through efforts such as supporting the defense of

Filipina nurses Narciso and Lenora Perez, who had been accused of murdering patients in Chicago.

These disjunctures and attempts to make connections between different cohorts of Filipinos in America represent a microcosm of what was occurring in Asian America at large. As the next chapter will show, the 1960s also marked a turning point of a demographic nature, of which Southeast Asian refugees, discussed in the previous chapter, were certainly a part. U.S. immigration reform and changes around the world would additionally set the stage for a dramatic new influx of Asian immigrants, transforming Asian America once again.

Notes

1   Karen Umemoto, "'On Strike!' San Francisco State College Strike, 1968–69: The Role of Asian American Students," *Contemporary Asian America: A Multidisciplinary Reader*, Min Zhou and James V. Gatewood, eds. (New York: New York University Press, 2000), 58.

2   Daryl J. Maeda, *Chains of Babylon: The Rise of Asian America* (Minneapolis: University of Minnesota Press, 2009), 81.

3   Ray Tasaki, "Wherever There is Oppression," Steve Louie and Glenn Omatsu, eds., *Asian Americans: The Movement and the Moment* (Los Angeles: UCLA Asian American Studies Center Press, 2001), 82.

4   Ibid., 82–3.

5   Ryan Masaaki Yokota, "Interview with Pat Sumi," Louie and Omatsu, *Asian Americans*, 18–9.

6   "Introduction—When We Wanted It Done, We Did It Ourselves," Louie and Omatsu, *Asian Americans*, xx.

7   Ibid., 77.

8   Warren Mar, "From Pool Halls to Building Workers' Organizations: Lessons for Today's Activists," Louie and Omatsu, *Asian Americans*, 40.

9   Ibid., 36.

10   Ibid., 39.

11   Bob Hsiang, "Growing Up in Turmoil: Thoughts on the Asian American Movement," Louie and Omatsu, *Asian Americans*, 112.

12   Quoted in Maeda, *Chains of Babylon*, 98.

13   Ibid., 99.

14   Yokota, "Interview with Pat Sumi", 19.

15   Ibid., 20.

16   Ibid., 21.

17   Maeda, *Chains of Babylon*, 98.

18   Louie, "When We Wanted It Done, We Did It Ourselves," xxii.

19   Yokota, "Interview With Pat Sumi," 25.

20   Ibid., 26.

21   Maeda, *Chains of Babylon*, 80.

22   Ibid., 3.

23   Yokota, "Interview with Pat Sumi," 24.

24   Carol Ojeda-Kimbrough, "Growing Up in Asian America as a Young Filipina American during the Anti-Martial Law and Student Movement in the United States," Louie and Omatsu, *Asian Americans*, 68.

25   Ibid., 71.

26   Umemoto, "On Strike!," 52.

27   Estella Habal, *San Francisco's International Hotel: Mobilizing the Filipino American Community in the Anti-eviction Movement* (Philadelphia: Temple University Press, 2007), 28.

28   Umemoto, "On Strike!," 52.

29   Maeda, *Chains of Babylon*, 79.

30 Grain of Sand, "We Are the Children," *A Grain of Sand: Music for the Struggle By Asians In America*, 1973, Paredon Records.

31 Hsiang, "Growing Up in Turmoil," 115.

32 Daryl J. Maeda, *Rethinking the Asian American Movement* (New York: Routledge, 2011), 96–104.

33 Merilynne Hamano Quon, "Individually We Contributed, Together We Made a Difference," Louie and Omatsu, *Asian Americans*, 212.

34 Daniel C. Tsang, "Slicing Silence: Asian Progressives Come Out," Louie and Omatsu, *Asian Americans*, 230.

35 Ibid., 223–24.

36 Ibid., 224.

37 Ibid., 227.

38 Ibid., 228.

39 Ibid., 234.

40 Umemoto, "On Strike!," 57.

41 Ibid., 56.

42 Ibid., 60.

43 Ibid.

44 They had previously served about 70%.

45 Umemoto, "On Strike!," 53.

46 Quoted in Umemoto, "On Strike!," 62.

47 Prior to the strike in the Spring, third world students and SDS members staged a sit-in at President Summerskill's office. This resulted in the granting of 412 slots for Third World students over the next two semesters, the creation of 10 faculty positions for TW professors with a student voice in hiring, rehiring of Juan Martinez in the history department. The SDS demand to expel ROTC from campus was denied. Ibid., 68.

48 Ibid., 63.

49 Ibid., 64.

50 Ibid., 55.

51 Ibid., 58.

52 Ibid., 62.

53 Ibid., 72.

54 Maeda, *Rethinking the Asian American Movement*, 44–51.

55 Umemoto, "On Strike!," 73.

56 Ibid., 74.

57 Corky Lee, "Untitled Photo Essay," Louie and Omatsu, *Asian Americans*, 130–31.

58 Habal, *San Francisco's International Hotel*, 36.

59 Beverly Kordziel, "To Be a Part of the People: The International Hotel Collective," Louie and Omatsu, *Asian Americans*, 244–45.

60 Harvey Dong, "Transforming Student Elites Into Community Activists: A Legacy of Asian American Activism," Louie and Omatsu, *Asian Americans*, 191.

61 Robert Sadamu Shimabukuro, *Born in Seattle: The Campaign for Japanese American Redress* (Seattle: University of Washington, 2001), 8.

62 Ibid., 25.

63 Ibid.

64 Ibid., 25–6.

65 Ibid., 29.

66 Quoted in Shimabukuro, *Born in Seattle*, 34.

67 Ibid., 35.

68 Quon, "Individually We Contributed, Together We Made a Difference," 216.

69 Shimabukuro, *Born in Seattle*, 41.

70 Ibid., 47.

71 Ibid., 73.

72 Ibid., 116.

73 Ibid., 116.

74 Habal, *San Francisco's International Hotel*, 121.

The Watershed of 1965 and the Remaking of Asian America

12

As discussed in Chapter 9, by the 1950s and early 1960s, a new orthodoxy of liberal multi-culturalism had come to characterize the national discussions about race relations, evidenced by celebratory rhetoric about immigration and assimilation as normative, even universal, aspects of the American experience. Rather than cast ethnic minorities as unwanted or inassimilable "others," new representations depicted them as vital participants in the American mosaic. In the world of Broadway musicals during the 1960s, for example, *West Side Story* showed Puerto Ricans claiming the American dream and a place in the U.S. melting pot, *Fiddler on the Roof* presented the saga of Jews fleeing the pogroms of Russia for new lives in the United States as a quintessentially American story, and *Flower Drum Song* domesticated the history of Chinese in America as a charming tale of generational conflict and cultural negotiation.

If these and other groups once deemed "foreigners" and "outsiders" were now part of the American fabric, and the United States was truly a nation of immigrants, then the national origins quota system established by the Johnson-Reed Act of 1924 seemed anomalous and out of sync with the times. Among its critics was the historian Oscar Handlin, who called it an "Unlovely residue of outworn prejudices."[1] To many Americans of southern and eastern European descent who had achieved a measure of visibility and influence in mainstream life, the national origins system was a reminder of an unpleasant era they wished to turn the page on.

Proponents of reform, moreover, argued that such a discriminatory policy undercut the United States' credibility in its crusade to defeat global Communism. As New York Congressman Emanuel Celler asked pointedly, "Is the way to destroy an iron curtain . . . to erect an iron curtain of our own?"[2] Finally, symbolism aside, the system simply was not working as it was designed to. Between the end of World War II through the early 1960s, the vast majority of new Chinese immigration was taking place outside of the quota system; from 1944 to 1960, 8,781 were quota admissions while 23,433 were nonquota.[3]

This chapter examines changes in U.S. immigration policy since 1965 and their impact on Asian America, reviewing demographic, social, and economic aspects of renewed Asian immigration in the late twentieth century. It comments on new challenges of adaptation that immigrants faced in a nation undergoing dramatic economic and political change and how they built their own lives and communities. Finally, the chapter explores how the post-1965 immigration gave new life to the model minority stereotype, which reemerged prominently in racial discourse and politics.

The Road to Reform

As criticism of the national origins system reached the highest levels of government and industry, legislative reform was not far behind. In 1958, then-U.S. Senator John F. Kennedy sarcastically remarked about Emma Lazarus' poem on the Statue of Liberty pedestal that anyone was welcome to enter the United States "as long as they come from Northern Europe, are not too tired or poor or slightly ill, never stole a loaf of bread, never joined any questionable organization, and can document their activities for the past two years."[4] The existing system was not just anomalous within the politics of multiculturalism, but it also made for bad diplomacy and economics. As the Japanese American representative from Hawaii Spark Matsunaga said in 1964, the discriminatory system was being used as Communist propaganda and "creat[ed] a suspicion among our Asian friends about the motives of the United States."[5] The Cold War and the "space race" had also exposed a domestic shortage of workers with technical expertise. In July 1963, President Kennedy urged Congress to overhaul the immigration system, and shortly thereafter, Emanuel Celler introduced a bill to the House, which he emphasized would attract "highly skilled aliens whose services were urgently needed."[6]

Kennedy would not live to see the passage of the immigration reform bill, which occurred under his successor, Lyndon Johnson. In a ceremony rich with symbolism, Johnson signed the Hart-Celler Act in front of the Statue of Liberty on October 3, 1965. He declared on the occasion that the legislation would "repair a very deep and painful flaw in the fabric of the American Nation." Formally taking effect on July 1, 1968, the Hart-Celler Act of 1965 set the overall immigration ceiling to 290,000 per year, with a cap of 170,000 for the Eastern Hemisphere and 120,000 for the Western Hemisphere. Previously, there had been no numerical limit on Western Hemisphere immigration. Eastern Hemisphere nations were given up to 20,000 annual visa slots, which would be distributed according to a preference system, with most categories favoring "family reunification." The idea behind family reunification was that immigrants who had been in the U.S. for a long time and separated from family members could reunite with them. Employment preferences were also included in the new system and were meant to ensure that any non-family based immigrants would add to the wealth and power of the United States.

The sentiment for reforming the immigration system by and large focused on eliminating its discriminatory characteristics, and not substantially changing the volume of immigration. As Oscar Handlin insisted before the Hart-Celler Act's passage, "The change [sought] in our immigration law will have only minor quantitative significance: Revision is important as a matter of principle."[7] President Johnson was also quick to emphasize that it was "not a revolutionary bill."[8] Although the immediate postwar years were an era of economic expansion accompanied by shortages of unskilled and skilled labor, Americans were nonetheless anxious about sustaining growth and avoiding another Great Depression. Toward these ends, they maintained that immigration ceilings would remain necessary.

The ensuing two decades revealed how off the mark Johnson, Handlin, and others were in their projections of future immigration. In the 1950s, average annual immigration was about 250,000, and by the end of the 1990s, it was about one million. Also by this time, the foreign-born made up 10 percent of the population. Equally dramatic were shifts in the sources of immigrants. In the 1950s, Europe provided 70 percent of immigrants, and forty years later just 16 percent. At the end of the 1980s, Mexico, the Philippines, and Vietnam were the top sending countries and no European countries were in the top ten. In 2000 Latin America accounted for about 50 percent of new immigrants and Asia 32 percent. Latinos, who at this time made up about 12 percent of the U.S. population, had surpassed African Americans as the nation's largest minority group.

Although many modifications have been made since 1965, the Hart-Celler Act provides the basic structure and principles of our current immigration system. Recent changes have included merging the separate hemispheric annual ceilings, altering the labor certification process to require applicants under the third and sixth preferences to have job offers in the U.S. before being given visas, and tightening the sibling sponsorship preference by requiring sponsors be at least twenty-one years old.[9] Additionally, the preferences for applicants with skills and in occupations that were in short supply in the United States changed as the occupational landscape shifted. For instance, health professionals, once a heavily favored group, were eventually removed as a category with domestic labor shortages.[10]

The Immigration Act of 1990 implemented significant changes, largely in response to economic needs, but again without altering the basic system. It raised the overall ceiling for legal immigration and increased employment based immigration, while also regulating it more tightly, but maintained family reunification as the main avenue of admission.[11] The Act also created a new category for investor immigrants that favored people who brought with them large amounts of capital.[12] Another important change it brought was altering how visa quotas were calculated, although they have stayed at around twenty thousand per country.

Although it was guided by the principle of equality, the new system created its own set of problems. Assigning each country the same quota, while reasonable in principle, quickly led to enormous backlogs for large nations like China and countries with historically close relationships with the United States, such as Mexico, South Korea, and the Philippines. On the other hand, small countries with little emigration never came close to filling their visa quotas. This problem gave rise to increased illegal immigration by people from oversubscribed countries, through methods such as overstaying visas, crossing borders clandestinely, and entering fraudulent marriages with U.S. citizens.

Remaking Asian America

The effects of the Hart-Celler Act of 1965 and subsequent modifications to the immigration system on Asian America were direct and profound. For one, they have transformed Asian America, as late as 2012, into a predominantly foreign-born population.[13] Between 1966 and 2009, about 9.5 million Asians immigrated to the United States, with the largest numbers coming from China, the Philippines, and India. In 1960, persons of Asian ancestry in the United States numbered less than one million, and forty years later this grew to 10.9 million, more than doubling every ten years. This dramatic rise emanated in large part from a multiplier effect of the preference system, an unanticipated result of the federal immigration law reform. By the late 1970s, it was evident that recent immigrants were utilizing the family preference categories to bring in large numbers of relatives and, ultimately, family sponsored immigrants took up the majority of allotted visas, not just from Asian countries, but overall as well. Additionally, a large number of people immigrated via non-quota categories. Once residents became citizens, they could sponsor relatives (spouses, children under twenty-one, and parents) without regard to visa limits. Although legislators had not anticipated that each admitted quota immigrant could open a path for non-quota immigration and additional family migration, the practice was perfectly legal within the system and ended up driving much of the growth of the Asian American population after 1965.

Socioeconomically, the post-1965 Asian immigrants were quite different from their pre-1965 predecessors. As described in earlier chapters, the newcomers of the nineteenth and early twentieth centuries were predominately men who arrived alone and did not plan to stay permanently. In the more recent waves, however, immigration has consisted largely of intact families coming with the intention of permanent settlement. About a third of the post-1965 immigrants, moreover, were professionals, a large share compared to those who arrived earlier. Educated and skilled immigrants, however, were concentrated in the first decade or so after reform, and from the mid-1970s on, due to family sponsorships—including the arrivals of so-called "poor cousins"—Asian immigration has become, on the whole, more socioeconomically diverse.[14]

To briefly discuss aspects of the post-1965 waves from the main Asian sending countries (except Southeast Asians who were discussed in Chapter 10), immigration from the Philippines, South Asia, South Korea, and China far eclipsed the flows of earlier decades, and among the major sending nations pre-Hart-Celler, only Japan has dropped off in its volume of emigration. With regard to the Philippines, economic woes and political instability in the country as well as labor demands in America drove large numbers of emigrants to the United States. Additionally, the Philippines in its post-independence period saw much political precariousness, including the imposition of martial law in 1972 by President Ferdinand Marcos, his ouster from government in 1986, and intense rivalries among succeeding governments. More crushing to the population was the country's poverty. Still a developing nation, the Philippines was weighed down by debt, dependency on exports, massive unemployment, and huge disparities of wealth. Many, thus, sought to work abroad in order to solve their unemployment or underemployment and would send a portion of their earnings to family still in the Philippines, money that has been crucial for the Philippine economy. By the 1990s, in the Middle East alone, about one million were employed as contract workers, and large numbers have also gone to Japan, Singapore, Hong Kong, and Europe. The jobs themselves were diverse, from entertainers to maids.

The United States was an appealing option because of its relatively high salaries (ten to twenty times higher than what they could earn at home) and because decades of U.S. influence had left Filipinos familiar with aspects of the country's culture. The Philippine government and education system were modeled after the United States' and most educated Filipinos spoke English. Furthermore, U.S. military installations, marriages between U.S. personnel and locals, and employment in American firms in the Philippines gave many would-be emigrants exposure that facilitated their adjustment in the United States. While in earlier periods, Filipino immigrant workers filled labor needs in unskilled positions, since

1965 they increasingly filled niches in skilled occupations. For example, the shortage of medical professionals following the establishment of Medicare in 1965 helped sustain the migration of Filipina nurses, of whom about fifty thousand were working in the United States by the 1990s.[15]

The circumstances that compelled emigration from South Korea were similar to and different from those affecting the Philippines. On the one hand, South Korea's economy expanded continuously after World War II until the 1990s, but there was, nonetheless, a growing sense among many that the country was backward and undemocratic.[16] Like the Philippines, South Korea—although never a U.S. colony—had been politically, militarily, and economically dependent on the United States, which gave would-be emigrants a level of familiarity with America and influenced their decision to come. As late as 1991, the United States had forty thousand troops in South Korea, and had also given the country billions of dollars in aid. As in earlier decades, a high proportion of post-1965 immigrants were Christian, and the widespread association of the United States with Christianity made it an appealing destination.[17] In terms of specific push factors, some sought to escape the military dictatorship of president Park Chung Hee (1961 to 1979), who instituted during his rule measures such as curfews, a strong police and military presence, the imprisonment of dissidents, the suppression of citizen unrest, and censorship in literary, intellectual, musical, and artistic life. With regard to economic conditions, while the nation, as mentioned above, was relatively healthy until the 1990s, it had its share of problems, including dependency on imports, a disorganized labor force, and high population density. Further, the country's astounding GNP growth and shift from an agriculturally based to industrial economy over the 1970s and 1980s occurred at the expense of working-class Koreans and exacerbated income inequalities. To alleviate these problems, the South Korean government had, since the early 1960s, promoted emigration by offering training programs to give potential emigrants skills in construction, equipment repair, hairdressing, and other fields that would make them employable outside the country.

Despite these problems, Korean emigrants were generally not drawn from the ranks of the impoverished, as these people typically would have not qualified for entry to the U.S. or possessed the resources to migrate. Instead, occupational preference programs, opportunities for students to adjust their status, and the advantages of having capital gave advantages to individuals from the higher socioeconomic echelons, and these were indeed overrepresented among new arrivals. Korean immigrants were generally people who wished to improve their class positions and material lives rather than escape dire poverty. With the growing importance of education for maintaining one's class position amidst an atmosphere of hyper-competitiveness, many parents decided that going to the United States offered the best prospects for their children's future. As one Korean woman in Los Angeles explained, "Educating my children in Korea was like a star in heaven, but here there was a chance."[16] Another immigrant living in Los Angeles reflected on the economic motivations involved in leaving Korea for the United States, saying, "The problem with Korea is that once you are stuck at the bottom there is nowhere to go . . . Our only path is to go to a regional city and then to Seoul, where discrimination pushes out of the country . . . We don't need to live in a place like that, so we come here, to a place of freedom."[19]

Chinese immigration also increased since 1965, expanding tenfold by 2000 and doubling each decade from 1970 to the end of the twentieth century.[20] These immigrants were very diverse, and included the most elite Taiwanese professionals as well as impoverished and uneducated refugees. The high volume of Chinese immigration was facilitated in part by the fact that the United States assigned separate quotas to Taiwan, Hong Kong, and the People's Republic of China (PRC). Hong Kong's quota, originally two hundred, was raised to five thousand in 1987 and then twenty thousand, making China's annual visa quota sixty thousand.[21] Adding further to the Chinese immigrant population were people who entered through non-quota categories as well as ethnic Chinese from other parts of the world, mainly Southeast Asia and Latin America.

International politics played a salient role in shaping Chinese immigration in the second half of the twentieth century. After the establishment of the PRC in 1949, the Nationalist government relocated to Taiwan (ROC), and from there until the late 1970s, nearly half of all Chinese immigrants to the United States came from Taiwan. After 1979, when the United States and the PRC established diplomatic relations, immigration from the mainland increased, although it was still exceeded by the ROC. Another political factor influencing immigration was the Tiananmen Square protests of 1989, after which President George Bush instructed the attorney general and secretary of state to provide protection to students fleeing the PRC in the aftermath of the Chinese government's suppression of the protesters.[22] Additionally, the Chinese Student Protection Act of 1992 gave all PRC citizens who were in the United States between June 1989 and April 1990 permission to apply for permanent residency. In the wake of the law's passage, some fifty thousand Chinese became permanent residents.

Immigration from South Asia has also grown dramatically. India and Pakistan are the largest sending countries in the region, but Bangladeshis have grown more numerous since the 1990s. Pakistani migration picked up after the Gulf War of 1991, as people sought refuge from the instability caused by that conflict by fleeing to places such as the United States and Europe. With regard to Indian immigration, from 1965 to the 1990s about 360,000 quota and 70,000 non-quota immigrants came to the United States.[23] Some of the new migration was a consequence of political developments, such as the Green Revolution in Punjab in the 1970s, which led many displaced families to seek refuge in places like California where they found work on farms. As with other Asian groups, in the initial years after U.S. immigration reform, Indian immigrants by and large skewed toward the elite, reflected in the high proportion of technical and employment based immigration. Between 1966 and 1977, 83 percent of those entering came under the occupational category of professional and technical workers. This included about twenty thousand scientists with Ph.D.s, forty thousand engineers, and twenty-five thousand doctors.[24] Such an impressive educational profile was in part a result of the promotion of the sciences by Indian Prime Minister Jawaharlal Nehru starting in the late 1940s as a way to uplift the country. Since the 1980s professional and technical immigration has declined while family based migration has increased, signaling a shift toward a more working class immigrant population. This has included a large number of sojourner men seeking work as taxi drivers and other low-paying occupations.

As mentioned, Japan is the only Asian country with close ties to the United States that has not sent large numbers of new emigrants since 1965. The relatively low rate of migration can be explained by Japan's industrialization and ability to provide its population with an adequate standard of living. As a result, the push factors were not as compelling as they were elsewhere in Asia. This is not to say Japanese immigration has come to an end, as about forty-six thousand quota and sixty-four thousand non-quota immigrants have entered from the 1960s to early 1990s.[25] These immigrants, however, were much different from those of the pre-1965 era, as they tended to be executives or employers with ties to multinational corporations.

Illegal Immigration

Immigration reform from 1965 on gave rise to a transformed and greatly enlarged Asian American population, but it did not open the door to all who sought entry. As a result, illegal Asian immigration has continued, although in recent decades it has received far less national attention than illegal immigration from Latin America. Despite a lack of extensive information about this population, undocumented immigrants are an integral part of Asian America, making up, for instance, a large share of workers in the lower tiers of the economy, in jobs such as garment workers, construction laborers, and domestic care providers.

Although they are found among all Asian groups, Chinese have been singled out as the largest Asian "illegal immigrant" problem. In 1990, the U.S. Census estimated there were 70,000 undocumented residents from China and 10 years later it was 115,000, although other estimates have been much larger.[26] These include visa overstayers as well as individuals who were smuggled or trafficked, and encompass people from the PRC, Taiwan, and Hong Kong. The issue of Chinese illegal immigration came to wide attention in the 1980s and early 1990s following several high profile smuggling discoveries. These operations resembled those from the era of Chinese exclusion, in which people in different nations collaborated to sneak in Chinese, most from Fujian Province, to the United States. Smugglers, or professional "snakeheads," who charged between $20,000 to $80,000 per head, took individuals from Hong Kong or Taiwan to Bolivia or Panama, and then to Mexico where the Chinese seeking entry would be led across the border, either in automobiles or on foot. A safer but more expensive method that some people employed was using fraudulently obtained documents to enter the United States, which would enable them to live as though they were legal immigrants and, thus, not have to remain in the shadows.[27] From the 1990s, an increasingly common avenue pursued by Chinese ineligible to enter through the regular system was to request political asylum. Many did so on the claim that they were victims of the country's one-child policy.

Toward the end of the twentieth century as concerns about national security became entwined with fears of illegal immigrants, abuses of the asylum system and other channels of entry have come under greater scrutiny, having effects on Chinese and other Asians. Government authorities, for instance, beefed up efforts to track down and deport visa violators after the 1993 World Trade Center bombing and the attacks of September 11, 2001, which has led to increased apprehensions of Chinese and other Asians.

As they had been during earlier periods, undocumented immigrants are a particularly vulnerable segment of Asian America. Not only do they face the constant risk of discovery and deportation, but they are also frequently exploited by co-ethnics. For instance, many undocumented immigrants turned to co-ethnic loan sharks for help entering the country, and remained indebted years after coming. Furthermore, because they could not legally work, often their only employment options were to work for co-ethnics in low-paying jobs and poor working conditions. To provide an illustration, a "Mrs. Lee," a middle-aged Chinese undocumented immigrant, worked with her three daughters and a son at a Chinese-owned garment factory in Brooklyn, New York. Between the four of them, the family income was about $100 per week.[28] In addition to the low wages, she was subject to various kinds of mistreatment at work, including the withholding of her wages. Because of her status, she had no legal protection or recourse.

Asian Americans and the New Economy

Garment factories may have employed large numbers of working class Chinese and other Asian immigrants—documented and undocumented—in recent years but, after the 1960s, manufacturing jobs were generally less abundant than they had been during earlier periods of Asian migration. Indeed, by the 1970s, the U.S. economy had been transformed profoundly by the forces of deindustrialization and the effects of capital flight and plant closings in traditional production centers. Furthermore, global competition sent many U.S. industries looking for ways to lower their operating costs or relocate overseas where labor was cheaper. While manufacturing overall declined, particularly in traditional heavy industries, it grew in high-tech industries (computers and biochemical products, for instance) and maintained production in certain low technology ones (like garment manufacturing).[29]

These and other structural changes have shaped the economic lives of Asian immigrants. Conditions have been particularly exploitative for the working class, a group to which many were permanently relegated due to language and other barriers. The difficulty of mobility was further compounded in recent decades, in both high and low-tech industries, by the decline of unions and accompanying lack of wage growth. This characterized the lot of many Korean immigrants during the 1970s, for instance, who were only able to find low paying jobs, often for co-ethnic employers. In garment factories, they labored in poor conditions, were paid by the piece, and received no paid vacations or benefits. Such poor conditions would lead many into entrepreneurship and running small business.[30] Working class Chinese immigrants also relied greatly on ethnic networks and employers for their livelihood. Between 1969 and 1982 about twenty thousand Chinese women in New York were employed in the garment industry, the majority in Chinese-owned factories.[31] They also turned to co-ethnics for help in other areas. Poorer newly arrived immigrants, for instance, often stayed in "family motels," or Chinese-owned temporary shelters in residences or apartments, and also depended on co-ethnic employment service firms, which grew considerably since the 1970s to accommodate the growing number of new immigrants.[32]

As a group, Asians participated in entrepreneurship at higher rates than the general U.S. population. This applied in particular to Vietnamese, Chinese, and Koreans but also significantly to South Asians and Filipinos.[33] Immigrants could engage in entrepreneurial activities because many had brought capital with them, although the amounts varied greatly, from modest savings to millions of dollars.

Entrepreneurship, furthermore, was an appealing option when limited abilities in English or non-transferable skills or education proved too high a barrier for obtaining good jobs with employers. For example, in 1973, only a third of Korean-trained nurses in Los Angeles held state licenses and about six hundred Korean physicians in Southern California could not practice medicine.[34] Additionally in the 1970s, there was little demand for Korean-speaking employees in law firms or corporations.[35] While many of these and other immigrants opened grocery stores, laundries, and other small shops in predominantly black and Hispanic neighborhoods in cities like Los Angeles and New York because these were areas increasingly neglected by the mainstream economy, they also launched businesses mainly serving co-ethnics that became the foundation of new Koreatown enclaves. According to a 1989 survey of Los Angeles, nearly 40 percent of employed Korean American men owned their own business.

Indeed, the figure of the Korean small shop owner captured the national media's attention by the 1980s, initially as fodder to extol the "American Dream" of rising by one's bootstraps. As *Time* stated in 1985, "Like previous generations of immigrants many Asians seek to realize their personal American dream not just by finding a good job but by starting their own business."[34] It furthermore singled out Koreans, saying the "entrepreneurial impulse runs strongest among" this group. For their part, many Korean immigrants were happy to trumpet their success. Peter Kim, a bakery owner in Gardena said: "Most Koreans would rather be self-employed than work for someone else. They're hardworking people."[37] Such stories, when they trickled back to Korea, encouraged others to follow in these footsteps. According to a 1986 survey of pre-departure Korean immigrants, over 70 percent of men said they expected to go into business, while just a fourth of them ran small businesses in Korea.[38]

Media accounts depicting Korean business owners as modern-day Horatio Algers, while inspiring, tended to paper over the harsh realities they lived. In reality, many were petty merchants with modest businesses who worked long hours seven days per week. For the large numbers who held college degrees and had professional backgrounds, running a small business represented a significant step down. "Yun" came to the United States in the late 1970s intending to pursue graduate studies in mathematics, but abandoned his plans because he needed to support his wife and child. He subsequently joined relatives in running a small store that sold trinkets, and even though he lived in an upscale suburb in Los Angeles, he considered himself a failure. "It is very embarrassing," he said.[37] Commenting on her father's disappointing fortunes in America, the daughter of an immigrant who had attended the prestigious Seoul National University only to run a dry cleaner in Los Angeles said, "I was shocked when I visited Seoul one summer to realize what it meant to be a Seoul National University graduate. Because so many of my father's friends went there I thought it didn't mean much, although my parents had always been so proud of my father's alma mater. Now I feel that I understand my father's frustration and sacrifice better."[39]

Another important development among Asian Americans since 1965 was the dramatic rise of professionals employed in the mainstream economy, a phenomenon tied to economic transformation and globalization. As mentioned, large numbers of Filipina nurses filled some of the demand for medical professionals. Additionally, the migration of Indian doctors to the United States as well as Great Britain began rising in the 1960s. Among Indians and other Asian groups, the professional migration has generally been spearheaded by health workers, but they were joined by other kinds of professionals in later years. This flow of people has also been called a "brain drain" of the most educated and talented people from their countries of origin.

In the United States, the restructuring of capitalism in the second half of the twentieth century saw, in addition to the decline of heavy manufacturing, the rise of the informational age, which has entailed product to process-oriented production and the flexibility of labor and capital. With the growth of high technology jobs in Silicon Valley and elsewhere, Asian immigrants helped fill labor demands for everything from engineers to assembly line workers. The proliferation of this industry from the 1980s on was an especially important force behind the rapid growth of the middle and upper class South Asian American population, mostly Gujarati Hindus and South Pakistani Muslims.[41] A large number of these were software engineers considered the "cream of India" and educated at the best Indian universities. The United States was the most favored destination for information technology (IT) workers due to its advanced infrastructure and favorable immigration policies for professionals. However, the development of a large IT sector in India prompted some return migration as well.[42]

The economic activities of the post-1965 Asian immigrants brought significant consequences into the areas in which they settled. Due to rising patterns of residential sub-urbanization and urban redevelopment, many of the self-sufficient Asian ethnic economies of the pre-World War II years disappeared, relocated, or became more geographically dispersed. In some cases, however, the old urban enclaves were revitalized as a result of new immigration. Old Chinatowns in cities like New York and San Francisco, for instance, were given a new lease on life by the arrival of post-1965 Chinese immigrants with capital who invested in Chinatown businesses such as sewing factories and helped to boost the local economies while providing employment to their co-ethnic counterparts. The development of a particular sector then gave rise to a proliferation of services—newspapers, legal services, real estate offices, dentists, etc.—which further fueled the revival of Chinatowns.

Other, especially newer urban ethnic enclaves, such as Los Angeles' Koreatown, fared much differently. Located near South Central Los Angeles, Koreatown emerged in the mid-1970s at a time when the area was reeling from deindustrialization and white flight. It nonetheless developed into a vital economic and cultural center for Korean immigrants in Southern California, benefiting from immigrant economic activity as well as infusions of South Korean capital. As far as the layout and social landscape, it developed much differently from dense, compact Chinatowns in places like San Francisco. Koreatown's population is multiethnic—in 1990 its population was 68 percent Latino—and the area also had a large number of businesses run by other Asians and Latinos.[43] Another way in which Koreatown differed from older urban ethnic enclaves, and this was generally true of recently established ethnic neighborhoods, is that it was spread out and lacked a distinguishable center. This has tended to make Koreatown seemingly invisible and illegible to surrounding residents. A *Time* magazine article from 1983 noted that a stockbroker from nearby Westwood did not even know that Koreatown existed, even though there were 150,000 Koreans living there.[44]

A separate but related phenomenon associated with post-1965 immigration and the arrival of investor immigrants was the influx of Asian capital into American cities. As mentioned, this was pivotal for the growth of new ethnic enclaves, but it was also channeled elsewhere. In San Francisco, for example, residents, entrepreneurs, and immigrant investors initially began purchasing business spaces outside of Chinatown, in places such as China Basin, due to the prohibitive cost of property in the former. After these kinds of investments showed positive returns, foreign capital started to pour in from East Asian countries that had experienced rapid growth in the 1950s and 1960s.[45] This Asian capital reconfigured Asian American communities by enabling their growth and enhancing residents' transnational orientations. It has also made its mark on the larger American landscape. Chinese investors, for instance, bought up hotels in Los Angeles such as the Universal Hilton, Beverly Wilshire, and Airport Hilton, and Taiwanese investors built a large commercial complex, the Evertrust Plaza, in New Jersey. Taiwanese investment in the United States in 1989 alone was about $1 billion.[46] Ironically, such urban investments by Asian investors have contributed to the problem of unaffordable housing for many longtime and working class Asian Americans.

The Suburbanization of Asian America and New Subcultures

Perhaps more striking than the revitalization of established Asian urban enclaves was the emergence of new ethnic economies where few Asians had lived or worked before, namely in the suburbs. Changes with regard to Chinese restaurants shed some light on this recent spatial shift. Indeed, Chinese restaurants were among the most visible and enduring symbols of Chinese American entrepreneurialism. Historically, these businesses served primarily co-ethnic customers but, from the 1960s on, found that they had to reach out to a broader and more diverse clientele in order to survive. Additionally, cultural and demographic changes led restaurants to start incorporating take-out, adding new dishes, including vegetarian options, and offering more than one regional cuisine.[47] These and other changes were also a function of Chinese restaurants' geographic expansion away from their traditional locations, particularly into the suburbs, where during the 1970s a greater number of upscale establishments emerged to meet residents' expectations for more high-end dining.

The movement and appearance of Asian businesses to the suburbs has both reflected and contributed to a wider geographic dispersion of Asian American communities and the "suburbanization" of Asian America. As shown in Chapter 9, this process was underway before 1965, but it would accelerate with the arrival of new immigrants. Some found it necessary to look to the suburbs, as existing urban ethnic enclaves were wiped out or squeezed due to urban renewal programs, impacting both residential and employment prospects. Thus, by the 1980s the shift toward the suburbs was being driven by jobs and affordability as well as the appeal of suburban living, and this gave rise to Asian American communities in which the working class—who might have relocated for jobs in hotels, restaurants, or domestic work—mingled with members of the middle and upper middle classes, and where long-time Asian Americans lived alongside very recent immigrants. Among Chinese, suburban enclaves began appearing as early as the 1950s, in inner-ring suburban neighborhoods like the Richmond in San Francisco and Flushing, Queens in New York. Nationwide, a smaller and smaller percentage of Chinese live in city centers—in 2000, for example, just 2 percent of Chinese in the Los Angeles metropolitan area lived in Old Chinatown—although they have by and large remained in major metropolitan areas.[48]

Even further outlying destinations at the edges of metropolitan areas—called ex-burbs—also became vital centers of growing Asian American communities. To take the example of Monterey Park, California, nicknamed the "first suburban Chinatown," this community's growth was driven by the arrival of people from Taiwan, Hong Kong, and the PRC. In 1980 Monterey Park became a "majority minority" city where Asians made up 35 percent of the population and, ten years later, they represented 56 percent.

Meanwhile, whites made up about a quarter of the population.[49] Similar transformations were occurring elsewhere, such as the San Gabriel Valley and Orange County, South Bay communities in Northern California, Queens and other New York boroughs, Houston, Texas and Orlando, Florida, as well as locations outside the United States such as Sydney, Australia and Vancouver, Canada. The Chinese community in Monterey Park grew out of the efforts of Frederic Hsieh, a realtor who had come from Hong Kong to the United States in 1963 to attend college. He arrived in the area in the early 1970s and envisioned the community becoming a "modern day mecca" for the "new Chinese" looking to relocate to the United States due to political uncertainty and desire to invest their money somewhere.[50] Hsieh understood that Los Angeles' Chinatown would not be attractive to affluent, educated, and skilled newcomers, so for several years he bought property in Monterey Park and promoted the area as the "Chinese Beverly Hills." Others soon followed suit, initially young engineers and other professionals, but by the mid-1970s, this shifted increasingly to Taiwan and Hong Kong businessmen. The arrival of immigrants was supplemented by infusions of Asian capital, as large numbers of Chinese-owned banks appeared over the 1980s. This money invigorated the business area of Monterey Park. Wesley Ru, a Monterey Park businessman, explained the transformation, "First it was the real estate people, and then trading companies, heavy investors, people that come with hundreds of thousands of dollars in cash."[51] Immigration and home purchases in the best neighborhoods drove up property values, which in turn triggered new development. Middle-aged white resident Howard Fry recalled a story he heard, saying, "He talked about an elderly Chinese gentleman riding his bicycle down the street with a satchel slung on one of the handlebars and if he saw anybody in the front yard, he would approach them and ask: 'Would you like to sell your house? I've got the money.'"[52]

Another prominent suburb identified with a particular Asian group that emerged in recent decades is Daly City, located just south of San Francisco, which has come to be known as the "Pinoy capital" of the United States and, according to Benito Vergara, is to many residents "indistinguishable from life 'back home.'"[53] Like Monterey Park, Daly City did not have a longstanding Asian presence and is very much a post-1965 phenomenon, but its make up differs significantly as its growth has not been accompanied by the appearance of wealth on the same scale. This community emerged after 1970, when Daly City was about 86 percent white. By 2008, Filipinos represented about 32 percent—or 32,720—of a population that was now majority Asian and foreign born. According to Vergara, proximity to San Francisco was a major factor leading to settlement in Daly City. It was an especially appealing option for upwardly mobile immigrants wishing to be homeowners. After the first few Filipinos settled, family sponsorship-based chain migration fueled the rapid growth of Daly City's Filipino population, and it soon became a site of first settlement for large numbers of subsequent newcomers. Like many other new Asian suburban enclaves, the Filipino American community in Daly City lacks a clear center and to many people is barely recognizable as a distinct enclave. However, Filipinos can be found congregating in the area's nondescript shopping centers and at events such as Filipino Cultural Nights. Additionally, evidence of their business presence can be found in Goldilocks restaurants and other establishments.[54]

South Asians have also participated in the suburbanization of Asian America. In the San Francisco Bay Area, large numbers of middle class and upwardly mobile immigrants were

Figures 12.1 and 12.2 Two images of Asian American enclaves in California, 2013. The first is a shopping mall, Cupertino Village in suburban Cupertino, California, which caters to a predominantly Chinese American clientele. The second photo is of a major intersection in Los Angeles' Koreatown. Such enclaves have emerged and grown dramatically with the rise in new Asian immigration since 1965. (Photograph of Cupertino Village by Shelley Lee. Photograph of Koreatown by Anthony Kim.)

especially drawn to suburbs of Silicon Valley in northern California, which soon became home to the largest South Asian population. This population, furthermore, was very diverse, including Punjabi Sikhs, Pakistani Muslims, Gujarati Hindus, Indo-Fijian Hindus and Muslims, Bangladeshi Hindus, Sri Lankans, and Nepalese.[55] South Asians were especially prominent in the community of Fremont, whose Asian population was nearly 40 percent in 2000. During the early 1990s, upper middle class South Asian families, many of whom were employed in the high technology industry, increasingly appeared in the new gated communities of this rapidly growing area.[56] For the South Asian residents, as well as other Asians moving there, living in large houses in the suburbs represented achieving the American dream and something that would have been unthinkable in their home countries.

The arrival of these relatively privileged immigrants also resulted in family and social formations that had not existed before. Transnational Asian families, for instance, took on a new character reflecting the resources and flexibility of immigrants and their varied interests in America. Many Asian investors, for instance, hoped to both make money in the United States and root their families there. A common means toward these goals was to come to America and establish a business and then bring family members and apply for permanent residence. If children were born in the United States, this gave the parents an automatic foothold. It was not uncommon in such families for businessmen husbands to settle their wives and children in the United States—in a community like Monterey Park— while they commuted back and forth across the Pacific. In some families, both parents stayed in Asia while the children were set up as students in the United States, and once the children obtained permanent residency, they sponsored their families.[57] The latter is known as the "parachute children" phenomenon, a term that describes students—disproportionately Chinese—who have come to the United States to attend school and live on their own, often admitted on F-1 student visas as teenagers or pre-teenagers.[58]

The concentration of Asians in suburban communities also gave rise to middle class Americanized ethnic youth subcultures among the 1.5 and second generations. In many cases, the lives of the children of post-1965 immigrants were framed by the fact that they were objects of their parents' deferred gratification. Among many Korean shopkeepers, for instance, as difficult and arduous as their own lives were, they held out hope that their children would do better. In turn, many of the children did not want to be shopkeepers and were driven to achieve prestigious and high-paying careers.[59] Children of upwardly mobile South Asian professionals in Silicon Valley attended the best schools in Bay Area and often went on to the most selective colleges where they studied for high tech, health, and other professional careers.

In areas with large concentrations of Asian immigrants, the children comprised a discrete cohort group whose lives and identities differed greatly from their parents'. In the 1980s and 1990s, for instance, a generation of South Asian teenagers and young adults had come to embrace "desi" identity. Desi is a Hindi term for "countryman" and slang for South Asians living outside the Indian subcontinent. It is an inclusive category that encompasses nation, religion, caste, ethnicity, language, and is also generationally specific, referring chiefly to young South Asians. According to Shalini Shankar, the term "signals a defining moment in the South Asian diaspora, during which a population that has steadily grown is emerging as a strong public presence."[60] The term's emergence also signaled a shift from South Asians as "immigrants longing to return to a homeland to public consumers and producers of distinctive, wildly circulating cultural and linguistic forms."[61] The subculture that they forged often revolved around school and social activities such as bhangra dance troupes.[62] In New York, the desi scene during the 1980s and 1990s consisted of parties, music mixes, and a transnational South Asian public culture.[63] While these were children who benefited from their parents' privilege vis-à-vis the immigration preference system, some came to be critical of their parents' emphasis on upward social mobility and found solace among like-minded peers.

The Place of Asians in America

The revival of Asian immigration to the United States did not just increase the size and diversity of Asian America; it also transformed the national landscape of American race relations. Asian Americans have achieved unprecedented levels of cultural visibility, socioeconomic mobility, and political power since the 1960s. As discussed in Chapter 9, Asian Americans began making notable strides in elected office from the local to national levels during the 1950s and early 1960s, and this continued into the 1970s and 1980s. In particular, on the mainland, where Asian Americans were not as numerous as they were in Hawaii, and, thus, could only form powerful voting blocs in select locations, achievements in electoral politics surfaced later. In 1974, Japanese American Norman Mineta won a seat in the U.S. House of Representatives and four years later he would be joined by fellow Californian and Japanese American Robert Matsui. Also in 1974, Chinese American March Fong Yu was elected secretary of the state of California. Although the number of elected Asian American officials remains very low overall, their presence has made a difference at crucial junctures on key issues, for instance with regard to the Japanese redress campaign.

Achievements aside, the educational and professional achievements of many post-1965 immigrants and their children tended to reinforce and magnify the model minority stereotype and gloss over Asian America's diversity. As Sucheng Chan has shown, various data, both anecdotal and statistical, were used to shore up the stereotype of the high-achieving, high income-earning Asian. For instance, according to the U.S. Census of 1970, Japanese and Chinese Americans outpaced whites in median family income.[64] Additionally, other research showed that in 1970 Chinese and Japanese American men had significantly more schooling than non-Hispanic whites. There are many problems with the use of such data to generalize about Asian American achievement. For one, the income information from the Census did not account for families in which more than one person worked. Further, "Hispanic" groups were lumped with whites, which likely brought down their income figure. Other studies, moreover, revealed that higher educational attainment had not directly resulted in higher median incomes for Asian Americans, and other data suggested that "returns to education" enjoyed by Asians were lower than for whites.[65] Also relevant was that most Asian Americans lived in metropolitan areas, where incomes tend to be higher. Asian Americans' relatively low unemployment rate disguised the common problem of underemployment. Further, while professional attainment is certainly notable, Asian American professionals tended to cluster in certain occupations (accounting, dentistry, nursing, health, engineering) while being underrepresented in fields such as law, teaching, administration, and social services.

Finally, there were wide differences across groups that lumping Asian ethnicities concealed. While Chinese and Japanese exhibited high levels of education and income, a 1970s study of the San Francisco Bay Area showed that Filipinos lagged significantly behind these two groups as well as whites in income and employment status. As shown in Chapter 10, Vietnamese and other Southeast Asian refugees—40 percent of whom in California were reliant on public assistance—also belied the model minority stereotype.[66] Taking such data into consideration, no unified picture emerges of Asian Americans' socioeconomic status, despite the certitude suggested by the model minority stereotype.

Also worth pointing out, as this often gets obscured in discussions about Asian American success and achievement, is that the privileged socioeconomic status and professional backgrounds that many immigrants possess is in significant measure the product of structural factors established by the Hart-Celler Act. In his critique of the model minority thesis with regard to South Asians, Vijay Prashad says that this group's success was "the result of state selection whereby the U.S. state, through the special-skills provisions in the 1965 Immigration Act, fundamentally reconfigured the demography of South Asian America."[67] This gave rise to another criticism of the law, that it promoted a professional "brain drain" from the developing world. As a writer for the *Commonweal* satirized about the issue in 1965, the Statue of Liberty should have read, "Give me your poor Ph.D.'s, your huddled graduate engineers."[68]

Another reality behind recent myths about Asian Americans that called for reexamination was the simmering, sometimes explosive, resentment that accompanied the arrival and visibility of upwardly mobile and successful immigrants. At times, they were blamed for problems associated with rapid commercial and residential growth, such as environmental concerns, poor public planning, and high costs of living. In the Monterey Park example, the seemingly sudden appearance of wealthy immigrants, Asian capital, and ubiquitous foreign-language signs struck many residents as a vulgar and unwelcome intrusion. What had in the not-too-distant past been a predominantly white, Christian community that revolved around the Methodist Church and service clubs had changed too abruptly. By the late 1970s, land speculation and construction in the community had inflated property values and increased rents, generating anti-growth sentiments among locals. In 1978 the city planning commission recommended a moratorium on the construction on multiple dwelling units, which typified a controversy about how the community was changing. Frederic Hsieh argued the recommendation was discriminatory toward Chinese immigrants.[69] Local resentment also turned on commercial development in reaction to the seemingly sudden appearance of Chinese restaurants, realtors, supermarkets, herb shops, bakeries, and mini malls. By the 1990s, Chinese were estimated to own between two-thirds and three-quarters of all business enterprises in Monterey Park.[70] Evidence of racial tension was everywhere: in 1985 3,000 Monterey Park residents signed a petition trying to get an Official English initiative on the municipal ballot, and cars displayed bumper stickers saying "Will the Last American to Leave Monterey Park Please Bring the Flag?"[71] In April 1986 the only non-whites on the city council, two Latinos and a Chinese, were defeated in a bid for reelection.

Another problem of the model minority stereotype, bolstered by the post-1965 immigrants, was that it tended to minimize racism directed at people of Asian descent. To be sure, the discrimination and nativism directed at Asians in more recent decades has been subtler than what they experienced in earlier decades. But nonetheless, as Vijay Prashad has argued, Asian professionals were praised and desired for their labor contributions, but were not wanted as permanent members of American society, signaling that less had changed than might have appeared. Reflecting this outlook was a marked shift during the 1990s toward non-immigrant visas (such as H-1B) in order to bring more people with needed skills. Under the H-1B visa, a worker can come to the United States for three years, but after this period must return home. Recent attempts by legislators such as Rep. Lamar Smith of Texas to limit new immigration only to those with skills and professional backgrounds while closing off certain family categories further illustrate this limited tolerance for Asians in America.[72] Prashad has, thus, characterized the legions of technology workers from China, India, Russia, and elsewhere, employed by firms such as Hewlett-Packard, as "high tech incarnations of the braceros of old."[73] In addition to large technology firms, supermarkets, department stores, and utility firms looked increasingly to foreign software programmers and other professionals as a way to hold down their costs.

Perhaps reflecting the disappointments faced by many post-1965 Asian immigrants as well as the diminishing luster of the "American Dream" in the late twentieth century, the rate of return migration among some groups increased while sentiments in favor of emigration declined. According to Binod Khadria, a significant return migration by IT professionals to India has emerged in recent decades. The good pay that jobs in India are able to offer and the country's developed technology sector—Bangalore for instance has been called the "Silicon Valley of India"—were incentives, but some also reported negative experiences in America such as isolation and "racial diatribes."[74] Another important factor was the development of Indian education, environmental issues, and social services. Since the 1980s for many Korean immigrants and would-be emigrants, South Korea's economic prosperity and growing freedoms cast doubt on the once certain notion that life was better in the United States, contributing to growing anti-emigration sentiments. As one immigrant said, "While Korea is old, but getting young, the United States is young, but getting old."[75] The rise of a new privileged class in Seoul was striking to Korean Americans who struggled just to maintain a foothold in the middle class. As another immigrant remarked, "We used to go to Korea and hold our heads high, people were jealous. Now we go and they tease us."[76]

Conclusion

The demographic transformation of Asian America since 1965 occurred against momentous changes in America and the world. Economic, social, and ideological developments had brought forth a new world of possibilities and problems. Working out what it means to be Asian American and who is Asian American became both murkier and more urgent. Taking the example of South Asians, there was an enormous cleavage between the elite—those with advanced degrees and professional occupations—and the working class and working poor. One Indian professional complained that South Asian cab drivers in New York City, who made up 50 percent of the city's cabbies, were "spoiling things for us," and "ruining our image."[77] Such internal differences and strategies of differentiation were not new to Asian America, as class, ideological, ethnic and other divides had always been present, but represented pressing issues into the late twentieth century.

However, America at the close of the twentieth century faced new frontiers against which race relations and racial politics also underwent seismic shifts. In a post-civil rights, post-industrial America, what was the role of race in the national scene? What were the lessons to be drawn from the 1992 Los Angeles riots, the 1982 killing of Chinese American Vincent Chin, the 1999 profiling and arrest of Taiwanese scientist Wen-Ho Lee, and other events in which racial suspicion or tension resulted in Asians being singled out for violence or persecution? The following chapter explores these and other developments in the late twentieth century, reflecting on the significance of recent Asian American history and its future.

Notes

1   Mae M. Ngai, *Impossible Subjects: Illegal Aliens and the Making of Modern America* (Princeton: Princeton University Press, 2003), 228.
2   Mae M. Ngai, "The Unlovely Residue of Outworn Prejudices: The Hart-Celler Act and the Politics of Immigration Reform, 1945–1965," Michael Kazin and Joseph A. McCartin, eds., *Americanism: New Perspectives on the History of an Ideal* (Chapel Hill: University of North Carolina Press, 2006), 110.
3   Madeline Hsu, "The Disappearance of America's Cold War Chinese Refugees," *Journal of American Ethnic History*, 31, no. 4 (Summer 2012): 20.
4   Vijay Prashad, *The Karma of Brown Folk* (Minneapolis: University of Minnesota Press, 2000), 74.
5   Ibid.
6   Ibid.
7   Quoted in Ngai, "The Unlovely Residue of Outworn Prejudices," 115.
8   Quoted in Roger Daniels, *Guarding the Golden Door: American Immigration Policy and Immigrants Since 1882* (New York: Hill and Wang, 2004), 135.
9   Sucheng Chan, *Asian Americans: An Interpretive History* (Boston: Twayne Publishers, 1991), 147.
10 Ibid.
11 It was raised to 700,000, then 675,000 from 1995 on. Philip Q. Yang, *Asian Immigration to the United States* (Cambridge: Polity Press, 2011), 109.
12 Investers must invest $1 million in urban areas, and $500,000 in rural areas to create ten or more jobs. Ibid.
13 http://www.pewsocialtrends.org/2012/06/19/the-rise-of-asian-americans/
14 Nancy Abelmann and John Lie, *Blue Dreams: Korean Americans and the Los Angeles Riots* (Cambridge: Harvard University Press, 1995), 77.
15 Chan, *Asian Americans*, 150.
16 Ableman and Lie, *Blue Dreams*, 68.
17 Ibid., 69.
18 Ibid.
19 Ibid., 74.
20 All told, about 460,000 have immigrated to the United States from the ROC and PRC between 1965 and the early 1990s and non-quota immigrants numbered about 150,000 from the same period. Chan, *Asian Americans*, 151. The 2000 Census recorded nearly three million people of Chinese ancestry. Zhao, *The New Chinese America: Class, Economy, and Social Hierarchy* (New Brunswick: Rutgers University Press, 2010), 22.
21 Peter Kwong and Dusanka Miščević, *Chinese America: The Untold Story of America's Oldest New Community* (New York: W.W. Norton, 2005), 316.
22 These were protests, largely led by students, calling for various reforms in China, such as economic freedom and freedom of the press. They were suppressed by the Chinese military.
23 Ibid.

24 Prashad, *The Karma of Brown Folk*, 75.

25 Chan, *Asian Americans*, 151.

26 Zhao, *The New Chinese America*, 24, 37. Elsewhere Zhao says illegal Chinese in the United States were estimated to number over 500,000.

27 Ibid., 26–7.

28 Kwong and Miščević, *Chinese America*, 330.

29 Abelman and Lie, *Blue Dreams*, 92.

30 Ibid., 128.

31 Kwong and Miščević, *Chinese America*.

32 To illustrate their growth, in 1970, in New York, there were two such firms that would send workers throughout the East Coast, and by 1980 ten were operating alone in Manhattan's Chinatown. Zhao, *The New Chinese America*, 90.

33 Zhao, *The New Chinese America*, 84.

34 Abelmann and Lie, *Blue Dreams*, 126.

35 Ibid.

36 Ibid., 121.

37 Ibid., 122.

38 Ibid., 129.

39 Ibid., 120.

40 Ibid., 125.

41 Shalini Shankar, *Desi Land: Teen Culture, Class, and Success in Silicon Valley* (Durham: Duke University Press, 2008), 36.

42 Binod Khadria, "Migration of Highly Skilled Indians: Case Studies of IT and the Health Professionals," OECD Science, Technology and Industry Working Papers (OECD Publishing, 2004/6), http://dx.doi.org/10.1787/381236020703, 5.

43 Abelmann and Lie, *Blue Dreams*, 105.

44 Ibid., 102.

45 Ibid., 324.

46 Ibid., 325.

47 Ibid., 81.

48 Kwong and Miščević, *Chinese America*, 339.

49 Timothy Fong, *The First Suburban Chinatown: The Remaking of Monterey Park* (Philadelphia: Temple University Press, 1994), 27.

50 Ibid., 29.

51 Ibid., 48.

52 Ibid., 38.

53 Benito Vergara, *Pinoy Capital: The Filipino Nation in Daly City* (Philadelphia: Temple University Press, 2008), 2.

54 See ibid., chapter 2.

55 Shankar, *Desi Land*, 32.

56 Ibid., 36.

57 Fong, *The First Suburban Chinatown*, 49.

58 Min Zhou, "'Parachute Kids' in Southern California: The Educational Experience of Chinese Children in Transnational Families," *Educational Policy* 12 no. 6 (November 1998): 682–704.

59 Abelmann and Lie, *Blue Dreams*, 129.

60 Shankar, *Desi Land*, 14.

61 Ibid., 17.

62 Ibid., 38.

63 Chan, *Asian Americans*, 168.

64 Ibid., 168.

65 Sunaina Maira, *Desis in the House: Indian American Youth Culture in New York City* (Philadelphia: Temple University Press, 2002).

66 Ibid., 170.

67   Prashad, *The Karma of Brown Folk*, 4.
68   The recommendation was ultimately rejected. Fong, *The First Suburban Chinatown*, 42.
69   Ibid., 44.
70   Ibid., 4.
71   Quoted in Ngai, "The Unlovely Residue of Outworn Prejudices," 111.
72   Prashad, *The Karma of Brown Folk*, 80.
73   Ibid., 81.
74   Khadria, "Migration of Highly Skilled Indians," 7, 18.
75   Abelman and Lie, *Blue Dreams*, 78.
76   Ibid., 79.
77   Ibid., 82.

Reckonings: 13

Asian America in the Late Twentieth Century

Toward the close of the twentieth century, Asian America was characterized by the persistence of long-running themes and the appearance of new challenges. Domestic and global developments gave rise to the return of "yellow peril" rhetoric that targeted persons of Asian ancestry, often with alarming consequences. At the same time, against the backdrop of liberal multiculturalism, Asian Americans, individually and collectively, continued to make strides and achieve historical milestones in mainstream life. Furthermore as the Asian population continued to grow and diversify, much of it due to new immigration, the category "Asian America" expanded and became more salient in the race relations landscape, although its meanings and boundaries became more elusive than ever.

This chapter discusses major developments in Asian America in the closing decades of the twentieth century, with a focus on how these events and themes underscored crucial reckonings, on the one hand for all Americans regarding race and intolerance in the United States and among Asian Americans themselves regarding their obligations toward one another, the meanings of solidarity, and their role in working toward a more racially just society. For all that had been attained and the progress achieved over the preceding decades, Asian Americans and the nation at large kept reaching familiar crossroads but against a constantly changing social and political backdrop, bringing to the fore new dilemmas. For instance, what were the meanings of anti-Asian violence at a time when Asian Americans had seemingly secured their status as model minorities? What place is there for racial and ethnic politics in a post-ethnic and post-racial America? What obligations do Asian Americans have toward one another and other racial minorities? And in an age of accelerated globalization and international competition, will Asian Americans continue to be stigmatized as "forever foreigners" despite their long presence in the United States? The chapter will explore these and other questions, with particular attention on the rise of racialized violence and the revival of Yellow Perilism, black–Asian conflict, the growth of the mixed-race Asian American population, and interethnic politics and conflict. While these developments have indeed underscored the continued salience of race, racism, and ethnic politics as a factor in Asian American experience, the changing landscape and cultural climate has simultaneously made it more challenging to discuss and address these matters, thus highlighting some of the major yet unresolved challenges facing this population into the twenty-first century.

The New Whiz Kids

As discussed in the previous chapter, one of the effects of the Immigration Act of 1965 was a greatly enlarged Asian American population with a prominent professional and educated class. Many of their children, furthermore, were high achieving students who excelled academically and gained admission to the nation's most selective colleges and universities. While such privileged and accomplished individuals were not representative of the Asian American population, they nonetheless came to dominate media representations of Asians in America. In this iteration of the "model minority," which gained traction by the mid-1980s, high-achieving Asian American students from the high school to college levels were especially visible and commented upon. Although their backgrounds were ethnically and socioeconomically diverse, they tended to be lumped in stories with headlines such as "The New Whiz Kids," as *Time* magazine proclaimed in 1987 and *Newsweek*'s "The Drive to Excel," from 1984.

In 1988 the cartoonist Gary Trudeau satirized about the high-achieving Asian American student in a comic strip in which a white high school student delivered a report to her class about the impact of Asian competition on the U.S. economy, which turned into a diatribe about Asian students in America. "And I agree with Mr. Gephardt's assertion that Asians are threatening our economic future . . . We can see it right here in our own school. Who are getting into the best colleges, in disproportionate numbers? Asian kids! It's not fair!"[1] At the conclusion of the presentation, the teacher chastised the student, saying, "Unfortunately it's racist," to which the student responded, "Um . . . Are you sure? My parents helped me." Here, Trudeau pointed out and made light of how people viewed U.S. prosperity and Asian success as mutually exclusive and antagonistic forces, even when the latter pertained to academic achievements by Americans of Asian descent.

The humor in Trudeau's comic strip spoke to a growing unease among Americans, white and non-white, about the heightened presence of Asian American students in U.S. schools, both as an overall proportion of student bodies and among the high achievers. In public school districts in major metropolitan areas, notable concentrations of Asian Americans had emerged with renewed immigration, student body diversification, and the rise of magnet schools designed to attract and retain students. At the same time, efforts to integrate schools sometimes resulted in discriminatory practices and negative attitudes against Asian students.

These nationwide trends played out in San Francisco, which in 1983 adopted a court-mandated consent degree aimed at facilitating the integration of its public schools. At the time, African Americans were the largest racial or ethnic group in the district, but demographic changes over the next few years dramatically altered the variables and stakes in the quest for desegregation. By the early 1990s, "white flight" had reduced white enrollment and immigration increased the presence of Asian Americans to approximately half of the student body.[2] At Lowell High School, the district's premier high school, officials following the diversity rationale became concerned not just with raising black enrollment, but also maintaining white enrollment and keeping down Asian American numbers. As Chinese students were the most numerous, officers implemented racial caps to limit them to no more than 40 percent of the student population, which Chinese parents vocally protested. The controversy at Lowell illustrated the complex nature of equal protection in a multicultural nation, specifically raising the question of what should happen when one racial minority no longer appeared to need preferential treatment, something that Asian Americans would increasingly confront with regard to the issue of affirmative action.

At the college level, admissions officials also started to use racial caps to limit Asian American enrollments, which occurred against the backdrop of dramatically changing student demographics and rising racial tensions over the increased presence of Asian and Asian American students, seen for instance in the nicknaming of UCLA as "University of Caucasians Lost Among Asians" and MIT as "Made in Taiwan." Under pressure by Asian Americans and others who charged that institutions were using quotas, several universities— among them Stanford, Harvard, Princeton and Brown—conducted in-house investigations of their admissions practices and conceded that their screening processes had made it more difficult for Asian American applicants to gain admission. For example, in Harvard's 1987 freshman class, the school accepted 15 percent of the overall pool of applicants, but only 12 percent of Asian Americans who applied. Additionally, in 1989, the Chancellor at UC Berkeley apologized for "disadvantaging" Asian students in admissions and Stanford University officials acknowledged the possibility of "unconscious bias" against Asians.[3]

As of 2012, research has continued to show that Asian American college applicants face a higher threshold when it comes to admissions, leading one scholar to call them "the new Jews on campus," a reference to historical discrimination that Jewish Americans once faced earlier in the twentieth century.[4] According to Thomas Espenshade, Asian American applicants need SAT scores 140 points higher than white students to get into college.[5] However, the newest round of research has looked beyond college admissions alone to connect this discrimination to underrepresentation in positions of power at institutions of higher learning. Despite their preponderance in the student bodies of Ivy League schools, as of 2012 there has been just one Asian American ever to lead an Ivy League institution, former president of Dartmouth Jim Yong Kim.

Racialized Violence against Asian Americans

Some of the resentment against high-achieving Asian Americans bubbled over into racialized violence, an increasingly pressing concern from the 1980s onward. To be sure, anti-Asian violence has a long history in the United States, some of which has been discussed in earlier chapters, but the issue took on new dimensions in the late twentieth century. For one, in the wake of the more recent occurrences of racialized violence, Asian Americans engaged in pan-Asian mobilization to demand justice and lobby for greater protections. Previously, anti-Asian violence tended to target particular ethnic groups, and those who belonged to different groups could, and often did, distance themselves from the victims. One of the more well-known examples of this was the practice by persons of Korean and Chinese descent wearing buttons to disidentify from Japanese Americans during World War II. Things changed in the late twentieth century, as racial incidents seemed to take on a more random or general character, and Asian Americans were, furthermore, better poised organizationally to take action through panethnic strategies.

Acts of what Bill Ong Hing terms "vigilante racism" against Asians occurred across the country toward members of different groups seemingly with alarming frequency. The following descriptions of a selection of incidents convey just a sense of the climate facing Asians in America during the 1980s and 1990s. In 1987, a group of white students at the University of Connecticut spat on and taunted eight Asian students on their way to a dance.[6]In 1989 Patrick Purdy, a white man who blamed Asians for taking jobs from native whites, shot to death five Asian children—mostly of Southeast Asian descent—at Cleveland School in Stockton, California. Also in the late 1980s, in Jersey City, New Jersey a gang of white youths calling themselves the "Dotbusters" terrorized South Asian residents through acts of vandalism and physical assault. Several victims were beaten into a coma. As members said in a public letter, "We will go to any extreme to get Indians to move out . . . If I'm walking down the street and I see a Hindu and the setting is right, I will just hit him or her. We plan some of our more extreme attacks . . . We use the phone book and look up the name Patel."[7]In 1997, a group of Asians was denied service at a Denny's restaurant in Syracuse and then beaten in the parking lot.[8]

Until the 1990s, the evidence of anti-Asian violence was mostly anecdotal, due to the limitations of hate crimes statistics gathering and the underreporting of incidents. However, some clear patterns started to emerge. For instance, in major cities such as Boston and Philadelphia by the mid-1990s, Asians were found to suffer the highest per capita rate of hate crimes.[9] According to Bill Ong Hing, these crimes reflected and perpetuated the "de-Americanization" of Asian Americans, in which attackers "base their assault on loyalty and foreignness . . . In the minds of the . . . self appointed enforcers of true Americanism, their victims are *immigrants* or *foreigners* even though they may in fact be citizens by birth or naturalization. Irrespective of the victim's community's longstanding status in the country, its members are regarded as perpetual foreigners."[10]

Often cited as a turning point after which Asian Americans, the media, and policy-makers began to take more seriously the issue of racialized violence was the 1982 killing of Vincent Chin. This crime occurred against the backdrop of domestic and international developments in which Asian Americans became increasingly vulnerable. Since the 1960s, Japan had been in the midst of a "postwar economic miracle" and became a major manufacturing power. Americans lauded this development, but by the late 1970s, some of Japan's industries were competing with U.S. producers. American manufacturers and trade protectionists complained that Japan was engaging in unfair trade practices and flooding U.S. markets with cheap exports. This economic protectionism often manifested as general anti-Japan sentiment, which in turn expressed itself as a generalized xenophobia against people of Asian ancestry in the United States, setting the stage for the Vincent Chin killing.

Chin was a Chinese adoptee whose father had served in World War II and whose mother had been a war bride. The family lived in Detroit, Michigan, home to a very small Chinese American community. In June 1982, the twenty-seven-year-old engineer went out with a small group of friends to celebrate his upcoming wedding. They went to a strip bar called the Fancy Pants where in the course of the evening they got into a physical altercation with two white locals, Ronald Ebens and his stepson Michael Nitz, both unemployed autoworkers. Witnesses in the club overheard Ebens say, "It's because of you motherfuckers that we're out of work," apparently believing mistakenly that Chin was Japanese. The fight went outside

Figure 13.1 Vincent Chin's mother, Lily, speaks at a rally for her son, circa 1984. Jesse Jackson is seated behind her. In 1982, Vincent Chin was brutally beaten during an altercation with two white men and died shortly afterward. A campaign for justice in the wake of the lenient sentences for the men politicized and rallied diverse Asian Americans across the country. (Photograph courtesy of Renee Tajima-Peña.)

into the street where Ebens and Nitz brutally beat Chin with a baseball bat. Chin was hospitalized and, several days later, he died.

Almost as shocking as the crime was the leniency with which Chin's attackers were treated. In the state criminal case, in which the judge expressed far more compassion toward Ebens and Nitz than Chin, the assailants received three years' probation and $3,000 fines. A subsequent federal civil rights trial in 1984 acquitted Nitz and convicted Ebens, but that decision was overturned on an appeal. A retrial in Cincinnati, Ohio three years later found Ebens innocent of all counts. Although it was small consolation, a 1987 civil suit was settled out of court in which Ebens and Nitz agreed to pay $50,000 (Nitz) and $1.5 million (Ebens) to Chin's mother for lost wages. Neither spent a day in jail for beating Vincent Chin to death.

Some of the consequences of the Chin killing and trial for Asian Americans are discussed below, but suffice it to say the brutality of the crime and callousness with which his life was treated, both by Ebens and Nitz as well as the courts, stunned and awakened many Asian Americans across the country. It was, explains Mae Ngai, "a stark counterpoint to the stereotype that Asian Americans were a 'model minority.'"[11] "The whole mood was total anti-Japanese," said activist Helen Zia, who lived in Detroit around the time of the Chin murder. "People who had Japanese cars were getting their cars shot at, and it didn't matter if they were white. And then if you were Asian, it was assumed that you were Japanese just like Vincent and there was personal hostility toward us . . . So, when Vincent was killed it was a confirmation to all Asian Americans there in Detroit, the antagonism that we were feeling. I felt totally like a moving target."[12]

Yellow Peril Redux

As mentioned, part of the backdrop of the Vincent Chin murder was growing concern and rhetoric about U.S.–Japan economic competition. Indeed through much of the 1980s and 1990s, incidents of anti-Asian racism in America frequently occurred against perceived threats about Asian global dominance or competition. Not only did such feelings contribute to the continued foreignization of Asian Americans, encouraging observers to link Asian Americans' activities and success in terms of foreign traits or agendas, but they also made them vulnerable to pernicious consequences of such racial profiling.

There were several signs of a resurgence of "yellow peril" fears in American life during the late twentieth century, with regard to U.S. economic strength as well as paranoia about Asian governments trying to infiltrate the American political process. In one episode from the 1970s, popularly referred to as "Koreagate," South Korean government officials were accused of bribing American legislators through lavish gifts and parties in the hopes of ensuring that the United States would continue to provide economic support to their country. Although other countries had engaged in similar lobbying, "the Koreans were different," said the *Washington Post*, "because of their persistence and their often heavy-handed methods."[13] Several individuals came under particular suspicion, including Suzi Thomson, a Korean American typist who worked for then-House Speaker Carl Albert, whose main misdeed, it seemed, was working in Washington, D.C. while Korean.[14]

"Koreagate," which allegedly exposed the vulnerability of American politicians to Asian influence, played out as anti-Japan economic nationalism was also on the rise. While Japan's economy flourished, America's struggled and had by the late 1970s incurred a large trade deficit to the former. Nowhere was sentiment against Japanese imports more intense than in the auto industry. As the U.S. auto industry spiralled downward, anxious autoworkers clinging to their jobs channeled their fears into "Buy American" campaigns, out of which an intense "generic fury" against Japan flowed.[15] Workers at United Auto Workers (UAW) picnics took turns gleefully bashing Toyotas and other Japanese cars with sledgehammers, people displayed bumper stickers ordering drivers of foreign cars to park elsewhere and, most unsettlingly, cartoons invoking Pearl Harbor with messages like "We Have to Beat the Japs" appeared.[16] In many instances, U.S. economic nationalism, which did spring from real concerns about job security and economic health, too easily slipped into rationalizing stereotyping and ridiculing Asian Americans, and then in the Vincent Chin case, violence and murder.

By the 1990s, the attention on Japan as a source of U.S. competition shifted as that country endured a painful economic slowdown. In its place emerged China as the newest Asian threat to American interests and wellbeing. By the 1990s, China was on an impressive economic trajectory, which fueled fears of competition and declining U.S. hegemony, and its rise was all the more menacing because it was ruled by a Communist regime. In 1996, allegations that President Bill Clinton's reelection campaign was soliciting donations from Chinese contributors in exchange for favors evoked China as a shadowy, malevolent force threatening the integrity of U.S. politics, illustrated in a *National Review* cover that labeled the Clintons and Vice President Al Gore as "The Manchurian Candidates."[17] Concerns had also circulated that China was building up a missile arsenal based on information leaked from the United States.

In 1999, this growing anxiousness about China had bubbled over into racial suspicion toward Americans of Chinese ancestry and led to the arrest and persecution of Wen-Ho Lee. In what became known as the "Los Alamos Incident," Lee, a sixty-year-old scientist employed at the lab, was accused of spying for China and immediately fired from his job and placed in solitary confinement pending a trial. Lee, a naturalized citizen who had been in the United States since 1965 and worked at the lab since 1978, pleaded guilty to one count of mishandling data (of the fifty-nine he was indicted for), although other scientists at the lab had engaged in similar illegal downloading. Nonetheless, a media frenzy ensued, intensifying the vilification of Lee, and for both the attorney general and court of public opinion, his Chinese ancestry and any connections or past travel to China—even though Lee himself was from Taiwan—sufficiently established his guilt.

Throughout his nine months of solitary confinement, Lee maintained his innocence and, as the government prepared its case, several key players who had accused him of lying recanted. From there the case unraveled. Even despite Lee's admission of mishandling information, there was no evidence that anything from Los Alamos made its way into Chinese hands. Lee was released, received an apology, and was paid $1.6 million. However, by then, the damage had been done. Lee paid dearly, but the debacle also had a chilling effect

Figure 13.2 Wen Ho Lee smiles after giving a statement upon his release outside the U.S. Courthouse in Albuquerque, New Mexico, September 13, 2000. His arrest was symbolic of the new yellow peril and foreignization of Asians in America. (AP Photo/Jake Schoellkopf.)

on other Chinese American scientists, who made up about 8 percent of the U.S. workforce in science and technology. As Cheuk-Yin Wong, the chairman of the Overseas Chinese Physics Association said, recalling the general suspicion cast on Japanese Americans in the wake of Pearl Harbor, "Without taking time to check the evidence, certain members of the media stated uncritically that the hundred thousand Chinese scientists working in this country provided ready targets for PRC intelligence gathering."[18]

Politicizing Asian America

These and other troubling developments, which served as reminders for some and wake up calls for others about Asian Americans' vulnerability and the persistence of racism led to a new wave of political activism. For many Asian Americans, this was the first time they had become potentially engaged, as they had come of age during the age of the model minority and believed that America had embraced a "postethnic" and "postracial" era. An event like the Chin killing and trial were particularly powerful because it demonstrated not just the vulnerability of all Asians, regardless of their specific ethnic background, but also how devalued their lives were in the legal system. "I think that the Vincent Chin case . . . was a watershed moment for all Asian Americans," said Helen Zia. "For the first time, we considered ourselves as a race, a minority race in America that faced discrimination and had to fight for our civil rights."[19]

Out of this episode came efforts aimed at toughening hate crimes laws while forging unity among Asian Americans. Existing Asian American civil rights organizations as well as new ones—such as the Asian American Legal Defense Fund, American Citizens for Justice, and Asian American Justice Center—worked to combat and bring attention to issues of anti-Asian violence and discrimination. Collecting data on hate crimes against Asian Americans, they found, for instance, that there had been a 13 percent increase in reported anti-Asian incidents between 1998 and 1999. South Asians, furthermore, had been the most widely targeted group, and vandalism was the most common form of anti-Asian discrimination. In 1994, the civil rights organizing of Asian Americans helped bring about the Violent Crime Control and Law Enforcement Act, which increased penalties for hate crimes committed on the basis of the actual or perceived race, color, religion, national origin, ethnicity, or gender of any person.

The politicization of Asian Americans around the issue of affirmative action and discrimination in school admissions was more complicated, as illustrated by the controversy over capping Asian admissions at Lowell High School, mentioned above. Specifically, the debate grew out of the district's implementation of the desegregation consent decree in 1983, in which each school was required to enroll at least four out of nine specified ethnic/racial groups and no single group could constitute 40 or 45 percent of the total enrollment.[20] At Lowell, which already had a very selective admissions process due to its reputation, Chinese applicants faced a higher bar so that their enrollment would not exceed 40 percent of the student body. In response to this practice, a group of Chinese Americans sued the school district. For the plaintiffs, this was a thorny situation because success in their lawsuit might mean dismantling racial preferences in admissions, which would most certainly hurt underrepresented minorities served by affirmative action. Chinese Americans were divided on the matter. State and local leaders including Henry Der and Leland Lee said the racial caps that limited Chinese American admission at Lowell were necessary to achieve desegregation, but on the other hand, the Chinese American Democratic Club argued that it was unfair that their group bore "by far the heaviest burden."[21] In addition, it pointed out, the consent decree in effect operated as a form of affirmative action for whites who did not have to meet the same standards that Chinese American students did. Members of the Chinese American Democratic Club said they did not wish to do away with affirmative action, and instead proposed two separate pools: one for non-disadvantaged students competing on merit and another for socioeconomically disadvantaged students, especially African Americans and Latinos.

Since the Supreme Court's 1978 ruling in the case of *Regents v. Bakke* the issues of racial preferences and caps have become volatile, placing Asian Americans in awkward, frequently divided positions. With regard to the Lowell High School controversy, the consent decree was overturned in 1996. While some cheered, such as the Asian American Legal Foundation, which had been formed in 1994 to support the lawsuit, other Asian American commentators condemned the development as well as Asian Americans against affirmative action as selfish and short-sighted. The Chinese Americans who embraced the anti-affirmative action cause, said writer Jeff Chang, were "on the wrong side." As Henry Der remarked, "This case is a tremendous setback for coalition politics."[22] The debate over affirmative action, also passionately fought over in colleges and universities, remains one of the most polarizing and pressing issues in Asian America.

Intra-minority Politics in a Post-Civil Rights Age

By the 1980s, issues such as admissions caps and affirmative action as well as socioeconomic achievement increasingly separated Asian Americans from the category of "disadvantaged minority," complicating the landscape of racial politics and Asian Americans' relationship with other non-whites. Were they fellow travelers? Or a successful minority who should help those with fewer advantages? While Asian Americans and other minorities had a common foe in racial discrimination and bigotry, structural, historical, and ideological factors in the late twentieth century had created new challenges in intraminority relations, becoming particularly salient in states like California, major cities like New York, and other places approaching "majority–minority" populations.

Rising intraminority tensions were not due so much to fundamental group differences but rather because of changing historical contexts and problems. The late twentieth century was a time of scarcity and cutbacks and the impact of deindustrialization on former manufacturing centers such as Los Angeles was devastating. As factories closed down and newer industries emerged but were located away from the old centers of production, once vital working class neighborhoods declined and suburbs flourished. Due to racial and economic barriers, these suburbs were very white (with some Asians), and the old city centers became increasingly black, Hispanic, and poor. Many Asian immigrants entered cities and metropolitan areas struggling with these economic shifts and residential reconfigurations, giving rise to new urban frontiers and intraminority concentrations.

To focus on the case of Korean–black relations, in several major cities, particularly New York and Los Angeles, the Korean population had grown dramatically since the late 1960s.

In Los Angeles their numbers had increased from 8,900 in 1970 to 145,431 in 1990.[23] As discussed in the previous chapter, the immigrants brought with them capital and skills, but cultural barriers led many into self-employment and entrepreneurship. Often times, they had enough money to start businesses and live in the nice emerging suburbs, but not enough to run establishments in prime locations. A feasible option, then, was to open businesses in the declining parts of the city, and this is where present-day Koreatown emerged. Additionally, many Korean businesses were located in South Central Los Angeles, which bordered Koreatown and had been all but abandoned by large-scale retailers.

In the meantime, many African Americans arrived in Los Angeles during the early and mid-twentieth centuries when jobs in manufacturing had been abundant and promised a degree of security. With deindustrialization and white flight, however, their once vital, dynamic neighborhoods and secure jobs fell by the wayside, giving rise to some of the current problems we see today in poor black communities. Added to this was the seemingly sudden appearance of immigrant shopkeepers from Asia who were unfamiliar with the struggles of African Americans, had not witnessed the civil rights movement, and had little inkling of the histories of the neighborhoods in which they were setting up shop.

Over the 1970s and 1980s, a narrative of Korean–black conflict took hold through the circulation of various news articles and editorials about Koreans "taking over" the black community in Los Angeles.[24] Scholars and writers sought to explain the nature of the racial tension between these communities. The Korean population had grown so rapidly and their presence near the city core at South Central seemed so sudden that some friction was perhaps inevitable. The vast majority were, furthermore, immigrants who had arrived after 1965 and just half had been in the United States for more than ten years.[25] As Helen Zia has explained, "In their pursuit of the American dream, the new immigrants seemed oblivious to the African Americans' long history of struggle for their unfulfilled dreams. In Los Angeles as well as New York and other cities, black people bristled over incidents of disrespectful treatment and false accusations of shoplifting."[26]

On the other side, African Americans' anger toward Koreans seemed to magnify through a series of violent encounters between Korean shop owners and black customers that received a great deal of media attention. These included a yearlong boycott of Family Red Apple Market in New York City's Flatbush starting in 1990 after an altercation between a black customer and a Korean proprietor who accused the customer of stealing. A particularly explosive encounter occurred in March 1991 in South Central Los Angeles. A teenager named Latasha Harlins entered Empire Liquor Market on South Figueroa. That day, Soon Ja Du, a middle-aged Korean immigrant, was working at the store because her son Joseph, who usually worked there, stayed home in fear of recent threats made toward him by members of the Crips gang after he had agreed to testify against them following a robbery attempt. Du accused Harlins of stealing from the shop, and an altercation between the two led to Harlins punching Du and knocking her down, after which Du shot Harlins in the back of the head, and killed her. Harlins was later found to have had juice from the store in her backpack and money in her hands. Young Kyu Yi, the owner of a store in South Central, said, "We should not lose our tempers over a bottle of orange juice."[27] Others empathized with Du, pointing out her religiosity and involvement in her church. Anger toward Korean merchants, however, bubbled over following this incident. The Los Angeles Sentinel ran an article in which they were called "poison pushing merchants who are apparently more outraged about being called names than they are about a dead Black child."[28] Black public sentiment against Korean-owned stores mounted, and in the wake of the shooting tragedy, Empire Liquor Store closed down. Afterward, the black organization Brotherhood Crusade placed a banner across its door that read, "Closed for Murder and Disrespect of Black People."[29]

Through the second half of the 1980s and into the 1990s, tensions between African Americans and Koreans, fed in large measure by the mainstream media, intensified until they reached a breaking point. It is important to note that, in addition to the run-ins between Koreans and African Americans in which the former displayed insensitivity toward the latter, Korean immigrants were also feeling besieged and vulnerable against a backdrop of rising incidents that targeted them. In 1986 alone, for example, four Korean storekeepers in Los Angeles were shot and killed by blacks in separate incidents. In 1991, forty-eight murders occurred in Koreatown, as well as 2,500 robberies. Koreans, furthermore, had been the number one target of anti-Asian hate crimes in the area.[30] By the early 1990s, the discourse of black–white conflict had crystallized. An indication of this was the appearance of the Korean shop owner in mainstream popular culture. Spike Lee's 1989 film *Do the Right Thing* featured a Korean shop keeping couple as minor, but pivotal, characters in this groundbreaking movie about race relations in New York. A year before the Harlins killing, the rapper Ice Cube released his track, "Black Korea," whose lyrics warned that if storekeepers did not respect blacks, their businesses would be burned. Korean Americans called for a boycott of the CD and members of the Korean American Grocers Association refused to sell the malt liquor that Ice Cube had endorsed.[31] In the meantime, some Koreans and blacks did work on healing the rifts between these communities. In 1986, in the wake of a rash of killings of Korean merchants, community leaders with the help of the Los Angeles County Human Relations Commission established the Black–Korean Alliance (BKA), whose objective was to maintain an ongoing dialogue between the two communities. It encountered problems from the start because merchant groups were fearful of drawing publicity about the killings and African Americans were reticent about rallying around this issue. However, the BKA did draw support from representatives from the NAACP, SCLC, merchants and shopkeepers from both communities. Chung Lee, the owner of Watts Market, was the first Korean merchant to join, and he expressed pride in the relationship he developed with blacks in Watts. He hired local workers, became involved in the African American community, and was one of the few Korean merchants willing to talk to the media. Illustrating the obstacles the BKA faced, many Koreans resented the publicity Lee received, and he eventually resigned from the organization due to negative pressure from co-ethnics.[32]

Despite these efforts and hopes for forging intraminority understanding, things quickly unraveled. With regard to the Harlins killing, BKA and the Human Relations Commission in Los Angeles tried to keep the issue from getting out of hand, but police released videotape of the altercation. Soon Ja Du was found guilty of manslaughter, but her sentence was suspended and she received five years' probation, $500 in fines, funeral costs, and community service. Asian American leaders were largely silent while black leaders could not contain their outrage.[33] Under siege and called "race traitors," the BKA disintegrated. According to Helen Zia, the fate of the BKA exposed some of the problems of pan-Asian unity and the inadequacies of an "old style multiracial coalition" to solve the problems of black–Korean relations. Stewart Kwoh, who was executive director of the Asian Pacific American Legal

Center and president of the Los Angeles City Human Relations Commission, had been asking mayor Tom Bradley for more resources to improve multiracial relations, to no avail. Additionally, thirteen days after the Harlins shooting, videotape of motorist Rodney King's beating at the hands of four white Los Angeles police officers was released and became major headline news.

An expression of uncapped, mounting anger, the Los Angeles riots erupted on April 29, 1992 after a jury announced that the police officers seen beating King were not guilty of assault. Known as the largest uprising of civil unrest in American history, much of the rioting and violence was captured by news helicopters and cameras on the ground. What they showed viewers ranged from the comic to horrific; shop owners defended their property Wild West style with uzis, motorists were pulled from their cars and beaten, and looters descended on stores seemingly with glee. As stores were looted and torched, police did little to stop the destruction of property. The governor of California called a state of emergency, sending in some six thousand National Guard troops as the rioting continued until May 4. In the course of these days, 58 people died, 2,400 were injured, and about 12,000 were arrested. The Los Angeles riots were a multiethnic affair; businesses and property owned by all ethnicities were destroyed and looters were of varied backgrounds, including some Koreans. However, Koreans were the primary victims who incurred the greatest losses in this uprising. Most of the 4,500 stores destroyed were Korean-owned or run and nearly every building in Koreatown had been damaged. Tens of thousands of Koreans instantly lost their livelihoods, suffering at least $500 million in damages.[34] Among those who lost their businesses was Chung Lee of the BKA who, despite his fifteen years of working to improve his relations with blacks, saw his store burn to the ground.[35]

The Los Angeles riots have been described in various ways; it was an urban rebellion, a protest against black and Latino disfranchisement, a food riot, an act of civil unrest. Many Koreans called it sa-i-gu, or April 2–9, while the Korean American journalist K.W. Lee described it as an American pogrom.[36] "For us it was like the Jewish last stand in Warsaw, or the internment of the Japanese Americans. Sa-i-gu was a convenient way for mainstream America to deflect black rage." Jan Jung-Min Sunoo of the Los Angeles County Human Relations Commissions said it was "our worst nightmare come true."[37] The riots exposed the precariousness of the success and economic achievements of Korean immigrants. They were also for Koreans in America, not just in Los Angeles but nationally, a moment of reckoning, which resulted in contradictory conclusions. To be sure, many realized and acted on the need to be more engaged with mainstream politics and affairs, but on the other hand, some groups devoted to interracial understanding dissolved in the aftermath of the riots because they showed that the problems seemed too insurmountable. Many Koreans, furthermore, opted to focus on rebuilding Koreatown and forgetting the trauma of sa-i-gu, while others fled the city. Since the riots, the Korean population around Koreatown has declined and grown in places like Orange County.

Intra-Asian Politics in Multicultural America

In the face of events like the Los Angeles riots as well as demographic and other changes in Asian America and the United States, people of Asian ancestry have been faced with a number of dilemmas and questions regarding the meanings of Asian American identity and belonging and their place in the wider multicultural and multiracial society. For example, were the Los Angeles riots fundamentally a Korean American problem, or something that should engage and involve all Asian Americans? Furthermore, what binds diverse Asians in America to one another? Do they have a shared culture? A set of ideological commitments? Does Asian American identity arise from a shared set of experiences? Does it only emerge in response to external events? How are ethnic, class, religious and other differences to be negotiated?

A number of recent developments have kept questions regarding the boundaries and meanings of Asian America at the forefront of discussion regarding identity. These include a movement among Filipino American activists to reclassify or at least disaggregate their group from the larger "Asian" category on the U.S. Census and debate over whether or not Pacific Islanders ought to be included in the larger Asian American grouping, and thus modify the category to "Asian Pacific American." Another prominent development has been the rise of the mixed-race Asian American population. The mixed-race population has been for some time the fastest growing segment of Asian America. They now comprise about 14 percent of the Asian American population and are projected to reach 36 percent by 2050. Their presence has a long history, but only recently have the political, demographic, and cultural implications of their increasing numbers emerged.

One of the major issues that the growth of the mixed-race population—and members' insistence on recognition as a discrete community—has raised has to do with enumeration and record-keeping. Organizations such as the Association for Multiethnic Americans (AMEA) and Project RACE (Reclassify All Children Equally), along with the Hapa Issues Forum—the latter specifically represented mixed-race Americans of Asian ancestry—emerged as prominent advocates of revising Census categories as well as recognizing mixed-race people as a distinct population. One of the AMEA's major concerns had to do with tracking hate crimes against multiracial people, something that could only be done by changing how population data was collected. The efforts of these groups paid off with the 2000 Census, which for the first time allowed individuals to check more than one box in describing their racial background.[38] This development drew mixed responses from major Asian American organizations. While the JACL supported it as an important step that would allow "multiracial persons to have the opportunity to respond truthfully and accurately," Chinese for Affirmative Action, and Asians for an Accurate Count opposed the check more than one box format.[39] As Rebecca Chiyoko King explains, "Many of these organizations asked if perhaps the Census was the appropriate place to work out racial self-esteem and self-identity issues. They, in effect, rejected the notion that census recognition was a civil right and reinforced the racialization of basing recognition on monoracial, mutually exclusive racial categories."[40]

Debates about the merits of changing how people self-identified aside, the 2000 Census was very revealing in how significant the mixed-race population had become as a subset of Asian America. The new approach gave the first reliable count of the number of multiracial Asian Americans. According to the census, 10,242,998 people identified themselves as entirely of Asian race (3.6 percent). Additionally, another 1,655,830 people identified themselves as being part Asian and part one or more other races. By far the largest group of multiracial Asians were half Asian and half white (52 percent), and of this group, the largest proportion had Japanese ancestry. Nearly 31 percent of those identifying as part Japanese were multiracial. They were followed by Filipinos, Chinese, Koreans, Asian Indians, and Vietnamese. Organization-building and cultural productions have further boosted the presence of mixed-race Asian Americans. The Hapa Issues forum, mentioned above, was formed at UC Berkeley in 1992, and became one of the first institutional expressions of the growing mixed-race population, whereby it sought to make itself a visible presence and a distinct voice in Asian America. Although it disbanded in 2007, a host of websites, blogs, art installations and publications have maintained and boosted the visibility of mixed-race people while redrawing the boundaries of Asian America.[41]

The growth of mixed-race Asian Americans and mixed-race Americans more generally has also given rise to broad discussions about race in America, whether or not the categories we rely on have much relevance anymore and if this population's presence means we are truly on our way to a post-racial society. Golfer Tiger Woods became the ultimate embodiment of this post-racial outlook. His emergence on the scene generated a great deal of excitement because of his talent and his mixed-race background, which includes Thai, African American, Native American, and Caucasian ancestries. Different communities tried to claim him and debated whether he was black, Asian American, or both. In the the midst of all this discussion, Woods himself declared in 1997 during an appearance on the *Oprah Winfrey Show* that he was "cablinasian," a term he invented to reflect his diverse ancestry, and furthermore asserted that race was not important to him. While this declaration was applauded by some who approved of Wood's refusal to play the "race game" and for using his celebrity to transcend race, others derided and ridiculed his gesture as rooted in utopian fantasy and out of step with reality. It remains to be seen whether the growth and visibility of mixed-race Americans will bring profound and lasting consequences to how we understand race in America. Although it is tempting to conclude that this development heralds our post-racial future, some of the events described in this chapter suggest that this is a long way off.

Debates regarding Asian American identity politics have also focused recently on intraethnic relations, inequality, and solidarity. A controversy during the 1990s over ethnic stereotypes and the responsibilities of Asian American writers served as a window to some of these issues. Much of this played out within the Association of Asian American Studies (AAAS), the main professional organization for teachers and scholars in the field of Asian American Studies. In 1994, the AAAS Board selected Lois Ann Yamanaka's *Saturday Night at the Pahala Theatre* for its Literature Award, which the Filipino American Studies Caucus immediately expressed its disapproval of. Referring to a Filipino character in the book, which struck some readers as an embodiment of negative ethnic stereotypes, caucus member Steffi San Buenaventura said, "I wish that the Filipino man had such power of the pen to say who he is, to speak back against the way he has been historically depicted."[42] Bennette Evangelista responded to Yamanaka's collection of poetry, saying, "Inasmuch as artists or writers have a right to free expression, we too have a right to express our outrage and anger," and compared Yamanaka's descriptions of Filipinos to Blackface and the degradation of black people.[43]

Four years later, in 1998, the association once again selected a book by Yamanaka for its fiction prize, this time the novel *Blu's Hanging*. A fierce controversy exploded in the wake of the selection that threatened to divide the association. As with her previous work, the outcry over *Blu's Hanging* emanated from the Filipino American community and others who objected to Yamanaka's portrayal of Filipino men, especially the character Uncle Paolo, a sexual predator who embodied existing stereotypes about Filipinos in Hawaii. Letters of protest had been sent to the association prior to the book's selection, and three Chinese American members of the committee went on to pick *Blu's Hanging* for the prize. After some discussion the association agreed to rescind the award, which resulted in a backlash among Yamanaka's supporters, who accused her critics and the association of practicing censorship. As the controversy played out, a larger story unfolded of a legacy in Hawaii of Japanese racism against Filipinos and other minorities, histories that were often kept under wraps in the interests of Asian American unity and cooperation. The controversy also brought up a hierarchy within Asian America in which Japanese and Chinese were "privileged readers who assume that these images have no power" and the "historical pain" they inflicted on fellow Asian Americans.[44] Also emerging from this, but still far from resolved, was an insistence that Asian American writings, creative work, and any kind of representation for consumption by a broader public must take care to balance individual expression and the collective interests of the wider Asian American community.

Conclusion

At the close of the twentieth century and into the twenty-first, the landscape of Asian American identity politics and the challenges of race relations have become perhaps more complicated than ever. The persistence of the model minority stereotype and push to embrace a post-racial politics has muddied the water, making many people, including Asian Americans, reluctant to even acknowledge, much less critically examine, issues of race and racism in American life. And as Asian Americans have made real strides in socioeconomic achievements and public visibility, the privileged positions they have attained have given rise to new challenges and controversies.

For their part, many Asian Americans have embraced the model minority designation. In 1987, they were featured in a famous *Time* cover story that was accompanied with the headline, "The New Whiz Kids." The article, to which a number of Asian American spokespersons provided quotes, celebrated the scholastic achievements of students of Asian descent, who were attending the nation's best universities in numbers significantly out of proportion to their representation in the general population. The article fell back on tired explanations, such as "Confucian ethics," and filial piety.[45] More recently, Yale law professor Amy Chua pursued a similar strategy of harnessing the model minority for notoriety and personal gain, through her self-orientalizing *Battle Hymn of the Tiger Mother*, which paid off handsomely in media attention and book sales.[46] However, equally striking has been the pushback against Chua by other Asian American commentators—a prominent blogger called Chua's *Wall Street Journal* piece that condensed a portion of the book, "a cringe-inducing, stereotype-laden proclamation"—thus illustrating, on the one hand, the diversity of ideas that exists among Asian Americans and the platforms on which they are able to express themselves, but on the other, how contested and explosive the terrain of intra-Asian racial and ethnic politics has become.[47] What it certainly indicates is that the stakes are very high.

Notes

1 Reproduced in Selena Dong, "'Too Many Asians': The Challenge of Fighting Discrimination against Asian–Americans and Preserving Affirmative Action," *Stanford Law Review*, 47, no. 5 (May 1995), 1028.

2 Ibid., 1032.

3 Dana Takagi, "From Discrimination to Affirmative Action: Facts in the Asian American Admissions Controversy," *Social Problems*, 37, no. 4 (November 1990), 578.

4 Jonathan Zimmerman, "Asian Americans, the New Jews on Campus," *Chronicle of Higher Education*, April 29, 2012. http://chronicle.com/article/Asian-Americans-the-New-Jews/131729/

5 Ibid.

6 Dongsheng Wang and Brian H. Kleiner, "Discrimination Against Asian Americans," *Equal Opportunities International*, 20 no. 5/6/7 (2001), 65.

7 Ronald Takaki, *Strangers from a Different Shore: A History of Asian Americans* (Boston: Little Brown, 1998), 481.

8 Wang and Kleiner, "Discrimination Against Asian Americans," 66.

9 Jerry Kang, "Racial Violence Against Asian Americans: The Nature of Prejudice," *Harvard Law Review*, 106 (June 1993), 2.

10 Bill Ong Hing, "Vigilante Racism: The De-Americanization of Immigrant America," *Michigan Journal of Race and Law*, 7 (Spring 2002), 4.

11 Mae Ngai, "The Legacy of Vincent Chin: A Twentieth Anniversary Commemoration," *Amerasia Journal*, 28, no. 3 (2002), 1.

12 Althea Yip, "Remembering Vincent Chin: Fifteen Years Later a Murder in Detroit Remains a Turning Point in the APA Movement," *AsianWeek*, July 5–13, 1997, 4.

13 "Koreans Lavished Largess on an Incurious Congress, " *Washington Post*, July 31, 1977, 1.

14 "Korean Agent or Merely a Hostess? Washington Woman is the Topic of Rumor and Unanswered Questions," *New York Times*, February 18, 1977, 17.

15 Dana Frank, "Demons in the Parking Lot: Auto Workers, Buy American Campaigns, and the 'Japanese Threat' in the 1980s," *Amerasia Journal*, 28 no. 3 (2002), 35.

16 Ibid., 33–5.

17 Robert Lee, *Orientals: Asian Americans in Popular Culture* (Philadelphia: Temple University Press, 1998), 1.

18 Cheuk-Yin Wong, "The Los Alamos Incident and Its Effects on Chinese American Scientists," Judy Yung, Gordon H. Chang, and Him Mark Lai, eds., *Chinese American Voices: From the Gold Rush to the Present* (Berkeley: University of California Press, 2006), 419.

19 The percentage depended on the type of school. Dong, "Too Many Asians," 1030.

20 Yip, "Remembering Vincent Chin," 4.

21 Ibid., 1033.

22 Jeff Chang, "On the Wrong Side: Chinese Americans Win Anti-Diversity Settlement—and Lose in the End," *Colorlines*, May 20, 1999. http://colorlines.com/archives/1999/05/on_the_wrong_side_chinese_americans_win_antidiversity_settlement_and_lose_in_the_end.html.e

23 Helen Zia, *Asian American Dreams: The Emergence of an American People* (New York: Macmillan, 2001), 173.

24 Ibid.

25 Ibid., 174.

26 Ibid.

27 Ibid., 179.

28 Ibid., 177.

29 Ibid., 178.

30 Ibid.

31 The liquor manufacturer persuaded him to apologize. Ibid., 177.

32 Ibid., 175.

33 Ibid., 180.

34 Other estimates are higher, as much as $800 million. Ibid., 183.

35 Ibid.

36 Ibid., 172.

37 Ibid., 182.

38 Rebecca Chiyoko King, "Racialization, Recognition, and Rights: Lumping and Splitting Multiracial Asian Americans in the 2000 Census," *Journal of Asian American Studies*, 3, no. 2 (June 2000): 191.

39 Ibid., 204.

40 Ibid., 205.

41 For example, see http://museums.depaul.edu/exhibitions/war-babylove-child-mixed-race-asian-american-art/; http://seaweedproductions.com/the-hapa-project/; and Kip Fulbeck, *Part Asian, 100% Hapa* (San Francisco: Chronicle Books, 2006).

42 Fujikane, "Sweeping Racism Under the Rug of 'Censorship': The Controversy Over Lois Ann Yamanaka's Blu's Hanging," *Amerasia Journal*, 26 no. 2 (2000): 168–69.

43 Ibid., 167.

44 Ibid., 168.

45 Kwong and Miščević, *Chinese America*.

46 http://online.wsj.com/article/SB10001424052748704111504576059713528698754.html. Amy Chua, *Battle Hymn of the Tiger Mother* (New York: Penguin Press, 2011).

47 http://blog.angryasianman.com/2011/01/your-permissive-western-parenting-is.html

Epilogue

The years since the turn of the twenty-first century have seen a number of momentous developments, both affecting the lives of Asian Americans and reshaping the major issues and debates among Asian American leaders, scholars, and the commentariat. One can only speculate about how the events of the last few years will appear in an Asian American history book ten or twenty years from now, but they surely indicate that this history is very dynamic and may look very different in the future.

That said, recent events have also been striking in how much they remind us of the adage, "everything old is new again." As much as we may wish to turn the page on the past, especially a past characterized by intolerance and discrimination against Asians in America, contemporary society has had a way of demonstrating how much we as a society still have to work through. The post-9–11 violence against Arabs, Muslims, and South Asians—the latter being mistaken for being Muslim, Arab or both—uncannily resembled the anti-Japanese backlash of the aftermath of Pearl Harbor.[1] And in 2012, a mass shooting at a Sikh temple just outside of Milwaukee, Wisconsin by a man with white supremacist associations and described as a "frustrated neo-Nazi" served as a chilling reminder of the persistence of racialized hatred toward Asian people.[2]

At the same time, the Asian America of today is vastly different from that of one hundred years ago. For one, the category "Asian American" is now a salient and meaningful one, the result of a long process of identity transformation and coalescence. It is also a category in which people of Asian ancestry have invested a great deal. Just how important its meanings are come into sharp relief every time an Asian American individual rises to national or international fame. At times, such as in the Amy Chua episode (discussed in Chapter 13), this results in intense debate and anger, and other times it gives a rallying figure and source of pride for the population. When professional basketball player Jeremy Lin skyrocketed to attention in early 2012, the reaction among Asian American commentators was nearly as stunning. "Jeremy Lin Makes Us All American," Eric Liu breathlessly declared, and variations of these sentiments followed.[3] More than just an expression of exhilaration at seeing a fresh, new athlete excel at his game, the Jeremy Lin hoopla also underscored that in 2012 race (and gender) still matter. His phenomenon, it seemed, tapped into many Asian Americans' desire to see people who look like them in the mirror of popular culture, thus underscoring a widespread sense of marginalization and invisibility in American life that persists to this day.

Another recent development that provides food for thought on the current state of Asian America and the politics of writing history in particular involves the revelation in a new book about the suppression of student radicals during the 1960s that Richard Aoki, a beloved figure from the Asian American movement, had been an informant for the FBI. Before the book was even released, the news unleashed a firestorm of reactions and attacks in all directions. Without venturing into whether or not the allegations are true or sufficiently supported, we can take away important points about the state and stakes of Asian American history. For some scholars, constructing an Asian American narrative revolves around valorizing individuals and using history to instill a sense of group pride. That the Aoki revelation generated such strong responses perhaps suggests that Asian American history has reached a point of development, that it has a known cast of characters and even "sacred cows," which is much more than we could say thirty years ago. And while the controversy has revealed that, for many, doing Asian American history remains an inherently political act, it also indicates that the field has evolved and grown to a stage in which scholars must recognize the extent to which all history is interpretive, a productive acknowledgement that will, I think, lead to richer and more nuanced scholarship.

While *A New History of Asian America* has sought to offer an updated history of Asian Americans, I recognize, even now, that much remains to be written as we move further into the twenty-first century and new scholarship continues to emerge. The second generation of post-1965'ers needs to be woven more prominently into history, and perhaps the entire post-1965 period can be broken down into discrete phases. If they cannot already, the impact of 9–11 and major developments since will also need to be historicized. As new histories are published at a rate with which I can scarcely keep up, new interpretations and narratives will emerge and continually transform how we understand Asian American history.

Notes

1   See for instance, http://newsfeed.time.com/2012/08/06/timeline-a-history-of-violence-against-sikhs-in-the-wake-of-911/.

2   Brian Louis, Henry Goldman and Chris Christoff, "Wisconsin Sikh Shooting Suspect Formed Skinhead Bands," *Bloomberg*, August 7, 2012. http://www.bloomberg.com/news/2012-08-06/wisconsin-sikh-shooting-probed-by-fbi-as-domestic-terror.html.

3   Eric Liu, "Jeremy Lin Makes Us All American," *Time*, February 13, 2012. http://ideas.time.com/2012/02/13/jeremy-lin-makes-us-all-american/

Bibliography

Secondary works cited

Abelmann, Nancy and John Lie. *Blue Dreams: Korean Americans and the Los Angeles Riots*. Cambridge: Harvard University Press, 1997.

Azuma, Eiichiro. *Between Two Empires: Race, History and Transnationalism in Japanese America*. New York: Oxford University Press, 2005.

Baldoz, Rick. *The Third Asiatic Invasion: Migration and Empire in Filipino America, 1898–1946*. New York: New York University Press, 2011.

Bonacich, Edna. "Asian Labor in the Development of California and Hawaii." In *Labor Immigration Under Capitalism: Asian Workers in the United States Before World War II*. Edited by Lucie Cheng and Edna Bonacich. Berkeley: University of California Press, 1984.

Bonacich, Edna and Lucie Cheng. "Introduction: A Theoretical Orientation to International Labor Migration." In *Labor Immigration Under Capitalism: Asian Workers in the United States Before World War II*. Edited by Lucie Cheng and Edna Bonacich. Berkeley: University of California Press, 1984.

Borstelmann, Thomas. *The Cold War and the Color Line: American Race Relations in the Global Arena*. Cambridge: Harvard University Press, 2001.

Brooks, Charlotte. *Alien Neighbors, Foreign Friends: Asian Americans, Housing, and the Transformation of Urban California*. Chicago: University of Chicago Press, 2009.

——. "In the Twilight Zone between Black and White: Japanese American Resettlement and Community in Chicago, 1942–1945." *Journal of American History* 84, No. 4 (March 2000): 1655–87.

Chan, Sucheng. *Asian Americans: An Interpretive History*. Boston: Twayne, 1991.

——. *Survivors: Cambodian Refugees in the United States*. Urbana: University of Illinois Press, 2004.

——. ed. *The Vietnamese American 1.5 Generation: Stories of War, Revolution, Flight, and New Beginnings*. Philadelphia: Temple University Press, 2006.

——. *This Bittersweet Soil: Chinese in California Agriculture, 1860–1910*. Berkeley: University of California Press, 1986.

Chang, Derek. *Citizens of a Christian Nation: Evangelical Missions and the Problem of Race in the Nineteenth Century*. Philadelphia: University of Pennsylvania Press, 2010.

Chang, Gordon H. "Emerging from the Shadows: The Visual Arts and Asian American History." In *Asian American Art: A History, 1850–1970*. Edited by Gordon H. Chang, Mark Johnson, Paul Karlstrom. Stanford: Stanford University Press, 2008.

——. *Morning Glory, Evening Shadow: Yamato Ichihashi and His Internment Writings*. Stanford: Stanford University Press, 1999.

———. "'Superman is About to Visit the Relocation Centers' and the Limits of Wartime Liberalism." *Amerasia Journal* 19, no. 1 (1993): 37–59.

———. "Whose 'Barbarism'? Whose 'Treachery'? Race and Civilization in the Unknown United States–Korea War of 1871." *Journal of American History* 89, no. 4 (March 2003): 1331–365.

Char, Tin-Yuke and Wai Jane Char. "The Chinese." *Ethnic Sources in Hawaii: Social Processes in Hawaii*. Edited by Bernard L. Hormann and Andrew W. Lind. New York: McGraw-Hill, 1996.

Chen, Yong. *Chinese San Francisco, 1850–1943: A Transnational Community*. Stanford: Stanford University Press, 2000.

Cheng, Lucie. "Free, Indentured, Enslaved: Chinese Prostitutes in Nineteenth-Century America." In *Labor Immigration Under Capitalism: Asian Workers in the United States Before World War II*. Edited by Lucie Cheng and Edna Bonacich. Berkeley: University of California Press, 1984.

Chiyoko King, Rebecca. "Racialization, Recognition, and Rights: Lumping and Splitting Multiracial Asian Americans in the 2000 Census." *Journal of Asian American Studies* 3, no. 2 (June 2000): 191–217.

Choy, Bong Youn. *Koreans in America*. Chicago: Nelson-Hall, 1979.

Choy, Catherine Ceniza. *Empire of Care: Nursing and Migration in Filipino American History*. Durham: Duke University Press, 2003.

Chung Simpson, Caroline. "Out of an Obscure Place: Japanese War Brides and Cultural Pluralism in the 1950s." *differences: A Journal of Feminist Cultural Studies* 10, no. 3 (1998): 47–81.

Cohen, Lucy. *Chinese in the Post-Civil War South: A People Without a History*. Baton Rouge: Louisiana State University Press, 1984.

Daniels, Roger. *Asian America: Chinese and Japanese in America Since 1850*. Seattle: University of Washington Press, 1988.

———. *Guarding the Golden Door: American Immigration Policy and Immigrants Since 1882*. New York: Hill and Wang, 2005.

———. *The Politics of Prejudice: The Anti-Japanese Movement in California and the Struggle for Japanese Exclusion*. Berkeley: University of California Press, 1962.

Dong, Selena. "'Too Many Asians': The Challenge of Fighting Discrimination against Asian–Americans and Preserving Affirmative Action." *Stanford Law Review* 47, no. 5 (May 1995): 1027–057.

España-Maram, Linda. *Creating Masculinity in Los Angeles's Little Manila: Working-Class Filipinos and Popular Culture, 1920s-1950s*. New York: Columbia University Press, 2006.

Fong, Timothy. *The First Suburban Chinatown: The Remaking of Monterey Park*. Philadelphia: Temple University Press, 1994.

Frank, Dana. "Demons in the Parking Lot: Auto Workers, Buy American Campaigns, and the 'Japanese Threat' in the 1980s." *Amerasia Journal* 28, no. 3 (2002): 33–50.

Friday, Chris. *Organizing Asian American Labor: The Pacific Coast Canned-Salmon Industry, 1870–1942*. Philadelphia: Temple University Press, 1994.

Fujikane, Candace. "Sweeping Racism Under the Rug of 'Censorship': The Controversy Over Lois Ann Yamanaka's *Blu's Hanging*." *Amerasia Journal* 26, no. 2 (2000): 168–69.

Fujita-Rony, Dorothy B. *American Workers, Colonial Power: Philippine Seattle and the Transpacific West*. Berkeley: University of California Press, 2003.

Fulbeck, Kip. *Part Asian, 100% Hapa*. San Francisco: Chronicle Books, 2006.

Gardner, Martha. "Working on White Womanhood: White Working Women in the San Francisco Anti-Chinese Movement, 1877–1890." *Journal of Social History* 33, no. 1 (Fall 1999): 73–95.

Griswold, Wesley S. *A Work of Giants: The First Transcontinental Railway*. New York: McGraw-Hill, 1962.

Gyory, Andrew. *Closing the Gate: Race, Politics, and the Chinese Exclusion Act*. Chapel Hill: University of North Carolina Press, 1998.

Habal, Estella. *San Francisco's International Hotel: Mobilizing the Filipino American Community in the Anti-eviction Movement*. Philadelphia: Temple University Press, 2007.

Hansen, Arthur A. "Peculiar Odyssey: Newsman Jimmie Omura's Removal from and Regeneration within Nikkei Society." In *Nikkei in the Pacific Northwest: Japanese Americans and Japanese Canadians in the Twentieth Century*. Edited by Gail Nomura and Louis Fiset. Seattle: University of Washington Press, 2005.

Hayashi, Brian Masaru. *Democratizing the Enemy: The Japanese American Internment*. Princeton: Princeton University Press, 2004.

Hing, Bill Ong. "Vigilante Racism: The De-Americanization of Immigrant America." *Michigan Journal of Race and Law* 7 (Spring 2002).

Howard, Robert West. *The Great Iron Trail: The Story of the First Transcontinental Railroad*. New York: G.P. Putnam's Sons, 1962.

Hsu, Madeline Y. "The Disappearance of America's Cold War Chinese Refugees." *Journal of American Ethnic History* 31, no. 4 (Summer 2012): 12–33.

——. *Dreaming of Gold, Dreaming of Home: Transnationalism and Migration between the United States and South China, 1882–1943*. Stanford: Stanford University Press, 2000.

Hurh, Won Moo and Kwang Chung Kim. *Korean Immigrants in America: A Structural Analysis of Ethnic Confinement and Adhesive Adaptation*. Rutherford: Fairleigh Dickinson University, 1984.

Ichioka, Yuji. "Dai Nisei Mondai." In Yuji Ichioka, *Before Internment: Essays in Prewar Japanese American History*. Edited by Gordon H. Chang and Eiichiro Azuma. Stanford: Stanford University Press, 2006.

——. *The Issei: The World of the First Generation Japanese Immigrants, 1885–1924*. New York: Free Press, 1988.

Iriye, Akira. *From Nationalism to Internationalism: U.S. Foreign Policy to 1914*. London: Routledge, 1977.

Irons, Peter. *Justice at War*. New York: Oxford University Press, 1983.

Jensen, Joan. *Passage from India: Asian Indian Immigrants in North America*. New Haven: Yale University Press, 1988.

Jung, Moon-Ho. *Coolies and Cane: Race, Labor and Sugar in the Age of Emancipation*. Baltimore: Johns Hopkins Press, 2006.

Jung, Moon-Kie. *Reworking Race: The Making of Hawaii's Interracial Labor Movement*. New York: Columbia University Press, 2006.

Kang, Jerry. "Racial Violence Against Asian Americans: The Nature of Predudice." *Harvard Law Review* 106 (June 1993).

Kelly, Gail. "Coping with America: Refugees from Vietnam, Cambodia, and Laos in the 1970s and 1980s." *The Annals of the American Academy of Political Science* 486, no. 1 (September 1986): 138–49.

Kim, Eleana. *Adopted Territory: Transnational Korean Adoptees and the Politics of Belonging*. Durham: Duke University Press, 2010.

Kim, Richard. "Inaugurating the American Century: The 1919 Philadelphia Korean Congress, Korean Diasporic Nationalism, and American Protestant Missionaries." *Journal of American Ethnic History* 26, no. 1 (Fall 2006): 50–76.

Klein, Christina. *Cold War Orientalism: Asia in the Middlebrow Imagination, 1945–1961*. Berkeley: University of California Press, 2003.

Kuhn, Philip A. *Chinese Among Others: Emigration in Modern Times*. Lanham: Rowman and Littlefield, 2008.

Kurashige, Lon. *Japanese American Celebration and Conflict: A History of Ethnic Identity and Festival, 1934–1990*. Berkeley: University of California Press, 2002.

Kurashige, Scott. "Pan-ethnicity and Community Organizing: Asian American United's Campaign Against Anti-Asian Violence." *Journal of Asian American Studies* 3, no. 2 (June 2000): 163–90.

——. *The Shifting Grounds of Race: Black and Japanese Americans in the Making of Multiethnic Los Angeles*. Princeton: Princeton University Press, 2008.

Kwong, Peter and Dušanka Miščević. *Chinese America: The Untold Story of America's Oldest New Community*. New York: New Press, 2005.

Lai, Him Mark. *Becoming Chinese American: A History of Communities and Institutions*. Walnut Creek: Alta Mira Press, 2004.

Lee, Anthony W. *A Shoemaker's Story*. Princeton: Princeton University Press, 2008.

Lee, Erika. *At America's Gates: Chinese Immigration During the Exclusion Era, 1882–1943*. Chapel Hill: University of North Carolina Press, 2003.

Lee, Erika Lee and Judy Yung, *Angel Island: Immigrant Gateway to America*. New York: Oxford University Press, 2010.

Lee, Mary Paik. *Quiet Odyssey: A Pioneer Korean Woman in America*. Seattle: University of Washington Press, 1990.

Lee, Robert G. *Orientals: Asian Americans in Popular Culture*. Philadelphia: Temple University Press, 1999.

Leonard, Karen Isaksen. *Making Ethnic Choices: California's Punjabi Mexicans*. Philadelphia: Temple University Press, 1992.

Leong, Karen. *The China Mystique: Pearl S. Buck, Anna May Wong, Mayling Soong, and the Transformation of American Orientalism*. Berkeley: University of California Press, 2005.

Lim, Shirley Jennifer. *A Feeling of Belonging: Asian American Women's Public Culture, 1930–1960*. New York: New York University Press, 2005.

Ling, Huping. *Chinese Chicago: Race, Transnational Migration, and Community Since 1870*. Stanford: Stanford University Press, 2012.

——. *Chinese St. Louis: From Enclave to Cultural Community*. Philadelphia: Temple University Press, 2004.

Lipman, Jana. "'The Face is the Roadmap': Vietnamese Americans in U.S. Political and Popular Culture, 1980–1988. *Journal of Asian American Studies* 14, no. 1 (February 2011): 33–68.

Liu, John M. "Race, Ethnicity, and the Sugar Plantation System: Asian Labor in Hawaii, 1850 to 1900." In *Labor Immigration Under Capitalism: Asian Workers in the United States Before World War II*. Edited by Lucie Cheng and Edna Bonacich. Berkeley: University of California Press, 1984.

Lopez, Ian Haney. *White by Law: The Legal Construction of Race*. New York: New York University Press, 1996.

Louie, Steve and Glenn Omatsu, eds. *Asian Americans: The Movement and the Moment*. Los Angeles: UCLA Asian American Studies Center Press, 2001.

Lui, Mary Ting Yi. *The Chinatown Trunk Mystery: Murder, Miscegenation, and Other Dangerous Encounters in Turn-of-the-Century New York City*. Princeton: Princeton University Press, 2005.

Maeda, Daryl J. *Chains of Babylon: The Rise of Asian America*. Minneapolis: University of Minnesota Press, 2009.

——. *Rethinking the Asian American Movement*. London: Routledge, 2011.

Maira, Sunaina Marr. *Desis in the House: Indian American Youth in New York City*. Philadelphia: Temple University Press, 2002.

Matsumoto, Valerie. *Farming the Homeplace: A Japanese American Community in California, 1919–1982*. Ithaca: Cornell University Press, 1993.

Mazumdar, Sucheta. "Colonial Impact and Punjabi Emigration to the United States." In *Labor Immigration Under Capitalism: Asian Workers in the United States Before World War II*. Edited by Lucie Cheng and Edna Bonacich. Berkeley: University of California Press, 1984.

McKeown, Adam. *Chinese Migrant Networks and Cultural Change: Peru, Chicago, Hawaii, 1900–1936*. Chicago: University of Chicago Press, 2001.

Melendy, H. Brett. *Asians in America: Filipinos, Koreans, and East Indians*. Boston: Twayne, 1977.

Molina, Natalia. *Fit to be Citizens?: Public Health and Race in Los Angeles, 1879–1939*. Berkeley: University of California, 2006.

Muller, Eric. *Free to Die for Their Country: The Story of the Japanese American Draft Resisters in World War II*. Chicago: University of Chicago Press, 2001.

Mumford, Kevin. *Interzones: Black/White Sex Districts in Chicago and New York in the Early Twentieth Century*. New York: Columbia University Press, 1997.

Nakano Glenn, Evelyn. *Issei, Nisei, War Bride: Three Generations of Japanese Women in Domestic Service*. Philadelphia: Temple University Press, 1986.

——. *Unequal Freedom: How Race and Gender Shaped American Citizenship and Labor*. Cambridge: Harvard University Press, 2002.

Ngai, Mae M. "The Architecture of Race in American Immigration Law: A Reexamination of the Immigration Act of 1924." *Journal of American History* 86, no. 1 (June 1999): 67–92.

——. *Impossible Subjects: Illegal Aliens and the Making of Modern America*. Princeton: Princeton University Press, 2004.

——. "The Legacy of Vincent Chin: A Twentieth Anniversary Commemoration." *Amerasia Journal* 28, no. 3 (2002): 1–6.

——. *The Lucky Ones: One Family and the Extraordinary Invention of Chinese America*. New York: Houghton Mifflin, 2010.

——. "The Unlovely Residue of Outworn Prejudices: The Hart-Celler Act and the Politics of Immigration Reform, 1945–1965." In *Americanism: New Perspectives on the History of an Ideal*. Edited by Michael Kazin and Joseph A. McCartin. Chapel Hill: University of North Carolina Press, 2006.

Oh, Arissa H. "From War Waif to Ideal Immigrant: The Cold War Transformation of the Korean Orphan." *Journal of American Ethnic History* 31, no. 4 (Summer 2012): 34–55.

Okihiro, Gary. *Cane Fires: The Anti-Japanese Movement in Hawaii: 1865–1945*. Honolulu: University of Hawaii, 1991.

——. *Margins and Mainstreams: Asians in American History and Culture*. Seattle: University of Washington Press, 1994.

——. *Storied Lives: Japanese American Students and World War II*. Seattle: University of Washington Press, 1999.

Patterson, Wayne. *The Ilse: First Generation Korean Immigrants in Hawai'i, 1903–1973*. Honolulu: University of Hawaii Press, 2000.

Pomerantz, Linda. "The Background of Korean Emigration." In *Labor Immigration Under Capitalism: Asian Workers in the United States Before World War II*. Edited by Lucie Cheng and Edna Bonacich. Berkeley: University of California Press, 1984.

Prashad, Vijay. *The Karma of Brown Folk*. Minneapolis: University of Minnesota Press, 2000.

Rhoads, Edward J.M. "The Chinese in Texas." In *Chinese on the American Frontier*. Edited by Arif Dirlik and Malcolm Yeung. New York: Rowman and Littlefield, 2001.

Robinson, Gregory. *A Tragedy of Democracy: Japanese Confinement in North America*. New York: Columbia University Press, 2009.

Rouse Jorae, Wendy. *The Children of Chinatown: Growing up Chinese American in San Francisco, 1850–1920*. Chapel Hill: University of North Carolina Press, 2009.

Said, Edward. *Orientalism*. New York: Pantheon Books, 1978.

Saxton, Alexander. *The Indispensable Enemy: Labor and the Anti-Chinese Movement*. Berkeley: University of California Press, 1971.

Shah, Nayan. *Contagious Divides: Epidemics and Race in San Francisco's Chinatown*. Berkeley: University of California Press, 2001.

——. *Stranger Intimacy: Contesting Race, Sexuality and the Law in the North American West*. Berkeley: University of California Press, 2011.

Shankar, Shalini. *Desi Land: Teen Culture, Class, and Success in Silicon Valley*. Durham: Duke University Press, 2008.

Sharma, Miriam. "Labor Migration and Class Formation Among the Filipinos in Hawaii, 1906–1946." In *Labor Immigration Under Capitalism: Asian Workers in the United States Before World War II*. Edited by Lucie Cheng and Edna Bonacich. Berkeley: University of California Press, 1984.

Shimabukuro, Robert Sadamu. *Born in Seattle: The Campaign for Japanese American Redress*. Seattle: University of Washington, 2001.

Sims, Robert C. "The 'Free Zone' Nikkei: Japanese Americans in Idaho and Eastern Oregon in World War II." In *Nikkei in the Pacific Northwest: Japanese Americans and Japanese Canadians in the Twentieth Century*. Edited by Gail Nomura and Louis Fiset. Seattle: University of Washington Press, 2005.

Sohi, Seema. "Race, Surveillance, and Indian Anticolonialism in the Transnational Western U.S.–Canadian Borderlands." *Journal of American History* 98, no. 2 (September 2011): 420–36.

Spickard, Paul. *Japanese Americans: The Formations and Transformations of an Ethnic Group*. New Brunswick: Rutgers University Press, 2009.

Starr, Paul D. "Troubled Waters: Vietnamese Fisherfolk on America's Gulf Coast." *International Migration Review* 15, no. 1/2 (Spring–Summer 1981): 226–38.

Sueyoshi, Amy. *Queer Compulsions: Race, Nation, and Sexuality in the Affairs of Yone Noguchi*. Honolulu: University of Hawaii Press, 2012.

Takagi, Dana. "From Discrimination to Affirmative Action: Facts in the Asian American Admissions Controversy." *Social Problems* 37, no. 4 (November 1990): 578–92.

Takaki, Ronald. *Pau Hana: Life and Labor in Hawaii, 1835–1920*. Honolulu: University of Hawaii Press, 1983.

——. *Strangers from a Different Shore: A History of Asian Americans*. Boston: Little Brown, 1998.

Tamura, Linda. *The Hood River Issei: An Oral History of Japanese Settlers in Oregon's Hood River Valley*. Urbana: University of Illinois Press, 1993.

Tchen, John. *New York Before Chinatown: Orientalism and the Shaping of American Culture*. Baltimore: Johns Hopkins Press, 2001.

Umemoto, Karen. "'On Strike!' San Francisco State College Strike, 1968–69: The Role of Asian American Students." In *Contemporary Asian America: A Multidisciplinary Reader*. Edited by Min Zhou and James V. Gatewood. New York: New York University Press, 2000.

Vang, Chia Youyee. *Hmong America: Reconstructing Community in Diaspora*. Urbana: University of Illinois Press, 2010.

Vergara, Benito. *Pinoy Capital: The Filipino Nation in Daly City*. Philadelphia: Temple University Press, 2008.

Walz, Eric. "From Kumamoto to Idaho: The Influence of Japanese Immigrants on the Agricultural Development of the Interior West." *Agricultural History* 74, no. 2 (Spring 2000): 404–18.

Wiebe, Robert. *The Search for Order, 1877–1920*. New York: Macmillan, 1966.

Wong, K. Scott. *Americans First: Chinese Americans and the Second World War*. Cambridge: Harvard University Press, 2005.

Wong, Marie Rose. *Sweet Cakes, Long Journey: The Chinatowns of Portland, Oregon*. Seattle: University of Washington, 2004.

Wu, Cynthia. *Chang and Eng Reconnected: The Original Siamese Twins in American Culture*. Philadelphia: Temple University Press, 2012.

Wu, Ellen. "'America's Chinese': Anti-Communism, Citizenship, and Cultural Diplomacy during the Cold War," *Pacific Historical Review* 77, no. 3 (August 2008): 391–422.

Wu, Judy Tzu-Chun. *Doctor Mom Chung of the Fair-Haired Bastards: The Life of a Wartime Celebrity*. Berkeley: University of California Press, 2005.

Yang, Kao Kalia. *The Late Homecomer: A Hmong Family Memoir*. Minneapolis: Coffeehouse Press, 2008.

Yang, Philip Q. *Asian Immigration to the United States*. Cambridge: Polity Press, 2011.

Yeh, Chiou-ling. *Making an American Festival: Chinese New Year in San Francisco's Chinatown*. Berkeley: University of California Press, 2008.

Yoo, David. *Contentious Spirits: Religion in Korean American History, 1903–1945*. Stanford: Stanford University Press, 2010.

———. *Growing Up Nisei: Race, Generation, and Culture among Japanese Americans of California, 1924–49*. Urbana: University of Illinois Press, 2000.

Yu, Henry. "The Oriental Problem in America, 1920–1960: Linking the Identities of Chinese American and Japanese American Intellectuals." In *Claiming America: Constructing Chinese American Identities during the Exclusion Era*. Edited by K. Scott Wong and Sucheng Chan. Philadelphia: Temple University Press, 1998.

———. *Thinking Orientals: Migration, Contact, and Exoticism in Modern America*. New York: Oxford University Press, 2001.

Yuh, Ji-Yeon. *Beyond the Shadow of Camptown: Korean Military Brides in America*. New York: New York University Press, 2002.

Yung, Judy. *Unbound Feet: A Social History of Chinese Women in San Francisco*. Berkeley: University of California Press, 1995.

Yung, Judy, Gordon H. Chang, and Him Mark Lai, eds. *Chinese American Voices: From the Gold Rush to the Present*. Berkeley: University of California Press, 2006.

Zhao, Xiaojian. *The New Chinese America: Class, Economy, and Social Hierarchy*. New Brunswick: Rutgers University Press, 2010.

———. *Remaking Chinese America: Immigration, Family, and Community, 1940–1965*. New Brunswick: Rutgers University Press, 2002.

Zhou, Min. "'Parachute Kids' in Southern California: The Educational Experience of Chinese Children in Transnational Families." *Educational Policy* 12, no. 6 (November 1998): 682–704.

Zia, Helen. *Asian American Dreams: The Emergence of an American People*. New York: Farrar, Straus, and Giroux, 2000.

Index